INCLUSION IN ACTION

INCLUSION IN ACTION

EDITED BY PHIL FOREMAN

THOMSON

Australia · Canada · Mexico · Singapore · Spain · United Kingdom · United States

Level 7, 80 Dorcas Street
South Melbourne, Victoria, Australia 3205

Email highereducation@thomsonlearning.com.au
Website http://www.thomsonlearning.com.au

First published as *Integration and Inclusion in Action* in
   1996 by Harcourt Australia Pty Ltd
Second edition published in 2001 by Harcourt Australia Pty Ltd

This edition published in 2005
10 9 8 7 6 5 4 3
08 07 06 05

Copyright © 2005 Nelson Australia Pty Limited.

National Library of Australia
Cataloguing-in-Publication data
Inclusion in action.

   Bibliography.
   Includes index.
   ISBN 0 17 011426 0.

   1. Mainstreaming in education – Australia. 2. Inclusive
   eduction – Australia. 3. Children with disabilities –
   Education – Australia. I. Foreman, Phil.

371.90460994

Editor: Elizabeth Watson
Project editor: Lucy Davison
Publishing editor: Rebekah Jardine-Williams
Indexer: Russell Brooks
Cover designer: Donna Kelly
Cover image: Photo Disc
Typeset in 10pt Sabon and Helvetica Neue by Sun Photoset Pty Ltd, Brisbane
Production controller: Carly Imrie
Printed in China by CTPS

This title is published under the imprint of Thomson
Nelson Australia Pty Limited ACN 058 280 149 (incorporated in
Victoria)
trading as Thomson Learning Australia.
The URLs contained in this publication were checked for currency
during the production process. Note, however, that the publisher
cannot vouch for the ongoing currency of URLs.

CONTENTS

Part A   Setting the scene

Part B Effective teaching practices

Part C Working with specific difficulties

Part D   Instigating change

PREFACE

Inclusion in Action has been developed from the previous two editions of *Integration and Inclusion in Action*, which has been widely used across Australia by teachers and by teacher trainees studying special education as part of their initial teacher education program. The change in title is small, but significant. The term 'integration' carries with it an implication of fitting students in to an abnormal or alien environment. The term 'inclusion' suggests that students are an expected part of the regular environment. This new edition has been revised and restructured, and there are new chapters on communication and use of resources.

The authors of the various chapters in this book have a strong view that special education is about good teaching. For this reason, much of this book is about teaching rather than about disabilities. Many of the concepts presented are about processes such as adapting curriculum to meet individual needs, planning teaching strategies, encouraging positive interactions and working collaboratively. These concepts are as applicable in regular education as in special education, and to students with a wide range of varying disabilities. The book's emphasis is not on specific disabilities but rather on an understanding of:

- the reasons why children with disabilities attend regular schools
- strategies that can be used to optimise the educational experiences of students with a disability in regular classes.

The approach does not attempt to relate a teaching approach to a particular type of disability. It is a myth that a named disability will indicate the type of teaching approach to be taken. For example to say that a child has cerebral palsy tells us nothing about that child's additional educational needs, which could be minimal or almost overwhelming. Certainly there are specialised teaching approaches for students with severe sensory disabilities, and they are not covered specifically in this text. Teachers can access information about specific disabilities when they have a child with that disability in their class – there is a special reference list in the back of this book for that purpose, and parents are often experts on their child's disability. However, for students with intellectual, physical or learning disabilities, the teaching approach is determined more by assessment of their educational needs than by knowledge of their disability.

The book is divided into four parts. The first part sets the scene by providing an overview of concepts, principles, legislation and policy related to inclusive practices. It also introduces the concept of inclusion in an early childhood setting. The second part examines effective teaching practices. The third part deals with specific difficulties in literacy, numeracy and communication. Finally, there is a section on instigating change, which looks at the role of teachers, the use of resources, and transition to adult learning.

The book can be used as the basis of a semester-based course for undergraduate students. An online instructors' manual is available. There is also an online course site for students, provided by the publishers.

Feedback from peers is very important in the development of a book such as this. I would particularly like to thank the following reviewers for their helpful and incisive suggestions on the outline and sample chapters:

- Dr Robert Andrew (University of Tasmania)
- Ms Margaret Dowrick (University of Western Sydney)
- Associate Professor David Evans (University of Sydney)
- Dr Ruth Fielding-Barnsley (Queensland University of Technology)
- Dr Brian Hemmings (Charles Sturt University)
- Dr Deslea Konza (University of Wollongong)
- Ms Julie Lancaster (Charles Sturt University)
- Dr Joe Murik (University of Canberra)
- Dr Paul Pagliano (James Cook University)
- Dr Diana Whitton (University of Western Sydney)
- Miss Lucia Zundas (Charles Sturt University).

I would like to thank the many parents, students, teachers, principals and other professionals who so generously provided case studies to develop and illustrate the concepts presented in each chapter. I would also like to thank student photographers from the University of Newcastle, Rebekah Smith, Cindy O'Keefe and Llawella Lewis, for their excellent contributions, and also to thank Gwen Tongé, Anne Porter and Rick Frost for their assistance with photography. Finally I would like to thank Publishing Editor Rebekah Jardine-Williams, together with my fellow contributors, for their expertise, commitment and unity of purpose.

Phil Foreman
2004

AUTHORS

Editor

Phil Foreman is Professor and Dean of Education at the University of Newcastle. He was Director of the University's Special Education Centre from 1986–99. He was editor of the *Journal of Intellectual and Developmental Disability* from 1992–2002, and remains an Associate Editor. He has had considerable involvement in community services for people with a disability and was foundation President of *Newcastle & Hunter Community Access* and *Disability Advocacy Service Hunter*. His current research interests are in the areas of severe intellectual disability and inclusion.

Contributors

Michael Arthur-Kelly is a senior lecturer in special education at the University of Newcastle, and has particular research-to-practice interests in instructional design and effectiveness, classroom management, and support for students with multiple and severe disabilities. His teaching background includes experiences in regular and special schools, and he is currently Editor of the journal *Special Education Perspectives*.

Susan Balandin trained as a speech pathologist in the UK and is currently a senior lecturer at the School of Communication Sciences and Disorders, at the University of Sydney. Her clinical work has focused on lifelong disability and complex communication needs. Her current research interests include interactions using augmentative and alternative communication (AAC), ageing with a lifelong disability and complex communication needs, and developing functional communication for people with a lifelong disability and complex communication needs.

Anne Carruthers is an educational consultant and has been a lecturer in Special Education. Previously she was a teacher in a regular school, she coordinated and taught in an early intervention program for infants and preschool children with disabilities, and she worked as an early childhood social educator with the Department of Health. She was also employed as a Senior Education Officer with the Department of School Education and was responsible for the Early Learning Project in the Hunter Region.

Robert Conway is Associate Professor and Director of the Special Education Centre at the University of Newcastle. He has taught in a variety of special education settings for students with intellectual, learning and behaviour difficulties. His research interests include the provision of educational services to students with behaviour difficulties and the adaptation of education settings to meet the needs of students with diverse needs. He has recently conducted a series of reviews of behaviour services and supported the implementation of schoolwide and system positive behaviour strategies.

Ian Dempsey is a senior lecturer in Special Education at the University of Newcastle. He has also worked as a high school teacher, a teacher of children and adolescents with autism, and as a coordinator of a respite care service for families with a member with a disability. Ian's research interests include community services for people with a disability, the education of students with intellectual disability, and parental empowerment.

Gordon Lyons has had more than 20 years experience as a teacher, school executive and education officer in special and regular education K–12, as an adult educator in the education and disability sectors, lecturer in special education, and as a guardian for adults with intellectual disabilities. His teaching experience has primarily been with students with intellectual disabilities and behaviour disorders. He recently completed his PhD at the University of Newcastle while on leave from the NSW Office of the Public Guardian. His current research agenda focuses on improving the quality of life of individuals with profound and multiple disabilities.

Janice North is currently employed as the Manager of Service Development at the Royal Institute for Deaf and Blind Children, Sydney, an organisation with which she has been associated since 1990. She holds teaching qualifications and a Master's degree in Education. Jan's primary interests have been in family-centred early education and use of investigative approaches to teaching young children. Jan has moved between special education and regular education and has occupied teaching and administrative roles in university, regular school, and special needs settings, and has been a school principal.

Greg Robinson is an Associate Professor at the Special Education Centre, University of Newcastle. He has worked with children and adults with learning disabilities and literacy problems for 28 years as a teacher, school psychologist and by providing a clinical/diagnostic service through the Special Education Centre. He has published and presented widely in the areas of underlying causes of learning disabilities and their effects on literacy, as well as on methods of providing support, especially through the training and use of parents as tutors.

Susan Spedding is Special Education Coordinator at the Central Coast Campus of the University of Newcastle and has lectured in special education for the past 14 years. She has been a teacher in a special school and in regular and support classes in infants, primary and secondary school. Her interests include learning difficulties, emergent literacy, and working collaboratively with parents and service providers to support the early literacy development of children in regional and rural areas.

Alison Sweep is currently a senior speech pathologist with the Department of Ageing, Disability and Home Care in NSW and coordinates a student unit. Alison holds an Honorary Clinical Associate title with the University of Sydney. Over the last 10 years she has worked with students aged from 3 to 19 years who have an intellectual disability and complex communication needs. She has provided services within special schools, support units, regular schools and home settings. Her area of interest is supporting teachers and parents to meet everyday, functional communication needs of students, including those who present with socially inappropriate or challenging behaviour.

PART A

SETTING THE SCENE

Chapter 1

Disability and inclusion: Concepts and principles

Phil Foreman

This chapter aims to:

- introduce readers to principles that have formed the basis of inclusive practices
- review the findings of research into the outcomes of inclusion
- locate inclusion as part of a range of possible responses to special educational needs
- explain terminology and concepts related to inclusion

- describe the special education settings available to students with a disability
- describe the concept of disability
- explain the appropriate use of language about disability
- explain some myths and misconceptions about disability
- provide an overview of the book's approach to teaching students with special educational needs in regular classes.

Teachers and disability

There was a time when most teachers, other than those who had chosen to be 'special education' teachers, were unlikely to have much contact with students with a disability. Many students with a disability either did not attend school or attended a 'special' school, if one was available. This was part of a general policy of keeping people with a disability separate from the so-called 'normal' community. In the nineteenth century and early twentieth century, a range of institutions was developed, some of them very large. A primary purpose of these institutions was to separate people with a disability from others, partly for their benefit and also, so it was thought, for the benefit of their families and the general community. It was common for the institutions to be physically isolated from the rest of the community and the treatment of residents was not always kind. Even people who remained with their families were often hidden away, or expected to mix only with other people with similar disabilities.

Since the *International Year of Disabled Persons (IYDP)* in 1981, it has become much more likely that people with a disability will seek and expect the same opportunities and lifestyle choices as people without disabilities. Although some institutions still operate, IYDP emphasised the right of people with a disability to make choices in the way they lived their lives – choices on such fundamental matters as where they lived, who they mixed with, where they worked, and how they spent their leisure time. Prior to this time, there was very little consideration given to the right of people with a disability to be part of an inclusive community. As a result, many people with a disability were separated from the general community in environments that gave them little opportunity to make any choices in their lives, even in the most routine of matters.

Principles underlying inclusion

Social justice and human rights

Changing attitudes to disability have been part of a much broader social justice movement which has led to changes for several minority or disadvantaged groups. Although there is still a long way to go, it is now less likely than in the past that people will have their lives restricted or determined by their gender, religion, race, ethnicity, sexuality or disability. It is now recognised that people with a disability want to be regarded as *people* first. They want to make decisions about their own lives, and they don't want these decisions to be based solely on the fact that they have a disability.

These changes in social attitude have been supported, and sometimes instigated, by legislation such as the *Disability Discrimination Act 1992* (Cwlth). This is discussed in more detail in Chapter 2. The changes that have occurred mean that classroom teachers at all levels are likely to have some students with a disability enrolled in their schools and in their classes. Parents, students and policymakers have all given their support to the view that attendance at the neighbourhood school is a valued option that should be open to all. This means that all teachers need to be able to adapt their classroom organisation and teaching methods to provide for a wide range of individual differences in students.

Normalisation

Normalisation is a social justice concept based largely on the writings of Bank-Mikkelsen (1969), Wolfensberger (1972, 1980) and Nirje (1970, 1985). It has formed the basis of the special education policies of most school systems. The concept of normalisation embraces the belief that people are entitled to live as 'normal' as possible a lifestyle in their community. Normal, in this context, is taken to mean what most other people in that culture do, or prefer to do. Taking this viewpoint, it could easily be shown that it is not 'normal' in western cultures for people to live permanently in a dormitory situation. It is not 'normal' for adults to have little choice about their daily activities or to be prevented from intimate sexual contact. Thus a residential institution that changed its dormitories into one- or two-person bedrooms, provided opportunities for residents to choose their own food, clothes and activities and allowed free interactions between people of both sexes would be acting consistently with the principle of normalisation.

In relation to education, the principle of normalisation suggests that all students should be able to choose to attend the neighbourhood school, in the same way that it would be expected that a student without a disability could go to their neighbourhood school, if that is what the student or the student's parents wanted, or to an independent school, if that was what was chosen. Wolfensberger has stated that he considers normalisation theory to have been 'subsumed by the broader theory of Social Role Valorization' (1995, p. 164). This theory looks at the various 'social roles' that people perform: husband, wife, friend, teacher, colleague, leader, and so on. Some social roles are obviously much more highly valued than others. The way others respond to our social roles affects the way we perceive ourselves.

Wolfensberger points out that the social roles of people with a disability tend to be poorly valued. If people with a disability are to be genuinely included in the community, it is important that their social roles are 'valorised'. This means they need to be given roles and opportunities that are valued by the rest of the community. Their living conditions, their education or work, and their everyday activities should not be greatly different from what is valued by the culture. For example, street begging is a very poorly regarded activity in almost every culture, with very low status. As such, it would be contrary to social role valorisation to have people with a disability raising money for charity by soliciting donations in the street.

Age-appropriateness

From a school's perspective, it is important that students with a disability are given roles that are valued by the school community. They need to be able to participate in the school's day-to-day activities and, wherever possible, perform roles that are seen as positive and valuable.

The principle of normalisation would say that students' activities should be appropriate to their age. Age-appropriateness suggests that teenage girls should not be given dolls to play with and teenage boys should not be listening to nursery rhymes. These activities would be seen as low status by others, and possibly by the students themselves. It is often possible to think of an age-appropriate activity or teaching material that can replace an inappropriate activity, but will provide the same, or better, learning opportunities. For example, it is better for older students to be given counting practice using objects such as pencils or coins rather than using childish objects such as blocks or counters.

The 'least restrictive environment'

The concept of the least restrictive environment is based on the philosophical principle that some environments are intrinsically more restrictive than others. People living in highly restrictive environments have very few choices about what they do each day, how they spend their leisure hours, what they eat, what they wear, when they sleep, whom they mix with, and so on. Most people prefer to live in non-restrictive environments, as we usually like to have choices.

Probably the most restrictive environment that we can imagine is a jail. There are good reasons why jails are restrictive, and why the inmates' choices are limited. Yet for many years, large residential institutions for people with a disability could be as restrictive as jails, perhaps even more restrictive than some jails! Because of the social changes referred to earlier in this chapter, many people with a disability in western countries now live with their families, in group homes or other alternative residential situations, or independently in the community, rather than in institutions. The institutions that continue to operate have generally made a large effort to provide more choice for their residents, a more normalised lifestyle, and fewer restrictions.

Most school systems provide a range of classes and schools to cater for students with special educational needs, and some of these have provided very restrictive environments. As with residential institutions, school systems have moved towards improved levels of personal participation and control for students. Whereas twenty years ago children with a disability were likely to have been placed in one of the first three settings listed below, they are now more likely to be in one of the second group of three settings (Dempsey & Foreman, 1997; Dempsey, Foreman & Jenkinson, 2002). Residential special schools are now very rare, and new segregated day schools are generally not being built. The only growth area for separate special schools is for students with emotional or behavioural disorders. The range of educational settings provided by school systems, from most restrictive to least restrictive, is as follows:

- residential school for students with a disability
- separate special day school
- separate special school on regular campus
- special unit (usually 2 or 3 classes) located in regular school
- single special class in regular school
- single special class in regular school, with part-time regular placement
- regular class.

There are, of course, many variations on the way students with special educational needs use these settings. Some students can attend a regular class with only minimal adjustments by the school, while others need to be provided with support such as equipment, full-time or part-time teachers' assistants, or specialist advisory services. Other students will be enrolled part-time in a special class and part-time in a regular class. The process of deciding the best possible educational placement for a child is often complex. Most school systems now recognise that this is a parental decision, based on advice from educational and health care professionals. However, many parents have a very clear view of what they would like for their child (see Box 1.1).

Box 1.1
Voices: Leanne and Emilio's dreams

We have a dream for our daughter's life and future.

We dream that she will have friends who will love and value her and include her in their lives.

We dream that she will be invited to birthday parties, outings and sleepovers.

We dream that she will be able to take part in school assemblies, school plays and concerts, sports and swimming carnivals, and excursions.

We dream that as she grows and matures life around her will also grow and mature. That her experiences will multiply, and her horizons expand. That she will experience life in all its fullness with its highs and lows.

We dream that she will love and be loved by others outside of her family.

>

Box 1.1 continued

We dream that she will be given opportunities that are available to all of us, and that she will have many and varied choices available to her.

We dream that she will continue to develop her strengths and self-sufficiency, and that her place and participation in life and her community will be valued.

We dream that her place in school, the community and later in the workplace will not be questioned but accepted as 'normal' and natural because she is an integral part of her community and in the lives of others.

We dream that she will never be lonely or alone; that she will be safe and healthy and surrounded by people who know and care about her.

We dream that she will be loved, challenged, cared for, taught, accepted and valued for the unique person that she is.

We dream that one day we will be able to go in peace knowing that she will be as safe, happy and content with her life as we have been, or more.

To many people these dreams are only 'natural' and so obvious they never even get thought about, let alone put down in writing. But it is only recently that we have been able to dream these dreams for our eldest daughter, and it is only through pursuing an inclusive education and life for her that we have any hope of making them a reality.

Our daughter is bright and bubbly; she has curly blond hair and the cheekiest grin. She loves the outdoors and going for walks. She has swimming lessons once a week and is learning to ride a bike. She enjoys books and music. She loves to have the wind blowing in her hair and watch it moving the leaves in the trees. She loves to tease her Poppy and try to steal his glasses, she thinks her Daddy is the most handsome man in the world, and her sister is hysterical. She also happens to have severe physical and intellectual disabilities, a hearing impairment and epilepsy, but she has more similarities to other children than differences. Despite that, all her life until now has been based on those differences, resulting in segregation for both her and us, as a family. This has always felt very unnatural to us. Isn't it more natural to live, work, and play with a wide range of people? Despite her differences, our daughter is still our daughter, a sister, a granddaughter, a cousin, a niece, a neighbour, a friend, so why shouldn't she also be a classmate or a student at her local school?

As the Rogers and Hammerstein song says:

You got to have a dream,
if you don't have a dream.
How you gonna have a dream
come true?

Inclusion has allowed us to dream for our daughter – we dream that one day parents of children with disabilities will also be able to take these things for granted as do parents of children with blue eyes.

Leanne and Emilio Dendaluce, parents of Ainhoa and Kaia

While the principle that a regular class is less restrictive than a special class usually applies, there are some exceptions to this. For example, if a student who uses a wheelchair is in a school that has very limited wheelchair access, then that student will be in a more restrictive environment than if they attend a school designed to accommodate wheelchairs. This does not imply that the ideal solution is for the student to attend a school for children with physical disabilities, which would be fully wheelchair-accessible. The implication is that all schools, like other parts of the community, should be wheelchair-accessible.

Making a school wheelchair-accessible can be a very expensive process. Because the number of students who use wheelchairs is relatively small, what many school systems do is to design new buildings to be as accessible as possible, and adapt the older school buildings as the need arises. Often, minor adjustments are all that is needed. A change in room timetable can mean that a class doesn't have to go upstairs or crisscross the playground after each lesson period. Most students who use wheelchairs are willing to put up with some inconvenience while they are waiting for things to be fixed up. What they find most important is that there is a welcoming and inclusive atmosphere, and an effort to make things work. They realise that it takes time for ramps to be installed, or for a piece of chair-lifting equipment to be transferred from another school.

All children can learn

Until the 1970s, public school systems in Australia provided programs only for students who were deemed capable of learning. Students with intellectual disability were classified as 'educable', 'trainable' or 'custodial', depending on their IQ scores. The public system provided programs for those who were 'educable' and possibly for those who were judged to be 'trainable'. Other students were regarded as medical 'cases' and were not usually accepted in the public education system. Since that time, there has been widespread acceptance that all children can learn and therefore that all children are entitled to an appropriate publicly-funded education program. Initially, these programs were invariably in segregated schools, especially for those with more severe disabilities. More recently, much education has occurred in more inclusive settings.

The learning that takes place is not the same for all students. For some students, learning to indicate when they are hungry or thirsty, or to show an activity preference, will have a significant positive effect on the quality of their lives. It is not typical school learning, but it is still learning that can be nurtured and developed by teachers and other school staff in school settings.

Towards inclusion in education

By the mid-1970s, most school systems had established segregated special schools for children with a disability. Typically, each school catered for one type of disability: usually intellectual, physical, vision, or hearing. Often there was further subdivision according to the level of intellectual disability or, for children with hearing impairments, according to the teaching approach. Thus there were schools for students with mild, moderate, or severe intellectual disability. There were schools for students with hearing impairments which used an oral approach while others used signed English. The development of the system of separate special schools was based on the notion that any child with a disability would benefit from being in a separate setting where it would be possible, at least in theory, to provide small classes and specialised teaching and equipment.

In 1994, the World Conference on Special Needs Education was held at Salamanca, Spain. Over 90 countries agreed on a statement that supported inclusion as the standard form of education for students with a disability. Article 2 of the Salamanca Statement said:

> Regular schools with this inclusive orientation are the most effective means of combating discriminatory attitudes, creating welcoming communities, building an inclusive society and achieving education for all; moreover, they provide an effective education to the majority of children and improve the efficiency and ultimately the cost-effectiveness of the entire education system.
>
> (UNESCO, 1994, p. ix)

This statement reinforced the view that education in a regular school should be available as a first option for all students. The statement has been endorsed by education systems in Australia and internationally, and has been widely used as a basis for policy development.

The Salamanca Statement referred to an 'inclusive orientation'. Some other terms used in relation to the process of education in regular schools are *integration*, *mainstreaming*, and *normalisation*. These terms have slightly different meanings, which will be explained later in this chapter. However, all the terms imply that students with a disability will use similar educational facilities to those used by students without disabilities. In this book, we will emphasise the concept of 'inclusion', as this has implications both about the process and the philosophy that underpins it.

Parents, educational administrators, politicians and educational theorists have all taken leadership roles in the move towards inclusive education. This has occurred for several reasons. First, there has been widespread acceptance of the right of all persons to participate fully in the mainstream community, if they choose to do so. Schools and school systems would be out of touch with community standards if they did not support inclusion. Second, research has failed to show clearly that separate special schools produce better social or academic learning outcomes than integrated settings. There is even evidence that some students with severe and multiple disabilities are more engaged with their environment and have more opportunities for communication in regular settings than in special schools (Foreman & Arthur, 2003; Rafferty, Piscitelli & Boettcher, 2003). In 1998, McGregor and Vogelsberg synthesised the findings of a large number of studies of the effects of various aspects of inclusive schooling, and concluded that the outcomes are generally beneficial. For the present chapter, other recent findings on the outcomes of research on inclusive education have been reviewed and are summarised in Box 1.2. The current review used the headings developed by McGregor and Vogelsberg as a starting point.

The consequence of such changes in thinking about inclusion is that some students who may previously have had to spend their entire school career in a segregated setting will now be in a regular class. It is therefore essential that class teachers are competent to teach all the students for whom they are responsible.

Terminology and concepts

Integration

Integration is a broad term used to refer to a student's attendance at or participation in activities at a regular school. The term can also refer to the *process* of transferring a student to a less segregated setting. A child who attends a regular school, but is in a separate special unit or class, can still be said to be integrated. This is sometimes referred to as an 'integrated class'. Although the student is in a special class, it is evident that, if that class is in a regular school, the opportunities to interact with other members of the general school community are much greater than if the student is in an isolated special school. The student may have siblings or neighbours at the school and is also likely to come into contact with schoolmates in out-of-school situations in the neighbourhood.

Box 1.2

Outcomes of research on inclusive education

Social outcomes for students with a disability*

- Students with a disability demonstrate high levels of social interaction in regular settings. However, placement alone does not guarantee positive social outcomes.
- Social competence and communication skills improve when students with a disability are educated in inclusive settings.
- Friendships develop between students with and without disabilities in inclusive settings.
- Teachers play a critical role in facilitating friendships between students with a disability and their peers without a disability.
- *Parents can play a role in facilitating friendships between students with a disability and their peers without a disability.*
- Friendship and membership are helped by long-term involvement in the classroom and routine activities of the school. *However, social interaction is difficult for some students with a disability.*

- *Students with severe multiple disabilities have more communicative interactions and communication partners in regular classes than special classes.*
- *Teachers' aides can have a negative influence on the social interaction of students with a disability.*

Outcomes for skill acquisition for students with a disability

- Students with a disability may demonstrate gains in curriculum areas, when they are educated in inclusive settings. *However, some studies do not show curriculum gains.*
- Interactive, small group contexts encourage skill acquisition and social acceptance for students with a disability in general education classrooms.

Impact on students without disabilities

- The *academic* performance of typically-developing students is not compromised

>

Box 1.2 continued

by the presence of students with a disability in their classrooms.

- *The classroom behaviour of typically-developing students is not generally affected negatively by the presence of students with a disability in their classrooms. However, some studies have suggested that there can be unwanted effects.*
- Typically developing students benefit from their involvement and relationships with students with a disability.
- *Typically developing students may perceive that adaptations and accommodations for students with a disability benefit their own learning.*
- The presence of students with a disability in the general education classroom provides learning opportunities and experiences that might not otherwise be part of the curriculum.

Impact on parents

- Parent support for inclusion is encouraged by experience with this approach to education, although experience alone does not shape attitudes.
- Parents of students with a disability are looking for positive attitudes, good educational opportunities, and acceptance of their child among educators.
- *Some parents of students with more severe disabilities are worried about the loss of the individual support of a specialised setting.*
- *Some parents of students without disabilities are worried about the impact of inclusion on their child's education.*

Impact on teachers

- Although many teachers are initially reluctant about inclusion, they become confident in their abilities with support and experience.
- *Teachers experience professional growth as a result of working in inclusive settings.*

- *Teachers experience increased personal satisfaction as a result of working in inclusive settings.*
- Support from other teachers is a powerful and necessary resource to empower teachers to problem-solve new instructional challenges.
- Facilitating the inclusion of students with a disability requires the sensitivity to make on the spot judgements about the type and amount of support to encourage participation, while not interfering with student interactions.
- *While many teachers see parents as a valuable resource, others prefer them not to volunteer to assist in the classroom.*

Role of teachers

- *Teacher attitude is a major factor in successful programs of inclusion.*
- *Training and experience assist teachers in successful implementation of programs of inclusion.*

Role of principals

- *Principals tend to be more supportive of inclusion than classroom teachers.*
- *Some principals are concerned about the logistics of planning for inclusion.*

Other factors

- *Factors such as program standards, financial support, and other logistic matters can impact on the success of inclusion.*
- *The number of students with a disability in any one classroom should not be excessive – it should be reflective of population numbers.*

*Headings and findings are based on McGregor & Vogelsberg, 1998, pp. 57–69. Findings have been updated, using research reports published after 1997. Findings in *italics* represent changes to or additions to the findings of McGregor & Vogelsberg. Findings in standard font are confirmatory of McGregor & Vogelsberg's original conclusions.

Many schools with special classes have specific programs to encourage interaction between students with and without a disability. For example, in some schools, children spend the mornings in a special class and afternoons in a regular class. Teachers and assistants from the special class are used to support placement in the regular class. Such opportunities for interaction, based on the principle of normalisation, are more likely to occur if the child is attending a regular school, even if in a special class or unit.

Mainstreaming

Students are mainstreamed while they are enrolled in or participating in a regular class. In the example given above, students were in an *integrated* special class in the morning, and were *mainstreamed* in the afternoon.

In Australia and New Zealand and other western cultures, mainstreaming is generally regarded as the most culturally normative placement; that is, it is the most usual type of placement in these cultures. Many parents and school systems consider that mainstreaming should be the standard placement for all students, except under exceptional circumstances. Box 1.3 provides an example of a school that has mainstreamed several students who have severe disabilities. These students, who would once have spent all their school lives in a special school, now have all of their education in a regular class. As you can see from Box 1.3, considerable planning and resources are sometimes needed to support a mainstream placement, but considerable planning and resources would be needed regardless of whether the students were in a special or regular school.

Inclusion

Inclusive education, while it leads to integration and regular class placement, comes from a different philosophical base than integration or mainstreaming. Indeed, inclusion is a concept that extends well beyond education to society itself. In education, inclusion is based on the philosophy that schools should, without question, provide for the needs of all the children in their communities, whatever the level of their ability or disability. Inclusive schools welcome and celebrate diversity in ability as well as in cultural, racial, ethnic and social background (Giorcelli, 1995). An essential difference between integration or mainstreaming and inclusion is that, with integration or mainstreaming, the school asks '*Can we* provide for the needs of this student?'. With inclusion, the school asks '*How will we* provide for the needs of this student?'. This question is asked in relation to students who are diverse socially, culturally, intellectually, or behaviourally. The school provides an inclusive and accepting environment, which caters for all members of its community. Inclusion will almost always lead to regular class placement, regardless of the type or level of disability (Brown, 1995).

Inclusion as a movement and a philosophy has been the subject of considerable debate (Fuchs & Fuchs, 1994; Wilton, 1994; Jenkinson, 1997). Some teachers will have strong views in favour of or against inclusion. However, regardless of these views, all teachers must now be prepared to provide for the needs of students with a disability in their schools, regardless of whether those students are 'integrated', 'mainstreamed', or 'included'.

Box 1.3
Inclusive education at Lambton Public School

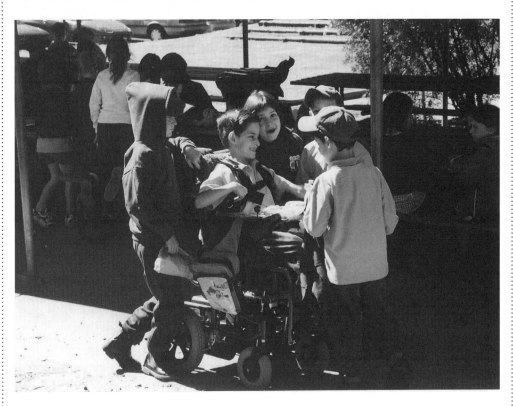

Lambton Public School aims to provide a quality educational program to all students in the local area. When the school becomes aware that a local child with special educational needs is approaching school age, the school counsellor contacts the parent and commences a process of needs assessment. In cases where the child is deemed eligible for a special placement other than within the regular school, or eligible for funding support or other special support within the school, the school counsellor, the school principal and, usually, the Stage 1 supervisor, attend a meeting with the child's parents to discuss the various options that may be available, and implementation of whichever options are decided upon. From this point, individualised learning outcomes are usually decided upon and the school proceeds to arrange

whatever physical facilities, special equipment and additional staffing are needed. If the child needs major building or grounds work to be undertaken for improved access, this process needs to start at least 12 months before the expected enrolment date. The school negotiates with the Department of Education and Training (DET) in arranging such facilities.

As the enrolment date approaches, the school builds a partnership with the child's parents, relevant health professionals and other agencies so that school staff and parents have shared expectations, understandings and goals. In this way all people working with and caring for the child form a *learning support team*. The learning support team directs the child's program on an ongoing basis and makes decisions about changes to the child's circumstances or

>

Box 1.3 continued

program, provision of special training for the child's teacher or aide, purchase of or alterations to equipment and materials, and so on. In every case, the learning support team attempts to establish a set of arrangements that allows the child to have the same opportunities as other students but also to receive whatever additional support is needed. The team also tries to arrange the child's program in such a way that it can be implemented by the teacher and other staff without overloading the teacher or other staff with extra demands and so that as much of the program as possible fits in with the general class program and regular school activities.

Students with disabilities who attend regular schools in New South Wales may be granted special funding from DET to assist with ongoing support. The school counsellor, in collaboration with health professionals from other agencies (and parents), assesses the child's needs and abilities. Under current arrangements, this assessment determines eligibility for funding. Members of the learning support team (parents, teacher, school counsellor, representatives of other agencies, school principal or representative) assess needs based on all available information, and submit the assessment results to DET for consideration. The child's needs in the areas of curriculum, communication, social competence, safety, personal care and mobility are described in this process. The manner in which funding granted is used is governed by the learning support team but funding is usually utilised to provide teacher's aide support for the child and teacher, additional teacher time, professional development and specialised training, and special equipment and materials.

The school principal and other members of the school executive team have a critical role in supporting inclusive education. It is essential that the executive establish a school climate that is professional, welcoming, flexible and reasonable and one in which all staff, students and parents are properly supported according to their own particular needs. The school executive must determine, for example, whether the school has, or could have, the capacity to provide an appropriate education for any particular student, and what must be done for an enrolment to be successful over the long term. The executive must build the school's capacity to address emergent needs, which means supporting and developing staff, employing appropriate personnel, and arranging any physical facilities that may be required, well in advance of enrolment. The school executive must ensure that all decisions and practices are governed by the principles of procedural fairness.

Inclusion in schools

Students with special educational needs in regular classes

Some teachers feel worried at the prospect of having children with special educational needs in their classes. Such concern is often misplaced. Many teachers find that a child with an identified disability can be less of a problem than some other children without disabilities. For example, consider the case of Damien. Damien is a 14-year-old boy with cerebral palsy, attending his local high school. He uses an electric wheelchair. His academic work is above average. He would like to work with computers when he leaves school.

There are some issues here that the school has to consider. How will Damien deal with the problem of stairs? Are there any obstructions to his wheelchair? Is there a wheelchair-accessible toilet? Does he need assistance in using the toilet, or accessing other school facilities? Are there special transport needs? How will he do assessments and examinations?

In most states, the education system will provide advice and financial support to help resolve these issues, and will have a procedure for assessing each child's needs. However, once these concerns have been dealt with, the chances are that Damien will cause his teachers fewer problems than many other children in the class. Yet there was a time when Damien would have spent his entire school-days mixing only with other children with physical disabilities, simply because the problems referred to above were regarded as insurmountable in a regular school. It is reasonable for Damien to choose not to be grouped according to one specific aspect of his humanity (his physical disability), just as it is reasonable for children not to be grouped according to their weight, ethnicity, hair colour or skin colour. The same comments apply to Ya'el, whose voice is heard in Box 1.6, towards the end of this chapter.

Of course, the enrolment of a child with a disability will sometimes require considerable effort on the teacher's part. Teachers and principals often worry that they will not have the teaching competencies or physical resources needed to include children with a disability in their classes (Bailey & du Plessis, 1998; Center & Ward, 1987; Center, Ward, Parmenter & Nash, 1985). There are students who will require individual programs and others who will require various levels of personal assistance. However, this statement can also be made about children without a disability, for example, students with challenging behaviour or who speak no English. It is not possible or reasonable to refuse to accept children in a school simply because they may be more difficult to teach, or have an identified disability. All employees have some part of their work which is more difficult than others, and which they would prefer to do without. Schools and teachers are expected to cater for their communities, and communities include people with disabilities and without disabilities, students who learn easily and those who need much assistance. The process of inclusion referred to in Box 1.3 required a lot of effort, planning and input from the principal, teachers, parents and education system. However, participants were happy to make the effort and are pleased with the outcome. Most schools and most teachers now accept that an inclusive school finds ways to cater for all of its community.

How many students have a disability?

There are various ways of defining a disability that will produce vastly different incidence rates. Consequently, the number of students with a disability depends on how we define a disability. For example, a very large number of people have a vision impairment to the extent that they need to wear glasses. At what point does a vision impairment become a disability? Probably the answer is when it interferes with everyday functioning.

In terms of numbers, we can say that the more severe the disability, the rarer it will be. Thus, there are many more children with a mild degree of intellectual disability than with a moderate degree of intellectual disability, and more children with a moderate disability than with a severe disability. Usually, the number of students who have a disability which, in the past, would have required placement in a special school, is stated to be around 1 to 2 per cent. Wilton (1998) estimated that 7 per cent of the school population have 'moderate learning or behavioural difficulties' (p. 6). Some publications report figures as high as 10 or 15 per cent. These figures would include students who are having difficulty learning to read or who have behavioural problems such as hyperactivity. Most of these children have always been in regular classes, and while it is expected that a school would continue to provide appropriate programs for these students, they cannot be looked on as an additional responsibility resulting from the inclusion process.

It is also wrong to think of disability as an 'all or nothing' concept. Everyone is at some point on a continuum for all their human characteristics: height, weight, intellectual ability, physical ability, physical fitness, and so on. Frequently, people who have a disability can be viewed as at a different point from others on one or more of the many continua of abilities and characteristics that make up an individual. They may be at the same point on some variables, and ahead of many people on others. For example, some students with cerebral palsy will be more intelligent than their classmates without cerebral palsy. Some students with learning difficulties will be as good as or better at sport than students without learning difficulties. Very often the similarities between people with and without disabilities will be greater than the differences. It is therefore not helpful to focus too much on the differences.

There has been some concern among teachers that inclusion means that special schools will close and that their classes will be overwhelmed by children with a disability. This fear is unfounded for three reasons. First, it is extremely unlikely that all special placements will close. Students who have moved out of special schools have tended to move into special classes and units (Dempsey & Foreman, 1995, 1997) and there is no suggestion that school systems will eliminate all special classes and units. Some parents want their children to attend specialised or segregated settings. Dempsey, Foreman and Jenkinson (2002) showed that, in NSW, the proportion of students in special schools and classes actually increased from 1.57 per cent of the school population to 1.76 per cent of the school population during the period 1986–98.

A second reason why teachers do not need to fear being overwhelmed by students with a disability is that the number of such students is relatively small. It would be unusual for there to be more than one or two children with a significant disability in any one class. And third, even though there are still a large number of students in special classes, the majority of students with a disability already attend regular schools (Dempsey & Foreman, 1995, 1997), so there is no influx waiting to happen.

In recent years, funding to support students with disabilities in regular classes has been extended to include students with low support needs. Thus the number of students receiving integration funding in NSW increased from 1135 in 1988 (McRae, 1996) to 16638 in 2002 (Vinson, 2002). This does not mean that there are 15 times as many students with a disability enrolled in regular classes. What it does mean is that schools are now receiving financial support to assist students with mild intellectual disability, language impairments, or emotional problems. These students have always been in regular classes but, in the past, did not attract integration funding support.

It could be seen as a distraction to debate what constitutes a disability and how many children with a disability there are. It is more helpful to focus on the particular support needs the student may have. The terms *children (or students) with additional educational needs* and *students with a disability* will be used throughout this book to refer to students who have educational needs that require some modification of standard curriculum, methods and/or equipment, as well as the emotional and social environment of the classroom and school, to obtain optimal benefit from their schooling. These are usually students with a physical disability, a learning difficulty, an intellectual disability or a sensory disability (that is, impairment of vision or hearing), or who have behaviour problems.

The emphasis on identification of support needs rather than disabilities has been embraced by most school systems in identifying those resources needed to support inclusion. This approach moves the emphasis away from identifying deficits in the child towards a statement of the responsibilities of the school or system. Mitchell (1995) outlines the range of levels of education support from Level 1 to Level 5. A student with *Level 1 Education Support* requires some adaptation of methods and materials that can be 'expected to be made by regular schools within existing resources' (Mitchell, 1995, p. 28). A student with *Level 5 Education Support* requires extensive modification of curriculum content, major adaptations to teaching methods and small group or individual teaching for the full day. Similar assessment systems have been developed in Victoria, Queensland and New South Wales (Foreman, Bourke, Mishra & Frost, 2001), and the best way of providing funding support remains a matter of debate (Wills & Cain, 2003). The common feature of the systems is that, whereas in the past, the question was 'What is wrong with this student?' the question has become 'What additional support does this student need to function well in a regular class?'. The use of resources to support inclusion is covered in more detail in Chapter 11.

Range and level of disabilities

Although this book is about teaching rather than about disabilities, it is useful for teachers to have some knowledge of the range and level of disabilities they are likely to see in their students. The usual ways in which disabilities are classified are as intellectual, physical or sensory disabilities, behavioural problems, or learning difficulties.

Intellectual disability

The term 'intellectual disability' refers to significant problems in reasoning and thinking. Former terms, no longer used in Australia and New Zealand and also becoming obsolete elsewhere, are *mental retardation, mental deficiency* and *subnormality*. Identification of intellectual disability is usually based on scores on an individual intelligence test. For school aged children this is frequently the Stanford Binet Intelligence Test (5th Edition) or the Wechsler Intelligence Scale for Children (WISC-III). The average intelligence quotient or IQ score is 100, with a score below 70 indicating a degree of intellectual disability. The level of disability is usually classified in the following way:

- 55–70 IQ: mild intellectual disability
- 30–54 IQ: moderate intellectual disability
- below 30 IQ: severe intellectual disability.

Some people also use the term 'profound' intellectual disability. However, this term has become less used in recent years because of the difficulty of assessing IQ levels below 30, and because of the negative implications of the term. The term multiple severe disabilities is sometimes used to refer to people who have a combination of severe physical, intellectual and/or sensory disabilities.

There have been many criticisms of the use of IQ tests to assess the educational needs of children. At best, they are a measure of performance on a particular test at a particular time. For example, it would obviously be silly to define someone's 'mathematical ability' for life on the basis of their performance in a maths test when they were six or eight years old, but this sort of determinism used to happen with intellectual ability. Most school systems now require additional measures of how a child is functioning, sometimes referred to as 'adaptive behaviour', before a child will be classified as having an intellectual disability, and functioning is reviewed on a regular basis.

Physical disability

The term 'physical disability' usually refers to a difficulty in mobility or movement, in particular, walking. However, it may also refer to a difficulty in the use of the hands or arms. Most physical disabilities are congenital, or present at birth. These may include disabilities such as spina bifida, which is obvious at the time of birth, and cerebral palsy, which is usually detected as the child's physical skill development starts to appear abnormal. Physical disability can also have a later onset, such as from a car accident or other form of injury either directly to the limbs, or indirectly to the brain. There are also some physical disabilities such as muscular dystrophy which, while present in the genetic structure from conception, are not apparent in the early years of life.

Some people wrongly assume that a severe physical disability is always associated with a severe intellectual disability. This error happens when the physical disability affects the person's speech. Some very intelligent people with cerebral palsy are treated as if they have an intellectual disability because their speech can be slow and distorted.

Although students with physical disabilities have typically been educated in separate special schools, they are often the easiest to include from the perspective of teaching and curriculum. For example, if the student does not have an intellectual disability, the teaching program may be exactly the same as that for every other child in the class, once their physical needs have been catered for.

Sensory disabilities

The term 'sensory disability' refers to impairment in vision or hearing, which in its most severe form is blindness or deafness. Students with mild vision problems have almost always been catered for in regular classes, sometimes with minor adjustments by teachers. Nowadays, students who have very low vision and even those who are blind, usually attend regular classes. They will require various types of support. This may include specialised lighting and equipment, and the assistance of a teacher's aide or a specialist itinerant teacher. Most school systems have procedures for providing materials in large print or Braille, and computers have hugely increased the access of blind students to a whole range of resources (see Chapter 11). Some people who meet the *legal* definition of blindness may still have some perception of light and colour and may even have quite good vision within a very restricted field.

Hearing impairments cover the range from a mild impairment that is not noticed by others to profound deafness, which can lead to impairments in the quality of speech, or may prevent the person from learning to speak at all. There has been considerable debate about whether deaf students should be taught through oral methods, or through the use of sign language, or through a combination of these methods. Usually students who are taught using sign language will be in a special class because of the need to have teachers who are expert in sign. Students who speak are more likely to be in regular classes, particularly as they move into the higher grades. However, there is often little other than mainstreaming in country areas, as sending children away to a residential special school is no longer an option.

Although many parents choose a regular class option for their child, profound deafness is a low-incidence disability, so the chance of having a signing student in a regular class is very small. If such a student were enrolled, the system would be expected to provide an interpreter, often in the form of a special teacher's aide who was proficient at sign. Some regular teachers have been very innovative and have learned to sign and have taught signing to the rest of the class as a second language. This greatly enhances communication between deaf students and their classmates, and could provide hearing students with a skill that would be useful if they met other people who signed.

Behaviour problems

There is some debate about the point at which 'unwanted' behaviour can be described as a behaviour problem. Indeed, there is debate about whether a behaviour problem is a disability. All children misbehave at some time. Often this is very situation-specific. That is, the child behaves well in some situations and poorly in others. Students who misbehave at school are very noticeable, because schools require a large amount of conformity and compliance. Chapter 6 contains a detailed discussion of problem behaviour and how to promote positive interactions in the classroom.

Learning difficulties

Some children find learning the basic skills of literacy and numeracy very difficult. This may be because they have an intellectual disability, which affects all areas of their learning. However, in other cases, students who function well in most areas will have difficulties in one area, often reading. This is sometimes referred to as a *specific* learning difficulty. The term learning *difficulty* is seen by many as preferable to learning *disability*, as it is usually assumed that a difficulty can be overcome with assistance, whereas a disability is less amenable to change. Chapter 7 provides a detailed account of problems in literacy and numeracy and Chapter 8 focuses on developing literacy and numeracy skills.

Language about disability

Usage and terminology

Language has a strong effect on the way we think about things. As a result, most people are careful about the use of discriminatory language. The most significant changes in language have occurred in relation to sexism. It has become widely accepted that schools have 'principals' rather than 'headmasters' and that politicians, judges and doctors are no longer always referred to as 'he'. Some people dismiss concerns about discrimination in the use of language as 'political correctness'. However, there are frequently important social justice issues at stake. Strong messages are conveyed in the language we use, and this is particularly the case in relation to people with a disability.

People who are different from the norm in any way frequently have these differences exaggerated by the way in which the language is used to describe them. In children, this sometimes leads to name-calling, but there are also ways in which we unintentionally use language that leads to inappropriate stereotyping, classifying or labelling of people with a disability.

A common problem is the use of language that suggests that all people with a disability are similar to each other. Expressions such as 'the disabled', 'the handicapped', 'epileptics', 'spastics', 'the blind' all imply that we are describing homogeneous groups. In reality, the people who are in the groups referred to by these words will be very different from each other.

The preferred use of language to avoid these problems follows the principle of *people first, disabilities second*. When we are referring to a disability, it is preferable to talk about *a person with a disability* or *a person who has a disability*, rather than a disabled person. This difference may seem inconsequential at first, but it is a significant one, and is very important to people with a disability. By saying 'people with ...' or 'people who ...', we convey the impression that the person's disability is just one of their many characteristics, just a part of their humanity. We still sometimes hear people say 'Sophie is a Down syndrome baby' or even 'Sophie is a Down syndrome'. In reality, Sophie is a baby with blue eyes, auburn hair, two brothers *and* Down syndrome. At first, it may seem awkward to always stick to this principle, but it becomes very natural after a while.

Another problem in the use of language about disability is the use of words that carry an implication of pity or suffering. We should not conclude that a person necessarily 'suffers' because of a disability. It is likely that Ruth Cromer has found that her Down syndrome has contributed to her career as a television actor (Cromer, 1999). It is unlikely that she would say that she *suffers* from Down syndrome or that she is a *victim* of Down syndrome. People who are deaf and use signing to communicate do not generally regard their deafness as a disability, but rather as an alternative culture, with its own language and communication system. They would be justifiably offended at the suggestion that they *suffer* from deafness.

Members of the deaf community do not usually like to be referred to as having a *hearing impairment*. They are generally proud of their deafness and are very happy with the terminology. That's why we have organisations with names such as the Adult Deaf Society. The deaf community distinguish between people who are deaf and communicate primarily through sign and those with a hearing impairment who communicate orally. Similarly, people who are blind (as opposed to those with some vision) do not usually refer to themselves as having a *vision impairment* and do not resist use of the word 'blind'. It is still preferable to use people first language such as 'John, who is blind, ...', 'My aunt, who is deaf, ...'.

People who have a disability usually find it offensive to hear their disability referred to gratuitously in conversation. Such references are not only hurtful but also stereotype certain characteristics in people with a disability. As professionals, teachers should avoid using expressions such as 'She'll have a fit when she finds out ...', 'Are you deaf or something?' 'He's as blind as a bat ...' or 'Blind Freddie could see that'. It is also offensive to use the word 'normal' as a way of comparing people with and without disabilities, for example, 'children with learning disabilities compared to normal children'. It is more accurate to say 'children with learning disabilities compared to children without learning disabilities'.

Another principle to observe in the use of language is that it is preferable not to refer to a person's disability unless the disability is relevant to the topic being discussed – it's a similar principle to referring to a person's religion or ethnic background. If the discussion is about cerebral palsy, it would be reasonable to say: 'Steady Eddie has cerebral palsy, and he's made a career as a stand-up comedian'. However, if the discussion is about comedians, then cerebral palsy is irrelevant and all that needs to be said, if that is what is believed, is that Steady Eddie does great stand-up comedy.

Some examples of appropriate and inappropriate use of language are given in Box 1.4.

Box 1.4
Use of language when talking about disability

Avoid expressions such as ...	*Use ...*
the disabled	people with a disability
the deaf	people who are deaf
spina bifida children	children with spina bifida
a haemophilia sufferer	a person with haemophilia
epileptics	people with epilepsy
the handicapped	people with a disability
his handicap is ...	his disability is ...
the cerebral palsied	people with cerebral palsy
a blind woman	a woman who is blind
a victim of blindness	a woman who is blind
mental retardation	intellectual disability
the retarded	people with intellectual disability
the intellectually disabled	people with intellectual disability
he is crippled	he has a physical disability
she has a visual impairment	she has a vision impairment
he suffers from Down syndrome	he has Down syndrome
she is wheelchair-bound	she uses a wheelchair
he had a fit when I told him	he was angry when I told him
my disabled sister	my sister
spina bifida people and normal people	people with and without spina bifida
blind Freddie could see that	anyone could see that

Impairments, disabilities and handicaps

The terms 'impairment', 'disability' and 'handicap' are sometimes used interchangeably, but there are important differences in meaning. The World Health Organization (1980) provided definitions of these terms, which have received wide acceptance. This is referred to as the International Classification of Impairments, Disabilities and Handicaps (ICIDH). The term *impairment* refers to an irregularity in the way organs or systems function. It usually refers to a medically-based or organic condition, for example, short-sightedness, heart problems, cerebral palsy, Down syndrome, spina bifida, deafness. A *disability* is the functional consequence of the impairment. For example, because of the impairment of spina bifida, a student may be unable to walk without the assistance of callipers and crutches. The *handicap* is the social or environmental consequence of the disability. The extent to which a person with a disability also has a handicap will depend on how well the environment caters for the disability. If a student who uses a wheelchair is unable to enter the school library, then that student will have a *handicap* in relation to library usage. If, on the other hand, the library and its equipment and contents are fully wheelchair-accessible, then the student does not have a handicap in using the library.

Sometimes an impairment can be treated in such a way that the person has no disability. A student who is short-sighted (impairment) may have excellent vision when wearing glasses, and therefore does not have a disability. Another student with a severe vision impairment may have the disability of very limited vision, even with glasses. Whether the person has a handicap will depend on whether the school can provide the specialised assessment, teaching and equipment the student needs. For students with vision impairments, this is achieved in most school systems through the provision of special equipment and itinerant teachers to work in regular classes.

These examples emphasise the fact that *handicaps* are often a function of the flexibility, resources and attitudes of the society in which the person is living. Schools are not often in a position where they can remove a student's impairment or prevent the disability. However, schools are perfectly placed to do something about the *handicapping* effects of a student's disability. A good position for a teacher to take would be to say: 'If I am aware that a child has an impairment that has led to a disability, I will try to prevent the disability from becoming a handicap.'

Of the three terms (impairment, disability and handicap), the most appropriate terminology to use about the students who are the subjects of this book is students with a *disability*. If the student has an impairment that does not have an associated disability, then the school need not be too concerned. However, if there is a disability, the school should be vitally concerned to ensure that the disability does not become a handicap.

Impairment, activity, participation and context: ICIDH-2

The World Health Organization has been working for some time on a revision of the *International Classification of Impairments, Disabilities and Handicaps*. This was initially known as *ICIDH-2: International Classification of Functioning, Disability and Health* and is now referred to as ICF. The revision involves a new conceptual framework. The previous WHO framework, although found useful by many practitioners, has been criticised for 'medicalising' disability (Pfeiffer, 1998). The new framework replaces the former terminology of impairments, disabilities and handicaps with the concepts of *impairment, activity, participation* and *context (environment)*. The aim is to be able to classify everything a person, or a body, can do. It does not classify people, or disabilities. Its purpose is to identify and describe the full range of human functions and any disturbance of those functions. While the ICF will help to reorder the way some people think about disabilities, it is unlikely, at least in the short term, to replace the current usage of the terms 'impairment', 'disability' and 'handicap' that are in such common use.

Gifted and talented students

This book does not deal with the issue of approaches to teaching students who are gifted or talented. There are several reasons for this. One is that the special class/regular class debate that has taken place about gifted students is quite unrelated to the special/regular debate about students with a disability. In the case of students with a disability, separate special schools and classes have, for many, been the only available option. In the case of gifted students, special 'opportunity' classes have been, for some, a desirable and sought-after alternative, which they have competed to enrol in. Gifted students have never been under threat of exclusion from regular schools because of their giftedness.

Another reason for not dealing with the needs of gifted and talented students in this book is that most school systems do not regard programs for these students as part of 'special education'. This is not to say that gifted and talented students do not have additional educational needs within the classroom. Indeed, an inclusive approach argues that the needs of all children should be catered for, regardless of their level of ability. For that reason, many of the concepts related to individualisation of instruction and catering for student needs will apply across the range of students, including those who are gifted and talented. However, readers seeking specialised information about teaching gifted and talented students are advised to consult the extensive literature and research on the topic.

Disability across the life-span

In the past, schooling was regarded as a period that covered the ages 5 to 15 years and dealt primarily with academic matters. Students with academic potential stayed on until 17 or 18 years. Some students with disabilities did not attend school at all. Even special schools focused on the traditional school years, and paid little attention to what happened to their students before they reached school age or when they finished with the education system. It was common knowledge and accepted practice that many students with a disability left school and spent the rest of their lives at home or, at best, in a sheltered workshop.

Gradually, this situation is changing. These changes have been brought about largely through parent initiatives, backed up by special education and disability research. Educational programs can start from the time the child is born, through early intervention programs, and may continue into adulthood.

Early intervention programs

Early educational intervention programs have been operating in Australia now for over 30 years. They have moved from the stage where there were a few university-based programs, attended by children whose parents were lucky enough to live nearby and to have access to information about them, to the situation where there is now some form of early intervention program available to most children with special needs.

In spite of the large research base in early intervention, methodological problems make it difficult to reach conclusions about outcomes. Certainly, there have been changes in our view of the educability of children with intellectual disability and of the capacity of all children to learn, if given the right level of support. However, we no longer try to evaluate early intervention in terms of its capacity to change the child's developmental pattern. Rather, early intervention is seen as part of an ongoing educational program that can begin in infancy and continue throughout life.

Teachers of school beginners need to be aware that the children in their class may be arriving with a significant educational history. The early childhood years are of major significance socially, cognitively and in all aspects of development. Issues related to early childhood programs are discussed in Chapter 3.

Post-school programs

School education is, for all children, both an important life activity and a preparation for future life. The importance of school in relation to future options is obvious for a student who is seeking a particular score to allow entry to a course of their choosing. However, schooling for students with a disability sometimes appears to lead nowhere, and there are examples of students who have finished 12 years of schooling having learned very few skills to help prepare them for their future environments.

Inclusive schools try to ensure that programs provided for students with a disability have relevance to their lives. A question that can be asked is: 'Is this subject matter of interest or importance to this student either now or in a likely post-school environment?' Because some children with a disability find it difficult to take what they have learned in school and apply it in a variety of settings, it is often necessary for teachers to consider what specific skills the student will need to be able to function well in a future environment. For example, it may be more important to teach skills in using a newspaper to access various types of information (such as understanding a TV guide) than to spend time teaching the student to appreciate a poem or short story. An able student can transfer skills learned through literature classes into a variety of other situations. A less proficient student may not be able to make these transfers unless they are specifically taught.

Another feature of modern educational and social systems is the provision of a wide range of post-school options. For people with a disability, these include training at technical colleges in both regular and specially designed programs, supported employment programs, and a diversity of community access and training programs. Most state systems now provide post-school options programs that extend educational and training support for students with a significant disability.

Chapter 12 provides information about transition from school learning to adult learning. The important factor is that education and training is seen as a life-span process. There is evidence, for example, that young adults with Down syndrome can benefit from a literacy program (Moni & Jobling, 2001), and there is no reason why this should not also apply to adults with other disabilities. People's needs will vary at different life stages and, for some people, education will be needed either continuously throughout life or at various times to help them achieve particular transitions and aspirations. This applies to people with and without disabilities, and life-long learning is a concept now embraced by many people. However, for people with a disability, some of the most important learning will take place after they have left formal schooling.

Myths and facts about disability

Generally held beliefs and myths

One of the potential benefits of inclusive schools is that they help to overcome many of the misunderstandings people have about disability, and can improve the attitudes of both teachers and students. There is often a fear of the unknown. Getting to know people who are different in some way can help to dispel myths and provide opportunities for a better understanding of differences. Most people can think of situations in which they were worried about how they might respond to a person or event, and later found their fear to be unjustified, or based on myths.

People who have a disability often report that the way they are treated is based on a misunderstanding of their disability. One of the strangest, yet most common, misunderstandings is the mistaken assumption that people who are blind or have a physical disability also have some form of hearing impairment. People who are blind or use wheelchairs often report that strangers use a much louder than normal voice when talking to them. Box 1.5 makes several statements about disability. It is suggested that these be discussed as a group activity. (The reasons why the statements are either true or false are given in the *Instructor's Manual*.)

Box 1.5

'Facts' about disability

True or false?

1 People who are blind have a strong motivation to learn to see and most people who are deaf would love to be able to hear.

2 People who are born blind have other innate abilities that compensate for their blindness.

3 Children with a disability are usually unaware that they are different in ability from other children.

4 If you meet a person with a disability, the best approach is to ignore it and pretend that it doesn't exist.

5 Cerebral palsy is a progressive disease, leading to increasing disability over time.

6 People who use sign language usually do so because they have a disability with their vocal chords.

7 People with a disability prefer to mix with their own kind.

8 Inability to speak, in a person with cerebral palsy, is an indication of intellectual disability.

9 Generally speaking, the greater the physical disability a person has the greater will be their intellectual disability.

10 You should avoid using the word 'see' when talking to a person who is blind.

11 Adolescents with intellectual disability are likely to be sexually promiscuous.

Myths about teaching students with a disability

One of the most widely-held myths about teaching students with a disability is the belief that a detailed knowledge of the child's disability is needed before a teaching program can be commenced. Teachers often say 'But I know nothing about Down syndrome' or 'I haven't studied cerebral palsy – how could I teach that child?'. Another myth is that teachers need special patience and special skills to be able to teach children with a disability. Research suggests that good general teaching skills and techniques are what is required to teach students with a disability. There is no need for special patience or unusual skills.

In the back of this book there is a bibliography of readings for teachers who would like to obtain information about various disabilities. However, detailed knowledge of specific disabilities is unlikely to provide much information about how to teach a particular student.

Children with a diagnosed disability may differ from each other as much as or more than they differ from children without a disability. Knowing that a child has Down syndrome tells us very little about how to teach that child. A 10-year-old child with Down syndrome may be a competent reader or may have few reading skills. What is required is a teaching program that is based on an analysis of that child's individual needs, just as it would be if the child did not have Down syndrome. In the future, there may be information about learning styles that will help us plan our teaching for students with particular disabilities (Fletcher & Buckley, 2002), but at present, knowledge of disabilities is not the most important requirement when preparing a teaching program.

This is not to say that we do not need to know about the particular student we are teaching. Parents are usually extremely knowledgeable about their own child, and can provide schools with a great deal of relevant information. They may be able to provide copies of written reports that will be helpful in planning. However, it is ultimately the student in the classroom who provides the most information. Later chapters in this book will suggest ways of approaching the planning and implementation of programs for children with special educational needs. These approaches are previewed in the section below.

Overview of approaches to teaching children with additional educational needs in regular classes

There are several ways in which education can be made relevant and useful to the lives of people with a disability. These include adapting the curriculum, planning for instruction and modifying classroom environments. These topics are treated in detail in Chapters 4 to 9.

Curriculum adaptations

There is no school system which mandates that all students should follow the same curriculum or achieve the same outcomes. If there is a standard, base curriculum or set of competencies, then the first preference would be for the student with additional educational needs to achieve similar outcomes to other students. However, this may not be possible and it may be necessary to adapt the curriculum to make it more relevant and more accessible to the student with a disability.

Sometimes students with a disability will be able to follow the regular curriculum with no modifications. For others, the student's degree of disability will be such that the standard curriculum has no relevance to the student's life. The teacher will then need to establish a different set of goals in consultation with the child's parents and other relevant personnel. It is important for teachers to recognise that, provided that a student is progressing in an appropriately planned curriculum, it does not matter if this is different from what is usually expected of the grade. For example, an 11-year-old student with moderate intellectual disability may not be reading at grade level, but may still be making excellent progress in relation to an appropriate curriculum centred on skills that are relevant to that child's life. Teachers need not say: 'How will I ever teach this child subtraction?' A more appropriate question is: 'How do I make the classroom experience relevant for this child?'

Planning for instruction

Planning is an important aspect of catering for the needs of students with a disability. The type of planning needed will vary with each student. Some students with a disability will have no difficulty progressing in the regular curriculum, and planning may revolve around the student's physical and mobility needs. For others it will be the content and methods of instruction that form the basis of planning.

An important first aspect of planning for many students with a disability is the need to individualise goals. A common procedure is to consider long-term goals, then further divide these into short-term goals, and perhaps further into teachable tasks. Chapter 5 goes into more detail about planning goals and strategies. Goals for students with a disability are usually set in consultation with the student's parents and, if possible, the student.

Partial participation

Partial participation is a concept that suggests that, although students may not be able to participate fully in a particular activity, ways can be found for them to partially participate. For example, many older students participate in ten-pin bowling as a recreational activity through use of a frame to hold and deliver the bowl. This is not the same as full participation, but still allows the person to participate in an enjoyable and age-appropriate activity. Students who have difficulty with the complexity of a full deck of cards may still be able to play cards with a deck from which some of the cards have been removed. For older students, this is preferable to playing with a children's deck.

The reason for partial participation should *not* be that no-one has bothered to make appropriate accommodations. For example, if the school library is only partly wheelchair-accessible, it is preferable for a student to partially participate in library activities rather than not to participate at all, particularly if the student has academic need to use the library.

However, what is required is for processes to be put into place to give the student full access to the library. This might involve providing a ramp or a chairlift or, if this is not possible, arranging for an aide or class peer to assist the student to locate and use inaccessible materials.

Modifying classroom environments

The environment of the classroom will have a significant effect on how handicapping a child's disability is. The classroom environment can be thought of under three headings: social, physical and academic.

The social environment of the classroom is often its most important aspect. In the ideal social environment, the student with a disability will be as valued as all other students. This will usually be a reflection of the attitude of the school principal, classroom teachers and other staff. The physical environment may need no modification or quite a lot. A child with a vision impairment may need special lighting and to be seated in a specific position. A student who uses a wheelchair may not be able to use a standard width aisle or sit at a standard height desk. An ideal academic environment is one in which the student experiences success and is learning skills that will be useful in a number of current and future environments. Several of the subsequent chapters in this book provide extensive information about modifying social, physical and academic environments.

Box 1.6 was written by Ya'el Frisch, a young woman with a significant physical disability who was educated very successfully in regular classes. Ya'el is now at university. At school, Ya'el's physical environment would have needed significant modification, but it is the social environment that had the major impact on her education and made a major contribution to her success.

Summary

Various concepts associated with the likely attendance of children with a disability in regular schools and classes were introduced in this chapter. A rationale for the study of disability by teachers of regular classes was provided, together with a brief overview of recent historical factors that have led to the likelihood that all teachers will, at some stage, be asked to provide programs for children with additional educational needs in their class. The chapter explained some of the principles underlying the inclusion process, including normalisation and the least restrictive environment. The range of possible special education settings was described, and specialised terminology, including mainstreaming, integration, and inclusion, was introduced and discussed. The chapter also defined terminology that will be used throughout the book and dealt with issues related to definition.

The chapter provided an overview of some myths surrounding disability and special education. These myths include the notion that extensive knowledge of disability is required to teach children with additional educational needs, and that children with a named disability are invariably more of a problem for the teacher than other children.

The chapter concluded with an outline of the book's approach to teaching children with additional educational needs in regular classes: that the essential skills for participating in the inclusion of students with a disability relate to programming, planning, and classroom management, rather than to the study of particular disabilities. These skills are treated in detail in later chapters of this book.

Box 1.6
Voices: Ya'el's story

I finished school last year and was always 'included' in mainstream schools, the only student with a physical disability. The word 'included' seems to assume that because I have cerebral palsy, I was lucky to be able to be in a class with everyone else. I *was* very lucky, but inclusion should be about right, not about luck. Being 'included' shaped my goals and expectations in life, and some of my peers learned to rethink stereotypes.

School should be about learning to respect difference. At the school I attended in senior years, I had friends of all cultures and religions, all of whom felt 'different' but valued. My disability was my 'difference', but my consciousness of it lessened because the school culture valued difference.

I did very well at school, but I strongly disagree with people who say that only 'smart' people with disabilities should be 'included'.

Students and teachers need to work with *all* students in the classroom. This is the way to understand that disability, and coping with it, is just a part of life. Everyone has obstacles; those faced by the student with a disability are just more visible.

I want to implore students and teachers to 'see the student, not the disability'. I've seen teachers and students 'freak out' on meeting me. They're well-meaning but nervous; they don't want to offend me, to do the 'wrong thing'. 'Relax guys' I want to say, 'you don't have to be an "expert" on me. Just treat me like anyone else and I'll explain how you can give me a hand.'

I may not be able to write, but I surprise everyone by being good at debating. I remember the rebuttal, and love the sense of empowerment debating gives me. I wouldn't have felt that empowerment if people had made assumptions about my abilities based on my disability.

It wasn't a completely rosy 13 years, but I think even those who weren't my friends have subconsciously become a little more broad-minded. My school was nervous about what was needed to include me. After I graduated, a deaf girl entered Year 7. Slowly, inclusion is becoming 'just the way it is'.

At the end of Year 12, I had to make a speech for assembly. I thought I'd talk about the importance of inclusion. I showed my speech to a friend, who asked in surprise 'Do you *only* see yourself as a person with a disability?'

She sees me as a person, a friend. Inclusion is working.

Ya'el Frisch

Discussion questions

1 What is the difference between inclusion, integration and mainstreaming? Give examples of each.

2 Give an example of a student who has been 'handicapped' by the school.

3 What changes have occurred in the lives of people with a disability as a result of the principle of normalisation?

4 Think about any contact you have had with people with a disability as classmates, students or in the community. How did you view those people? In retrospect, could you have got to know and understand them better?

5 Read Box 1.3. What actions are taken by the staff of Lambton Public School to provide an inclusive environment for students with a disability? What is the involvement of the principal and executive, school staff, parents, the education system, health care professionals and other advisers in planning for inclusion? (You don't have to limit your answer to what is in the box.)

Individual activities

1 Collect some newspaper articles or record a news report about people with a disability. How are those people depicted? What type of language is used in describing them? Does this stereotype or patronise them in any way? Are they infantilised or socially devalued?

2 Each of the following newspaper headlines/captions contains language that may be considered discriminatory by people with a disability. Write an alternative headline or caption:
   a LOCAL DEAF GIRL MISSING, BELIEVED DROWNED
   b CEREBRAL PALSY VICTIM COMPLETES CITY-TO-SURF
   c *Jane Brown, who is wheel-chair bound, demonstrates her driving skills on the Albert Park circuit*
   d EPILEPTIC MISSING IN KAKADU
   e BLIND TENOR ARRIVES IN AUSTRALIA
   f *Pictured is 35-year-old James, who suffers from Down syndrome, with fellow workers at McDonald's, Ms Jenny Brown and Mr Michael Smith*
   g NEW LAW FOR THE DISABLED
   h HOME FOR THE RETARDED TO CLOSE

3 Rewrite the following statements so that they are expressed in a better way:
   a I taught a Down's boy last year.
   b My sister's a spastic.
   c My brother's friend is a victim of spina bifida.
   d Her uncle is deaf and dumb.
   e Don't tell your mum – she'll have a fit!
   f He's crippled as a result of a car accident.

Group activities

1   Read Leanne and Emilio's story in Box 1.1. As a group, consider the extent to which their hopes for their daughter reflect socially valued roles and experiences. How might their daughter's life be enriched by attending the same school as her sister?

2   As a group, come to a conclusion about whether each of the statements in Box 1.5 is true or false, and provide reasons why.

3   As a group, discuss the following scenarios. Use the sample grid (see below) to prepare answers to the questions about each scenario.

Scenario 1

Daniel is a 10-year-old boy with a moderate to severe intellectual disability. He has been attending a special school some distance from the town in which he lives, but hopes to commence at the local school next year. The school he will attend is a large country primary school, with an enrolment of 240 children in 10 classes.

Scenario 2

Penny is 6, and her family has recently moved from interstate. She has severe, bilateral hearing loss and has aids for both ears. Her parents are hearing. Penny communicates through oral methods (residual hearing/lip reading/speech). She has attended a regular preschool since she was 3, with specialised support from an Institute for Deaf and Blind Children. Her speech and language are as expected for a student with a severe hearing impairment, with some problems with articulation and some language delay in receptive and expressive areas. She will enrol in a regular class.

Scenario 3

Bradley is re-commencing Year 9 after having nearly a year off school following a car accident which left him with quadriplegia. He has some use of his hands and uses an electric wheelchair for mobility. He writes using a laptop computer.

For each of these scenarios, to ensure that the students get maximum benefit from their schooling, what adjustments might need to be made to:
a   attitudes/knowledge of staff?
b   attitudes of students?
c   physical characteristics of the school?
d   timetable?
e   curriculum?
f   available resources and equipment?
g   teaching/learning arrangements and other aspects of school organisation?

Use the following pro forma to consider the adjustments that could be made to assist these students.

Area	What needs to be done?	Who should be involved?	What resources (people or material) can be used to assist?
Staff attitudes/knowledge			
Student attitudes			
Physical characteristics of school			
Timetable			
Curriculum			
Available resources and equipment			
Teaching/learning arrangements			

References

Bailey, J. & du Plessis, D. (1998). An investigation of school principals' attitudes towards inclusion. *Australasian Journal of Special Education, 22*, 12–29.

Bank-Mikkelsen, N. E. (1969). *Normalization: Letting the Mentally Retarded Obtain an Existence as Close to Normal as Possible.* Washington, DC: President's Committee on Mental Retardation.

Brown, R. (1995). *Dynamics of Inclusion: Emotions and Practices.* Paper presented at the 19th Annual Conference, Australian Association of Special Education, Darwin, July.

Center, Y. & Ward, J. (1987). Teachers' attitudes towards the integration of disabled children into regular schools. *Exceptional Child, 34*, 41–56.

Center, Y., Ward, J., Parmenter, T. & Nash, R. (1985). Principals' attitudes toward the integration of disabled children into regular schools. *Exceptional Child, 32*, 149–61.

Cromer, R. (1999). *It's My Way, It's My Life*. Keynote Address, 35th Annual Conference, Australian Association for the Study of Intellectual Disability, Sydney, September/October.

Dempsey, I. & Foreman, P. (1995). Trends and influences in the integration of students with disabilities in Australia. *Australasian Journal of Special Education, 19*(2), 47–53.

Dempsey, I. & Foreman, P. (1997). Trends in the educational placement of students with disabilities in New South Wales. *International Journal of Disability, Development and Education, 44*, 207–16.

Dempsey, I., Foreman, P. J. & Jenkinson, J. (2002). Educational enrolment of students with a disability in New South Wales and Victoria. *International Journal of Disability, Development and Education, 49*, 31–6.

Fletcher, H. & Buckley, S. (2002). Phonological awareness in children with Down syndrome. *Down Syndrome Research and Practice, 8*, 11–18.

Foreman, P. J. & Arthur, M. (2003). *A Comparison of the Experiences of Students with the Most Severe and Multiple Disabilities in Special and Regular Schools, Using Behaviour State Assessment*. Paper presented at the International Conference on Inclusive Education, Hong Kong Institute of Education, December.

Foreman, P., Bourke, S., Mishra, G. & Frost, R. (2001). Assessing the support needs of children with a disability in regular classes. *International Journal of Disability, Development and Education, 48*, 239–52.

*Fuchs, D. & Fuchs, L. S. (1994). Inclusive schools movement and the radicalization of special education reform. *Exceptional Children, 60*, 294–309.

Giorcelli, L. (1995). An impulse to soar: Sanitisation, silencing and special education. Des English Memorial Lecture. In *Forging Links*, Keynote Papers from the 19th Annual Conference, Australian Association of Special Education, Darwin, July.

Jenkinson, J. C. (1997). *Mainstream or Special? Educating Students With Disabilities*. London: Routledge.

*McGregor, G. & Vogelsberg, R. T. (1998). *Inclusive Schooling Practices: Pedagogical and Research Foundations*. Baltimore: Paul H. Brookes.

McRae, D. (1996). *The Integration/Inclusion Feasibility Study*. Sydney: NSW Department of Education.

*Mitchell, D. (1995). New Zealand special education: Policies and systems. In D. Fraser, R. Moltzen & K. Ryba (Eds), *Learners with Special Needs in Aotearoa/New Zealand*. Palmerston North: Dunmore Press.

Moni, K. & Jobling, A. (2001). Reading-related literacy learning of young adults with Down syndrome: Findings from a three year teaching and research program. *International Journal of Disability, Development and Education, 48*, 377–94.

Nirje, B. (1970). The normalization principle: Implications and comments. *British Journal of Mental Subnormality, 16*, 62–70.

Nirje, B. (1985). The basis and logic of the normalization principle. *Australia and New Zealand Journal of Developmental Disabilities, 11*, 65–8.

Pfeiffer, D. (1998). The ICIDH and the need for its revision. *Disability and Society, 13*, 503–23.

Rafferty, Y., Piscitelli, V. & Boettcher, C. (2003). The impact of inclusion on language development and social competence among preschoolers with disabilities. *Exceptional Children, 69*(4), 467–79.

UNESCO, (1994). *Salamanca Statement and Framework for Action on Special Educational Needs.* Paris: United Nations.

Vinson, T. (2002). *Inquiry Into the Provision of Public Education in New South Wales: Final Report.* Sydney: New South Wales Teachers Federation. Online at http://www.pub-ed-inquiry.org/ reports/final_reports/

Wills, D. & Cain, P. (2003). Conceptualising a coherent funding model to support school communities to build inclusive capacities. *Interaction, 16,* 35–7.

Wilton, K. (1994). Special education policy for learners with mild intellectual disability in New Zealand: Problems and issues. *International Journal of Disability, Development and Education, 41,* 143–58.

Wilton, K. (1998). Special education policy for children with moderate learning or behavioural difficulties in New Zealand: Does 'inclusion' really mean 'exclusion'? *Australasian Journal of Special Education, 22,* 5–11.

Wolfensberger, W. (1972). *The Principle of Normalization in Human Services.* Toronto: National Institute on Mental Retardation.

Wolfensberger, W. (1980). A brief overview of the principle of normalization. In R. J. Flynn & K. E. Nitsch (Eds), *Normalization, Social Integration, and Community Services* (pp. 7–30). Baltimore: University Park Press.

Wolfensberger, W. (1995). An 'if this, then that' formulation of decisions related to social role valorization as a better way of interpreting it to people. *Mental Retardation, 33,* 163–9.

World Health Organization. (1980). *International Classification of Impairments, Disabilities and Handicaps.* Geneva: Author.

------

*Recommended reading for this chapter

Chapter 2

Legislation, policies and inclusive practices

Ian Dempsey

This chapter aims to:

- describe relevant legislation associated with the inclusion of students with special needs
- describe the important features of educational policies for students with special needs in the states and territories in Australia and in New Zealand
- discuss the ways in which this legislation and policy impacts on educational services for students with special needs.

Principles, policies and practice

At both the private and the professional level, our day-to-day behaviour is a reflection of our beliefs, our obligation to follow the law, and the requirements associated with organisations such as the workplace and educational institutions. For example, in the situation of a university teacher education program, our relations with staff and other students are 'coloured' by our personality and by our personal beliefs, they are constrained by the limits of legal behaviour, and they are influenced by university policies designed to prevent behaviour such as plagiarism and cheating and to encourage an enjoyable learning experience. In the situation of a school environment, our behaviour is similarly influenced by personal beliefs (for example, what we think is important for students to learn and how they should learn it), by legislation (for example, child protection laws), and by organisational policy (for example, the need to be accountable to head teachers and to principals).

An awareness of the relationships between these principles, laws, policies and practices can assist us in understanding how our behaviour, and the behaviour of others, comes about. Such an understanding is important in the context of this book. One of the main aims of this book is to provide practical advice about how to effectively support students with a disability in the regular classroom. Consequently, supporting these students (the practice), will be influenced by our attitudes and beliefs (the principles), and by laws and organisational guidelines (the legislation and policies). In turn, how well we do at the practice will also influence future changes in the principles, legislation and policies. The relationship between these variables is shown in Figure 2.1.

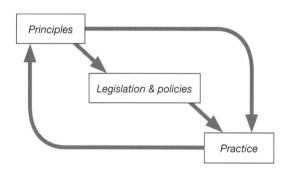

Figure 2.1 The relationship between principles, legislation and policies, and practice

Let's begin to explore this relationship by focusing on principles and practice. As explained above, our personal beliefs and philosophies can be expressed as principles that directly or indirectly influence practice. Chapter 1 introduced and discussed several of these principles as they are relevant to students with a disability. Examples of these principles are normalisation, 'people first', least restrictive environment, all children can learn, and partial participation. A way in which the principle of least restrictive environment could be implemented in schools is that students with a social or behaviour problem who require assistance in anger management would be withdrawn from the regular classroom only for as long as was required to receive instruction in this area from a specialist teacher. In other words, their withdrawal from the regular classroom is the minimum required, because their long-term segregation, among other things, may negatively impact on their self-esteem and their ability to keep up with the work in the classroom. In this case, the principle (least restrictive environment) directly impacts on classroom practice.

In other cases, the principle may impact first on laws or policies, which, in turn, may influence practice. To illustrate this, bear in mind that the core of our present belief system about the education of students with a disability is reflected in the ideas of human rights, equity and social justice. The principle, 'social justice', is difficult to define because the term can mean different things in different contexts. For most educators, however, social justice means the elimination of injustice to students with a disability, and to other disadvantaged groups of students, by ensuring equity in access to education for these groups. Unfortunately, such injustice in educational settings may be more common than we wish to acknowledge. For example, a 2002 inquiry into the education of students with a disability in Australia concluded that:

> The first concern is that children with a disability and their parents are not being given the support they need in the education systems ... Social justice demands that students with disabilities should have equal access to education. Commonwealth, state and territory anti-discrimination legislation support this fundamental principle, yet there still appear to be marked disparities in the quality of educational opportunities offered to students with disabilities ...
>
> (Employment, Workplace Relations and Education References Committee, 2002, p. xix)

This view illustrates the manner in which principles (for example, social justice), directly influence legislation (that is, anti-discrimination legislation), which in turn is designed to influence practice (that is, quality education for students with a disability). However, as the quotation demonstrates, a change in practice is not always guaranteed, despite clear principles, legislation and policy.

The education of students with a disability is based on a number of beliefs and principles. These beliefs and principles are responsible for the way in which western society presently supports these students. As the last chapter demonstrated, our views of disability and difference have changed considerably in the past century. Consequently, our present views of disability should not be seen as static. These views represent our society's current interpretation of disability and special needs, and these views may change in the future. Regardless, these principles have been responsible for the development of legislation that influences school services for students with a disability. This legislation is now discussed.

International legislation and policy

The United Nations Educational, Scientific and Cultural Organisation (UNESCO) has stated that regular schools with an inclusive orientation are the most effective means by which discriminatory attitudes towards students with a disability may be combated. UNESCO has called on all governments to adopt an inclusive education policy by enrolling all students in regular schools (UNESCO, 1994).

The Special Needs Mission Statement of UNESCO (1998) states that:

> Inclusion and participation are essential to human dignity and to the enjoyment and exercise of human rights. Inclusive education has evolved as a movement to challenge exclusionary policies and practices and has gained ground over the past decade to become a favoured adopted approach in addressing the learning needs of all students in regular schools and classrooms.

All children should learn together wherever possible regardless of difficulties, disabilities or differences.

More recently, a UNESCO (2001) World Education Forum argued that:

> The need to think inclusively in education, as in other areas of society, has never been more important. Inclusive thinking is a reminder that education must be as concerned with the sustenance of communities as with personal achievement and national economic performance. Thinking inclusively about education allows us to recognise the undermining effects on social cohesion and the consequent economic costs of a narrow technical focus in education, where the sole concern is with 'what works' to increase average school attainment, narrowly conceived in terms of academic results.
>
> (UNESCO, 2001, p. 46)

These consistent statements by a major agency of the United Nations demonstrate that inclusion is much more than an isolated western phenomenon. Inclusion is supported by all members of the United Nations and it is relevant to the 113 million officially recorded children of school age who are excluded from regular schools and classes, and the many millions more who either drop out or whose progression through the school system is impeded (UNESCO, 2001).

Such international policy statements are reflected in the legislation and policy of a wide variety of individual countries. Legislation and policy in the United States and Great Britain is included in this chapter (see below), because it has attracted international attention and because it has had some impact on policy development in other countries, including Australia. However, it would be incorrect to assume that educational policies about students with special educational needs are identical in other countries. As the ensuing sections of this chapter show, there are differences in legislation and policy across countries, and across states and districts within countries.

United States

In the United States, support for an inclusive approach has a relatively long history that is based on a comprehensive and detailed piece of legislation, Public Law 94–142, the *Education for All Handicapped Children Act 1975*. Its name changed to the *Individuals with Disabilities Education Act* (IDEA) in 1990, was modified in 1997, and was further amended in 2004. These Acts ensure that an educational service is provided to all students, regardless of the nature of their disability or learning needs, that the characteristics of this education are relatively consistent across all states, and that students with a disability are included in national assessments. In the USA, disability includes students with learning disabilities and behaviour problems, who are typically not included in disability categories in Australian schools (Office of Special Education Programs, 2003).

The USA Acts entitle parents to be involved in the educational process from initial assessment to annual reviews of the student's placement. The Acts also attempt to address the quality of educational programs delivered to students by specifying that an individualised education program (IEP) must be provided for all students with special needs. This IEP comprises information about the student's educational needs and educational goals and objectives, specifies the educational and other services (for example, physical therapy services), that will be provided to the student, and defines how the educational goals and objectives will be evaluated. One outcome of this legislation is that the proportion of students with a disability who are both educated in regular schools, and in regular classes in these schools, has increased considerably (US Department of Education, 2001).

In the area of early childhood special education, PL 99–457 has had a major impact on educational services to infants with a disability. An important feature of this Act is the use of an individualised family support plan to determine the family's needs, strengths and resources. This feature is an example of a movement away from child-centred support, to family-centred support for young children with a disability. The community-based companion to these examples of legislation is the *Americans with Disabilities Act* (PL 101–476). It extends civil rights to the community by giving access for people with a disability to such services as employment, transport and communications.

Great Britain

There have been several pieces of legislation in Great Britain that have addressed the provision of educational services to students with a disability. This legislation is less prescriptive than its American counterpart, and it has allowed educational authorities to interpret the legislation in a variety of ways (Carpenter, 1997).

The *Warnock Report* (1978) and the subsequent *Education Act* in 1981 were primarily responsible for raising the profile of special education in Great Britain in recent decades. One outcome of the Act was a change in the language used to describe students with special needs and a move away from 'deficit' explanations of student behaviour. For example, students who were previously referred to as 'remedial' or 'educationally subnormal', are now described in Britain as 'children with learning difficulties'.

More recently, the 1988 *Education Reform Act* and a 1993 amendment to the *Education Act* recognised, among other things, the need to provide access to the national curriculum for all students. Exemption from the national curriculum for students with a disability is reviewed every six months in an attempt to maintain access to the regular curriculum for as many students as possible. The 1993 legislation specified that Local Educational Authorities have a duty to include a child with a disability in a regular school, so long as the child's needs are being adequately met, resources are used efficiently, and parents are in agreement. The Act also extended parents' rights to participate in the educational planning for their son or daughter with special needs.

In 2001, the *Special Educational Needs and Disability Act* extended the responsibility of schools by specifying that children '… must be educated in a mainstream school unless that is incompatible with the wishes of his parent, or the provision of efficient education for other children' (Her Majesty's Stationery Office, 2001). The proportion of students enrolled in English special schools decreased slightly from 1.39 per cent in 1997, to 1.32 per cent in 2001 (Centre for Studies on Inclusive Education, 2003). However, there were considerable variations in the extent of inclusion across the local education authorities.

At the wider community level, the *Disability Discrimination Act 1995* originally addressed discrimination in employment, and gaining access to goods, facilities and services. However, a 2002 amendment to the Act requires schools not to treat students with a disability less favourably than other students, and to make reasonable adjustments to avoid disadvantaging these students (Riddell, 2003).

Legislation in Australia and New Zealand

Many states in Australia have legislation that indirectly relates to the education of students with learning problems. For example, there is the *Anti-Discrimination Act 1982* (NSW), the *Disability Services Act 1993* (WA), and the *Anti-Discrimination Act 1991* (Qld). In addition, the *Disability Discrimination Act 1992* (DDA) (Australian Government Publishing Service, 2003) is a piece of federal legislation that indirectly covers the area of education and effectively ensures that educational services are provided to students with a disability. In New Zealand, both the *Education Act 1989* and the *Human Rights Act 1994* also guarantee an education to students with disabilities. However, none of this legislation mandates, to the extent of the United States, the way in which this education should be provided.

There are a number of features of the Australian DDA that are unique and that have impacted, and continue to have the potential to impact significantly, on school students. The first of these features is that the DDA defines disability as including a range of more traditional impairments (for example, physical, intellectual, psychiatric and sensory), as well as some impairments that are typically not recognised as disabilities in educational settings in Australia (for example, learning disabilities, behaviour problems, attention deficit hyperactivity disorder and physical disfigurement). In addition, the DDA recognises disabilities that individuals may presently experience, may have had in the past, or may have in the future. Because the original legislation addressed enrolment, and not educational services in schools, there has been little incentive for school systems to broaden their definitions of disability beyond the traditional, medically-based categories. Indeed, for many education departments there has been a powerful disincentive to broaden their definition of disability. It has been a concern that if the definition is expanded then it may place excessive resource demands on their budgets in meeting the needs of a perceived additional group of students. However, these education systems already provide a range of extensive supports to such students as those experiencing difficulties with their reading and social skills.

A second important feature of the DDA is that it provides the opportunity to develop education standards to assist schools in understanding what their responsibilities are in avoiding discrimination against students with a disability. The development of these standards has had a 'chequered' history. At the time of writing, although standards to support the DDA have been developed in the area of public transport, it has taken from 1996 until 2002 for a second set of draft education standards to be released (Human Rights and Equal Opportunity Commission, 2003). The education standards address enrolment, participation, curriculum, student support services, and elimination of harassment and victimisation. An extract from these draft standards, as they relate to participation, appears in Box 2.1. Despite the delay in ratifying the education standards, they have the potential to significantly influence schools' responses to disability. As discussed in the paragraph above, the standards will impel schools to embrace a wider definition of disability than they may currently use. In addition, schools will now be legally obliged to provide a minimum level of educational support to students with special needs (Nelson, 2003). Just how schools interpret this level of service will, no doubt, be open to interpretation and perhaps subject to legal challenge.

Box 2.1

Extract from Draft Australian Disability Standards for Education 2003

Participation standards

1. The education provider must take reasonable steps to ensure that the student is able to participate in the programs provided by the educational institution, and use the facilities and services provided by it, on the same basis as students without disabilities and without experiencing discrimination.

2. The provider must:

   a. consult the student, or an associate of the student, about the impact of the student's disability on their ability to participate in the programs for which the student is enrolled and use the facilities or services provided by the provider; and

   b. in the light of the consultation, decide whether an adjustment is necessary to ensure that the student has substantive equality with students without disabilities in participating in those programs and using those facilities or services; and

   c. if:
      - an adjustment is necessary to achieve the aim mentioned in paragraph (b); and
      - a reasonable adjustment can be identified in relation to that aim

      make a reasonable adjustment for the student in accordance with Part 3.

3. The provider must repeat the process set out in subsection (2) as necessary to allow for the changing needs of the student over time.

>

Box 2.1 continued

Measures for compliance with standards

Measures that the provider may implement to enable the student to participate in the course or program for which the student is enrolled and use the facilities provided by it on the same basis as students without disabilities, include ensuring that:

a   the course or program activities are sufficiently flexible for the student to be able to participate in them; and

b   course or program requirements are reviewed, in the light of information provided by the student, or an associate of the student, to include activities in which the student is able to participate; and

c   adjustments and appropriate programs necessary to enable participation by the student are negotiated, agreed and implemented; and

d   additional support is provided to the student where necessary, to assist him or her to achieve intended learning outcomes; and

- where a course or program necessarily includes an activity in which the student cannot participate, the student is offered an activity that constitutes a reasonable substitute within the context of the overall aims of the course or program; and

- any activities that are not conducted in classrooms, and associated extracurricular activities or activities that are part of the broader educational program are designed to include the student.

Sourced from Human Rights and Equal Opportunity Commission, 2003

That the legislation in Australia and New Zealand has not been as prescriptive as USA legislation about the nature of special educational services can be seen as both a weakness and a strength in meeting the educational needs of students. Supporters of stronger legislation say that laws guarantee a minimum standard and that they may create the circumstances by which attitudes to students with a disability in the general and teaching communities may change in a positive direction. Those critical of legislation point out that there is a difference between 'following the letter of the law', and acting in the best interests of students and their families. They contend that litigation can be a counterproductive process and that policymakers and bureaucrats, with the assistance of anti-discrimination legislation, are best placed to implement the prevailing community perspective. Whatever the view taken on legislation, the reliance in Australia and New Zealand on educational policy to ensure educational services for students with a disability is a reflection of both countries' cultural standards and historical precedent.

Policy in Australia and New Zealand

At a national level in Australia, the Commonwealth government exerts some influence over educational policies in the states and territories through agreements it has reached with them, as well as providing targeted funding for students with additional needs. The Commonwealth government's priorities for schooling are aimed at '… ensuring that all students are allowed to realise their full potential, so that they leave school with the knowledge, skills and attitudes appropriate to their post-school destinations, and they have a sound foundation for undertaking further education and training, participating successfully in the workforce, and contributing to and benefiting from Australian society' (Commonwealth Department of Education, Science and Training, 2002, p. vi).

At the time of writing, the most recent national agreement about schooling in Australia is the Adelaide Declaration on National Goals for Schooling in the Twenty-First Century (Ministerial Council on Education, Employment, Training and Youth Affairs, 2002). The Declaration followed a meeting of state, territory and Commonwealth ministers of education in 1999. One of the goals agreed at the meeting (Goal 3.1), relates specifically to students with a disability. It states that 'schooling should be socially just, so that students' outcomes from schooling are free from the effects of negative forms of discrimination based on sex, language, culture and ethnicity, religion or disability; and of differences arising from students' socio-economic background or geographic location'.

Although all Australian states and territories provide educational services for students with special needs, these services are provided at the discretion of these states and territories. There is some diversity in their special education policy statements and this diversity illustrates the extent to which arguments for inclusive education may have influenced service provision in these states and territories (Dempsey, Foreman & Jenkinson, 2002; Employment, Workplace Relations and Education References Committee, 2002).

All the special education policies of the states and territories in Australia recognise the ability of every student to learn, they recognise the need to focus on students' strengths and needs, not just on their weaknesses, and they recognise that instruction must be individualised to the extent necessary for the educational experience to be positive for the student. There is also agreement that students with a disability should be placed in the least restrictive environment. Many states and territories interpret 'least restrictive environment' as the regular classroom, at least as a first option for the initial school placement of students with a disability.

In Tasmanian government schools, regular classroom placement has had a relatively long history where, 'placement of students with disabilities in regular schools is the preferred educational option … To the fullest extent possible, students with disabilities should be educated in the company of their age peers while also being provided with curriculum and support that effectively meet their needs' (Department of Education Tasmania, 1997). In a similar vein, the Department of Education Victoria (2003) states that 'a key component of quality education is the provision of inclusive education so that students with special education needs are able to participate fully in educational programs provided by schools'.

Many of the educational jurisdiction's policies make strong statements about equity. The 'Values and Purposes Statement' from the Department of Education Tasmania (2000), recognises equity as a core value for all school students. Equity is defined as including 'developing tolerance and a commitment to social justice, acknowledging diversity, respecting difference and encouraging distinctiveness'. In New Zealand, the Ministry of Education's (2003) Education Priorities state that '… having special needs or a disability are not reasons why someone should fail in education or have fewer learning opportunities'.

One of the common features of special education policy in Australia is the desire for meaningful involvement from parents. In South Australia, for example, 'educators will negotiate goals with students and families as much as practicable and bring to the negotiation their professional expertise as well as their knowledge of a particular student's current level of development. Goals should be set so as to provide a challenge to students to stretch themselves beyond their current level of skills but not so far ahead as to be daunting or impossible to achieve within a reasonable time frame' (Department of Education, Training and Employment, South Australia, 2002). The importance of being aware of parents' perspectives is illustrated by the description of Jacob's and Alex's inclusion in Boxes 2.2 and 2.3.

Box 2.2
Voices: Jacob's story

My son Jacob is 10 years old; he is in Year 5 at the local school; he has a great bunch of friends who like to hang out with him; he has interesting things to do – recently performing in the *StarStruck* concert. At school expectations are high and Jacob is progressing well. Jacob's life is pretty good and in many ways is very typical of any 10-year-old.

Jacob also has disability – he has severe cerebral palsy and a hearing impairment. His disability impacts significantly on his development and Jacob needs a high level of support in every aspect of daily life. He uses a wheelchair and he is not able to speak, but communicates using signs, gesture, vocal sounds, picture symbols and a voice device.

Traditionally kids with disability have been placed in separate units and separate schools. We, like many parents of kids with a disability, have defied this tradition and have chosen an inclusive education for Jacob. For our family *inclusion* is about the kind of life we want for Jacob.

When Jacob was very young, I was so fearful for his future because his future looked bleak. We have all grown up in a society that excludes people with disability – no one had to tell me about special schools, special units, sheltered workshops, or group homes. I had seen people with a disability on community access bussed in like tourists and bussed out again, and I already knew institutions were terrible places. And this was the existence prescribed for my son – life long segregation, and exclusion. But this was not the life we wanted for Jacob.

Our dream or vision for Jacob's future is that he should enjoy a life that is typical for most people. I want Jacob to have friends and real relationships, to be part of the community and to be accepted and treated with respect. I want Jacob to have an interesting learning environment where expectations are high but realistic. And, of course, I want Jacob to be happy, healthy and safe. This is not unusual. Most parents share a similar vision for their child, it's just when your child has a disability that this vision does not happen automatically.

With this vision for Jacob, naturally we chose inclusive education and sought to enrol him in the local school. However, choosing an inclusive education and actually achieving it … let's say the process was by no means easy. While the rhetoric was that I had a choice in educational setting, the reality was that I couldn't implement my choice (Jacob's enrolment was rejected by two schools). Always, I was directed to send Jacob to special school. And eventually I relented – literally I did what I was told – and placed Jacob in a special school.

Jacob was at special school for one year. As a frequent visitor to the special school I saw Jacob's abilities significantly underestimated. All the children in the class spent most of their time unoccupied as they waited for *their turn* with the teacher. The peer support that is natural to every regular class was absent, because all the children at the special school needed support, so they all were totally dependent on teachers as communication partners and to support all their learning and play. For example, in the regular class Jacob has 30 kids who are potential communication partners. There are kids to talk to, kids to support him, and he supports

>

Box 2.2 continued

their learning too. But this cannot happen in special classes and schools.

Jacob was bored at special school. He became grumpy and his behaviour deteriorated. There were other issues as well, such as the time spent travelling to and from school (some children on Jacob's bus spent two hours travelling to school, and two hours travelling home). It was just blatantly obvious that there was no educational or social advantage in a special school education for Jacob. These criticisms, however, are not levelled at this special school specifically, but rather, are issues inherent in all segregated education settings.

After a year at special school Jacob transferred to a regular class. Finally my tenacity had paid off and I found a school in our area where Jacob was welcomed. Since then Jacob has had five very successful years at school. There has never been any major problem and any issues that arise are resolved easily. Jacob's enrolment is never questioned, he is seen as a valued member of the school. Once he joined the regular class his behaviour improved (like magic), he was happier, he showed initiative.

Jacob is an enthusiastic learner and enjoys the friendship with the kids.

Socially school has always been great, often people are surprised that disability is not a barrier to friendship. Children enjoy Jacob's friendship, they look out for him and problem solve to find ways for Jacob to participate and be involved in what they are doing. Kids see his strengths and skills and I feel confident things are going well for Jacob at school because if they weren't I would hear about it from the other students. Parents have commented on the gifts Jacob brings to the school and how their child benefits from Jacob's inclusion.

Despite all the good things about Jacob's inclusion at school, it is not always perfect. Inclusion in the classroom fluctuates dramatically year to year depending on the teacher. Some teachers have struggled with the idea of inclusion and have left curriculum adaptation and modification entirely to the teacher's aide. But other teachers have embraced Jacob as a class member and strive to include him in all aspects of the class and school life.

Jacob's mother

Box 2.3
Voices: Alex's story

A special school or special class was never even considered for Alex. His life, we believe, should involve the same kinds of experiences, opportunities, places and people as any other kid's life. He should be known and valued for his own personal qualities, not defined by his deficits. So he has always been in a regular class, and is now in Year 7 at high school.

The level and nature of his disabilities are such that most people would assume he could not participate in an ordinary class environment. There is always an idea in people's minds that being in an ordinary classroom means 'keeping

up' with the grade level. But this idea of 'keeping up' is totally out of the question for Alex. His multiple disabilities include a severe intellectual disability and autism. His goals are completely different from anyone else's in his class. This does not translate in practice to a separate individualised program. He has high support needs, but he doesn't work one-on-one with an aide very often, or in a separate corner or resource room. This would defeat the purpose of his being in the ordinary class at all.

For the vast majority of his time, Alex works with classmates in pairs or groups where he

>

Box 2.3 continued

participates in a class exercise, but with different goals or contributions from the other students. Others may be working together to make a mind-map that summarises a topic. Alex may be working on making eye contact with others in the group, attempting to repeat or approximate words, or working on a range of other personalised goals. So, he can be an active participant in the lesson, while also having opportunities to form relationships with other kids and for them to get to see who he really is.

There are implications in this approach for the role of the teachers and teachers' aides. Alex's teachers do not need to write some lengthy individualised program each week for him, but to look at planning the class lesson in a way that provides a place and a contribution for Alex. The aide may help to set up a group exercise, may perhaps 'coach' some peers about how to interact with Alex or sometimes provide hands-on help, but on many occasions also, she will 'fade out' once kids are providing natural support to Alex and assist other groups, or do some other form of preparation for the teacher. Some teachers and aides do this better than others.

As a family we could get caught up in judging the success of Alex's schooling by how well particular teachers manage, or by the good and bad days Alex may have. We definitely have some problems to solve along the way, like how to communicate with 10 teachers at high school instead of just one. But the small day-to-day details are not the 'bottom line' for us. Alex makes progress on his goals. He is very popular at school and friends see him as someone worth knowing. He is known in his community by his name, not as some kid with a disability. We think these are the bottom line issues.

Alex's mother

Another important feature of special education policies in Australia and New Zealand is the provision of specialist staff to assist regular class teachers. In Queensland, an example of specialist support staff are Advisory Visiting Teachers (AVT) whose main role '… is to support school staff in enabling students with disabilities to access and participate in the curriculum' (Education Queensland, 2003a). This model of support can provide professional development activities for staff, give advice on developing teaching programs, assist in implementing programs and in evaluating their success, providing specific information on particular learning needs or disabilities, and assisting education staff and families to access support networks. For classroom teachers, this type of assistance can be useful in developing support strategies that can continue to be used in the future. This will likely necessitate the specialist staff member spending time with the teacher and the student in their classroom. For example, the AVT may observe several lessons and provide the teacher with feedback, they may team teach with the teacher, they may run an in-class program with the student with special needs and other students, or they may develop a program for use by the teacher. Whatever approach is taken, the aim is to leave the classroom teacher with skills they can use to continue to assist the student with a disability. A similar model operates in New Zealand, where Resource Teachers (Teaching and Learning) work to assist schools to develop support strategies for students with behaviour and/or learning problems. They are also involved in providing training for regular classroom teachers (Thompson et al., 2003).

A further key feature of educational policy for students with a disability is the collaboration of a variety of individuals to coordinate support for these students. In the Northern Territory, this is achieved through Special Education Advisory Support Teams (NT Department of

Employment, Education and Training, 2003). In NSW, these are called Learning Support Teams (NSW Department of Education and Training, 1998). As in the Northern Territory, the core members of these teams comprise the student, the student's parent or caregiver, the classroom teacher, and other specialist support (for example, school counsellor, itinerant or visiting teachers). Support teams will consider the student's needs within the context of the regular classroom, how to coordinate support resources within and outside of the school, and the development of specific planning for classroom activities. The advantage of this approach is that the responsibility for supporting the student with additional needs is seen as a shared, school-wide responsibility. Further examples of resources and supports that are available to regular classroom teachers are examined in Chapter 11.

If education systems are genuinely interested in including students with a disability in all school activities, then at first glance the inclusion of all students in testing and assessment may appear to create difficulties. Presumably, the reason why students with additional needs have been identified as such is because they may have experienced difficulty following testing and assessment. This line of thinking may lead one to conclude that exposure to standard testing for many students with a learning problem will exacerbate their differences and may be detrimental to their self-esteem. However, just as inclusion may be justifiably achieved with modifications to the learning experience, so too can assessment be modified to include students with special needs. This can also be done without compromising the assessment. As Education Queensland explains:

> Assessment is an integral part of effective teaching and learning. Schools need to ensure that their means of assessment are fair and equitable to all students. For students with disabilities, learning difficulties and learning disabilities this may mean the application of special consideration to ensure they have an equitable opportunity to demonstrate their knowledge and skills. Special consideration does not provide the students with an advantage over their peers but enables them to demonstrate the full extent of their learning.
>
> (Education Queensland, 2003b)

Special consideration in assessment is supported by most educational authorities as a means of promoting equity (Johnson et al., 2001; Thurlow & Bolt, 2001). Box 2.4 provides examples of the many ways in which special consideration can be provided to students with diverse additional needs.

Box 2.4

Examples of special consideration in assessment

Using appropriate technology

- Braille machines
- Laptops with voice input
- Assistive listening devices
- Augmentative and alternative communication devices
- Use of CD-ROM, audio or video
- Closed circuit television
- Talking or large print calculators

Using time flexibly

- Negotiate additional time for tests and assignments
- Provide rest breaks during longer testing
- Schedule exams when students may be more alert

>

Box 2.4 continued

Allowing variations in the response

- Accept different formats (for example, audio, signing)
- Use concrete materials and computer presentations

Changing the presentation

- Increase font size
- Change colour of paper
- Audio tapes
- Pair written word with symbols and graphics
- Simplify the questions without changing the meaning

Considering the environment

- Check lighting (for example, natural versus fluorescent)
- Check seating (for example, free from distractions)
- Allow oral presentation

Providing reasonable assistance

- Allow scribes, interpreters and readers
- Consider safety implications (for example, science)
- Help with planning and research for assignments

There is some diversity in the special education policies of the states and territories in Australia, and this diversity has resulted in some differences in the extent to which students with a disability are included across Australian schools. There is also evidence to show that a large number of students have moved from special to regular schools, and that there are increasing numbers of students with a disability being identified in regular classes. This evidence is detailed in the next section.

The practice of inclusion

The extent of inclusion

Apart from Victoria, which has effectively eliminated special classes in public schools, Australian educational jurisdictions provide three main types of enrolment options for students with a disability. The vast majority of these students will be educated in regular classrooms and will have their needs adequately met by regular classroom teachers, with assistance from specialist support staff as required. A smaller group of students with a disability are enrolled in either special classes in regular schools, or in special schools. As explained in Chapter 1, an important principle to follow in the enrolment of students with additional needs is to provide the least restrictive environment. That is, provide the environment that most closely parallels the regular classroom.

The number of students with a disability who were enrolled in special schools in Australia decreased dramatically during the 1980s and 1990s (Dempsey, Foreman & Jenkinson, 2002). In 2001, 369 of all the 9596 schools in Australia (3.85 per cent) were special schools. Traditionally, government schools have been the main institutions providing specialist services to students with a disability. However, by 2001, 15.2 per cent of all special schools in this country were provided by the non-government sector (Productivity Commission, 2003).

In the past two decades there have also been dramatic changes in the number of students with a disability who are enrolled in regular classes. Figure 2.2 shows the number of students with a disability who were enrolled in NSW public special schools, special classes, and regular

classes. Following an increase in the mid-1990s, there has been a more recent stabilisation of the number of students in segregated settings. In contrast, the number of students with a disability in regular classes has significantly increased, such that the number of these students now challenges the number of students in special schools and special classes. This trend in NSW is also consistent with the situation in other states and territories, including schools in the non-government sector (Dempsey, Foreman & Jenkinson, 2002; Dempsey, 2001; Employment, Workplace Relations and Education References Committee, 2002).

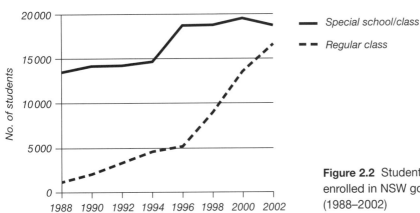

Figure 2.2 Students with a disability enrolled in NSW government schools (1988–2002)

(NSW Public Education Inquiry, 2002)

Clearly, the large increase in students with a disability being identified in government schools in NSW, and elsewhere, cannot be explained by a movement of students from segregated to inclusive settings. Instead, there are at least two good explanations for the increase. First, beginning in the early 1990s, the Commonwealth government provided additional funding to schools for identified students with a disability. This funding has probably provided an incentive to both government and non-government schools to identify students who were always enrolled in regular classes but who may have been overlooked in the past (Dempsey, 2001).

A second explanation for the increase is that schools, and the general community, have become more aware of both special needs in general and of specific disabilities in particular. The *Disability Discrimination Act* has played a role in raising an awareness of disability because the legislation obliges schools to act in an equitable manner to these students. As well, a range of additional needs, such as attention deficit hyperactivity disorder and Asperger syndrome, have received considerable coverage in the press as well as the professional literature in the past decade. For these reasons, schools and teachers are much more aware of disability and special needs than they were in the past.

Table 2.1 shows the proportion of students identified with a disability and other special needs in Australian government schools. The diversity in the number of students identified with a disability in the states and territories reflect the different ways in which disability is defined in different departments, and some differences in policy about the identification and support of students with a disability.

Table 2.1 Percentage of students identified with a disability in Australian states and territories.

Jurisdiction	Proportion of students
New South Wales	4.7% of students in NSW public schools were identified as having a disability in 2002
Victoria	4.3% of the total school population were identified with an impairment or disability in 2001 An estimated further 10% of all students may have a learning disability
Queensland	2.87% of the total student population in 2002 – that is, 12617 school-aged students with high support needs Students with learning difficulties and learning disabilities represent approximately 12% of students
South Australia	5.9% of the school population were identified with a disability in 2002
Western Australia	3.3% of the student population defined as having a disability in 2001
Tasmania	0.79% of the school population were identified as 'Category A' students, or students with the most severe level of disability in 2002 Other students with a disability are supported at the school, or support service level, and are not centrally identified
Northern Territory	Close to 20% of the 32000 students in the territory's government schools access special education programs Students with severe or multiple disabilities in special schools account for 0.5% of the school population
Australian Capital Territory	3.9% of school students were identified with a disability in 2001

(Sourced from ACT Department of Education, Youth and Family Services, 2002; Education Queensland, 2002; Northern Territory Department of Employment, Education and Training, 2002; NSW Public Education Inquiry, 2002; Department of Education, Training and Employment, South Australia, 2002; Tasmanian Department of Education, 2003; Department of Education and Training, Victoria, 2002)

At one end of the spectrum are states such as Tasmania which have minimised the labelling of students with a disability, and attempted to maximise the extent to which these students are included in regular classes. This state took a decision over a decade ago to limit the identification of students with a disability to the most severe level of disability. These students are known as 'Category A' students, they have high support needs, and they are placed in both segregated and inclusive settings. The vast majority of students with a disability in Tasmania are enrolled in regular classes.

At the other end of the spectrum there are states such as the Northern Territory and South Australia who report much higher rates of disability. These education departments have taken the position that it may be in the best interests of students, their families, and schools that those students with significant learning problems are identified and labelled, and as a consequence of this process of identification that the students are able to access appropriate support. In addition, the higher proportion of Indigenous students in schools in those states has also influenced the number of students identified with special needs.

Key players in inclusion

The legislation and policies discussed in this chapter have had their greatest impact in the way in which education is provided to students with a disability. However, it would be a mistake to assume that educational practice in this area is influenced by these principles and policies alone. Other potential influences on educational services to students with a disability are discussed in this section. Examples of key players in the debate about and the practice of inclusion are teachers, academics, parents, lobby groups, politicians and the media.

Public and professional opinion can also influence practice. For example, for the past two decades there has been an ongoing debate about the adequacy of existing educational placement for students with a disability. Many academics and professionals have argued that there is no place for segregated settings and that these students have a right to be educated not just in a regular school, but in a regular class along with other students.

The basis of this proposal is that a unified and coordinated education system is likely to provide better educational support to all students than two separate education systems, that is, regular education and special education. Rather than categorising students using psychometric tests and then assigning them to a service, students would be assessed on the basis of their curriculum needs and would be supported as far as possible in the regular classroom. This support would be supplemented by specialist teachers as necessary.

There are several arguments used by the inclusion movement to support their case (see Cole (1999) for an extensive discussion of arguments for and against inclusion policies for students with disabilities). First, it is claimed that there are not two types of students in the education system – regular and special. Instead, there is a single body of students eligible for education and these students will differ in their abilities and needs along a variety of continuums. Consequently, it is the responsibility of regular schools to meet the needs of these students by providing the necessary support.

Second, it is argued that having two education systems is inefficient. To some extent, special education has developed by 'tacking on' new services to existing services, and this has not always been done in a coordinated way. A potential problem with this approach is that these new services may bear little relationship to each other and to the general education system, and they may overlap existing services. An alternative is to service all students from a single education system that is planned in an organised manner.

A third argument for inclusion is that having a separate education system leads to the development of inappropriate attitudes and beliefs. For example, having a separate system may maintain the misconception among some teachers that they do not have the skills needed to support students with additional needs. Further, it emphasises that special education is indeed 'special', because it uses a range of teaching strategies that are very different from those used in mainstream classes. While teachers in special education may use some teaching practices in a more systematic way than teachers in regular education, the principles of good teaching practice are essentially the same, regardless of the setting. Later chapters in this book will explore this issue further.

A final argument for inclusion is that maintaining some students in special schools and support classes is discriminatory and cannot be justified on the basis of equity. It is claimed that it is fundamentally unjust not to allow all students, regardless of the severity of their disability, access to a regular class. Supporters of inclusive education suggest that with appropriate levels of peer and staff support, and with appropriate levels of curriculum modification, the education of students with very high support needs in regular classes can be a meaningful experience for those students and for their peers.

Not surprisingly, some people see inclusive education as an extreme option for many students with a disability. For example, educators and academics such as Kauffman, Bantz and McCullough (2002), Mock and Kauffman (2002), and Kauffman (1999), have argued that special education has 'lost its way' in recent years by being overly influenced by philosophical arguments associated with inclusion. They argue that special education grew from a recognition that the regular education system did not meet the needs of students with learning problems. Consequently, to deconstruct segregated placements for such students, particularly for students with severe behaviour problems, is seen as illogical.

The role of politics, the media and 'pressure groups' influencing educational policy and practice for students with a disability cannot be overlooked. One example of the interplay between press reports, government policy and interest groups relates to Aboriginal education in NSW. In January 2003, the Minister of Education, John Watkins, stopped an independent review of Aboriginal education policy because departmental data on statewide testing and school suspension rates were very poor (Doherty, 2003). However, the motivation for stopping the review, according to the NSW Teachers Federation, was to prevent the damaging results of the review becoming public in the lead up to a state election. Incidentally, NSW Department of Education and Training data show that the number of Aboriginal students who were suspended rose from 5115 students in 1999, to 6934 students in 2001. While Aboriginal students comprised 4 per cent of the government school population in 2001, 40 per cent of the girls suspended from kindergarten to Year 2, and nearly one-quarter of the boys in this age group were Aboriginal (Doherty, 2003).

Another important group of stakeholders in the practice of inclusion is parents and caregivers. Some parents of students who are currently educated in special schools feel worried at the prospect of the closure of these schools if inclusion policies were comprehensively implemented. The issue is certainly an emotive one. However, the wholesale closure of special schools and classes is highly unlikely. The main reason is that such a closure requires the support not only of administrators and academics, but also the students, families and teachers involved.

Community support for inclusive education is reflected in a variety of organisations such as the parent–professional advocacy groups of *The Association for Persons with Severe Handicaps* (TASH) in the United States, *Family Advocacy* in New South Wales (for parents seeking to enrol their child with a disability in regular classes), and *SPELD Vic.* (for parents of children with specific learning difficulties). Box 2.5 gives some background to the mission of Family Advocacy and the issues that it sees as being important to address in achieving inclusion. A consequence of the development of advocacy and lobby groups is that the debate about inclusive education has extended from the school to the wider community. An indication of this change is that it is now common for political parties to develop a policy on inclusion, and in some states, the area of disability is recognised as a government portfolio in its own right.

Box 2.5
Family Advocacy, NSW

Family Advocacy is an advocacy agency that promotes and protects the rights, needs and interests of children and adults with developmental disability in New South Wales. Its mission is:

> to attain positive social roles for people with developmental disability through the development of advocacy by families and through strengthening the role, knowledge and influence of the family.

The organisation has a priority to undertake advocacy on behalf of people with developmental disability who have very high support needs. It does this through a strong systems advocacy function combined with advocacy development work with families in all parts of the state.

One of the first valued roles that children with disability can assume is the role of student in the regular class of the local neighbourhood school. This valued status can only be achieved through inclusive education.

Some of the work undertaken by Family Advocacy to achieve inclusive education includes:

- supporting parents across NSW to gain inclusion for their sons and daughters

through information, one-day and weekend workshops, and individual support
- auspicing the *Kids Belong Together* campaign at the 1995 state election calling for a change of education policy
- coordinating the *Action for McRae Report Coalition* to provide a unified voice in negotiating educational reform
- active involvement in the State Integration Reference Group including Chair of the Training and Development Working Party and active membership of the Policy, Physical Access and Curriculum working parties; leadership of the Coalition for Inclusive Education.

Current issues in inclusive education

1 Understanding the value base of full inclusion

Inclusive education is premised on the right of all children to be full members of regular classes of local neighbourhood schools. Each child is valued for who they are – for the contributions they bring and for the growth and development they can expect as a result of membership of a valued group.

>

Box 2.5 continued

Inclusion is different from integration. Integration assumes that classes are made up of 'normal' children and children who in any way do not fit this 'normality' must secure additional resources in order to be *allowed* to become members of the class. The extra resources are used to stabilise the child into a class and a school that fundamentally remains unchanged.

Inclusive education, on the other hand, springs from the assumption that everybody belongs. Rather than seeking to minimise difference, inclusion values the richness of diversity and seeks to transform schools in order to respond to the diversity of learners.

The biggest challenge facing schools in Australia today is to move from an integration approach to an inclusive education approach.

2 Implementing the totality of full inclusion

The significantly increased number of students on integration programs confirms the improved opportunities for children with disability to be enrolled in regular classes. The challenge today is to implement the totality of inclusion, in a physical sense, socially and through the curriculum.

Wills and Jackson (2001) outline the breadth of inclusion in terms of:

- Physical inclusion – attending the local neighbourhood school, playing in the same playground, being in the same classrooms as well as having access to opportunities offered by the school at the same time as same-aged peers without disability.
- Social inclusion – the personal and social welcoming of children within the social milieu of the school. Social inclusion involves policies and practices to promote a welcoming social environment for *all* students, including promoting personal friendships, caring for one another, discouraging and addressing bullying and all other forms of social isolation of students.
- Curricular inclusion – the involvement of all students in the regular curriculum of the school. All children have individual skills and needs that must be addressed by all teachers. The child with the disability highlights this issue for all children.

A more strategic focus on social and curricular inclusion will benefit children with and without disability.

3 Bending over backwards for the most vulnerable

Under the current integration approach, schools have accepted that an increasing range of students is allowed to participate in the regular class. Simultaneously, they have more clearly defined groups of students that are much less welcome (for example, those with challenging behaviour), and have created new support classes and special schools in response. The enrolment of these children in the regular class becomes less certain and depends on the vision and advocacy of their parents. In a school system based on an inclusive education policy, a major thrust of activity would be to understand 'what it takes' to enable all students (including those with challenging behaviour), to be full members of the regular classroom.

4 Understanding some of the elements of 'what it takes'

To make inclusion work, we need a fundamental change in education policy and in teacher education. Slee (2001) sees the problem for schools as 'working out how to fit different kids in with a minimum of disruption'. He argues that a transition is required in teacher education to 'explore new forms of knowledge about identity and difference and to invite students to consider the pathologies of schools that enable or disable students' (pp. 173–4). This will lead to a re-conceptualisation of teaching practice.

>

Box 2.5 continued

The most pressing work must relate to building the capacity of schools. Currently, the majority of integration resources are turned into teachers' aide time, and while many students benefit from an aide, the over reliance on often untrained staff cannot move us towards classrooms and schools in which all children learn.

What students with a disability need most is quality teaching from teachers skilled for mixed ability classes, and who are confident with grouping processes that enhance all students' self-esteem and educational outcomes.

Belinda Epstein-Frisch, Advocate,
Institute for Family Advocacy & Leadership
Development Assoc. Inc.

Some schools and sections of the wider community continue to debate the merits of including students with a disability. However, currently the debate centres on the degree to which this inclusion should occur (rather than whether it should occur at all), and the strategies that should be employed to support this inclusion. Perhaps the most important thing that should occur in this process is that students and their families must be given choices in the educational placements offered to them.

Providing supportive environments

Meeting a diversity of needs in the classroom is a challenge. The demands of teaching in mixed ability classrooms, of changing instruction to meet individual needs, teaching to reduce prejudice, of working with others in the classroom, and of taking time out of the classroom

to meet with other professionals, are considerable. However, as UNESCO (2001) points out, it is also an opportunity to enrich learning and social relations. From this perspective, the challenge is an institutional one, rather than an individual problem. Meeting this challenge means reforming schools and education systems and organising classroom activities so that students with additional needs achieve success in the activities provided to them. However, the focus is not just on the student with special needs. The focus is on providing good teaching; teaching that will benefit all the students in the classroom.

A traditional way of meeting a disability in the classroom has been to attend to real or perceived 'deficiencies' in the student. For example, the assumption may be that the student is unable to achieve at the same level as their peers because of faulty cognitive or perceptual processing. That is, the student with learning difficulties who reads at a level five years behind their peers does so because of a cognitive impairment. Assessment of the student would concentrate on identifying the nature of the impairment and perhaps in quantifying it (for example, through an IQ test).

This approach has its limitations because it does not provide the classroom teacher with much useful information. For example, providing the teacher with an IQ score for a student tells the teacher nothing about the strengths, interests and needs of the student. While IQ test results are reasonable predictors of a student's academic performance, there is a range of other important variables that are also relevant (for example, motivation, family support, personality). Indeed, overly relying on test scores can have the unfortunate consequence of raising preconceived ideas about what students can and can't do. For example, knowing that a student has an IQ score of 73 may lead some to assume that the student may not be capable of much in the regular classroom. Importantly, this student may be capable of achieving much in the classroom if their learning experiences are positive.

A much more useful way of thinking about special needs in the classroom is to focus on what it is that the student has difficulty doing. If the student has difficulty reading, then what aspect of the reading activity is the problem (for example, the length of the passage, the difficulty of the words)? If the student has difficulty with some mathematical tasks, then what aspect of this activity is the problem (for example, a lack of understanding of a more basic maths concept)? It is here that working collaboratively with specialist staff, as many of the state and territory special education policies expect regular classroom teachers to do, can assist us. Such specialist staff will have a good understanding of the reading process, and of maths skills, and they can make suggestions about ways in which we can modify teaching activities for students with special needs.

Such modifications, which are discussed in some detail in later chapters, are part of a broader strategy in relation to students with additional needs. This strategy sees the environment that the student functions in as being crucial to the success of that student. The environments that we are most interested in as teachers are the classroom and school environments. Crucially, these environments comprise a variety of components that interact with each other to influence the learning experience and its outcomes. Box 2.6 lists some important components of classroom and school environments.

At the level of the school, the leadership provided by the principal and other executive staff can have a profound impact on the behaviour of staff and students. For example, the principal arguing for the benefits of inclusion in staff meetings, and providing opportunities

Examples of components

School and classroom environments that impact on the inclusion of students with a disability

- Leadership by the school executive
- School policies on inclusion
- Resources and facilities
- Experience with students with a disability
- Attitudes of staff

- Attitudes of students without a disability
- Curriculum
- Teaching strategies
- Characteristics of students with a disability

for students with a disability to be included in school assemblies, will send a clear message to the school about inclusion. At the level of the classroom, the leadership provided by the teacher can also have a profound impact on the behaviour of students and others. For example, teachers who provide opportunities for all students to achieve success show the class that cooperation and acceptance are valued in the classroom. So our goal at the classroom level is to create and maintain a supportive environment that will assist all the students in the class, including students with a disability.

There are a number of strategies that schools can take to check how successful their inclusive practices are. One approach is to reflect on the degree of match between best practice and reality. Table 2.2 lists key indicators from the Index for Inclusion produced by the Centre for Studies on Inclusive Education (2002). Teachers and schools can use these indicators to analyse their beliefs, policies and practices and to identify the barriers to learning and participation that may occur within each of the identified areas.

Table 2.2 Indicators of best practice in inclusion.

A Creating inclusive cultures	
A1 Building community	A2 Establishing inclusive values
• A1.1 Everyone is made to feel welcome • A1.2 Students help each other • A1.3 Staff collaborate with each other • A1.4 Staff and students treat one another with respect • A1.5 There is a partnership between staff and parents/carers • A1.6 Staff and principals work well together • A1.7 Local communities are involved in the school	• A2.1 There are high expectations for all students • A2.2 Staff, principals, students and parents/carers share a philosophy of inclusion • A2.3 Students are equally valued • A2.4 Staff and students recognise that each has an important role • A2.5 Staff seek to remove barriers to learning and participation in all aspects of the school • A2.6 The school strives to minimise discriminatory practices

continued

Table 2.2 continued

B Producing inclusive policies	
B1 Developing the school for all	B2 Organising support for diversity
• B1.1 Staff appointments and promotions are fair • B1.2 New staff are helped to settle into the school • B1.3 The school seeks to admit all students from its locality • B1.4 The school makes its buildings physically accessible to all people • B1.5 New students are helped to settle into the school • B1.6 The school arranges teaching groups so that all students are valued and encouraged to achieve	• B2.1 Support for all students (including ESL and Indigenous students) is coordinated • B2.2 Staff development activities help staff to respond to student diversity • B2.3 School policies reflect the principles of inclusion • B2.4 Pastoral care and behaviour support policies are linked to curriculum development and learning • B2.5 Pressures for disciplinary suspension are decreased • B2.6 Barriers to attendance are reduced • B2.7 Bullying is minimised
C Evolving inclusive practices	
C1 Orchestrating learning	C2 Mobilising resources
• C1.1 Teaching is planned with the learning of all students in mind • C1.2 Lessons encourage the participation of all students • C1.3 Lessons develop an understanding of difference • C1.4 Students are actively involved in their own learning • C1.5 Students learn collaboratively • C1.6 Assessment contributes to the achievements of all students • C1.7 Classroom discipline is based on mutual respect • C1.8 Teachers plan, teach and review in partnership • C1.9 Teachers are concerned to support the learning and participation of all students • C1.10 Teaching assistants support the learning and participation of all students • C1.11 All students take part in activities outside the classroom	• C2.1 Student difference is used as a resource for teaching and learning • C2.2 Staff expertise is fully utilised • C2.3 Staff develop resources to support learning and participation • C2.4 Community resources are known and drawn upon • C2.5 School resources are distributed fairly so that they support inclusion

(Adapted from Centre for Studies on Inclusive Education, 2002)

Acting ethically

At a basic level, ethics involves a consideration of the 'correctness' of actions or practices in a given situation (Freakley & Burgh, 2002). Ethics is closely associated with moral conduct, and services for students with additional needs are founded on some basic moral concerns. Examples of these concerns are a desire to prevent repetition of past injustices to these students (for example, exclusion from education and the provision of irrelevant curriculum), and a belief that affirmative action may be required for this population.

Given, as demonstrated earlier in this chapter, that our educational services to students with special needs are influenced by our principles (such as the moral principles identified in the paragraph above), and by policy and legislation, one might ask: why do we need to consider ethics in our day-to-day work as teachers? The following analogy may assist in answering this question.

The legislation and educational policy that is related to students with a disability can be likened to a safety net. That is, individual laws and policies act as the webbing on the net, and their purpose is to prevent students from falling through the net (that is, missing out on services and supports, or experiencing discrimination). To make the net failsafe, in terms of stopping any students from falling through, would require an extensive range of laws and policies to cover every possible situation. Unfortunately, this extent of coverage is not practical (it would create a maze of confusing procedures), or desirable (control over teaching would move from educators to lawyers and administrators). Instead, what we have in Australia is some general legislation that relates to students with a disability, which is supplemented by more specific policy statements in the different education systems.

So, a consideration of ethics is a relevant activity in the work of teachers because laws and policies will not always provide us with all the guidance we need. In addition, the following excerpt shows that existing practices and prejudices can work against the spirit of the legislation and policy being implemented.

> Without the development of inclusive policies in education or an analogous strategy to include all learners, who have a basic human right to education, education for all will not be achieved. The reason is that all systems, even those overtly committed to education for all, have a tendency to exclude, sometimes directly and sometimes indirectly, sometimes consciously, sometimes inadvertently, through the construction of religious, ethnic, racial, gender, linguistic, educational, intellectual and other barriers to participation.
>
> (UNESCO, 2001, p. 4)

Box 2.7 gives some examples of situations that teachers may encounter that raise ethical issues related to equity, honesty and fairness.

Box 2.7

Ethical issues raised by teaching experiences involving students with additional needs

Examples

A   Julia

Julia is a high school student who is reading at a level four years behind her peers. She struggles to understand much of the content presented in her English, Maths and Science lessons, but she has learned to stay quiet in class to prevent being asked by the teacher to answer questions. Sitting near the back of the class on her own has been a useful strategy for her to achieve this objective. There are several very disruptive students in these classes who occupy much of the teachers' time. From the teachers' perspective, these classes are in the lower stream and are difficult to manage. They complain that many of the students don't want to be there and aren't interested in the work. Meanwhile, Julia hands in another topic test with less than half the questions attempted.

>

Box 2.7 continued

B Raymond

Raymond is retiring in a few years after 33 years of continuous service as a regular class teacher. He has let most of his colleagues know that he's had enough of what he regards as the grind of working in a system that doesn't value teachers' work and a system that is responsible for falling standards of student respect for teachers. A particular gripe for Raymond is the difficulty of the system to 'get rid of' students who shouldn't be there (for example, students with behaviour problems and students with a disability). The classroom is increasingly seen as a 'battleground' by Raymond where survival for another few years is vital. Keeping on top of students with sarcasm and ridicule has been an effective strategy that he continues to use. Students are occasionally reduced to tears in his classes for violating class rules. His colleagues feel uncomfortable with his attitudes, but they respect his ability to control the behaviour of the students in his classes.

A way to deal with the problem of a difference between educational practice and educational policy is the development of codes of ethics, and codes of conduct, for employees by their employers. Briefly, codes of ethics give general advice about ethical principles that should be followed. Codes of conduct give much more specific advice about what should and should not be done in specific situations. For example, the code of conduct for teachers used by the NSW Department of Education and Training (1997) states, in part, that all staff must:

- treat students equitably, including those with disabilities or other special needs
- meet the individual learning needs of students and assist each student to maximise their learning outcomes
- perform their duties efficiently and effectively and with honesty, integrity and fairness at all times.

While such documents can be helpful to staff, the development of a code is just the start for an organisation in encouraging ethical behaviour. Ultimately, a code will be worth no more than the paper it is written on unless the code is 'owned' by its members, and it is reinforced and supported by management.

Clearly, supporting students with diverse needs in the classroom can be challenging. However, these students have a legal right to enrol in regular classes, and teachers and schools have a legal responsibility to provide quality educational experiences for them. In meeting this responsibility, it is not helpful to regard students with a disability as a separate group to the other students in the school. All the students in the school, including those who may be gifted, will differ along a continuum of abilities and interests. These differences are a given in any school and they reflect the differences we experience when we interact with others outside of the school setting.

The argument over whether inclusion works is ended. Inclusion does work when key components of the classroom and the school environment are in place, and legislation and policy now demand that teachers and schools ensure that these components are enacted. In doing so, some students will need some changes and modifications to what might normally occur in the classroom. Later chapters, particularly the chapters in sections two and three of this book, will explore the wide range of options that teachers have in changing classroom practice to support students with diverse additional needs. The next chapter, 'Inclusion in early childhood', examines how this support occurs with young children with a disability, and how these children are assisted to transition to school.

Summary

This chapter discussed the legislation and educational policies associated with the inclusion of students with a disability. Some countries have relied mainly on legislation to ensure that the rights of these children are maintained. While Australia has national legislation to prevent discrimination against people with a disability, and education standards are likely to have an increasing impact on services for students with a disability, individual state and territory policies have been the main vehicle by which educational services for students with special needs have been maintained. Both laws and policies have their limitations, and they provide no guarantee that inclusive practices will be followed by all schools. Consequently, achieving inclusion for students with additional needs is the responsibility of a variety of key players that include regular classroom teachers, the parents of these students, the schools the students attend, and the education systems of which the schools are a part.

Discussion questions

1   Debate the following statements:
    a   The rights of teachers are just as important as the rights of students with a disability.
    b   All educators are special educators.
    c   Inclusion is a natural process that will eventually lead to all students being enrolled in their local school.
    d   Meeting the needs of students with a disability in the regular classroom is incompatible with meeting the needs of other students.

2   What are the ramifications of the following extract from the UNESCO (2001) quotation that appears on page 38 of this chapter?

    Inclusive thinking is a reminder that education must be as concerned with the sustenance of communities as with personal achievement and national economic performance.

3   Discuss the suggestion that inclusion is much more than just the physical placement of a student with a disability in a regular school.

4   Using the descriptions in Box 2.7, identify the ethical issue(s) in these scenarios, and discuss ways in which the issues could be resolved in a manner that meets the needs of all relevant stakeholders.

Individual activities

1   Conduct a review of some of the literature on inclusion to determine what views parents, teachers and the community hold.

2   Examine policies related to students with a disability in your state, territory or region. What does this policy say about the rights and responsibilities of:
    a   students with a disability?
    b   regular classroom teachers?

c   the families of these students?

d   the teachers of these students?

e   the schools that these students attend?

Group activities

1   Brainstorm the issues associated with the inclusion of students with a disability from the perspective of students, parents, teachers, and the community.

2   Using the education standards that appear in Box 2.1, develop a list of issues that teachers and schools would need to address to ensure that the standards are being met.

References

ACT Department of Education, Youth and Family Services (2002). *Annual Report 2001–2002.* Canberra: Author.

Australian Government Publishing Service (2003). *Disability Discrimination Act 1992.* Online at http://www.austlii.edu.au/au/legis/cth/consol_act/dda1992264/

Carpenter, B. (1997). The interface between the curriculum and the code. *British Journal of Special Education, 24*(1), 18–20.

Centre for Studies on Inclusive Education (2003). Decrease in segregation in special schools. Online at http://inclusion.uwe.ac.uk/csie/stats02.htm

*Centre for Studies on Inclusive Education (2002). Index for inclusion: Developing learning and participation in schools. Online at http://inclusion.uwe.ac.uk/csie/indexlaunch.htm

Cole, P. (1999). The structure of arguments used to support or oppose inclusion policies for students with disabilities. *Journal of Intellectual and Developmental Disability, 24*(3), 215–26.

Commonwealth Department of Education, Science and Training (2002). *Finance Assistance Granted to Each State in Respect of 2000 States Grants (Primary and Secondary Assistance) Act 1996.* Canberra: Author. Online at http://www.deetya.gov.au/schools/publications/Green/2000GreenReport1.pdf

Dempsey, I. (2001). Students with a disability in Australian non-government schools. *Special Education Perspectives, 10*(2), 3–6.

*Dempsey, I., Foreman, P. & Jenkinson, J. (2002). Educational enrolment of students with a disability in New South Wales and Victoria. *International Journal of Disability, Development and Education, 49*(1), 31–46.

Department of Education Tasmania (1997). *Inclusion of Students With Disabilities in Regular Schools.* Online at http://connections.education.tas.gov.au/Nav/StrategicPolicy.asp?ID=00000189#PolicyStatement

Department of Education Tasmania (2000). *A Statement of Values and Purposes.* Online at http://www.education.tas.gov.au/ocll/publications/valuespurposes.pdf

Department of Education Victoria (2003). *Program for Students With Disabilities 2004, booklet 1.* Online at http://www.sofweb.vic.edu.au/wellbeing/pdf/disabil/Handbook_2004.pdf

Department of Education and Training, Victoria (2002). *Submission to the Inquiry Into the Education of Students With Disabilities Australian Senate Employment, Workplace Relations and Education References Committee.* Online at http://www.aph.gov.au/senate/committee/eet_ctte/ed_students_withdisabilities/submissions/sublist.htm

Department of Education, Training and Employment, South Australia (2002). *Submission to the Inquiry Into the Education of Students With Disabilities Australian Senate Employment, Workplace Relations and Education References Committee*. Online at http://www.aph.gov.au/senate/committee/eet_ctte/ed_students_withdisabilities/submissions/sublist.htm

Department of Education, Training and Employment, South Australia (2002). *Negotiated Education Plan*. Adelaide: Author. CD-ROM resource.

Department of Education, Training and Employment, South Australia (1997). *Administrative Instructions and Guidelines, Section 3: Student Matters*. Adelaide: Author.

Doherty, L. (2003). State fails Aboriginal students. *Sydney Morning Herald*, 17 February, 4.

Education Queensland (2002). Submission to the Inquiry Into the Education of Students With Disabilities Australian Senate Employment, Workplace Relations and Education References Committee. Online at http://www.aph.gov.au/senate/committee/eet_ctte/ed_students_withdisabilities/submissions/sublist.htm.

Education Queensland (2003a). *Specialist Staff Services*. Online at http://education.qld.gov.au/curriculum/learning/students/disabilities/staff/avtservices.htm.

Education Queensland (2003b). *Guidelines for Special Consideration in Assessment*. Online at http://education.qld.gov.au/curriculum/learning/students/disabilities/policy/guidelines.html.

Employment, Workplace Relations and Education References Committee (2002). *Education of Students With Disabilities*. Canberra: Commonwealth of Australia. Online at http://www.aph.gov.au/senate/committee/eet_ctte/ed_students_withdisabilities/report/report.pdf.

Freakley, M. & Burgh, G. (2002). *Engaging With Ethics: Ethical Inquiry for Teachers*. Katoomba: Social Science Press.

Her Majesty's Stationery Office (2001). *Special Educational Needs and Disability Act 2001*. Online at http://www.hmso.gov.uk/acts/acts2001/20010010.htm

*Human Rights and Equal Opportunity Commission (2003). *Disability Standards and Guidelines*. Online at http://www.hreoc.gov.au/disability_rights/standards/standards.html

Johnson, E., Kimball, K., Brown, S. O. & Anderson, D. (2001). A statewide review of the use of accommodations in large-scale, high-stakes assessments. *Exceptional Children*, 67(2), 251–61.

Kauffman, J. M. (1999). Commentary: Today's special education and its messages for tomorrow. *The Journal of Special Education*, 32(4), 244–54.

Kauffman, J. M., Bantz, J. & McCullough, J. (2002). Separate and better: A special public school class for students with emotional and behavioral disorders. *Exceptionality*, 10(3), 149–70.

Ministerial Council on Education, Employment, Training and Youth Affairs (2002). *The Adelaide Declaration on National Goals for Schooling in the Twenty-First Century*. Online at http://www.curriculum.edu.au/mceetya/adeldec.htm.

Ministry of Education (1998). Special education 2000. Online at http://www.minedu.govt.nz/

*Mock, D. R. & Kauffman, J. M. (2002). Preparing teachers for full inclusion: Is it possible? *Teacher Educator*, 37(3), 202–15.

Nelson, B. (2003). *Most state and territory education ministers vote against disability standards*. Media release, 11 July. Online at http://www.dest.gov.au/ministers/nelson/jul_03/minco703.htm

New Zealand Ministry of Education (2003). *Education Priorities for New Zealand*. Online at http://www.beehive.govt.nz/mallard/priorities/priorities.pdf.

Northern Territory Department of Employment, Education and Training (2002). *Submission to the Inquiry Into the Education of Students With Disabilities Australian Senate Employment,*

Workplace Relations and Education References Committee. Online at http://www.aph.gov.au/senate/committee/eet_ctte/ed_students_withdisabilities/submissions/sublist.htm.

Northern Territory Department of Employment, Education and Training (2003). *Assisting Students With Special Needs*. Online at http://150.191.80.32/pages/assisting.shtml.

NSW Department of Education and Training (1997). *Code of Conduct*. Retrieved 9 September 2003 from http://www.det.nsw.edu.au/policies/behaviour/schools/media/schools_code.pdf.

NSW Department of Education and Training (1997). *Enrolment of Students in Government Schools: A Summary and Consolidation of Policy*. Sydney: Author.

NSW Department of Education and Training (1998). *Special Education Handbook*. Sydney: Author.

NSW Public Education Inquiry (2002). *Report of the Independent Inquiry into Public Education in New South Wales*. Online at http://www.pub-ed-inquiry.org/.

NSW Teachers' Federation (1997). *Memorandum to Members*, 25 October.

Office of Special Education Programs (2003). *Legislation and Policy*. Online at http://www.ed.gov/offices/OSERS/OSEP/Policy/.

Productivity Commission (2003). Report on Government services, 2003. Canberra: Commonwealth Government. Online at http://www.pc.gov.au/gsp/2003/index.html.

Riddell, S. (2003). Devolution and disability equality legislation: The implementation of part 4 of the Disability Discrimination Act 1995 in England and Scotland. *British Journal of Special Education, 30*(2), 63–9.

Slee, R. (2001). Social justice and the changing directions in educational research: The case of inclusive education. *Journal of Inclusive Education, 5*, 2–3, 173–4.

Tasmanian Department of Education (2003). *2001–2002 Annual Report*. Online at http://www2.education.tas.gov.au/

Thompson, C., Brown, D., Jones, L., Walker, J., Moore, D. W., Anderson, A., Davies, T., Medcalf, J. & Glynn, T.L. (2003). Resource teachers learning and behaviour: Collaborative problem solving to support inclusion. *Journal of Positive Behaviour Interventions, 5*(2), 101–11.

Thurlow, M. & Bolt, S. (2001). *Empirical Support for Accommodations Most Often Allowed in State Policy* (Synthesis Report 41). Minneapolis: University of Minnesota, National Centre on Educational Outcomes. Retrieved 16 December 2002 from http://education.umn.edu/NCEO/OnlinPubs/Synthesis41.html.

United Nations Educational, Scientific and Cultural Organisation (1994). *Salamanca Statement on Principles, Policy and Practice in Special Needs Education*. Paris: Author.

United Nations Educational, Scientific and Cultural Organisation (1998). Special Needs Education Mission Statement. Online at http://www.unesco.org/education/educprog/sne/index.html.

*United Nations Educational, Scientific and Cultural Organisation (2001). *Inclusion in Education: The Participation of Disabled Learners*. Paris: Author. Online at http://unesdoc.unesco.org/images/0012/001234/123486e.pdf.

U.S. Department of Education (2001). *Twenty-third Annual Report to Congress on the Implementation of the Individuals with Disabilities Education Act*. Online at http://www.ed.gov/offices/OSERS/OSEP/Products/OSEP2001AnlRpt/TOCandEXSUM.pdf.

Wills, D. & Jackson, R. (2001). Report card on inclusive education in Australia. *Interaction, 14*, 2–3, 5–12.

---

*Recommended reading for this chapter

Further recommended reading

Allan, J. (Ed.) (2003). *Inclusion, Participation, and Democracy: What is the Purpose?* Dordrect; Boston: Kluwer.

Beloin, K. & Peterson, M. (2000). For richer or poorer: Building inclusive schools in poor urban and rural communities. *International Journal of Disability, Development and Education, 47*(1), 15–24.

Byrnes, M. (2002). *Taking Sides: Clashing Views on Controversial Issues in Special Education.* Guilford, CT: McGraw-Hill/Dushkin.

Cutts, S. & Sigafoos, J. (2001). Social competence and peer interactions of students with intellectual disability in an inclusive high school. *Journal of Intellectual and Developmental Disability, 26*(2), 127–42.

Dore, R., Dion, E., Wagner, S. & Brunet, J. (2002). High school inclusion of adolescents with mental retardation: A multiple case study. *Education and Training in Mental Retardation and Developmental Disabilities, 37*(3), 253–61.

McLeskey, J. & Waldron, N. L. (2002). Inclusion and school change: Teacher perceptions regarding curricular and instructional adaptations. *Teacher Education and Special Education, 25*(1), 41–54.

Osler, A. & Osler, C. (2002). Inclusion, exclusion and children's rights: A case study of a student with Asperger Syndrome. *Emotional and Behavioural Difficulties, 7*(1), 35–54.

Rose, R. (2002). Special and mainstream school collaboration for the promotion of inclusion. *Journal of Research in Special Educational Needs, 2*(2), 1–22.

Salend, S. J. & Duhaney, L. M. G. (2002). What do families have to say about inclusion? How to pay attention and get results. *Teaching Exceptional Children, 35*(1), 62–6.

Smart, J. (2001). *Disability, Society and the Individual.* Gaithersburg, Maryland: Aspen.

Chapter 3

Inclusion in early childhood

Jan North and Anne Carruthers

This chapter aims to:

- focus on family and service provider perspectives on inclusion
- examine early education of children with disabilities – enabling maximum access to mainstream environments
- consider the preparation of inclusive environments with reference to administrators, staff and the physical and social environments

- focus on transition to early childhood programs and school, including potential issues and possible courses of action
- examine implementation of inclusive preschool practices
- address the options for the education of young children and parent choice.

Introduction

Adults who are to become parents hold many expectations for their unborn infants. One basic expectation, while not often openly expressed, is that their children will attend a regular school from age 5 to 16–18 years in preparation for later life. This is a reasonable expectation given that school attendance is compulsory in most developed countries, and the vast majority of the population attend regular schools. It is common for the parents of a child born with a severe disability to articulate their concern about the possibility their child will not meet this expectation by raising as one of their first questions: 'Will my child be able to go to regular school?' To the outsider, this may appear to be an unusual question given that the child could be just a few days old. However, this reflects the parents' desire to have their child follow the same road through life as the majority of other children.

For the families of children with disabilities, the initial stages of the child's life will bring many emotions, issues, challenges and adjustments that will not be encountered by the majority of families. The events of these early years, possibly filled with hospitalisations, medical appointments and hours of specialist services will shape the child and the family for the future. All personnel involved with the child during these years play a role in the development of the child and family, whether they be medical personnel, other health professionals, teachers, support workers or family and friends.

Over the past 30 years, most western countries have developed educational systems designed to provide support for families in these early years, with the understanding that children with disabilities should be given every available assistance to participate fully in the regular life of the community. The majority of these families will therefore take advantage of early intervention programs while their children are infants and toddlers. They will then expect to enrol their children in regular day care or preschool programs, and will want them to progress to regular school.

The development of early intervention services in Australia and New Zealand has parallelled the development in the USA where legislation has underpinned practice. The *Individuals with Disabilities Education Act* (IDEA, 1991) established mandatory practice in the USA for early intervention programs (children aged 0–3). The legislation is underpinned by two principles that are central to the provision of early education of young children with disabilities in Australia. The first is the concept of 'family centred practice' and the second is that of the education of children in 'natural environments'. Understanding of the principles of 'family centred practice' and 'natural environments' will assist the reader to understand why parents ask questions about schooling when a child is a few days old, why families effectively commence the process of preparing their children for schooling from the time of diagnosis, why it is important for teachers to have an understanding of each child's early history, and how best to cater for the child and family in inclusive settings.

Family centred practice

The concept of family centred practice has developed from the field of early intervention. Family centred practice is based on the following understandings:

- Families are part of complex systems that influence the child. Systems include the immediate and extended family, friends, and community organisations and members, all of which impact on the family.
- Families know their children and are very aware of the factors that impinge on their lives.
- Families have many decisions to make about their lives and the lives of their children. These will be best made when families have a sense of control over the decision making process.
- Families will be more committed if they make decisions themselves and are involved in the implementation of those decisions.

This gives rise to an approach that seeks to place as much of the child's education as possible under the direct control of the family. To achieve this end, early intervention personnel seek to:

- consider the whole family rather than viewing the child in isolation
- be respectful of and responsive to family diversity, recognising the varying family structures, cultural backgrounds and values of each family
- treat parents/carers as capable and competent individuals and promote this view
- build family strengths rather than focus on weaknesses
- work in partnership with families, recognising and respecting the contribution of each member of the partnership in all aspects of service delivery
- work in ways that are enabling, empowering and strengthening of families.

(See McBride 1999, for a fuller explanation of these concepts.)

The relationships that workers try to create with families are characterised by openness and trust, collaboration, empathy, mutual respect, agreed goals and clear responsibilities. While early intervention programs do not always interpret family centred practice in the same way, generally one would expect that families will approach any future educational setting with a history of being involved in a 'family centred' manner. This will affect their expectations of all future interactions with educational personnel.

Natural environments

IDEA (1999) mandates that, to the maximum extent appropriate, children should be educated in 'natural environments', where natural environments are defined as 'settings that are natural or normal for the child's age peers who have no disabilities' (IDEA, 34 CRF Part 303.18). In the early intervention years these natural environments may be homes, child care settings or neighbourhood playgroups. IDEA states that provision of early intervention in a setting other than a natural environment can occur 'only if early intervention cannot be achieved satisfactorily for the infant in a natural environment'. The premise behind the natural environment concept is effectively the same as the premise behind the concept of inclusion, that is, to the maximum extent appropriate, children with and without disabilities should be educated together in environments that are 'the norm' for the community.

Early intervention

In Australia, as in the United States, early intervention (in Australia now named early childhood intervention) refers to the provision of a range of services to babies and young children who have been identified as having intellectual, physical, emotional and/or sensory disabilities, or who are at risk of having developmental problems. Early childhood intervention services are delivered by a range of personnel, including occupational therapists, physiotherapists, special educators, speech therapists, medical personnel, psychologists, social workers, audiologists, orthoptists, orientation and mobility instructors, and technology teachers. They may work in individual and/or small group settings, often with related services such as transport, respite care, support groups, and service coordination.

Early intervention programs also vary in their location (usually home or centre based), size of group served (individual or small group), amount of inclusion in regular programs, delivery methods, and core philosophy.

Most babies and young children with severe disabilities in Australia now have access to early childhood intervention programs based on the belief that:

- development can be significantly influenced by environmental input
- early learning is critical for all future development
- early intervention ultimately is beneficial to society
- early intervention provides support for families
- early intervention helps prepare children for mainstream environments.

A typical early intervention program would meet with parents, discuss the family's aspirations and concerns for their child, and collaboratively establish an IFSP (Individual Family Service Plan). The IFSPs used in Australia usually resemble those required by the USA legislation contained in the *Individuals with Disabilities Education Act* (IDEA, 1991) which requires:

- statement of child's present level of development
- statement of family resources, priorities, and concerns in relation to the child

- statement of the expected outcomes to be achieved by the child and family
- a list of services necessary to meet the needs of the child and family and how these will be delivered
- dates for beginning services and approximate length of time to receive these
- a statement of the places in which these services will be provided
- name of a service coordinator
- steps to be taken to assist in the child's transition to preschool services (that is, a transition plan).

Children with a disability and their families can be involved with intensive early intervention services from birth (if their disability is immediately obvious), until preschool entry, that is, for up to three years. During this time children probably will have undertaken continuous therapy and teaching sessions designed to promote their optimal development. Families often will have undertaken endless hours of information gathering, working with professionals and with their child, attending medical and educational visits, and managing the emotions and tasks that follow the initial diagnosis of the disability. They will have worked intensively to enable their child to be as ready as possible for entry to the next educational program.

Inclusion in early childhood environments

The majority of young children in Australia and New Zealand attend preschool or day care environments in the years before they enter formal schooling. Although there has been uncoordinated policy development with regard to inclusion in the early childhood years, Australian early childhood policymakers generally have valued the practice of including children with additional needs in mainstream education, and have expected that this will occur at the earliest possible opportunity. Policymakers have viewed mainstream early childhood settings as appropriate environments for all children irrespective of their abilities, and this has translated into a high level of acceptance of inclusive practices in Australian early childhood centres. The acceptance of inclusive practices in school settings has proceeded more slowly, but continues to gain impetus, and increasingly has resulted in positive experiences for children.

The rationale for inclusion has been clearly outlined in earlier chapters. However, it is clear that, if children with a disability are perceived to be equally valued members of mainstream environments from birth, inclusion can become a natural process which can continue in the early years of schooling.

For a number of reasons, inclusion is generally more successful with younger children. Families interact with mainstream communities and participate in the activities of those communities prior to the birth of their child with a disability. They continue to be part of those communities once the child with a disability or any other child enters the world, even though the 'early intervention journey', filled with emotion, onerous medical, educational and related services, sometimes sets families apart for a time.

Once the child moves from early intervention to a mainstream early childhood setting, the mainstream environment is generally more accommodating than at later ages. A number of factors contribute to this situation. Early childhood staff are trained to focus on individual needs and are more concerned with stages of development than age related development.

Teachers and child care workers observe and assess the developmental skills of each child in their classes, and plan individual programs that are implemented and carefully monitored. Teachers generally allow children to work at their own level, with demands to perform to a group standard being relatively low. Implementation of early childhood programs is characterised by great responsiveness, that is, teachers are able to capitalise on incidental opportunities that arise to teach particular skills, making programs highly flexible and responsive to individual needs.

Early childhood teachers are trained to observe children closely and identify areas of concern for all of their charges. They are successful at identifying all manner of delays and issues as the basis for programming to ensure the optimal development of each child. This approach suits the child with additional needs, and means that all children are perceived in the same way as having strengths and areas of need. This leads to a greater tolerance of a range of behaviour, in particular, an acceptance of behaviours that are not always socially appropriate, as this often is seen as a developmental issue rather than a long-term problem. In short, young children display a wide range of behaviours that may be deemed to be part of 'growing up'. Additionally, preschool teachers often find that the child identified with a disability on entry is not the most difficult child in the class to accommodate.

The individualised program approach of early childhood educators is complemented by pupil/teacher ratios that are generally much lower than for formal schooling, enabling more individual attention to be provided to each child, and individualisation to be more readily encouraged and supported.

The early childhood years are also a time of maximum family involvement. The ability of family and preschool to work closely together maximises the chance of success for the child by promoting understanding and consistency between both parties and environments.

The provision of specialist support, for example, speech pathology, has been a feature of inclusion in early childhood facilities. The services generally are welcomed by teachers, who are eager to cater for the individual needs of children and understand that specialist support is sometimes necessary. Early childhood environments are accustomed to the involvement of many adults, whether they be parents, volunteers or teaching staff, and the more informal early childhood environments are conducive to unobtrusive intervention by additional specialist staff.

As children with additional needs grow, differences in appearance and development can become more evident, making inclusion somewhat harder in the later years. In general, early childhood staff appear to recognise that the early years provide the opportunity for children with or without a disability to be educated in inclusive settings and to take advantage of all that such an arrangement has to offer.

The benefits of inclusion have been presented in Chapters 1 and 2, but are worth restating in the context of early childhood. Educational policymakers have generally supported the inclusion of children with disabilities in early childhood programs, and the practice has become widespread in the USA and Australia. The majority of efficacy studies on inclusion in the early childhood years have been conducted in the USA where positive outcomes are reported for children with disabilities and for their typically developing peers in inclusive settings (Odom, 2000).

Advantages for the child and the family

There are many advantages for the child and family if their child is educated in an inclusive setting. The child and family are able to have similar preschool experience to other families and children (that is, being close to home, part of the community, establishing local friendships, which can be commencement of long-term relationships). The child is exposed to role models resulting in skill development across all domains. The child is educated in a language-rich environment. Promotion of language is the key to cognitive development.

Inclusive environments constantly present 'incidental' demands to 'perform' (that is, the child will be drawn into activities by peers and teachers in a way that they would not have been in a segregated environment). Staff maintain high levels of expectations for the child, based on the skills and behaviours of peers. The child develops confidence to function in community environments because opportunities to acquire social competence and communication skills continually arise in this setting.

Parents want their children to be included in a mainstream early childhood program for similar reasons to other parents such as to 'help them reach their potential', for 'socialisation', to 'make friends', to 'learn to live in the real world', to 'make them productive citizens'. Additionally, they value the role models of the other children for behaviour, speech and social skills (Hanson et al., 1998).

Advantages for other children and families

It can be argued that inclusion has potential benefits for other children and families at the early childhood centre. Inclusion fosters an understanding, acceptance and enjoyment of the range of differences in people (Peck, Carlson & Helmstetter, 1992). Acquaintance with children with disabilities fosters knowledge about communication methods and disabilities (Diamond & Hestenes, 1994; 1996).

Other children can also benefit from the additional resources that have been applied to accommodate the child with additional needs. Program suggestions from special education and related professionals can be helpful for other children with minor problems. In addition, some children learn altruism and empathy while helping and encouraging those with different abilities from themselves.

In general, research has found that families of children who do not have disabilities in inclusive settings have been positive to inclusion. Community parents are generally accepting of the inclusion of children with disabilities unless there are behavioural issues that they believe may impinge on the safety or education of their children (Odom, Schwartz & ECRII Investigators, 2002).

Advantages for teachers and staff

Teachers in early childhood settings often report benefits from the inclusion of children with a disability in regular settings. Teachers have the opportunity to improve their teaching skills and to acquire knowledge from special educators and personnel from other disciplines who may be involved with children with disabilities.

Despite these potential benefits, it is clear that there is a host of variables affecting the outcome of inclusion. Successful inclusion is related to the implementation of programs that are both child and situation specific.

Transition to a regular early childhood environment

The transition from an early intervention program to a community preschool or early childhood centre is a significant milestone for the child and family. It is a major step towards autonomy and is associated with more independence and greater challenges for the child. Children with disabilities and their families will not only be faced with the adjustments that all children make when they enter the new environment but will also encounter additional challenges that are related to their disability. These could include being without the primary carer; functioning within a group; adjusting to an unfamiliar, sometimes confusing, 'busy' environment; learning to respond to group rather than individual directions; relating to a number of new adults; becoming more independent; learning to initiate own activities; and/or carrying out tasks with less adult help and attention.

Careful and comprehensive preparation involving the family, the child, and service providers is important in ensuring success, as everyone involved in the transition needs time to share information, obtain special resources, learn new skills and become familiar with the unfamiliar (Minor, 1997). This necessitates becoming aware of the role, the needs, concerns and aspirations of each of the other parties.

The first approach to a regular service

It is to be recognised that families and service providers will enter the 'inclusive relationship' with different backgrounds, and agendas. Some of the contrasts between families and early childhood staff are listed below.

- The primary concern for families is *their* child. Their goal will be to secure the best possible education for this child, and other children will be of much lesser concern. *Early childhood staff will be concerned about many children and will be balancing the needs of all of the children in their care.*
- Families are concerned about their child for the whole of life. Early childhood staff are concerned for a relatively short time (that is, the period the child is in their class or educational setting). *Service providers will cease to have responsibility for the child and will not need to be concerned with the long-term outcomes for the child.*
- Families of children with disabilities will have undergone a myriad of highly intense experiences prior to seeking entry to an inclusive early childhood environment. This may have included the establishment of a diagnosis, ongoing medical and therapy treatments, involvement in early intervention, family and lifestyle adjustments, and altered relationships with family friends and community members. *Early childhood staff initially will have no knowledge of the range and depth of the early experiences encountered by the family and their child.*
- Families will be intimately concerned with all aspects of their child's life and will see them in many roles and situations. *Early childhood staff primarily will be concerned with the aspects of the child's life that relate to their education.*
- Families know about all aspects of their child's development. *Early childhood staff know about general child development.*

- Families may know little about the funding, administrative, management, and functional arrangements of the preschool. *Early childhood staff will be intimately concerned about these issues.*
- Families arrive with vastly different backgrounds including culture, socio-economic status, family structure etc., which will have some bearing on how they relate to staff, how they view different aspects of the program, etc. *Early childhood staff are also influenced by their backgrounds and experiences, which may vary from those of parents.*

(This list is adapted from personal communication with Deborah Fullwood, 2003.)

Additionally, families approach the educational setting with a host of worries. The parents of a child with a disability may experience both excitement and anxiety about the prospect of their child's first entry to an educational setting. These emotions are common to all parents as they watch their child take the first independent steps into the community. Often they worry about the child's capacity to cope with unknown children, new adults and a foreign environment. The families of children with disabilities usually undergo a more intense experience, partially because of the vast amount of energy that has been expended to enable their child to reach the current level of development. Despite the mammoth efforts made, the parents will be conscious of the differences in development between their children and the community of children into which they are being placed.

Parents may be concerned whether:
- their child will be admitted to the program
- staff will support their child and 'treat them in the same way as others' (for example, will their interactions be as positive to their child as they are to all the others?)
- staff will treat their child with respect
- staff will refrain from talking about the child in front of them
- this is the right place for their child
- the child is ready to participate in this kind of program
- their child will be safe
- other children will respond to their child and interact positively with them
- their child will be able to cope without the parents
- staff will be willing to take on the additional responsibilities and duties associated with their child's additional needs
- the teacher will provide honest feedback about their child's progress in the program
- the program will be able to provide the special education teaching and other support their child needs
- the parents of other children will be positive towards their child and them.

Administrators may be concerned about the:
- safety of the child
- allocation of the appropriate teaching staff and the grouping of children
- adequacy of teacher training and skills
- extent of other demands placed on teachers
- provision of support to teachers, including other professionals
- organisation of inservice for teachers/staff members
- maintenance of funding once it is secured

- adequacy of funding
- reaction of other families
- organisation of relief staff if informed staff members are absent
- recruitment of aides.

Teachers may be concerned about:

- their lack of special education training, particularly in the area of programming
- their knowledge of disabilities and the implications, particularly the medical aspects and how to manage these
- the safety of the child
- the amount of time needed for preparation, implementation, and evaluation of programs
- the amount of time needed to meet with parents and involved professionals
- the level of competence needed to relate to parents about the child's complex issues
- issues associated with working with an aide (for example, time spent in training, liaison, supervision)
- the adequacy of the physical environment
- the impact on the other children in the class
- the reactions of the parents of other children in the class
- the extent of specialist support.

The concerns of the various parties can create tensions and may result in negative interactions. It is not uncommon for relationships among parents and administrators to be characterised by lack of trust, respect and shared values (Erwin et al., 2001), which is not in the best interests of the child. Administrators and teachers who are aware of, and ready to accommodate, the different world views of the parties involved in the inclusion process will be well placed to embark on a successful start to inclusion.

The initial meeting

The initial meeting will be an important first step in the building of positive relationships between the family and the centre. Such relationships have been found to be crucial for successful inclusion (Beckman, Hanson & Horn, 2002).

- When the parents approach the centre to request enrolment for their child the director/ principal (administrator) generally will organise a meeting time that is convenient for all participants. It is advisable to ensure that sufficient time is allocated to fully undertake the initial discussions, unrushed and uninterrupted.
- Parents should be encouraged to bring the child to the meeting as this will enable the administrator to observe the child, gain a cursory understanding of the child's needs, assist the child to become familiar with the new environment, allow the administrator to pay positive attention to the child and convey to the family that the child will be a valued member of the class.
- The family should be encouraged to bring all relevant reports to the meeting to inform the staff and enable them to think about their planning.
- Every attempt should be made to create a friendly, relaxed atmosphere in which parents feel comfortable. This will facilitate the exchange of information and commence relationship building between the family and the centre.

- Consultation with the parents will provide information about the child's history, the culture, family structure, number and ages of the siblings, language used at home, the value system and socio-emotional climate of the home.
- Relevant medical issues and needs should be discussed.
- Parents will be able to provide information about the child's likes and dislikes, favourite activities, what motivates the child, physical care needs, safety issues, food preferences, etc.
- It will be important to find out which particular skills or competencies the family would like to be prioritised in the child's program.
- Parents can also often provide valuable information about the teaching strategies they have found to be effective. It is important to create an understanding that the child's program is an enterprise that the staff and parents share, one in which they learn from each other.
- The family should be encouraged to talk freely about their child and about their aspirations for the child in the new environment.
- The administrator should accompany the family on a tour of the educational facility. The family can then visualise the child in the environment and, as a result, may or may not proceed to seek enrolment. The administrator can gauge the parents' reaction to certain aspects of the program and incorporate this information into future planning.
- The parents should be encouraged to ask questions and voice concerns.
- The administrator should be open and honest about the way in which the program operates.
- Together the family and administrator should determine the next steps in the quest for inclusion.

Preparing the inclusive environment

Administrators

As part of the enrolment process the administrator will seek parental approval to examine the child's reports and discuss program needs with the service providers who have previously worked with the child, organise another formal assessment to ensure the child qualifies for funding (if necessary), apply for funding, think about allocation of staff, and commence preparation of the physical environment. The administrator will seek to determine:

- the extent of the need for specialist services (for example, early childhood special educator, physiotherapy, speech therapy etc.) and how they can be incorporated into the program while including the child with the group as much as possible
- consultancy needs
- necessary adaptations to centre layout, furniture, and equipment, both inside and outside
- need for additional equipment
- need for additional staff – it is preferable that this is determined before the child is enrolled
- staff needs in terms of information and inservice training
- support needs for the parent of the child
- decisions about the child's attendance schedule
- whether parents wish to be directly involved in the program
- how progress will be measured, recorded and reported
- management of health and/or emergency procedures (for example, care of hearing aids, what to do if the child has a seizure, etc.).

Once the child has been accepted for enrolment, the creation of positive staff attitudes towards the inclusion of the child will be the primary task. Staff will feel more confident that they can be successful and will manage better if they feel they have the commitment of the administrator and their full support. All staff in the facility should be involved in the preparation as they will all be involved in the care and education of the child (Lieber et al., 1997).

Teachers

Upon enrolment, teachers will begin to plan for the child by attempting to ascertain the child's needs from reports, discussion with the director, the parents, and staff who have worked with the child. Soodak et al. (2002) have highlighted the need for administrators and educators who are open and eager to collaborate with parents, confident they can contribute to system change, work hard to implement changes, and are committed to professional growth and continuous improvement.

Including the child in the regular program is more likely to be successful if staff:

- feel the child has the same right to a place as all other children, that is, the child belongs
- understand that the child's additional needs will require adjustments to program planning, content, teaching methods and/or the time taken to plan and implement programs
- are willing to share responsibility for the child
- demonstrate that they value the child

- empathise with parents
- are willing to spend considerable time consulting with parents
- work in partnership with parents
- work as a team
- are eager to share with other disciplines and have skills in collaborative working
- recognise their limitations and seek assistance.

The families of children with disabilities will come from a diverse range of backgrounds and have undertaken a wide variety of experiences. Some of the family background factors that will need to be considered when staff are interacting with the parents of the child with additional needs include:

- language background, which may mean that the family has difficulties with English requiring use of interpreters and translated written information
- culture, which may impact on attitudes to disability, the role of family members in the child's educational program, feeling of lack of empowerment in Australian society
- the level of confidence with school systems, which may be influenced by previous experiences
- support networks in the community
- intra-family support and friendship networks
- the role of the child in the family
- the parents' feelings of control over various situations they encounter
- past experiences with the child
- child characteristics
- parents' desires to 'get on with their life' balanced with the needs of the child
- the value attributed to education and the aspirations held for the child
- the presence of other children in the family
- emotional factors relating to the child
- experience with early childhood special education
- knowledge of their own child but parents will probably know very little about assessment and programming in this setting.

Parents who have been involved with an early intervention program and more individual skill-based programming will need to learn about how children will be encouraged to learn new skills in a naturalistic program.

Parents of the child with a disability

Parents will need to be assured that teachers care about and like their child. They will need to be reassured that teachers will provide the best possible programs for their child. They will need to understand how this will be implemented within the activities organised throughout the day. Parents may have little understanding of the roles of various staff members and their preservice training and may need information to reassure them. They will need to realise that the centre staff have many responsibilities in the classroom and will not be able to focus on their child at all times. Parents may sometimes need some help to understand that staff have to balance all their responsibilities without sacrificing the needs of any of the children in their care.

After the parents have been fully informed about the program, decisions will need to be made about how communication between them and the centre will be conducted, the special considerations being made for their child, a strategy for addressing problems, and how they can assist the teacher.

Parents of other children

The administrator, staff and the child's parents may collaboratively decide that it is in the best interests of the child with the disability if the other parents in the child's class have knowledge of the child's needs on, or soon after, enrolment. In this case they will ascertain a strategy and a time for talking with parents. On the other hand, the parents might prefer that their child enters the school on the same basis as any other child, that is, with known and unknown needs and may see informing the parent community as unnecessary. However, the findings of Chadwick & Kemp (2003), studying kindergarten classes, demonstrated that of the many possible school preparation factors they explored, only one, 'the preparation of the other parents in the child's class for the integration of the child, demonstrated a significant relationship with successful integration'. It is possible that these results are also applicable to inclusive preschool environments.

Other children

The teacher and parents may decide it would be wise to talk with children about individual differences, including those of the child with a disability, as a way of creating understanding and empathy among peers. Sometimes, if a child has an obvious difference, it is helpful to use an explanation such as 'John is still learning to talk, but he likes to play just the way you do'. On the other hand, teachers may find that modelling positive interactions is the best way to promote understanding and acceptance of the child with a disability.

Physical environment

The disabilities of the children seeking entry to early childhood environments may be the result of physical, sensory, intellectual and/or behavioural/emotional problems. It cannot be assumed that the child's disability label will provide the key to determining the accommodations needing to be made to the physical environment, for example, a child labelled 'hearing impaired' may have a severe impairment and be using signed communication, or may use a hearing aid or cochlear implant, and communicate solely through listening and speaking. The child with cerebral palsy may have restricted limb movement and use a wheelchair for mobility, or may have little impairment. A full assessment of the child's needs and the physical environment should be undertaken to ensure that the appropriate modifications can be made. This is usually best conducted by a specialist or specialists in the area, for example, physiotherapist, orthoptist, occupational therapist, or access consultant, in collaboration with the teacher. As with all aspects of the child's inclusion, parent consultation will provide valuable information to assist in the preparation of the physical environment.

Equipment and materials

Some children will require use of specific prosthetic equipment and some will require adaptations to the physical environment, for example, furniture arrangement. However, the usual age-appropriate toys and equipment provided in preschool environments will generally be appropriate for children with diverse additional needs.

Early days

Once the child is enrolled in the early childhood setting, the process of 'settling in' and adapting to the new environment commences. After familiarising themselves with the child's history, the teaching staff begin assessing the child to facilitate program planning. The assessment process will take some weeks. In early childhood programs, as at all other levels of education, there are different types of assessment for different purposes. In general, early childhood educators glean the majority of their information for the purposes of program planning from discussions with the parents and direct observation of the child, in conjunction with direct input and reports from other professionals. The initial assessment will need to be more comprehensive than later assessments so that a detailed Individual Education Plan (IEP) can be formulated.

It is suggested that observations in the preschool setting be carried out over a period of time, within a broad range of activities and that all developmental domains are included. It is useful to involve all staff members with the observations while bearing in mind that children with additional needs may take longer than other children to adjust to and become familiar with a new environment and unfamiliar adults and peers.

The objective of observation is to obtain a better understanding of the child's strengths, interests and abilities in order to assist programming and teaching. The following issues can form a basis for observing the child.

General issues

- The objects and activities that seem to interest the child
- The activities the child enjoys
- The names of other children approached most often by the child
- The activities within which interactions take place
- The names of children who approach or interact with this child
- The way in which the child responds to the various activities and approaches of other children
- The staff member to whom the child relates most positively
- The way the child communicates wants, needs, pleasure, discomfort

Environmental issues

- The child's ability to access all activities
- The child's ability to find their way to the toilet
- The amount of assistance the staff need to provide
- Whether the child knows where various activities are located and their purpose

Behavioural issues

- Self-esteem and confidence
- Ability to make choices
- The child's capacity to attend to adults and/or peers, and/or tasks

- Whether the child can follow directions and at what level – simple or complex
- The way the child approaches a task
- The way the child communicates with other children and adults
- The child's capacity to concentrate on a task and persist with the activity
- The child's level of awareness of, and interest in, their surroundings including other children in the group
- The ability of the child to initiate an activity
- The social appropriateness of the child's behaviour
- The extent to which the child generalises learned behaviour to other activities in social and non-social environments

Developmental skills

- Gross motor
- Fine motor
- Communication
- Social skills
- Self-help skills
- Cognitive skills

After the first few weeks of consultation and observations the teacher is ready to prepare the IEP in consultation with a collaborative team, including the centre staff, parents, relevant professionals who are, or who have been, involved in the child's care and/or program, and early intervention teachers. It will incorporate the parents' aspirations, and priorities in the home setting and information from previous medical and developmental assessments.

The child's individual program should include the specific learning goals that have been agreed upon for the child with a disability. These will be functional and relevant in the context of the child's home and culture, as well as the centre environment They should be aimed towards independence, be developmentally appropriate, measurable, purposeful for the child, and promote the acquisition, generalisation and maintenance of skills (Bricker & Woods Cripe, 1992; Bricker, Prette-Frontczak & McComas, 1998).

The program should include relevant details about the strengths and learning approaches used by the child and detail some strategies that teachers will use and how these will be adapted to fit in with different activities. There needs to be a method of recording progress each day to be used by all staff members, and an evaluation plan. There should also be information about the child's preferences and motivators, determined through observation and parent interview.

Implementation

Most early childhood researchers and professionals support the view that infants and preschool children will develop, learn skills, and acquire knowledge and information when provided with a stimulating, responsive, and supportive environment. This environment is designed to provide opportunities for play, interaction with peers, lots of stimulating, challenging and developmentally appropriate experiences and materials, with the encouragement of supportive adults who are knowledgeable about stages of development. This type of program is recommended by the revised Developmentally Appropriate Practice in Early Childhood

Programs (Bredekamp & Copple, 1997), which is based on the developmental theories of Piaget (1963) and Vygotsky (1978), promoting the theme that learning occurs through play. Teachers ensure that children acquire knowledge and skills relevant to their age, stage of development and needs for the next educational environment through rhymes, songs, activities, and experiences.

The environment that this type of program provides has also proved to be an appropriate learning environment for children with a disability, but these children will require additional individualised programming and instruction to achieve functional and developmental goals (Bredekamp & Rosegrant, 1992.) The provision of activities and equipment is also guided by an awareness of cultural backgrounds, age appropriateness and individual differences in personality, growth, interests and experiences. The progress of the children is carefully monitored, generally through observations during play, with individual goals updated on a regular basis to ensure that development proceeds.

One of the main advantages of inclusion for the child with a disability is that they will be part of the mainstream environment of their age group. In a well-organised program, children will have the opportunity to interact with a variety of materials, other children and adults. This creates the opportunity for greater emphasis to be placed on the acquisition of age-appropriate social competence and social interaction skills in a non-directive manner. It helps if all activities are arranged so that opportunities for teaching social interaction in the context of other activities can occur in a natural way with minimal teacher prompts. Although it is recommended that all staff are involved and responsible for the implementation of the program plan, as is the case with other children in the group, one teacher will be chosen to be primarily responsible for ensuring that the program is carried out daily and that results are recorded each day the child attends.

When therapists and/or an early intervention teacher are to be involved in the program implementation, it is preferable for that person to work with the child within the classroom where there are lots of opportunities for the child to practise new skills in the regular program within a small group. This is usually possible in early childhood environments because children are often in small groups in the classroom and playground during the usual activities of the day. If it is necessary to withdraw the child, perhaps another child could also be included.

Goals for a home program are also sometimes established, but it is as well to remember that parents are often busy. A home communication book is a useful idea. A brief note in the book can let parents know about things that happen at preschool. Parents can also inform teachers if there are home issues that are of relevance in the school environment.

Teaching strategies

A number of different strategies have been used to address the individual learning goals of children with disabilities within the routines and activities of the regular centre without separating them from the group. It is important that the focus child participates in all activities at some level. Many opportunities arise in activities and routines to teach new skills and the opportunity to practise these in naturalistic and functional settings. Different teaching strategies work for different children and different situations. Sometimes a combination of different strategies works best.

There are a number of strategies that fall within the ambit of naturalistic teaching strategies where *naturalistic teaching strategies* are defined as systematic approaches that use typical routines and activities in natural environments as the teaching context (Noonan & McCormick, 1993).

The common features of these approaches are:

1 They occur in the child's natural settings (for example, play and activities occurring in the classroom).
2 The teacher identifies times during the day when a child has the opportunity to engage in an activity where the desired skill can be incorporated.
3 The teacher organises the activity so the opportunity occurs and provides the support necessary.
4 The natural consequences of participating in the learning opportunity are fun and rewarding for the child.

(Odom et al., 2002)

These strategies have various names but are much the same as the intuitive strategies mothers use when teaching their infants and young children. Mothers model language and behaviour and, without conscious thought, match it to the child's developmental level and needs of the moment. They use *teachable moments*.

Example

The child waves goodbye to Dad in the morning and says 'daddy go work'. His mother will reinforce what they have said but also extend it a little saying 'Yes! Daddy's going to work *in the car*'. She will usually repeat it and prompt the child to imitate 'Daddy's gone to work in the … *car*. He went in the …'

Embedding is described as a procedure in which children are given opportunities to practise individual goals and objectives that are included within an activity or event in a manner that expands, modifies or adapts the activity/event while remaining meaningful and interesting to children (Bricker, Prette-Frontczak & McComas, 1998, p. 13). The teacher includes the opportunity to learn or practise a skill in a regular preschool activity that the child is likely to enjoy. The teacher provides support to ensure the child is successful, thus encouraging confidence while building on the child's interest.

Example

Learning goal – understanding and use of spatial terms

Activities for the day could include embedding of the learning goal as follows:

• Sand play with little cars making hills to go over and shoe box bridges to go under.
• In home corner objects to be put and found 'in', 'on', 'under', etc.
• 'Tidying up time' could also provide the same kind of opportunities with child having to 'find' or pick up objects 'under' chair or table, etc.
• Dressing skills can be incorporated into dress-up corner, labelling of objects can be part of playing shops or setting the table in home corner.

It's important to ensure that the child knows exactly what they need to do to get a positive outcome.

Scaffolding is a term used by Bruner (1982) that aptly describes an interaction where the teacher unobtrusively assists with the first stages of an activity or task and encourages the child to assist or finish the last step. The teacher gradually withdraws assistance and support as the child manages more of the task independently. This is also sometimes referred to as *backward chaining* and is usually very effective as the child initially has to complete only one small step before having the satisfaction of success.

Example

Learning goal – develop hand–eye coordination through bead threading

Step 1:   Teacher puts her hand over the child's hand grasping plastic tubing and pushes tubing through the bead held in her other hand. Teacher guides child's hand to slide bead towards stopper at the end of the tubing, gradually removing guiding hands.

Step 2:   With the next bead teacher gradually reduces pressure letting child guide tubing through hole and push bead along.

Step 3:   Repeat, gradually reducing guidance until child completes the activity alone.

Time delay is an effective tool in a situation where a child wants or needs something that is necessary for the next step in a behaviour chain.

Example

Learning goal – naming objects

Home corner activity – putting doll to bed. Teacher holds doll, sheet, blanket, and baby bottle and withholds each object till verbally requested.

Physical and verbal prompts are excellent tools that teachers use frequently. However, remember to recognise the need to give children the time and dignity to solve their own problems when they can. Ensure that they participate in problem solving situations during play and routines etc.

Incidental teaching was defined by Warren and Kaiser (1988) as 'the interactions between an adult and child that arise naturally in an unstructured situation'. They maintain that incidental teaching can teach target skills effectively in the natural environment and assist in the generalisation of these skills across settings, time and persons, resulting in gains in the formal and functional aspects of language (Kaiser, Hendrickson & Alpert, 1991).

Teachers who are very aware of individual goals make use of teaching opportunities that arise during daily routines and activities. The interventions are brief and typically respond to the child's behaviour and result in naturally occurring consequences.

Example

Learning goal – requesting needs

At morning tea time children are waiting for their drink. The teacher serving the drink holds jug over each child's cup 'What do you want?' 'Do you want a drink?' Child replies 'Drink please'. When it's the turn of the focus child the correct response has been modelled a number of times and they will probably imitate and be rewarded with the drink. Any approximation or attempt is rewarded to begin with, but closer approximations are expected each time.

Other naturalistic strategies suggested by Bricker and Woods Cripe (1992), but also often used by mothers, include:

*   *Forgetting* – the teacher pretends to have forgotten some piece of equipment or an important component of an activity, for example, no cups for juice time or paint brushes

for painting. The goal is for the children to recognise that something is wrong and ask questions, look for material and problem solve.

- *Visible but unreachable* – the teacher puts objects that will be wanted within sight but out of reach. This can stimulate language and problem solving. It is advisable to make sure an adult is nearby and ready to respond to the verbal request or to provide help, and ensure safety if problem solving is the goal.
- *Violation of expectations* – children find incongruity amusing when something is changed in a well known activity or routine and this provokes communicative and problem solving responses, for example, putting blocks on children's plates for morning tea.
- *Piece by piece* – this is useful in an activity with a number of pieces of equipment, for example, setting the table or creating a collage. Teacher holds pieces and gives them to the child but only when named.

Teachers also prepare the activities and equipment with individual children's program needs in mind. For example, if fine motor skills are a priority for a number of the children who attend on Tuesday, teachers could prepare finger paint and playdough activities and select toys that involve manipulative skills. They could provide little bags of sultanas for morning tea, and demonstrate eating them one by one. Wet sand instead of water play may be prepared giving children who need to develop fine motor skills the opportunity to develop these skills in an incidental way.

Children without disabilities explore their environment and experiment with the functions of objects and equipment that they find around them. Children with disabilities will often need to be explicitly shown the functions of objects and their use demonstrated. They may need to be specifically taught many of the skills other children learn incidentally. Play skills and the ability to invite another to play and to respond to another's invitation to play are very important skills for success in the playground at school, and should be the focus for specific teaching. Many children with disabilities have not had the opportunity to interact and play informally with other children before going to school. This may be for a number of reasons, such as health care regimes, appointments, parental concern and, sometimes, fragility. They have often learned to interact quite well with adults and this may obscure their inability to relate to peers.

Although most children learn many of the skills mentioned incidentally, teachers will need to specifically program for these skills for children with additional needs, and use a direct teaching approach.

There are also some general teaching strategies that have proved to be useful in working with young children with additional needs. Individual teaching interactions are more likely to be effective if they are brief and spread throughout the day. The position of the teacher is also important. Children are more responsive when approached at eye level so that they are spoken 'with' rather than 'at'.

Effective communication and positive social interaction skills are important for all preschool children but are vital for the successful integration of children with disabilities into the broader community. Children with special needs should be included in all preschool activities. Giving them a role of some kind in all activities is necessary for genuine inclusion. The teacher should take every opportunity to encourage social interaction and group involvement.

A most valuable and effective motivator is success. Ensure that a task for a focus child within a group activity is adapted to their ability level, for example, if a group of children is cutting out pictures, the focus child could snip and fringe a paper mat or tear strips and contribute to making a collage. Goals need to be revised when necessary. It may become obvious that they are too low, too high, or even inappropriate.

Use encouragement and recognition of effort rather than unspecified praise. For example: 'You built a very big castle!' is better than 'You're a good boy!'. Acknowledgement of the child when they begin a task without a prompt is important, as is acknowledgement for completion. Remember that success must be measured against IEP goals, not against peers or chronological age.

Many children with disabilities will have shorter auditory memory and concentration spans than same-aged children. Short sentences and instructions spoken a little more slowly than usual give the child longer to process information before making a response. Repeating phrases and exaggerating key words can help. Ask open-ended questions that require more than a 'yes' or 'no' response.

It is important to have high expectations, which may not always be easy to maintain. However, this is critical if children with a disability are to reach their potential.

Assessment and monitoring

Activities, even when well planned, will not guarantee that children will learn new skills or generalise these skills to new situations. The learning objectives should be evaluated each day and the objective and the teaching strategies adjusted, and decisions made concerning activities for the next session the child will attend. More comprehensive assessments and meetings with parents and other agencies involved should be held each term to discuss and monitor progress and make decisions about the next step.

During the year before children move on to school, individual programs will focus on the skills and competencies that will assist their transition to the new environment and prepare them for a more teacher directed, curriculum oriented, formal academic program. A number of studies have focused on the identification of the skills that are important for success in the school environment (Carruthers, 1986; 1995; Johnson et al., 1995; Green & Kemp, 1998; Hains et al., 1989; Salisbury & Vincent, 1990). The skills identified in these studies are similar. They relate to independence, social competence, following classroom routines and directions, self-help, functional communication and play skills, rather than pre-academic skills. The preparation for school for the child with a disability will be enhanced if the teacher responsible for the child's program in the preschool has an understanding of the specific environment into which the child will be placed, and the skills the child will need to cope in that environment. The preschool teacher should visit the receiving classroom to observe the program in progress and discuss needs with the classroom teacher. Opportunities to teach the identified skills and routines should then be planned and incorporated into the child's program within the general activities of the preschool program, thus providing the opportunity for generalisation.

Box 3.1
Voices: Mainstreaming Joshua

When Joshua was young, I had my heart set on him going to a regular preschool. At the appropriate time I phoned up the local preschool to put his name down, as I had done with my other children. When I mentioned that Joshua had an intellectual disability, I was told that it would be a very different process for him. Joshua would have to undergo a battery of psychometric tests and then someone from the Department of Education would advise us of the best setting for him. After the testing I was told that (in their opinion) the best place for him was the special school. When I asked about the possibility of him going to the local preschool, I was told that there were no places available.

I decided to make my own inquiries and discovered that there were, in fact, two places available at the government preschool in my street. I begged the preschool teacher to support a trial enrolment. She was extremely hesitant, but eventually, I wore her down and she agreed to 'give it a go'. I had to promise that if she wasn't happy, I would remove him.

So, after intense negotiations with everyone concerned, Joshua started preschool with his neighbourhood peers. His teacher was extremely concerned about his developmental delay and initially focused on the things he couldn't/wouldn't do and his differences. I spent a lot of time at the preschool each week, helping out on the fruit and cleaning rosters, which gave me the opportunity to tell the teacher what a great job she was doing and how happy I was that he was there. In time, Joshua settled into preschool and his teacher relaxed. Joshua's differences and delays became less noticeable. The other children had never really noticed in the first place. He was invited to birthday parties and was included in every way. He belonged.

>

Box 3.1 continued

When it came time for him to go to school his preschool teacher showed me a draft of her report on his progress. It was about half a page outlining the things he couldn't do – his poor fine motor skills, his communication problems, his short attention span, difficult behaviour, inability to master pre-reading and pre-writing tasks and so on. Everything in her report was true. But there was not one positive thing on the page. I asked her 'What things can he do now that he couldn't do at the start of the year?' She thought about this for a minute. And then she said, 'Well, he doesn't run away any more, and he can sit with the group for longer. He participates more … and his fine motor skills have really improved'. I talked to her for about an hour by which time she had written a page and a half of things he could do and the skills he had developed. It was a very positive report. And everything in it was true.

The transition to school was a very stressful one. Not for Joshua but for me. I had so many questions. Would we be able to enrol him in the school of our choice? What would the barriers be? Would the teachers accept him? Would they have the skills to teach him? Was Joshua ready for school? How could we best prepare him? And how would the school deal with the myriad of problems – communication, toileting, running away?

Some of the answers surprised me. And when I didn't get what I desperately wanted for him (for example, a place at the school his sisters attended) the alternatives often turned out to be more than satisfactory.

The school had organised the necessary resources (and more) and put in place all of the required supports, but they were still very nervous. His teachers seemed to believe that if he couldn't achieve the same things as the other students it was somehow their fault, they hadn't taught him properly. Their goals and expectations were very high. Initially, I believed that Joshua had to change to fit the school, he had to be 'good enough' to go there. But I came to realise that really the school needed to change their attitudes and practices to accommodate him, which in time they did. In time we all learned that his differences could be accommodated and that it was OK for him to achieve at his own pace.

Joshua was included in his neighbourhood preschool and school. He was well liked by his peers. He developed confidence in himself and his surroundings and was happy. He learned to communicate and socialise with others and they learned to communicate and socialise with him. His Year 2 report sums up his experience of mainstreaming: 'Joshua is a very popular boy … He really likes it best when he is doing what everyone else is doing. Joshua gets his cues from other class members and tries to fit in. He does this so well. Joshua is to be commended on a mighty fine semester.'

Joshua's mother

Transition to school

Despite intensive preparation, children with disabilities will face many challenges when commencing school (Richardson, 1997; Briggs & Potter, 1995; Meier & Schafran, 1999; Pianta & Kraft-Sayre, 1999; Wood & Bennett, 1999). There will be some children with additional needs who have yet to acquire the prerequisites for academic learning. The regular classroom program will need to be modified for these children. Some children will not have acquired the necessary social and communication skills to ensure successful inclusion.

Some of the adjustments that school beginners must make include being part of and functioning within a larger educational environment; becoming more independent of adult attention, response and guidance; learning new rules and coping with more regimented routines; relating to different adults; adjusting to more formal interactions with adults; getting to know a different group of children and making new friends; attempting new tasks in an unfamiliar environment; adapting to a shift in curriculum emphasis from a discovery child-centred approach to a more subject-dominated program with specific learning goals; and separating from the primary caregiver into a new environment.

The parents of children with a disability are usually aware of the necessity to plan for school but may need to be prompted to begin the process of transition. Ideally the process needs to begin early in the year before the child goes to school. Parents need to be well informed to participate effectively. They will need to have some understanding of the way the Department of School Education in their state operates, what policies, funding arrangements, rules and procedures control the processes of integration and transition to school. They should also investigate options available in the non-government schools in the area. They also benefit from being aware of relevant policies and legislation that will support their choice for inclusion.

There are several factors that can inhibit effective parent participation in the transition process. Some parents are not aware that they are entitled to attend meetings concerned with their child's placement before beginning school, and to attend meetings that review the child's progress and placement after enrolment. Language can also be a barrier. Parents who can speak and understand English sufficiently well for everyday interactions may need an interpreter to ensure that they can understand unfamiliar terminology and processes discussed at meetings. Even parents whose first language is English can be confused by the use of professional jargon and unfamiliar acronyms during meetings, or by the presence of a large number of very confident professionals. It is also very confusing for parents if they are not informed about the role and/or responsibility of other participants in the process.

Education authorities have recognised the contribution successful transitions to school make in ensuring continued success for the child in the educational environment. It has become accepted that a planned transition process is the key to success. A number of different models have been developed and trialled in the USA and in Australia. The formation of a 'transition team' has been recommended as a useful initial step in the process (Conn-Powers, Ross-Allen & Holburn, 1990; Rous, Hemmeter & Schuster, 1994; New South Wales Department of School Education, 1997). Each of the personnel responsible for some aspect of the child's care and education is invited either by the parent or one of the service providers, with the parent's permission, to meet and plan for the child's transition to school. The functions of this team would include:

- ensuring that the family is informed about the school options that are available in the area
- supporting the family in their interactions with the education system and/or personnel from non-government schools
- organising visits to schools and meetings with school executives and facilitating the exploration and consideration of these options

- providing the opportunity for families to examine the advantages and disadvantages of the options available for their child
- developing a plan to prepare the child and their family for school that will include orientation activities in cooperation with the school
- ensuring that relevant assessment information is compiled cooperatively into a report for school personnel
- ensuring that relevant information about the transition process is shared with parents and service providers
- assisting parents with the collection of medical and developmental history relevant to the child's enrolment and/or program, and the transfer of this information to the proposed school
- ensuring that parents are informed as soon as possible about enrolment and support decisions
- organising for a relevant expert to address the staff and/or the parent group about the disability of the child to be integrated if and when this is appropriate or required
- establishment of an integrated program with shared goals that will be implemented in a coordinated and cooperative manner.

The team and its various functions need to be coordinated. The parents may choose to do this themselves, but may prefer that another member of the team take this responsibility. Personnel from the child's current and future environments will be invited to join the team during the year. It is suggested that team members meet at least three times before school begins. The coordinator will take responsibility for organising meetings, information collection, distribution and sharing when necessary. In Australia, the processes have been published in guidelines for families and educators. For example, the New South Wales Department of School Education has developed guidelines (1997) and made them available to early childhood programs, early intervention programs and schools.

Successful transitions can increase parents' confidence in their ability to deal with organisations and can assist them in their role as advocates for their child in the future. There is an awareness that the inherent stress of transition for children and parents can be alleviated to some extent by ensuring that changes are introduced gradually where possible and by allowing plenty of time for adjustment to a new situation.

During the transition process the child may need to be assessed for entry to school. The process of assessing children for school entry is more regulated than for preschool entry. Several different assessments, some formal, some informal, are carried out. The first round of assessments is designed to determine the best school option for the child, and to ensure that the limited resources available are used in the most equitable and effective manner. Sometimes a formal assessment using a norm-referenced test is a requirement, often leading to an IQ score. Parents sometimes find these tests distressing (Shotts et al., 1994), particularly if they are the primary source of information for decision making about placement. The results tend to be expressed in numerical terms that determine the labelling of a child with a category or degree of disability.

The use of such tests with young children remains unpopular with some early childhood educators who feel that a 'one off' test, often administered by an unfamiliar adult in an unfamiliar environment, does not yield results that reflect the true abilities of the child. The more unique the child, the less valid the results are likely to be. Parents are often distressed when their child fails to perform to their best during the testing process. More comprehensive data collection, involving observation, parent and professional input and developmental checklists, usually provides information which parents and preschool teachers feel is more reliable and more valid for decision making about the child. Such an approach is supported by the National Association for the Education of Young Children (1991).

Entry to school will bring similar issues to those experienced on entry to preschool. Faced with the prospect of school, parents often reassess their child in terms of the skills and competencies of other children of the same age without disabilities, rather than in terms of their child's individual progress. This adjustment often results in another period of grieving and adjustment similar to that usually experienced by parents when they first become aware of the child's impairment. Consequently, while other parents may be excited about the prospect of school, parents of children with a disability may be experiencing great levels of anxiety and stress.

Professionals who are helping with the transition process will need to approach parents in a sensitive and understanding manner, realising that parents will react and cope with this occasion in different ways. The emotions of the parents may be reflected in their behaviour, for example, they may appear aggressive and demanding, or perhaps timid and frightened, about what will happen to their child.

When children move into the local school, parents will sometimes miss the informal relationship with staff that developed in preschool early childhood programs. Parents and staff generally use first names in preschool, and parents are encouraged to either observe or join in the program activities whenever they wish. The higher staff-to-child ratio in preschool early childhood programs makes it easier for staff members to be available to parents, and the informality of the relationship can be very supportive.

Getting to know the parents of the other school beginners and being involved in the school community will be important for parents of children with disabilities and should be actively encouraged. Regional groups for the parents of children with additional needs, integrated into regular schools, could provide mutual support and the opportunity to share experiences, problems and to generate solutions. Parents may also find the support groups in the community that are concerned with particular disabilities very informative and helpful.

As in preschool, parents will be worried about whether their child will be safe in the 'big school' environment, particularly in the playground. They will also be concerned about the attitude of the classroom teacher to having a child with a disability in the class; other children's interactions with their child; the reactions of the parents of other children about the presumed extra teacher-time the child with a disability will need; their child's ability to cope and their happiness in the situation; knowing what is happening in the classroom; having the opportunity to ask questions and share problems and problem-solving with teachers; whether teachers will give them honest information about the child's day and include positive as well as negative reports; whom they should approach if they have concerns; whether the expression of concerns or complaints might put at risk their child's continued enrolment at the school; being unaware of how best to prepare their child to participate effectively and happily in the kindergarten classroom.

Parents may have been very involved in their child's early intervention or preschool program and be aware of the child's developmental profile, of what best motivates the child, of teaching strategies and management strategies that have worked well for their child. It is therefore difficult to cope with suddenly having no active part in the child's program, and having the school ignore the knowledge and expertise they have acquired during the last five years. Lehr (1992) points out that parents like to be invited to help solve problems and to share what they know.

Separation for parents who may have hitherto never had the opportunity to leave their child with another caregiver can sometimes be even more difficult. Even those parents who now are ready to entrust their child and the program to the school, enabling them to pursue a career or other interests, will usually find the transition process difficult. School personnel will need to understand some of the stresses facing parents to enable sensitive collaborative relationships.

Options in inclusion

When the term 'inclusion' is used by parents, administrators and teachers, there is a tendency to assume this means immediate, full participation in preschool or school for the child with a disability. In reality, however, there is a range of options for children who have additional needs, and families may take advantage of different options at different times in the child's

---

Box 3.2
Voices: Being a parent

A parent expresses her feelings

My experience has been that being a parent of any child is an important, tiring, constant, though fulfilling job; being the parent of a disabled child is also important, even more tiring and more constant, but, on the whole fulfilling; but being the parent of a disabled child integrated into a regular preschool or school is so exhausting and constant that you haven't the time or energy to spell the word important let alone consider the various meanings of the word fulfilling. It's the hard option.

It's hard to be the parent of the child who is seen as different in the school when all the other children are seen as similar. It's hard to keep the teachers happy, confident and feeling supported. It's hard to find some support yourself. It is hard to keep the hovering professionals informed, coordinated and providing the sort of support the class teacher wants. It's hard trying not to appear too knowledgeable about your child. It's hard being a 'good' parent with all the usual school duties – and believe me the pressure to be a good parent is immense. It's hard being the parent of the child who other parents blame for anything at all – bad habits in their child, poor speech in their child, class unrest, teacher exhaustion.

It's lovely though being the parent of the child who wins the sack race, even if it's only because his legs are so short he doesn't have to shorten his stride. It is lovely being the parent of the delighted child who gets invited to his first 'non-disabled birthday party'. It is lovely being the parent of the child who has learned to read and who got an 'A' for manners.

Deborah Fullwood

---

life. The reasons families may select a particular option will be complex and unique to their circumstances. Families may consider factors such as travel arrangements, out of school hours care, opportunities for socialisation, the cultural values of the school community, as well as program and other related issues.

In preschool programs the range of decisions could involve: number of days of attendance, long day care/preschool placements, the possibility of part-time attendance (to prepare child and school for full attendance), or a mix of preschool and early intervention.

When entering school, options may include private or public school; special class/regular class with or without support, short-term placement in special school to prepare the child for inclusion, and part-time placements.

Whatever the option, families should make their choice using the most comprehensive information available about the benefits and potential limitations of each option. This can only be done in collaboration with those involved in the child's present and potential placement. In the words of Anne Naylor (a parent):

> Most parents make choices in the very best interests of their child. If it has been researched, informed and carefully thought out, then that must be seen as the best choice for those parents. The unique set of beliefs, understandings, reasons and motivations they may have are central to their point of view, and consequently their decision. When I am making a choice for my child, I hope that other people understand and respect my right to do so, irrespective of whether they agree with me or not.

Summary

Children with disabilities usually commence their educational journey by attending early intervention programs. Two basic principles guiding early intervention are the implementation of 'family centred practice' and including children in 'natural environments'.

When children enter preschool and school education it is expected that 'family centred practices' already established in early intervention will continue to be implemented. Fully involving families in the early years of their child's education is perceived to be the best way to secure optimum outcomes for the child.

The understanding that, wherever possible, children with disabilities should be included in environments that are most 'natural' for their non-disabled peers, means the majority of families will seek enrolment in mainstream preschool educational environments and mainstream 'big' schools for their children. Attending preschool education and 'big' school for the first time are important steps in the child's autonomy and independence. Research and practice have demonstrated that the stress associated with the process can be lessened and the chances of successful inclusion enhanced if the process is well planned and characterised by collaboration between all the stakeholders in the process.

Once the child enters the educational program it is incumbent upon educators to carefully assess the child and the environment, to plan comprehensive programs and to implement and evaluate those programs in a way that affords the child the best opportunities for growth.

Sometimes inclusion will be relatively easy, while at other times there will be many adjustments to be made and continual issues to be faced. Inclusion can take many different forms, from full-time permanent inclusion to part-time temporary attendance in mainstream school. Whatever the attendance pattern, it is clear that the early childhood years provide the best opportunity for children with disabilities to attend inclusive educational environments and be educated alongside their peers.

Discussion questions

1 Why is it generally easier to include a child with a disability in a preschool early childhood environment than in a regular school environment?

2 As the director of a preschool, what information would you be seeking when interviewing a family as a basis for programming?

3 Why is it generally recommended that the focus of special education be on the child rather than the child's disability?

4 Why do teachers need to be sensitive in their interactions with the parents of children with disabilities?

5 Why should early childhood teachers collaborate closely with parents?

Individual activities

1 The following professionals are integral to special education, particularly during infancy and early childhood. Briefly outline the role of each, in the context of early childhood special education.
   a Physiotherapists
   b Occupational therapists
   c Speech pathologists
   d Audiologists
   e Psychologists
   f Social workers
   g Orthoptists
   h Interpreters

2 Describe some of the challenges that a child with a disability may face when beginning 'big' school.

3 Read the following scenario and, using the table opposite, note the learning skills the child exhibits under the heading 'child's behaviour'. Note some thoughts that may assist you with further assessment and programming under the heading 'implications'.

Scenario

Sophie entered the preschool playroom for the first time. She stood in the middle of the room showing no interest in the play activities that had been set up, nor the children in the room. The teacher approached her and directed her to the water trough. Sophie stood motionless. The teacher showed her how to pour water onto the water wheel making it spin. Sophie picked up a cup of water and poured it onto the water wheel. However, there was insufficient impact to make the wheel spin because she had poured the water on the side of the wheel. She threw the cup onto the ground and began to splash the water with her hands. The teacher gently asked Sophie to pick up the cup, but was ignored. A second time the teacher demonstrated how to make the wheel spin. Sophie ceased splashing and tried once again to pour water onto the wheel. Again she poured water onto the side of the wheel, which meant it didn't spin as intended. This time Sophie picked up the wheel and threw it, almost injuring another child. She then ran off.

Learning skills	Child's behaviour	Implications
Communication		
Imitation		
Problem solving behaviour		
Following directions		
Initiative		
On-task behaviour		

Group activities

1 List reasons why collaboration between service providers is important.

2 List some barriers to communication and cooperation between service providers.

3 The diversity of backgrounds and the vast range of experiences of parents of children with disabilities may impact on their relationships with personnel and/or their child's program in the preschool or school. List 10 factors that may influence the family's capacity to participate in and take advantage of inclusion.

4 Teachers may have many concerns when informed that a child with a disability will be included in their preschool or school class. List and discuss the relevance and legitimacy of these concerns.

5 What are some adjustments to the environment that may be necessary to accommodate a child with:
  a a physical impairment that necessitates the use of a wheelchair or walking aids?
  b a severe vision impairment?
  c hearing impairment?

6 List some ways behaviour problems can be addressed in early childhood programs.

References

Australian Early Intervention Association (NSW Chapter) (1992). *Transition. Report of Workshop at Early Intervention Conference (NSW Chapter)*. Sydney: Author.

Beckman, P. J., Hanson, M. J. & Horn, E. (2002). Family perceptions of inclusion. In S. L. Odom (Ed.), *Widening the Circle: Including Children With Disabilities in Preschool Programs* (pp. 98–108). New York: Teachers College Press, Columbia University.

Bredekamp, S. & Rosegrant, T. (Eds). (1992). *Reaching Potentials: Appropriate Curriculum and Assessment for Young Children 1*, 92–112. Washington, DC: National Association for the Education of Young Children.

Bredekamp, S. & Copple, C. (Eds). (1997). *Developmentally Appropriate Practices in Early Childhood Programs* (rev. edn). Washington, DC: National Association for the Education of Young Children.

Bricker, D. & Woods Cripe, J. (1992). *An Activity-Based Approach to Early Intervention*. Baltimore, MD: Brookes.

*Bricker, D., Prette-Frontczak, K. & McComas, N. R. (1998). *An Activity-Based Approach to Early Intervention* (2nd edn). Baltimore, MD: Brookes.

Briggs, F. & Potter, G. K. (1995). *Teaching Children in the First Three Years of School* (2nd edn). Melbourne, Vic: Longman Cheshire.

Bruner, J. (1982). The organization of action and the nature of the adult–infant transaction. In E. Tronick (Ed.), *Social Interchange in Infancy: Affect, Cognition and Communication* (pp. 23–35). Baltimore, MD: University Park Press.

Carruthers, A. (1986). *The Perceptions of Kindergarten Teachers/Year 1 and Preschool Teachers in the Hunter Region of NSW and the Brisbane West Region of Queensland as to the Most Essential Skills for a Child to Have in Order to Survive in the Kindergarten/Year 1 Classroom*. Unpublished thesis, University of Newcastle.

Carruthers, A. (1995). *Adaptive Behaviour Skills Necessary for Survival and Social and Academic Success in the School Environment*. Paper presented at Early Intervention Conference (NSW Chapter), Pokolbin, August.

*Chadwick, D. & Kemp, C. (2003). Factors in successful transition to mainstream for preschoolers. *Australasian Journal of Special Education, 26*(1/2), 48.

Conn-Powers, M. C., Ross-Allen, J. & Holburn, S. (1990). Transition of young children into the elementary education mainstream. *Topics in Early Childhood Special Education, 9*, 91–105.

Diamond, K. & Hestenes, L. (1994). Preschool children's understanding of disability: Experiences leading to elaboration of the concept of hearing loss. *Early Education and Development, 5*, 300–9.

Diamond, K. & Hestenes, L. (1996). Preschool children's conceptions of disabilities: The salience of disability in children's ideas about others. *Topics in Early Childhood Special Education, 16*, 458–75.

Erwin, E., Soodak, L., Winton, P. & Turnbull, A. (2001). 'I wish it wouldn't all depend on me': A critical analysis of research on families of children with disabilities and inclusive early childhood settings. In M. Guralnick (Ed.), *Early Childhood Inclusion: Focus on Change* (pp. 127–58). Baltimore, MD: Brookes.

Fullwood, D. (1986). *Early Intervention: The Parents' Viewpoint*. Paper presented at 4th annual conference of New South Wales Early Intervention Association, 22–51.

Green, I. & Kemp, C. (1998). Transition: Support issues for teachers integrating young children with disabilities into mainstream classes. *Special Education Perspectives, 7*(1), 4–16.

Hains, A. H., Fowler, S. E., Schwartz, I., Kottwitz, E. & Rosenkoetter, S. (1989). A comparison of preschool and kindergarten teacher expectations for school readiness. *Early Childhood Research Quarterly, 4,* 75–88.

*Hanson, M. J., Wolfberg, P., Zercher, C., Gutierrez, S., Barnwell, D. & Beckman, P. (1998). The culture of inclusion: Recognising diversity at multiple levels. *Early Childhood Research Quarterly, 13*(1), 185–209.

IDEA (Individuals with Disabilities Education Act Amendments) 1991, PL102–19 (October 7, 1991). Title 20, U.S.C. 1400 et seq: U.S. Statutes at Large, 105, 587–608.

IDEA (Individuals with Disabilities Education Act) 1999, PL 105–17.

Johnson, L. J., Gallagher, J., Cook, M. & Wong, P. (1995). Critical skills for kindergarten: Perception from kindergarten teachers. *Journal of Early Intervention, 19,* 15–49.

Kaiser, A., Hendrickson, J. & Alpert, K. (1991). Milieu language teaching: A second look. In R. Gable (Ed.), *Advances in Mental Retardation and Developmental Disabilities IV,* 63–92. London: Jessica Kingsley.

Lehr, S. (1992). Integration from a parent's perspective: Yesterday was a long time ago and tomorrow isn't here yet. In K. A. Haring, D. L. Lovett & N. G. Haring (Eds), *Integrated Lifecycle Services for Persons With Disabilities: A Theoretical and Empirical Perspective* (pp. 340–57). New York: Springer-Verlag Inc.

Lieber, J., Beckman, P. J., Hanson, M. J., Janko, S., Marquart, J. M., Horn, E. & Odom, S. L. (1997). The impact of changing roles on relationships between professionals in inclusive programs for young children. *Early Education and Development, 8,* 67–82.

*McBride, S. L. (1999). Family-centered-practices. *Young Children,* May, 62–8.

Meier, D. & Schafran, A. (1999). Strengthening the preschool-to-kindergarten transition: A community collaborates. *Young Children,* May, 40–6.

Minor, L. (1997). Effective practices in early intervention. In D. Chen, (Ed.), *Infants Whose Multiple Disabilities Include Both Vision and Hearing Loss.* Northridge, Cal: California State Library.

*National Association for the Education of Young Children (1991). Guidelines for appropriate curriculum content and assessment in programs serving children ages 3 through 8. *Young Children, 46*(3), 21–38.

*New South Wales Department of School Education (1997). *Transition to School for Young Children With Special Needs.* Sydney: Author.

Noonan, M. J. & McCormick, L. (1993). *Early Intervention in Natural Environments.* Pacific Grove, CA: Brooks/Cole.

*Odom, S. L. (2000). Preschool inclusion: What we know and where we go from here. *Topics in Early Childhood Special Education, 20*(1), 20–37.

Odom, S. L. (2002). Learning about the barriers to, and facilitators of inclusion for young children with disabilities. In S. L. Odom (Ed.), *Widening the Circle: Including Children With Disabilities in Preschool Programs* (pp. 1–9). New York: Teachers College Press, Columbia University.

*Odom, S. L., Schwartz, I. S. & ECRII Investigators (2002). So what do we know from all this? Synthesis of points of research on preschool inclusion. In S. L. Odom (Ed.), *Widening the Circle: Including Children With Disabilities in Preschool Programs* (pp. 155–74). New York: Teachers College Press, Columbia University.

Odom, S. L., Zercher, C., Marquart, J., Li, S., Sandall, S. R. & Wolfberg, P. (2002). Social relationships of children with disabilities and their peers in inclusive classrooms. In S. L. Odom (Ed.), *Widening the Circle: Including Children With Disabilities in Preschool Programs* (pp. 61–80). New York: Teachers College Press, Columbia University.

Peck, C. A., Carlson, P. & Helmstetter, E. (1992). Parent and teacher perceptions of outcomes for typically developing children enrolled in integrated early childhood programs: A statewide survey. *Journal of Early Intervention, 16*, 53–63.

Piaget, J. (1963). *Play, Dreams, and Imitations in Childhood*. New York: Norton.

Pianta, R. C. & Kraft-Sayre, M. (1999). Parents' observations about their children's transitions to kindergarten. *Young Children*, May, 47–52.

Richardson, L. (1997). Review of transition from home to school. *Australian Journal of Early Childhood, 22*(1), 18–22.

*Rous, B., Hemmeter, M. L. & Schuster, J. (1994). Sequenced transition to education in public schools: A systems approach to transition planning. *Topics in Early Childhood Special Education, 14*(3), 374–93.

*Salisbury, C. L. & Vincent, L. J. (1990). Criterion of the next environment and best practices: Mainstreaming and integration 10 years later. *Topics in Early Childhood Special Education, 10*(1), 78–90.

Shotts, C. K., Rosenkoetter, S. E., Streufert, C. A. & Rosenkoetter, L. I. (1994). Transition policy and issues: A view from the states. *Topics in Early Childhood Special Education, 14*(3), 395–411.

Specialist Child and Family Services (1992). *Early Intervention. Practices and Procedures in Victoria*. Melbourne: Author.

*Soodak, L. C., Erwin, E. J., Winton, P., Brotherson, M. J., et al. (2002). Implementing inclusive early childhood education: A call for professional empowerment. *Topics in Early Childhood Special Education, 22*(2), 91–104.

Vincent, L. J. (1994). Foreword. In S. E. Rosenkoetter, A. H. Hains & S. A. Fowler, *Bridging Early Services for Children With Special Needs and Their Families: A Practical Guide for Transition Planning* (pp. xi–xii). Baltimore: Paul H. Brookes Pub. Co.

Vygotsky, L. (1978). *Mind in Society: The Development of Higher Psychological Processes*. Cambridge, MA: University Press.

Warren, S. F. & Kaiser, A. P. (1988). Research in early language development. In S. L. Odom & M. B. Karnes (Eds), *Early Intervention For Infants and Children With Handicaps: An Empirical Base* (pp. 89–108). Baltimore: Paul H. Brookes Pub. Co.

Wood, E. & Bennett, N. (1999). Progress and continuity in early childhood education: Tensions and contradictions. *International Journal of Early Years Education, 7*(1), 5–16.

---

*Recommended reading for this chapter

Further recommended reading

Chen, D. (Ed.). (1997). *Infants Whose Multiple Disabilities Include Both Vision and Hearing Loss.* Northridge Cal: California State Library.

Cook, R. E., Tessier, A. & Klein, M. D. (2000). *Adapting Early Childhood Curricula for Children in Inclusive Settings* (5th edn). Upper Saddle River, NJ: Prentice-Hall, Inc.

Thorburn, J. & Corby, M. (2002). *The ECE Inclusion Handbook. Practical Guidelines for Early Childhood Teachers Working With Children Who Have Special Needs.* User Friendly Resource Enterprises Ltd.

PART B

EFFECTIVE TEACHING PRACTICES

Adapting curriculum, teaching and learning strategies

Robert Conway

This chapter aims to:

- examine the concepts of curriculum and pedagogy and the effects on teaching students with additional needs in classrooms
- introduce the concept of the classroom as an ecosystem in which the teacher, students, curriculum and resources, and physical factors interact to create a learning and teaching environment for all students in the class
- examine issues relating to curriculum instructional practices that can reduce the ability of students with additional needs to access the taught curriculum

- discuss methods of adapting syllabus topics, including the preparation of adapted worksheets, adapted textbooks and adapted units to address syllabus topics for students with learning and/or behaviour difficulties, and students with mild intellectual disabilities in the mainstream classroom

- discuss methods of including students with high additional needs in classroom curriculum and teaching activities

- examine issues in assessment for students with additional needs in classroom instruction

- examine staff cooperation and collaboration to increase curriculum and teaching adaptation skills.

Introduction

This chapter focuses on the role of learning, curriculum and pedagogy in the school and the effects of regular curriculum on the diversity of students with additional needs in classrooms. Strategies that allow for multiple curriculum approaches and alternate approaches are examined, although the chapter acknowledges that teaching within the regular school is very much governed by the curriculum of the class, school or jurisdiction. Hence learning and teaching approaches in this chapter recognise that teachers may perceive that they have limited flexibility in providing learning activities that include students with additional needs. This chapter provides clear evidence that students with additional needs can be included in classroom learning activities, regardless of their additional need, although this takes belief, commitment, and effort on the part of the teacher. While the difficulties of adapting curriculum to meet the learning needs of all students appear greater in secondary schools, there is still the clear opportunity to do so, as will be seen in the examples and activities.

The Australian national curriculum framework

Key learning areas (KLAs)

In Australia, the 1980s saw a concerted move towards a national curriculum, largely at the instigation of the Commonwealth government (Lokan, 1997; Pascoe, 2001). This decision was reversed in 1994 with the Commonwealth passing responsibility back to the jurisdictions. Two key decisions by ministers of education through MCEETYA set the current course of the current national framework. These were the Hobart and Adelaide Declarations (Department of Education, Science and Technology (DEST), 2002).

The Hobart Declaration in 1997 identified eight key learning areas (KLAs) that were to become the foundations for a nationally common set of learning outcomes. Each of the eight areas of the national curriculum has both statements and profiles (McGaw, 1995; O'Leary & Shiel, 1997). The statements provide strands that indicate content and process and a sequence for developing knowledge and skills across the first 10 years of schooling. The profiles provide, for each strand, eight broad levels that describe the progression in learning outcomes typically achieved by students. Hence, the determination of what knowledge students will be expected to gain within KLAs determines the structure of the profiles that will emerge.

There has been considerable criticism of efforts to continue this approach. One of the strong criticisms is that the selection of eight learning areas reflects some arbitrary amalgams of content areas, particularly in the areas of technology, society and environment, and the arts (Kennedy, 1995). This affects the determination of the knowledge and skills that will represent these areas. While this appears conceptually logical, Kennedy argues that the developmental levels provided in the national standards do not reflect the reality of the classroom and are naive. Consequently, assessment measures based on profiles that have been constructed with little regard for classroom learning realities will be of limited value in measuring student achievement.

For students with additional educational needs in mainstream settings, the concept of a developmentally sequenced set of learning tasks that can be measured through a series of levels of outcomes on each of the profiles, presents considerable difficulties. Many students with additional needs are unable to learn curriculum topics at the same rate as other students and, particularly in the case of students with intellectual disability, they may be unable to attempt profile assessment tasks even at Level 1.

The Adelaide Declaration in 1999 endorsed a set of three national goals for schooling. These goals were couched in terms of the full development of students' talents and capacities. First, students were to leave school with a set of defined skills and qualities. Second, the curriculum should be balanced and comprehensive through the compulsory years of schooling and be based on the agreed eight KLAs. Finally, schooling should be socially just. This last goal identified the removal of discrimination in education, including on the grounds of disability, and that educationally disadvantaged students should have improved learning outcomes over time that matched those of other students.

The future of a national curriculum with statements and profiles remains uncertain. The topic has produced considerable political debate and has exposed the concept of curriculum as a major political issue, not simply an education issue.

Assessment and the national goals of schooling

One of the consequences of the national perspective on KLAs and nationally agreed benchmarks for learning is the movement towards national benchmarks for academic skills, particularly literacy and numeracy. While jurisdictions remain responsible for assessment formats and administration (Zammit, Meiers & Frigo, 1999), the Commonwealth seeks to have nationally recognised reporting of literacy and numeracy levels. Apart from the difficulties of creating nationally comparable data from disparate data collection sources, the difficulties for students with additional needs is the failure to adequately report their involvement in national results. While students are reported by gender, language background and whether they identify as Indigenous or not, there is no identification as to whether they have a disability or not. A complicating factor is that many students with disabilities are excluded from the testing and reporting (Ministerial Council of Education, Employment, Training and Youth Affairs (MCEETYA), 2002), ranging from 0.6 per cent in Tasmania to 3.7 per cent in the Northern Territory. The issue of exclusion of students with disabilities from the reporting is symptomatic of the development of curriculum and assessment models that are beyond the ability of some students with additional needs. The considerable emphasis placed on literacy skills in the current Australian educational context also means that students with additional needs in mainstream classes will have added pressure placed on them as school results are scrutinised at local, state and national levels for educational and political purposes.

This pattern is reflected in the wide discrepancies in the involvement of students with additional needs in statewide assessments in the United States (Quenemoen et al., 2001) and in the United Kingdom's National Curriculum (Zammit, Meiers & Frigo, 1999), where much greater emphasis is placed on annual student performance on standardised measures. There needs to be considerable discussion on the value of including students with additional needs in national testing if the outcome serves only to reinforce their exclusion from mainstream education because they lower the school's scores.

The movement to a pedagogy-focused model

While there has been widespread acceptance of the eight KLAs across Australian educational jurisdictions, there has been an increasing move towards seeing student learning from a pedagogy perspective rather than a curriculum perspective. In this model, pedagogy is seen as the core business of teaching (NSW Department of Education and Training (DET) Professional Support and Curriculum Directorate, 2003) and 'pedagogy focuses attention on the processes through which knowledge is constructed, produced and critiqued' (p. 4). The DET document goes on to say that 'crucially, the term pedagogy recognises that how one teaches is inseparable from what one teaches, from what and how one assesses and from how one learns' (p. 4).

The model commenced in Queensland under the Productive Pedagogies Model, developed through the findings of the Queensland School Reform Longitudinal Study (QSRLS) (Lingard et al., 2001a). The Productive Pedagogies identified in that study (Lingard et al., 2001b) included four dimensions: intellectual quality; connectedness; supportive classroom environment; and, recognition of difference. The model, termed New Basics, developed from these pedagogies and organises the curriculum into four clusters: life pathways and social futures (*Who am I and where am I going?*); multiliteracies and communications media (*How do I make sense of and communicate with the world?*); active citizenship (*What are my rights and responsibilities in communities, cultures and economies?*); and, environments and technologies (*How do I describe, analyse and shape the world around me?*) (Education Queensland, 2000). Activities are sampled from the content of the eight nationally agreed KLAs, although they are not seen as such. Rather they are used as examples for applying the New Basics.

Assessment is through 'rich' tasks that are undertaken at the end of three-year cycles (unlike the two year stages of the KLA model). These assessment tasks are seen as the culmination of the three year's work that has occurred in the classroom learning based around that task (Hinton, 2003). Hinton points out that the New Basics project operates in a comparatively small number of schools as a pilot, while the pedagogies are expected to be adopted by all Queensland schools. While the model has been hailed as an alternative to traditional KLA-based instruction, the model is still in its early stages with the first set of pilot schools completing Year 3 of the pilot in 2003. Data from that pilot will inform the future status of the approach.

While the concepts of New Basics and Rich Tasks may be in their pilot phase, the model of productive pedagogies has been taken up by a number of other jurisdictions in various forms including NSW, Northern Territory and Tasmania. The NSW model, termed *Quality teaching in NSW public schools* (NSW DET Professional Support and Curriculum Directorate, 2003), is based on the concept of productive pedagogies, although it is couched in terms of three dimensions of pedagogy: intellectual quality; quality learning environment; and, significance. While the document speaks of supporting the Adelaide Declaration *National Goals for Schooling in the Twenty-first Century* (DEST, 2002), there is no mention of the KLAs agreed to in the Hobart Declaration and restated in the Adelaide Declaration.

The Essential Learnings Framework (ELF) currently being implemented in Tasmanian Schools (Tasmanian Department of Education, 2003) provides the clearest statement that the traditional KLA approach to learning in schools will be replaced by a pedagogy-focused curriculum model. Five essential learnings are identified: thinking; communicating; personal futures; social responsibilities; and world futures. Again each has key elements that reflect activities in schools. The model has stages or standards from birth to age 16 and each standard forms the basis of whole school planning, assessment, monitoring and performance (p. 7). The model is designed to encompass all students, including students with additional needs, although there is no specific reference to students with additional needs in the documents.

One advantage of the move towards a pedagogy-based curriculum model is that skills are more easily identified and traditional curriculum content is used as examples for the development of the skill. For students with additional needs in the classroom, this provides the opportunity to practise those skills in a range of tasks, rather than focus on curriculum content. It is important to understand that, regardless of the approach taken to curriculum, students with additional needs will be part of the learning and teaching that takes place in the classroom and their needs are a legitimate concern that must be addressed.

What is inclusion?

The concept of inclusion has many meanings and interpretations. One that encompasses the key concepts is Mastropieri and Scruggs's (2000) view that students with disabilities are served in the regular classroom with instruction provided by the regular class teacher. It requires the provision of adaptations and accommodations to the classroom curriculum so that the student benefits from the placement rather than just being there. As Wolfe and Hall (2003) note, it doesn't require that the student with additional needs performs at the same level as their peers without disabilities. Particularly in the case of students with severe disabilities, inclusion provides many challenges to teachers to include them appropriately in curriculum content areas.

The inclusive curriculum in Australia

One feature of the move towards a pedagogy-based curriculum framework should be the ability to include students with additional needs in the teaching. While many jurisdictions don't directly acknowledge students with additional needs in their documentation, two jurisdictions make specific reference to an inclusive curriculum.

The ACT Department of Education (2002) released a discussion paper to encourage schools to consider the assumptions underlying inclusivity and to promote more inclusive practices in schools. Inclusivity was seen as understanding and catering for the different potentials, needs and resources of students in schools through effective learning and teaching. Importantly the inclusive curriculum is not just for students with additional needs but also for all students. The paper argues that inclusivity arises both from the objective of improving educational outcomes for students and from the broader social justice considerations of equity, access and participation.

While this notion of social justice is important, Wolfe and Hall (2003) provide the warning that 'the social integration focus of inclusion negates the opportunity for the student with disabilities to receive instruction in content areas' (p. 56). The argument is that including students with severe disabilities in regular classrooms without a clear focus on their learning needs, not just their social justice needs, will result in failure of the placement. We will return to this issue later in the chapter.

The Northern Territory in its model of Essential Learning has attempted to blend KLA and outcomes-based learning within a curriculum model that includes all students. Their definition is based on the concept that a curriculum is inclusive when all that goes on in school reflects and responds to the needs and rights of all students and places value on students as individuals. All student needs should be encompassed by providing broad, balanced and appropriate programs. The definition is important as the framework used combines both KLAs and a model of essential learning outcomes based on outcomes expected at specific points in the process. Importantly there is no separate special education curriculum, as curriculum activities can be identified for all students, particularly as the curriculum has 'drilled down' at Stage 1 to include activities for students with additional needs.

Providing alternative curriculum for students with additional needs

An alternative model is to supplement the existing mainstream curriculum approach with an alternative model based on the same KLAs but with different learning outcomes and assessment activities. This model is used in NSW where students with disabilities can undertake a life skills curriculum in secondary. For example, the Stage 6 Life Skills program of study is designed to operate as part of the transition-planning process for students across Years 11 and 12 that provides them with both a transition process from school to adult life as well as a formal qualification in the Higher School Certificate. The Board of Studies NSW (2001) provides case studies to assist teachers identify activities within the KLAs that will obtain the required outcomes. As the model has been extended, alternate Life Skills curriculums are being developed for students in Stages 4 and 5 (Junior Secondary). While students in mainstream settings are able to access these programs, their main focus is students in special classes and schools.

The classroom as an ecosystem

Any understanding of the classroom as a teaching and learning environment in which curriculum is implemented requires an understanding of the dynamics of that room and how a student with additional needs impacts on those dynamics.

Any classroom is an ecosystem. It has certain inputs and outputs but within the room there are four key factors that influence what happens. These are: teacher factors; student factors; curriculum and resources factors; and physical setting factors (Figure 4.1). All interact constantly in the classroom at any moment of time, and all are critical to the teaching and learning outcomes. Previous chapters have introduced some of the factors that make up the ecology of the classroom, while others have also introduced factors in different ways, such as teacher attitudes and student attitudes. The important point in this chapter is that the four factors constantly interact to impact on the learning outcomes.

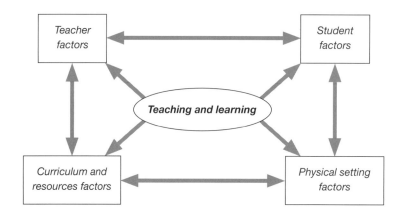

Figure 4.1
The classroom ecosystem as a model for teaching and learning in an inclusive classroom

Teacher factors include preparedness to teach students with additional needs as part of their overall instruction, their knowledge of the skills and prior knowledge of the students, their attitudes towards having the student with additional needs in their classroom, and their visible acceptance or otherwise of the student as a model for others in the class. Other factors include the teacher's knowledge and beliefs about teaching and learning and instructional techniques, particularly those that relate to students with additional needs. Teachers have been shown to be willing to employ strategies that require little adaptation and which will assist the majority of the class not just those with additional needs (Scott, Vitale & Masten, 1998). Instead, today teachers need a continuum of teaching interventions and specialised strategies to support students with additional needs in the classroom (Schmidt, Rozendal & Greenman, 2002).

Student factors include the abilities and skills of the student with additional needs and other students in the class, their attitudes and willingness to have the student with additional needs as part of their learning environment. Metacognitive skills and collaborative instruction skills are important for successful inclusion. Metacognitive skills provide the ability to monitor performance and reduce the level of teacher assistance required. The ability to work collaboratively is one of the key skills needed by students in a classroom (Schmidt, Rozendal & Greenman, 2002), whether that is through peer tutoring or other cooperative learning activities. In this way the social and academic skills of the students is integrated and enhanced.

Curriculum and resource factors include the mainstream and any alternative curriculum used in the classroom, the selection of content and vocabulary to be taught and the methods and resources such as textbooks, worksheets and other materials used. It also includes whether the students with additional needs will take part in the curriculum content of the class or whether they will be accessing different curriculum tasks. Importantly, there needs to be differentiation of the curriculum materials for students with additional needs rather than a watering-down of what is presented to the remainder of the class (Westwood, 2001).

Physical setting factors include the layout of the classroom, whether there need to be adaptations to accommodate wheelchairs and a desk for a teacher's aide or how the implementation of the curriculum will need to be adapted in terms of accommodating all students in the class.

The critical point is that in the room there will always be learning and teaching occurring. The concept of teachers teaching and students learning no longer reflects the classroom: teachers teach and learn, students teach and learn. Utilising all factors in the classroom effectively enhances the opportunities not only for the student with additional needs, but for all students and teachers. We will return to each of these factors throughout the chapter and in Chapter 6.

Another, similar ecological approach to considering the classroom educational environment is to look at the four domains of instruction that can be readily modified by the teacher (Welch, 1997). Welch identifies from earlier studies *materials, activities, teacher behaviours and student groupings* (MATS) as the key to adapting the classroom. Welch provides forms that assist the teacher and the collaborative consultant, such as a special education teacher, to identify ways in which each of these factors can be managed to best assist the student with additional needs in the class.

Regardless of the approach that is taken in considering the educational environment, the major focus is on inclusion in the curriculum.

Needs, expectations and resistance

If you are told that inclusion of students with additional needs in a classroom is a simple matter that requires little preparation and effort, then you are likely being misled. As discussed below, where students have higher additional needs, there are considerable pressures on teachers, parents and students to ensure that inclusion is both academically and socially effective. Even where the student has minimal additional requirements, there is a need to ensure that the learning and teaching engage all students in the class. After looking at the concerns and issues, we will examine ways of overcoming them both at the individual teacher, school and system level.

Teachers

Teachers have often reported that having students with additional needs in their classes causes additional stress, particularly when the student has a moderate or severe intellectual disability (Engelbrecht et al., 2003; Forlin, 2001). Engelbrecht et al., in a study of South African teachers, identified administrative issues such as lack of knowledge in how to adjust unit planning and competence issues such as sustaining an active learning environment, the inability to teach others in the class while focusing on the student with additional needs, and a lack of appropriate training both preservice and inservice. They also reported difficulties with the short attention span of the students and their poor communication skills.

In a similar study among teachers in Queensland, Forlin (2001) found that teachers were challenged by a wide range of programming, teaching and assessment tasks for students with intellectual disability. These included: interpreting the student's Individual Education Plan (IEP) within the curriculum framework of the class; developing and modifying

specific curriculum objectives; modifying curriculum and teaching methods; individualising instruction; preparing teaching materials; managing the student's teaching program in the context of teaching all students; teaching the student self-help; social and coping skills; and, assessing and reporting student performance relative to the class peers.

Westwood and Graham (2003) also identified a broad range of issues for teachers in assisting students with additional needs in classrooms in South Australia and New South Wales. They identified three categories of challenges for those teachers: *Key problems encountered* including lack of time, need for constant supervision of the student with additional needs, balancing demand of the student with additional needs with those of the whole class, knowing how to program effectively, access to appropriate personnel and resources; *Operating the classroom program* including time to work with and supervise the student with additional needs, interruptions and disruptions, management of student behaviours, not keeping up with the set work, additional required preparation, others not getting enough attention, and lack of materials and resources; *Preservice and inservice training* including no required preservice training in South Australia and only one unit in NSW. Only between 29 and 39 per cent of teachers reported they received inservice training on assisting students with additional needs in the classroom.

The issue of preservice training of teachers is an interesting one. Many of the readers of this chapter will be completing an undergraduate course on inclusion or special education. A Queensland study (Campbell, Gilmore & Cuskelly, 2003) has shown that student teachers taking part in courses on inclusion and additional needs changed their attitudes to disabilities and people with disabilities.

The degree of heterogeneity of the classroom also affects the decisions on who will receive support/assistance in the classroom and the amount of time spent with individual students (Fields, 1999). Fields found that the more heterogeneous the class the greater the chance that the student with additional needs will receive assistance.

Having identified the numerous difficulties that teachers face in inclusive classrooms, there is a process of change that can occur (Fullan, 1991, cited in Buly & Rose, 2001). The three steps in the change process involve:

- the processes leading up to and including the decision to change
- the first experiences of attempting to put the ideas into practice (this can continue for a number of years)
- determining whether the change continues or disappears.

Importantly, the authors acknowledge that the process is almost always accompanied by anxiety. Where the change is mandated, the range of emotions across a staff can consist of staff wanting to resist change, those who are fearful of change, those who are open to implementing change but who privately remain uncertain, and those who are able and willing to implement change: 'Regardless of the change vehicle, some teachers will view the change from the outside in and others from the inside out' (Buly & Rose, 2001, p. 5). In the case of inclusion of students with additional needs, the full range of teacher responses exists in many schools.

Parents

Many parents who come to the inclusive classroom in primary school have already experienced mainstream education in early childhood settings, where there is a much stronger commitment to inclusive practices (see Chapter 3). They come to primary school with great hopes that inclusion will work for their child but can quickly become concerned at the lack of adaptation in mainstreamed school settings and the resistance of administrators to enrolment of their child with additional needs. Parental expectations of continued mainstreaming, particularly at the secondary level, are often not realised when modifications and adaptations are not made to the curriculum or teaching strategies and their child slips further behind others in the class. As a result, parents are forced to return to more restrictive settings, having been met by strong resistance to inclusion by some educators (see Box 4.1 for Gail's story). Gail raises many issues, interestingly as both a parent and as an educator.

Students

Fields (1999), in a study of Queensland schools, identified that low achieving students, in comparison to more able students:

- are provided with fewer modifications to instruction
- receive less direct teacher instruction and supervised practice
- receive less teacher interaction
- are more criticised for failures.

This doesn't mean that students will receive more attention or a 'better education in a segregated special setting'. Wehmeyer et al. (2003) found that students with an intellectual disability in inclusive settings were working on tasks related to a curriculum standard for 90 per cent of the time compared to 50 per cent for students in a special class. Students in special classes worked more on specific IEP tasks rather than general curriculum tasks, with limited exposure to the broader curriculum. Wehmeyer et al. (2003) argued that by having a more open curriculum with open-ended standards, students with an intellectual disability can have greater access to the curriculum and hence to inclusive settings. They also found that teachers were supportive of students with higher support needs accessing the regular curriculum as that would raise student expectations.

An issue not often addressed specifically is the need to be more sensitive to the needs of girls with learning difficulties as they have more maladaptive attribution patterns than boys (Ring & Reetz, 2000). Hence there is a need to provide them with accommodations and graded adaptations. This is important as students who perceive themselves as capable are more willing to work on a task. Conversely if they are debilitated by the task, they are more likely to give up and fail as a consequence. Ring and Reetz liken the process to the reversal of 'learned helplessness' (2000, p. 39).

Clearly there is a need to provide students with additional needs with the skills to be able to work within the inclusive classroom, including the metacognitive skills as well as the attributional skills that will enhance their involvement.

Box 4.1

A parent's view of teaching a child with additional needs in a regular school

Gail is the parent of a child with Down syndrome who now attends a special class in a regular high school. Prior to placement in a special unit in primary and high school, he attended an infants class in a regular school. Gail is also a teacher and currently the principal of a school.

As part of her advice to regular and special education teachers based on her experiences as a parent, Gail suggests:

- Concentrate on what our children *can* do not what they *can't*. If you grade them against the 'norm' they will always fail. It is hard to look forward to a report card that emphasises what your child can't do.
- Don't stereotype children with disabilities – not all children with Down syndrome are 'loving' or musical. Certainly *some* children with Down syndrome have *some* things in common, but they are just as individual as anybody else.

- Don't overlook the possibility of talents (even children with an intellectual disability). Our son has an amazing sense of humour, knows more about rugby league than most people I know, has an accurate throw and is a born mimic.
- Don't assume that our children respond best to a 'behaviourist' approach. This seems to be the favourite teaching method promoted in special education training. Our children are not animals to be taught to perform on demand.
- Accept that children with disabilities go through the same stages as other children do. We went through so much unnecessary heartache for two years because teachers were unwilling to accept that adolescents with an intellectual disability have the same difficult times as other adolescents. Things would have been much easier if we had had the support and understanding of the school.

>

Box 4.1 continued

- Have reasonable expectations! Be consistent! Be fair!

The story of Gail's son and his difficulties with teaching and learning demands, seen from the eyes of a parent and educator, provides an insight into the frustrations that parents and teachers have in gaining appropriate educational access for their children.

The final word on teaching and learning is best said in Gail's words:

Realise that parents of children with a disability may be overly vocal in defence of their children. This is not because they are more protective, but more because their children are less likely to have teachers or adults who are willing to champion their cause.

Problems with existing instructional materials and approaches

The difficulties teachers face in presenting content in the classroom is not restricted to students with additional needs. As many teachers will attest, a large number of students have difficulty in understanding curriculum content. This has been attributed to a number of factors directly related to what we teach and how we teach it. Particularly in secondary schools, there is a reliance on textbooks as a source of learning (fortunately nowhere near the level that exists in the USA where the textbook is the curriculum) and hence the readability level of written materials and the differences in instructional levels within the classroom becomes important.

Readability, text structure and conceptual analysis

Readability is a concept that is often talked about in schools, particularly in relation to meeting the needs of students with learning difficulties. Terms such as 'high interest/low vocabulary' or 'modified' suggest that the original material has been adapted to meet the needs of students who are unable to read at the appropriate developmental or grade level. Often these books will be coded to show a readability level.

Readability, in its crudest form, is based on two components: the sentence length and the difficulty of the individual words. Longer sentences are considered more difficult as they include more information and often join a number of pieces of information together. Words with more syllables are considered to be more difficult to read and hence the readability level is higher. While this is generally the case, there are multisyllabic words that students are very familiar with, such as 'television' or 'McDonald's'. Usually the two components are combined into a readability formula.

Box 4.2 shows an example of a secondary science worksheet. The readability level of the passage is high as a result of the number of long and complex sentences and the complexity of the vocabulary. The passage contains only one sentence with fewer than 12 words, and one has over 30 words. The average sentence length is 24 words. Another feature of the sentences in the passage is that they often contain additional comment or contradictory comments that confuse the weak reader. Assessing the level of difficulty of the vocabulary using the number of syllables in a word (1.86 on average in Box 4.2) can be misleading in secondary subject areas, due to the number of technical words that are used. Nevertheless, it does give a general indication of vocabulary complexity.

Box 4.2

Science worksheet

Chromite in alpine-type intrusions, however, is widespread and virtually ubiquitous. There is hardly an orogenic belt, particularly in post-Precambrian terrains, devoid of 'serpentine', and there is probably no known serpentine belt that does not have, somewhere along its length, chromite concentrations of sufficient size and richness to constitute ore. In addition, even those ultramafic lenses with no actual ore deposits contain conspicuous chromite, including local concentrations, which though rich, are of insufficient size to be economic. The largest known deposits are those of the ultramafic belts of the Ural Mountains in Russia, the Philippines, and Turkey. Substantial deposits are well known in the ultramafic belts in Cuba, New Caledonia, India, Pakistan, Eastern Europe (Yugoslavia and Greece), and Brazil. Minor deposits are known in the ultramafic belts of California-Oregon, the Maritime Provinces of the United States and Canada, and the Paleozoic belts of eastern Australia.

1 Circle the correct answer:
   a How frequently does chromite ore occur in orogenic belts?
   Never / Sometimes / Usually / Always
   b Chromite concentrations do not occur in a serpentine belt.
   True / False

2 What does economic mean in the passage?

_____

_____

_____

_____

3 How is it that chromite can be conspicuous yet not be an ore deposit?

_____

_____

_____

_____

Author and date unknown

Readability can be measured in a number of ways including the use of a readability formula, by the teacher estimating the level based on experience, or by having the students read the text and then explaining the content in their own words. Readability formulas require the teacher to count the variables used in the formula, such as the number of words, sentences and syllables, and then use the data in a mathematical formula. Teacher estimates are quick and may assist teachers in primary grades to select possible readers for students. However, the most successful readability measure is the student – the consumer of the text.

One method is to have students read part of the text and explain the content. Translation of teacher language into student language indicates that the student has not only read the content, but has been able to make sense of it. An alternative way is to use a cloze technique in which each fifth word is left blank and the student inserts the missing word. Care needs to be taken in technical passages.

It is important to sample from different parts of any text in assessing readability, as books often do not have a consistent readability level. It is also important to apply the same readability formula to each passage or book in order to make valid comparisons.

Recently there has been a move beyond readability analysis to examining text structure and conceptual analysis (Harniss et al., 2001). The text structure can contribute to the difficulty of a text or passage through lack of coherence. Often textbooks lack both the global coherence (integration of ideas) and local coherence (text unity at the sentence and paragraph levels) needed for passages to be clearly understood by the reader.

Conceptual analysis relates to whether the textbook actually teaches and reinforces the key concepts behind the content, or only a series of facts and superficial points. Harniss et al. (2001) point to analysis of texts in the USA which found that only 13 to 25 per cent of the fundamental concepts were included in a series of textbooks in social studies. Relying on texts to provide coverage of the key concepts in any curriculum area can mean lack of coverage of those concepts. Where teachers identify the key concepts and then seek materials to address those concepts, or develop the materials themselves, there is greater likelihood that students will be exposed to all key concepts. This is particularly important for students with additional needs where teaching may need to be more explicit. Hence there is a need to consider not only the readability of the text or written material, but also its text structure and conceptual analysis.

Differences in the instructional levels in the classroom

Discrepancies exist between the three instructional levels that exist in the classroom: the material instructional level, the teacher instructional level and the student instructional level. Figure 4.2 shows the relationship between the three levels in a Year 8 subject classroom, assuming that the students have been streamed and the class is in the lowest stream.

The *material instructional level* is determined by the readability level of the text. Textbooks are written to sell as broadly as possible and to meet the syllabus requirements. Most are not written for students with learning difficulties and none are specifically written for students with additional needs. As adults write them, they frequently have a readability level above their targeted grade level. Even some texts written for modified level courses have readability levels well above the ability levels of their target audience. In the hypothetical class in Figure 4.2, the textbook has been identified as being at a Year 10 level of readability, two years above the grade level.

The *teacher instructional level* is the level at which we communicate with students. For secondary school teachers, the youngest grade level they will normally have taught is Year 7. Teachers use a certain level of sentence complexity and a vocabulary level, based on their detailed knowledge of the curriculum topic. Hence teachers could be said to have an instructional level in their oral presentation in class.

The *student instructional level* is the level at which the students are operating. Students have two instructional levels: one is the level at which they comprehend the spoken word from the teacher and the other is the comprehension level of the written word (textbook or worksheets). Because the spoken word often contains explanations and restatements

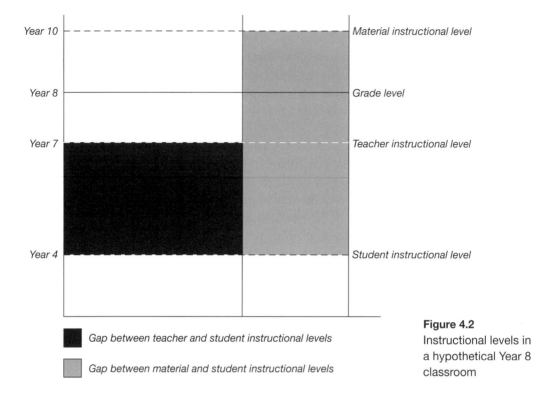

Year 10 ------------------------------- Material instructional level

Year 8 ──────────────────────────── Grade level

Year 7 ─ ─ ─ ─ ─ ─ ─ ─ ─ ─ ─ ─ ─ ─ Teacher instructional level

Year 4 ─ ─ ─ ─ ─ ─ ─ ─ ─ ─ ─ ─ ─ ─ Student instructional level

Gap between teacher and student instructional levels

Gap between material and student instructional levels

Figure 4.2
Instructional levels in a hypothetical Year 8 classroom

and doesn't require reading skills, it is easier for students to understand. In the example in Figure 4.2, the student instructional level is shown at a Year 4 level, which is roughly equivalent to a functional reading level. In reality, a classroom will contain students operating at a wide range of instructional levels, particularly in mixed ability classes.

The problem for the teacher and students in Figure 4.2 is that the discrepancy between the student instructional level and the material instructional level is six grades and between the teacher instructional level and the student instructional level it is three grades. This means that the students can understand neither the textbook nor the teacher and effective communication of curriculum content cannot be achieved.

What can be done to address the problem? Clearly it is not possible to instantly increase the instructional level of the students, although teaching of cognitive and metacognitive skills and work-related behaviours may achieve some increases. Teacher instructional levels can be reduced by using language structures that students understand, by reducing the use of technical vocabulary where it is unnecessary, as well as through the use of learning experiences other than 'chalk and talk'. The prime area for attention, however, is in the area of reducing the complexity and difficulty of written materials such as textbooks and worksheets.

Textbooks – difficulties and strategies

As discussed earlier there is a reliance, particularly in the secondary school, on textbooks to provide content information, student activities, and assessment tasks (Harniss et al., 2001). Textbooks that contain lots of facts but few concepts place greater demands on the learner and for students with additional needs there is a need for teachers to scaffold information through

teaching strategies (Jitendra et al., 2002). These and other authors have s
range of strategies for assisting students with additional needs to access text

One of the issues identified in texts is that often only the teacher edition has
of strategies for students with additional needs – the student editions rem
same (O'Connell, 2001). Most teacher editions provide generic suggestions
in general and rarely in relation to any specific sections of the textbook. Her
left to make any adaptations themselves.

Dyck and Pemberton (2002) suggest five options for adapting textbooks for use in inclusive classrooms: bypass reading; decrease reading; support reading; organise reading; and, guide reading. *Bypass reading* involves the student listening to the text on tape with the advantage that understanding is not reduced by reading difficulties. Reading can be completed by another student or through adaptive technology such as Kurzweil 'reading' the print to tape. *Decrease reading* includes rewriting sections of text, altering the vocabulary, and using only portions of the text (see boxes later in this chapter for examples). *Support reading* requires the addition of material to the text to assist understanding, such as providing definitions of key terms in the margins, and adding cues and signals to the text, such as underlining or highlighting key terms. *Organise reading* involves the use of graphic organisers such as hierarchical trees, compare and contrast charts and concept maps. *Guide reading* involves the use of summaries, structured notes instead of commercial study guides and graphic organisers. Importantly Dyck and Pemberton urge that when textbooks are adapted for struggling students, teachers consider adapting assessment as well. We will return to the issue of assessment later. Specific examples of the adaptation of texts across curriculum areas is also provided in *Reading and Writing Quarterly* Vol. 17 (2001) where, in addition to the Harniss et al. (2001) paper on history texts, there are examples of adaptations for geography and science, among others. While the examples apply to US texts, they can easily be applied to any textbooks.

Difficulties in presentation formats

Apart from textbooks, there are several other curriculum presentation formats that also cause difficulty, particularly student worksheets. The science worksheet in Box 4.2 is an example of a material that is inappropriate for students to work on unassisted. First, it does not ask science questions. The first question (1a) focuses on semantics of 'widespread and virtually ubiquitous'; the second (1b) asks the student to respond in the negative to a negatively worded question, to gain the positive fact in the text; the third question (2) asks a definition of the term 'economic'; and the fourth question (3) asks the student about the viability of mining. Second, students with additional needs (and many others) would be unable to comprehend either the text or questions.

Other inappropriate presentation formats for mainstreamed students include the use of some videos that have been produced for general audiences on television, rather than being tailored to student needs, overheads and stencils that have been hurriedly prepared and/or poorly copied so that students cannot read them, and the board filled with teacher written notes that are to be copied into workbooks. The outcome of the last approach is often a set of inaccurate, incoherent words. Heavily teacher-dominated lessons in which there is no opportunity to use student language or to work cooperatively also places strain on mainstreamed students. Lessons that focus on content facts, with no emphasis on strategies

...erstanding processes also present difficulties for mainstreamed students, particularly ...en there is a need for additional time to process and internalise information, such as occurs for students with intellectual disability.

Participation by all students in the regular curriculum

One way to conceive the level of participation of students in the regular curriculum is to see it as one of three options (Giangreco, Cloninger & Iverson, 1992). These include:

- *same* – the same curriculum focus, objectives and activities
- *multilevel* – the same curriculum activity but at a different level (for example, addition less than 10, while the class is completing multiple column addition)
- *curriculum overlapping* – the same activity but with a different curriculum focus (for example, a social skills focus of working in a group rather than the academic aim of the history lesson).

An alternative model is to conceive a cascade of options (Wolfe & Hall, 2003, p. 57). In this approach, five options are possible, four of them in the regular classroom:

- *Unadapted participation in the general curriculum* (same activities, same objectives, same setting). Can the student complete the activities as written for the general education classroom? Do one or more of the lesson objectives match the student's IEP?
- *Adaptations to the regular curriculum* (same activities, different (related) objectives, same setting). Can the student meet the lesson objectives with minor modifications (time, response mode)?
- *Embedded skills within the general curriculum* (same activity, different (related) objectives, same setting). Are there components of the activity that can be met by the student, even if not the central objective of the lesson but match an IEP objective?
- *Functional curriculum in the general education classroom* (different activities, different (related) objectives, same setting). Are the class activities greatly unrelated to the student's IEP? Are there IEP objectives that could be met in the same setting?
- *Functional curriculum outside the general education classroom* (different activities, different (unrelated) objectives, different setting). Are the class activities greatly unrelated to the student's IEP? Are IEP objectives better met in a different setting?

These approaches are applicable at both primary and secondary levels. We wi. explore these broad options by examining first strategies for students with low support n in the inclusive classroom and then students with higher support needs.

Students with low additional education support needs in the classroom

A number of methods to adapt the regular curriculum have been suggested, including ways in which to restructure curriculum content, ways to enhance presentation of the curriculum topics, and additional skills training that will assist curriculum content understanding. The methods are summarised in Box 4.3. In the following sections a number of these approaches are discussed in detail, and examples are given of how they can be developed.

There are three main options in developing curriculum units that better meet the needs of students in the classroom. Teachers can:

- *adapt* existing materials
- *adopt* alternative materials
- *create* new materials
- use a combination of adapting, adopting and creating.

These options can occur whether the teacher wishes to maintain the existing curriculum topic or whether an alternative curriculum topic is used. Many teachers are required to maintain the same curriculum content, and any adaptations are to increase the involvement of students rather than to produce alternative topics.

Adapting content materials: Improving the readability level

The aim of adapting text is to increase student understanding of the content. One way of achieving this is through improving the readability of the text by rewriting it at a level that can be comprehended by students. This involves adapting both the sentence structure and the vocabulary, the two main components in readability. Box 4.4 shows the same piece of text, before and after rewriting.

The two versions of the text shown in Box 4.4 contain the same information. While students working at a Year 6 level could read the original version with ease, the adapted version could be read by students working at a Year 3 level. The value of the alternative version is that it allows students operating at a younger developmental level to participate in the lesson. In this case the readability level has been lowered through the use of reduced sentence complexity (more short sentences) and the substitution of alternative vocabulary (for example, 'civilisation' is replaced by 'people could live'). Notice that the adapted version is longer than the original version, due to the use of several short sentences rather than connectives. This is not a problem, as the students will persist in reading text that is within their reading ability.

This approach was used by Lesley Heath, a primary teacher, who adapted a syllabus topic in the New South Wales K–6 English syllabus (Box 4.5). She rewrote one of the recommended texts to allow a group of students of lower ability in the Year 5 class to work on the same content as the remainder of the class. As the topic was to be integrated across the Key Learning Areas (KLAs), it was important that all students could access and understand

of adapting curriculum content and ion

	Methods
Curriculum content	<ul><li>Streamline the sequence of content</li><li>Use a different curriculum format</li><li>Embed a skill in an activity</li><li>Modify the rate and presentation of the curriculum</li><li>Make sure that the tasks are developmentally appropriate and not beyond the ability of the student</li></ul>
Presentation methods	<ul><li>Require limited but specific participation by student with additional needs</li><li>Use alternative materials</li><li>Use learning centres</li><li>Use the same activity but targeting different skills</li><li>Make the presentation of content relevant to the experiences of the learner</li><li>Provide more time for learning a task</li><li>Use memory assistance such as charts and checklists where memory of a task is not essential</li><li>Allow the use of aids such as calculators</li><li>Use project work, preferably through cooperative learning activities</li><li>Where possible, use explicit direct teaching of both academic skills and cognitive skills</li><li>Use individualised learning kits</li><li>Use discovery learning to encourage mental effort, group work, student language and transfer but be careful not to make activities too unstructured as students with additional needs may become lost in the process</li><li>Allow time for students to think through the question and then respond</li><li>Involve language skills in lessons and encourage students to use student language</li><li>De-emphasise the use of textbooks</li><li>Modify the assessment requirements to be consistent with teaching approaches</li><li>Provide structure and be explicit in all assignments</li><li>Highlight the critical features of the content being presented</li><li>Make worksheets clear, well spaced and unambiguous, and print in a readable font</li></ul>
Additional skills training to assist curriculum content understanding	<ul><li>Teach cognitive strategies to encourage self-monitoring, problem solving and increased self-reliance</li><li>Teach structures such as essay writing skills</li><li>Teach test-taking skills</li><li>Teach general study skills</li><li>Teach strategic learning or process skills that focus on thinking about, completing and evaluating curriculum tasks</li></ul>

the environmental messages of the text. The adapted vocabulary in the adapted text was followed through into the worksheets and the teacher's oral presentations. (Note: Stage 2 is Years 3 & 4; Stage 3 is Years 5 & 6).

At the secondary level, it is often more difficult to simply rewrite the text, including all content. In order to increase the readability, decisions may also need to be made on reducing the amount of content to be included. Box 4.6 shows both the original and adapted versions of a passage from a secondary textbook.

The rewritten text has more, shorter sentences to reduce the amount of information within each sentence. This has the effect of reducing the complexity of the sentence and increasing the readability level. The result is that the difficulty of the passage is lowered. The average sentence length of the adapted version is 12.3 words, compared to the original version's 26.0 words. The original text contained one short and two long sentences (>30 words), while the adapted text contains four short and no long sentences.

The vocabulary has been altered to remove difficult words that reduce meaning, without removing the specific content vocabulary needed. For example, 'the number of people who

---

Box 4.4

Simplification of language

Original version

About 4000 years ago, it seemed that civilisation was possible only in river valleys. Such valleys were flooded once a year. People learned to use the floods for irrigation by digging canals or catchment basins. Irrigation made it possible to produce surplus food. With a surplus of food, came the division of labour and the growth of cities. As people settled down, they developed new areas of knowledge and new forms of government. Each early society that developed a civilisation went through this order or change.

Could civilisation develop in other environments? We know that people had been growing crops long before they found out about irrigation.

Adapted version

About 4000 years ago, it seemed that people could live only in river valleys. Each year the valleys were covered with water when it rained a lot. People learned to use the water in a new way. They would dig holes in the ground to catch the water. They saved the water. Later, the water helped to grow more food. They had more food than they needed. With more food they could give people different kinds of work. The cities began to grow. People stopped moving. They stayed in the one place for a long time. They made new kinds of government. Each of the early people changed in this way.

Could people live in other places? We know people had been farming long before they found out about catching and saving water.

Feature	Original version	Adapted version
Number of sentences	9	15
Average length of sentences	12	9
Number of words	106	132
Words not commonly known at a Year 5 level	22	3

Source unknown

---

have died' has replaced 'mortality'. The use of terms such as 'eighteenth century' has been replaced by '1700s'. Some terms such as 'industrial revolution' have been retained as the section of text is about the effects of the industrial revolution. As a result of adapting the vocabulary, the level of difficulty of the vocabulary has been reduced.

The overall effect of the adapted text is that, while it is shorter in total length, it contains more, shorter sentences because each concept appears in a separate sentence, rather than being linked within one longer sentence. It is also possible that an adapted version may be longer than the original text because of this (see Box 4.4).

Box 4.5
Vocabulary changes in a KLA syllabus topic

Windows on the environment: An English KLA unit

Teacher: Lesley Heath

I have taken the New South Wales K–6 English syllabus and have used one of the recommended texts for Year 5 students: 'Cry me a river' by Rodney McRae. The main group in the class is working towards Stage 3 English outcomes, while one group is working towards Stage 2 outcomes. In adapting a unit of work for the Stage 2 students, I have prepared a workbook of the text in which modified vocabulary is used throughout. In addition, the worksheets for this group also use the modified vocabulary.

The vocabulary on the right has been substituted for the vocabulary on the left.

shimmering	shining
chiselled features	shaped face
brittle tussocks	broken clumps of grass
amber	yellow
welled	rose
cascaded	fell
soothed	calmed
moist	damp
thicket	bushes
abounded	lived
soothing	calming
quenching	water
flourished	grew
fruits	result
discharged	flowed
nourished	grow
smelly	putrid
indifference	people who don't care

Box 4.6

Adaptation of text

Original version

As mortality has fallen over the last century so have birth rates, although birth rates have lagged behind mortality decreases. In pre-industrial societies, that is, those of the years before the industrial revolution of the eighteenth century, it was common for death and birth rates to be approximately even, so any increase in population occurred slowly. Industrial societies, however, show a decline in both birth and death rates. Social scientists have studied the reason for this, but while declining death rates can be attributed to improvements in medical science and hygiene, for example, the reasons for declining birth rates are not as clear-cut.

Adapted version

The number of people who have died in the past 100 years has dropped. So has the number of people who have been born. Before the industrial revolution in the 1700s, the number of people who died was the same as the number of people who were born. Scientists have studied this. They found that less people are dying because hygiene has improved. They are not as sure why less people are being born.

Feature	Original version	Adapted version
Number of sentences	4	6
Average length of sentences	26.0 words	12.3 words
Number of short sentences	1	4
Number of long sentences	2	0
Number of words	104	74
Syllables per word	1.71	1.32
	(Vocabulary may be too advanced for most readers)	(Most readers could understand the vocabulary based on the number of syllables per word)
Flesch Readability Score	36	83
	(Difficult for most readers)	(Easy for most readers)

Making decisions on what to include in adapted written material

Content

Some teachers would argue that the adapted version has less information than the original version, and students will miss out on the amount of content they need to learn the task. While it is true that the amount of content has been reduced, the overall understanding by students will increase because they are focused on the essential content and not distracted by additional, less vital information. This is best illustrated by the concept of a target (Figure 4.3).

Knowledge in a specific topic can be divided into at least three categories: *must know*; *should know*; *could know*. The *must know* is the information essential to that topic, without which the student could not be said to have mastered the key knowledge. While the *should*

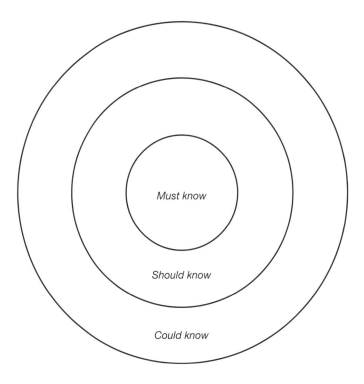

Figure 4.3 Content decisions

know and *could know* material is also important for students, these categories provide additional knowledge that may confuse the student working at an earlier developmental level. Where the concern of the teacher is that all students work on the same syllabus topic at this same time, the concept of levels of content provides a method of catering for the variety of student performance levels in the class.

Vocabulary

In the same way as the content needs to be categorised, the vocabulary needs to be assigned to one of three categories: essential; alter; delete (Box 4.7). Some vocabulary from the content in Box 4.6 has been used to demonstrate the three categories. Another example of altered vocabulary in geography would be to replace the term 'precipitation' with 'rain', although technically rain is only one form of precipitation. Where the text uses vocabulary that students already have in their repertoire, it allows additional time to concentrate on the content.

Box 4.7
Adapting vocabulary

Essential	Alter		Delete
	Original	*Replacement*	
Industrial Revolution	century	100 years	medical science

It is important to realise that essential vocabulary does need to remain, particularly technical, subject-specific vocabulary, such as the names of pieces of equipment. However, there is a tendency for specialist teachers to believe that all terminology in their subject is vital, when many terms can be expressed in student language without reducing understanding. An important point to remember about adapting vocabulary in the text, is that adaptation also needs to occur in notes, overheads and in teacher oral language. Where essential vocabulary exists, it should be introduced at the time it is needed and through deliberate practice of the concept in the worksheets, not through a discrete spelling list given in isolation.

Another way to ensure that vocabulary skills are incorporated into the unit is to have students look both at their own meanings and at the dictionary meaning of the word. This is important, as students often have a different interpretation of the meaning. Through the use of student language, the teacher gains insight into the student understanding of the vocabulary. Box 4.8 shows an example for a science and technology unit.

Box 4.8

Adapting vocabulary within a syllabus topic

Dinosaurs unit

Teacher: Naomi Pex

Within a unit for Year 5 on dinosaurs in the science and technology KLA, I have attempted to include the vocabulary in a variety of ways that emphasise the relationship between the essential vocabulary of the unit and the students' own language. An example of this is in a language skills worksheet in Lesson 3 where students are encouraged to think about the vocabulary terms rather than be given them as a set of words to know. This will also form the basis of a personal dictionary for the unit that can be used in the writing exercises that follow.

Let's talk words

Word	What I think it means	What the dictionary says

Box 4.9 shows how a teacher has ensured that students acquire the vocabulary within an English topic, by incorporating the benefits of peer tutoring and mastery learning into the learning process. The accompanying worksheets show how a variety of activities can be included on one language activity sheet. Notice that jumbled words are not included. For students with learning difficulties or intellectual disability, seeing a jumbled word can often leave the impression of that format rather than the correct one.

Producing worksheets that incorporate the selected content and vocabulary

Once the content and vocabulary for a specific worksheet or sub-unit have been decided on, the worksheet can be prepared. Any worksheet needs to use language and reading activities at the students' level to access the topic content. Worksheets need to be in a form that can be clearly followed by students, particularly if they are to work unassisted. Box 4.10 shows how worksheets can be adapted to meet the needs of differing groups but on the same task.

Another important strategy to consider for students with special educational needs is to relate curriculum activities to their own experiences. This is particularly important for subjects such as history, where events are outside any experiences they have had. A way to overcome this on a history worksheet on life in medieval times is to relate the medieval daily eating patterns to students' own experiences, through mapping of their own eating pattern below those of the medieval nobleman and serf.

A final reminder of the need to adapt the teaching and presentation of content for students with additional needs, particularly those who are working within the regular curriculum of the classroom, is the difference in readability and ease of learning of the two worksheets presented in Box 4.11. Worksheet A represents a standard textbook approach. However, Worksheet B shows the same topic reduced in terms of content, vocabulary and presentation. All activities are presented spaced out to fill one page, including instructions and recording. Worksheet B provides a clear summary of what has been learned and at a level that can be understood. Worksheet A can continue to provide a learning approach for capable students.

Box 4.9
Incorporating vocabulary into a syllabus unit
The hippopotamus race

Teacher: Michelle Clark

I have developed an English KLA unit for Year 3, based on Lurie's book *The twenty-seventh annual African Hippopotamus Race* (1977) and a suggested implementation unit by Pam Olney (1993). I have produced an alternative version of the book for students with learning difficulties in the class and those who are unable to read at grade level. As part of the unit, I have incorporated a large variety of language activities that emphasise the vocabulary needed to complete the adapted version of the text.

One technique I have used is to have peer tutors to assist students and to check that vocabulary terms are known. The method for this is to have a list of twelve vocabulary words and ask the tutor and student to do the following:

- Peer tutor listens to the student read the twelve sight words each day and tick those that are correct. When the word has been ticked three times it is mastered.
- Peer tutor plays a flashcard game – snap, memory, board games.
- Student practises writing the vocabulary word using a look, cover, write, check approach.
- Complete associated worksheet.

For list 1 an example worksheet is shown on page 127. I have also extended the use of peer support by asking that the research lessons in the unit be conducted in pairs to ensure that no single student is left to find the information alone.

>

Box 4.9 continued

Vocabulary Worksheet LIST 1

{1} Put these words in alphabetical order.

• trunks, African, measured, race.

_____

• grandfather, President, Zamboola, swim

_____

{2} Fit these words into the shapes below.

(weighed)   (measured)   (trunks)

(Edward)   (swim)

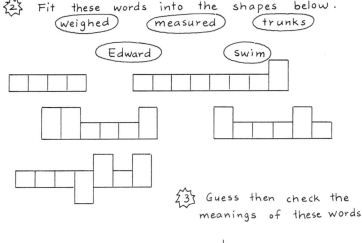

{3} Guess then check the meanings of these words

• annual : guess _____
         check _____

• trunks: guess _____
         check _____

Box 4.10

Using a task to achieve involvement of students at differing levels of ability in the classroom

Communication worksheet

Teacher: Kate Goldman

I used the following two worksheets with a group of students with learning difficulties. One provides a series of visual cues to assist the student find the correct word in the list. The other has no cues and has an additional task to extend the student. This allows me to involve all students in the group but at their instructional level.

>

Box 4.10 continued

Name: _____

COMMUNICATION

There are many different ways we can communicate with others. Label the pictures below, then draw and name four more ways to communicate.

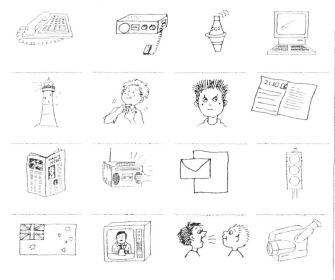

Telephone

Lighthouse

Flags

Facial expressions

Television

Traffic lights

CB Radio

Sign language

Conversation

Diary

Tape recorder

Emergency beacon

Newspaper

Computer

Letter

Video Camera

Classify these by colouring the **nonverbal** ones **red** and the **verbal** ones **blue**.

Choose one of the above and briefly describe its purpose and how it works.

_____

_____

_____

_____

_____

Box 4.10 continued

Name:

COMMUNICATION

There are many different ways we can communicate with others. Label the pictures below, then draw and name four more ways to communicate.

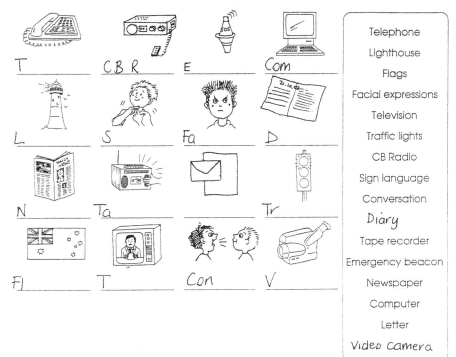

T _____   C B R _____   E _____   Com _____

L _____   S _____   Fa _____   D _____

N _____   Ta _____   _____   Tr _____

Fl _____   T _____   Con _____   V _____

Telephone
Lighthouse
Flags
Facial expressions
Television
Traffic lights
CB Radio
Sign language
Conversation
Diary
Tape recorder
Emergency beacon
Newspaper
Computer
Letter
Video Camera

Classify these by colouring the **nonverbal** ones **red** and the **verbal** ones **blue.**

Box 4.11

Making activities relevant to students through adapting curriculum content and presentation

Worksheet A (original)

Do the following activities. Use correct scientific method in your write-up.

1 Which materials can be charged?

    a Tear a piece of paper about 10 cm × 10 cm into little pieces.

    b Use the piece of cloth given to you by your teacher to rub a glass stirring rod and see if it will pick up your little pieces of paper. Try holding the rubbed rod next to your hair and see what happens.

    c Try using various other objects such as a pencil, a biro, comb and a metal rod.

    d In your book write a list of objects that became charged and a list of objects that did not.

2 What materials are attracted by an electric charge?

    a Make a pile of small pieces of several kinds of materials; for example, paper, aluminium foil, birdseed, sawdust, plastic lunch wrap.

    b Rub a perspex rod on a piece of silk.

    c Hold the charged end of the rod (the end you rubbed on the silk) near each pile in turn and write down what you see happening.

    d Repeat using an ebonite rod rubbed on a piece of wool.

    e What else can a charged rod attract – experiment with things around you (hint: try your hair, a fine trickle of water, etc.).

3 Two kinds of electric charge: Work with a partner in this activity.

    a Stick a small amount of plasticine on either side of a large watch glass.

    b Charge a perspex rod by rubbing it on a piece of silk and balance it on your watch glass as shown in Figure X below:

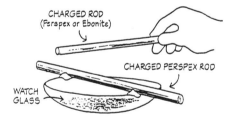

Figure X How do charges behave?

    c Charge a second perspex rod in the same way and bring its charged end near the charged end of the first rod – record what you see.

    d Replace the rod on the watch glass with a charged ebonite rod.

    e Repeat (b) and (c).

    f Do you think perspex and ebonite receive the same charge when they are rubbed? If perspex becomes negatively charged, what happens to ebonite when it is rubbed?

    g Make a general statement about how positively and negatively charged substances behave.

>

Box 4.11 continued

Worksheet B (adapted)

Experiment: Electric force/static electricity
Aim: To find out what material can be charged.
You need:

1 Tiny pieces of paper
2 Silk cloth
3 Glass rod

Method:

1 Put the pieces of paper on the desk.
2 Rub the glass rod with the silk cloth.
3 Bring the rod close to but not touching the pieces of paper. What happened?

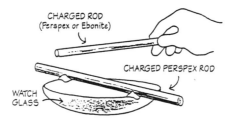

4 Bring the glass rod close to but not touching your hair. What happened?
5 Now try rubbing the following objects: a pencil, a biro, a comb and a metal rod and bring each one close to the pieces of paper.
6 Complete the table below to show what happened:

Object	What happened
Pencil	
Biro	
Comb	
Metal rod	

Monitoring of student performance

There are many monitoring strategies that can be employed before, during and after the lesson and through both formal and informal methods. Methods identified from a review of the literature by Schumm, Vaughn and Sobol (1997) include:

- *Informal member checks* – checking with each student intermittently to see that the key issues are understood.
- *Student summaries of the main points* – asking the student to summarise the main points during the lesson to see that they are on the right track.

mary of directions – after giving instructions, asking the student to repeat

lers – encouraging students to ask questions that 'take a risk' rather than only stions where the answers are known.

ction sheets – students write a brief reaction to the lesson in response to such as 'what did you learn?' or 'were there any parts you didn't understand?'.

- *K-W-L* – a three-column sheet to use at the end of a lesson to highlight what the student Knows about the topic, Wants to learn more about, and has Learned in the lesson.
- *Learning logs* – a type of journal in which the student records entries about their learning in class. This can be as structured or unstructured as needed.
- *Think-Pair-Share* – rather than having to work alone, students are encouraged to think about the topic for a few minutes before then forming into pairs to share their knowledge, followed by pairs sharing with the class.
- *Collaborative open-note tests* – using student notes in assessment tasks is helpful, particularly for students with learning difficulties for whom memory is a problem. The notes are gained from a small group summarisation activity at the end of a lesson. These notes are then used to answer a question about the lesson topic. Notes can be revised or added to.
- *Fake Pop Quiz* – a short two-to-five question quiz that is given by the teacher unexpectedly and which has no effect on the student's grade. It can be used to gauge what has been learned so that further teaching or revision can be undertaken.

Many of the methods discussed above provide examples of cooperative learning between students, and the opportunity to use student language to translate from the teacher's lesson input to student understanding. While monitoring strategies are important, the assessment process is often where students with additional needs are most disadvantaged.

Adapting assessment methods to reflect adapted worksheets

An important issue in adapting content and vocabulary is to ensure that adaptations within the unit are carried through to adaptations within the assessment tasks. This can occur in a number of ways. One is to use progressive assessment throughout the unit, through evaluating worksheets and other activities, and/or including short progressive assessment tasks at the end of each sub-unit. If there needs to be an end of unit assessment, this should reflect the adapted approach to the unit.

Box 4.12 shows how this can operate within a secondary science unit. Notice that the assessment format reflects the worksheets during the unit. Matching the unit and assessment approaches ensures that assessment measures what has been taught, not what is expected at the grade level. This is important and reflects the problems that exist at secondary level in cross-grade assessment strategies that assess to a standard, rather than assess what the students have attempted. Cross-grade assessment tasks which indicate that a considerable minority of students have failed the topic test really show that they have not been taught the content adequately.

Other methods of assessment avoid the necessity of paper and pencil responses, such as oral responding or through multimedia presentations, use of cooperative learning outcomes where other students prompt and share the workload (Dyck & Pemberton, 2002) and teacher observation.

Box 4.12

Relating curriculum assessment to teaching in a unit on energy

A Unit worksheet

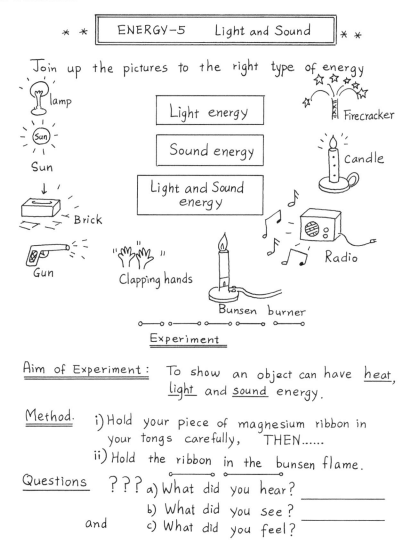

Adaptations of syllabus topics

To this point the focus has been on adapting individual passages and worksheets. Many teachers may wish to unify the approach to cover a complete unit or syllabus topic. This has the advantage of ensuring that the complete unit, rather than single worksheets or vocabulary exercises, meets student needs. Jitendra et al. (2002) argue that content literacy and understanding are essential in determining success in content specialist classes, and hence

Box 4.12 continued

B Unit assessment

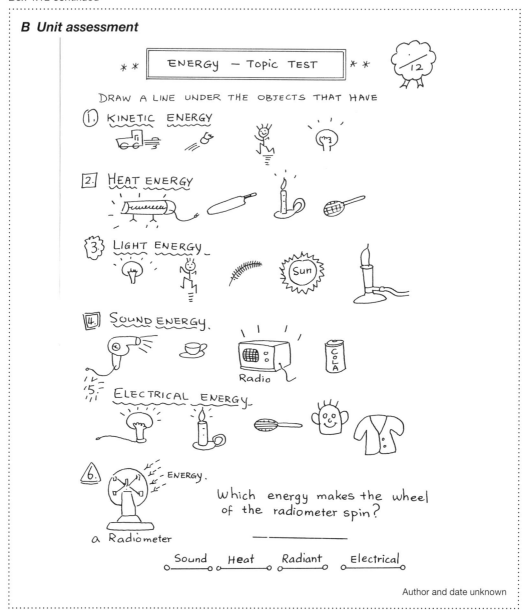

** | ENERGY — Topic TEST | ** /12

DRAW A LINE UNDER THE OBJECTS THAT HAVE

1. KINETIC ENERGY

2. HEAT ENERGY

3. LIGHT ENERGY

4. SOUND ENERGY

Radio

5. ELECTRICAL ENERGY

6. _____ ENERGY.

a Radiometer

Which energy makes the wheel of the radiometer spin?

_____

Sound   Heat   Radiant   Electrical

Author and date unknown

assistance in providing a cognitive structure for integrating prior knowledge with the new information in a topic is important.

While individual teachers can adapt units or topics by themselves, this is a skill perhaps best accomplished in a cooperative program with other teachers. Particularly at the secondary level, individual teachers will not be able to adapt all units for all classes they teach. A strong recommendation is to tackle one unit first and see how that succeeds, and then use that experience in developing another unit. The procedures for cooperative adaptation are discussed in the following sections under staff training. Chapter 10 deals further with the topic of collaborative consultation.

Preparing an adapted unit of work

The following section is based on the assumption that the syllabus topics are fixed and a specific number must be completed in the term. This applies more particularly in secondary schools, where the syllabus is set beyond the school's control.

The preparation of an adapted unit of work follows a sequence of steps that highlight the techniques discussed above:

- *Background:* Read through the syllabus unit including any support information. Gather all materials that may be available including textbooks, previous worksheets and activities and other resources, even if these seem too difficult. Make a decision whether the entire unit is to be adapted for one ability level, or whether it will be used for multiability groups in the class. The latter is the most likely, even where you have a streamed class. It also increases the opportunity to use the materials with other groups later.

- *Content decisions:* Using the diagram in Figure 4.3, decide what content is essential (*must know*). The *should know* and *could know* material can be included in extension activities or in group-work activities. Be realistic about what can reasonably be covered in the time. Divide the unit into sub-units to have manageable teaching blocks. Informing students of the sub-units allows them to have a clearer idea of the sequence and to monitor progress.

- *Vocabulary decisions:* Using the grid in Box 4.7, decide what vocabulary will go into each category. Specific technical terms should be retained where they are important. Remember that any alterations or deletions to vocabulary need to be carried through worksheets, notes, overheads and teacher oral language. Where mixed ability groups are used, language activities can reflect differing levels of vocabulary through different activities.

- *Incorporate language and reading activities into worksheets:* In preparing worksheets, group activities and notes, remember to include activities that increase student understanding through doing rather than receiving. Remember to watch sentence length, incorporate vocabulary as it is needed, and have variety in activities. Parts of many commercial materials are suitable for use in adapted units, or may provide useful ideas that can be adapted. Use some of the presentation methods listed earlier in the chapter.

- *Assessment:* The assessment methods also need to be adapted. Avoid assessing all students in the grade using the one assessment test as it really doesn't assess what the teacher has taught. Where possible, have assessment as an amalgam of methods, rather than leaving the assessment to one final measure. This gives students a clearer measure of their progress and allows remediation of skills not mastered in each sub-unit.

- *Check the adapted materials:* Once you have adapted the content, vocabulary, presentation methods and assessment, check to make sure that you have not left out material that needs to be covered or activities that are needed. It may be useful to have another staff member check the unit as well.

In order to set out the unit and cover all of the aspects set out above, the framework in Box 4.13 may be useful.

An alternative model is to develop a semantic map of the topic (Jitendra et al., 2002). In this approach the information (big ideas) is set out much like a mind map and the content for each lesson mapped against the content. A separate statement on the content outcomes, vocabulary, modifications and adjustments is prepared as well as the ongoing and final assessment tasks. Assessment is seen as the opportunity for the student to understand how the knowledge relates to prior learning and future learning not the assessment of a set of facts in isolation. This, of course, should apply to all students in the class. While the example used by Jitendra et al. is based on an American history example, the model is useful for Australasian teachers to consider.

Box 4.13

Framework for adapting a unit of work

A Cover information

Adapted unit of work

Topic: _____

Grade: _____

Sub-topics: _____
_____
_____

Key content: _____
_____

Vocabulary: _____

General: _____

Specific to sub-topic: _____

B Sub-topic preparation details

Sub-topic: _____

Lesson number	Topic	Lesson content sequence	Resources	Specific vocabulary

---

Implementing the unit

A number of methods exist for implementing an adapted unit. The example that follows emphasises its adaptability to mixed ability classes. The method (Figure 4.4) provides the opportunity to teach sub-units and then have a short period of enrichment and remediation for students who have, and have not, mastered the sub-topic. Within the activities for each sub-unit, students would be able to operate at a number of levels through same ability groups, mixed ability groups and individual worksheets and homework. An additional benefit of this approach is that the more capable students are able to cover more of the *should know* and *could know* content through the enrichment activities. With a series of sub-units, it is possible for the teacher to use a variety of teaching strategies across the sub-units, thus increasing student participation.

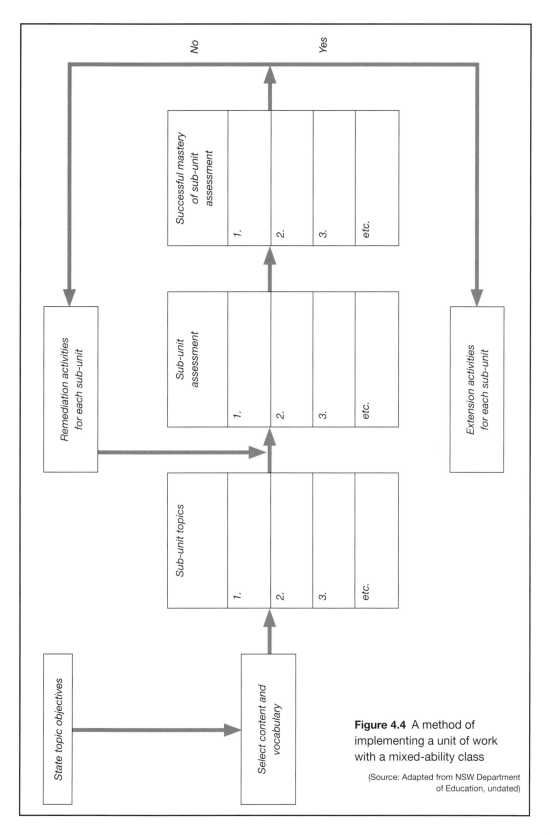

Figure 4.4 A method of implementing a unit of work with a mixed-ability class

(Source: Adapted from NSW Department of Education, undated)

Students with high additional education support needs in the classroom

Including students with high additional education needs in a classroom learning and teaching environment requires a greater commitment to innovation and effort. Having said this there are many ways in which this can very successfully occur.

The key to successfully including a student with high additional education support needs in the classroom is a process based on collaborative planning (Wolfe & Hall, 2003) or consensus building (Dowrick, 2002). The outcome is a learning support plan to support involvement in the classroom, not a separate program. The planning process identifies: the support needs of the student; the specific learning goals for that student; the adjustments that may be required to enable the student to access the curriculum and participate actively in the life of the class and school; and, the identification of additional personnel who may have a role in providing information and advice to support the class teacher.

The adjustments that may be needed are part of the legal requirement that schools do not discriminate against students on the grounds of disability (Australian Parliament, 2003), and because these changes and alterations assist students to maximise their access to the broadest range of class and school activities. These adjustments can occur at the school level or the classroom/curriculum adjustment level (Access and Participation Team Disability Programs NSW DET, 2003).

Examples of adjustments to enhance access and participation in the broader school may include:

- physical access considerations such as building modifications
- organisational considerations such as location of classes, and flexible timetabling
- peer support, playground support, social support groups
- provision of advice and information for staff, students and parents
- provision of support staff
- training and development for schools.

Examples of more specific classroom/curriculum adjustments can include:

- grouping of students
- use of modified materials, for example, scissors
- use of technology to bypass difficulty of task and to facilitate access and participation within the curriculum – this may include use of notetakers, use of word prediction software, use of alternative and augmentative communication devices, use of switches to activate electrical equipment
- specialised seating/positioning equipment
- use of specific teaching strategies, for example, use of visual supports, explicit teaching strategies
- identification of appropriate outcomes and indicators
- identification of alternative assessment tasks
- training and development for school staff
- assistance with curriculum planning/programming
- access to information for staff, parents and students.

The planning process for students with high support needs

The collaborative planning process is based on five specific steps:

- identification of student needs/strengths/challenges
- identification of priority learning goals for the student
- identification of adjustments required to achieve the goals
- identification of additional consideration (for example, medical/health considerations, behaviour support considerations, therapy considerations)
- identification of key personnel to assist in classroom implementation, not as separate programs but embedded in the classroom activities.

This collaborative process and the adaptations to the classroom and curriculum activities are best illustrated in two case studies developed by the Access and Participation Team Disability Programs of the NSW Department of Education and Training (DET). The team works extensively with schools and teachers across NSW and provides consultancy on a wide range of resources and programming strategies for students with complex disabilities. The first case study (Box 4.14) is of Stephanie who is transitioning from Year 6 (Stage 3) in primary to Year 7 (Stage 4) in her local high school, while the second case study (Box 4.15) is of Ben, a nine-year-old boy in Stage 2.

Stephanie

As seen in Box 4.14, Stephanie has a severe intellectual disability and hence will need considerable adaptation to the learning and teaching strategies used in the room so that her particular learning needs can be met. These include her non-verbal language, her moving around the room, her lack of interest in peers and her reluctance to use her hands unless the object is motivating. Notice that the team that works with Stephanie during the transition to high school is a multidisciplinary team and includes Stephanie's mother. If Stephanie were able to contribute directly to the planning, she would be involved in the process as well.

From the four priority goals of the meeting, the school can then identify the adjustments that need to be made both at the school level and at the classroom/curriculum levels. These are reflected in the Learning Support Plan (LSP), which reflects the learning needs and adjustments. Part of the LSP is shown in Box 4.14 with the English, maths, technical and applied studies (TAS), creative arts and science section illustrated. Adjustments are required to all classroom activities and these are shown in Table 1 in the box. Notice how both the adjustments as well as the relevance to Stephanie are shown to assist understanding of the process. To further assist, the Access and Participation Team has provided pictorial examples of how these adjustments might look.

To bring the case study to a specific curriculum activity, the Team has provided a programming template for a unit in the HSIE (human society and its environments) KLA, environments and the specific topic of Antarctica. On the left is the whole class planning for the topic, while on the right is the individual planning for Stephanie. Examples in Box 4.14 illustrate the actual resources used in the lessons. Note the use of the voice output device (both the Bigmack and the Step-By-Step are illustrated) and these reflect the use of technology in supporting students with additional needs in classroom learning. The tactile map allows the student to feel the topography of Antarctica, while Boardmaker allows the student to select known symbols to match to the specific Antarctic tasks.

Notice also that there is built-in assessment of the topic. This is critically important as students with high support needs must have a clear link between the learning tasks and the measurement of performance. Notice particularly the outcomes for the main classroom cohort and the outcomes for Stephanie and the indicators of successful completion of the learning outcomes. Also see the final notes on the adjusted geography assignment on assessing the student's work. The Observation Sheet provides a clear mechanism for recording the assessment of both priority goals and curriculum goals across all teachers, consistent with the LSP.

Box 4.14
Stephanie

Stephanie is a 12-year-old student transitioning from a primary class setting into Year 7 at her local high school. Stephanie has a severe intellectual disability. Stephanie has a younger brother and a younger sister. Stephanie likes music (especially R&B), dancing, things that feel soft or sticky, swimming, being outside, ice cream, animals, playing with musical instruments, and looking at photographs. She doesn't like loud noises, sitting still, or walking on sloping or uneven terrain.

Stephanie communicates non-verbally. Her communication consists of natural body language and instinctive behaviours. For example, when she doesn't like something she will move away from it and when she likes something she will reach for it. Stephanie responds to her name and will make eye contact when it is used. She enjoys being busy and is happy to be guided to do activities. She has just begun to imitate basic movements (like clapping). When she is not being directed, Stephanie tends to leave her seat and wander around the classroom. She tends not to use her hands to pick things up or hold things unless she is directed to or they are very motivating items. Stephanie is not able to independently manage self care tasks. She doesn't demonstrate a lot of interest in her peers.

The family's vision for Stephanie

Stephanie's family members each identified their own vision for Stephanie's future.

- *Stephanie's mother*: I'd like Stephanie to be a happy, valued, contributing member of her neighbourhood and to have the same typical life experiences as her brother and sister and her peers.
- *Stephanie's father*: I'd like Stephanie to be happy, have friends, have some independence, and to be able to communicate, especially with her family.
- *Adam* (Stephanie's brother, aged 7): To learn to play cricket with me, and to climb trees.
- *Sophie* (Stephanie's sister, aged 10): To do sister things with me, and to have friends, and to have a good job, a nice home and a boyfriend when she grows up.

Planning for Stephanie

To facilitate the collaborative planning process a Learning Support Team (LST) was identified to guide the transition planning process and develop a learning support plan. Members of this team included:

- Head Teacher Welfare
- Year 7 advisers (2)

>

Box 4.14 continued

- Stephanie's mum
- District Support Teacher (transition).

The local therapy team and her Year 6 teacher provided additional input.

Stephanie's speech pathologist and occupational therapist attended the initial planning meeting and developed the following therapy goals:

- *speech pathology* – making choices from real objects, beginning to make choices from photographs, responding to photograph timetables, using a Bigmack to initiate communication
- *occupational therapy* – using her hands to pick up and grasp objects, crossing the midline with her hands; managing uneven terrain, especially up and down stairs.

Identification of priority goals

From this information, a number of priority goals were developed. These were:

- for Stephanie to use object symbols and photographs to communicate her needs and wants
- for Stephanie to develop greater independence in her self-help skills
- for Stephanie to interact meaningfully with her peers
- for Stephanie to use her hands more purposefully.

As part of the collaborative planning process a number of adjustments were identified that would facilitate Stephanie's access and participation. This also included the identification of support required by staff (for example, training and development).

Identification of adjustments

- Whole school:
    - Location of roll call class to be on ground floor
    - Identification of appropriate safe playground area
    - Information to Stephanie's roll call class, which included involving them in identifying how she can be included in class activities
    - Information to staff
    - Training and development for all staff
    - Painting of lines on stairs to enable Stephanie to manage stairs more easily
    - Risk management planning on use of high risk areas such as woodwork and kitchen area
    - Identification of, and training for, Stephanie's subject teachers
    - Flexible timetable considerations
    - Playground peer support program – training for peers involved with this
- Classroom/curriculum:
    - Given Stephanie's support needs, a decision was made by the LST for Stephanie to participate in a Life Skills pattern of study. This meant that Stephanie would be working towards relevant Life Skills outcomes that would enable her to attain a Year 10 credential (School Certificate) and then a Year 12 credential (Higher School Certificate).
    - Stephanie would be attending Year 7 classes but would be working towards different outcomes to other students in the class, while participating in the same or similar learning activities, with adjustments.

The Life Skills outcomes for Stephanie are represented in her Learning Support Plan (Table 1).

>

Box 4.14 continued

Who can assist?

Given the complexity of Stephanie's support needs, support from additional personnel was identified as necessary to enable staff to develop confidence and skill in meeting her particular needs. This included teacher aide support, support from the district support teacher transition and support from the local therapy team.

Identifying curriculum adjustments: Training for staff

Staff wanted to know how to adjust class activities to enable Stephanie to participate meaningfully. They were particularly concerned about subjects like HSIE, English and maths, which require extended periods of reading, writing and talking. Staff training looked at alternative ways for Stephanie to access these activities while working towards her individual goals (see Table 2).

A programming template and examples of learning and teaching adjustments

The mapping of the priority goals for Stephanie onto a classroom HSIE unit on Environments is shown in Table 3. It also shows the specific learning activities that can be used to ensure that Stephanie is both learning in the context of relevant classroom tasks as well as having resources that fit her learning needs. These activities are explained in detail in Table 3.

Assessment

Suggestions for general assessment indicators are set out in the LSP and the specific indicators for the HSIE unit on Environments are set out in the Programming template. The way in which the activities Stephanie undertakes can be linked to the class goals for Stage 4 Geography are shown in point 7 of the Antarctica assignment. Hence we can identify both the specific assessment indicators for Stephanie's LSP as well as how they map onto the regular curriculum outcomes.

Staff were encouraged to select outcomes from across the KLAs when planning activities and assessment for Stephanie. For example, during an HSIE activity on Antarctica, Stephanie could be working towards English, science and creative arts outcomes.

Stephanie's outcomes were summarised onto an observation sheet (Table 4) to make it easy for staff to quickly select appropriate outcomes from the full range identified in Stephanie's LSP.

Box 4.14 continued

Table 1 *Learning support plan*

Name: Stephanie		Stage: 4	Date:	Review:
Priority goal	**Teaching strategies and adjustments**	**Curriculum outcomes**	**Indicators**	**Comments**
What knowledge/skills does the student need to learn?	*Which adjustments can be made to help the student to achieve this goal?*	*Which outcomes is the student working towards? What is the purpose of the learning experience? Do the learning experiences relate to the student's existing knowledge and skills? Expand on learn to and learn about in programming.*	*What are the indicators of the student's learning that you would expect to observe?*	*What are the student's strengths? What are the student's current achievements? What are the areas of concern?*
		Stage 4/5: Life Skills		
For Stephanie to use object symbols and photographs to communicate her needs and wants	Use photographs to show Stephanie what activity is going to happen next Offer Stephanie choices across the day using real object symbols When possible, pair the real objects with photographs Reinforce Stephanie's choice-making by providing the requested object or activity immediately	ENG E1 Recognises individual photographs, pictures, symbols or words for personal use E2 Responds to the attention of others E3 Communicates basic needs and wants E4 Follows one step commands E5 Communicates to make basic choices across a range of environments	• Reaches for desired objects when offered a choice • Doesn't reach for non-desired objects when offered a choice • Demonstrates anticipation when shown a photo of her next activity (moves towards activity, looks at equipment needed etc.)	Use photos to teach turn-taking skills

continued

>

CHAPTER 4 ADAPTING CURRICULUM, TEACHING AND LEARNING STRATEGIES   **143**

Box 4.14 continued

Table 1 *Learning support plan* (continued)

Name: Stephanie		Stage: 4	Date:	Review:
Priority goal	**Teaching strategies and adjustments**	**Curriculum outcomes**	**Indicators**	**Comments**
		Stage 4/5: Life Skills		
		MATHS		
		M1 Accesses physical activities involving space and/or measurement in a range of environments	• Places items beside each other when cutting and pasting • Aligns things from right to left when cutting and pasting	
For Stephanie to develop greater independence in self-help skills	Encourage Stephanie to request assistance by not always anticipating her needs (that is, give her the walkman and tape but don't put the tape in the walkman) Wait until she looks at you, then shape her to use the 'help' symbol Call Stephanie's attention to important symbols in her environment (ladies toilets, stop signs etc.)	TAS T1 Uses technology to increase participation in and control over the environment T2 Operates appropriate technology for daily living and leisure	• Uses a Bigmack without prompting • Independently operates walkman, stereo • Accesses the computer	

continued

Box 4.14 continued

Table 1 *Learning support plan* (continued)

Name: Stephanie		Stage: 4		Date:	Review:
Priority goal	Teaching strategies and adjustments	Curriculum outcomes	Indicators		Comments
		Stage 4/5 Life Skills			
For Stephanie to use her hands purposefully.	Motivate Stephanie to use her hands by incorporating some sensory (soft or sticky) materials into activities Encourage Stephanie to point to objects or symbols to communicate Encourage Stephanie to access the computer (cause and effect software, PowerPoint)	CREATIVE ARTS	CA1 Accesses materials for the sensuous appeal of working with the media CA4 Accesses activities involving making music sounds CA6 Recognises familiar music that they listen to and experience	• Engages in craft activities without requiring hand-over-hand prompting • Imitates rhythms using musical instruments • Consistently selects preferred music when offered a choice	Music is a strong motivator for Stephanie
For Stephanie to interact meaningfully with her peers	Use photo-timetables to develop Stephanie's turn-taking skills Encourage Stephanie to use the Bigmack: • to provide feedback to the class after group activities • for greetings • to ask questions Encourage peers to record their voices on the Bigmack	SCIENCE	S1 Uses one or more of their senses to explore their environment S2 Identifies changes in their environment that require a response	• Demonstrates an awareness of cause and effect by deliberately accessing a Bigmack or computer to elicit a response	

∨

Box 4.14 continued

Table 2 *Adjusted reading, writing, and communication activities*

Activity	Adjustment	Relevance to Stephanie	How this might look
Talking	Encourage Stephanie to express an opinion by looking at or looking away from an object. Encourage Stephanie to make choices when shown two real objects. Encourage Stephanie to use a Bigmack for greetings, providing feedback after groupwork, and asking questions	Stephanie has a wide range of instinctive communication behaviours. Her speech therapy goals are aimed at teaching her that these behaviours can be used meaningfully across the day to bring about a desired outcome. Offering Stephanie choices will help teach her this concept	Offer Stephanie a choice by showing her two objects or symbols and encouraging her to reach for the one she wants
Listening	Sit quietly during group work. Wait for her turn to participate, using photos to show her who is talking and when her turn will be	Becoming aware of her peers is an important first step in establishing peer relationships for Stephanie. Using photos to highlight when a peer is talking and when it's Stephanie's turn to talk will promote Stephanie's turn-taking skills	A turn-taking timetable can be used to promote Stephanie's awareness of her peers

continued

∨

Box 4.14 continued

Table 2 *Adjusted reading, writing, and communication activities (continued)*

Activity	Adjustment	Relevance to Stephanie	How this might look
Writing	Pasting items on paper Combining photos/symbols on paper	Although combining symbols to communicate is a long-term goal for Stephanie, this provides some initial experience for her in pre-writing skills such as attending to print/writing from right to left Cutting and pasting are new skills for Stephanie to learn and will meet the OT goal of using her hands more purposefully Cutting and pasting tactile items taps into something that is motivating and enjoyable for Stephanie	Stephanie can participate in writing activities by cutting and pasting symbols Encourage a peer to caption the final product
Reading	Looking at and responding to familiar symbols (timetables, symbol for ladies toilets, walk/don't walk signs etc.) Looking at books/photographs Using PowerPoint to create individual books	Recognising common symbols and symbols that are relevant to her will be an important element in preparing Stephanie to have some independence in the community Stephanie enjoys looking at pictures in books and magazines This is an important leisure skill for Stephanie Extending this activity to PowerPoint books provides opportunities to add sounds, music or narration and to encourage Stephanie to use her hands to access the computer	Using a switch and PowerPoint Stephanie can look at and listen to information about the class topic The presentation could be developed by a peer as part of the assessment process

Box 4.14 continued

Table 3 *Example of programming template for HSIE: Environments*

Whole class planning HSIE: Environments			Individual planning			
Unit outcomes	**Content/teaching/ learning activities**	**Resources**	**Life skills outcomes**	**Indicators**	**Content/teaching/ learning activities**	**Resources**
Identifies and gathers geographical information Organises and interprets geographical information Uses a range of written, oral and graphic forms to communicate geographical information Demonstrates a sense of place about environments outside Australia	Student demonstrates geographical research skills by selecting a country, and prepares a report including the following terms: • a map identifying the main geographical features • information about the climate • information about plants and animals • culture and customs of the people • dwelling places The report is to feature a range of media including text, pictures and diagrams/graphs	Videos Textbooks Library books Internet	Uses technology to increase participation in and control over their environment Uses a range of skills to access living, work and leisure environments Accesses materials for the sensuous appeal of working with the media Makes artworks responding to their own experiences and the appeal of working with the media Responds to sounds of music	Accesses a variety of switches to activate equipment Accesses a variety of electronic equipment Follows sequenced instructions to achieve a goal Uses colour with help Responds to tactile qualities/ colours of craft materials Uses senses to be aware of music in a range of settings	The student produces a report on Antarctica by completing the following activities: *Tactile map:* The student pastes a range of sensory craft materials onto a map of Antarctica *Environment:* The student selects a 'descriptive' symbol and a picture of Antarctica to paste into her book — a peer then writes a sentence about the two symbols *Animal chart:* The student selects and pastes animal pictures into her book; by varying the number of pictures of each animal type available to the student, the chart could become a 'free form graph' representing the relative proportions of the animal populations	Class resource materials The Internet Topic board featuring descriptive words (make this very general so it can be used across subjects) A voice output device Craft materials Switch and Powerlink Animal noises (often found in new age music)

continued

Box 4.14 continued

Table 3 Example of programing template for HSIE: Environments (continued)

Whole class planning HSIE: Environments			Individual planning			
Unit outcomes	**Content/teaching/ learning activities**	**Resources**	**Life skills outcomes**	**Indicators**	**Content/teaching/ learning activities**	**Resources**
	The written report will be accompanied by an oral presentation to the class		Uses hands to complete a range of activities		*Animal multimedia:* The student uses a switch to activate a tape featuring animal sounds — she could select a sound to record on a voice ouput device to be played to classmates at an appropriate time *Dwelling places:* Matches (with assistance) symbols of animals and their dwellings by drawing lines between them — consider various ways for the student to make lines (paintbrush, roller, finger painting etc.) *Presentation:* The student uses a voice output device to present her report to the class.	

Box 4.14 continued

Table 4 Observation sheet

Things Stephanie can do:	Things I can do to help Stephanie:
• Show that she likes/wants something by reaching for it • Show that she doesn't like something by moving away from it • Imitate simple physical movement (clapping, hitting a drum) • Listens to music on her walkman • Likes to look at magazines and books	• Offer her choices between real objects or familiar photos • Encourage her to look at photographs that relate to classroom topics • Encourage her to use her hands during class activities (she enjoys cutting and pasting) • Incorporate sensory materials into her activities (things that feel or smell nice) • Provide Stephanie with extra time to walk between classrooms, especially when stairs are involved

Priority goals	Assessment date	Comments
To communicate her needs and wants		
To develop greater independence in self-help skills		
To use her hands more purposefully		
To interact meaningfully with peers		

Curriculum outcomes

E1 Recognises individual photographs, pictures, symbols or words for personal use		
E2 Responds to the attention of others		
E3 Communicates basic needs and wants		
E4 Follows one-step commands		
E5 Communicates to make basic choices across a range of environments		

continued

Box 4.14 continued

Table 4 *Observation sheet* (continued)

Priority goals	Assessment date	Comments
M1 Accesses physical activities involving space and/or measurement in a range of environments		
T1 Uses technology to increase participation in and control over their environment		
T2 Operates appropriate technology for daily living and leisure		
CA1 Accesses materials for the sensuous appeal of working with the media		
CA2 Makes artworks responding to their own experiences and the appeal of working with the media		
CA3 Responds to material qualities of artworks		
CA4 Accesses activities involving making music sounds		
CA5 Responds to sounds of music		
CA6 Recognises familiar music that they listen to and experience		
CA7 Accesses movement and dance activities		
S1 Uses one or more of their senses to explore their environment		
S2 Identifies changes in their environment that require a response		

v

Box 4.14 continued

Sample adjusted geography assignment – Antarctica

Purpose of activity: Students will engage in the same learning activity as their classmates while achieving their individual goals and identified outcomes (life skills pattern of study).

Individual goals may include:

- independently choice making from a selection of objects or pictures
- using their hands to participate in a range of activities
- using technology to promote their communication and leisure.

Resources required	Suggestions
Pictures of Antarctica for cutting and pasting 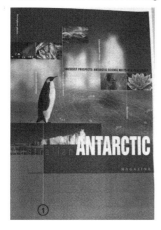	Class resource materials The Internet: The Australian Antarctic Division website has a wide range of pictures available for educational purposes – for speed and convenience, it is also possible to download and print the 'Australian Antarctic Magazine' (pictured left), which would provide pictures and valuable reference material for the entire class
Topic boards featuring descriptive words	Use BoardMaker or pictures from magazines to develop a topic board that features descriptive words Make the topic board very general rather than specific to Antarctica – this will mean it can be reused during future lessons or assignments
A voice output device	A Bigmack or Step-by-Step communicator would allow students to present their report to the class
Textured craft materials	Fabrics sent from home Materials from around the school (tissues, bubble wrap, cottonwool, corrugated cardboard)

Suggested activities

Tactile map

Students could paste a map of Antarctica into their books, then use craft materials to show the geographic features of Antarctica (for example, tissues or cottonwool for snow, bits of corrugated cardboard for mountains, feathers for penguin rookeries). It doesn't really matter where they stick the items – Antarctica is covered in snow, mountains, and penguins!

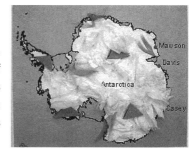

Box 4.14 continued

Describing the environment

Students could use their choice-making skills to select descriptive words from their topic board to stick into their workbooks. Teaching staff or a peer could then help them to select a picture that relates to each descriptive word. Because the topic board is general rather than specific to Antarctica, some creative interpretation may be needed!

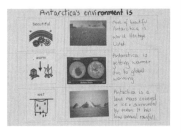

Plants and animals

- Animal collage: Encourage students to select and paste animal pictures into their books. A variation may be to provide students with an assortment of pictures that represent the populations of each animal (for example, there are many penguins, but only a very small number of huskies).
- Students may enjoy listening to whale sounds (often found in relaxation music) as they work.
- Animal noises could be recorded onto a voice output device to be played to classmates at an appropriate time.

Dwelling places

Select pictures or symbols of animals and their dwellings, and encourage students to match them up by drawing lines between them. Consider various ways for students to make lines (for example, using a toy car or small massage toy to roll paint lines between pictures).

Culture and customs of the people

Students could demonstrate how people dress in Antarctica by gluing clothes onto a scientist. All you need to do to prepare for this activity is cut up a picture of a person in Antarctic clothing – you can paste them onto a stick figure. Alternatively, you could use PCS symbols.

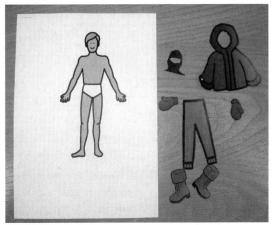

(These pictures were taken from the website <www.secretsoftheice.org>)

Box 4.14 continued

Presenting the assignment to the class

Students could use a voice output device to present their reports to the class.

A Bigmack (single message)

A Step-by-Step communicator
(multimessage)

Assessing student work

When assessing students' work, consider each student's individual priority learning goals rather than the class assignment criteria. These goals can also be linked to relevant stage 4 geography outcomes. For example, is there evidence of:

• independent choice making
• use of technology
• independent hand use.

If there is, the student has achieved the learning goals intended for the assignment.

This case study was developed by the Access and Participation Team,
Disability Programs NSW Department of Education and Training (DET). The team consists of Julie Hook,
Sarah Mottarelly, Valda Stephenson-Roberts, Sarah Humphreys, Anne Temple, and Garry Smith.

Ben

The case study of Ben (Box 4.15) provides a common example of a student with high support needs attending a regular primary school with his siblings. Technology again features strongly to support his communication needs, in this case the use of Picture Communication Symbols (PCS) to respond to adult questions. He also uses the computer for enjoyment. Hence the PCS is commonly used throughout the individual planning for Ben. The science KLA topic for Ben is the same as that for the class, with Ben having a number of adaptations to the tasks so he can participate in the group activities. In this example both the outcomes for all students and Ben's specific outcomes are provided. Again the assessment of Ben's performance is documented in the LSP and in the individual activities in the topic.

Ben

Ben is a 9-year-old student with Down syndrome and autism spectrum disorder. Ben also has a moderate intellectual disability.

Ben has an older sister and a younger brother. His family decided that Ben would access a regular school setting so that he could attend the same school as his siblings.

Ben communicates non-verbally using gesture and facial expression. Staff are using photographs and some picture communication symbols (PCS) to show Ben his daily timetable and to offer him choices within activities. He recognises about 25 symbols that represent objects and activities he accesses regularly. Ben does not initiate the use of photographs or symbols to communicate and only uses them in response to an adult's question.

Ben uses behaviours such as screaming, hitting or kicking to express frustration, anxiety or confusion. These are mainly seen when he is left alone in the playground.

Ben is able to independently engage in activities that he finds highly motivating. These include using the computer and playing with noisy books and toys. Ben's engagement with these items is at a cause-and-effect level – he enjoys pushing a button and watching what happens. Ben also likes music, especially country and western, and enjoys adult attention.

Ben has low muscle tone and experiences difficulty with a range of gross and fine motor activities. He requires adult assistance for most other activities throughout the day. These include toileting, unwrapping his lunch, and deskwork. If left unattended in the classroom, Ben will leave his desk to access more motivating activities.

Ben recognises his name, but can't yet write it. Staff are currently providing him with hand-over-hand assistance during handwriting activities.

Ben has been assessed by a local therapy team. Speech pathology and occupational therapy recommendations have been provided to the school.

Individual planning for Ben

Ben's learning support team consists of his teacher, a support teacher integration, his parents, and the school principal. The occupational therapist and speech pathologist also attended the initial LST meeting to assist with integrating therapy goals into Ben's classroom activities.

Ben's parents wanted him to experience the full range of learning opportunities offered at the school. They didn't have any concrete expectations about how much they wanted Ben to achieve academically, but they stated that they would like him to be able to communicate effectively, complete familiar activities independently, to have friends, and to be able to read and write.

The LST used these family priorities as a basis for selecting individual learning goals for Ben. The goals were intended to represent an 'umbrella' of priority skills that Ben could work towards while engaged in class activities across all of the KLAs (see Table 1).

Programming

Staff were encouraged to program for Ben by starting with the class activity, and making the smallest adjustment necessary to allow Ben to participate meaningfully.

Table 2 is an example of a detailed planning format that lists a student's individual adjustments beside the whole class activities. It is an effective example for teachers who are new to making individual adjustments.

As the teacher becomes more accustomed to adjusting class activities, it is likely that the adjustments could be noted directly onto the original class planning format.

>

Table 1 *Learning support plan*

Name: Ben	**Grade: 2**	**Date:**	**Review date:**

Planning team: Classroom teacher, support teacher integration, Ben's parents, speech pathologist, occupational therapist

Strengths and achievements	Family priorities	Priority goals	Strategies and adjustments
Can concentrate for about 10 minutes	To be able to communicate effectively	1 To increase his ability to complete activities independently	Use photos/symbols as much as possible when providing instructions.
Enjoys cause-and-effect toys	To be as independent as possible		Continue to use the daily timetables
Enjoys noisy books	To learn to read and write		Begin to introduce mini-timetables within each activity that show the stages of the task
Imitation skills	To have friends		Cue Ben through each stage of the task by pointing to the symbols
Responds well to routine and repetition			Encourage him to do the same
Enjoys the computer			Begin to reduce the amount of verbal prompting
Matches pictures and colours			Praise Ben when he is on task
Enjoys music			Use a reward system that Ben will be able to achieve, for example, at the end of each activity
Indicates 'no'			Develop a range of leisure/learning activities that Ben can request and use independently (this could be done using a 'requesting shelf")
Knows colours			
Can make a clear choice when offered a choice of four		2 To develop his 'writing' and 'reading' skills across all KLAs (encouraging him to combine symbols to convey meaning)	Introduce a range of 'writing' possibilities across the day, for example:
Recognises his name in print			• cutting and pasting PCS
			• cloze procedure
			• circling symbols on a topic board

continued

∨

Box 4.15 continued

Table 1 *Learning support plan* (continued)

Name: Ben	Grade: 2	Date:	Review date:

Planning team: Classroom teacher, support teacher integration, Ben's parents, speech pathologist, occupational therapist

Strengths and achievements	Family priorities	Priority goals	Strategies and adjustments
		3 To indicate to adults and/or peers that he has finished an activity or game	Introduce a finished symbol for Ben to point to or bring to the teacher as an additional or alternative way to communicate that he is finished Encourage Ben to use symbols to tell you what he wants to do next (for example, read a book, listen to music)
		4 To contribute to a class discussion/initiate communication using language and/or visuals	Model language – to extend number of single words/ combination of words Have symbols available and accessible Set up situations where Ben is expected to initiate (that is, try not to anticipate his needs)
		5 To participate in group activities	Use of social story – talking turns

>

Box 4.15 continued

Table 2 *Other curriculum support considerations*

Occupational therapy	Left arm requires a splint to provide additional support – encourage Ben to use both hands as much as possible, for example, catching a ball, holding page with left hand while he colours with right hand OT report suggests strategies for promoting pencil grip, scissor use etc.
Speech pathology	Talk to Ben with symbols as well as speech Encourage Ben to point to symbols to indicate needs and wants Trial Go Talk Oromotor activities – as reward at end of activity Speech activities (for individual sounds) – at home
Behaviour support	Use of visual supports/social stories

Science unit of work: Out and about (stage 2)

Outcomes and learning experiences are from the NSW Science and Technology K–6 document. Students will know and understand that:

- environments are sometimes modified to fulfil new and different requirements
- simple machines can make moving loads easier
- materials are joined, formed, shaped and finished.

Students will:

- demonstrate that investigation can take many forms
- recognise that designs are constrained by time, skills, tools and materials
- justify the selection of processes, tools, equipment, materials, products and software to meet the requirements of the task.

Activity: Class discussion about commonly used means of transport

Important goals for Ben during this activity include sitting with his peers, and using symbols to communicate.

- During class discussions, use a transport topic board (a page featuring a range of symbols about a topic). As students mention various types of transport, call Ben's attention to the relevant symbol on the topic board. This introduces the important vocabulary (the 'metalanguage') of the unit to Ben in symbolic form.
- When it is Ben's turn to answer a question, provide him with a choice of only two symbols to tell you how he came to school. Encourage him to look at and point to his choice.

Ben told us he came to school in a car today!

Assessment for Ben from this activity would involve observation of his choice making skills looking for evidence of Ben examining both choices before making a selection. The responses provided through Ben's choice making will allow the teacher to evaluate his understanding of the metalanguage of the unit (for example, does Ben provide the correct answer when he makes a choice?).

>

Box 4.15 continued

Table 3 Example of programming template for science: Out and about (stage 2)

Whole class planning Science: Out and about (stage 2)			Individual planning			
Unit outcomes	Content/teaching/learning activities	Resources	Individual goals/outcomes	Indicators	Adjusted content/teaching/learning activities	Resources
Students will know and understand that: • environments are sometimes modified to fulfil new and different requirements • simple machines can make moving loads easier • materials are joined, formed, shaped and finished	Students conduct a survey to determine their most commonly used means of transport — draw diagrams of the vehicle, labelling parts Design solutions to problems associated with the use of student's transport (small groups) • groups brainstorm advantages and disadvantages of most common types of transport — include safety, environment • students devise a plan to address identified problem (that is, community campaign about bicycle helmets)	Clock Meccano Lego Cardboard Textas Papercraft materials	To increase his ability to complete activities independently To develop his 'writing' and 'reading' skills across all KLAs (encouraging him to combine symbols to convey meaning) To indicate to adults and/or peers that he has finished an activity or game To contribute to a class discussion/initiate communication using language and/or visuals	Follows a visual timetable to complete an activity and/or to achieve a reward Uses a finished box to cue himself through the stages of a task Combines symbols to create a sentence in literacy activities Points to symbols on a topic board to comment	Students conduct a survey to determine their most commonly used means of transport • Uses topic board to participate in class discussion (use turn-taking schedule to assist him to anticipate his turn) • Participates in survey using his Go Talk • Uses symbols to record results of survey Design solutions to problems associated with the use of student's transport (small groups) • Looks at road safety social story	Go Talk PCS Turn-taking chart Social story Road safety sign photos Visual schedule for writing task Finished box

continued

Box 4.15 continued

Table 3 *Example of programming template for science: Out and about (stage 2) (continued)*

Whole class planning Science: Out and about (stage 2)			Individual planning			
Unit outcomes	Content/teaching/learning activities	Resources	Individual goals/outcomes	Indicators	Adjusted content/teaching/learning activities	Resources
Students will: • demonstrate that investigation can take many forms • recognise that designs are constrained by time, skills, tools and materials • justify the selection of processes, tools, equipment, materials, products and software to meet the requirements of the task	• students evaluate their plan by consulting with other groups, parents and staff about their opinions Investigate how gears/cogs make things move • class investigates cogs/gears in: bicycle, clock with face removed (whole class) — talk about where else cogs/gears might be found		To participate in group activities	Uses PCS to request a change in activity Points to a symbol in response to a question Uses a Go Talk during class discussions Uses PCS to request assistance or items Tolerates being part of a small group Uses PCS to show whose turn it is	• Identifies road safety signs during class discussion by pointing when asked • Uses PCS to write about road safety (to make a chart about things to remember when crossing the road) Investigate how gears/cogs make things move • Assistance tracing cogs • Writes own name on cog tracing (attempts B) • Looks at models of moving cogs on the computer	

continued

Box 4.15 continued

Table 3 *Example of programming template for science: Out and about (stage 2) (continued)*

Whole class planning Science: Out and about (stage 2)			Individual planning			
Unit outcomes	Content/teaching/ learning activities	Resources	Individual goals/ outcomes	Indicators	Adjusted content/ teaching/learning activities	Resources
	• students use Meccano/Lego to explore how cogs work together — encourage students to substitute cogs of different sizes to explore how this changes the movement • students trace their construction onto paper, and add arrows to show the path of movement Use gears to design and make a moving toy (small groups) — decorate as appropriate				Use gears to design and make a moving toy (small groups) • Uses PCS symbols to make contributions to groupwork (deciding on the colour) • Plays a role in construction (takes turns dabbing glue on construction)	
Assessment strategies:			**Assessment strategies:**			

∨

Box 4.15 continued

Activity: *Conduct a class survey of types of transport used by students*

The primary goal in this activity is to encourage Ben to use a voice output device (VOCA) to initiate communication. His use of the VOCA will provide positive reinforcement for Ben by eliciting a verbal response and actions from his peers.

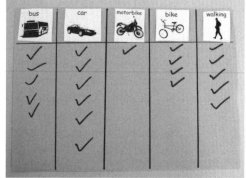

- Using a VOCA to ask the question 'How did you travel to school today?', Ben can independently conduct his own investigation. Use symbols from the transport topic board to create a retrieval chart. Ben can take the retrieval chart to his peers, and use the VOCA to ask them to tick the appropriate column.
- When everyone has answered, he can use copies of the symbols to make a graph. A range of numeracy concepts can be incorporated into this task including matching, one-to-one correspondence, counting, and concepts like more and less, or many and few.

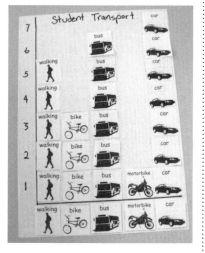

Ben's participation in the survey activity will enable him to work towards the stage 2 science curriculum outcome of understanding that investigation can take many forms. This would occur at the same time as he is working towards his individual communication goals.

Activity: *Design solutions to problems associated with the use of students transport*

- Take digital photographs of Ben using different types of transport – sitting in the taxi, sitting on a bike, walking along the road. Laminate each page to make a book. Encourage him to look at each page and draw a circle around the item that will keep him safe (using a whiteboard marker).

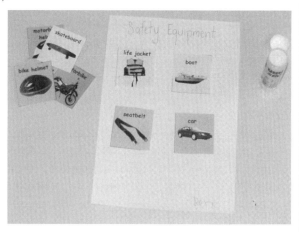

- Ben can use symbols to write about safety measures. Use a mini-timetable to show Ben the steps of the task so that he can complete the task independently.

Ben's completion of this task will enable him to work towards the stage 2 science outcome of understanding that environments are sometimes modified to fulfil different require-ments, as well as working towards his individual goals.

Box 4.15 continued

Class activity: Investigate how gears/cogs make things move; use gears to design and make a moving toy

Adjustments

- This activity does not need significant adjustment to enable Ben to participate, however it provides a good opportunity to embed Ben's individual goal of working in a group by using a turn-taking timetable to assist him to anticipate, take and complete his turn.

- Have a range of visuals available to promote Ben's communication when it is his turn. These could include symbols for colours and real object choices for construction materials.

During this task, Ben is working towards the stage 2 science outcomes of understanding that materials are joined, formed, shaped and finished, and recognise that designs are constrained by time, skills, tools and materials.

This case study was developed by the Access and Participation Team, Disability Programs NSW Department of Education and Training (DET). The team consists of Julie Hook, Sarah Mottarelly, Valda Stephenson-Roberts, Sarah Humphreys, Anne Temple, and Garry Smith

Adapting curriculum for students with high support needs in practical lessons

The discussions above have focused on lessons relating to curriculum activities in the classroom. Adaptation of practical activities such as in physical education can, and should, also occur. One of the difficulties faced by PE teachers of mainstreamed classes is the traditional approach of teachers selecting a task, goals and teaching strategies, and then ensuring that students learn the skill. The Board of Studies NSW (1999), in a set of support documents for including students with additional needs in personal development/health/physical education, highlighted the need to modify equipment or use adapted procedures to ensure physical participation. For a student with a hearing impairment this may involve other students using and interpreting sign language to support the student with additional needs as a participating member of the class. For a student with high physical support needs, this may require assistance from a physiotherapist in enhancing wheelchair mobility to increase access and participation in a dance lesson.

Both the above examples and the case studies emphasise the importance of working as a team rather than having the class teacher work alone on the adaptations. This emphasises the collaborative nature of aiding students with high education support needs in the classroom.

Using technology in learning and teaching

Technology is increasingly used in assisting student learning and there are few schools or even classrooms that do not have computer technology. For students with additional needs, technology usage has become increasingly more sophisticated and has moved well beyond the earlier applications in remediation or compensation. Remediation for students with learning difficulties in reading, mathematics and spelling was frequently undertaken using computer-aided instruction (CAI). The attraction was that CAI provided personalised instruction, sequenced instruction and direct and immediate feedback (Chan & Dally, 2001). Recent advances in the form of CD and DVD technology has permitted a greatly enhanced role for CAI with the opportunity to explore virtual worlds rather than use remediation exercises that resemble traditional worksheets.

Today we often use the term adaptive technology, which covers any device used to increase, maintain, or improve the functional capabilities of children with disabilities (based on the IDEA definition cited in Parette & McMahan, 2002). This extends from simple communication boards to sophisticated electronic communication devices, computers and their peripherals, and mobility aides. For the purposes of this section, we will focus on computer-related technologies.

The World Wide Web (www) has provided the greatest advance in curriculum modification. Where the material is available as electronic text, it can be adapted through changing its size, appearance and layout to meet specific additional learning needs (Castellani & Jeffs, 2001). It can also be augmented with screen readers, text readers such as Kurzweil and other speech synthesisers. Text-reading software enables written text to be scanned and provides auditory feedback. Castellani and Jeffs also note the Web allows graphics, sound, video and animation to be accessed to further increase student motivation. They demonstrate a range of uses of computer technologies in reading including the development of flowcharts and writing guides.

Rather than focus on traditional technologies that can be seen in the case studies in the chapter, the remainder of this section focuses on some new and innovative ways technology can be used to enhance learning and teaching through a variety of accommodations and modifications.

The development of e-books (Cavanaugh, 2002) has changed the way we consider text access. E-books consist of three parts, the e-book file, a software file to read the e-book and a hardware device to read it on. Their role in accommodations is that they have adjustable text size, can have multicoloured highlighting of key points, can have bookmarks, and can use text to speech for auditory as well as visual input. For students with physical disabilities, the use of e-books on palm (handheld) computers enables students to use a stylus to operate any of the above features. The same can be achieved by using peripherals on a regular computer. In addition, the accommodations can be made by the teacher in advance or by the student during the task. Cavanaugh also provides specific examples of how to access e-books and develop accommodations.

Other uses of palm (handheld) computers include self-monitoring of behaviour, self-recording of grades, and communicating between parents and school as a communication device (Bauer & Ulrich, 2002). A key advantage of palm computers is that the information is immediately accessible rather than relying on access to a standard computer. Information is also personalised and not stored on a general computer where other students may have access.

Technology can also play an important role for teachers in developing programs and evaluation records for students with additional needs. Denham and Lahm (2001) used adapted peripherals including switches and an IntelliKeys overlay constructed using the Overlay Marker program (IntelliTools, 1996) to involve students with moderate and severe disabilities in the curriculum choice making and the development of their learning portfolio. The format and accommodations were specific for each student. Denham and Lahm also provide specific advice on customising overlays for students and provide examples. Implementation included teacher training in the procedures and the use of a peer buddy (see Chapter 6 for further information on peer buddies). The result was that individual students were able to increase their level of independence in responding from 4 to 35 per cent in four trials.

Another use of technology by teachers in accommodating additional educational needs is the widget (Miller, Brown & Robinson, 2002). Widgets are learning tools that are small self-contained instructional activities that are created using software which can be stored on the computer. They are not designed to be used as drill and practice or even independent use (although they can be used for that purpose). They are mediational software programs to be used by the teacher interacting with a student on a learning task. The teacher determines the content input, level of difficulty, and speed of learning, not the widget software. Miller, Brown and Robinson (2002) used the widgets to assist students with a mild intellectual disability acquire mathematics skills. Again, they provide examples of widget screens in their paper.

While educators see technology as a major source of accommodations and adaptations to learning and teaching in schools, the views of parents and their expectations have not be well explored. Parette and McMahan (2002) found that family feelings about assistive technology are often heavily influenced by cultural and linguistic backgrounds, with clear differences between groups. Some parents do not want technology to be used in the home or in public places, while others are concerned that the technology may draw attention to their child. While these issues have not been explored in Australian schools, it should not be assumed that all parents would want their children to access specific adaptive technology. Involving the parents in any decisions about technology may overcome any perceived difficulties and may ensure their support for its use.

Staff working cooperatively on curriculum adaptation and implementation

For many teachers of students with high additional needs, the thought of having to adapt curriculum presentation is too daunting. There is commonly the need for additional support in planning, and implementing the learning and teaching adaptations discussed above. This support can come from specialists within the school or from a broader range of specialists within the education jurisdiction or beyond.

Specialist support

The case studies of Stephanie (Box 4.14) and Ben (Box 4.15) both emphasised the importance of specialist support in the development of learning and teaching adaptations for their full involvement in the classroom. Both had input from a speech pathologist and an occupational therapist in the development of their LSP. This support addressed both their communication and motor skill needs within the curriculum activities of the classroom.

Support in adapting curriculum may come from school-based specialist staff, most often the support teacher (learning difficulties) or equivalent, although assistance can also come from special education teachers who may have assisted in the mainstreaming process in some cases where the student has been previously in a special class. A support teacher (learning difficulties) can provide assistance, both in terms of understanding student ability level and in strategies for adapting content. The role of the class teacher is to provide the content knowledge and vocabulary. It must be remembered that any specialist support is designed to assist the classroom teacher – the support teacher provides ideas and assistance, the class teacher always remains the professional in charge of the student's learning.

In the section on preparing an adapted unit of work above, the support teacher could provide assistance in adapting content and vocabulary, in developing worksheets and alternative teaching/learning strategies, and in assessment tasks, based on knowledge of student needs and ability. Support teachers can also provide assistance to faculties, grades and the total school staff on adaptation strategies. Support teachers can also assist with assessment requirements including planning, evaluation of existing assessment tasks, and supervision and assistance with assessment procedures such as reading the test or recording answers (Hallinan, Hallinan & Boulter, 1999).

Another possible support person is the special teacher's aide or the integration aide. While these staff can provide assistance in carrying out the curriculum adaptation made by the class teacher and specialist teachers, it is not their role to adapt curriculum. One important factor in using integration aides is to ensure that they work towards the incorporation of the student with additional needs within the class curriculum, rather than providing alternative academic tasks that increase a sense of academic isolation.

It is important when another adult assists, either in the adaptation of the curriculum content or in its presentation, that the ownership of the curriculum, the teaching strategies and the student's education remain the responsibility of the class teacher. The role of the class teacher is to teach; the role of the support person is to assist.

Collaborative planning

One way in which collaboration can enhance learning and teaching is through the process of collaborative planning (Jitendra et al., 2002; Kennedy, Higgins & Pierce, 2002). Collaborative planning is a team effort in which each member of the team supports the others in developing appropriate instructional plans and in designing differentiated learning and teaching activities for students with additional needs. The aim is to ensure the student's active involvement in the classroom learning environment. Collaboration is best defined as *how* teachers work together rather than what they do and is seen as an intangible process based on the interaction styles professionals use to accomplish their shared goals (Cook & Friend, 1993; Friend & Bursuck, 2002, cited in Kennedy, Higgins & Pierce, 2002). Collaboration is seen as a long-term process built on a common and shared understanding of the needs of both students and teachers.

Collaborative planning requires high levels of support from the school executive for the development of the skills of interacting and working as a team, and then the time to implement those skills for specific students. Without these two conditions being fulfilled, there is little likelihood that collaborative planning (as measured by student outcomes) will succeed (Villa & Nevin, 1994, cited in Schmidt, Rozendal & Greenman, 2002).

Interestingly, although Kennedy, Higgins and Pierce (2002) focus on the needs of students who are both gifted and who have a learning difficulty in the regular classroom, the processes and procedures are the same as for all students with additional needs in the classroom. In addition they provide a range of proforma that are appropriate for students with low additional needs as well. The discussions above on the development of learning and teaching adaptations for students with high support needs such as Stephanie and Ben also reflect the importance of collaborative planning and implementation.

Co-teaching

It should not be assumed that teaching staff working together would necessarily be successful. In a study of co-teaching, or cooperative teaching, conducted in the states of Queensland and Pennsylvania (USA), Rice and Zigmond (2000) found that the approach had limited success in secondary schools in both locations. Co-teaching was defined as 'a restructuring of the teaching procedures in which two or more educators work in a co-active and coordinated fashion to jointly teach academically and behaviourally heterogeneous groups of students in integrated educational settings' (Brauwens & Hourcade, 1995, p. 46, cited in Rice & Zigmond, 2000). Rice and Zigmond point out that, while the cooperative teaching model is often seen as synonymous with students with additional needs being retained in the regular classroom, it provides all students with a wider range of instructional alternatives than would be provided by one teacher and combines expertise to meet the needs of all students. For students with additional needs, it enhances the opportunities for full class membership, and increases the opportunities for improved learning outcomes.

The study found that no classroom accurately reflected the definition of co-teaching and that the special education teacher invariably undertook a subordinate role with planning based on the subject teacher's decisions on curriculum pacing and the specialist teacher's

role being to adapt the assignments and materials for the students with additional needs. Six themes are identified by Rice and Zigmond (2000) that give guidance to improving teaching practice in classroom:

- effective implementation of co-teaching requires schoolwide acceptance of inclusive policies and co-teaching as a viable support option
- co-teaching arrangements bring benefits to all teachers and students
- teachers rate professional and personal compatibility highly in preferred co-teaching partners
- special education teachers are seldom given equal status in co-teaching partnerships
- special education teachers most often prove themselves capable of making a unique and substantive contribution
- implementing co-teaching in secondary schools often involves overcoming entrenched attitudes and administrative barriers.

Critical among the themes is the need for school executive support for co-teaching and teachers having the opportunity to train in the skills of co-teaching. Like so many strategies that exist for increased involvement of students with additional needs in the classroom, teachers need support from the school executive, skills to make the strategies work, and the ability to choose whom to work with rather than this being imposed.

School staff development

The responsibility for curriculum adaptation cannot be seen as the sole responsibility of individual teachers or even the responsibility of faculties; it lies with the entire school. Successful curriculum adaptation at a whole school level requires first the support and personal commitment of the principal, followed by the support and commitment of the staff, students and parents. Given Slee's comment 'that schools are less than satisfactory for increasing numbers of young people who are not considered disabled' (1995, p. 7), any adaptation of curriculum for students with additional needs should be seen as a part of a rethinking of the way we approach curriculum implementation in a wider sense.

One of the critical issues relates to the way teachers are trained. While many employing authorities now require a mandatory course (subject) in special education, often on inclusion, the influence of training in content specialist areas can outweigh any knowledge of inclusion techniques that are learned in special education courses. Some teachers will not use strategies such as problem solving and modelling that have been shown to be useful for students with additional needs, because they do not fit with the approaches learned in their initial subject preparation. This may be because the lecturers in those specialist content areas are unaware of the strategies for adaptation and modification of curriculum to assist students with additional needs. Inclusion of subject specialist lecturers as tutors in special education courses is a valuable way of assisting their understanding of the issues and, in special education terms, promote the maintenance and generalisation of the strategies discussed in this and other chapters. As Buly and Rose (2001) noted, some will observe change from the inside, while others will do so from outside the process.

Any training in curriculum adaptation at a school staff level must address these gaps in teacher strategy repertoire, and point to the value of changing existing practices before change for students will occur. As Westwood and Graham (2003) found, additional training was identified as an important issue for teachers who had students with additional needs in their classes. This theme they noted was common among teachers in previous studies, both in Australia and overseas.

These staff training needs can be accomplished in a combination of ways. Staff development training packages are available in a number of jurisdictions. In addition, support teachers (learning difficulty), or their equivalent, may provide staff seminars on techniques of adaptation, including specific examples. Where staff prefer outside involvement, this can occur by involving specialists such as integration consultants. However, the best method is to visit and to invite as speakers, staff from schools where successful curriculum adaptation and modification has occurred.

Summary

This chapter has focused on the role of the regular school curriculum and related syllabuses that heavily influence mainstream classroom teaching. The approach has been to examine ways in which the curriculum can be adapted to meet the needs of students with additional needs, rather than developing discrete curriculums or teaching models that may exacerbate differences rather than increase inclusion. Strategies that have been examined include the adaptation of individual worksheets through altering the readability and through the inclusion of language and reading activities that are appropriate to the students' instructional levels. The difficulties of using textbooks and the challenges of finding suitable alternatives have been acknowledged in the light of the heavy reliance placed on them, particularly by secondary teachers.

The development of units of work to provide a more restricted amount of content, coupled with focused vocabulary, has been suggested as an appropriate approach for mainstreamed classes. While such an approach is time-consuming for the individual teacher, the involvement of groups of teachers and whole faculties can reduce the burden on each teacher. Adapted curriculum presentation has the potential to increase student involvement and reduce disruptive behaviour through teaching at the student instructional level.

The more specific adaptations and modifications required for students with high support needs require a greater level of support for classroom teachers. This is perhaps best undertaken through collaborative planning to ensure maximum participation in classroom learning and assessment.

Finally the chapter looked at staff training needs at individual and whole staff levels, emphasising the need for executive and whole staff support in any coordinated approach to adaptation and modification of learning and teaching. The following chapter will explore further the interrelated areas of social integration and management of the inclusive classroom.

Discussion questions

1 What topics would you include in a half-day staff development session on adapting curriculum for students with additional needs in your regular education school?

2 How can you make assessment tasks relevant for all students in the class?

3 Inclusion of students with high additional needs in the classroom requires greater collaboration between professionals. What is collaborative planning and what are the key principles that underlie this process?

Individual activities

1 Take a topic in your subject area and identify the 'must know' content and the vocabulary that should be placed in each of the three categories. Compare your results with those of a colleague.

2 Take a worksheet you have used previously and adapt it for use by students with a student instructional level at least three grades below the grade level the worksheet was originally designed for.

3 Name five technology-based teaching strategies that would assist a student with additional needs learn a curriculum topic. Show how you would use that strategy for a specific topic.

4 For each of the following from Box 4.3, identify three strategies that could be used and describe how they can be used for students with specific additional needs. Try to identify ones additional to those listed in the chapter:
   a curriculum content adaptation
   b curriculum presentation methods
   c additional skills training to assist curriculum content understanding.

Group activities

1 As a small group, take a curriculum topic and work through the process of identifying the critical curriculum content, adapting the vocabulary and then developing a series of sample worksheets for the topic that demonstrate the importance of adapted curriculum, reduced vocabulary, appropriate presentation styles. Also prepare an adapted assessment task for the same topic. Share the outcomes with other groups in the same or different curriculum areas.

2 Using the five steps of the collaborative process of planning and implementing learning and teaching adaptations and modifications, show what occurs at each step for either Stephanie or Ben in the case studies in Boxes 4.14 and 4.15. What other strategies could be used? How could these vary or be similar in another curriculum area?

References

Access and Participation Team Disability Programs NSW DET. (2003). *Planning for Students With Complex Disabilities*. Unpublished notes. Sydney: Author.

ACT Department of Education. (2002). *The Inclusivity Challenge. Within Reach of Us All: A Discussion Paper for School Communities*. Canberra: Author.

Australian Parliament. (2003). *Draft Disability Standards for Education*. www.dest.edu.au/rresearch/docs/july03/draftstandards2003pdf

*Bauer, A. M. & Ulrich, M. E. (2002). 'I've got a palm in my pocket': using handheld computers in an inclusive classroom. *Teaching Exceptional Children*, 35(2), 18–22.

Board of Studies NSW. (1999). *Personal Development, Health and Physical Education K–6: Support documents for students with special education needs*. Sydney: Author.

Board of Studies NSW. (2001). *Stage 6 Special Program of Study: Case studies*. Sydney: Author.

Buly, M. R. & Rose, R. R. (2001). Mandates, expectations, and change. *Primary Voices K–6, 9*(3), 3–6.

Campbell, J., Gilmore, L. & Cuskelly, M. (2003). Changing student attitudes towards disability and inclusion. *Journal of Intellectual and Developmental Disability, 28*(4), 396.

*Castellani, J. & Jeffs, T. (2001). Emerging reading and writing strategies using technologies. *Teaching Exceptional Children, 33*(5), 60–7.

*Cavanaugh, T. (2002). EBooks and accommodations: Is this the future of print accommodation? *Teaching Exceptional Children, 35*(2), 56–61.

Chan, L. K. S. & Dally, K. (2001). Instructional techniques and service delivery approaches for students with learning difficulties. *Australian Journal of Learning Disabilities, 6*(3), 14–21.

*Denham, A. & Lahm, E. A. (2001). Using technology to construct alternate portfolios of students with moderate and severe disabilities. *Teaching Exceptional Children, 33*(5), 10–17.

Department of Education, Science and Technology (DEST). (2002). *National Goals and Adelaide Declaration*. Retrieved 27 November, 2003, from http://www.dest.edu.au/schools

Dowrick, M. K. (2002). A model for assessing learning outcomes for Australian students in special schools. *British Journal of Special Education, 29*(4), 189–95.

Dyck, N. & Pemberton, J. B. (2002). A model for making decisions about text adaptations. *Intervention in School and Clinic, 38*(1), 28–35.

Education Queensland. (2000). *New Basics: Theory Into Practice*. Brisbane: New Basics Unit.

Engelbrecht, P., Oswald, M., Swart, E. & Eloff, I. (2003). Including learners with intellectual disabilities: Stressful for teachers? *International Journal of Disability, Development and Education, 50*(3), 293–308.

Fields, B. A. (1999). The impact of class heterogeneity on students with learning disabilities. *Australian Journal of Learning Disabilities, 4*(2), 11–16.

*Forlin, C. (2001). Inclusion: Identifying potential stressors for regular class teachers. *Educational Research, 43*(3), 11–21.

Giangreco, M. F., Cloninger, C. J. & Iverson, V. (1992). *Choosing Options and Accommodations for Children (COACH): A Planning Guide for Inclusive Education*. Baltimore: Paul H Brookes.

*Hallinan, P., Hallinan, P. & Boulter, M. (1999). Enhancing student learning: Inclusive practice at a Queensland High School. *Australian Journal of Learning Disabilities, 4*(1), 10–17.

Harniss, M. K., Dickson, S. V., Kinder, D. & Hollenbeck, K. L. (2001). Textual problems and instructional solutions: Strategies for enhancing learning from published history textbooks. *Reading and Writing Quarterly, 17*, 127–50.

Hinton, L. (2003). Productive pedagogies: The link between new basics and philosophy in schools. *Primary and Middle School Educators, 1*(1), 7–12.

IntelliTools (1996). *Overlay Maker*. Novvato CA: Author.

Jitendra, A. K., Edwards, L. A., Choutka, C. M. & Treadway, P. S. (2002). A collaborative approach to planning in content areas for students with learning disabilities: Accessing the general curriculum. *Learning Disabilities Research and Practice, 17*(4), 252–67.

Kennedy, K. (1995). National curriculum statements and profiles: What have we learnt? In C. Collins (Ed.), *Curriculum Stocktake: Evaluating School Curriculum Change* (pp. 153–71). Canberra: The Australian College of Education.

Kennedy, K. Y., Higgins, K. & Pierce, T. (2002). Collaborative partnerships among teachers of students who are gifted and have learning disabilities. *Intervention in School and Clinic, 38*(1), 36–49.

Lingard, B., Ladwig, J., Mills, M., Bahr, M., Chant, D., Warry, M., Ailwood, J., Capeness, R., Christie, P., Gore, J., Bayes, D. & Luke, A. (2001a). *The Queensland School Reform Longitudinal Study*. Brisbane: Education Queensland.

Lingard, B., Ladwig, J., Mills, M., Bahr, M., Chant, D., Warry, M., Ailwood, J., Capeness, R., Christie, P., Gore, J., Bayes, D. & Luke, A. (2001b). *The Queensland School Reform Longitudinal Study: A Strategy For Shared Curriculum Leadership – Teachers' Summary*. Brisbane: Education Queensland.

Lokan, J. (1997). Overview of developments with the national statement and profiles to 1993. In J. Lokan (Ed.), *Describing Learning: Implications of Curriculum Profiles in Australian Schools 1986–1996*. ACER Research Monograph No. 50. Melbourne: ACER.

Lurie, M. (1977). *The Twenty-Seventh Annual African Hippopotamus Race*. Melbourne: Puffin.

Mastropieri, M. A. & Scruggs, T. E. (2000). *The Inclusive Classroom. Strategies for Effective Instruction*. Upper Saddle River, NJ: Merrill.

McGaw, B. (1995). Outcome specification in curriculum design. In C. Collins (Ed.), *Curriculum Stocktake: Evaluating School Curriculum Change* (pp. 73–87). Canberra: The Australian College of Education.

*Miller, D., Brown, A. & Robinson, L. (2002). Widgets on the web: Using computer-based learning tools. *Teaching Exceptional Children, 35*(2), 24–8.

Ministerial Council of Education, Employment, Training and Youth Affairs (MCEETYA). (2002). National Report on Schooling in Australia: Preliminary Paper. National Benchmark Results: Reading and Numeracy: Years 3 and 5. Retrieved 6 June, 2003, from http://www.curriculum. edu.au/mctyapdf/2000_benchmarks.pdf

NSW Department of Education and Training. (2003). *Quality Teaching in NSW Public Schools*. Sydney: Author.

O'Connell, K. (2001). Looking at textbooks. *Journal of Special Education Technology, 16*(3), 57–8.

*O'Leary, M. & Shiel, G. (1997). Curriculum profiling in Australia and the United Kingdom: Some implications for performance-based assessment in the United States. *Educational Assessment, 4*(3), 203–35.

Olney, P. (1993). *Suggestions for implementing 'The Twenty-Seventh Annual African Hippopotamus Race'*. North Richmond: Author.

*Parette, P. & McMahan, G. A. (2002). What should we expect of assistive technology? Being sensitive to family goals. *Teaching Exceptional Children, 35*(1), 56–61.

Pascoe, S. (2001). *Generic Verses Content-Driven Assessment*. Paper presented at the 2001 annual conference for the Australian Curriculum Assessment and Certification Authorities. Retrieved 16 December, 2002, from http://www.boardofstudies.new.edu.au/manuals.pdf.doc/ pascoe.pdf

Quenemoen, R. F., Lehr, C. A., Thurlow, M. L. & Massanari, C. B. (2001). *Students With Disabilities in Standards-Based Assessment and Accountability Systems: Emerging Issues, Strategies and Recommendations. NCEO Synthesis Report 37*. Washington: National Centre on Educational Outcomes.

*Rice, D. & Zigmond, N. (2000). Co-teaching in secondary schools: Teacher reports of developments in Australian and American classrooms. *Learning Disabilities Research and Practice*, *15*(4), 190–7.

Ring, M. M. & Reetz, L. (2000). Modification effects on attributions of middle school students with learning disabilities. *Learning Disabilities Research and Practice*, *15*(1), 34–42.

Schmidt, R. J., Rozendal, M. S. & Greenman, G. G. (2002). Reading instruction in the inclusive classroom. *Remedial and Special Education*, *23*(3), 130–40.

*Schumm, J. S., Vaughn, S. & Sobol, M. C. (1997). Are they getting it? How to monitor student understanding in inclusive classrooms. *Intervention in School and Clinic*, *32*(3), 168–71.

Scott, B. J., Vitale, M. R. & Masten, W. G. (1998). Implementing instructional adaptations for students with mild disabilities in inclusive classrooms. *Remedial and Special Education*, *19*, 106–19.

Slee, R. (1995). Education for all: Arguing principles or pretending agreement? *Australian Disability Review*, *2–95*, 3–19.

Tasmanian Department of Education. (2003). *Essential Learnings: Introduction to the Outcomes and Standards*. Hobart: Author.

Wehmeyer, M. L., Lattin, D. L., Lapp-Rincker, G. & Agran, M. (2003). Access to the general curriculum of middle school students with mental retardation. *Remedial and Special Education*, *24*(5), 262–72.

Welch, M. (1997). The MATS form: A collaborative decision-making tool for instructional adaptations. *Interventions in School and Clinic*, *32*(3), 142–7.

*Westwood, P. (2001). Differentiation as a strategy for inclusive classroom practice: Some difficulties identified. *Australian Journal of Learning Disabilities*, *6*(1), 5–11.

*Westwood, P. & Graham, L. (2003). Inclusion of students with special needs: Benefits and obstacles perceived by teachers in New South Wales and South Australia. *Australian Journal of Learning Disabilities*, *3*(1), 3–15.

*Wolfe, P. S. & Hall, T. E. (2003). Making inclusion a reality for students with severe disabilities. *Teaching Exceptional Children*, *35*(4), 56–61.

Zammit, S. A., Meiers, M. & Frigo, T. (1999). *Assessment and Reporting of Student Achievement for Students With Specific Educational Needs Against Literacy and Numeracy Benchmarks*. Melbourne: ACER.

*Recommended reading for this chapter

Further recommended reading

Mercer, C. D. & Mercer, A. R. (2001). *Teaching Students With Learning Problems* (6th edn). Columbus: Charles E. Merrill.

Vaughn, S., Bos, C. S. & Schumm, S. (2003). *Teaching Exceptional, Diverse and At-Risk Students in the General Education Classroom*. Boston: Pearson Education.

Westwood, P. (2003). *Commonsense Methods for Children With Special Needs: Strategies for the Regular Classroom*. London: Routledge Falmer.

Chapter 5

Planning effective teaching strategies

Michael Arthur-Kelly

This chapter aims to:

- examine aspects of curriculum, teaching and the learning environment relevant to the education of all students, including individuals with special needs

- introduce a model of classroom planning that is practical and relevant to the needs of teachers working in regular schools and the students they teach

- explain several key concepts and strategies that support the design of effective teaching interventions, including curriculum-based assessment, mastery learning and task analysis.

Introduction

As suggested in the earlier chapters of this book, students with special educational needs are not vastly different from their peers who do not have a disability. In fact, it is much more helpful to consider similarities between the two groups rather than differences. The same point is true for the approaches effective teachers use when including students with differing levels of ability in the one class. The design and implementation of class programs that meet the needs of all students is a process grounded in the very principles of effective teaching and learning familiar to all teachers.

Figure 5.1 shows some of the factors that play a part in the achievement of effective teaching and learning for students, under the headings of *curriculum issues*, *instructional issues* and *aspects of the learning context*. The points that have been listed in this figure are not exhaustive and it may be useful to develop other topics for further consideration and follow-up reading.

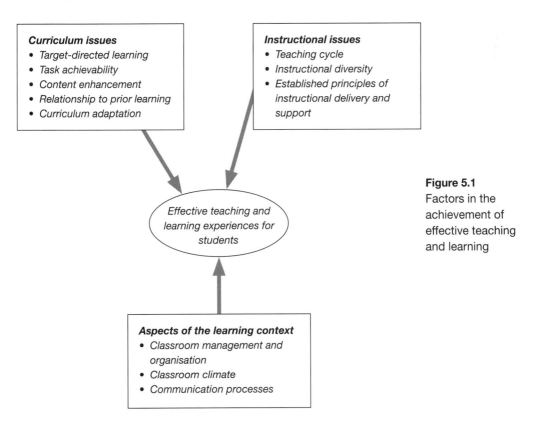

Figure 5.1
Factors in the achievement of effective teaching and learning

Curriculum issues

A number of the factors identified in this aspect of Figure 5.1, such as task achievability and curriculum adaptation, have already been discussed in Chapter 4. These factors are underpinned by the quality of the relationship between the learner and the curriculum on offer in the school. For example, the effective teacher will consider questions such as:

- To what degree does the student recognise the link between current and past learning experiences and lesson content?
- How achievable is the material or task presented to the student?
- Can the student identify the goal of the task and recognise its relevance and application (target directed learning)?

Example

Natalie is in Year 9 and is struggling to maintain an interest in the subjects she is completing. Boredom, hormones, a lack of achievement and little connection between what happens in class and everyday life have combined to produce a sense of disillusionment and frustration. Natalie is increasingly in trouble with teachers for talking constantly and wasting her time and that of her friends and received a very poor report in the mid-year assessments. Although her family have expressed concern for her school work, classroom behaviour and poor results, Natalie is finding it very difficult to break this emerging pattern of failure and possible resentment.

As suggested by this example, an underlying theme in any analysis of curriculum is the level of personal motivation to engage in learning new content and skills and the degree to which individual needs are met by such experiences. The nature and relevance of school curriculum has been the subject of much discussion in the last decade, and several authors have examined the relationship between the satisfaction of personal and academic needs in the school setting (Arthur, Gordon & Butterfield, 2003; Glasser, 1998). In this context, the teacher is concerned with the interaction between school curriculums and student variables; the nature of what is taught to students, and the impact for the individual. Equally important is the question of how this material is taught and the complex relationship between curriculum and instruction.

Instructional issues

In the past two decades, educational research in the area of effective instruction has blossomed (Good & Brophy, 2000; Westwood, 2003; Wolfe, 1998; Algozzine, Ysseldyke & Elliott, 1997). In exploring the many linkages between curriculum (what to teach) and instruction (how to teach), teachers continue to generate creative approaches to program design (Rosenshine, 1995), including those centred on cognitive and metacognitive techniques such as strategy instruction (Deshler et al., 2001), student-directed learning (Agran et al., 2003), cooperative learning (Goor & Schwenn, 1993; Jenkins et al., 2003), and the principles of behavioural analysis (Alberto & Troutman, 2003; Duker, Didden & Sigafoos, 2004). At the heart of such diversity, however, is an instructional design that remains constant.

In Figure 5.2 a basic instructional cycle, perhaps typical of a daily lesson, is set within the larger process of instructional design. The outer cycle describes the key phases all teachers go through when designing instruction, while the inner cycle represents one of a number of approaches to the delivery of instruction in a daily lesson. Both cycles reflect the same process on a macro and micro scale. The themes raised in this figure are not new and have been discussed by many writers in the area of instructional effectiveness (Algozzine, Ysseldyke & Elliott, 1997; Christenson, Ysseldyke & Thurlow, 1989; Rosenshine, 1995; Wolfe, 1998). However, current literature (and common sense!) suggest that instruction and curriculum (the how and the what of teaching) are best considered as part of an integrated approach to effective teaching and learning (Arthur, Gordon & Butterfield, 2003).

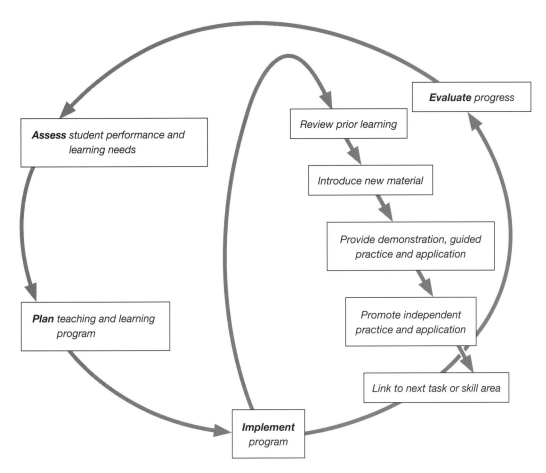

Figure 5.2 A typical instructional cycle embedded in the process of instructional design

Hudson, Lignugaris-Kraft and Miller (1993), for example, drew attention to the ways in which teachers can link content enhancements such as advance organisers and mnemonics with various instructional stages, including the presentation of new material, guided and independent practice, in order to optimise student learning outcomes. A review by Walberg (1990) discussed the research base for teaching and highlighted the relationship between particular curriculum areas and specific methods of instruction. For example, phonic approaches to early reading instruction are reported to be more effective than other methods such as repeated reading, a debate that is considered in detail in Chapters 7 and 8. Rosenshine (1995) drew attention to the research evidence for the critical linkage between an individual learner's cognitive processing patterns and the features of instruction designed to support the learning process.

Finally, a range of factors related to the quality of instructional delivery and support must also be considered in any discussion of effective teaching and learning. Examples include (but are not limited to) pacing, types and amounts of feedback and reinforcement available, the strategic use of prompting strategies, provision of adequate learning time, and specific techniques such as teacher cueing, question distribution behaviours and grouping arrangements employed (Bauer & Shea, 1999; Christenson, Ysseldyke & Thurlow, 1989;

Duker, Didden & Sigafoos, 2004; Rieth & Evertson, 1988; Rieth & Polsgrove, 1994; Vaughn et al., 2001). Schloss et al. (1995) provided a review of a number of established principles and strategies for teaching, including prompting, chaining, modelling and shaping. These approaches are central to good teaching and provide a foundation for student learning and motivation. As indicated in the next section, the quality of instruction achieved in a classroom is also a function of several contextual variables, such as climate and communication, which effectively set the scene for meaningful student participation in the learning process.

Aspects of the learning context

The learning context provided for students is a crucial factor in the achievement of productive and effective learning outcomes. Teachers face the daily challenge of establishing and supporting a rich learning environment that is both stimulating and efficient. Although many aspects must be considered, three interrelated themes can be identified. First, issues in classroom management and organisation including the development of classroom routines, seating arrangements and rules (Bauer & Shea, 1999; Blankenship, 1988; Porter, 2000; Smith & Misra, 1992). Second, the classroom climate, typically described as the 'feeling' or atmosphere experienced by both class participants and visitors. This feature is usually related to the types of expectations teachers have of students, the variety of curricular and instructional approaches used in the promotion of learning and the degree of encouragement provided to students. Finally, communication processes have an integral role in the provision of a supportive classroom context. Factors to be considered may include the teacher's use of effective listening skills and the recognition that communication is a multimodal and complex process (Arthur, Gordon & Butterfield, 2003; Smith & Laws, 1992).

The quality of the classroom context is central to the promotion of learning and behaviour, and readers are encouraged to pursue this area in greater depth. Several writers have discussed the contribution of careful programming and teaching to the prevention of misbehaviour and the development of positive patterns of behaviour, emphasising the proactive role of the classroom teacher and the importance of understanding the ecology of the individual (Blankenship, 1988; Arthur, Gordon & Butterfield, 2003; Smith & Misra, 1992). Chapter 6 examines a range of strategies for encouraging appropriate behaviour in students. The interested reader may also wish to review papers by Daniels (1998) and Maag (2001) when they are identifying issues and strategies relevant to the practical management of disruptive behaviour in inclusive classrooms.

The case study of Hayley's secondary schooling experiences (Box 5.1) illustrates many of the curricular, instructional and organisational aspects of effective teaching and learning discussed in the chapter to this point. The reader should note the interactive use of the principles and procedures described in Figure 5.1. For example, flexible organisational structures are used, including a variety of student grouping and team teaching arrangements, in direct relation to the type of lesson content, available resources and, primarily, Hayley's learning needs.

Box 5.1
Hayley's secondary schooling

After Hayley's primary school years (see Arthur, 2001, pp. 148–9) we moved to Coffs Harbour. Hayley began her secondary school education in the Catholic school system in the Diocese of Lismore. I mention the specific Diocese because personally, I consider their inclusive practices and how they use their government funding to be far superior to another Diocese I worked with before. This opinion I offer based purely on personal experiences, as a teacher, an advocate and a parent support person for the ACT Down syndrome Association.

We chose John Paul College (JPC), a school of over a thousand students ranging from Year 7 to Year 12, in Coffs Harbour. JPC was chosen for two reasons – their willingness to enrol Hayley regardless of her disability and the fact that I was offered a position in Special Education at the same school. Of course, the fact that I would be partly responsible for Hayley's educational program with an experienced and 'open-minded' teacher had nothing to do with it!

Hayley hit Year 7 at JPC in a flurry of new buildings, new uniforms, new peers, new teachers, new expectations and a new six-period-a-day timetable. She was readily accepted by all and was lucky to acquire a particularly 'cool' and understanding tutor teacher. This tutor teacher only came looking for me once in the whole of the first year and this was because he had lost her! At the time I was unconcerned, as Hayley sometimes 'zigged' when she should have 'zagged', getting around the school, and would always take herself to the front office to seek directions. Surprisingly, after a few weeks, Hayley had the timetable 'nailed' and she only found herself lost if there was a change to the timetable, either because she hadn't listened or because she misunderstood the details of the change. Hayley got on with her peers, who

treated her well. She was particularly close to her tutor group peers, who looked out for her, and who occasionally came to visit me if they thought something needed my intervention because she had a problem, or needed 'talking to' because she had been a 'Drama Queen', or was seen to be behaving in an inappropriate manner. Not once did I see or hear of Hayley being mistreated by one of the students, which didn't surprise me as JPC was very much a 'community minded' school and students were expected to treat each other with respect.

During Hayley's two years at JPC, her education program consisted of four core subjects – English, maths, science and social science. Other subjects included PE/health, religion and an elective chosen each semester – Japanese, technology/computing, cooking, drama and music. Hayley participated in Thursday sport afternoons and experienced many different types of sports. She was expected to be on the right bus at the right time, with her gear and money, ready to be transported to and from these sports, as were her peers. The only hiccup we had was when Hayley decided to do 'surf skills' as her sport for the term. Hayley being a 'water baby' from way back, always tended to spend more time being a mermaid under the waves, than a human above. Once she hit the water the teacher panicked a few times, when she thought she'd lost her! We quickly changed this sport for beach volleyball, for *everyone's* peace of mind! All Hayley's subject teachers were expected to modify her work accordingly and mostly did so successfully. Some teachers actively sought and received help with certain content and activities, from the Special Education teachers. Hayley was expected to complete and hand in all her assignments on time and lost marks if she didn't. There

>

Box 5.1 continued

were no Teachers' Assistants at JPC at this time, so her peers were sometimes used to support Hayley in some of her classes. We Special Education teachers always supported her in classes of high need, mainly for safety reasons, for example, technology/computing and cooking. Hayley always carried a folder of work she was able to complete without help to each of her classes. If the class teacher found that they could not work out an appropriate modification or work was considered to be beyond her needs, Hayley could use her folder and work without assistance. While Hayley was integrated for most of her classes, we Special Education teachers knew she also needed more explicit teaching for English and maths. For three out of the four lessons for each of these subjects, one of us would withdraw her either on a one-to-one basis or in a group situation, to work on programs designed specifically for her needs. We sometimes used additional periods to help her with her assignments. These practices were in place for other students that required similar support, although Hayley's academic skills were far lower than any other student with Special Needs at JPC at the time.

Some of the highlights of Hayley's stay in Coffs Harbour were:

- Offering an impromptu prayer at the first Year 7 Mass (we were all surprised!).
- Being a guest speaker at the Early Intervention Centre during Down syndrome Week in 2000.
- Winning 'Best Couple' with a good friend at the first school disco.
- Completing a Modelling and Etiquette Course and modelling in a Fashion Parade.
- Sunday activities with the Saint Vincent de Paul, run by some older students from JPC.
- School camps, school sleepovers, discos and numerous other school functions.

- Getting her photo in the JPC Year Book a couple of times.
- Last, but not least, her first 'serious' kiss!

While all of this sounds wonderful, there was one major concern we parents had. Although Hayley was happy and 'popular' at school, she had no 'real' close friends. We did some major soul-searching and came to the conclusion that really close friends usually have common interests and yes, 'similar abilities'. A mainstream setting has its definite advantages but if you don't have one or more close peers to share it with, it can be lonely. Hayley was often 'alone' at school and took to talking to imaginary friends and playing games she'd made up to fill in time.

We felt that if there had been a couple of students in the same year with similar intellectual ability, this 'problem' may not have occurred. This and her lack of future prospects in this particular NSW coastal town helped us make up our minds to move back to the ACT. During these two years, Hayley had grown into a confident, assertive teenager, but we felt she needed more socially, to help her acquire the skills needed to become a successful, independent and valued working member of society.

In 2002, we moved back into our original home and Hayley was enrolled in Caroline Chisholm High School, of which her original primary school was a feeder school. Two added bonuses were that we lived directly across the road from the school itself, which allowed Hayley to walk independently to and from school, and one of Hayley's closest friends, Jessica, who also had Down syndrome, was in the same year, at the same school. Hayley had a good year at Caroline Chisholm High School but not necessarily a 'great' year. We were pleased with her progress and the skills she attained but felt that she had lost a lot of her independence and some of her identity. Hayley was in Year 9

>

Box 5.1 continued

with two other girls with Down syndrome, who were managed and seen as one entity. They attended nearly all of their classes together and were withdrawn from mainstream classes more often than not, working with two very dedicated Special Teachers' Assistants (STAs). Hayley sat in the same place every day for lunch and recess, under the watchful eyes of office staff, and did not socialise much with her other peers because this would sometimes make her unpopular with the other two girls she spent her lessons with. This, coupled with the fact that three is not always a good number, motivated us to move schools the following year.

I had been working at Kambah High as a Special Education teacher and had slowly begun to realise that Hayley needed to experience what Kambah had to offer, especially since she was starting college the following year. We knew at Kambah, Hayley would be challenged, independent and have many friends, as roughly 10 per cent of the school population of approximately four hundred, had 'special needs' and that 'integration' was part of the school ethos of acceptance and dignity for all students. Hayley had always accepted change enthusiastically and was very excited to move schools. She hadn't always been happy and motivated at Caroline Chisholm High, although she knew she'd miss her friend Jessica. Hayley has had a very exciting and successful year at Kambah High. She is greeted enthusiastically by her many 'close' friends each morning as she arrives to school. She has been challenged academically everyday, by both her special education and mainstream teachers. She has been to many sleepovers, birthday parties, movies and outings during the weekends with her friends. Hayley has had several 'boyfriends' and has asked one of her 'close' friends to be her partner for the Year 10 Formal. Like any teenager, she spends a lot of time on the phone, gossiping and organising her social life. We haven't regretted the many changes during her secondary school years, as these have helped Hayley become the well-adjusted person she is. She is off to college next year and that will be another story!

Prepared by Jenny Bottrell,
Kambah High School, ACT

Designing effective teaching interventions (DETI)

An overlay linking student learning and teaching effectiveness

An implicit theme in Box 5.1, and in current educational policies (see Chapter 2) is the individualisation of support for all students, including those with special needs. Although this support may be delivered in a group setting, the teacher has the responsibility of ensuring that individual goals and learning experiences are relevant and achievable. In Figure 5.3 a practical model of class-level support for students with special needs (DETI) is presented that will form the basis of much of the remainder of this chapter. At each decision point, a focus question is presented as a way of highlighting the most important point for consideration by the teacher.

Like Figure 5.2, Figure 5.3 emphasises the dynamic and cyclical nature of effective teaching interventions. In such programs, assessment, planning, teaching and evaluating are integrally linked with each other in an ongoing process. In the discussion to follow, four related concepts and strategies that assist the classroom teacher in individualising student support are introduced, along with a number of practical steps to follow in the design of programs. These concepts are:

- the identification of curriculum priorities and long-term outcome goals
- curriculum-based assessment
- task analysis
- mastery learning.

The phases outlined in Figure 5.3 should be considered in the light of this information.

Identification of curriculum priorities and long-term outcome goals

There are a number of possible sources for the curriculum priorities and long-term outcome goals that form the basis of class-level programming designed to include a student with special educational needs. First, in the context of the key learning areas (KLAs), syllabus documents and program directions for the whole class, the teacher may identify specific areas of need for an individual student. For example, a primary school teacher may be generally aware of the difficulties experienced by a Year 5 student in the area of producing different text types, in the light of various work samples and the stages, learning outcomes and indicators described in syllabus documents (NSW Board of Studies, 1998a, 1998b, 1998c). The teacher may then decide to use a particular screening test to confirm this suspicion. Of course, parents may also alert the teacher to difficulties the student is having in consolidating and generalising the skills outside the classroom. Second, the established long-term goals, often viewed as an annual target, will usually reflect the needs of students in both their current and future situations. These goals are usually expressed in the form of an individualised educational program or plan (IEP) (Bateman & Linden, 1998; Bauer & Shea, 1999; Rodger, 1995; Schulz & Carpenter, 1995). An IEP is simply a written statement of the target curriculum areas, intended learning outcomes and necessary supports for an individual, and usually involves input from the student, regular and special education (support) teachers, parents and other personnel such as counsellors and speech pathologists. In some cases, such decisions may be the result of formal review or team meetings. In other situations, they may be agreed upon more informally. The importance of teamwork and collaboration in the design of effective teaching interventions will be reviewed later in this chapter, and in Chapter 10. At this point, it is critical to note that the process of reviewing student needs and developing an IEP is a fluid yet vital part of effective planning for teaching success, and informs curricular, instructional and contextual supports for students with special needs. There is evidence of improved student learning outcomes when a plan of support is developed and implemented by a unified and collaboratively-focused team (Hunt et al., 2003).

Regardless of the manner in which such priorities and goals are established, the classroom teacher is centrally responsible for their implementation and evaluation. Accordingly, it is vital that both regular and special education classroom teachers contribute to and support the planning processes and intended outcomes for students. The curriculum priorities and long-term outcome goals for a student with special needs may be very similar to those planned for the majority of students in the class (see the examples below), or they may involve modified or alternative curriculums (Chapter 4).

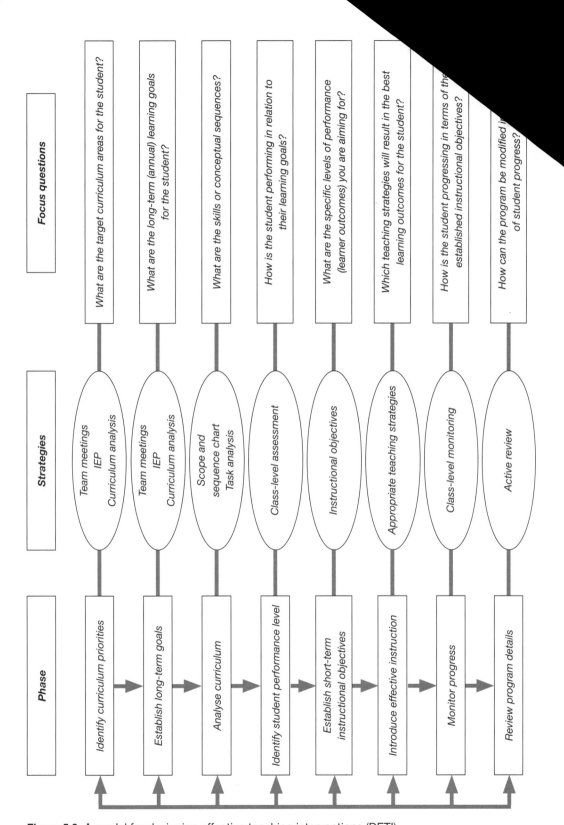

Figure 5.3 A model for designing effective teaching interventions (DETI)

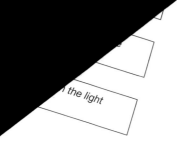

...me goals

...ge of algebraic equations

... the library to gather information about the use of mathematical

...reader fluently

...are a basic meal

...dependently within a 3-centimetre boundary

...ions with peers in the playground without prompting

...wing case study of Meredith (Box 5.2) highlights the importance
of ... ...rative approach to planning and delivering educational programs
that address ... ...eeds.

Box 5.2
Meredith's secondary school program

Now 14 years old and in Year 8, Meredith is a student with moderate intellectual disability whose parents chose to enrol her in the mainstream high school. Consequently, Meredith is eligible for and receives substantial support from the NSW DET funding support program. The money from this program is used for: the release of teachers from class for professional development, program development, preparation of learning materials, and participation in Individual Learning Support Team (ILST) meetings regarding Meredith's needs; and to employ a Teachers' Aide Special (TAS).

Meredith interacts well with her peers and is a high-functioning student, socially. The significant delay she experiences with her cognitive skills, however, makes it very unlikely that she will achieve the same outcomes as her mainstream peers. For this reason the ILST decided that Meredith should be provided with a special program of study incorporating a life skills curriculum. This, of course, meant the development of an Individual Education Plan (IEP) and an Individual Learning Program (ILP) for each of the classes that Meredith attends.

The development of the IEP was the relatively easy part as Meredith was already enrolled in her classes and had been issued with a timetable. The ILST was, therefore, able to use the existing life skills curriculum to highlight some priority outcomes for each of the KLAs. The IEP, then, was used as the basis of professional development sessions for each teacher where they were shown how to plan and develop ILPs for each unit of work in their discrete KLAs. This, and the implementation of the ILP, were the most difficult and time-consuming aspects of the differentiation process.

For example, Meredith's English teacher had planned to use the book *Storm Boy* as the foundation of a coastal theme. Meredith's IEP identified an increase in the number of sight words and a greater range of concepts she could use in interactions with peers as priority long-term outcome goals. A curriculum was devised that took the IEP priorities into account but which also had elements in common with the coastal theme to be studied by the rest of the class.

A summary of Meredith's English ILP for Storm Boy *and the coastal theme*

- *Long-term outcome goal:* Development of a sight word vocabulary that will enable Meredith to recognise and name features associated with the coast.

>

Box 5.2 continued

- *Sight word list:* Beach, sand, waves, wind, swimming, flags, life saver, sea gull, ocean, boat, surf, fish, shark, sun, sunburn, sand dune, hat, towel, sun cream, pelican, wind.

Instructional sequence

- Familiarisation with coastal features and concepts associated with the story.
- Watch the video of the story.
- Class reading of the story.
- Learning activities:
  - find pictures of beaches, boats, pelicans, etc. (see word list)
  - paste pictures into exercise book and label
  - talk to somebody in the class about your favourite part of the story
  - copy phrases/sentences from the story that include words from the list
  - draw and/or write about the least favourite part of the story.
- Assignment:

  On a large map of Australia, locate the place where the story is set, colour it yellow and paste a picture of a pelican near that part of the map. Locate at least one other beach you know, colour the spot yellow and paste a picture of your choice near that part of the map.

The classroom teachers have been assisted in the development and delivery of the ILPs by the coordinator of the school's LST, an executive trained in special education by the Support Teacher Learning Difficulties (STLD) and by the TAS who was employed to support the teachers. The coordinator assisted the teachers with an orientation to the life skills expectations and outcomes, and supported them in their professional learning about program differentiation. The STLD assists the teachers with the modification of materials and with withdrawal sessions where Meredith is helped to pre-learn facts and concepts that the class will be looking at in up-coming lessons. The TAS helps the teachers in class by enabling them to spend more time with Meredith where necessary, helping Meredith directly with some parts of the learning program as directed by the teachers, and assisting the teachers with the preparation of learning materials.

Meredith's ILST has a core membership of student, parent/s, year adviser, counsellor, and coordinator. It meets regularly, once each month to discuss her IEP and to identify issues pertinent to the ongoing development of her ILPs. Individual classroom teachers are invited to participate as issues relevant to their particular KLA arise.

A summary of Meredith's IEP priorities for each KLA and the differentiated ILP goals

	Maths	*PD/H/PE*	*Hospitality*
Class:	Measurement	Basketball	Catering
ILP:	Money	Catch–bounce–pass	Mixing ingredients

Prepared by Paul Hunt, Singleton High School

Having identified appropriate curriculum priorities and long-term outcome goals for the student, the teacher uses the principles of curriculum-based assessment to design and implement a teaching program that aims for student success.

Curriculum-based assessment

Essentially, curriculum-based assessment (CBA) is a framework for class level testing of student performance, and the use of this information in programming and teaching decisions. Unlike standardised testing, where individual student performance is compared against that of the wider population, the teacher who employs curriculum-based assessment effectively generates a profile of the learner in the context of the specific curriculum goals and experiences of that individual. Blankenship and Lilly (1981) have defined curriculum-based assessment as 'the process of obtaining direct and frequent measures of a student's performance on a series of sequentially arranged objectives derived from the curriculum used in the classroom' (p. 81).

Several features of this definition are important to note. First, CBA is a process, rather than an isolated testing event. Second, such measures are direct and frequent, and occur in the classroom. Third, student performance is considered in terms of a sequence of objectives. This implies that lesson content is analysed, and targeted student performance is clearly stated. Finally, the curriculum followed in the classroom forms the basis for assessment. Of course, these curriculums will often reflect the prescribed content set out in syllabus documents adopted for use in KLAs. Alternatively, as discussed earlier, long-term teaching and learning goals for a student with special needs may be derived from an individualised educational program. However, the distinguishing feature of CBA in this context is the emphasis on measuring student performance on material that is individually relevant and part of a class-level program (Blankenship, 1985). Although there has been some discussion in the literature about various terminologies and areas of emphasis (for example, curriculum-based measurement (CBM) as opposed to CBA, see Fuchs & Deno, 1991), the use of systematic data to inform the teaching and curriculum decisions made by the teacher is one of the hallmarks of the CBA approach (Jones, Southern & Brigham, 1998).

Curriculum-based assessment, then, helps the teacher to clearly identify students' instructional needs by pinpointing what the students can presently do as well as the skills and knowledge they need (Choate et al., 1995; Fuchs & Fuchs, 1998; Howell & Nolet, 2000; Jones, Southern & Brigham, 1998; Whinnery & Fuchs, 1992). In the following discussion, the five main steps involved in CBA are described, along with examples of the application of these procedures.

Key steps in applying curriculum-based assessment

Step 1: Identify the scope and sequence of the curriculum

The first step in using curriculum-based assessment in the classroom is to analyse the curriculum (What should the learner be able to know or do?) and sequence that information (What is the logical order of this content or set of skills?). This information is often presented as a scope and sequence (or continuum of learning) chart for organisational purposes, thus allowing the teacher to organise content into a series of cumulative teaching modules or stages (see examples in Carnine, Silbert & Kame'enui, 1990; Kame'enui & Simmons, 1990; NSW Board of Studies, 1998a, 2003; Silbert, Carnine & Stein, 1990).

In a sense, the scope and sequence chart describes, at a glance, what is to be learned. While, on the one hand, it may describe in fine detail the content and ordering of a curriculum area, it may also reflect the broad sweep of curriculum content and coverage in schools and classes. On a very large scale, the levels and outcome statements contained in various profile documents used to report on student progress in Australian states (National Curriculum and Assessment Committee, 1993) are an example of the latter application.

Example

Figure 5.4 provides a simple example of a scope and sequence chart for the language skill(s) of writing simple sentences.

Figure 5.4 emphasises three related points. First, content is broken up into a sequence of modules that are linked to each other and are not taught on a rigid timeline. That is, one module does not equal one 40-minute period. Second, learning is cumulative, with previously taught and reviewed material serving as a base for new skills and content. Finally, the visual display allows the teacher to analyse and summarise curriculum and identify skills or content that need to be further refined. This strategy is commonly referred to as task analysis.

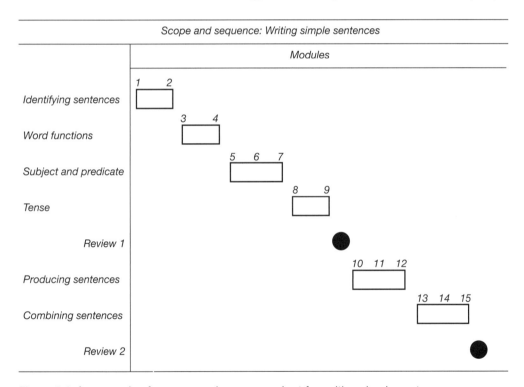

Figure 5.4 An example of a scope and sequence chart for writing simple sentences

(Source: Developed by Paul Sleishman, St Laurence Centre, Catholic Schools Office)

Task analysis

Task analysis, as the name implies, is the strategy of breaking down a task (or activity) into its component parts. Typically, a task will be made up of content (knowledge, concepts, facts) and strategies (what to do with the content) (Howell, Fox & Morehead, 1993). A task analysis can assist the regular teacher to answer the question: 'What is involved in Student A successfully completing that task, or demonstrating that skill?' In the following example, note the sequencing of steps and the role of prerequisites in the overall completion of a task.

Example

Task analysis for the use of a calculator to check four-digit addition problems

Prerequisites: Fine motor control in order to grasp and activate the calculator, and press appropriate keys.

1 Turn calculator on
2 Read through the written problem on the sheet, including solution
3 Key in the first number
4 Press addition symbol
5 Key in the next number
6 Press addition symbol
7 Key in the next number
8 Press addition symbol
9 Key in the next number
10 Press equal sign
11 Compare totals on the written sheet and on calculator display

This type of analysis allows the teacher to view, from the perspective of the learner, the complexity of a learning task. In the example above, prerequisites, sub-tasks, concepts and strategies built into the task include fine motor control (computer use), numerical and operational key recognition and selection, and comparison of results when presented in two formats. Of course, it may not be necessary to analyse such a task in this way for many students in the class. In addition, such an exercise can take up a considerable amount of time. However, for a small number of students, task analysis has a wide range of applications, from the broad ('What comprises successful grade-level writing?') to the specific point of focus ('What is the skills sequence for designing a basic computing program?'). It can be used for academic, social and activity skills (see discussion questions at the end of this chapter) and provides the classroom teacher with information that is useful in three phases of teaching (Kemp, 1992). First, as an assessment device, the task analysis helps the teacher to decide where, in a given activity or skill, the student is having difficulty. Second, the teacher can then pinpoint the area of need and write appropriate teaching objectives. Finally, a task analysis clearly identifies the teaching sequence and allows the teacher to deliver and adjust instruction that builds on previous learning (Kemp, 1992).

In practical terms, there are several ways to conduct a task analysis. The teacher may slowly perform a target skill or task, writing down each step in its logical and natural order. In this way, the teacher gains a clear understanding of what is involved, including the sequential and cumulative aspects of the task. Another approach is to watch somebody else performing the skill, while recording the steps and prerequisite sub-skills demonstrated for successful completion of the task or activity. Finally, a teacher may choose to work backwards through a task, from completion to the very first step. In this way, information is gained regarding the complexity of the task, the cumulative use of skills and the chaining of one skill with the next, in a logical order. This sequencing information is especially useful when the teacher is deciding how to work on a difficult task with a student.

For example, a teacher may be working with a student on the activity of accurately cutting along a line. It may be appropriate to commence by focusing student effort on the very last step of the task (the student independently cuts for the last 2 centimetres, having been assisted with the earlier tasks of grasping the paper, coordinating the scissors and so on). Gradually, and dependent on student performance, the student is encouraged to attempt more of the steps in the task, in reverse order, as their success and confidence develops. Referred to as 'backward chaining', this strategy is a simple and effective use of the principles of task analysis. There are many other variations of this approach, including forward chaining (working forward through a task, providing assistance at the first point of need) and completion of the whole task, with teacher support on any and all areas of difficulty. The interested reader is referred to an excellent paper by Carter and Kemp (1996) that reviews the different types of task analysis and outlines the implications of a task analytic approach to assessment, planning and teaching approaches relevant to the education of students with and without disabilities.

This section has discussed the integral role of curriculum analysis as the first step in curriculum-based assessment and introduced the strategies of IEPs, scope and sequence charts and task analysis. The next step in the process is to gather specific information on student performance within the curriculum.

Step 2: Assess the current performance level of the student on the curriculum

In Figure 5.5, three levels of assessment are described in the context of learning processes and outcomes. Level 1 reflects aspects of student performance that are considered daily. Level 2 introduces key considerations for the teacher in the medium term, while Level 3 is concerned with the larger time frame and the overall relevance of curriculum and learning for the individual.

In reality, teacher assessments of student performance and needs combine elements of Levels 1, 2, and 3. However, in terms of daily programming, Level 1 is the natural starting point. The teacher is concerned with gaining a picture of student ability in terms of the curriculum content being covered in the class, sometimes referred to as a pre-test or baseline. As noted earlier in this chapter, and in Chapter 4, these curriculums may be drawn from a vast array of subject areas, may involve modified or enhanced content and follow a set of objectives outlined in a personalised educational plan (IEP).

What to assess

Notwithstanding the diversity of curriculums on offer in classrooms, the teacher is particularly interested in two related dimensions of student behaviour: the process (*how* the student performed the task); and the outcome (*how well* the student performed the task) (Figure 5.5). In the first area, the learning process, task analysis should be considered as a useful means of describing student performance. Two alternatives should be considered: first, devising a task analysis prior to the lesson and noting how a student performs in relation to this sequence; second, observing the process followed by the student, recording the sequence of steps and the specific areas of difficulty. The observation of the process allows the teacher to analyse errors and pinpoint areas for remediation (Gable & Hendrickson, 1990).

In the second area, learning outcomes, the teacher collects information about individual performance in terms of designated behaviours (for example, putting hand up to speak) or permanent products (for example, number of correct simple sentences written in one minute). One useful way to consider the quality of student learning outcomes is to evaluate the stage of learning the student appears to be functioning within for that task or area. These stages are often described as the phases of acquisition, fluency, maintenance and generalisation (Figure 5.5). In the acquisition phase, the student is learning how to do the task and so is, of necessity, building up speed, confidence and understanding. Fluency refers to the use of a skill or content quickly and efficiently. In the maintenance phase, the learner retains the skill over time, while in the generalisation stage, the skill or content is adapted to suit new needs as they arise (Alberto & Troutman, 2003; Snell & Brown, 2000). For example, a common way for a teacher to assess student fluency of a skill is to count how many maths facts or sight words a student is able to recall in one minute (see Chapter 8). In contrast, another teacher may be interested in the number of times a student independently perseveres in a conversation with peers in the playground. The nature of the task, then, will determine how such assessment is carried out.

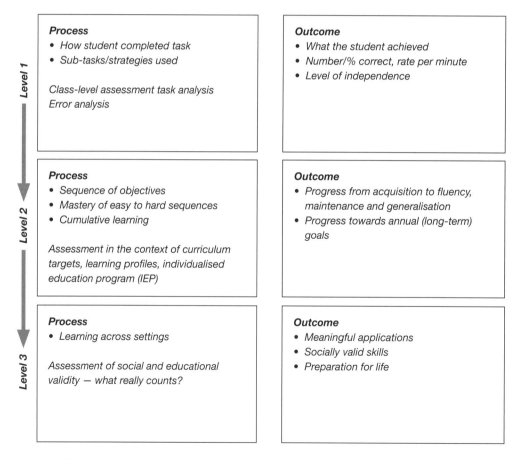

Figure 5.5 Considering processes and outcomes in assessment – a three-tiered model

How to assess

Teachers assess student performance in many ways, depending on the skills or content being considered and a range of other factors, such as the amount of time and the level of teaching support available. Some of the most common methods are:

- pencil and paper tests
- informal work samples that serve as indicators of skill development
- portfolios – a collection of student work over a period of time
- checklists
- running records, in which the teacher writes down as much as possible about student performance as it occurs, typically as a continuous description
- systematic observational records
- rating scales.

On many occasions, teachers use several sources of information in order to fully assess student behaviour, as illustrated in the example below. This assessment information is then used to establish specific teaching objectives.

Example

Mr Pascoe, Year 10 English teacher, was concerned about Julie's skills in the area of reading comprehension. In group work, Julie appeared to be heavily reliant on other students for answers to questions requiring direct recall, and was totally nonplussed when required to evaluate even short passages of text. When Mr Pascoe was able to hear Julie read a sample piece of text on her own, it soon became obvious that the student was unable to extract meaning from the print because of her slow rate of reading. Further testing using a common sight word list and primary school readers confirmed that Julie was three years behind her peers in overall reading rate and sight vocabulary. This explained her lack of confidence and dependence on others in reading comprehension tasks.

Having gathered appropriate classroom level assessment information, the teacher turns to the task of establishing specific performance objectives in the area. This becomes Step 3 in the curriculum-based assessment process.

Step 3: Establish short-term instructional objectives for the student(s)

Having analysed the curriculum and assessed student performance within it, the next step for the teacher using curriculum-based assessment is to program for student progress. By developing a series of objectives that reflect the specific learning needs of the individual, ensuring that small progress steps are built in and regularly checking the quality of student performance, the teacher is using the principles of mastery learning (Bloom, 1980; 1984).

Mastery learning

The teacher using mastery learning seeks to avoid student failure on the curriculum by allowing adequate time for the individual to master the target content, and ensuring that formative, ongoing assessment is used to guide teaching decisions and support given to the student, including corrective instruction as appropriate (Bloom, 1980; 1984). At the heart of a mastery learning approach is the principle that only small amounts of new information should be taught and that the student should not be introduced to more complex skills or content until the criterion for mastery of earlier work has been reached. In the example below, the value of careful curriculum analysis and the introduction of mastery learning principles is highlighted with reference to the language skills of a Year 8 student, Justin. Following this example, the development of short-term instructional objectives for use in the regular classroom is discussed.

Example

Justin has been struggling in Year 8 mathematics for some time and class level assessment has indicated the need for specific work in the area of algebraic addition and subtraction tasks and written story problems involving these calculations. Justin has received teaching support in the form of individualised instruction, peer modelling and worksheets, enabling him to successfully identify the various types of number tasks when presented in written or oral form. Before moving onto the strategy of story problem writing (including deriving numerical concepts from text and speech), Justin must independently achieve 80 per cent correct on three consecutive sets of tasks that involve the skill of writing or stating simple number sentences comprising an algebraic addition or subtraction. Justin's confidence has increased markedly as a result of the opportunity to master these basic numeracy skills.

Designing short-term instructional objectives

In order to be able to carefully monitor student progress and change teaching and learning programs as necessary, a very clear statement of intended student performance can be designed (see Alberto & Troutman, 2003 for further information on this aspect of programming). As noted in the overview of mastery learning, progress is then measured against this objective, allowing the teacher to make informed decisions about whether, for example, to introduce the next skill in the sequence (or section of content), or alternatively, to revise student understanding and application in the present area.

Short-term instructional objectives (sometimes referred to as teaching, performance or behavioural objectives) should reflect small progress steps for the student based on the performance information gathered in the class level assessment phase. As demonstrated in the two examples that follow, these very specific statements of intended student performance have four features, expressed in a variety of ways (see Alberto & Troutman, 2003). These are:

Features	Example
Student name	Paul will, …
The conditions under which the behaviour will occur	when provided with the cue 'Paul, write your name', …
Statement of intended behaviour	legibly write his name within 2 cm boundary lines …
Criteria for successful performance	on three consecutive occasions over two days.

This example describes an academic skill that is important for Paul, identified from direct assessment of his classroom behaviour and a curriculum sequence. Many teachers write similar objectives for social behaviour, as demonstrated in the next example (Alberto & Troutman, 2003; Arthur, Gordon & Butterfield, 2003; Jones, 1996). Note that this example relates to the performance of the whole class, rather than an individual student:

Example

Class 4H, on hearing the teacher's request for silence, will be sitting quietly without noise within 10 seconds on five consecutive occasions.

The short-term instructional objective is a precise statement of expected student performance, based on what the student(s) can do and needs to be able to do. It does not, however, specify how to teach students. The next section introduces the important topic of instructional strategies (Step 4), as a means of assisting students to achieve targeted levels of performance.

Step 4: Introduce effective instruction

In this section, an overview of several instructional strategies is presented. Further material on teaching strategies is presented in Chapter 8 and the reader is directed to the sources listed at the end of this chapter for more detailed information. Books by Westwood (2003), Kame'enui et al. (2002), Henley, Ramsey and Algozzine (2002) and Mastropieri and Scruggs (2004) may be especially useful in this context. It is important to emphasise that the established principles of instructional delivery and support (Figure 5.1), discussed earlier in this chapter, provide a necessary framework for the successful introduction of more specific teaching strategies. That is, the effective teacher continually evaluates the impact of factors such as reinforcement and prompts on the learning processes and outcomes achieved by students, along with the effectiveness of particular approaches, such as those described in the following section.

The techniques described below represent examples from a wide range of strategies teachers may select and use in classrooms. In fact, the strength of a model such as DETI, based on the principles of curriculum-based assessment, is the emphasis on active review of programs and the opportunity for changes in the light of student progress, including the selection of new teaching methods when others are not effective. Teacher preferences, communication styles and the levels of additional support available are examples of the factors that may influence a decision to use a particular approach. In addition, as highlighted in many of the suggested readings, particular curriculum areas lend themselves to certain instructional methodologies. The aim of a programming overlay such as DETI is to provide the teacher with a means of effectively designing and delivering teaching and learning programs that maximise student outcomes by enhancing the learning process. The selection of appropriate teaching strategies is an important step in this process. As we note in the following discussion, it may well be necessary in some situations to systematically combine strategies in order to optimise student engagement and learning outcomes (Copeland et al., 2002).

Cooperative learning

Cooperative learning strategies (sometimes referred to as team learning methods) have been the subject of much research and discussion over the past few decades (Jenkins et al., 2003; Nelson, Johnson & Marchand-Martella, 1996; Putnam, 1998; Slavin, 1996). Using a problem-solving focus, students with a range of ability levels work together to achieve learning outcomes through a process of planned interdependence. Rewards can be based on individual or group changes in performance, and many variations on the basic theme, such as Jigsaw, Student Teams Achievement Divisions, and Think-Pair-Share have been developed. (For a practical discussion of the key aspects of several models and a range of instructional considerations when using cooperative approaches, see Goor & Schwenn, 1993. For a recent analysis of teacher perceptions about the use of cooperative learning techniques, see Jenkins et al., 2003.)

Cooperative learning has a great deal of potential for promoting the inclusion of students with special needs, with an emphasis on the social process, positive learning outcomes and relevance to a wide variety of student needs highlighted in current literature (Gillies & Ashman, 2000; Piercy, Wilton & Townsend, 2002; Putnam, 1998). However, cooperative learning is considerably more than simply placing students into groups and providing a task for them to complete. For example, Goor and Schwenn (1993) emphasised the importance of preparing students for cooperative learning, including the clear definition of roles, and monitoring progress closely as the group works together. In one study, Jenkins et al. (1994) discussed the role of group dynamics (for example, establishing, as far as possible, which students will be compatible, before the activity) in the successful introduction of cooperative learning strategies in the classroom. While this method may have a great deal to offer, then, in terms of promoting student acceptance of individual differences and improving student learning outcomes, the time involved in carefully structuring and over-viewing such a program may be regarded by some teachers as a definite limitation to its practical use in schools and classes.

Peer tutoring as one example of peer-mediated approaches

The involvement of peers in some form of instructional arrangement has burgeoned in the past decade and is often referred to as the peer-mediated range of strategies (Utley, Mortweet & Greenwood, 1997). One example, perhaps most commonly known and used by teachers,

is peer tutoring. As the name suggests, peer tutoring is a general descriptor for teaching strategies that involve one student helping another with specified content or tasks. Typically, these may be referred to as same-age or cross-age tutoring arrangements. In the first type, the tutor is usually in the same age-bracket (or class) as the tutee, while in cross-age tutoring, the tutor is older than the tutee. The tutor may have several roles, including modelling, explaining skills or content, and encouraging the tutee, and so training and monitoring of the tutor is an important issue for the supervising teacher. (For an excellent discussion of several critical considerations in the effective use of peer tutoring and peer-centred strategies, see Jenkins & Jenkins, 1985; 1987; Topping & Ehly, 1998; for an overview of peer-mediated approaches, including peer tutoring, see Utley, Mortweet & Greenwood, 1997.) Tutoring may produce important affective and skills-based improvements for both the tutor and tutee (Utley, Mortweet & Greenwood, 1997), and promote the achievement of individualised support in inclusive settings (Jenkins et al., 1994). As noted earlier, teachers may decide to combine strategies in order to best meet the needs of their students. In a recent study, Spencer, Scruggs and Mastropieri (2003) utilised peer tutoring with strategy instruction in the skill of summarising paragraphs. They found that not only did the targeted students with emotional or behavioural problems enjoy this format when compared with more traditional lesson types, but they demonstrated important improvements in their on-task behaviour and their achievement in some content testing.

Like all teaching strategies, peer tutoring has several potential strengths and weaknesses. One of the major contributions of the approach is the use of peers as an additional instructional resource, providing an opportunity for individualised student practice and skill development. On the other hand, peer tutoring may only lend itself to certain curriculum areas or topics and be overly demanding in terms of preliminary student training as well as ongoing teacher monitoring. Teachers who plan to use peer tutoring do well to explore the tutor training aspects associated with the strategy, in order to avoid the problem of tutees practising errors or diverting off-task due to poor tutor support.

Cognitive and metacognitive approaches

Teachers play a central role in facilitating and supporting the cognitive ('thinking') and metacognitive ('thinking about thinking') processes taking place in their students. To this end, approaches such as process-based instruction (Ashman & Conway, 1993), reciprocal teaching (Palincsar & Herrenkohl, 2002; Palincsar & Klenk, 1992) and strategy training (Deshler, Ellis & Lenz, 1996; Deshler et al., 2001) have received increasing attention in the research and practice literature. Deshler et al. (2001), for example, discussed a series of intervention levels for teachers working with secondary students who are experiencing problems in mastering content-area reading. They explored various means of maximising instructional resources at the system, school and class levels, as well as the importance of tapping into and enhancing the information processing experiences of students (Deshler, Ellis & Lenz, 1996). In other words, in addition to maximising daily learning outcomes, teachers using approaches such as strategy training (and other similarly focused cognitive and metacognitive techniques) try to empower students with a learning framework that can be used independently and in a generalised manner. The goal of this form of intervention is to assist students to make connections among the skills, knowledge and concepts they learn, and to be able to independently tackle new and challenging tasks in school and beyond. Examples of these strategies include overt and covert self-instruction, monitoring, evaluation and reinforcement (Agran et al., 2003). In reciprocal teaching, similarly, students are encouraged to use a series of steps to tackle the meaning in texts they are presented with, by questioning, summarising, clarifying and predicting (Palincsar & Herrenkohl, 2002; Palincsar & Klenk, 1992).

Direct instruction

Direct instruction (DI) involves highly structured and explicit teaching of content and strategies to students, using similarities and differences between examples as a central instructional tool (Darch, 1990; Engelmann & Carnine, 1982; Kinder & Carnine, 1991). The teacher using DI employs specified prompt and reinforcement techniques, curriculum analysis and the principles of mastery learning to promote student learning. Teachers who use the materials based on this approach (for example, *Reading Mastery 1*, by Engelmann & Bruner, 1988) are expected to deliver scripted cues and instructions to their students and make regular program decisions in the light of individual performance levels and established criteria.

DI places a great deal of emphasis on the clear transmission of information to the learner, and student success on the learning tasks (Gersten, 1992). These points, coupled with a strong research base indicating the effectiveness of the approach (Darch, 1990), have contributed to the popularity of DI materials and techniques in many areas. On the other hand, the focus on teacher direction and the careful structuring of content and lesson delivery has also attracted criticism. Heshusius (1991), for example, critically analysed the fundamental assumptions of curriculum-based assessment and DI, suggesting that, among other concerns, the over-emphasis on measurement in these models may detract from the validity of learning outcomes for the individual. Clearly, DI continues to evoke controversy, both in terms of how it is used and the principles upon which it is based. Perhaps, as Gersten (1998) notes, explicit instruction, of which DI is an example, is best viewed as part of an array of instructional approaches that teachers can call upon in order to maximise student engagement, cognition and retention of critical skills and knowledge.

Computer-assisted instruction and technological supports

The role of computers in educational programs is ever-changing, as technology opens new doors, and access to hardware, software and peripherals improves (for a detailed discussion of this area, see Burtch, 1999; Lankshear, Snyder, & Green, 2000; Mull & Sitlington, 2003). In addition to providing augmentative and alternative means of communication for students with severe physical or intellectual disabilities (Hustad, Morehouse & Gutmann, 2002), computers and computer programs can be used to enhance and support teaching and learning programs in a multiplicity of ways. The potential roles and contributions of computers and other technologies in instructional programs may include improving student attention to and concentration on tasks, individualised practice and drill opportunities, improved levels of motivation and enhanced thinking and problem-solving skills (NSW Department of Education, 1988). Of course, the quality of peripherals such as scanners, digital cameras and videos and relevant instructional software (Higgins, Boone & Williams, 2000) will determine the degree to which technology supports make a positive and sustained impact upon student learning and participation. However, it is fairly self-evident that computers cannot replace

teacher-directed instruction, given the constant need for teacher explanation of concepts, linkages to previous and new materials and the complex levels of information processing exhibited by students in classrooms everyday. Researchers continue, however, to explore ways in which computers can support and maximise individual learning processes and outcomes in various educational contexts (see a useful case study on the use of computers with students who have special needs in New Zealand, in Boyd, 1999).

As indicated in Figure 5.3, after appropriate teaching strategies are selected, the next step in the design and implementation of effective teaching interventions involves the systematic and frequent review of program effectiveness and student outcomes.

Step 5: Actively monitor student progress and adjust program features in the light of progress information

The effective classroom teacher is constantly reviewing student progress and fine-tuning teaching programs in order to maximise student participation and learning outcomes. The use of ongoing monitoring procedures, such as observational records, work samples and the development of portfolios (discussed earlier), allows the teacher to decide whether specific instructional objectives have been attained. For example, the support documents for literacy and communication in the English K–6 syllabus (NSW Board of Studies, 1997a; 1997b) and other more recent syllabus documents identify a wide array of indicators of student learning in relation to specific student outcomes. (For a useful paper relating to monitoring procedures in early childhood education, the reader is referred to Schwartz & Olswang, 1996.) Alberto and Troutman (2003) and many other special education books provide excellent examples of monitoring forms, and many teachers find that it is easiest to adapt an existing format or design one to meet their particular needs.

Example

Ms Chapin was concerned to monitor the conversational turn-taking behaviours of Sam, a boy with severe intellectual disability in her Year 1 class, when working in paired activities. With 29 students in her class, the most practical method was the incidental use of anecdotal records during observations as the whole class set about tasks from various subject areas. It soon became apparent that the target student tended to respond to his partner, but rarely initiated interactions. Ms Chapin decided to provide Sam with specific modelling to emphasise the importance of leading into a conversation, as well as helping his peer to delay initiating on some occasions to allow Sam enough time to start the process of interaction.

On the basis of information gained from observations, the teacher may decide to introduce a new or revised student objective, conduct a further task analysis of the skills or content to be learned, change the teaching strategies employed, or cancel the program. Table 5.1 provides some examples of common program changes made in the light of progress information.

Table 5.1 Examples of typical program changes in the light of progress information

Progress information	*Program change*
Student struggling to achieve short-term instructional objective	Revise objective Review instructional methods Conduct further task analysis of the target skill
Short-term instructional objective achieved	Identify new objective in light of skills sequence and task analysis
Long-term goal achieved	Establish new long-term goals Monitor mastered skills
Student appears to be bored with task	Review objective for mastery Evaluate instructional methods and change if necessary

Synthesis

The DETI model introduced in Figure 5.3 raises many issues related to the design of effective teaching interventions, and in the limited space available it has been possible to introduce only key ideas and strategies. The reader is strongly encouraged to follow up the suggested readings at the end of the chapter, all of which extend the basic concepts introduced above. The following case study (Box 5.3) exemplifies many of the key elements raised in this chapter and emphasises the importance of team work in the design, implementation and ongoing evaluation of individualised educational programs for students with special needs. This case study also demonstrates that inclusion is not an 'all-or-nothing' matter. Some special school and special class settings can still have a focus on inclusion to ensure that their students are, as far as possible, part of regular society. A major theme to emerge in this case study (Box 5.3) is the importance of effectively involving other personnel when planning and delivering class-level support – an issue that is now briefly considered.

Involving other personnel in teaching and learning programs

A look around any school will quickly illustrate the number and range of people who are involved in some aspect of the school community. The challenge for the teacher who is setting out to address the varied needs of the students in a regular classroom is to effectively match the people available, including parents and other students, to the teaching and learning plans and programs on offer (Hunt et al., 2003). One major issue is the need for cooperation and collaboration, discussed in detail in Chapters 10 and 11 of this book. Another aspect relates to the time that is needed to adequately train support people in the teaching strategies being used, such as peer tutoring (discussed earlier). The complex issues relevant to the wider involvement of people in your classroom, including aides, parents and volunteers, are discussed in several sections of this book, including Chapters 8, 10 and 11.

Box 5.3

Inclusive practices in New Zealand schools

Students with special needs in New Zealand are provided with funding through the Ongoing and Reviewable Resourcing Scheme (ORRS funding). The level of funding depends on the student's level of need and applies irrespective of where the student attends school. Parents have the choice as to where they want their children to attend school; however, the small population and expanse of rural areas often limit choices in many areas. Schools for Specific Purposes tend to be limited to cities such as Auckland, Hamilton or Rotorua in the North Island, and some larger towns often have satellite classrooms, or classes specifically for students with special needs, in one school within the towns. Many students are integrated into their mainstream classes at their local schools and assistance for their teachers consists of employment of teacher aides to work within the classroom and support from a district specialist services team.

One special school that demonstrates an excellent blend of inclusion and special programs for their students is Arohanui Special School in West Auckland. The school caters for approximately 150 students with a wide range of special needs, from mild developmental delay to multiple and complex disabilities and also

students with autism and Asperger syndrome. The school is organised with a base school where the students with special needs are enrolled and the specialist teachers and therapists are employed. This enables speech and language therapists, occupational therapists, psychologists and cultural liaison staff to be on site and available for consultation with teachers. It also enables a definite team approach to working with the students to develop, as all staff and families are involved in the decision making and goal setting processes and there are many opportunities for classroom interactions.

There is also a team of senior teachers available for consultation with staff on programming or behaviour management issues. The base school has a small number of classrooms on site, mostly for the oldest students, who are often participating in transition to work or community programs. The level of inclusion in community life has seen a number of students become involved with many facets of setting up and operating a worm farm business. The remaining classes are situated at local primary and secondary schools, with teachers and teacher aides employed by the special school. This situation provides an excellent opportunity for students to participate in a variety of the

>

Box 5.3 continued

mainstream school programs, both on an individual and group level, while still maintaining the benefits of small group specialist programs.

The range of inclusive practices is able to change as necessary to accommodate student needs. Teachers are able to continually evaluate the benefits of different situations and relate to students' IEP goals. There are many opportunities for mainstream students and students with special needs to participate in lessons together. Some specific examples include: classes attending whole school activities such as assemblies, fitness/sport, and library lessons; small groups of mainstream students working as buddy readers, individual students integrating into classes for specific interest lessons, such as music and art; as well as students gradually integrating into mainstream classes in preparation for mainstream enrolment, when their skills, behaviour and confidence are adequate to cope and learn in the large classroom setting. Organised lunchtime playground activities also benefit students in meeting on a social level as well as helping to eliminate behaviour problems for some students in the unstructured environment of the playground.

The inclusion of special education classes at the local schools also provides an excellent opportunity for teachers of all students to share information and ideas about programs, teaching and learning activities, behaviour support strategies and an understanding of individual needs. It is also an ideal situation for students to learn from one another and develop empathy and an understanding of other people's needs. This is enhanced by periodically teaching disability awareness programs. This enables mainstream students to learn specifically about different disabilities by being given information appropriate to their level of understanding and providing the opportunity for them to ask questions.

The special class within the regular school provides the ideal learning environment for many reasons. As well as the inclusion in regular programs as outlined above, a number of features of the teaching programs in the special classes greatly enhance student learning. The small group situation and high student to staff ratio are an excellent combination for providing one-to-one assistance and also for teaching skills, such as social skills, or enabling therapists to work effectively within the classroom. Class programs are based on the same KLAs as mainstream programs with each student having specific goals in their IEP, which are reviewed twice yearly. This ensures that programs are individualised to cater for each student's level of need, as well as providing a balanced and comprehensive class program that builds on the student's skills or interest areas. It also assists students who are involved in integration to mainstream classes to adapt to the regular teaching program. For example, a shared reading lesson may be providing the opportunity to extend the literacy skills of one student in the group, develop another student's attending skills and assist another student to follow directions, as well as encouraging all students' enjoyment of reading.

Teachers tend to utilise strategies that follow a whole class introduction using verbal and visual explanations and modelling of expected behaviours and task outcomes. Hands-on activities are then completed in small, relatively homogeneous groups of three to four students. This enables each group to have an adult nearby to assist students if necessary. Activities generally have quite specific outcomes to enable students to follow through to completion. Students are frequently able to choose a favourite activity from a choice board when finished. This encourages students to make independent choices and to adopt a positive approach to new or less preferred tasks. All classes utilise visual communication systems for timetables, labelling, student interactions and activity-based learning.

>

Box 5.3 continued

This is extremely effective for providing structure to the class program, visual cues for students who are often more visual than aural learners and a consistent means of communicating for people with non-verbal skills.

Teachers also use visual systems to consistently inform students of the timetable of events throughout the day. Each session begins with the teacher reading across a visual display of symbols for activities or events to the group, for example, reading, art, occupational therapy, music, and lunch. Then as each activity is completed, the students regroup, the symbol is removed from the timetable, shown to the students and they are told that the task is finished. Then the next symbol is shown before the next lesson begins. Simple sign language is also incorporated into classroom practices, especially during these structured explanations, again to enhance the learning and communication opportunities for these students.

The large number of teacher aides working in the classrooms means that teachers need to be extremely well organised and as much a team organiser within their classroom as an educator of students. Fortnightly team meetings are necessary as well as specific daily directions being given by teachers to ensure the classroom runs smoothly. It is important that teacher aides work with a number of students within the class and that the teacher always maintains a leadership role in terms of student learning outcomes and discipline. Throughout the year, teacher aides also undertake inservices, highlighting such things as the importance of assisting students, but not completing work for them, hence maintaining and encouraging as much independence as possible. It is also important for the teacher aides to develop an understanding that for many of the students, the process involved in the learning is more significant than the final product. This team approach to the classroom has many benefits for students' learning, including the daily opportunity to learn to relate to many people.

The size of the special school and the number of host schools involved in inclusive practices provides a challenge for all staff to maintain communication. This is managed through a number of systems. Dividing the school into three schools: complex school – classes mainly for students with multiple disabilities; general school – classes mainly for students with mild or moderate disabilities; and the autistic school – classes for students with autism spectrum disorder. Senior staff in each of these areas regularly visit classrooms and maintain contact with host schools.

There is also a good system of newsletters, staff meetings and a resource room onsite, which ensure staff visit the base school on a regular basis. With the large number of students with special needs enrolled at Arohanui Special School and the wide range of programs available to the students, it is evident that options for inclusive practices are almost as many and various as the number of students involved. By providing a flexible approach to student learning opportunities and regularly evaluating learning outcomes, the students and teachers at this school are able to achieve a 'best of both worlds' situation where special and mainstream schools can operate for the greatest benefits for everyone.

Prepared by Michelle Pointon, Arohanui Special School, West Auckland

Summary

This chapter has provided an introduction to several important programming and teaching strategies that allow the involvement and inclusion of all students into the learning environments of the local neighbourhood school. The practical questions of *what to teach* and *how to teach* were discussed, along with some aspects of classroom management relevant to effective program implementation.

Some of the key principles and approaches relevant to the design of individualised teaching interventions, including curriculum-based assessment, mastery learning and task analysis, were discussed in the context of a model designed to foster student success by exploring aspects of assessment, programming, instruction and evaluation. A number of case studies highlighted the ways in which all students can be active participants in classrooms based on effective teaching and learning principles and strategies.

The following chapters continue to explore the practical aspects of class-level support for and inclusion of students with special needs. In Chapter 6, a range of approaches in the development of pro-social participation by students is explored, with emphasis on the purpose and contexts of behaviour. Chapter 7 provides an overview of the problems commonly experienced by students in the areas of literacy and numeracy. In Chapter 8, specific instructional strategies that target these basic skills are introduced and discussed. Although these approaches are particularly relevant to programs of support for students with learning difficulties, they may be used effectively in the design and implementation of teaching and learning programs for all students. Chapter 9 focuses on the invigoration of communication processes in the inclusive classroom.

Discussion questions

1 Discuss the instructional cycle presented in Figure 5.2. What are the potential constraints and advantages of continuously monitoring program and student outcomes?

2 Read the case study presented in Box 5.1. In light of Hayley's experiences, what do you consider to be the most important aspects of a full and inclusive educational experience?

3 How useful is the strategy of task analysis for the regular classroom teacher? What are the possible applications and problems associated with this approach?

4 How does the concept of mastery learning differ from other approaches to classroom assessment, programming and instruction, such as outcome-based education?

5 How can the classroom teacher involve other personnel in programs designed to optimise learning outcomes for all students? What are some difficulties and some benefits that may be encountered by a class teacher when attempting to collaborate with parents and other partners in the educational field?

6 On the basis of your reading and experience, are there particular teaching strategies that may best assist in the participation and inclusion of students with special needs in the regular classroom? If so, what are they and how can they be implemented most effectively?

Individual activities

1 Select a unit of work in your area of specialisation and design a scope and sequence chart for it, perhaps using Figure 5.4 as a guide. How can this exercise assist the classroom teacher in the task of planning and delivering teaching programs?

2 Identify an everyday activity, such as catching a bus, brushing your teeth or making a cup of coffee. Using one of the strategies discussed earlier in this chapter, task analyse the activity, writing out each step in a logical sequence. As a follow-on activity, conduct a similar analysis for an academic task, such as the early reading skill of sounding out and blending words.

3 Using one of the case studies presented in this chapter (Boxes 5.1, 5.2, 5.3), along with your reading and experience to date, identify five issues that are of particular importance for the classroom teacher who is aiming to include and support a student with special educational needs in daily teaching and learning programs and activities.

4 Visit one or more of the following websites and navigate around the various technology-focused resources and links. How will the information you find in these sites assist you in enhancing the inclusion of students with special needs in your classroom?
- www.mup.unimelb.edu.au/click
- www.library.jcu.edu.au/Educ/special.html
- www2.edc.org/NCIP/library/toc.htm
- www.abilityhub.com

Group activities

1 Identify and discuss ways in which particular aspects of curriculum, instruction and features of the learning context (Figure 5.1) play a role in the provision of effective teaching and learning programs that are inclusive of all students.

2 Identify a hypothetical student and develop some examples of long-term goals and short-term instructional objectives in a relevant curriculum area. How could you monitor individual progress towards these targets, given that you may have 30 other students in your class? Design a method (that is practical for you) of tracking and evaluating student learning outcomes in your selected curriculum area.

3 Design and implement either a peer tutoring or cooperative learning procedure, such as Jigsaw. Discuss the strengths and constraints of the techniques(s) you trialed.

References

Agran, M., King-Sears, M. E., Wehmeyer, M. L. & Copeland, S. R. (2003). *Student-Directed Learning*. Baltimore: Paul. H. Brookes.

*Alberto, P. A. & Troutman, A. C. (2003). *Applied Behavior Analysis for Teachers* (6th edn). New Jersey: Merrill/Prentice Hall.

Algozzine, R., Ysseldyke, J. E. & Elliott, J. (1997). *Strategies and Tactics for Effective Instruction*. Longmont, CO: Sopris West.

Arthur, M. (2001). Designing effective teaching interventions. Chapter 5 in P. Foreman (Ed.), *Integration and Inclusion in Action* (2nd edn). (pp.139–68). Melbourne: Thomson Learning.

Arthur, M., Gordon, C. & Butterfield, N. (2003). *Classroom Management: Creating Positive Learning Environments*. Melbourne: Thomson Learning.

Ashman, A. F. & Conway, R. N. F. (1993). Teaching students to use process-based learning and problem solving strategies in mainstream classes. *Learning and Instruction*, 3, 73–92.

Bateman, B. & Linden, M. A. (1998). *Better IEPs* (3rd edn). Longmont, CO: Sopris West.

Bauer, A. M. & Shea, T. M. (1999). *Inclusion 101: How to Teach All Learners*. Baltimore: Paul. H. Brookes.

*Blankenship, C. S. (1985). Using curriculum based assessment data to make instructional decisions. *Exceptional Children, 52*, 233–8.

Blankenship, C. S. (1988). Structuring the classroom for success. *Australasian Journal of Special Education, 12*(2), 25–30.

Blankenship, C. S. & Lilly, M. S. (1981). *Mainstreaming Students With Learning and Behavioural Problems: Techniques for the Classroom Teacher*. New York: Holt, Rinehart & Winston.

Bloom, B. S. (1980). The new direction in educational research: Alterable variables. *Phi Delta Kappan, 61*, 382–5.

Bloom, B. S. (1984). The search for methods of group instruction as effective as one-to-one tutoring. *Educational Leadership*, May, 4–17.

Boyd, S. (1999). *All Keyed Up: The Use of Computers, At Home and At School, by Children with Special Needs*. SET Special, Wellington: New Zealand Council for Educational Research.

Burtch, J. A. (1999). Technology is for everyone. *Educational Leadership, 56*(5), 33–4.

Carnine, D., Silbert, J. & Kame'enui, E. J. (1990). *Direct Instruction Reading* (2nd edn). New York: Merrill.

*Carter, M. & Kemp, C. R. (1996). Strategies for task analysis in special education. *Educational Psychology, 16*(2), 155–70.

*Choate, J. S., Enright, B. E., Miller, L. J., Poteet, J. A. & Rakes, T. A. (1995). *Curriculum-based Assessment and Programming* (3rd edn). Boston: Allyn & Bacon.

*Christenson, S. L., Ysseldyke, J. E. & Thurlow, M. L. (1989). Critical instructional factors for students with mild handicaps: An integrative review. *Remedial and Special Education, 10*(5), 21–31.

Copeland, S. R., Hughes, C., Agran, M., Wehmeyer, M. L. & Fowler, S. E. (2002). An intervention package to support high school students with mental retardation in general education classrooms. *American Journal on Mental Retardation, 107*(1), 32–45.

Daniels, V. I. (1998). How to manage disruptive behavior in inclusive classrooms. *Exceptional Children, 30*(4), 26–31.

Darch, C. (1990). Research on direct instruction. Chapter 3 in D. Carnine, J. Silbert & E. J. Kame'enui, *Direct Instruction Reading* (2nd edn). New York: Merrill.

Deshler, D. D., Ellis, E. S. & Lenz, B. K. (1996). *Teaching Adolescents With Learning Disabilities: Strategies and Methods* (2nd edn). Denver: Love Publishing

Deshler, D. D., Schumaker, J. B., Lenz, B. K., Bulgren, J. A., Hock, M. F., Knight, J. & Ehren, B. J. (2001). Ensuring content-area learning by secondary students with learning disabilities. *Learning Disabilities Research and Practice, 16*, 96–108.

Duker, P., Didden, R. & Sigafoos, J. (2004). *One-to-one Training: Instructional Procedures for Learners With Developmental Disabilities*. Austin, TX: Pro-Ed.

Engelmann, S. & Bruner, E. (1988). *Reading Mastery 1*. Chicago: SRA.

Engelmann, S. & Carnine, D. (1982). *Theory of Instruction: Principles and Applications*. New York: Irvington.

Fuchs, L. S. & Deno, S. L. (1991). Paradigmatic distinctions between instructionally relevant measurement models. *Exceptional Children, 57*, 488–500.

Fuchs, L. S. & Fuchs, D. (1998). Building a bridge across the canyon. *Learning Disability Quarterly*, *21*, 99–101.

Gable, R. A. & Hendrickson, J. M. (Eds). (1990). *Assessing Students With Special Needs: A Sourcebook for Analyzing and Correcting Errors in Academics*. New York: Longman.

Gersten, R. (1992). Passion and precision: Response to 'Curriculum-based assessment and Direct Instruction: Critical reflections on fundamental assumptions'. *Exceptional Children, 58*, 464–7.

Gersten, R. (1998). Recent advances in instructional research for students with learning disabilities: An overview. *Learning Disabilities Research and Practice, 13*(3), 162–70.

Gillies, R. M. & Ashman, A. F. (2000). The effects of cooperative learning on students with learning difficulties in the lower elementary school. *The Journal of Special Education, 34*(1), 19–27.

Glasser, W. (1998). *Choice Theory: A New Psychology of Personal Freedom*. New York: Harper Perennial.

Good, T. L. & Brophy, J. E. (2000). *Looking in Classrooms* (8th edn). New York: Longman.

Goor, M. B. & Schwenn, J. O. (1993). Accommodating diversity and disability with co-operative learning. *Intervention in School and Clinic, 29*, 6–16.

*Henley, M., Ramsey, R. S. & Algozzine, R. F. (2002). *Characteristics of and Strategies for Teaching Students With Mild Disabilities* (4th edn). Boston: Allyn and Bacon.

Heshusius, L. (1991). Curriculum-based assessment and Direct Instruction: Critical reflections on fundamental assumptions. *Exceptional Children, 57*, 315–28.

Higgins, K., Boone, R. & Williams, D. L. (2000). Evaluating educational software for special education. *Intervention in School and Clinic, 36*(2), 109–15.

*Howell, K. W., Fox, S. L. & Morehead, M. K. (1993). *Curriculum-based Evaluation: Teaching and Decision-making* (2nd edn). Belmont: Brooks/Cole.

Howell, K. W. & Nolet, V. (2000). *Curriculum-based Evaluation: Teaching and Decision Making* (3rd edn). Belmont, CA: Wadsworth/Thomson Learning.

*Hudson, P., Lignugaris-Kraft, B. & Miller, T. (1993). Using content enhancements to improve the performance of adolescents with learning disabilities in content classes. *Learning Disabilities Research and Practice, 8*, 106–26.

Hunt, P., Soto, G., Maier, J. & Doering, K. (2003). Collaborative teaming to support students at risk and students with severe disabilities in general education classrooms. *Exceptional Children, 69*(3), 315–32.

Hustad, K. C., Morehouse, T. B. & Gutmann, M. (2002). AAC strategies for enhancing the usefulness of natural speech in children with severe intelligibility challenges. Chapter 13 in J. Reichle, D. R. Beukelman & J. C. Light (Eds), *Exemplary Practices for Beginning Communicators: Implications for AAC* (pp. 433–52). Baltimore: Paul. H. Brookes.

Jenkins, J. R., Antil, L. R., Wayne, S. K. & Vedas, P. F. (2003). How cooperative learning works for special education and remedial students. *Exceptional Children, 69*(3), 279–92.

Jenkins, J. & Jenkins, L. (1985). Peer tutoring in elementary and secondary programs. *Focus on Exceptional Children, 6*, 1–12.

Jenkins, J. & Jenkins, L. (1987). Making peer tutoring work. *Educational Leadership, 44*, 64–8.

Jenkins, J., Jewell, M., Leicester, N., O'Connor, R., Jenkins, L. & Trouser, N. (1994). Accommodations for individual differences without classroom ability groups: An experiment in school restructuring. *Exceptional Children, 60*, 344–58.

Jones, V. F. (1996). In the face of predictable crises: Developing a comprehensive treatment plan for students with emotional or behavioral disorders. *Teaching Exceptional Children*, Nov/Dec, 54–9.

*Jones, E. D., Southern, W. T. & Brigham, F. J. (1998). Curriculum-based assessment: Testing what is taught and teaching what is tested. *Intervention in School and Clinic*, 33(4), 239–49.

Kame'enui, E. J., Carnine, D. W., Dixon, R. C., Simmons, D. C. & Coyne, M. D. (Eds). (2002). *Effective Teaching Strategies that Accommodate Diverse Learners* (2nd edn). New Jersey: Merrill/Prentice Hall.

*Kame'enui, E. J. & Simmons, D. C. (1990). *Designing Instructional Strategies: The Prevention of Academic Learning Problems*. Columbus: Merrill.

Kemp, C. (1992). Designing and implementing instructional programs. Unit 5 in *Teaching Students With Special Needs in the Regular Classroom (K–6)*. Sydney: Department of Employment, Education and Training.

Kinder, D. & Carnine, D. (1991). Direct Instruction: What is it and what is it becoming. *Journal of Behavioral Education*, 1, 193–213.

Lankshear, C., Snyder, I. & Green, B. (2000). *Teachers and Techno-literacy: Managing Literacy, Technology and Learning in Schools*. Sydney: Allen and Unwin.

Maag, J. W. (2001). Rewarded by punishment: Reflections on the disuse of positive reinforcement in schools. *Exceptional Children*, 67(2), 173–86.

Mastropieri, M. A. & Scruggs, T. E. (2004). *The Inclusive Classroom: Strategies for Effective Instruction* (2nd edn). New Jersey: Pearson.

Mull, C. A. & Sitlington, P. L. (2003). The role of technology in the transition to postsecondary education of students with learning disabilities: A review of the literature. *The Journal of Special Education*, 37(1), 26–32.

National Curriculum and Assessment Committee (CURASS) (1993). *The Use of Profiles*. Canberra: AEC.

Nelson, J. R., Johnson, A. & Marchand-Martella, N. (1996). Effects of direct instruction, co-operative learning, and independent learning practices on the classroom behavior of students with behavioral disorders: A comparative analysis. *Journal of Emotional and Behavioral Disorders*, 4(1), 53–62.

New South Wales Board of Studies (1997a). English key learning area interim support document: Communication. Sydney: Author.

New South Wales Board of Studies (1997b). English key learning area interim support document: Literacy. Sydney: Author.

New South Wales Board of Studies (1998a). English K–6 Syllabus. Sydney: Author.

New South Wales Board of Studies (1998b). English K–6 work samples. Sydney: Author.

New South Wales Board of Studies (1998c). English K–6 modules. Sydney: Author.

New South Wales Board of Studies (2003). Personal Development, Health and Physical Education: Years 7–10 Syllabus. Sydney: Author.

New South Wales Department of Education (1988). *Potential Unlimited*. Sydney: Author.

Palincsar, A. S. & Herrenkohl, L. R. (2002). Designing collaborative learning contexts. *Theory Into Practice*, 41(1), 26–32.

Palincsar, A. S. & Klenk, L. (1992). Fostering literacy learning in supportive contexts. *Journal of Learning Disabilities*, 25(4), 211–25, 229.

Piercy, M., Wilton, K. & Townsend, M. (2002). Promoting the social acceptance of young children with moderate-severe intellectual disabilities using cooperative-learning techniques. *American Journal on Mental Retardation*, 107(5), 352–60.

Porter, L. (2000). *Student Behaviour: Theory and Practice for Teachers* (2nd edn). Sydney: Allen & Unwin.

*Putnam, J.W. (Ed.). (1998). *Co-operative Learning and Strategies for Inclusion: Celebrating Diversity in the Classroom* (2nd edn). Baltimore: Paul H. Brookes Pub. Co.

Rieth, H. J. & Evertson, C. (1988). Variables related to the effective instruction of difficult to teach children. *Focus on Exceptional Children*, 20(5), 1–8.

*Rieth, H. J. & Polsgrove, L. (1994). Curriculum and instructional issues in teaching secondary students with learning disabilities. *Learning Disabilities Research and Practice*, 9(2), 118–26.

Rodger, S. (1995). Individual education plans revisited: A review of the literature. *International Journal of Disability, Development and Education*, 42(3), 221–39.

Rosenshine, B. V. (1995). Advances in research on instruction. *The Journal of Educational Research*, 88(5), 262–8.

*Schloss, P. J., Alper, S., Robertson, J., Sher, H. & Henley, J. (1995). Supporting regular early childhood teachers in integrating young children with disabilities: A power continuum. *Australian Journal of Early Childhood*, 20(4), 19–29.

Schwartz, I. S. & Olswang, L. B. (1996). Evaluating child behavior change in natural settings: Exploring alternative strategies for data collection. *Topics in Early Childhood Special Education*, 16(1), 82–101.

Schulz, J. B. & Carpenter, C. D. (1995). Developing individualized education programs. Chapter 6 in J. B. Schulz. & C. D. Carpenter. *Mainstreaming Exceptional Students: A Guide for Classroom Teachers*. Boston: Allyn & Bacon.

Silbert, J., Carnine, D. & Stein, M. (1990). *Direct Instruction Mathematics* (2nd edn). Columbus: Merrill.

Slavin, R. (1996). Research on co-operative learning and achievement: What we know, what we need to know. *Contemporary Educational Psychology*, 21, 43–69.

Smith, D. & Laws, K. (1992). The communicating role. Chapter 3 in C. Turney, N. Hatton, K. Laws, K. Sinclair. & D. Smith. *The Classroom Manager*. Sydney: Allen & Unwin.

Smith, M. A. & Misra, A. (1992). A comprehensive management system for students in regular classrooms. *The Elementary School Journal*, 92(3), 353–71.

Snell, M. E. & Brown, F. (2000). Development and implementation of educational programs. Chapter 4 in M. E. Snell & F. Brown, (Eds). *Instruction of Students With Severe Disabilities* (5th edn). New Jersey: Merrill.

Spencer, V. G., Scruggs, T. E. & Mastropieri, M. A. (2003). Content area learning in middle school social studies classrooms and students with emotional or behavioral disorders: A comparison of strategies. *Behavioral Disorders*, 28(2), 77–93.

Topping, K. & Ehly, S., (Eds). (1998). *Peer-Assisted Learning*. New Jersey: Erlbaum.

Utley, C. A., Mortweet, S. L. & Greenwood, C. R. (1997). Peer-mediated instruction and interventions. *Focus on Exceptional Children*, 29(5), 2–23.

Vaughn, S., Hughes, M. T., Moody, S. W. & Elbaum, B. (2001). Instructional grouping for reading for students with LD: Implications for practice. *Intervention in School and Clinic*, 36(3), 131–7.

Walberg, H. J. (1990). Productive teaching and instruction: Assessing the knowledge base. *Phi Delta Kappan*, February, 470–8.

*Westwood, P. (2003). *Commonsense Methods for Children With Special Educational Needs* (4th edn). London: Routledge.

Whinnery, K. W. & Fuchs, L. S. (1992). Implementing effective teaching strategies with learning disabled students through curriculum-based measurement. *Learning Disabilities Research and Practice*, *7*, 25–30.

Wolfe, P. (1998). Revisiting effective teaching. *Educational Leadership*, *56*(3), 61–4.

———

*Recommended reading for this chapter

Further recommended reading

Algozzine, R. & Ysseldyke, J. E. (2003). *Tips for Beginning Teachers*. Longmont, CO: Sopris West.

Calhoun, M. B. & Fuchs, L. S. (2003). The effects of peer-assisted learning strategies and curriculum-based measurement on the mathematics performance of secondary students with disabilities. *Remedial and Special Education*, *24*(4), 235–45.

Gable, R. A., Enright, B. E. & Hendrickson, J. (1991). A practical model for curriculum-based assessment and instruction in arithmetic. *Teaching Exceptional Children*, *24*, 6–9.

Howell, K. W. & Nolet, V. (2000). *Curriculum-based Evaluation: Teaching and Decision Making* (3rd edn). Belmont, CA: Wadsworth/Thomson Learning.

Jones, V. F. & Jones, L. S. (2004). *Comprehensive Classroom Management: Creating Communities of Support and Solving Problems* (7th edn). Boston: Pearson.

Kozloff, M. A. (1994). *Improving Educational Outcomes for Children With Disabilities: Principles for Assessment, Program Planning and Evaluation*. Baltimore: Paul H. Brookes.

Marston, D., Deno, S. L., Kim, D., Diment, K. & Rogers, D. (1995). Comparison of reading intervention approaches for students with mild disabilities. *Exceptional Children*, *62*(1), 20–37.

Mastropieri, M. A., Scruggs, T. E. & Graetz, J. E. (2003). Reading comprehension instruction for secondary students: Challenges for struggling students and teachers. *Learning Disability Quarterly*, *26*(2), 103–16.

Schulz, J. B. & Carpenter, C. D. (1995). *Mainstreaming Exceptional Students: A Guide for Classroom Teachers*. Boston: Allyn & Bacon.

Wills Lloyd, J., Forness, S. R. & Kavale, K. A. (1998). Some methods are more effective than others. *Intervention in School and Clinic*, *33*(4), 195–200.

Chapter 6

Encouraging positive interactions

Robert Conway

This chapter aims to:

- establish a clear link between managing learning and managing social interactions in classrooms as being interrelated parts of learning and teaching for all students in the classroom ecosystem

- examine what is meant by social behaviour and how it can become problem behaviour

- examine the factors behind inappropriate social behaviour and their effects on students in mainstream classes

- discuss social aspects of mainstream classes and why some students with additional needs have difficulty
- discuss management strategies both for students with additional needs as well as other members of the class
- examine ways in which positive social interactions can be developed and enhanced.

Positive interactions

This chapter is about encouraging positive interactions. It has deliberately not been called a chapter on behaviour management or classroom discipline, as the methods of achieving positive interactions are far broader that either of those terms. Positive interactions are affected by student behaviour, teacher behaviour, the curriculum, teaching strategies, the classroom and the school community, and the ways in which all these ingredients combine to produce positive learning environments. If these terms sound familiar it's because, as in Chapter 4 on curriculum adaptations and modifications, the concept of the classroom or school as an ecosystem is critical to understanding ways of enhancing positive social environments. Throughout the chapter there are references to the importance of social skills being addressed in the context of the learning and teaching that takes place in the classroom. Where teaching and learning are productive, behavioural problems are reduced and positive social inclusion is enhanced. Where there is little appropriate learning in the inclusive classroom, positive social skills are left to develop in isolation.

Social skills, together with academic skills, provide the two great challenges to inclusion of students with additional needs. Many teachers tend to focus on the perceived lack of social skills of students with additional needs, particularly those skills associated with a lack of peer acceptance, and work-related behaviours such as keeping on-task or completing work with minimum assistance. These issues are addressed in this chapter through examination of approaches that have been shown to be effective in increasing classroom involvement, such as social skills training programs, cooperative learning experiences and positive teacher management strategies.

Social behaviour and schooling

To understand the ways in which positive interactions can occur, it is necessary to focus briefly on what factors can contribute to negative interactions within the classroom and school environments. Unlike other areas of special need involved in inclusion, the issue of student behaviour and its management has been an area that has met strong resistance from mainstream school teachers and executive (Conway, 2002). The inclusion of students with additional needs brings to the regular class additional challenges. Students with a primary disability such as intellectual disability or a sensory disability may have an associated behaviour problem or may have difficulty adjusting from a special setting to the regular class, with its different learning–teaching factors. If a student with a special need has always been a part of the regular school environment, these difficulties are substantially reduced.

While the initial discussion that follows focuses on students in general, the discussion on teacher and curriculum variables is also critical in planning for positive interactions for all students in the mainstream class.

What is behaviour and when does it become 'problem behaviour'?

In determining when behaviour becomes problem behaviour, we need to consider a number of variables including the *frequency*, *intensity* and *duration* of the behaviour, as well as where the behaviour occurred (*location*). Other variables include *socio-economic* and *cultural* influences, and the issue of *age appropriate* behaviour as introduced in Chapter 1.

The issue of when behaviour becomes problem behaviour can best be summed up in the following definition that highlights that all children, and all adults, demonstrate problem behaviours at times. While the definition may be dated in terms of when it was published, it remains one of the clearest definitions.

> What makes behaviours disordered is when they are exhibited in the wrong place, at the wrong time, in the presence of the wrong people, and to an inappropriate degree.
>
> (Apter, 1982)

This definition brings together the issues of frequency, intensity, and duration, together with location and the socio-economic and cultural values of the observer. It also highlights the importance of the observer in defining problem behaviour. Most students are identified by teachers, parents and others as having a problem behaviour because it offends, annoys or irritates them as observers of the behaviour. This is important to consider when looking back on the terms used so far, such as *inappropriate* behaviour and *unacceptable* behaviour, which reflect the label that others place on the behaviour and the student. With the exception of attention-seekers, few students define themselves as behaviour problems.

Why do students misbehave?

One of the clearest ways to identify the cause of problem behaviour is to focus on the grid that is often used in functional behaviour assessment or FBA for short (see CECP, 2000 or there is free access to the FBA manuals on the website at www.air.org/cecp). We will return later in the chapter to consider the process of FBA and positive behaviour improvement plans (BIP) in detail.

Within the FBA process, all behaviour is seen as having a purpose: to get something; to avoid something; or to communicate something. This can occur either internally or externally. The grid is used to identify the relationship between getting and avoiding, and provides possible functions of the behaviour.

An example may be in a classroom when a teacher hands out a worksheet to each student. One student with learning difficulties or a mild intellectual disability screws up the paper and throws it across the room and yells out: 'I'm not doing this (expletive) work'. The teacher responds: 'You can't speak to me like that, get out of the room and sit in the corridor!'.

Table 6.1 Relationship between getting and avoiding

Student	Internal	External
Gets	A sense of satisfaction that they have told the teacher off	Kudos from their classmates that they have told the teacher off
Avoids	Having to do a task that is beyond their ability	Classmates seeing that they can't do the task

Let's examine the reasons for the behaviour using the FBA grid method. What does the student get and avoid through the problem behaviour? The student avoids doing the task by being sent out of the room, and avoids others seeing that they can't do the task. It may well be the case that each time they are confronted with tasks they can't do, they adopt that same behaviour because they know what the teacher's reaction will be and can orchestrate the teacher behaviour of having them removed. If this is the case, then it is the student who is managing the behaviour, not the teacher.

In behavioural terms, both are negatively reinforced by the teacher reactions. By the student displaying the behaviour and the subsequent teacher actions, the teacher is negatively reinforced by having peace in the room and the student out of the room. The student is reinforced by getting out of the work and the room. Importantly, the student has communicated that the work is beyond their ability, and this should be noted by the teacher, particularly if the student doesn't have the skill to communicate frustrations in other ways.

From a social skills perspective, students who display these behaviours are considered to have interfering problem behaviours (Gresham, 1998). Gresham sees these as being in three categories:

- social skills acquisition deficits – they do not have appropriate skills in their repertoire
- social skills performance deficits – they have the behaviour and either choose not to use the behaviour, or don't realise that they need to use the skill
- social skills fluency deficits – they use the behaviour in the setting in which it is reinforced but fail to use it in other situations.

We will return to the issues of social skills again later in the chapter as they are critical in ensuring the social inclusion of all students, particularly those with additional needs.

Types of behaviours causing concern in students with additional needs

The most common behavioural categories of student with additional needs that concern mainstream teachers are: issues of attention and work habits, such as not being able to work unassisted and inability to complete tasks without additional assistance; coping with the attitudes and behaviours of others towards them; and, the establishment and maintenance of peer relationships (Fad & Ryser, 1993).

Work habits include the expectation by teachers that students will attend classes and comply with teacher requests within that class. Some of the behaviours identified as of concern here include failure to complete homework, not completing class work on time, refusing or failing to make corrections, not following teacher requests promptly and not coming to class prepared to work. Many of these behaviours are associated with reduced academically engaged time, which is a source of annoyance to teachers. Studies have shown that students with learning and behaviour difficulties have significantly less academically engaged time than do higher performing students. Providing appropriate learning experiences would be a simple method of addressing many of these issues.

Coping skill behaviours of concern to class teachers include inability to express anger appropriately, inability to cope in acceptable ways when something is taken belonging to the student, and problems with coping following an insult or when being bossed or when being blamed unfairly. Again, acquisition of the alternative behaviour in each case would be seen as positive characteristics.

Peer relationship behaviours difficulties include failure to maintain friendships over time, being thought of as a social isolate, not knowing how to join in group activities, not being able to end a conversation and failing to interact with a variety of peers. As failure in peer relations and poor behaviour patterns are linked to poor academic performance, skill acquisition in these areas is important for successful maintenance of mainstream placement.

Students with behaviour problems can be found in every classroom and the management of student behaviour has been recognised internationally as the major source of worry for beginning teachers (LaMaster et al., 1998; Moeller & Ishii-Jordan, 1996). LaMaster et al. (1998), in a study of USA beginning specialist physical education teachers in elementary school, found that the greatest concern of those teachers was working with students whose special education needs included behavioural difficulties. They also reported fear of verbal or even physical abuse by some students with additional needs towards other students or staff. Recent events both in the USA and Australia would suggest that staff working with students with additional needs who have a behavioural component might be at risk of injury. Moeller and Ishii-Jordan (1996) identified that trainee teachers did not have the training to facilitate appropriate interactive behaviours of students with and without additional needs in the regular education environment.

In a study of inclusion of students with additional needs in South Australian and NSW schools, Westwood and Graham (2003) identified that time to work with and supervise students was the greatest problem created by students with additional needs. Other problems were interruptions and disruptions of other students' work, the inability of students with additional needs to keep up with class work, and the need for constant behaviour management. Addressing the issues above may assist in increasing academically engaged time in class. The study found that 47 per cent of NSW teachers in the survey identified the emotional and behaviour needs of students as the second highest concern of having students with additional needs in the classrooms. Interestingly, South Australian teachers did not identify this issue at all. The NSW results reflect the concerns raised by teachers on the behaviours of students in the Vinson Report (Vinson, 2002), where the six most common behaviour problems identified for all students were: swearing, disobedience, clowning, refusal to cooperate, confronting, and disruption of the teaching and learning process.

A study of behaviour difficulties of students in western Sydney schools found that the most common behaviour problems were distraction, problems with listening, physical aggression, demands for teacher attention, inability to remain on-task, and disruption of others (Stephenson, Linfoot, & Martin, 2000). Given that these were regular students and not students with additional needs, the behaviour issues are common across both students with additional needs and their regular class peers and not the province only of students with additional needs.

Despite this there is concern by many teachers that students with additional needs will add to the management problems that already exist in the class. This is a valid concern as shown in the Westwood and Graham (2003) study and it must be addressed through ensuring that adaptations and modifications of the learning–teaching environment assist students with additional needs to function to their full potential in the class.

Home and school factors

The home

Students come to school with a set of values and attitudes that cannot be left at the school gate. Family perceptions of school and the value of schooling play an important role both in the student's attitude to school and its management practices, and in the degree of support teachers can expect from the home in promoting school management practices. While school behaviour problems cannot be directly attributed to family factors, a number of home issues can exacerbate school problems. These include the type of disability, single-parent families, marital discord, low socio-economic status and disturbed child–parent relationships.

Particularly in the case of students with mental health needs, there is a clear link between their mental health needs and the home situation. The National Health and Wellbeing Survey (Sawyer et al., 2000) conducted across Australia found that approximately 14 per cent of all Australian children and youth aged 4 to 17 years had mental health problems and that among the key variables were:

- unstable relationships with parents or carers
- death of a parent
- inadequate parenting skills
- family discord, violence, separation or family breakdown
- parents with serious mental health problems, alcohol/drug problems that affect parenting.

While schools are not designed to address home issues, increasingly schools are forced to address issues that stem from homes. Many school programs for students with behaviour and mental health needs have provided parenting programs, although these have met with limited success.

For parents of students with additional needs, the home environment plays a critical role in supporting the work of early intervention programs (Bentley-Williams & Butterfield, 1996). When these students arrive at school, the transition process has added importance to ensure their social inclusion. There is a clear need for the process to occur over a protracted period involving school, parents and the child (Kemp, 2003) and where this occurs in a formalised, coherent manner, there is greater likelihood that the student with additional needs will maintain a regular class placement. Even with a planned transition process, the process of social inclusion is still fraught with difficulties. Kemp found that of children with moderate intellectual disability transitioning to kindergarten from an early intervention program in Sydney, the majority of teachers still found the inclusion process difficult, even with support of early intervention staff and other services.

The school

The school contributes to behaviour difficulties of students whether they have additional needs or not. As discussed in Chapter 4, what we teach and the way we teach can provide a catalyst for behaviour problems. Among the factors are the curriculum, the way in which we teach, the physical features of the classroom, and the timetable structure. Each is discussed in the following sections.

Curriculum

The curriculum is a major source of school-related behaviour problems and this is exacerbated for students with additional needs. Where the curriculum content is well above the ability level of students, there is little incentive for students to learn. For example, if students are in Year 8 and attempting simultaneous quadratic equations when they have not yet mastered the basic operations, there is little incentive to pay attention. The failure cycle is based on failure to learn followed by misbehaviour, followed by failure to learn, until students become trapped in an academic and social failure cycle from which they cannot escape. Where the individual teacher perceives they have little control over the topics that are taught, as in some secondary schools, there is a need to ensure that all students are involved in the learning process, not only those students capable of attempting the set topics. This becomes a major area of concern for students with additional needs, particularly those with learning difficulties or mild intellectual disability, where the academic performance level of the student may be well below the grade level, but the student is required to participate in the regular curricular topics with no modifications or adaptations.

Teaching methods

Other school factors include the way in which teachers teach. Teachers cannot compete with a colour television or interactive videos, but they can ensure that they have variety in their lessons, that they are prepared to teach the lesson and that they are able to make learning interesting. As discussed in Chapter 4, being able to teach the curriculum is important, but being positive and being able to interact with all students and treat them as people is also important. Again, the clear link between social and academic issues cannot be overlooked.

This is illustrated in the findings of Good and Brophy (2000) that over 70 per cent of the academic day is spent on independent work rather than on interaction between teacher and student. It is in these periods of independent work that teachers report the occurrence of social behaviour difficulties that arise from the frustration associated with inability to successfully complete independent practice (Gunter, Coutinho & Cade, 2002). Importantly, Gunter, Coutinho and Cade (2002) note that students can use the undesirable behaviour to terminate the academic activity. For students with additional needs, the frustration level is quickly reached in classes where there is little or no adaptation or modification of the tasks to meet their instructional needs. Gunter, Coutinho and Cade sum up the finding of the optimal blend of academic and social activities as: 'We believe that the key is to find a ratio of positive, desirable interactions that produces effective teaching and learning for both teachers and students' (2002, p. 129). In that way both student and teacher needs are met.

The physical classroom

The physical features of the classroom can also have an affect on behaviour. Classrooms that are poorly maintained, with no stimulating features, as often found in some secondary schools, do not create an environment in which students are encouraged to learn. In contrast, some early childhood and primary classrooms are so stimulating that students are constantly distracted by the many things around them. For some students this may exacerbate inattentive or distractible behaviours, especially for students with attention deficit hyperactive disorder (ADHD).

The layout of the room also has an effect on the management of student behaviour. Some secondary teachers prefer desks to be in single rows, with minimum contact between students. In contrast, many primary classrooms are arranged with groups of desks and work areas for different subjects. Both layouts have advantages for classroom management. Rows of single desks may reduce behaviour disruptions and increase on-task time for both primary and secondary students. If, however, the aim is to promote discussion and increase cooperative work skills, as is often the case for students with additional needs, small groups of desks will be more appropriate. Alternatively, for social and academic support, pairs of desks allow a buddy system to operate.

Where the student requires considerable space in the room, such as a student with severe physical disability, the needs of that student may in fact determine the layout of the room for the remaining students. The layout of desks selected by the class teacher will also depend on the level of direct control the teacher wants to have, the communication the teacher wants to have with the class, the level of communication the teacher wants to occur between students, and the types of learning activities that are to take place in the classroom.

Timetabling

The timetable can provide both support and difficulties in managing classroom behaviour. Where high schools are streamed or graded, timetabling the lower ability classes to complete difficult academic subjects late in the afternoon, with more active subjects such as physical education or design and technology in the initial periods of the day, creates difficulties for both the students and the teachers. In addition, where high schools timetable very active subjects such as PE followed immediately by subjects such as mathematics that may require sustained individual work, there is the potential for students with behaviour problems to have great difficulty in adjusting from active to passive behaviour in a short time. Such a timetable also presents considerable difficulties for students with additional needs who have mobility restrictions that prevent quick movement around a school. Timetabling must be sensitive to these needs to ensure that all students have access to all social as well as academic activities during the school day.

Students who have limited ability to complete academic tasks may find great difficulty concentrating on academic tasks late in the day. For example, a primary class teacher may assign mathematics tasks late in the day because the class didn't manage to complete them before recess. Students who have great difficulty concentrating on new mathematical skills at that time of the day, may have their inattention seen as a behaviour problem, when inappropriate timetabling caused the problem.

Teachers

Kauffman (2001) provided a list of the major ways in which teachers contribute to the development of inappropriate behaviour. Included in the list were actions such as being insensitive to the individuality of the students; having inappropriate expectations of the students; being inconsistent in managing student behaviour; giving inappropriate reinforcement; teaching irrelevant skills; and, providing undesirable models of behaviour. Inappropriate models of behaviour can include the way we dress, the way we speak to students and the way we present work to students, either on the board or in worksheets. Although these actions can be applied to all students, they have particular significance in relation to students with additional needs, in the light of research that demonstrates that teachers' attitudes to students with additional needs are often typified by these very actions (see Shulz & Carpenter, 1995, pp. 393–7). We will return to these issues at the end of the chapter.

As teachers spend considerable time with their students, it is essential that any discussion on management of behaviours, both for existing students and students with additional needs, focuses on the perceptions of teachers.

One problem that occurs with teacher perception of behaviour problems is that we all choose to see behaviour from our own point of view. In a study of teachers' perception of behaviour, Olsen (1995) asked teachers to rate nine possible causes of a student's misbehaviour in their class using the introduction 'A student is misbehaving in your class'. Teachers rated inability to do the work, inability to control their own behaviour, not being accepted by classmates, and lack of parental control as the four main reasons. A few days later the teachers were given the same task with one difference. The initial wording was now 'Your child is misbehaving in class'. The four main responses were now student inability to do the work, lack of teacher control, encouraged by classmates, and unable to control own behaviour. Lack of parental control had slipped from fourth to eighth place as a reason. However, lack of teacher control had increased from seventh place to second place.

What does this tell us? It says that for our own children, we see that the cause of the behaviour problem will lie with the teacher's management skills and other students encouraging poor behaviour. However, for students in our class the misbehaviour will be caused by students being unable to control their own behaviour and lack of parental control. Importantly for both scenarios, the inability of the student to do the work is rated as the first reason, again reinforcing the link between academic performance and misbehaviour.

Teachers have reported both frustration and stress from attempts to meet the behavioural needs of students in the classroom, particularly where students with additional needs and behaviour problems are present. Part of the difficulty for teachers may lie prior to their entering the classroom. Teacher preparation for the classroom management of behavioural difficulties has been shown to be inadequate (Vinson, 2002).

Classroom control as 'good' management

Teachers have often expressed concern that having a student with additional needs in a class will reduce their ability to control a class (Westwood & Graham, 2003). Control is seen as an important quality and this is reinforced often by administrators who see a quiet class as an indicator of a good teacher. A fear of loss of control frequently forces teachers to adopt a more rigid and confrontational management style that is often inconsistent with the needs of students, particularly those with additional needs. More importantly, confrontational behaviour by the teacher often exacerbates the likelihood that the student will react with even more severe behaviours (Colvin, Ainge & Nelson, 1977). Students with additional needs may require a more supportive, cooperative learning environment in which they can develop coping, learning and social skills with teachers modelling positive rather than confrontational behaviours.

What is social inclusion?

Social inclusion is concerned with the interactions of teachers and students within the classroom. Social inclusion factors include peer acceptance, friendships, and participation in group activities. Equally important are the teacher's interactions with the student with additional needs.

Three components of social inclusion have been identified (Shulz & Carpenter, 1995). The first is an *affective* component that focuses on the way peers and teachers feel about or perceive mainstreamed students. The second or *cognitive* component is concerned with understanding individual differences and disability in general. The third component is *behavioural* and covers the verbal, non-verbal and physical actions of students towards their peers. To the last component, the role of teacher behaviour needs to be added. The teacher's verbal, non-verbal and physical actions are also important as the teacher acts as a role model, both for the students with additional needs, but also for the way other students in the class interact with those students.

Difficulties of social inclusion for students with additional needs

Placing students with additional needs within a general education setting does not guarantee that they will establish and maintain desirable social contacts or develop social support networks. Many of these students, particularly adolescents with moderate and severe disabilities, remain socially isolated (Abery & Simunds, 1997).

A review of early intervention for children with a dual developmental and behaviour disability found that behaviour problems occur far more frequently in this group than in the general early childhood population (Roberts et al., 2003). Among the behaviours reported in studies were non-compliance, aggression towards others, destructiveness, tantrums, self-injury and self-stimulation. The behaviours were identified as stable over time and persisting into adolescence and adulthood. Early childhood intervention was seen as the best opportunity to address the behaviours through positive family-focused interventions based on social learning theory and applied behaviour analysis. Without such interventions, the behaviours can lead to more serious and stigmatising challenging behaviours that may ultimately result in exclusion from community settings. Early intervention within the school education sector through FBA and BIP strategies are seen as important for competent management. We will return to these later in the chapter.

Sale and Carey (1995), in a study conducted in a full-inclusion model school, argued that placing students with additional needs together with regular class students for 100 per cent of the day doesn't alter how they are reported to be liked or disliked by their same-age peers. The study included students with perceptual/communication disorder, emotional disability and physical disability in primary schools. In terms of social preference scores, students with emotional disability were the least socially acceptable, while those with physical disability were the most acceptable. Sale and Carey (1995) concluded that, although there are clear benefits from full inclusion, there is a need for further study of the social benefits for students with additional needs.

In a study of social inclusion for adolescent students with physical disabilities, Mpofu (2003) found that higher achieving students with additional needs were more socially acceptable than those who were low achieving. As found in the Sale and Carey (1995) study, just attending the same classes doesn't enhance social status but those assigned socially desirable school and classroom roles did have a higher sense of social acceptance. They were found to have reinforced confidence and increased social capital. Teachers and students saw social acceptance as important for academic achievement, school retention and adjustment.

Integrating behaviour and academic skills

Prior to examining the methods of focusing on social skills, it is important to stress again the strong interrelationship between social and academic skills (McEvoy & Welker, 2003). In this context, it is necessary to understand that classrooms are a teaching–learning environment. Both teachers and students teach in a variety of ways, some of them appropriate and some not. By the same token, teachers and students learn from each other. The concept of teachers teaching and students learning in a one-way flow of knowledge and control is a historic myth, sometimes perpetuated in models of discipline that suggest that teachers must be assertive and take charge, or use teaching practices that emphasise a control focus. As discussed in Chapter 4, the focus of modern Australian curriculums is that students learn from a wide variety of experiences and that teachers guide learning and learn from student output. Hence behaviour change must be seen in the context of a web of learning and teaching for all students in the mainstream class. Another way of conceiving the close relationship between management of social/behavioural needs and academic needs is to look for clear parallels.

As Glasser (1969) suggested in his early model of ten steps to discipline with disruptive students, the first three steps we need to follow in changing students' behaviour should be directed at ourselves: What am I doing? Is it working? Make a plan. These steps are aimed at assessing whether we can change our behaviour and, particularly, whether we can change what we teach and how we teach it. It also emphasises the need to do something positive in our interactions with students when they are not being disruptive, such as greeting them or smiling at them.

Kauffman (2001) asks teachers to reflect upon the relationship between curriculum presentation and behaviour problems. While Kauffman acknowledges that not all behaviour problems can be solved by changing the learning–teaching environment, such changes may avoid the need to embark on specific management programs.

The importance of linking academic and behaviour/social skills has been highlighted already in the research of Mpofu (2003), and Gunter, Coutinho and Cade (2002). In both cases, the social and academic outcomes for students with additional needs were enhanced through the inter-linking of academic and social skills. Similarly, Williams and Reisberg (2003) emphasise the importance of embedding the teaching of social skills in the teaching of curriculum content. They use the example of a history unit for secondary students in which the social skills are identified and programmed to be used within sub-topics. For example, they will explicitly include small groupwork with and without teacher involvement, pairs, independent in-seat work and large groups at different times throughout the topic with each deliberately programmed alongside the curriculum content decisions. We will return to this study when we consider the use of cognitive strategies.

Advice on linking academic and behaviour skills also comes from government directions. Within the pedagogy approaches being supported by most jurisdictions there is a clear focus on the role of a positive learning environment (see, for example, NSW Department of Education and Training, 2003). The dimension *Quality learning environment* includes a series of elements that focus on a caring, safe and supportive learning environment. These include engagement, social support, self-regulation and student direction.

In a review of research regarding best practice for optimising learning for students with additional needs in inclusive classrooms, Moeller and Ishii-Jordan (1996, p. 299) identified a number of significant elements. Most of these are directly related to classroom management:

- consistent structure, routine and predictability
- explicit rules co-constructed with student input
- variety of teaching approaches and techniques (for example, contract, project approaches)

- address all learning styles (haptic, aural, visual) – 'helping children learn all the way'
- high expectations
- classroom atmosphere conducive to active learning and building a trusting relationship
- memorisation, application, analysis and synthesis
- constant positive reinforcement
- reward system in place (both external and internal motivation techniques)
- constant assessment (both traditional and alternative)
- multisensory approach to teaching
- small group and cooperative group work
- frequent interactions with students
- connection of school work to student interests, experiences and community.

What is also important is that the list reflects good sound classroom management, regardless of whether there are students with additional needs.

Preparation and lesson delivery by teachers

The level of preparation by teachers for each class has an important effect on the behaviour of all students during lessons, but most particularly for students with additional needs. If teachers have a number of students with additional needs in their mainstream classes, there is a need to ensure that adequate activities are prepared, particularly if those students are to attempt tasks that are different from those being attempted by the majority of the class (see Chapter 4, Boxes 4.14 and 4.15). If the teacher is unable to supervise directly at all times, teacher management difficulties will increase if the students are unable to complete the tasks with minimum assistance. Similarly, if there is inadequate preparation for the main group in the class, again the opportunity for behaviour problems increases, this time from the students without additional needs.

One issue often spoken about in special education literature, but to a lesser extent in regular education literature, is *academically engaged time*, or the amount of time spent in productive learning by each student. In some classes, both special and regular, the amount of academically engaged time can be very little, particularly when time spent on interruptions, handing out of materials and disciplining students is totalled. Students who are academically engaged are, by definition, engaged in appropriate behaviours.

The way in which teachers communicate with students can also affect both the presentation of the lesson and the behaviour of students. In South Australia, problems of authoritarian teacher management style were found to have impeded the development of trust and relationships between teachers and students (Kingdon, 1995). The solution was to ensure that teacher preparation for lessons was thorough, as well as ensuring that teachers had a clear management plan to cover all students throughout the lesson.

What skills are appropriate to focus on in increasing social acceptance of students with additional needs?

A number of suggestions have been made on the specific skills to focus on as part of making the classroom a more positive place in which to work. As discussed earlier, the three areas of work habits, coping skills and peer relationships are important areas to focus on, particularly for students with higher levels of learning needs.

Bowd (1990) has suggested a broad approach to grouping skills, rather than focusing on very specific skills. He suggests that teachers consider adapting methods of instruction and classroom management to accommodate the areas. The five broad areas, which are still very relevant today, are:

- learning to cope with anxiety, fear of failure and fear of rejection
- developing feelings of self-worth both in class and in the wider school
- learning to accept reasonable direction and guidance from teachers including asking for help and following directions
- developing behaviours that are likely to increase acceptance by other students
- developing good work habits such as listening, and positive attitudes towards schoolwork.

Clearly the role of the class teacher is to ensure that positive learning situations can occur in the classroom, as well as encouraging the development of these social skills.

Managing disruptive behaviours in the classroom

Daniels (1998) provides a clear sequence of ten questions to ask in managing the disruptive behaviour of students in inclusive classrooms. She commences with the important question of whether misbehaviour could result from inappropriate curriculum or teaching strategies, the issues raised in Chapter 4, which looked at the relationship between academic content and student management. The ten questions posed by Daniels are shown in Box 6.1. The teacher matches each question to potential actions with adaptations for the Australian context.

Box 6.1
Questions to ask in managing disruptive behaviour in inclusive classrooms

	Questions to ask	Possible actions
1	Could this misbehaviour be the result of inappropriate curriculum or teaching strategies?	Identify the blockages to learning (curriculum content, resources and equipment). Adapting teaching and learning can reduce the occurrence of student misbehaviour.
2	Could this misbehaviour be the result of the student's inability to understand the concepts being taught?	Use task analysis to check prerequisite skills, learning styles and ability to determine the functional level of students and assist them in moving to mastery of relevant skills.
3	Could this misbehaviour be an underlying result of the student's disability?	A knowledge base of the disability and potential behaviour problems is useful (for example, autism).

continued

Box 6.1 continued

Questions to ask	Possible actions
4 Could this misbehaviour be a result of other factors?	The ecology of the classroom is important beyond the instructional issues in Q1 above. This includes how students and teachers interact and respond to the included student.
5 Are these causes of misbehaviour that I can control?	The level and forms of feedback to the student are important.
6 How do I determine if the misbehaviour is classroom based?	Again the classroom ecology is important and conducting a functional assessment may be useful, including identifying events, variables and circumstances that contribute to the problem.
7 How do I teach students to self-regulate or self-manage behaviour?	Teaching students to self-instruct, self-monitor and self-reinforce has been shown to be successful in reducing behaviour problems.
8 How do I determine what methods of control are appropriate without violating the rights of students with disabilities?	Under the Australian Commonwealth and state Disability Discrimination Acts, certain management procedures may be illegal. In addition, use of physical restraint may not be permitted in some educational services. Remember to be positive in feedback, including the use of words, facial expressions, closeness, activities and rewards.
9 How do I use reinforcement strategies to reduce disruptive behaviour?	Reinforcement needs to be systematic over time. Reinforcing alternative positive behaviours and incompatible behaviours has been found to be useful.
10 Is it appropriate for me to use punishment?	Punishment does not have to be physical. It includes time out, loss of earned rewards (response cost), restitution and overcorrection. Any punishment should be paired with reinforcement of positive behaviours and within school policy. It should not be the first or prime management strategy.

Adapted from Daniels, 1998

Approaches to managing behaviours in mainstreamed classes

Prior to discussing some of the specific approaches that are available to teachers in mainstreamed classes, it is important to realise that the range of approaches is open to all teachers. There is no mystical set of strategies that operate in managing behaviours of students with additional needs. The strategies are the same as operate for all students. The difference is in the level of management and the consistency of monitoring the chosen management strategy.

Responding to the levels of behaviour requires a corresponding level of teacher response. Hence:

- low-level or infrequent misbehaviour requires a low-level teacher response
- moderate or frequent misbehaviour requires a consistent teacher response
- high-level or dangerous misbehaviour requires a strong, consistent teacher response.

At the low misbehaviour level, strategies may be dealt with using techniques such as reflecting, 'I' statements (for example: 'When you do that I feel …'), redirecting, checking class rules and asking the student 'What are you doing?' and 'What should you be doing?'. At this level, there is no need for specific management programs. Appropriate management at this level may avoid the necessity of moving to more defined management strategies. For many students, a reminder of the rules (previously established and understood by all) and a redirection to work may be sufficient to maintain appropriate social skills.

At the moderate misbehaviour level, consistent reminders of rules or consequences such as having to make up lost working time after short in-class timeout may be useful. At the major or repeated misbehaviour level, specific assessment of the behaviour through a formal assessment of the function of the behaviour and a formal management plan may be required. This is discussed in detail later in the chapter.

Another approach is to see the behaviour needs from the perspective of what the teacher does. In this model, the categories would be prevention, defusion, and follow-up (Colvin, Ainge & Nelson, 1997):

- *Prevention* – focus is on teaching desired behaviours and providing effective learning activities. The aim is to develop a positive classroom climate with productive pro-social behaviours.
- *Defusion* – focus is on addressing the behaviours after they have commenced. The goal is to arrest the behaviour before it escalates and to assist the student to resume classroom activities.
- *Follow-up* – focus is on providing consequences for the behaviour and assisting the student to terminate the behaviour and engage in appropriate behaviour on subsequent occasions.

Clearly the first approach is most effective in preventing behaviours, although all approaches will need to be used at some time.

Three key factors in any management program

Three important points need to be remembered in regard to any behaviour management approach:

- the students must want to change their behaviour if a behaviour management program is to work effectively
- the development of the process of change requires the active, ongoing involvement of the student
- the process of change must occur within the teaching–learning context.

These points are important because they re-emphasise the necessity of ensuring active involvement of students and the relationship between academic and social skills within the teaching–learning environment.

The following sections provide a discussion on possible approaches to addressing behaviour needs of all students, including those with additional needs, starting with specific management approaches for students with high behaviour support needs.

Developing specific behaviour plans

If students with additional needs require additional assistance in managing their behaviours over and above the classroom and school discipline systems, a specific behaviour management program may be needed. This may be either for a specific behaviour, such as increasing on-task behaviour or staying in seat, or for a cluster of behaviours, such as work habits or working cooperatively in the classroom. Any specific behaviour management program must be designed with the aim of incorporating the student into the normal management practices of the class and school to the greatest extent possible. This is important both for increasing the social acceptance of the student and for reducing the necessity for operating additional programs that reduce teacher time available for curriculum adaptations and attention to teaching strategies.

For some students in mainstreamed classrooms, initial behaviour management programs may not be in keeping with the principle of students wanting to change behaviours. It is recognised that the establishment of a foundation of acceptable classroom behaviour, particularly for students with behavioural/emotional problems, may require teacher-established programs, without student concurrence. It is important, however, that as soon as possible the student moves onto a behaviour management program that does involve their active willingness to participate.

The process of developing a specific behaviour program is based on a sequence of FBA leading into a BIP. The process comes from the intellectual disability literature and was originally used for students with challenging behaviours where the teacher was unable to gain information from the student directly because of communication and intellectual impairment. Hence the teacher was concerned to understand the function of the behaviour in order to develop an appropriate behaviour management plan. In recent years the FBA process has been used widely with students with emotional and behaviour problems in both regular and special settings. Until recently it was a mandated process in the American education system as part of the 1997 amendments to the Individuals with Disabilities Education Act (IDEA). Under these provisions, all students with additional needs in regular classes were required to have both a full FBA and a BIP developed if their behaviour in the regular class was identified as an issue in retaining their placement in regular education. While it has increased in use in Australian schools, there is no mandatory requirement for its use. As a result, the process has the advantage in Australia of being able to be adapted to current needs rather than having to be completed as a legal requirement.

The process is based on ten steps. Each is set out below with a description of what occurs in the process. The manuals for both FBA and BIP written by the Centre for Effective Collaboration and Practice (CECP) in the USA are available free of charge from their website. The three manuals cover an introduction to the FBA and BIP process (CECP, 1998a); conducting an FBA (CECP, 1998b); and, the development and implementation of

BIPs (CECP, 2000). There is also a vast range of American training manuals, videos, and workbooks available.

A clear example of the process for a student with additional needs in a regular classroom is provided by Hudson (2003). This will provide a clear illustration of the process in real life.

Functional behaviour assessment (FBA)

Functional assessment of challenging behaviours is critical to the design of effective interventions to decrease challenging behaviours in students with severe intellectual disability (Horner & Carr, 1997; Stephenson, 1997). Functional assessment is aimed at understanding the functions, or reasons, for the behaviours. In particular, it looks at factors in the environment that precede (antecedents) or reinforce (consequences) the occurrence of the behaviour. Functional assessment may include interviews, questionnaires, descriptive analysis followed by direct observation to confirm hypotheses (see Rosenberg et al., 2004 for a detailed description of techniques).

FBA involves examining the behaviours of the student before, during, and after the behaviour occurrence with the key aim of establishing the function of the behaviour. It covers the first six steps of the sequence. The process is normally conducted by a team rather than individual teachers as the process is extensive and requires up to two weeks to complete for students with severe behaviour problems.

- Step 1: *Describe and verify the seriousness of the problem behaviour*
  In this step the aim is to identify and define both the positive and problem behaviours through observation and discussion. Observation at this step may avoid the need for a full assessment or a behaviour plan if the teacher is able to make changes to the teaching process. If an FBA is still appropriate, the team moves to the next step.
- Step 2: *Define the problem behaviour*
  A succinct definition of the problem behaviour is essential. For example 'remain in seat' is an observable, measurable and modifiable behaviour while 'enjoy being in the class' is not. Only a precise definition allows consistent measurement of the behaviour. Information is needed on when and where the behaviour occurs, the conditions under which it does and doesn't occur, who is present, events that occur before, during and after the behaviour and any other behaviours that are associated with the behaviour.
- Step 3: *Collect information on possible functions of the behaviour*
  Data is collected from a wide variety of sources including direct observation in all settings where the behaviour occurs, interviews, logbooks, and educational and medical records. A wide variety of direct observation recording formats are available including ABC charts, scatterplots, and classroom observation sheets (see CECP Manual 2 for examples). A wider range of data collection procedures is also available in Rosenberg et al. (2004). A data collection sheet developed for use by local support teachers (behaviour) is shown in Box 6.2 and provides the opportunity to use momentary time sampling, in which the behaviour is observed at a specific time interval (in this case every 15 seconds). The observer looks at the student only at that instant of time and records the behaviour on a data sheet. The systematic data collection method ensures that an accurate pattern of the behaviour is obtained without bias. Again it is always useful to have another teacher or assistant carry out the data collection, as you are an integral part of the classroom

environment. If another person is not available you may be able to keep a record of the behaviour by putting marks on a piece of paper and then tallying up the frequency across the lesson. Remember that this self-collection method is subject to bias, as you are a player. Any systematic data collection needs to be supplemented by anecdotal recording of classroom interactions. As a behavioural approach is based on the cycle of antecedents-to-behaviour-to-consequences, systematic collection doesn't allow the teacher to note the

---

Box 6.2

Data collection sheet

Part A: Classroom observation

Fifteen minutes

This observation uses a 15-second momentary time sample. You should observe the target student on the fifteenth second and record the code for what he or she is doing. Code 1 refers to on-task behaviour, that is, the student doing what is expected of the class at that time. Codes 2 to 5 should be determined in discussion with the class teacher and should be the student's main presenting problems, for example, 'out of seat', 'physical aggression to other student' etc. Code * is used for behaviours not on the list and can be amplified in the comments section.

Student _____ Year _____ Teacher _____

School _____ Lesson _____

Observer _____ Date _____ Time _____

Observation   No. 1   No. 2   No. 3

Behaviours   Tally   Tally

1 .... _____   4 .... _____

2 .... _____   5 .... _____

3 .... _____   *Other .... _____

Other negative behaviours _____   Other positive behaviours _____

Codes   **Comments**

One line per minute × 15 minutes[†]

15"	30"	45"	60"

[†] Only 8 minutes shown on this sheet

>

Box 6.2 continued

Part B: Classroom observation

This observation takes place for the 15 minutes after the Part A, and comprises detailed notes on classroom interactions and classroom behaviours. Where possible note antecedents, behaviours and consequences.

_____
_____
_____
_____
_____
_____
_____
_____
_____
_____
_____
_____
_____
_____
_____
_____
_____
_____
_____
_____
_____
_____
_____
_____
_____
_____

classroom events that may precipitate classroom disturbances, such as teaching methods, outside disturbances, and classroom seating arrangements. By recording all activities in the room, some of the antecedents and consequences of the behaviour can be measured. The important point is that multiple data sources are used to ensure that a total picture emerges of the behaviour and its function.

- Step 4: *Analyse assessment data*
  The data collected in Step 3 is analysed by the team using either a data triangulation chart or a problem pathway analysis (see CECP, 1998b). The aim is to identify the precipitating events and the maintaining consequences, as well as the function of the behaviour. As discussed earlier in the chapter, the function is most often seen in terms of getting and/or avoiding something as a result of either a skills or performance deficit. It is also possible

through problem pathway analysis to map the behaviour from setting events to antecedents to the behaviour to the consequences that maintain the behaviour.

- Step 5: *Generate a hypothesis statement regarding the probable function of the behaviour*
  In this step a concise summary of the behaviour is developed, based on the information obtained during the FBA. This will provide the basis for the development of a BIP, if required.
- Step 6: *Test the hypothesis*
  A behaviour plan should not be commenced until the hypothesis statement is tested by implementing the actions on at least five consecutive occasions. If the behaviour changes as a result of the adaptations made, there is no need to proceed to the specific behaviour plan. However, if the hypothesis is confirmed, the plan can be developed and implemented.
  As a result of the functional assessment, there should be four outcomes:
  - an operational definition of the behaviour(s)
  - identification of the variables that predict both the occurrence and non-occurrence of the behaviour
  - identification of what maintains the behaviour
  - verification of the predictors and maintainers of the behaviour.

Behaviour improvement plan (BIP)

The BIP is designed to provide a positive intervention that will develop appropriate behaviours while reducing or eliminating the challenging behaviours that prevent successful learning in the class. These are addressed in Steps 7–10 of the FBA–BIP process (see CECP, 2000).

- Step 7: *Develop the plan*
  The same team that conducted the FBA should develop the plan. It should have specific behaviour expectations to meet the skills or performance deficits of the student, be built on the experiences of previous interventions and of course be positive in focus. The plan will contain both long- and short-term goals.
- Step 8: *Monitor the faithfulness of the plan's implementation*
  The monitoring provides a check on the consistency and accuracy of the plan's implementation by the staff. This is often done through a checklist completed by team members at the BIP team meeting.
- Step 9: *Evaluate the effectiveness of the plan*
  Comparing the baseline data collected in the FBA with BIP performance data provides a demonstration of behaviour change. It also provides a measure of the movement through short-term goals towards the long-term goal.
- Step 10: *Modify the plan*
  The plan is considered to be complete when the long-term goal is met or, in the case of the goal not being met, the plan is no longer appropriate. Data from Steps 8 and 9 will provide the evidence for decisions in Step 10. If the behaviour has not changed in the desired direction, it may be necessary to conduct a new FBA based on the new data and develop a further plan or a revised plan.

The discussion above provides a brief introduction to the methods of establishing a specific intervention to develop or increase positive social behaviours, not only for students with challenging behaviours, but for any student in the class whose behaviour is of serious concern.

The steps in the FBA and BIP are reflected in the case study developed by Student Management Consultants in the ACT (Box 6.3). Tim is a young boy entering kindergarten whose behaviour, resulting from a special need, required an FBA and the development of a BIP. Notice that the FBA identified information from the grandparent that can be incorporated into the activities of the school. The large number of failed foster care placements and disruptive parenting can be used in considering the function of the behaviour and in developing an appropriate BIP.

Box 6.3

Case study: Tim

Tim entered kindergarten (the first year of school in the ACT system) eagerly this year. He loves to play and delighted in all the manipulatives and puzzles that were new to him and tended to play alone for the first week. Tim was new to the area, and hadn't gone to preschool with the other children, so his teacher predicted that it might take some time for him to get to know everyone. One play session, early in the second week of school, Tim was confronted by another child who wanted to use the Mobilo set. Tim yelled at the child and threw a large wooden block at his head. The child cried, went to the teacher, and Tim continued playing happily with the Mobilo as if nothing had happened.

Many more of these aggressive incidents were to follow. The situation had worsened such that Tim was violent nearly every day, would not participate in any activities except playing alone with a toy of his choice, and sometimes ran away from school. Tim is a good climber and tended to spend time scaling trees, drainpipes and walking along the roof of school buildings. The school had started suspending him, which Tim didn't mind either. Tim's teacher was in her first year of teaching, so was starting to panic. Tim wouldn't talk to her or anyone else about his behaviour. Those who persisted were kicked, bitten or spat at. The school could see

they needed assistance working out a plan for Tim, so they made a referral for behaviour support.

A team was set up to conduct a Functional Behavioural Assessment. Each person had clear roles towards gathering information towards analysis and developing an Individual Learning Plan within the month. Tim's class teacher went about tracking patterns on a simple timetable, coding different behaviours. She determined that Tim's aggressive behaviours were worse in the literacy block and at recess. Hardly any incidents ever occurred at lunchtime when Tim played happily on the library computers. The Deputy Principal and Student Management Consultant undertook a structured interview with Tim's grandmother, ascertaining that she was indeed his prime carer, while his mother and father were in jail for drug offences. She divulged that she didn't believe Tim had a bond with anyone, had hardly ever seen his parents and just lived from moment to moment, doing what he had to meet his need at the time.

Tim had also experienced six foster care placements, all of which had broken down. The Student Management Consultant undertook direct observations with a view to determining some simple strategies that could be used to engage Tim in positive social and academic experiences.

>

Box 6.3 continued

The information led the team to formulate a simple plan, with a two-week review period. Also, a crisis management plan was written, detailing the steps to be taken if Tim was violent. The initial positive goals were to engage Tim in Guided Reading each day for five minutes, and to ask for permission when leaving the room. A Special Teacher's Assistant was employed to support the teacher in engaging Tim during the literacy block. To begin with, the plan was highly behaviourist. Tim's favourite toys were put out of sight and he was shown a smiley face chart and a sand timer. If he could sit with the kids for five minutes, he would get until the next break with the toys. Stamp charts were used and highly desirable rewards to get through the two weeks. However, the real breakthrough came with a strategy we called 'time with Tim'. Each day, the class teacher sat with Tim between 8:45 and 9 am talking to him about her life, asking questions about his interests and reinforcing his daily goals. It was through these conversations that the class teacher found out crucial information like the fact that he hardly ever ate breakfast. She began letting him eat when he was hungry as long as he stayed in class.

Gradually, Tim spent more time in class. He started to like his teacher and wanted to be near her. For play times, the Deputy Principal developed and resourced an alternative play program, which looks like a highly supervised playroom with a focus on incidental social skilling through modelling and giving children feedback on their interactions. Tim's teacher was released from playground duties in order to accompany Tim to the program, then gradually reduced her involvement. Tim still uses this program, and has started allowing other children to be near him when he plays.

Tim's mum is out of jail now and he lives with her in a treatment oriented half-way house. She continues to receive support in developing parenting skills and Tim is the happiest anyone has seen him. He has even started taking readers home and can write his name.

Tim is now diagnosed as having an attachment disorder. Those working with him know that he will need support for some time to come. However, through supports put in place at the school level, Tim has learned that people care, and the people around him have learned that all the hard work is definitely worthwhile.

Specific techniques used in increasing positive behaviours

Positive reinforcement

This is the most common approach used because it both increases the likelihood of the positive behaviour occurring and also promotes positive relationships between the teacher and the student. The important point about reinforcement is that it must follow the demonstration of the target behaviour. Reinforcement is given immediately after the behaviour occurs for maximum reinforcement, then faded (gradually reduced) to delayed reinforcement as the behaviour takes shape.

Reinforcers commonly come from three main groups: tangible (food, toys), social (praise, attention) and activity (free time, early marks). The biggest difficulty is that the reinforcer must be sufficiently powerful for the students to want to change their behaviour, but still remain realistic for the degree of behaviour change required. One way of ensuring this is to involve the students in the selection of the reinforcer, while another is to provide a menu of reinforcers that the student can select from. If this is the case, all reinforcers must be available to select from and the student allowed freedom of choice.

The complication is that a reinforcer used in a behaviour program for an individual student may cause resentment in other students when they do not have access to the reinforcer. If this occurs, the teacher can either allow the focus student to earn reinforcers for the whole class or, if this is inappropriate, offer the remainder of the class other reinforcers at appropriate times. However, having the target student earning reinforcers for the class can sometimes have the undesired effect of that student 'controlling' the class through control of the rewards.

Student developed improvement plans

A technique that is very effective for students who are able to be involved in the behaviour process is to allow them to develop a plan for behaviour improvement. This places ownership for the process directly with the student. As will be discussed later in the chapter, having the student state in their own words (student language – see Chapter 4) personalises the planning process. Having students rate their performance also ensures they are active and realistic in their assessment of their own behaviour. To assist the student the teacher may run a parallel rating scale in the initial weeks of the program to scaffold the monitoring process. Figure 6.1 provides an example of a self-monitoring sheet for a student. The plan provides for up to four positive behaviours (identified with the teacher as part of the BIP) as well as a signed commitment to achieve the goals. The format provides for daily monitoring by the student.

Figure 6.1 My plan for improvement

Source: Olga Nisbet, School Counsellor NSW

Reducing negative behaviours

Reducing negative or inappropriate behaviours can occur through extinction, response cost, or through the use of aversives.

Extinction

This is a procedure that is often poorly used in classrooms. Also called planned ignoring, it involves not providing reinforcement for particular behaviours. For example, if a student is calling out in class, the teacher may choose to ignore the behaviour until it stops. This will work only if:

- the student is aware that the teacher is ignoring the behaviour
- the teacher genuinely can continue to ignore the behaviour until it is extinguished
- no other class members pay attention to the behaviour
- teacher attention is a reinforcer for the behaviour.

Such a combination of factors is usually not possible, and the extinction procedure fails. The other main problem with extinction is that it doesn't teach any positive behaviours, it only reduces an undesirable one. This problem can be overcome if the teacher rewards positive behaviours concurrently with the extinction procedure.

Response cost

Response cost can be part of a token economy. A token economy operates when the student earns points for positive behaviour, which can be exchanged later for a reinforcer (delayed reinforcement). Response cost occurs when the student loses a predetermined number of points for not complying with the behaviour program. For example, a student earns ten points for completing work on time and an additional five points for it being neat and five more points for it being correct. The student may also lose five points if the work is not completed on time. The latter is the response cost.

It is essential that response cost not be used in the initial stage of a token economy, for two reasons. First, at the initial stage the aim is to develop positive behaviours, and response cost involves a punisher. Second, there is a danger in the initial stages of the program that the student may lose more points than have been gained, and a token economy cannot operate in a deficit!

Aversives

Aversives are often portrayed as being a type of physical punishment, yet they include many strategies that we take for granted in regular school discipline models. These include the use of timeout (isolation) and reprimands. It is important to remember that timeout must be timeout from reinforcement and that the student should not receive reinforcement from either the teacher or other students. Timeout does not occur when the teacher continually reminds the student that he or she is not part of the group and will not be listened to. For some students, this only reinforces and maintains the behaviour.

Timeout can take three main forms in school behaviour management programs: in-seat timeout; timeout in another part of the classroom; and, time out of the classroom. The simplest form of timeout is for the student to remain in-seat and not receive reinforcement. In this way the student continues with the task. Timeout in the classroom involves the student being sent to a separate area of the room where the student plays no part in the class activities. In many primary classrooms, this may be an area behind a storage shelf where the student is unsighted by the remainder of the class.

Timeout in a separate area of the school is commonly used in school discipline policies, particularly where the school uses a Glasser approach. The greatest problem is that many schools forget that timeout is designed to provide no stimulation, so that the student wants to return to the classroom and receive reinforcement from the teacher and students. If the classroom provides an environment that is not academically or socially stimulating for the student, the concept of timeout fails. As a technique within a specific behaviour management program for younger students, where the bond between teacher and student is greater, timeout can be an effective tool provided it is used infrequently and for short periods.

Reprimands are commonly used as a management tool both within specific management programs and in general teaching, as it is one of very few in-class management techniques available to class teachers. However, reprimands are very ineffective if the reprimand is continued over time or the reprimand becomes the beginning of a power struggle. Reprimands have been shown to be very ineffective if they are used as a form of nagging, or as the main type of teacher interaction with students. Studies have shown that students with behaviour problems often receive more teacher attention than other students, but that attention is negative and brief. Constant harping reprimands such as 'Sit down', 'Get on with your work', 'I told you to start work', are more likely to maintain the behaviour through attention than to reduce it. Reprimands can be used effectively when they are simply and clearly stated, and not open to discussion. Remember that the reason for constant reprimands may result from the learning and teaching in the room not engaging the student, and the student may be communicating this through inappropriate behaviour.

Behaviour management in inclusive classrooms: Meeting the needs of a diverse range of students

A clear example of the procedures for managing difficult behaviours of students with additional needs in the class is provided in Carpenter and McKee-Higgins (1996). In a class of 25 students, six had additional needs including speech/language delays, learning difficulties, hearing impairment and emotional/behavioural problems. The arrival of an additional student with emotional disturbance (Alex) provided the catalyst for the breakdown in the classroom management program.

Carpenter and McKee-Higgins describe how the chronic minor behaviour problems such as out-of-seat, speaking out of turn and over the top of others, and touching other students developed from minor to major proportions that threatened the positive atmosphere of the classroom as well as the effectiveness of instruction (1996, p. 198). When the teacher examined the problems by systematically gathering data on the behaviours and the environmental factors that preceded or followed the undesired and desired behaviours, Alex was found to contribute 50 per cent of the off-task behaviours. The teacher also identified that the main off-task behaviours occurred in large group instruction lessons. She also found that most teacher interactions were corrective and negative, averaging 6:1 negative to positive statements. Using a systematic behaviour management approach similar to the methods discussed above, the teacher was able to identify reinforcers for the student and also to

increase her rate of positive responses to Alex. The outcomes for Alex were that he was able to reduce his off-task behaviour and remain in class for the whole day.

There are three important outcomes from this study that highlight the issues for students with additional needs in a classroom:

- When behaviour management programs only marginally meet the needs of students without additional needs in a classroom, the inclusion of students with additional needs may amplify existing problems.
- Although teachers may know about classroom management methods, they may be too close to challenging behaviour situations to see clearly what is happening. Having a collaborative or support person assist in both the FBA process and as a critical friend in the BIP implementation can assist in improving outcomes for both the teacher and students.
- We need to use known and effective practices to be more responsive to all students' learning characteristics.

Preventing escalation of behaviour

One of the most difficult teacher skills in a classroom is the prevention of behaviour escalation and confrontation with individual students (Colvin, Ainge & Nelson, 1997). Escalation of behaviour often occurs without the teacher being aware that the process is occurring until the cycle of confrontation is underway.

Behaviour escalation is defined as an occasion where a group of problem behaviours occur in a sequential pattern in which successive responses are of increasing severity or intensity (Shukla-Mehta & Albin, 2003). The sequence usually begins with less severe problems that can be responded to more easily. Through behaviour escalation, however, more severe responses by the teacher and student replace the initial behaviours and the result can be behaviours that are dangerous to people and/or cause property damage. The result of behaviour escalation is the cessation of learning in the classroom and the modelling of inappropriate behaviours to the class.

The behaviour of some students with behaviour-focused additional needs is designed to develop a specific response from the teacher and they will ensure that the teacher provides that response. This will lead to refusal to comply, which will then be escalated into more serious behaviours and confrontation. Here the intent is deliberate on the part of the student. For students with special learning needs, who may escalate behaviours out of frustration or lack of alternative management skills, behaviour escalation is often used as an argument for their permanent removal from the class. The aim for the classroom teacher should be to focus on developing positive behaviours that avoid behaviour escalation rather than responding to it after it occurs.

Shukla-Mehta and Albin (2003) provide 11 strategies that may assist teachers in avoiding behaviour escalation and confrontation:

- reinforce calm and on-task behaviour
- know the triggers
- pay attention to anything unusual about the student's behaviour
- do not escalate along with the student
- offer students opportunities to display responsible behaviour
- intervene early in the sequence
- know the functions of problem behaviours
- use good judgement about which behaviours to punish
- use extinction procedures wisely
- teach students socially appropriate behaviours to replace the problem behaviours
- teach academic survival skills and set students up for success.

Each of these approaches provides a strategy for the teacher. However, the combination of strategies for individual students will be based on the specific situation the teacher is dealing with, particularly whether the confrontation is with a student with behaviour-focused additional needs or learning-focused additional needs.

Teaching social skills

What are social skills? They are complex and include overt, observable behaviours as well as problem-solving behaviours; they often occur in difficult social situations (Elksnin & Elksnin, 1998). Elksnin and Elksnin have documented the changes that have occurred in our approach to teaching social skills from the time when schools saw the responsibility for teaching social skills as being a parental role to the realisation that academic success depends to a considerable extent on the social skills of students. Elksnin and Elksnin identify six main types of social skills (Table 6.2).

As discussed earlier, social skills deficits can be seen as resulting from one of three categories (Gresham, 1998):

- social skills acquisition deficits (students do not have appropriate skills in their repertoire)

- social skills performance deficits (they have the behaviour and either choose not to use the behaviour, or don't realise that they need to use the skill)
- social skills fluency deficits (they use the behaviour in the setting in which it is reinforced but fail to use it in other situations).

Table 6.2 Types of social skills

Interpersonal behaviours	These behaviours are 'friendship-making skills', such as introducing yourself, joining in, asking a favour, offering to help, giving and accepting compliments, and apologising
Peer-related social skills	These are skills valued by peers that are associated with peer acceptance – examples include working cooperatively, asking for and receiving information, and correctly assessing another's emotional state
Teacher-pleasing social skills	These are behaviours associated with school success and include following directions, doing your best work, and listening to the teacher
Self-related behaviours	These skills allow a student to assess a social situation, select an appropriate skill, and determine the skill's effectiveness Other self-related behaviours include following through, dealing with stress, understanding feelings, and controlling anger
Assertiveness skills	These behaviours allow students to express their needs without resorting to aggression
Communication skills	Communication skills include listener responsiveness, turn-taking, maintaining conversational attention, and giving the speaker feedback

(Source: Adapted from Elksnin & Elksnin, 1998, p. 132)

For some students with additional needs, where the social skill is not part of their repertoire, there may be a need for explicit teaching of that skill at the individual level prior to incorporating the skill into the general classroom setting. The challenge for teachers of students in the second category lies in those who have the skill and choose not to use it. Here the key issue is that reinforcement for appropriate use of the strategy is critical. Returning to the concept of the function of the behaviour discussed earlier, unless the student 'gets' or 'avoids' better with the social skills you wish to promote, they will maintain the existing social skills. In the last category are those students where the social skills are demonstrated only in specific situations, those where they are expected and reinforced. The critical issue for some students with additional needs is to use those skills across situations and without prompting or reinforcement.

Teaching social skills

Teaching social skills has long been considered a critical factor for all students, but particularly those with additional needs. There are two main approaches to teaching social skills. The first is to teach social skills as a specific curriculum, including the use of cooperative learning activities. The second approach suggested is to blend social and academic skills through the use of cooperative learning activities in which the social skills are not explicitly taught but develop within the implementation of the academic program. As discussed above, the type of social skill to be learned, the type of deficit the student demonstrates, and the resources available will determine the chosen approach.

Most social skills instructional curriculums use a format of (Williams & Reisberg, 2003):

- advanced organiser – explanation of the skill and the steps in the learning of the task
- model – modelling of the skill by the teacher or other students
- guided practice – the teacher guides the student through the skill, acting as a coach and reinforcing the self-instruction of the student
- independent performance – the student practises the skill alone with the teacher observing the skill but without the level of guidance
- generalisation – performance occurs in a variety of situations to reinforce the use of the skills in those settings not just the initial instructional setting.

The format emphasises some key instructional components. First, there is a strong emphasis on the transfer of the skill from the teacher to the student through scaffolding. At the initial step, the teacher poses the skill and throughout the steps of the procedure, that skill is transferred to the student. Scaffolding is a very powerful instructional tool for social skill acquisition, particularly as the teacher can slow down or speed up the rate at which that transfer of skill can occur. For students with high level additional needs in the class the process can take a considerable time. Another critical ingredient is the role of teacher or other student demonstration of the skill, as modelling is a powerful tool to demonstrate appropriate behaviours, particularly when the model is another student. Finally, the use of self-instruction is important as it provides the student with the ability to talk through the steps in the skill. One word of caution: if possible, have students use their own words for the steps in the social skill, rather than the teacher's words. By using their personal student language, the steps have greater meaning and lead to a sense of ownership of the process, rather than being the teacher's steps.

Social skills training programs have been used to teach a wide variety of skills, although the outcomes have often been less than optimal (see Gresham, 1998; Gresham, Sugai & Horner, 2001). Programs range from the teaching of specific behaviours such as eye contact and facial expressions, to broader, more complex social skills such as making friends. While earlier studies sought to teach these skills in isolation and then generalise them to social settings in the classroom, recent studies have incorporated cognitive and environmental influences in programs. One of these is self-efficacy or the belief we have that we can do a task successfully. As many mainstreamed students have had negative social experiences in classrooms, their self-efficacy may be lowered and hence they are unwilling to persevere if obstacles or rejection occurs.

A number of commercial programs are available to teach social skills. These include Walker's *ACCEPTS* (Walker, 1983) and *ACCESS* social skills curriculum (Walker et al., 1988) and Goldstein's Prepare Curriculum (Goldstein, 2000), *Skillstreaming the adolescent* (Goldstein & McGinnis, 1980) and *Skillstreaming the elementary school child* (McGinnis & Goldstein, 1984). All of these programs are American. Many teachers prefer not to use packaged programs for social skills training, often because of their somewhat artificial format and their American approach. As a result, teachers use ideas from a variety of sources and develop a program that meets their own needs. Kauffman et al. (1995) suggest that any teacher-developed program should be scrutinised using the following questions:

- What are the skills that need to be learned?
- Am I actually teaching social competence through requiring students to interact?
- Am I teaching skills explicitly?
- Can I generalise the skills to other classroom settings?
- Is the approach I am using meeting the needs of the mainstreamed students?

Training in social competence and social skills does not have to take place in the classroom. Gow, Balla and Calvez (1995) examined the social integration of students within a leisure club. Such a non-school environment provides the opportunity to interact in less structured settings in which students can choose their own directions in open-end activities. In this way, Gow, Balla and Calvez (1995) argue, students are more likely to develop personal and social competencies because they are interacting at a variety of levels rather than at the one level, as may occur in the classroom.

An excellent series of Australian resources is that by McGrath (see McGrath, 1997; McGrath & Edwards, 2000; McGrath & Francey, 1991; McGrath & Noble, 1993). As a result, teachers use ideas from a variety of sources and develop a program that meets their own needs. An excellent American website with practical ideas for teaching social skills is <www.cccoe.net/social>, which provides access to many teaching ideas.

The final word on the teaching of social skills is best stated by Walker, Stieber and Bullis (1997, p. 304):

> Our belief is that most social skills interventions are offered for far too short a time and in an inconsistent instructional manner in order to shape positive behaviour. To be truly effective, social skills interventions should be planned and offered in a similar fashion as any other academic course of study and should be considered in terms of years rather than weeks, as is now the norm.

Enhancing peer acceptance through classroom activities to involve all students

Throughout this chapter, the theme of increasing social integration of students with additional needs in mainstream classes has focused on strategies to overcome demonstrated lack of social skills by students with additional needs, either through management programs or through skills training. Development of positive social interactions in the class will be best achieved by: developing cooperation and support between students; teaching students the specific work-related skills and social skills needed; and, consistently monitoring the application of those skills.

This section focuses on methods of ensuring that other students have the skills of accepting these students in their class and hence prevent the rejection and isolation that mainstreamed students can face.

Cooperative learning activities

Cooperative learning is based on three key ingredients: small groups of students working together; making explicit efforts to help each other learn; and, share in the evaluation of learning through group evaluation (Jenkins et al., 2003). In their review of cooperative learning and students with additional needs, Jenkins et al. found that the approach is used widely in elementary schools, particularly in reading and mathematics. Like all learning–teaching strategies used in regular education, its success with students has been mixed from a research perspective, although Jenkins et al. found that teachers were much more positive about its use. Jenkins et al. quote a wide variety of teacher comments. The key benefits identified by teachers were improved self-esteem, the security that comes from being a member of a group, and the higher success rate and improved quality of completed work. This comes as part of the cycle of improved self-esteem leading to stronger efforts, leading to improved learning outcomes, as the students were not on their own and not singled out. The group provided the support they needed in areas they were weak in and they were part of the successful outcome of the group. Interestingly, teachers commonly did not use individual accountability or assessment when students with additional needs were included in the tasks, although this is recommended in the literature (Antil et al., 1998).

One advantage of cooperative learning strategies is that they provide the opportunity for students with additional needs to interact with other students on a less formal level than occurs in the normal classroom learning environment. Other benefits from cooperative learning activities include less rejection by other students, increased motivation to work with other students, increased socialisation with peers, and the development of higher order thinking skills that are related to acting in the role of teacher and facilitator rather than recipient, as more commonly occurs in classrooms.

Another important strategy that occurs within cooperative learning situations is the opportunity to use student language. A difficulty many mainstreamed students have in the regular classroom is understanding the middle class language structures and vocabulary used by the class teacher (see Chapter 4). Small group work provides the opportunity to use student language, which employs the language structures and vocabulary of the students. This translation of teacher language may increase the understanding of content and provide the mainstreamed student with an opportunity to communicate at a less formal level.

There are a number of cooperative learning activities that can be used in the classroom such as Student Teams Achievement Divisions (STAD), Team Accelerated Instruction (TAI), Jigsaw, Think-Pair-Share and Group Investigations (see Arthur, Gordon & Butterfield, 2003, p. 46). Each approach varies the method of involvement of the individual students. In some cases, individual students contribute information to the group, while in others the group divides the workload. Students should have experience in as wide a variety of roles as possible, depending on their ability. Hence a student with additional needs may be responsible for timekeeping rather than for reporting the findings of the group's work. In many cases, students with additional needs may require a coach or a team member who assists by supporting them within the group. The findings of Jenkins et al. (2003), however, suggest that teachers often don't use structured approaches or modifications, leaving the group members to make the adjustments and modifications themselves within the framework of 'cooperation' in learning.

Cooperative learning is not a panacea for students with additional needs in regular classes, particularly in the case of those students who will not work in a small group environment. One teacher-perceived disadvantage of cooperative learning activities is the potential to lose control of the class. As discussed earlier, some teachers fear a loss of control when they do not have direct management of all students. Interestingly, in the case of the teachers in the study, there was recognition that no other strategy worked more effectively. Clearly, for students to work in cooperative learning activities, there may need to be direct and explicit teaching of the skills before cooperative learning, rather than relying on the group to teach those skills.

Using cognitive and metacognitive strategies

Cognitive and metacognitive approaches operate on the assumption that students are aware of their environment and are able to make behaviour decisions based on the information they obtain. For some students with additional needs, the decisions they make are based either on using incorrect information or through incorrect interpretation of the information. Hence a mainstreamed student who mistakes a teacher's expression of annoyance as being supportive has made a cognitive error and will likely suffer negative consequences. While these errors could be corrected through a specific behaviour management program or through a social skills training program, they could also be addressed through a cognitive or metacognitive behaviour program.

Cognitive strategies

Cognitive programs rely on teaching students a specific series of steps, which they learn and then apply themselves. Scaffolding is often used, as is verbal self-instruction as discussed in the earlier section on social skills instruction.

Self-management approaches can also be used with students with developmental disabilities. Koegel, Harrower and Koegel (1999) reported on a study of two students with severe language and cognitive disabilities in kindergarten classes in separate schools. One student was taught by a support person and then prompted by that support person to use a self-management strategy of placing an X in a printed box each time he was successfully engaged in a task. Reinforcement by a support person was continuous at first and then faded to the point where the student could complete the self-reinforcement task alone. The task is considered as cognitive self-reinforcement because the technique was determined by the adult, taught and reinforced by the adult until the student could perform the skill without adult assistance or reinforcement.

Mnemonics have also been used successfully used with students (Williams & Reisberg, 2003). Anger management was taught concurrently with an academic using the mnemonic CALM:

C   Can you tell when you are starting to get upset and angry?
A   Are there any techniques you can use to help yourself calm down?
L   Look at those, choose the best one, and try it!
M   Monitor yourself – is it working? If it is – great! If not, try again or try another one. (p. 208)

In this case the strategy has a self-monitoring component also, but still relies on a teacher to train the strategy initially.

Self-management

The involvement of self is an important skill for all students, but particularly for students with additional needs as it takes the responsibility for management of the behaviour support away from the adult and places it on the student. Importantly this cannot occur without the training and scaffolding discussed previously.

Self-management is any set of purposeful and systematic responses by an individual that changes or maintains some aspect of the student's repertoire of behaviours (Daly & Ranalli, 2003). It includes self-monitoring (including self-recording and self-observation), self-instruction and self-reinforcement (Schloss & Smith, 1998). Studies of students with additional needs (see Daly & Ranalli, 2003, p. 31) have shown that positive academic and social changes can occur through the use of self-monitoring. When students are engaged in self-monitoring of social behaviours, research has shown that they tend to improve that behaviour, even if there are discrepancies in the accuracy of the data collected.

The inability of some students with additional needs to self-regulate and self-determine is a characteristic that distinguishes them from other students in the class. Mithaug (2002) taught a group of students with a variety of multiple additional needs to use self-regulation skills in completing academic tasks. Students were taught to set goals of the amount of independent work they completed in a set time period on a choice card, self-record the number of tasks completed and self-evaluate their performance by comparing the number of tasks chosen with the number of tasks completed. Data collected by Mithaug demonstrated that students' correct self-regulation was highest when they made choices rather than during baseline or teacher's choice phases, as were the percentages of work units completed. Importantly, as well as promoting positive work habits, independence and increased on-task time, it also allows the teacher more time to interact with other students.

Earlier in Figure 6.1 we saw how students can track their performance as part of a self-monitoring procedure. The advantages of this approach include a clearer and more immediate picture of the behaviour improvement, a stronger reinforcement, the involvement of the student in the selection of the behaviours to be monitored and, perhaps most importantly, a measure against their own behaviours rather than against others'.

Metacognitive approaches

The difference between cognitive and metacognitive approaches is that metacognitive approaches place greater responsibility on the student to plan a strategy and to monitor its implementation. While a cognitive approach teaches specific steps for the student to work through, a metacognitive approach places emphasis on the student developing a plan for behaviour change, initially with teacher guidance.

One Australian metacognitive approach is the concept of Process Based Instruction (PBI) (Ashman & Conway, 1998). The approach is based on the student, assisted by the teacher, developing a plan to modify specific behaviours. The importance of a plan is that it must provide a series of actions and checking steps that will allow the student to work through the plan unassisted. In a sense, the plan is like a staircase and the student works through the plan in a similar fashion to an object rolling down the stairs. The concept of a plan includes four components: cueing, acting, monitoring, and verifying. The monitoring step provides the metacognitive feature in that students are responsible for checking their progress. An important feature of this approach is that it uses student language in the plan, rather than using a predetermined set of steps with fixed terminology, as occurs in a cognitive approach.

The use of cognitive and metacognitive approaches to teach positive social interactions to mainstreamed students may need to be preceded by more specific approaches such as those discussed earlier in the chapter. In this way students can progress through stages of growth in social skills. Not all students will reach the point of being able to plan and monitor their behaviour change, although it is important to have access to the broadest range of strategies.

Peer tutoring

Peer tutoring has been widely used both for social and academic support of students with additional needs. Traditionally students with additional needs have been assisted as tutees in the model, with benefits across a wide range of academic content areas. However, the benefits do not flow only from receiving tutoring. Students with low additional needs can improve their self-esteem through serving as tutors, as they are engaged in the task and are also developing their social skills at the same time (Fulk & King, 2001). The guided practice sessions with peer tutoring are particularly important as they maximise student involvement in the subject content.

The key implementation guidelines recommended by Fulk and King (2001) include:

- explaining the purpose and rationale for the technique, stressing the opportunity for practice and on-task behaviour
- stressing collaboration and cooperation rather than competition
- selecting the content and materials for the tutoring sessions
- training the roles of tutor and tutee, particularly feedback, correction and data recording
- modelling appropriate behaviours
- providing practice of the tutor and tutee skills with feedback
- supervising and reinforcing appropriate student roles.

While the skills of peer tutoring are often implemented in academic subjects, the strong positive social skills component is the critical factor in the success of peer tutoring. Again it stresses the critical link between academic and social skills.

Buddies

A more general relationship between students with additional needs and their class peers is the use of peer buddies. Buddies support can be used for a wide range of activities. Copeland et al. (2002) identified a range of buddy activities such as:

- teaching class routines
- reading tests and recording answers
- paraphrasing text
- helping with augmentative communication device
- modelling joining an activity
- teaching the use of a picture sequence
- showing how to surf the net
- taking notes for the buddy and discussing them
- supporting during cooperative learning activities
- getting the buddy involved in general activities out of class.

In a study conducted with teachers in secondary schools, Copeland et al. (2002) found that the majority of the benefits of peer buddies noted by special education teachers were social-related including increased opportunities for interaction, and acquisition of age-appropriate skills. Regular class teachers more commonly reported benefits that related to academic or functional skills, the concept of 'learning useful skills' (p. 17). This difference is important, as it reflects differing priorities teachers have for social inclusion, and needs to be understood in planning activities to support positive social inclusion. However, all teachers did see increased positive relationships, enhanced personal growth and fewer disruptions as a result of the buddies program.

As discussed earlier, peer buddies facilitate increased opportunities for students with additional needs to form positive relationships. As one teacher in the study commented: 'Prior to receiving peer supports these students tended to isolate themselves from the general education students. I have noticed that they are now more willing (and seeking) to contact students outside their special education group.' (Copeland et al., 2002, p. 19).

Importantly Copeland et al. (2002) identify that peer buddy roles need to be based on the individual requirements of the student with additional needs so that the relationship is not one of supporter and supportee, but one of a buddy. Hence the reverse role of the student with additional needs as the tutor is also important.

Secondary teachers provided a number of challenges and warnings on the use of buddies. Planning and timetabling the peer buddy time was difficult, particularly if the student with additional needs was withdrawn from class for frequent or lengthy periods of time. Having the student with additional needs in and consistently involved in the regular program was seen as important. Preparation of buddies was required to overcome a wide range of difficulties such as buddies not knowing the content well enough to provide support, not trying to be over-helpful in doing the tasks for the buddy, failing to monitor the buddy's performance and not turning up to provide the support when required. If these issues were managed, teachers were very positive about the effects of peer buddies in secondary schools.

Friendship activities

Developing friendships is an important way of maintaining positive social relationships in the classroom. Friendship will not always develop spontaneously and may need to be actively encouraged or taught. Ways of doing this include: fostering relationships by using cooperative learning strategies or pairing students to work together; encouraging support in the class through discussing ways of helping a new class member settle in; teaching peer support and friendship skills; encouraging all students to recognise individual differences in their lives; and, providing good role models.

Box 6.4 provides a case study of Simon, a boy with additional needs in secondary school, who has considerable difficulties in developing friendships with other students as a result of anxiety. The strategies that were developed focused on both an individual program for Simon as well as a classroom focus on social justice issues and bullying. The aim is not to change Simon's behaviours completely but to work towards his being engaged with the curriculum in the classroom. The development of one friend is the beginning of a longer process that may lead to greater involvement in the school. It also demonstrates the need for teacher friendship and trust.

Box 6.4

Case study: Simon

Simon is 13 years old. He lives at home with his older brother, mum and stepfather. He likes the Internet and electronic games and can spend hours playing on the computer. He has a mild intellectual disability and hasn't been performing well at school, skipping most classes each day. He wears glasses, which get broken a lot and he can't work effectively without them. He can talk for a long time about subjects of interest to him.

Simon is in Year 7 at his local high school. The school's Student Welfare Coordinator recommended behaviour support after a series of incidents in which Simon was aggressive towards other students. On the referral form, it was written that Simon had knocked a student over resulting in a broken arm, and had also thrown a garbage bin at a student in the playground.

By observing Simon in each of his classes and the playground, it became apparent that he had no real friends at school. Through chatting informally, Simon was happy to talk about his 'cyberspace friends' and showed no interest at all in making connections with young people in his grade. Also of concern was the frequency of derogatory comments directed at Simon by other students.

The school counsellor suggested that Simon had an anxiety problem, and possibly depression, centring on his feeling of rejection by peers. Each of his violent incidents had been a response to being humiliated in front of others. As a result, Simon often ran away from classes and hid. He spent most lunchtimes playing on a computer in the library. His mother reported that Simon often said he wanted to kill himself.

A major focus of the support put into place for Simon was around promoting his feeling of safety and belonging at school. A team was formed incorporating a selected group of adults in Simon's life (his mother, his home group teacher, the Student Welfare Coordinator, the student management consultant and the school counsellor). Members of this group met

>

Box 6.4 continued

approximately every three weeks with Simon to discuss progress, concerns and articulate goals. Only one goal at a time was highlighted, and strategies were always discussed with Simon in planning meetings. Goals over the course of the program included going to two classes a day, talking with an adult about his feelings each day and interacting with at least one classmate each lesson.

Simon himself monitored the plan by filling in a matrix in conjunction with the Student Management Consultant, who visited twice a week for a review discussion with him. Strategies such as self-removal to a designated, yet supervised place when anxious and saying one genuinely nice thing each lesson to a peer replaced Simon's usual strategies of 'going berko'. His classmates began to notice that their provocations didn't have as much of an effect in producing the show they were used to from Simon. The Home Group teacher took Simon's case as an opportunity to implement class discussions focusing on social justice issues. The Student Welfare Coordinator began a whole-school blitz on bullying. Simon's mother saw this as a huge show of support and supported the move by reinforcing each goal with Simon at home.

By involving Simon in every step of the 12 week behaviour support program, from the initial meeting, through the observation phase, the development of goals and strategies and reviews of his progress, he developed ownership and ultimately, much more responsibility for his behaviour. Simon has not been suspended for two whole school terms, and now manages to attend nearly every class each week. He has made one friend, who has similar interests to him. While he has no interest in developing friendships with most of his peers, he can at least be in the same classroom or playground without experiencing major anxiety. He has three adults in the school whom he trusts, and makes sure he connects with at least one of them each day for a chat.

Recently, Simon expressed interest to his teacher in doing extra practice work in maths. The team celebrated this action, as it was an indicator of a major achievement: the re-engagement of Simon with the school curriculum.

As seen in the case study of Simon, it is possible that friendships may not develop and students should not be forced into friendships that they do not want. Importantly, the development of friendships in the mainstream class should not prevent students with special educational needs from maintaining contact with special needs or specific disability groups, as these may provide a sense of identity as well as the opportunity to mix with people with similar characteristics and interests. For example, a student may attend a regular secondary school, but still be a member of the Spina Bifida Association.

Ways in which schools have developed friendships include the use of friendship games in which students with disabilities are paired with regular students across grades and classes, and the inclusion of friendship as a specific educational objective in the student with additional needs' individualised educational plan (IEP). In the case of the friendship games, the aim is to gain a shift in regular class students' attitudes to disability and the development of friendships that can be maintained beyond the games.

The *Circle of Friends* program (Frederickson & Turner, 2002) specifically aims at enhancing interactions between students with and without additional needs. The lower social attractiveness of students with disabilities may be due to the limited opportunities that students with additional needs may have to interact with a broader range of students.

Programs such as *Circle of Friends* try to overcome this difficulty by structuring positive activities.

Another method of developing friendships and social skills in younger students is through the use of academic content, including the use of children's literature (Cartledge & Kiarie, 2001; Degeroge, 1998). In this approach, teachers use books based on themes of friends, socialising, conversation and playing together. Such methods incorporate both academic and social skills as well as fun and involvement by all students in the class. There are opportunities to explore the ideas of friendships and to practise skills in other group situations in class.

Overcoming loneliness

The sections above, and the case study of Simon, highlight the importance of addressing the issue of loneliness of students with additional needs. Students with additional needs are more vulnerable to feelings of loneliness than their peers without additional needs, for two main reasons (Pavri, 2001). First, they may have difficulty in reading and processing the social cues and developing social relationships leading to rejection from social groups. Second, they may not have the opportunity in the regular school to fully participate in activities that promote a sense of belonging and acceptance. Pavri recommends a multipronged approach to assisting students who are lonely which combines many of the strategies discussed above. Five areas of support and training are recommended:

- teach social skills – assertiveness training, initiating, maintaining and terminating interactions, conflict resolution skills, social problem solving skills and dealing with aggressive behaviours
- create opportunities for social interaction – participating in extra curricular activities, structured recess activities, use of cooperative learning and peer tutoring
- create an accepting classroom climate – developing rapport with students, promoting class membership and belonging, promoting awareness of additional needs
- teach adaptive coping strategies – a range of coping skills, using alternative strategies, changing self-perceptions and attributions through counselling
- enhance student self-esteem – using positive reinforcement, encourage risk taking, assigning classroom jobs and responsibilities.

Many of these strategies were incorporated in the program for Simon (Box 6.4). The list also provides a clear summary of the variety of strategies that can be used to assist all students with additional needs increase their social inclusion in the class and school, not only those who are lonely.

Using technology in promoting positive relationships

Although the use of technology has traditionally focused on the academic aspects of classroom learning and teaching (see Chapter 4), technology can also be used with a specific focus on management of behaviours as well as in friendship and relating skills.

One application for increasing student involvement in self-management of behaviour is self-graphing on computers. Gunter et al. (2002) developed a method of student graphing of data based on the use of Excel (Carr & Burkholder, 1998). The procedure allows the teacher and student to establish the format and even a trendline to show the rate of development required to meet the desired social or academic goal.

A very different use of technology is found in the area of friendships. Hobbs et al. (2001) observed students with and without additional needs engaging in computer play, both structured and unstructured. Structured play consisted of predetermined group-based activities in which a student with additional needs was included. An adult worked with each group and directed activities and provided reinforcement. In free-play students were free to choose who they worked with and what computer activities they chose. Adults limited their activities to general supervision.

Inclusive play occurred on 90 per cent of occasions during structured play and between 40 and 67 per cent in unstructured play. Importantly, inclusive computer play increased over the study time and persisted beyond the training. Some useful strategies for inclusive computer play include: have lots of adult assistance at the start; put students with similar technical and game skills together; have a highly structured limited time session; and have a short wind-down activity after the computer activity to transition to other activities. Other important issues for inclusive computer activities include making certain that students are proficient before encouraging free play, use older or more computer-proficient students as helpers, and tolerate a higher noise level as students have fun.

Another approach to friendships through the computer is that of e-buddies where students with and without additional needs can communicate through an email friendship program. This enables students to expand their interactions with other students without the need to have face-to-face contact. The program is an American commercial one and information can be found at <www.ebuddies.org>.

Computers have often been used as rewards for student cooperation through free time activities. While this is an effective reward for many students, it also provides a period of time for the teacher to work with other students in the class. Care needs to be taken that students with additional needs do not rely on the computer to replace friendships and interactions with other students. Students with additional needs may rely on computers to avoid, or to replace, interactions with other students (see Box 6.4). Where students have specific skills in the use of technology, these can also be used to assist others, particularly in peer or buddy strategies or in other cooperative learning tasks.

Highlighting specific skills of the student with additional needs

Where students with additional needs have a specific skill, their opportunities for social acceptance are greatly increased. This may include sporting skills, computer skills, or some leisure activity they are particularly good at. Encouraging sharing of these skills may assist in the development of peer acceptance and the social status of the student. Alternatively, students with particular skills in the class may be able to teach these to other students in the class or school.

Mentoring by teachers

Another method, this time using staff rather than students, is to develop the concept of mentors who can provide individual students with assistance from a non-threatening adult (Christiansen, Christiansen & Howard, 1997). Mentors can provide support to students with additional needs by the mentor taking a special interest in that student and developing a nurturing, facilitating relationship. Mentors can come from within the school or from the community. They may teach specific skills or act as a general adult support. Benefits of such programs include increased self-esteem, increased attendance and improved academic performance.

Using staff and other personnel

One of the key issues in the ongoing integration/mainstream debate relates to the amount of additional support required to maintain an inclusive placement. All teachers welcome additional appropriate support through the use of support teachers, teachers' aides and parents. If they are used effectively, additional personnel can provide an extra set of hands and eyes to give individual attention, modify the teaching methods, give additional practice and revision, and provide additional teaching–learning ideas. However, as discussed in Chapter 4, collaborative teaching requires careful planning to ensure that all staff have a common understanding of the aims and implementation of the program (see Rainforth & England, 1997).

Collaborative staff teams

The use of a collaborative team of staff to support social inclusion has been highlighted in the earlier section on developing a positive behaviour plan. The most appropriate approach to developing and implementing a social behaviour program was identified as being a team approach. In a model of regular education and special education staff collaboration, Hunt et al. (2003) found that students with severe disabilities in regular classrooms improved their academic performance but, more critically for the focus of this chapter, they substantially reduced the amount of non-engaged time, and greatly increased the occasions on which they initiated social interactions. Staff and students' parents involved in the process reported gains in self-confidence, assertiveness and social interactions with classmates. The importance of full and equal involvement of parents in the planning, implementation and evaluation of the program was seen by all as essential for the success of the student plans. Another important finding of the study was that, not only must teams be established, they need time to meet regularly to reflect together. Hunt et al. (2003) highlight the importance of school executive ensuring that time is made available for this to occur as well as ensuring that the required resources are made available. This last need was addressed by ensuring that any support staff in the classroom worked with all students, not only those with additional needs.

Preparing teachers and students to support social inclusion

The placement of students with additional needs in a mainstream class will not guarantee their social integration. While it is important to prepare students with additional needs for placement in mainstream classes, it is also important to prepare the class teacher and students.

Teachers

Teacher preparation needs to include the areas of attitudes, competency and expectations. Studies of attitudes to inclusion have shown that teachers are often the least enthusiastic

(Forlin, 2001; Westwood & Graham, 2003), which is not surprising given that they are ultimately the group that has to implement the process. Attitudes are often stereotypic and, although many studies demonstrate that having students with additional needs in the classroom reinforces negative attitudes, other studies have shown a positive change in attitude. McEvoy and Welker (2000) summed up these concerns in noting that current levels of teacher preparation, the placement of beginning teachers in difficult classes, the lack of mentoring of new teachers, and the use of untrained staff to run programs, works against the success of social practices. As discussed in Chapter 4, trainee teachers can improve their inclusion attitudes and skills during training (Campbell, Gilmore & Cuskelly, 2003).

Preparation in the area of competency could include developing classroom teaching skills to make the social aspects of inclusion work. These could include the use of strategies such as cooperative learning, the use of buddies, friendship groups and how to teach students appropriate learning-related skills. Finally, preparation in the area of expectations would include avoiding stereotypic responses to specific disability labels, responding to the individual social needs of students, and addressing the limitations of students as they adapt to a regular education environment.

Mentoring of staff

As discussed earlier, many new and inexperienced teachers are placed in classes with a diversity of students, including often those with a variety of additional needs, and often those with behaviour difficulties. Mentoring of beginning teachers is a critical professional role of experienced school staff, supported by the school executive and at higher levels in the education system. In a paper on mentoring of beginning teachers in Australia, Eves (2001) sees mentoring as vital, given that teacher training provides much less time on sustained practicum during their teacher training and many new graduates enter teaching with limited management skills. Mentoring provides these teachers with practical advice; it reduces the stress of beginning teaching, and provides a broad support network. The outcomes identified by Eves (2001) for teachers she has mentored include:

- a change in the behaviour of individual students allowing more effective work with that student and the remainder of the class
- an increased relationship between the teacher and the class
- an increased concentration on academic programs
- increased peer acceptance of the student with additional needs in the class and a better working environment in the class
- positive behaviour strategy feedback by the teacher leading to a more positive learning and teaching environment
- less class teacher stress
- the class teacher's style is a positive role model with positive problem solving.

The strategies suggested by Eves and the positive outcomes have the potential to increase the satisfaction of beginning teachers with the initial classroom appointments.

Students

As with teachers, student attitudes to, and knowledge about, disability need to be improved so that they will be comfortable having students with special educational needs as classmates.

Attitudes are often a result of ignorance and this leads to preconceived patterns of social interaction. An important social aspect of inclusion is not to avoid the issue of disability as this gives the impression that it is something to hide. Preparation of regular class students through the use of stories about disability or the use of games that simulate disability may increase empathy for students with disability and hence increase the possibility of positive social interactions. These strategies are explored further in the following section.

Involving parents

Any efforts to increase positive social interactions in the classroom have limited value for the student with special educational needs if they are not generalised. A key part of the generalisation comes from communication with parents. There are six key reasons to involve parents in enhancing social relationships. These include (adapted from Porter, 2000, p. 280):

- they have the most important and enduring relationship with their child
- children learn more from the home environment
- parent involvement assists development of their child's attitude to learning
- parent involvement promotes understanding between home and school
- parents make a valuable contribution to school
- accountability is more open when parents are involved.

Many parents of students with additional needs have played a vital role in securing assistance for their child since birth (see Chapter 3). They have often been actively involved in early education programs and in seeking an appropriate education placement. Where their child has been in an early education intervention setting, prior to mainstream placement, they were probably involved in the planning of educational goals, through IEP or Individual Family Service Agreement (ISFA) meetings (Bentley-Williams & Butterfield, 1996; Kemp, 2003). They should not be forgotten in developing social skills in a mainstream placement.

The role of parents needs to be a cooperative one, in which the teacher seeks assistance in supporting the social skills programs of the school. This can be achieved through parent–teacher meetings, brief notes home to parents and encouraging parents to visit the class (Ramirez-Smith, 1995). Conveying good as well as bad news will also increase parental involvement.

One specific technique used for communication between schools and home is the communication book. Hall, Wolfe and Bollig (2003) reported on the use of a communication book between home and school for students with severe disabilities. The key advantages of the approach is that the book provides a permanent record of communications and the opportunity to express in writing views and ideas that can't always be expressed face-to-face. There is also the opportunity for teachers to incorporate parent information in programming and to review changes in comments and feedback over time.

Maintaining positive interactions in the wider school context

While much of the concentration of programs for enhancing positive social behaviours has focused on the classroom, the broader school situation also holds both opportunities and pitfalls for students with additional needs. Earlier discussion of the school discipline policies points to the need for all teachers in the school to be supportive and consistent in their management of students with additional needs.

One particular area of difficulty is the playground where the actions of other students and teachers may exacerbate social difficulties. While the development of positive social interactions may be achieved in class, the opportunity for other students to bully or threaten students in the playground or between school and home, requires a positive social skills program in the wider school, covering many of the issues raised earlier. The development of friendships in the class, or across the school through peer support, may assist students in their playground interactions.

Socially valid outcomes and behavioural change

Throughout this chapter the focus has been on supporting the social inclusion of students with additional needs in the mainstream class and many strategies have been identified that can be used. In reviewing these approaches, it is important to consider three important questions relating to the social validity or quality of life outcomes of what we are doing (Carpenter, Bloom & Boat, 1999). These are:

- Are the goals of the intervention socially significant?
- Are the outcomes of the program socially important?
- Are the procedures used socially acceptable?

The same questions can also be asked of any academic program. Carpenter, Bloom and Boat (1999) believe that methods such as cooperative learning, peer tutoring, and peer support networks are methods that can assist all students in an inclusive classroom to increase their quality of life through socially valid activities.

Summary

This chapter has focused on the importance of developing positive social interactions in mainstream classrooms, and the role a variety of social skills play in that process. Together with academic skills, social skills are critical if the student with additional needs is to maintain a mainstream placement. As has been discussed, social and behaviour problems are likely to occur in any class and are certainly not the sole province of students with additional needs. The initial section outlined the reasons why all students can demonstrate behaviour problems and suggested that many of the practices we adopt in schools exacerbate those behaviour problems. Despite the obvious concerns teachers have about student behaviour in schools, students with additional needs are often rejected in the mainstream class by both teachers and students because they do not have the interpersonal skills or the work-related skills expected of other students. The chapter has discussed the reasons for this, including teacher and student characteristics.

In addressing ways to develop social skills and positive interactions, the chapter has discussed a variety of approaches that can be used, including specific behaviour management programs, cognitive and metacognitive strategies, social skills programs, cooperative learning methods and friendship/peer support programs. These approaches need to address the issues at both the classroom and the wider school levels.

Social interactions assume a two-way process. Hence, the development of social skills should focus not only on students with additional needs, but also on peers and the class teacher, and ultimately on the school.

Discussion questions

1   What are the variables that need to be considered in determining when behaviour becomes problem behaviour? Give an example of each from your teaching or student experiences.

2   What classroom variables can exacerbate behaviour problems for students with additional needs? Give an example of each from your teaching or student experiences.

Individual activities

1   What are the 10 steps in implementing a functional behaviour assessment and a behaviour improvement plan? For each, record the key function of the step, the actions that take place and why they are important.

2   What types of social skills needs exist? Provide an example of each.

3   For each of the following, explain how the strategy is used for students with additional needs and provide an example of how it can be used in the school setting:
    a   cooperative learning
    b   direct instruction
    c   cognitive and metacognitive instruction
    d   self-monitoring
    e   buddies
    f   peer tutoring.

Group activities

1   Three key areas for social inclusion are work habits, coping skills and peer relationships. Within the group each take one area, outline the skills identified as potential weaknesses in each, and suggest techniques to turn these into positive behaviours. Share the findings with the whole group.

2   A major difficulty for teachers is the escalation of behaviour in a confrontation. Record the 11 strategies to assist in avoiding confrontation and for each record why the strategy is important.

3   The use of buddies can be very effective for students with additional needs as well as for regular students. Record some specific activities that involve buddies.

References

*Abery, B. & Simunds, E. (1997). The yes I can social inclusion program: A preventative approach to challenging behaviour. *Intervention in School and Clinic*, *32*(4), 223–34.

Antil, L. R., Jenkins, J. R., Wayne, S. K. & Vadasy, P. (1998). Cooperative learning: Prevalence, conceptualizations, and the relation between research and practice. *American Educational Research Journal*, 35, 419–54.

Apter, S. J. (1982). *Troubled Children/Troubled Systems*. New York: Pergamon Press.

Arthur, M., Gordon, C. & Butterfield, N. (2003). *Classroom Management: Creating Positive Learning Environments*. Southbank: Thomson.

Ashman, A. F. & Conway, R. N. F. (1998). *Cognitive Education: Theory and Application*. London: Routledge.

Bentley-Williams, R. & Butterfield, N. (1996). Transition from early intervention to school: A family focused view of the issues involved. *Australasian Journal of Special Education*, *20*(2), 163–80.

Bowd, A. (1990). *Exceptional Children in the Class* (2nd edn). Melbourne: Hargreen Publishing Company.

Campbell, J., Gilmore, L. & Cuskelly, M. (2003). Changing student attitudes towards disability and inclusion. *Journal of Intellectual and Developmental Disability*, *28*(4), 396–9.

Carpenter, C. D., Bloom. L. A. & Boat, M. B. (1999). Guidelines for special educators: Achieving socially valid outcomes. *Intervention in School and Clinic*, *34*(3), 143–49.

*Carpenter, S. L. & McKee-Higgins, E. (1996). Behaviour management in inclusive classrooms. *Remedial and Special Education*, *17*(4), 195–203.

Cartledge, G. & Kiarie, M. W. (2001). Learning social skills through literature for children and adolescents. *Teaching Exceptional Children*, *34*(2), 40–7.

Carr, J. E. & Burkholder, E. O. (1998). Creating single-subject design graphs with Microsoft Excel. *Journal of Applied Behavior Analysis*, *31*, 245–51.

Center for Effective Collaboration and Practice (CECP). (1998a). Addressing student problem behavior Part 1: An IEP team's introduction to functional behavioral assessment and behavior intervention plans. Washington DC.

Center for Effective Collaboration and Practice (CECP). (1998b). Addressing student problem behavior Part 2: Conducting a functional behavioral assessment (3rd edn). Washington DC.

Center for Effective Collaboration and Practice (CECP). (2000). Addressing student problem behavior—Part 3: Creating positive behavioral intervention plans and supports (2nd edn). Washington DC.

Christiansen, J., Christiansen J. L. & Howard, M. (1997). Using protective factors to enhance resilience and school success for at-risk students. *Intervention in School and Clinic*, *33*(2), 86–9.

Colvin, G., Ainge, D. & Nelson, R. (1997). How to defuse confrontations. *Teaching Exceptional Children*, July/Aug, 47–51.

*Conway, R. N. F. (2002). Behaviour in and out of the classroom. In A. F. Ashman & J. Elkins (Eds), *Educating Children With Diverse Abilities* (pp. 172–236). Sydney: Prentice Hall.

Copeland, S. R., McCall, J., Williams, C. R., Guth, C., Carter, E. W, Fowler, S. E., Presley, J. A. & Hughes, C. (2002). High school buddies: A win–win situation. *Teaching Exceptional Children*, *35*(1), 16–21.

*Daly, P. M. & Ranalli, P. (2003). Using countoons to teach self-monitoring skills. *Teaching Exceptional Children*, *35*(5), 30–5.

*Daniels, V. I. (1998). How to manage disruptive behaviour in inclusive classrooms. *Teaching Exceptional Children*, Mar/Apr, 26–31.

Degeroge, K. L. (1998). Friendship and stories: Using children's literature to teach friendship skills to children with learning disabilities. *Intervention in School and Clinic, 33*(3), 157–62.

Elksnin, L. K. & Elksnin, N. (1998). Teaching social skills to students with learning and behaviour problems. *Intervention in School and Clinic, 33*(3), 131–40.

*Eves, C. (2001). Assisting beginning teachers in managing inappropriate classroom behaviour through mentoring. *The Primary Educator*, *1*, 3–15.

Fad, K. S. & Ryser, G. R. (1993). Social/behavioural variables related to success in general education. *Remedial and Special Education*, *14*(1), 25–35.

*Forlin, C. (2001). Inclusion: Identifying potential stressors for regular class teachers. *Educational Research*, *43*(3), 11–21.

Frederickson, N. & Turner, J. (2002). Utilizing the classroom peer group to address children's social needs; An evaluation of the circle of friends intervention approach. *Journal of Special Education*, *36*, 234–45.

Fulk, B. M. & King, K. (2001). Classwide peer tutoring at work. *Teaching Exceptional Children*, *34*(2), 49–53.

Glasser, R. (1969). *Schools Without Failure*. New York: Harper & Row.

Goldstein, A. P. (2000). *The Prepare Curriculum: Teaching Prosocial Competencies*. Champaign IL: Research Press.

Goldstein, A. P. & McGinnis, E. (1980). *Skillstreaming the Adolescent*. Champaign, IL: Research Press.

Good, T. L. & Brophy, J. E. (2000). *Looking in Classrooms* (8th edn). New York: Addison-Wesley Longman.

Gow, L., Balla, J. & Calvez, M. (1995). A study of social integration: The development of a qualitative methodology. *Australian Journal of Remedial Education*, *27*(3), 20–2.

Gresham, F. M. (1998). Social skills training: Should we raze, remodel or rebuild? *Behavioral Disorders*, *24*(1), 19–25.

Gresham, F. M., Sugai, G. & Horner, R. H. (2001). Interpreting outcomes of social skills training for students with high-incidence disabilities. *Exceptional Children*, *67*(3), 331–44.

Gunter, P. L., Coutinho, M. J. & Cade, T. (2002). Classroom factors linked with academic gain among students with emotional and behavioral problems. *Preventing School Failure*, *46*(3), 126–32.

Gunter, P. L., Miller, K. A., Venn, M. L., Thomas, K. & House, S. (2002). Self-graphing to success. *Teaching Exceptional Children*, *35*(2), 30–4.

Hall, T. E., Wolfe, P. S. & Bollig, A. A. (2003). The home-to-school notebook: An effective communication strategy for students with severe disabilities. *Teaching Exceptional Children*, *36*(2), 68–73.

Hemphill, S. A. (1996). Characteristics of conduct-disordered children and their families: A review. *Australian Psychologist*, *31*, 109–18.

Hobbs, T., Bruch, L., Sanke, J. & Astolfi, C. (2001). Friendship on the inclusive playground. *Teaching Exceptional Children*, *33*(6), 46–51.

Horner, R. H. & Carr, E. G. (1997). Behavioural support for students with severe disabilities: Functional assessment and comprehensive intervention. *The Journal of Special Education, 31*, 84–104.

*Hudson, P. (2003). Behavioural intervention plan: Reducing challenging behaviour through academic skills instruction. *Special Education Perspectives, 12*(3), 35–64.

*Hunt, P., Soto, G., Maier, J. & Doering, K. (2003). Collaborative teaming to support students at risk and students with severe disabilities in general education classrooms. *Exceptional Children, 69*(3), 315–32.

*Jenkins, J. R., Antil, L. R., Wayne, S. K. & Vadasy, P. (2003). How cooperative learning works for special education and remedial students. *Council for Exceptional Children, 69*(3), 279–92.

*Kauffman, J. M. (2001). *Characteristics of Emotional and Behaviour Disorders in Children and Youth* (7th edn). Columbus: Charles E. Merrill.

*Kauffman, J. M., Lloyd, J. W., Baker, J. & Riedel, T. M. (1995). Inclusion of all students with emotional or behavioural disorders? Let's think again. *Phi Delta Kappan, March*, 542–46.

Kemp, C. (2003). Investigating the transition of young children with intellectual disabilities to mainstream classes: An Australian perspective. *International Journal of Disability, Development and Education, 50*(4), 403–29.

Keogel, L. K., Harrower, J. K. & Koegel, R. L. (1999). Support for children with developmental disabilities in full inclusion classrooms through self-management. *Journal of Positive Behaviour Interventions, 1*(1), 26–34.

Kingdon, M. (1995). Student behaviour management: Addressing the issues for teachers of Languages Other Than English (LOTE). In R. N. F. Conway & J. Izard (Eds), *Student Behaviour Outcomes: Choosing Appropriate Paths* (pp. 86–91). Melbourne: ACER.

LaMaster, K., Gall, K., Kinchin, G. & Siedentop, D. (1998). Inclusion practices of effective elementary specialists. *Adaptive Physical Activity Quarterly, 15*(1), 64–81.

McEvoy, A. & Welker, R. (2000). Antisocial behaviour, academic failure and school climate: A critical review. *Journal of Emotional and Behavioral Disorders, 8*(3), 130–40.

McGinnis, E. & Goldstein, A. P. (1984). *Skillstreaming the Elementary School Child: Teaching Prosocial Skills to the Preschool and Kindergarten Child*. Champaign IL: Research Press.

McGrath, H. (1997). *Dirty Tricks: Classroom Games for Teaching Social Skills*. Melbourne: Longman Australia.

McGrath, H. & Edwards, H. (2000). *Difficult Personalities: A Practical Guide to Managing the Hurtful Behaviours of Others (and maybe your own!)*. Marrickville, NSW: Choice Books.

McGrath, H. & Francey, S. (1991). *Friendly Kids, Friendly Classrooms: Teaching Social Skills and Confidence in the Classroom*. Melbourne: Longman Cheshire.

McGrath, H. & Noble, T. (1993). *Different Kids, Same Classroom*. Melbourne: Longman Cheshire.

Mithaug, D. K. (2002). Yes means success: Teaching students with multiple disabilities to self-regulate during independent work. *Teaching Exceptional Children, 35*(1), 22–7.

Moeller, A. J. & Ishii-Jordan, S. (1996). Teacher efficacy: A model for teacher development and inclusion. *Journal of Behavioural Education, 6*(3), 293–310.

Mpofu, E. (2003). Enhancing social acceptance of early adolescents with physical disabilities: effects of role salience, peer interaction, and academic support interventions. *International Journal of Disability, Development and Education, 50*(4), 435–54.

NSW Department of Education and Training (2003). *Quality Teaching in NSW Public Schools*. Sydney: Author.

Nichols, P. (1992). The curriculum of control: Twelve reasons for it, some arguments against it. *Beyond Behaviour, 3*(2), 5–11.

Olsen, G. (1995). Teacher perceptions of student behaviour. Unpublished manuscript. University of Canberra.

Pavri, S. (2001). Loneliness in children with disabilities: How teachers can help. *Teaching Exceptional Children, 33*(6), 52–8.

Porter, L. (2000). *Student Behaviour: Theory and Practice for Teachers* (2nd edn). Sydney: Allen & Unwin.

Rainforth, B. & England, J. (1997). Collaboration for inclusion. *Education and Treatment of Children, 20*(1), 85–104.

Ramirez-Smith, C. (1995). Stopping the cycle of failure: The Comer model. *Educational Leadership, 52*, 14–19.

Rietveld, C. M. (1994). From inclusion to exclusion: Educational placement of children with Down syndrome. *Australasian Journal of Special Education, 18*(2), 28–35.

Roberts, C., Mazzucchelli, T., Taylor, K. & Reid, R. (2003). Early intervention for behaviour problems in young children with developmental disabilities. *International Journal of Disability, Development and Education, 50*(3), 275–92.

*Rosenberg, M. S., Wilson, R., Maheady, L. & Sindelar, P. T. (2004). *Educating Students With Behavior Disorders* (3rd edn). Boston: Pearson Education.

Sale, P. & Carey, D. M. (1995). The sociometric status of students with disabilities in a full-inclusion school. *Exceptional Children, 62*(1), 6–19.

Sawyer, M. G., Arney, F. M., Baghurst, P. A., Clark, J. J., Graetz, B. W., Kosky, R. J., Nurcombe, B., Patton, G. C., Prior, M. R., Raphael, B., Rey, J., Whaites, L. C. & Zubrick, S. R. (2000). *The Mental Health of Young People in Australia*. Canberra: Mental Health and Special Programs Branch Commonwealth Department of Health and Aged Care.

Schloss. P. J. & Smith, M. A. (1998). *Applied Behavior Analysis in the Classroom* (2nd edn). Needham Heights, MA: Allyn & Bacon.

*Schulz, J. B. & Carpenter, C. D. (1995). *Mainstreaming Exceptional Students: A Guide for Classroom Teachers*. Boston: Allyn & Bacon.

Shukla-Mehta, S. & Albin, R. W. (2003). Twelve practical strategies to prevent behavioral escalation in classroom settings. *Preventing School Failure, 47*(4), 156.

Stephenson, J. R. (1997). Dealing with the challenging behaviour of students with severe intellectual disability. *Special Education Perspectives, 6*(2), 71–80.

Stephenson, J., Linfoot, K. & Martin, A. (2000). Behaviours of concern to teachers in the early years of school. *International Journal of Disability, Development and Education, 47*(3), 225–35.

Vinson, T. (2002). *Inquiry Into the Provision of Public Education in NSW*. Sydney: NSW Teachers Federation and Federation of P & C Associations of NSW.

Walker, H. M. (1983). *The Walker Social Skills Curriculum: The ACCEPTS Program*. Austin TX: Pro-Ed.

Walker, H. M., McConnell, S., Holmes, D., Todis, B., Walker, J. & Golden, N. (1988). *ACCESS: Adolescent Curriculum for Communication and Effective Social Skills*. Austin TX: Pro-Ed.

Walker, H. M., Stieber, S. & Bullis, M. (1997). Longitudinal correlates of arrest status among at-risk males. *Journal of Child and Family Studies, 6*(3), 289–309.

*Westwood, P. & Graham, L. (2003). Inclusion of students with additional needs: Benefits and obstacles perceived by teachers in New South Wales and South Australia. *Australian Journal of Learning Disabilities, 8*(1), 3–15.

Williams, G. J. & Reisberg, L. (2003). Successful inclusion: Teaching social skills through curriculum integration. *Intervention in School and Clinic, 38*(4), 205–10.

---

*Recommended reading for this chapter

Further recommended reading

Friend, M. P. & Bursuck, W. D. (2002). *Including Students With Special Needs: A Practical Guide for Classroom Teachers.* Boston: Allyn & Bacon

Smith, T. E. C. (2004). *Teaching Students With Special Needs in Inclusive Settings.* Boston: Allyn & Bacon.

Vaughn, S., Boss, C. S. & Schumm, J. S. (2003). *Teaching Exceptional, Diverse and At-risk Students in the General Classroom.* Boston: Pearson Education.

PART C

WORKING WITH
SPECIFIC DIFFICULTIES

Chapter 7

Understanding literacy and numeracy

Greg Robinson

This chapter aims to:

- develop an awareness of the negative effects of literacy problems on confidence, motivation and self-esteem
- provide an understanding of literacy as an interactive process
- provide an outline of underlying learning disabilities that may hinder literacy development

- outline the basic word attack and comprehension skills and their influence on reading development

- develop an understanding of the nature of spelling and likely spelling problems

- provide an outline of basic numeracy skills and methods to develop these skills.

Literacy

Problems with literacy have received a great deal of attention, because difficulties with reading and writing influence all areas of school achievement. Most school tasks require the finding and presenting of information, and reading and writing is the main way this is accomplished (Cawley, Miller & Carr, 1991). Doyle (1993) found that 83 per cent of the school day is directed to paper and pencil activities which involve reading. Even mathematics in later primary and high school years involves word problems that require very detailed reading (Jitendra et al., 1998) and a higher level of comprehension skill than other reading tasks (McGregor, 1989).

Not only are literacy skills important, but also large numbers of students have reading and writing problems. Masters and Forster (1997) found that approximately 30 per cent of children at Years 3 and 5 level in the National Schools English Literacy Survey (1997) did not meet an acceptable standard in reading and writing. Rohl and Milton (2002) report a survey that estimated 16 per cent of the primary school population in Australia had learning difficulties. Brent, Gough and Robinson (2001) claim that up to 30 per cent of Australian children enter high school with reading and writing difficulties, while Kearsley (2002) found only 66 per cent of Year 7 students in Queensland were confident with their reading competence.

These estimates mean that literacy difficulties are by far the largest area of disability in our community. Combined estimates for all other areas of disability do not approach this figure. The large estimates of literacy difficulty also mean that all teachers are likely to be involved with students with literacy problems during their careers. It is not an area that teachers can ignore in the hope that they will not have to deal with it; all teachers need to understand how children with problems in literacy feel and how to support them.

Literacy problems are not 'visible'

Often literacy problems are not effectively identified and assisted because they are not 'visible' or noticeable. Other disabilities, such as behaviour problems, developmental delays and physical impairments, are more easily 'seen' (Fitzgerald & Paterson, 1995). These more obvious disabilities are often identified at an early age, with special support provided. Potential literacy problems are usually not identified until the end of the first year of school, at the earliest. Many children who are having difficulties with initial reading and writing may be able effectively to conceal the problem till later grades by their good use of oral language, their good behaviour in class or by getting assistance from their friends. This is especially likely to be the case when the difficulty is not severe, and reading is not impossible, just more difficult. McLeskey (1992) found that only 42 per cent of students with such disabilities were identified by Year 3, while an Australian survey by Sugai and Evans (1997) found that teachers judged only 7 per cent of students to be at high risk for academic problems. If students with literacy problems are not identified and supported until Year 3 or later, they may have experienced significant and prolonged failure and would be unlikely to bridge the academic gap between them and their peers (Foorman et al., 1998; Kame'enui & Simmons, 1999; Torgesen, 2001).

Students with moderate difficulties will read if forced to, but do not usually read for pleasure, and may become frustrated when confronted with reading tasks at home or at school. This reluctance or frustration can easily be seen as the cause of the problem, rather than as one of the effects of the problem because their negative behaviour is usually very visible. The student might be seen as just 'lazy' or having a behaviour problem, rather than being reluctant and frustrated because the task is very difficult. In such situations, attempts to make students 'try harder' when they feel they have made a genuine effort could lead to resentment or demotivation, as they feel their efforts are not being rewarded (Smith et al., 1997; Riddick, 1995; Cordini, 1990; Groinick & Ryan, 1990).

In the situation described above, students can easily get caught in a downward learning cycle. Their difficulties with literacy can lead to lack of achievement, which in turn may cause lack of motivation or confidence, leading to even further lack of achievement (Hunter-Carsch, 2001), as shown in Figure 7.1.

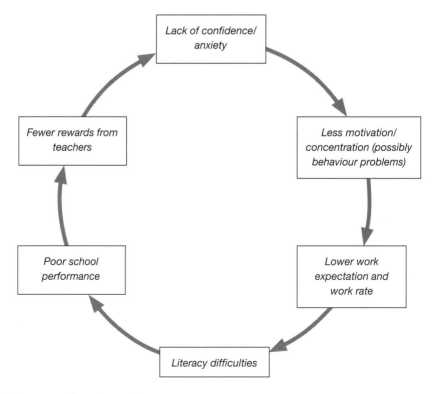

Figure 7.1 Downward learning cycle

Adams (1990) claims that students with reading problems are less likely to practise reading at home, and are reading fewer words at school because they are not reading when the teacher is not helping them. They are also more likely to be reading in a 'round robin' situation, which emphasises accuracy and oral reading more than comprehension. Juel, Griffith and Gough's (1986) longitudinal study of good and poor readers found good readers in Year 1 were reading an average of 18 600 words per annum, about twice as many as poor readers. By Year 4, the difference was 178 000 per annum versus 80 000. Nathan and Stanovich (1991) cite evidence to suggest that a child at the 90th percentile in terms of reading skill is likely to read in eight days what a child at the 10th percentile might take a full year to read. This very large difference in practice alone would lead to differences in skill level, and if difficulties are not identified at an early age, then the practice gap between good and poor readers may be too wide to catch up. Shaywitz, Fletcher and Shaywitz (1994) claim that if such children are not identified and provided help by the age of 9, then 74 per cent of them will still have difficulties through high school.

Literacy problems lead to a lack of confidence and motivation

If a child has difficulty reading at school and completing school tasks, their friends may see them as being 'dumb' or at least 'different'. In order to cope and feel good about themselves, such children might devalue the importance of school achievement (Cordini, 1990; Smith et al., 1997).

Repeated failure, denigration and frustration can result in an aversion to reading and hostility to school (Chan, 1991; Hummel, 2000). Behaviour problems are frequently associated with learning disabilities (Prior et al., 1999). Students with literacy problems are at risk of developing apathy towards learning, which has been called a learned helplessness (Bruce & Robinson, 2002; Reid, 2003). These students may feel they are incapable of success, with poor school achievement being considered inevitable and beyond their control, and any success attributed to luck or help from the teacher. They may not bother to try, as there is no point; whatever happens will be out of their control. This lack of confidence and learned helplessness might be accelerated at high school level for children with literacy problems, as frequent changes of class and teacher may make it more difficult to identify students with problems, and support them. Self-esteem at this age is likely to be a significant problem (Filozof et al., 1998), with Alvermann (2002) claiming that for adolescents, the potency of their belief about self is phenomenal. At this age, students may not want to be identified as having a disability and needing help. If children with literacy problems are to be helped, they first need to feel they can have control over their learning and that success is possible. Worthy et al. (2002) found the most important factor in tutor success for struggling resistant readers was the tutor's willingness to take personal responsibility for the student's progress, tailoring instruction to the student's interests and spending whatever extra time it took to motivate their students to read. Following is a list of ways to help develop confidence and commitment:

- Reduce failure to a minimum:
  - ensure students get success at the beginning of the program
  - have small incremental steps to show them they are capable of learning
  - reinforce success situations immediately.

- Provide a supportive class environment:
  - work *with* the student, sharing their problems and successes
  - establish a good rapport before undertaking special work
  - be willing to try a variety of techniques until success is achieved
  - do not highlight differences between low- and high-ability students.
- Encourage feelings of competence and control:
  - keep tasks and materials meaningful (Kame'enui & Simmons, 1999)
  - provide self-control by structuring lessons which allow *students*, where possible, to make some choices about activities (Reetz & Hoover, 1992).
- Emphasise students' strengths and use them to the maximum.

Literacy problems run in families

There is a growing amount of evidence to suggest that literacy problems have a high family incidence (Nopola-Hemmi et al., 2002). A long-term study of families with literacy problems (Scarborough, 1990) found 65 per cent of children from these families had developed reading problems. Similar high estimates of incidence come from Lewis (1990), whose examination of four families found 68 per cent of the nuclear family affected. Robinson, Foreman and Dear (1996; 2000) investigated family incidence of visual processing problems and found the chance of either one or both parents showing similar symptoms was over 80 per cent, with over 50 per cent of siblings being similarly affected.

This high family incidence may have some advantages for teachers who have to identify and support children with literacy problems:

- An investigation of family incidence may help to identify children likely to have difficulties at an early age. Such early identification means help can be provided before significant problems with literacy occur, thus preventing the downward learning cycle described in Figure 7.1. Children who are identified at a later age are less motivated to improve and may be deeply imprisoned in faulty learning habits (Paris & Oka, 1986).
- Investigation of family incidence may lead to more understanding and support being generated within the family. If one of the parents is made aware of the fact that they have similar symptoms then they should have more empathy with the child's difficulties. The parent may also be more confident to act as an advocate for the child, and the child may gain some comfort from the fact that they are not the only one to have problems. If parents are aware of the symptoms, they are also more likely to identify other children in the family with similar symptoms at an earlier age.

Literacy/reading as an interactive process

There has been a great deal of discussion and argument about how children learn to read, with three major explanations commonly used:

- The bottom–up approach emphasises the learning of associations between letters and their sounds to identify words (phonic analysis and synthesis).
- The top–down approach introduces reading by exposing children to stories and whole words, with associations between letters and sounds being largely learned incidentally.
- The interactive approach states that both whole words/stories and letter–sound association are important and are used interactively in learning to read.

Bottom–up theories state that the initial emphasis needs to be on analysis of sounds in words so that children have a basis for working out new words by themselves. Once these letter–sound associations are mastered, they will have more ability to teach themselves new words and should readily progress to learning whole words and using patterns of words (phrases) to help develop meaning.

Top–down models stress the similarity between learning to read and learning language. A child learns language by being repeatedly exposed to words and conversations. This repeated exposure allows the child to learn word meanings, pronunciation and grammar. Reading (or language in print) is seen as an extension of oral language, and thus the same process of learning by repeated exposure to language should apply. Reading is seen as a constructive process in which meaning is built up by using word patterns (phrases, sentences) to understand what the author is saying (Smith, 1997).

The interactive model views both top–down and bottom–up processes as important (Stanovich, 1980), with readers alternating between the two strategies according to the degree of difficulty of reading material for them. If words are difficult to recognise or the word patterns are unfamiliar, the reader may use a more bottom–up strategy. If the words are easy to recognise and word patterns familiar, a more top–down approach may be used. In the early stages of learning to read, a more top–down style may be used initially so that the student can recognise that print is a visual form of language. Once this understanding has developed, then effort may need to be directed to a bottom–up strategy of learning letter–sound associations. This bottom–up phase may be very short for children with no learning problems, but may take longer for children with auditory or visual difficulties who may need very structured teaching. Once children are familiar with letter sound patterns, a top–down emphasis on using whole words and phrases to develop meaning should again become prominent.

An outline of the possible processing stages in reading that can help explain the three approaches is shown in Figure 7.2.

Good readers spend most of their time at the top levels of Figure 7.2, where words and phrases are instantly recognised and a high level of comprehension is achieved (Samuels, 1999). Understanding of what is being read can also be used to predict what will be said next, thus saving time in word recognition. Occasionally, good readers may be faced with a topic where the words are not familiar, and the grammar used is different (such as a legal document or, possibly, a medical article). In this situation, they may need to revert to a bottom–up process of reading, using letter sounds to identify words and rereading to understand word patterns.

Poor readers are likely to spend most of their time at the bottom levels of Figure 7.2, where more effort and attention is directed to recognising or decoding single words. If too much attention has to be directed to recognising words, then less attention is likely to be available to develop an understanding of what is being read (Andrews, 1989), and meaning may be lost. It is hard for good readers to understand the frustration of not comprehending what they are reading, as it only occurs rarely, when they may have to read in new topic areas or if they have to read more technical and scientific material, such as research journals. To help good readers appreciate the frustration of being confronted with words or language patterns that are not familiar, the following example from medical literacy has been included. Most people find, on first reading of this passage, that attention is directed to the difficult words and the thread of meaning can be lost. Usually repeated rereading is required to gain some sense of word patterns (phrases) and thus meaning. It is important to remember that good readers tend to spend most of their reading time at the higher levels of Figure 7.2, where reading is meaningful and useful, where it is related to previous experiences, and where the meaning gained can be used to help word identification (Kim & Goetz, 1994). However, poor readers are likely to spend more time at the bottom stages of Figure 7.2, where meaning is less evident, and reading is more an exercise in word identification.

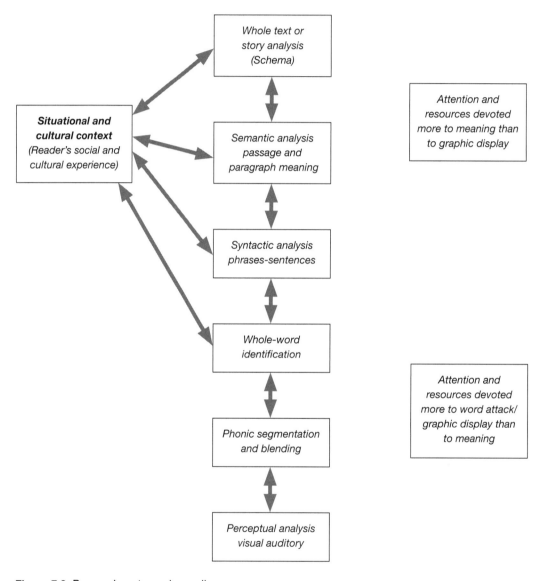

Figure 7.2 Processing stages in reading

(Source: Based on Kintsch, 1977)

Example

Consistent with differences in synaptotagmin immunolabeling between ribbon-style and conventional synapses, physiological studies indicate that the calcium dependence of phasic neurotransmitter release between ribbon-style and conventional synapses can be quite different. For example, the calcium dependence of phasic neurotransmitter release in the goldfish Mb bipolar cell is an order of magnitude lower (Heidelberger et al., 1994; Heidelberger, 1998) than that reported for phasic release at a conventional central synapse, the calyx of Held (Bollmann et al., 2000; Schneggenburger & Neher, 2000), and does not match the calcium-binding profile of the C2A domains of the conventional vesicular synaptotagmins (Li et al., 1995; Sugita et al., 2002).

(Source: Heidelberger, Wang & Sherry, 2003, p. 44)

As readers progress further up the stages of the model outlined in Figure 7.2, words are identified more quickly and automatically and reading starts to become more like a language conversation, in which meaningful phrases and sentences are easily identified. This easy recognition of phrases helps the reader to identify unknown words. If the reader is not sure of a word, then knowledge of word patterns used in phrases or sentences (often in conjunction with some letters in the word) will help the reader identify the word (Liubinas, 2000; Stanthorpe, 1989). This skill is shown in the following sentence where the first letter of the missing word can be combined with the general meaning of the sentence to work out what the word is:

Example

They all went to t— beach.

In the higher levels of the model outlined in Figure 7.2, there is much more interaction between the emerging story and past personal experience relevant to the story to help construct meaning. Word identification then becomes even more automatic and does not demand much attention. The following example shows how emerging meaning can help quick and easy identification of words:

Example

It was hot, so they all went to the beach for a s—.

The words 'hot' and 'beach' help predict the final word.

Studies of developmental stages in reading suggest that readers alternate between a top–down and bottom–up learning style, as discussed in the interactive model of reading (Kamhi & Catts, 1999; Collins, 1998; Watson, 1990; Lovett, 1987; Harding, Beech & Snedden, 1985). Beginning readers may be more likely to use a top–down approach, as they initially need to understand that reading is a visual form of the oral language. Once this connection is made, they may need to spend some time learning how to identify or work out words. This would involve a bottom–up approach, where visual analysis and sound analysis to identify words is likely to be more predominant. In the third stage, as word attack skills become more proficient and word identification is more automatic, it is more likely that a top–down strategy will again be used with greater attention directed towards the construction of meaning.

Methods of teaching reading in the regular classroom have alternated between a top–down approach and bottom–up emphasis. The top–down approach was prominent during the last two decades, but has recently lost favour due to a large and growing body of evidence identifying the importance of the bottom–up strategy of analysing and blending sounds to make up words. The interactive approach, which combines elements of both other approaches, is also becoming increasingly accepted.

Underlying learning disabilities and literacy

The model of reading outlined in Figure 7.2 emphasises the need for children to have automatic and swift recognition of words so that reading can 'flow' in much the same way as oral language. If this language 'flow' is achieved when reading, then knowledge of word patterns in language (such as meaningful phrases) can be readily used to help interpret the reading message. However, many children do not reach this automatic word identification stage because of underlying learning disabilities.

While the nature of underlying learning disabilities influencing reading is not fully understood, there are at least two areas of disability that have been consistently researched and reported in the literature over the years. These are:

- vision and visual perception/processing problems
- hearing and auditory processing problems.

In addition to these two areas of underlying learning disability, there are other disabilities that can indirectly influence reading achievement, such as Attention Deficit Hyperactivity Disorder (ADHD), Attention Deficit Disorder (ADD) or Oppositional Defiance Disorder (ODD). These disabilities make learning to read difficult due to lack of concentration (ADD; ADHD) or due to poor behaviour (ADHD; ODD). These disabilities may overlap with the two underlying disabilities likely to influence reading identified above. There are a large number of children, for example, who may have ADD or ADHD, as well as a significant reading disability called dyslexia (Parry, 1996), which may mean that multiple treatments are required (Hardman & Morton, 1991). However, if a more 'visible' disability, such as ADHD or ODD, is diagnosed and treated, the possibility that there are other disabilities needing treatment may not be considered. Treatment for ADHD or ADD may lead to improved behaviour and concentration, but there may still be problems with reading if there are difficulties seeing print (vision problems) or identifying sounds in words (auditory processing problems).

Vision and visual perception

The level of visual detail on a page of print is usually much greater than any other visual pattern. Most pages in this book have far more visual detail than maps, diagrams or plans, with hundreds of letters and words arranged in a large number of sequences. Not only is there a great deal of detail, but also it must be processed very quickly, at hundreds of words per minute. If a complex design or diagram were to be interpreted, much more time would be allowed. Even the larger and well-spaced print in early reading texts is much more complex than most other visual patterns a child at that age is required to interpret.

As a result of this detail, even minor visual problems can make reading a very difficult activity and may lead to a loss of confidence and an avoidance of reading. If a pattern of demotivation and avoidance becomes established, then the student will soon fall further behind, as outlined in the downward learning cycle of Figure 7.1. In Box 7.1, the print has been distorted to show how it might look to a person with visual problems. A person who saw print in this way would find it difficult to read, and would avoid reading tasks. To a teacher working with a student who saw print in this distorted fashion, it could appear that the student was reluctant for no apparent reason, as the teacher would see the print clearly and would assume that the student is seeing the print in the same way as they are. Even the person with the problem may not be aware that the print should be clearer, as it may have always looked this way to them. If students do not complain and the teacher can find no reason for the reluctance, an easy interpretation may be that they are just 'lazy' or 'lack concentration'.

Box 7.1

There have been two main areas of investigation of underlying visual problems: optical difficulties and visual–perceptual or processing difficulties.

Optical difficulties

Optical difficulties are concerned with standard vision problems and the use of prescription glasses. Difficulties in this area are assessed by optometrists or ophthalmologists (eye doctors). The most common problems that may cause difficulties with reading (Liubinas, 2000) include the following:

- *Long sightedness:* Objects are clear at a distance, when copying from the board, but not at near point when reading and writing.
- *Short sightedness:* Objects are clear at near point (reading and writing) but not at a distance.
- *Astigmatism:* Optical clarity may be different through one eye than through the other, which may cause stress when reading and writing.

- *Eye teaming problems:* Both eyes may not focus at the same point, causing a doubling of letter and word images.
- *Focusing or accommodation problems:* The eyes may have difficulty re-focusing from one point to another, such as from the board to a writing page.

Evans (2000) claims that about 5 per cent of children are long sighted, 10 per cent short sighted and 5 per cent have astigmatism.

Table 7.1 Checklist for visual problems

Directions: For accuracy, observation of the child should occur for at least two to three weeks. Do not mark a symptom if the item is inappropriate for the age of the student.

Symptoms of possible problems	Frequently	Occasionally
1 Does the student complain of headaches?	❏	❏
2 Does the student complain of nausea?	❏	❏
3 Do the eyes become inflamed?	❏	❏
4 Do the eyes appear to water?	❏	❏
5 Does the student complain that eyes burn or itch?	❏	❏
6 Does the student complain of dizziness?	❏	❏
7 Does the student cover an eye(s) with hand?	❏	❏
8 Does the student mention 'spots' before the eyes?	❏	❏
9 Does the student complain that eyes are tired?	❏	❏
10 Does the student mention seeing double?	❏	❏
11 Do bright lights hurt the student's eyes?	❏	❏
12 Does the student have difficulty seeing the blackboard?	❏	❏
13 Does the student complain that print blurs?	❏	❏
14 Does the student mention seeing two lines of print when reading?	❏	❏
15 Does the student squint while looking at books or while reading?	❏	❏
16 Does the student use facial contortions or blink while doing close work?	❏	❏
17 Does the student seem to close their eyes during work sessions?	❏	❏
18 Does the student hold their work very close or far away?	❏	❏
19 Does the student shade their eyes during reading?	❏	❏

If two or more of the above symptoms appear under the column marked 'Frequently' or four or more of the above symptoms appear under the column marked 'Occasionally', referral should be considered.

Even minor problems with any of the above areas may make extended reading and writing activities difficult, which, in turn, might encourage children to avoid reading and writing activities. The observation checklist could be used as an initial screen for vision problems. This checklist should not be used as an accurate indicator of vision problems, but could be used as a basis for referral to a vision specialist for further examination.

Visual–perceptual problems

Visual perception is the ability to identify or interpret what is seen. With visual perceptual problems, the image a person is getting at the eye may be clear, but the person may not be able to recognise what the image is. An analysis of a large range of studies in this area found that 14 per cent of the variance in reading skills can be accounted for by visual perceptual skills (Siedermann, 1980). Howell and Peachey (1990) use survey evidence in Victoria to suggest as many as 19 per cent of children may have visual perceptual problems.

Recognising letters and words

The most common example of visual perceptual problems in reading involves identifying letters of the alphabet. Children with visual processing problems have no difficulty seeing letters such as 'b' and 'd', but have problems recognising the difference between them. Terepocki, Kruk and Willows (2002) found that individuals with a reading disability made more letter orientation confusions than average readers, even at the age of 10.

Many letters in the alphabet have the same shape, but are placed in a different direction or orientation. This can be seen with the following letters:

Example

b – d p – q w – m n – u h – y f – t

If capital letters are included, there is also a problem. When we use capitals and lower case, some letters that look different are actually the same, as shown below:

Example

g – G e – E d – D q – Q

There are also letters that look similar, but which are different:

Example

a – o c – e n – r u – v

Children at the beginning stages of reading, or children with visual processing problems, may see letters clearly, but may be confused about the recognition of some letters, because they do not understand the critical distinguishing features, such as direction (b – d), or orientation (p – d). Letters that change identity merely by changing direction cause the most problems, as most things we look at are not identified by the direction they face. Direction is usually ignored as a clue in determining identity. For example, a cup or a chair can face any direction and be still recognised as a cup or a chair, as shown in the following diagram:

If a child has learned to ignore direction in identifying objects, then identifying letters will be difficult, especially b, d and p, which appear frequently in English words. They must learn that the distinctive features which determine the identity of these letters is related to direction and orientation (Gerber, 1993). This problem with direction can also explain confusions in recognition of words such as 'was' and 'saw', or 'on' and 'no'. It may also help to explain why some children confuse words that have the same initial letters, such as 'when' and 'where'.

Behavioural (developmental) optometrists

Some students may have difficulty with poor eye tracking across a line of print, which is assessed by behavioural optometrists who look at a variety of eye skills, in addition to those normally examined by a regular optometrist or ophthalmologist. Problems assessed by behavioural optometrists include the following:

- *Eye movement/tracking*, including tracking of the eye across lines of print or moving the eye from one point in space to another, such as from the board to the page when copying.
- *Eye coordination/teaming*, which covers a variety of conditions in which the eyes tend to drift inward, upward or outward. If both eyes do not focus on exactly the same place when reading, then double images of words may be seen.
- *Eye focusing*, which is the ability to contract or relax the eye-focusing muscles to quickly cope with changes in the focus situation from near point to far point. There may be difficulty focusing quickly from a worksheet to the board and back again.
- *Laterality and direction*, which involves a poor awareness of left and right. This problem could cause difficulties with identifying the correct direction of letters such as b and d or words such as was and saw.

Behavioural optometrists claim that exercises can be given to children to help overcome the above difficulties, and a number of studies in optometry journals argue for the benefits of vision training for people with literacy problems. However, other studies of the degree to which such training may help reading have been mixed, with some showing a positive response (Fischer & Hartnegg, 2000; Pavlidis, 1985), and others finding no response (Halveston, 1987; Keogh & Pellard, 1985), or casting doubts on many of the methods used (Evans, 2000; Catts & Kamhi, 1999). It should be remembered that such exercises may help visual efficiency, but do not teach reading, and may need to be accompanied by reading tuition.

Use of coloured filters

Another visual processing disability that can cause problems with rapid sequential processing of print has been called Irlen Syndrome (Irlen, 1991) or visual discomfort (Conlon et al., 1999). Symptoms reported by people with Irlen syndrome while reading include a blurring and shadowing of letters and words, a doubling or movement of print, eye strain, restricted span of focus and problems focusing for an extended period of time (Irlen, 1991). These symptoms are not related to skills normally assessed by an optometric examination (Simmers, Gray & Wilkins, 2001; Scott et al., 2002). According to Irlen (1991) the symptoms can be treated by individually diagnosed coloured overlays or coloured lenses to filter out the specific colours of the white light spectrum to which the person is sensitive.

It has been suggested that the symptoms relate to a sensory after-imaging effect in which images, such as words, could stay in the eye longer for children with this disability than for average readers (Willows, 1998). If this were to occur, there would be an overlapping of words between consecutive eye fixations when reading (Demb et al., 1998). If the words from one focus point in reading persist after the eye has moved to a new focus point, there could be confusing or doubling of words. This confusion is more likely to occur in reading than in other visual tasks because of the rapid eye movement involved.

The problem of overlapping visual images has been related to a deficit in the visual neurological pathway called the magnocellular pathway (Boden & Brodeur, 1999). This pathway is claimed to suppress any potential overlapping of images, and the effect has been called saccadic (eye movement) suppression (Hussey, 2002). A number of studies have identified difficulties in the magnocellular pathway for poor readers (Romani et al., 2001; Talcott et al., 2001), and coloured filters have been found to influence the functioning ability of this pathway (Whiteley & Smith, 2001; Chase et al., 2003).

A large number of controlled studies have reported improvements with the use of coloured plastic overlays (for example, Wilkins et al., 2001; Scott et al., 2002) and with coloured lenses (for example, Lightstone, Lightstone & Wilkins, 1999; Robinson & Foreman, 1999b; Robinson & Conway, 2000; Bouldoukian, Wilkins & Evans, 2002). However, while the majority of studies have reported improvements in reading, not all studies have had positive results (Martin et al., 1993; Robinson & Foreman, 1999a). Some negative studies are to be expected as the reported improved print clarity may assist learning to read, but it will not teach word recognition skills and supplementary reading support may be needed. If words are clearer, for whatever reason, it will make word recognition easier, but it will not allow a person to read words they do not know. People with reading difficulties are likely to avoid reading practice (Stanovich, 1986) and as a consequence may not have developed a large vocabulary of instantly recognisable words, or have had regular practice in blending sounds to make words. Developing such skills should be easier if print is clearer, but assistance and regular practice will still be needed.

Box 7.2
Logan

I am a Resource Teacher: Literacy (RT: Lit.) and have been in this position for almost two and a half years. There are 112 RT: Lits in New Zealand and our role, as specialist teachers of literacy, is to work with the hardest to teach children in Years 0–8. Often this involves working with the school and teachers to implement a program rather than teaching individual children but we also have a small number of individual children who receive 1:1 assistance three to four times per week. Pupils are referred to our service by the schools – usually after there has been an intervention program by the school with little or no improvement shown by the child.

Logan was referred to me in May 2002 at age 7 years, 3 months although I had discussed his progress with the Special Needs teacher, Catherine Birt, at his school on numerous occasions. Catherine runs the Reading Assistance program at the school and takes, on a daily basis, small groups of targeted children for additional support in reading. Logan had been included in a very structured, well-planned program during 2001 and the first half of 2002 and although he had progressed from a pre-reader to reading at Orange (6-year-old level) he had a very poor view of himself as a reader/writer and was still well over a year behind his peers and knew it.

>

Box 7.2 continued

He disliked coming to school and had a low self-esteem although he is a terrific sportsperson and excels in almost all sports as well as being popular among his peers. Logan's oral language is strong and he has a very good vocabulary. He enjoys being read to but struggles with both reading and writing independently.

Logan came on to my roll in July of 2002 and initially I felt it was best to concentrate on lifting his reading level. He had good comprehension of text at a 5½-year-old level and although his item knowledge was reasonable (letter identification, concepts about print etc.) he still had letter reversals and some confusion with basic sight words. His handwriting was a hindrance as many letters were incorrectly formed and were not easily distinguished. Logan had difficulty hearing sounds in sequence when writing and wrote few basic sight words independently. Logan's biggest hurdle was his intense dislike of reading and of writing.

He was included as a member of a small group and had half hour lessons three to four times per week. As mentioned, we initially focused on boosting the reading level and enthusiasm of the group. I provided a wide range of previously unseen texts, allowed student choice where possible, taught strategies to solve unknown words and employed incentives for increasing reading mileage. Although Logan complied with all that was asked of him, he showed no greater enthusiasm for reading than he had previously. His reading was consolidated at the 6 year level but he was too fragile a reader to push beyond that. At the end of the third term I decided to change my own strategy and to instead concentrate on writing and ensure that they read everything they wrote. I continued to provide incentives for increasing reading mileage but mainly worked on structuring stories, writing reports (basic ones) and learning strategies for spelling unknown words. We also worked on a program called 'Chunk, Check, Cheer' (CCC), which teaches pupils to use known chunks (usually rhymes) to solve unknown words in both reading and writing.

At the same time Catherine Birt was completing a study on children's literature and conducted a mini research project on helping children to progress in reading through reading library books (on a contract type system). She included Logan in this study – which he thoroughly enjoyed and this showed as an increase in his reading level.

By the end of 2002 Logan was reading at Light Blue (6½–7 year level) and was reading more independently. He was using the CCC method independently in our group sessions but had not transferred much of this back to the classroom. At this stage Logan was now aged 7 years 9 months so still lagged behind his peers. He was beginning to use more of the visual information on the page rather than rely on memory for text – which was his previous strategy.

At the end of the year I recommended that Logan have some further assistance to consolidate what he had learned and to further encourage him to use visual information independently. As his attitude and his skill level had improved I believed reading mileage and involvement in a tape-assisted reading program (TARP) would be beneficial. I also recommended that whatever assistance Logan receives be in-class, as he disliked being withdrawn from the class program.

This year Logan had a few carry-over lessons with me but these were discontinued due to Logan's dislike at being withdrawn and my own workload, which had increased substantially. Logan had a very supportive teacher – as he had had throughout his schooling – and she was willing to assist him within the class program.

I was still concerned that he was not attending to visual information and knew he

Box 7.2 continued

needed to do this if he was to move on to more complex text without supporting pictures.

At the end of term 1 this year I trained as an Irlen screener and several aspects pointed towards Logan having Irlen Syndrome. First, he had a discrepancy between his level of achievement in oral language in comparison to his achievement in written language (both reading and writing). He also did not attend to visual information – rather he attempted to 'remember' what the story was about or tried to use cues from the pictures. He did not enjoy reading for long periods of time, often blinked, looked away from the page and misread words and sentences.

I screened Logan for Irlen Syndrome in August 2003 and although he displayed a large number of symptoms, I was unable to find a coloured overlay that alleviated these symptoms and made it easier for him to see the words on the page. I was unsure of whether to refer him on to an Irlen diagnostician for a full analysis, as I had not experienced this before. Usually one or more coloured overlays improved the perceptual ability of the person being tested but this was not so with Logan. I discussed this with Mary Cubie, our local diagnostician and she advised sending him for further testing as she had a much greater range of tints to try.

Logan went for further testing and again displayed a high number of symptoms. He was then diagnosed as needing tinted lenses and they made an enormous difference to his reading ability. For the first time he read a paragraph without stumbling whereas previously he struggled over just a few sentences.

Logan now proudly wears his tinted lenses at school and all involved in his case have noticed changes. His teacher said his confidence has improved greatly and he has *almost* become cheeky (a fact she is pleased to see as for Logan this is proof of his improved belief and confidence in himself). He is also happier about reading and is showing an improvement in his level of achievement in written language. Logan says the difference for him with his lenses is that he 'can see the words better', 'it's easier' and he reports that he now reads some 'chapter books' at home. This has been a big boost to his self-esteem.

To continue with this growth, Logan now takes home curiosity kits (theme based packs containing books, magazines, artefacts and activities around a central theme – dinosaurs/cars/mammals/trucks/sports etc.) and these he thoroughly enjoys. They enable him to interact with other family members with high interest reading material.

I believe the enormous amount of assistance that Logan has received over his first 3½ years at school has given him many strategies to help him with reading and writing. Now that his difficulty with visual perception has been corrected he will be able to apply those strategies and, if given access to material that is high interest, he should continue to make progress and enjoy the reading/writing process.

Linda Savage, Resource Teacher: Literacy, Gisbourne Intermediate School, Gisbourne, New Zealand

Visual problems and inappropriate reading strategies

The difficulties caused by visual perceptual problems may be aggravated by the methods children use to cope with the problem. In particular, they may develop a strategy for reading that avoids processing the visual detail of letter patterns by using some of the following strategies:

- looking at pictures in the text for clues to the story
- guessing words on the basis of what they expect the word to be (use of story context)

- guessing words from the initial or final letter in a word
- guessing using both story context and letters in a word.

It has been claimed that poor readers may not develop effective strategies for reading (Wong, 1998). If print is unclear they could develop ways of trying to understand the story (such as guessing), which may not help them to learn letter shapes and letter sound patterns (Prior et al., 1995). The strategies described above avoid looking at visual details, which makes it less likely that letter shapes and patterns and their relationship to sounds would be learned (Pratt, Kemp & Martin, 1996; Waring et al., 1996). If such strategies persist through primary school, they will exaggerate any initial difficulties caused by minor vision problems. If students avoid looking at details of letter–sound patterns for many years, they can be expected to be years behind their peers in the recognition of such patterns.

Accommodations that could assist students at all school levels with visual or visual processing problems include the following (Irlen, 1991; Mailley, 2001):

- Markers – if a student has difficulty staying on a line then use of a marker such as a finger or ruler may assist.
- Comfortable lighting – some students who are light sensitive may need to sit away from lights and windows. Hats or visors with dark brims may also be helpful.
- Paper colour – recycled or coloured paper may help reduce strain from bright lights, especially in exams.
- Extended time in exams and for assignments – some students may need to rest their eyes by periodically looking away from a book. Allow for regular breaks and consider providing extra time for reading test questions and writing legible and accurate answers.
- Checking tests – check that errors have not occurred because of misreading test questions.
- Help with copying from board – errors may be made when reading or copying from boards or overhead projectors. Students may need more time for this task or need another student to copy the work for them.

Hearing and auditory perception

As well as requiring a high level of visual processing, readers also require a high level of auditory processing. A student must learn to attend to the often minor differences in sound that distinguish certain letters or letter patterns. When reading, there is no pause between each word read. This could make the discrimination of separate words as well as sounds in words very difficult. In particular, this discrimination may be a difficult task for early level readers, and they may have to be trained to identify these differences.

As with visual processing, it may need only a small hearing or auditory perception problem to make letter–sound discrimination and identification a very difficult task. This would, in time, make the student more vulnerable to failure, and more likely to avoid sound analysis in reading and spelling, possibly relying instead on memorising words by sight, or guessing. There is also the difficulty that minor auditory problems may be undetected for many years. By this time, the child may be well behind the rest of the class in many word attack skills involving sound analysis.

The most common areas of difficulty for auditory skills seem to be minor hearing problems or auditory perceptual difficulties, especially phonemic awareness.

Minor hearing problems

A large number of children have minor hearing problems related to middle ear infection (otitis media). It is called a conductive hearing loss because inflammation of the middle ear combined with a build up of fluid and mucus means that sounds cannot be efficiently conducted along the ear canal to the sound analysis system. The degree of hearing loss associated with this problem may vary from 30 decibels (which is the noise level of a whisper) to 60 decibels (which is a noise level just below normal conversation level). This loss may last from a few days to a few months.

The problem is quite common, which means that large numbers of children may have difficulties in sound analysis, and this could make learning to read more difficult. Moore (1994) reported a survey of 2- to 5-year-olds, in which one in three experienced a 35-decibel loss on the day of the test. Bishop (2000) claimed that the incidence of middle ear infection in children from advantaged populations is 5 per cent, but among Indigenous students, especially in remote communities, it can range from 40 to 70 per cent.

School-aged children with otitis media will be further handicapped by the background noise levels found in schools (Burnip, 1994). This could include minor conversations, neighbouring class noise, paper rustling and desks scraping. If the teacher has a voice level of 65 decibels, the normal background class noise level of 40 to 50 decibels would reduce the teacher's voice to the level of a whisper, which would not be heard by a student with a minor hearing loss of 30 decibels.

In such conditions, it would be particularly difficult to hear low-level sounds such as 'p', 't', 'k' and 'f'. Such people may also miss plural endings such as 's' and 'es', or final position sounds such as 'th' or 'sh' (Reichman & Healey, 1983). The problem may be further aggravated by distance from the teacher. If the student is at the back of the room, there may be a further 10 to 20 decibel lowering of the teacher's voice, which could lead to vital instructions or explanations being misunderstood. It could also mean that the detailed processing or analysing of sounds in words that the teacher is demonstrating becomes a much harder task.

Speech and language therapists have found that children who had delayed language development were having to contend with large amounts of background noise such as radio, television, traffic and washing machines (Townend, 2000). When mothers were asked to turn everything off in the house for one hour a day, there was impressive progress in spoken language. Townend also reported an unpublished study which found that children who lived under the flight path of a New York airport were less competent when measured on tests of reading, phonological processing and knowledge of words.

An observation checklist that could be used as an initial screen for hearing problems has been included (Table 7.2). This checklist should be used only as a brief initial screen for hearing problems. Referral to a hearing specialist for a fuller examination would be needed if problems are suspected.

Auditory perceptual difficulties/phonemic awareness

In addition to minor hearing problems, some people may also have difficulties in processing (identifying) different sounds within words. This skill has been called phonemic awareness, or the ability to identify sounds in words and the sound structure of spoken words (Center & Freeman, 1998). Phonemes in words are considered to be the smallest units of spoken language and thus phonemic awareness is the ability to identify these component sounds (phonemes) and be able to intentionally manipulate them to make up words (Gonzalez, Espinal & Rosquette, 2002).

A child may be sensitive to sounds and rhyme at an early age because of exposure to language. However, the focus is on meaning, not separate sounds, when a person is listening or speaking. As a consequence, separating the sounds of speech from whole words into individual phonemes is an abstract concept with no meaning, and difficult for a child to comprehend (Griffith & Olsen, 1992). Developing phonemic awareness is thus likely to require explicit and systematic instruction. Problems with phonemic awareness may lead to difficulties in some of the following skills:

- discrimination of the differences between word sounds (for example, cat and bat)
- identification of sounds in words (for example, beginning, middle or ending sounds in the word 'saw')
- counting sounds in words (for example, how many sounds in the word 'dish'?)
- identification of rhyming words (for example, does 'mat' rhyme with 'bat'?)
- linking sounds to letters or letter groups (for example, what sound is made by the letters 'sh'?)
- deleting a sound from a word – what does it say now? (for example, say 'dish' and now say it without the 'd')
- substituting sounds in words – what does it say now? (for example, say 'mat' and now say it with 'c' instead of 'm')
- segmentation of sounds in words (for example, what are the three sounds in 'dish'?)
- blending separate sounds to make up words (for example, 'c'–'a'–'t'. What word is this?).

There are many assessment methods available to identify deficiencies in phonemic awareness skills, with Torgesen (1999) providing details of a large number of these methods. In Australia, the Sutherland Phonemic Awareness Test (Neilson, 1999) is frequently used.

This test is easily administered and effectively identifies deficiencies in a comprehensive range of phonological skills.

Table 7.2 Checklist for hearing problems

Directions: This checklist should be used only after observing the child for two to three weeks. Do not mark a symptom if the item is inappropriate for the age of the student.

Symptoms of possible problems	Frequently	Occasionally
1 Does the student mention earaches?	❏	❏
2 Does the student have colds?	❏	❏
3 Does the student tend to rub and pick at ears?	❏	❏
4 Does the student lean forward while listening?	❏	❏
5 Does the student turn one ear towards the speaker?	❏	❏
6 Do the student's ears discharge?	❏	❏
7 Does the student have monotonous or unnatural pitch to the voice?	❏	❏
8 Does the student have faulty pronunciation and lack of clear and distinct speech?	❏	❏
9 Does the student appear inattentive?	❏	❏
10 Do the student's ears seem to have an excessive accumulation of earwax?	❏	❏
11 Does the student have difficulty breathing or breathe through the mouth?	❏	❏
12 Does the student make requests for questions or statements to be repeated?	❏	❏
13 Does the student complain of a blocked feeling in the ears?	❏	❏
14 Does the student watch the speaker's lips closely?	❏	❏
15 Does the student lack confidence in responding to questions?	❏	❏
16 Does the student frequently say, 'I don't know'?	❏	❏
17 Does the student fail to turn when called?	❏	❏
18 Does the student seem to dislike listening to oral reading?	❏	❏
19 Does the student seem to dislike music and musical activities?	❏	❏
20 Does the student appear to have difficulty following directions?	❏	❏

If two or more of the above symptoms appear under the column marked 'Frequently', or four or more of the above symptoms appear under the column marked 'Occasionally', referral should be considered.

If children have difficulty identifying and blending sound units in words, they may be restricted to developing their reading by trying to memorise words by sight, as they cannot use phonological cues and blending to help identify them. They may also be forced into rote memorisation of spelling lists, as they cannot use knowledge of letter–sound cues as an aid to memory (Snow, Burns & Griffin, 1998). A large number of studies have indicated that phonemic awareness is important for literacy development (Torgesen, 1999; Snowling, 1998). Torgesen (1999) describes phonemic awareness as a most crucial language skill, which directly influences the acquisition of word recognition skills, as well as contributing to the growth of a wide vocabulary of words identified by sight. Longitudinal studies have found that tests of phonemic awareness and tests of alphabetic coding ability are both strong predictors of later achievement in reading (Greaves et al., 1998). Ehri et al. (2001) analysed 52 research studies from 1976 to 2000 and found phonemic awareness training helps children read words by using sound blending, and by matching sounds with letters and letter combinations. They also emphasised the importance of being able to manipulate sound units when spelling and writing.

Training in phonemic awareness has been shown to significantly improve reading performance, especially for those with reading difficulties (Vellutino et al., 1996; Torgesen, 1999; O'Connor, 2000; Ehri et al., 2001). There could also be a mutual benefit, with the development of phonemic awareness leading to improved reading skills and greater reading practice, which in turn helps to further develop phonological processing (Munro, 1998). McCutchen et al. (2002) conducted a long-term study of the effect of giving teachers strategies to develop phonological awareness skills, and found improved reading and spelling scores in students on a two-year follow-up. Olsen (2002) suggested that it is important to provide phonological awareness training before formal reading, so it can be more effectively incorporated into later automatic reading processes.

It should be noted, however, that some children at risk do not appear to respond to phonological awareness training (Gonzalez, Espinal & Rosquette, 2002), possibly because they have persisting phonological problems, or because their underlying learning disabilities are in the visual perceptual or language processing area. Oloffsen (2002) reviewed evidence which found phonological processing problems persist in adults who had problems reading in childhood, even when their adult reading skills are normal. They revisited a study 20 years later and found that the people in the study still had phonological deficits, as well as deficits in visual processing.

For training in phonemic awareness, Munro and Munro (1991) suggested that the following activities may be useful:

- rhyming and alliteration activities:
  - paired reading of rhymes and rhyming stories (*The Cat in the Hat*)
  - categorising words according to rhyme or alliteration (children naming pictures such as hat, mat, bat, hen, and selecting the odd word out)
- listening games:
  - clapping or doing other actions each time a particular sound is heard
  - counting the number of sounds in a word
  - tapping sounds as they are heard
- blending:
  - what word am I saying – 'b-a-t', 'm-a-t'?

Older students could be encouraged to explore sound patterns in words, invent new words based on sound patterns, reflect on how they may manipulate sounds and practise doing this:

- some activities to develop these skills could include:
  - sound-to-word matching, for example: Does 'fish' start with 'f'? Does 'bat' end with 't'?

- isolation, for example: What is the first sound in 'gate'? What is the last sound in 'man'?
- deletion of a phoneme, for example: Say 'fish'. Now say it without the 'f'
- specifying which phoneme has been deleted, for example: Say 'seat'. Now say 'eat'. What sound was left out in the second word?
- phoneme substitution, for example: Say 'seat'. Now say it with 'f' instead of 's'.

There is now a wide range of phonemic awareness programs available. Some have been developed by school education systems, but others are available as published books of classroom activities. Good examples of books of activities are Adams et al. (1998) and Goldsworthy (1998), which provide a variety of practical tasks that are well sequenced for teaching. Torgesen (1999) provides good descriptions of a wide range of kits, computer products and teacher strategies for use in the regular classroom and in small group situations.

Auditory problems and reading strategies

Auditory processing problems may lead to the child lacking confidence in sound analysis tasks and avoiding them. If sound analysis is effectively avoided, it will not be learned, as is evidenced in the fact that older students and adults with significant reading problems often lack phonics skills (Kitz, 1988; Snowling et al., 1997; Oloffsen, 2002). Such people have often obtained lower grades throughout their school career (Felsenfeld, Broen & McGue, 1994).

Apart from specific training in phonemic awareness, accommodations that could assist students at all levels with hearing or auditory processing problems include the following:

- gain the listener's attention by some action before beginning the conversation
- look directly at the person when you are speaking and be on the same level where possible – the speaker's face should preferably be in clear light
- speak normally and clearly without over-emphasis of mouth movements, which could make lip reading more difficult
- cut down or avoid background noise and do not talk from another room
- give visual cues by using body language and facial expression
- get to the point or say something another way if you haven't been understood – if necessary, write it down.

Basic word attack and comprehension skills

Emphasis has been placed on the need for recognition of words to be 'automatic' (Samuels, 1999). This need was highlighted by Figure 7.2, which suggests that early readers and poor readers may direct most of their attention to decoding or identifying words rather than to extracting meaning from what is read. As word recognition becomes more 'automatic' it is more likely that attention will be directed to meaning, thus providing more understanding of what is read.

Word recognition needs to be 'automatic' so that language patterns are readily identified and the reader is at meaning level of the reading continuum (Figure 7.2). The nature of word recognition skills that would allow this fluency and automaticity to develop is discussed below.

Whole word recognition (sight vocabulary)

This is the ability to recognise a word on sight with no analysis of letter sounds or use of language cues to help in identification. Knowing common or key words by sight is an important skill for readers (Ehri, 1997; 1999). Fluent readers have a large sight vocabulary of high frequency words (Worthy & Broaddus, 2002). Assessing student knowledge of the most frequent words used may have the following advantages:

- The words that appear frequently in reading are words that the student most needs to learn. Most books use a relatively small number of key words frequently, so pre-teaching of these key words may make an important difference to automatic word identification (Holmes, 1996; Samuels, 1999).

- Learning the words that are going to be used frequently in all reading could provide fairly immediate success for the reader. Lists have been developed of words that are used so frequently they will consistently appear in any reading material. Learning these words thus guarantees frequent success in word identification. In addition, many of these common words cannot be easily identified by blending their letter sounds (for example, 'the', 'one', 'would'), so they need to be known by sight.

- It is easy to involve parents in practising these words at home. This could significantly extend the amount of practice time with such words. School remedial lessons may be available only two or three times per week, while parents may be able to practise more frequently than this. Learning lists of words is not a complex task, and it should not be too difficult for parents to assist.

- Increasing the number of words identified by sight reduces the frequency of hesitations and mistakes, and thus allows more fluency, which, in turn, will make it easier for students to use language patterns in print to help identify new words.

Developing sight words would allow students to gain confidence and enjoyment in reading because they are getting more meaning from what is read (Tan & Nicholson, 1997). If they like reading, they may read more, which is likely to lead to a greater number of words being recognised on sight because of greater exposure to the words (Barker, Torgesen & Wagner, 1992; Torgesen et al., 2000). As a consequence, there may be an upward spiral of improvement, with greater sight vocabulary leading to more reading, more knowledge of language patterns in print and thus even greater ability to identify new words and eventually learn these by sight.

The importance of knowing the common words used by sight has resulted in the publication of many lists of sight words, based on surveys of words frequently used in children's literature. Most lists have only 200 to 400 words (Broomfield & Combley, 1997; Eeds, 1985; Spencer & Hay, 1998), so not a huge amount of learning is required to master them and make reading much easier. The words commonly found on these lists are shown in Box 7.3.

Box 7.3

Words commonly included on lists of frequently used words

a	all	am	an	and	are
as	ask	at	be	because	but
by	came	can	come	could	did
do	does	eat	far	find	for
from	go	good	has	had	have
he	here	his	I	if	in
is	it	let	made	me	my
not	no	of	on	one	or
our	ran	said	saw	see	she
so	some	soon	tell	that	the
they	this	to	try	up	us
very	was	we	when	who	why
with	would	yes	you	your	

Lists of common words usually have to be supplemented by personal words, which may not be on common lists, but which students find they are frequently using. These words (usually nouns) most often relate to a particular book being read, and may be introduced during regular school activities prior to the book being used in class. At secondary level, such lists must also include words common to particular topics being taught. It could be possible for teachers in subject areas to identify words frequently used in topics. These words could be pre-tested both for understanding of their meaning and for reading recognition. Words not understood or recognised would need to be taught prior to the topic being introduced, as teacher explanations about the topic, or reading for assignments on the topic, would be limited if the words were not known.

At secondary level, parents could be asked to identify and help pre-teach topic words that are difficult for their children. The regular secondary teacher may not have time to consistently pre-test and teach words for individual students, while parents usually have the motivation and a one-to-one learning situation that could make this possible. Involving parents may also help to relieve their anxieties and frustrations concerning the child's progress, as they are doing something positive to overcome the problem.

Sound analysis and blending (phonics)

This word attack skill involves the ability to blend sounds in a word so that it can be recognised as a word used in spoken language. This ability is an extension of phonemic or phonological awareness skills discussed earlier in this chapter. Phonological awareness involves the ability to identify and manipulate component sounds in words while phonics involves the ability to blend the component sounds to make words. This skill is considered to be a very important component in the development of successful reading skills. The extensive review of research by Ehri et al. (2001) found that systematic phonics instruction helped children learn to read better than all other forms of instruction to which it was compared. They recommended that it should be used in programs to teach beginning reading, as well as in programs to assist students with reading difficulties.

The development of phonics skills is usually difficult in the English language because of the lack of correspondence between sounds and letters of the alphabet. The lack of correspondence means that letters and letter clusters may represent more than one sound (for example, the sound of the 'ough' letter pattern in the words 'rough', 'cough', 'bough', 'through' and 'though'). Sounds may also be represented by more than one letter or letter group (for example, the 'oo' sound in 'moon', 'canoe', 'threw', 'two', 'blue', 'who', 'manoeuvre'). As a consequence, the student must learn more than just sounds of letters of the alphabet. For example, blending of the single letter sounds, 'k-n-i-f-e', does not even approximate the sound of 'knife' in our language, nor does blending of the single letter sounds 't-h-e' approximate the sound of 'the'.

The gradual development of knowledge of letter sound patterns in English and their irregularities may be possible over the first three years at school, when a significant amount of time is devoted to instruction in word attack skills. However, these skills may be quite difficult to develop later in a remedial situation, which may be restricted to only a few short lessons per week (Fields & Kempe, 1992). By late primary or secondary level, students with literacy difficulties are likely to lack motivation and confidence in their ability to learn to read, as outlined in Figure 7.1. If they are introduced to the confusions of our sound–symbol system with little practice or learning time, it may reinforce their belief that learning to read is too difficult and reinforce their self-perception of being an inadequate learner. While such a skill may be difficult to learn, it still needs to be developed, for the following reasons:

- Skill in phonics will make it more likely that students will be able independently to learn new words (Badenhop, 1992). If they do not have the capacity to use letter–sound patterns to help identify new words, they may be restricted to learning new words only when a teacher or parent is available to identify them.

- As a student progresses through school, an increasing range of new topics and areas of study will be introduced, and it is unlikely that all new words related to these topics will be learned immediately by sight. In such situations, phonics skills may be needed for effective initial word identification. After new words are initially identified using phonics, frequent use should help them develop into sight words.

- A high level of proficiency in phonics helps generate the 'automaticity' and 'fluency' in word identification required to recognise language patterns in print and to allow attention to be directed to meaning (Perfetti, 1986; Torgesen, 1999; Chard, Vaughan & Tyler, 2002).

It could be said that learning phonics in English is a difficult and complex task (although a necessary one) because of the irregularity between sound and symbol. The 26 letters of the alphabet have to represent the 44 sounds that are used in the English language. This leads to letters and letter combinations representing more than one sound, or sounds representing more than one letter, as discussed above, with the 44 phonemes represented by 1200 letters and letter combinations (Landerl, Wilmer & Trinity, 1997).

Training in phonics skills usually occurs in conjunction with developing reading for meaning, and with the development of other reading skills such as sight vocabulary (Greaney, 2001; Torgesen et al., 2000). In such circumstances, it may be more effective to teach letter–sound patterns as they are needed in day-to-day reading rather than by drilling of patterns in isolation. Students will then see their relevance to reading, and introducing them gradually on a needs basis may not be too overwhelming. Parents and children could help identify patterns causing difficulty by writing them down for the teacher. The teacher may then mark the sounds taught on a chart of letter–sound patterns used in reading, such as that developed by Badenhop (1992), shown in Box 7.4. The chart could be used as a guide to provide practice with sound patterns that are similar to those identified as causing a difficulty. Evidence suggests that when children become aware of letter–sound patterns, they are more likely to generalise this awareness to the learning of new letter patterns (Gaskins et al., 1988). Marking letter-sound patterns that have been taught on a chart would also allow the teacher to periodically review sounds that may again need attention.

In recent years, structured training in phonics has again become an important part of regular school activities. This has resulted in a wide variety of structured phonics training material being available. There are also games (including phonics crosswords) that allow training to be more interesting. There are also books with stories that frequently use a particular letter–sound combination and thus provide frequent practice with this sound while reading (for example, O'Carroll, 1992). Stories that are oriented to a particular letter–sound combination help make its relevance to reading seem more evident (Adams, 1990), and frequent practice of this combination facilitates retention (Colteart & Leahy, 1996).

While the gradual introduction of sounds when they are relevant to reading may enhance their learning (Ehri, 1999), the development of phonics skills may still be a difficult and confusing task for students, especially those with a serious learning disability or those with significant developmental delay. Several studies have shown that phoneme segmentation is a difficult task for young students (Solomons, 1992). There is also a great deal of evidence suggesting that both children and adults with learning disabilities have difficulties with phonics (Oloffsen, 2002; Kitz, 1988; Stanovich, 1986). If this skill is introduced at an early stage in the reading process, especially for students with a developmental delay, it may merely convince them that reading is too difficult to learn. In such cases, it would be more effective to concentrate on the development of sight vocabulary for immediate reading and social needs.

Box 7.4

A teaching sequence for basic sounds

Step 1:	5 unvoiced and voiced pairs	
	p, b; t, d; k, g; s, z; f, v	

Step 2:   5 short vowels
           a, e, i, o, u

Step 3:   3 similar sound groupings:
           m, n, ng (nasal sounds)
           h, w, wh (windy sounds)
           l, r (tongue lifting sounds)

Step 4:   3 unvoiced and voiced pairs
           th, th
           sh, zh (treasure)
           ch, j

Step 5:   Early double vowel sounds
           ee, ea (meat), ai, ay, oo, oo

Step 6:   Remaining letters that borrow sounds
           c = /k/or/s/
           x = /ks/
           qu = /kw/
           y = /ee/yoke, jelly
           /ie/sky
           /i/gym

Step 7:   Initial and final consonant blends
           Initial: sp st sc sk sm sn sl sw tw dw bl cl gl fl pl pr br tr dr cr gr fr
           Final: st ft lk ld pt sp ct lp lt xt nd nt nch mp nk
           3 letter blends: thr, spr, squ, spl, shr, str, scr

Step 8:   Long vowel sounds
           Long e spellings: ee, ea, e-e, y
           Long a spellings: ai, ay, a-e
           Long o spellings: oe, ow, oa, o-e
           Long u spellings: ew, ue, u-e
           Long i spellings: ie, i-e, y

Step 9:   Remaining diphthongs and r-controlled vowels
           ar, or, er, ir, ur
           oi, oy; ow, ou; au, aw

From Badenhop, 1992

Use of language (context) cues

Use of context cues in reading involves the identification of language patterns in print and then using knowledge of these patterns to assist in word identification and meaning (Ehri, 1999). Knowledge of sentence structures and the meaning they are providing the reader can serve to narrow down the set of alternative words and meanings the reader expects. This also applies to patterns of letters in words. For example, if the first letter of a word is 'b', there are only eight possible letters that will follow, and this number of possible letters is narrowed further as one goes to the next letter in the word. Other examples can include the letter 'q' which is always followed by 'u' and the fact that a letter combination such as 'ck' is more likely to occur at the end than at the beginning of a word. Similarly, language structures help to predict the order of words in sentences, the likely meaning of words and likely story patterns. Children come to the reading situation with a knowledge of language patterns, which they would have used to help understand oral conversations. They are thus likely to use such patterns when confronted with language in print (Breznitz, 1997; McKay & Neale, 1991). A study of preferred word identification strategies used by teachers in New Zealand (Greaney, 2001) found that while teachers encourage students to use a variety of cues to identify unknown words, the predominant initial cue selected was related more to context-based information. The author also noted that early reading texts facilitate prediction (based on predictable sentence patterns) and teachers tend to encourage children to rely on this source of information.

In particular, use of context cues may help in the following reading situations:

- They may allow a reader to anticipate a word, which could assist quick word recognition.
- They may aid identification of unknown words, especially if used in conjunction with some letters in the word, for example: 'The girl sw— across — river.'
- Context cues may be needed to determine the pronunciation of many words, for example, the word 'bow' in the following two sentences: 'They had to bow to the queen.' 'They had to make a bow and arrow for the king.'

A good reader may be able to use language patterns as a means of 'skimming' over sections of print where the meaning is predictable (Adams, 1990). If this skimming leads to occasional errors, good readers will quickly identify that an error has been made because of problems with meaning, and reread to correct the problem. The sentence below shows it is easy to skim over sections of print, identifying only some of the letters or words, but still retaining meaning. There are many letters missing in the sentence, but the meaning can still be obtained.

Example

'Sh– p–t t— d–ll— in the ba—.'

There are two common interpretations for this sentence, which centre on whether the fourth word is 'dollars' or 'dollies'. If the word is read as 'dollars', then one would expect the last word to be 'bank'. If the last word was 'bath', then a quick reread would interpret the fourth word as 'dollies'. Competent readers become highly skilled at using language patterns, as can be shown by reading the extract below, which was submitted to the *Times*

Educational Supplement to prove that use of such patterns should be considered a part of the reading process. In this extract, a large number of letters are missing from words, or letters are placed in an incorrect order, and yet the passage can still be understood. The title is 'The Real Books Debate is Pointless'. This title should give you enough background to read the rest of the extract with reasonable fluency and good comprehension.

Example

Whxn wxll thx rxxl bxxks xrgxxmxnt xnd? Sxrxly xt mxst bx clxxr thxt chxldrxn usx a vxrxxty of strxtxgxxs tx rxxd prxnt xnd thxt xn xndxrstxndxng xf thx rxlxtxxnshxp bxtwxxn lxttxrs xnd sxxnd xs xnly xne xf thx strxtxgxxs.

It muts be fairyl obvoius to aynone raeding thsi lettre that raedres draw on thier konwledeg of how lagn uaeg wroks, thier abitily to recgonise wrods on sihgt and theri capacity to ues contextaul cleus to enabel them to maek senes of what has goen befoer and perdict what is cmoing next.

If Kenne-Cl-and Ma-Tu-can re-th-let- they mu-agr-tha-a mix-appro-is nec-. If th-ar-no-abl-to re-thi-let-the-mu-be-stu-or cra-,'

Peter Donnelly
General Advisory Teacher
5 Dockings Lane
Cambridgeshire

A letter to the editor, *Times Educational Supplement*, 29 March 1991

Donnelly is using the extract to demonstrate that neither the 'top–down' nor 'bottom–up' approach to teaching reading (as discussed earlier in this chapter) can be seen as the only relevant method. He is trying to prove that a mixed approach is required.

While good readers may use language patterns to speed up word identification and enhance comprehension (Bowey, 1996), poor readers may have to rely on such patterns just to compensate for inadequacies in word identification (Fink, 1996). If a word is not known by sight and phonics skills are limited, then the only alternative might be to try to identify the word from language patterns. However, such patterns may be hard to identify for students with a literacy problem, due to their lack of reading fluency and reading practice (Adams, 1991). Less skilled readers often find themselves reading grade-level materials that are too difficult and the contextual cues from language patterns are thus less available to assist in word recognition and comprehension (Bruce & Robinson, 2002). They may be forced to guess word patterns based on only a few recognised words, or to use only some letters in a word as a basis for its identification. This may result in words being guessed that do not fit the meaning of the sentence pattern, or words being guessed which fit the meaning of the sentence pattern but are not the right word. Poor readers have been found to be less aware of the processes involved in reading, less likely to be aware of strategies used and less likely to monitor and regulate such strategies (Spedding & Chan, 1994).

Reading comprehension – a conversation with only one person present

Able readers are usually highly proficient at word identification and easily identify language patterns in print needed for comprehension (Hummel, 2000). These word identification skills also allow them to easily reread, to create a repetition of what is said, as is frequently used in oral language to help gain meaning. It is useful to think of reading as being similar to a language conversation, but with only one person present. When people are engaged in a conversation, there needs to be a good overlap between what the speaker means and what the listener understands. If the meaning is unclear, the listener will ask the speaker for a further explanation. Similarly, in reading, there needs to be an overlap between the reader's and the author's meaning, with strategic readers using an inner conversation to help them make sense of what they read based on their own thoughts and experiences (Harvey & Goudvis, 2000). If there are difficulties understanding what the author means, the reader cannot directly ask the author about the intended meaning, but can use rereading or reading ahead as a substitute. The slow reading style of poor readers may not allow this rereading to occur easily. They may not enter into an interactive dialogue with the author that involves monitoring meaning, questioning, and accepting/rejecting the interpreted meaning of the author (Galbraith & Clayton, 1998; Smith & Elkins, 1992).

If students do not go through a process of monitoring and reflecting upon what is read, then they may 'read' each word on a page without understanding or remembering what was read. Everyone has at some stage in their student career 'read' a page while thinking of something else and had to reread for meaning. There is a need to actively monitor what is read, to see whether it makes sense and satisfies the purpose for reading. If this purpose is not being achieved, as can be the case with poor readers (Chan, 1991), then they must be able to use compensatory strategies, such as rereading.

Unsworth and Lockhart (1994) found a very small percentage of teacher time for reading comprehension is spent on specific instruction strategies to monitor meaning. The emphasis in comprehension tasks is more likely to be on the answers obtained than on the processes used to obtain the answers (Cairns, 1989). Teachers need to ask questions such as those outlined below to assess whether students have developed effective comprehension monitoring skills:

- Do students know when they are not comprehending?
- Can they locate the source or difficulty?
- Can they modify reading strategies to correct the problem?
- Can they identify information relevant to a theme or assignment objective?
- Can they identify statements that agree with or contradict their own opinions?

Metacognition

Asking questions about monitoring of comprehension such as those outlined above help a student to assess and control their understanding of what they are reading. This strategy is frequently called a metacognitive approach to learning. Metacognition is defined as awareness and control of one's learning or thinking activities by becoming conscious of the skills and strategies required to perform a task effectively (Caldwell, 1995). Students are trained to regulate the use of these skills and strategies by effective planning, monitoring and modifying when appropriate (Cuevas, Fiore & Oser, 2002; Wong, 1985). Haller, Child and Walberg (1988) identified three clusters of metacognitive skills:

- awareness of level of understanding by identifying inconsistencies and inaccuracies while reading
- monitoring that goals for reading are achieved and that effective strategies are being used to achieve these goals

- regulating the use of strategies to ensure that they assist faltering comprehension (for example, rereading, self-questioning).

A variety of activities has been used to help develop metacognitive skills, with Mastropieri and Scruggs (1997) and Manning and Payne (1996) providing detailed overviews of good practice for promoting metacognition and reading comprehension. It is important to choose strategies that help students create meaning, to formulate hypotheses as they read, and to stop them focusing on the words and move their attention to the meaning (Hummel, 2000). Strategic readers know how to think with text (Peterson & Van der Wege, 2002). Some of the more common techniques are outlined below.

- *Text completion:* This requires the reconstruction of meaning of certain sections of a passage that have been deleted. It can include activities such as the cloze procedure, involving the deletion of single words from a passage, and text frame filling, which involves removal of larger sections of text such as phrases.
- *Graphic organisers – imagery, modelling and mapping:* Imagery involves students developing in their mind a picture of the situation being read about. Modelling or mapping involves converting this image into a graphic form, such as a drawing, a map, a plan, a chart or a diagram.
- *Questioning – reciprocal questioning:* Questioning is a class activity that encourages the effective monitoring of meaning. This activity can include reciprocal questioning, in which the pupil and teacher take turns to ask and answer questions. Class groups may also set questions for other class groups to answer. Questions can be used to monitor comprehension.
- *Marking of text:* This activity could involve underlining sections of text that are critical for understanding, such as key words or phrases. The activity again helps facilitate a monitoring of meaning, as the student must understand what they are reading to identify key words or phrases. This technique also means the student must develop an effective schema or meaning structure of what is being read.
- *Prediction and sequencing:* Students are required to predict what might happen next, or to make an estimation of the order of events in a selection, which ensures that they reflect on what is being read. It is most effective when dealing with steps in an instruction manual, in undertaking an experiment or in the development of a plot. Sequencing can also involve cutting the text up into sections, which have to be re-ordered to make sense, or presenting sections of a text and asking students to predict what would happen next.

Hummel (2000) provides a good review of a large number of the strategies described above. Strategies shown to be effective for students with learning disabilities include graphic organisers, especially story mapping, and self-questioning (Gardill & Jitendra, 1999; Hummel, 2000).

Comprehension and text structure

Good comprehenders can identify words quickly and accurately, have a good knowledge of vocabulary, are able to activate their relevant background knowledge, are aware when they do not understand and use sentence structure to help fill in gaps in word identification and comprehension (Bluestein, 2002; Jitendra, Hoppes & Xing, 2002). They are also able to use knowledge of text structures or story grammar, which involves identification of principal components of a story or a text and using these components as an organisational guide when reading (Gersten et al., 2001). A number of different text structures have been identified to use as guides, including structures for reports, discussions, explanations, narratives, recounts and drama. For narrative text types, students get to know the structure of stories and are able to make predictions that help comprehension (Bakker & Whedon, 2002). For students in the first year of secondary school and those with literacy problems, expository texts that present facts, theories and dates may not be familiar and the structure and organisation of the text is less predictable (Bakker & Whedon, 2002). Students at secondary school level are likely to have increased reading demands, an increase in the difficulty of concepts they have to understand and an increase in the variety of different literacies or text structures, all of which have specific concepts, terminology and understanding.

Spelling

While good spelling may not be as important to school success as good reading, spelling difficulties may still cause problems with written assignments and exams (Knight & Smith, 1998). Good spellers may be able to effectively maintain meaning and coherence while writing, as they are less likely to be distracted by uncertainty about spelling (Fryburg, 1997; Westwood, 1999), or disrupted by the need to use a dictionary for spelling. Good spellers are also likely to be viewed more favourably by teachers who are marking assignments or examination papers.

As with reading difficulties, the main reason for spelling difficulties appears to be the inconsistencies between letters and sounds in English. These inconsistencies have developed largely because the English language has acquired words from many other languages. In most cases, the original spelling of these words has been left intact, but pronunciations have gradually evolved to be more 'comfortable' to say in English, which means that words like 'knife' and 'knight' are now pronounced without the 'k'. In addition, some letters were once sounded but have fallen silent (for example, 'e' in love, 'w' in answer). In other countries, such as France and Spain, committees have been set up to regularise and simplify spelling, but this has not happened in English-speaking countries.

The problem of inconsistencies in English spelling has been further aggravated by different regional pronunciations (dialects), especially as it has only been in the last few hundred years that words were thought to have a 'correct' spelling (Hawkins, 1984). Until the advent of the printing press, language was controlled by scribes who were responsible for writing books by hand, one at a time. They often used different spellings to represent different dialects. By the nineteenth century, the advent of the *Oxford English Dictionary* formalised spelling, and people were expected to spell according to the dictionary.

For many children, the complex and confusing relationship between letter patterns and sounds in English may not be properly learned unless specific teaching of these patterns is provided (Knight & Smith, 1998; Ehri et al., 2001). Peters (1985) suggests that good readers and spellers usually work out these patterns as they learn to read and practise writing, with their spelling attempts becoming progressively closer to being correct. Poor spellers, however, may need to be specifically taught these patterns. Spelling 'instruction' in schools, however, may merely involve presenting a list of words to be learned, without any analysis and teaching of common letter–sound patterns. The good spellers might become aware of such patterns and get to know them, but poor spellers may need such common patterns to be identified.

If specific instruction is needed, it should preferably include the following aspects:

- a lot of writing – children who do not write are less likely to be good spellers
- personal writing – children who can see a purpose for writing and become involved in the process are more likely to develop a wider spelling vocabulary than those who write only when required
- drawing attention to letter structures and sound groupings while writing
- providing motivation to write by encouraging attempts at words and not penalising for errors.

James et al. (1991) and Sipe (2002) also claim that improving self-esteem and developing a positive attitude towards spelling can be important. James et al. (1991) used peer counsellors to support poor spellers, and while these counsellors gave no specific tuition in spelling skills, there was a significant improvement in spelling achievement.

Spelling problems

Poor revisualisation

Revisualisation involves the ability to identify visual patterns in words and retain them. It usually involves the ability to consistently look for common letter patterns in words until these patterns (and their sounds) are familiar. For example, good spellers in English know that 'q' is followed by 'u', or that the letter combination 'ck' is more likely to be at the end rather than the beginning of a word. This skill was outlined by Peters (1985), who claimed that good spellers are more likely to 'image' what they have spelt than poor spellers, and poor spellers are more likely to develop incorrect images (Frith, 1980).

The ability to revisualise is one that teachers can consciously develop by giving children a strategy for learning to spell new words. The most common strategy is the 'look, say, cover, write, check' technique, outlined below:

- *look* – look at the word – note letter patterns and peculiarities
- *say* – say the word, spell out the letters
- *cover* – cover the word and see if the letter patterns can be visualised
- *write* – write the word and say the letter as it is written
- *check* – check to see if it is correct.

A variety of similar techniques are suggested in the literature, all of which attempt to help the child to visually analyse the word and become aware of its structure. These activities include the following (Westwood, 1999):

- shutting the eyes and trying to picture the word
- tracing the letters in the air with eyes closed
- using your eyes like a camera to imagine you can see the word.

Underlying learning disabilities

A teacher who has a child with significant spelling problems should look for signs of visual processing difficulties (reversals of letters and words, incorrect letter order, letters added or omitted) or auditory processing deficiencies (sounds not known, sounds omitted, sounds added, confusion of similar sounds). In addition, there may be fine-motor coordination problems resulting in incorrectly or poorly-formed letters (Gregg & Mather, 2002). If any difficulties are evident, a fuller assessment of hearing, vision or motor coordination may be warranted. For children with such problems, multisensory methods involving looking, saying, writing and tracing the letters in the word are often used (as outlined above).

Spelling irregular words

A large number of commonly used words are difficult to spell correctly using letter–sound analysis because they are phonically irregular (for example, 'receive'). These words are hard to learn and yet they are so frequently used they need to be known. Poor spellers may avoid using them and this could restrict the range of words they use in their writing.

Lists of these common but irregular words have been developed (Sipe, 2002), and they often overlap with common sight word lists in reading. As with reading, many such lists have been developed. Examples include those by Graham, Harris and Loynachan (1994) and Westwood (1999).

Such lists can have many uses, including the following:

- as a core list to be learned for all writing situations
- as a supplement to personal word lists developed from spelling errors in writing
- as a check to ensure that students are not avoiding common words that are difficult to spell.

One must be careful, however, not to introduce words on such a list at too rapid a rate for students with spelling problems (Sipe, 2002), with possibly only three words a day being given (Gordon, Vaughan & Schumm, 1993). As with sight lists in reading, it needs to be remembered that such lists cover only the most common words and do not cover specific interest words identified in personal writing. Problem words identified in personal writing are not only important to learn, but students may be more motivated to learn them. Such lists also do not usually group words with similar sound structures together (for example, words ending in 'ould', 'ight' or 'ck'), which would help the child understand common letter–sound patterns and help generalise these patterns to the spelling of new words.

Box 7.5
John

Most teachers cannot remember learning how to read and assume that reading and writing are naturally occurring phenomena. As very few students with severe literacy based learning disabilities take up careers in teaching, educators are usually unaware that reading and writing can be such a challenge. Instead, it is sometimes assumed that poor reading and writing skills are caused, in part, by factors within the student such as poor motivation and practice. John, a 43-year-old male who is the subject of this case study, contradicts the view that problems with reading and spelling are caused by laziness and that children will 'grow out' of their difficulties.

As you examine John's writing samples consider that in spite of his literacy difficulties John has a well-paid job and is a highly respected member of the community. Not surprisingly,

>

Box 7.5 continued

John goes to great effort to hide his difficulties, however as the following card sent to 'Deb', his wife, to wish her 'all the best' shows, his spelling is very weak. John agreed to be the subject of this case study so that teachers would understand what it is like for the children in their classes who have literacy based learning disabilities.

While there was no evidence of a family history of learning disabilities, John was born prematurely and initially failed to thrive. As a young child he was particularly accident-prone and though most incidents were unremarkable, particularly in the case of young boys, two cases of serious head trauma were reported. At the age of 3, John fell down a hole in the backyard and hit his head on a metal bucket, leaving him unconscious for a brief period. In the second incident, he was hit from behind with a cricket bat and the blow knocked him unconscious.

John had unexpected and enduring difficulties acquiring literacy skills in primary and secondary school. As is often the case, John's earliest recollections of feeling different

> To Ded.
>
> *Congratulations-*
> *Prepare to celebrate!*
>
> all the pest
> dont vorry be happy.
>
> Love John.
> The dogs L CAT

Box 7.5 continued

was Year 3 when he refused to read out aloud in class because he was aware of his problems with fluency and word recognition. Up until this point, John had managed to guess the words from the pictures and remembered some whole words but in Year 3 pictures in texts begin to disappear and informational texts, rather than easier to predict narrative texts, are introduced.

According to John, reading was always difficult and rarely enjoyable. In Year 2 John wished that one morning he would wake up and be able to read because he felt it did not make any difference how hard he tried at school. By Year 3 John had all but given up hope. Given he believed he had 'missed out' on learning to read, John did not enjoy school and remembers the embarrassment of feeling that he was 'dumb'. When John's teachers gave him easier work or colouring in to do while the rest of the class completed academic tasks, he felt different. John quickly developed a repertoire of negative behaviours to avoid literacy related tasks and was frequently punished. Had it not been for the firm stance his mother took on attendance, John would have happily stayed at home.

John can remember a special reading group being established at the secondary school he attended, however, places were limited and he was unable to fit into the class for Year 8 or part of Year 9. He finally gained entry when he was ready to leave school at 15 years of age. John's reports show that he did well in Manual Arts and Physical Education and 'tried hard' in most subjects. Several teachers commented that homework tasks were 'not completed' and that John 'refused to answer questions in class'. John explained that he was often unable

to read the instructions for homework tasks and could not pronounce words correctly and felt embarrassed speaking in front of the class.

John has worked in a variety of labour intensive industries but has been unable to realise his hopes of joining the army because of the literacy requirements. Indeed, there have been many instances when John has been recommended for a promotion, but has been unsuccessful because he cannot pass the written examination. To make up for his literacy difficulties John has developed some compensatory skills and as the note below shows, he makes several attempts to spell the word 'barrier' phonically before writing 'border with the doors'. While John's substitution is close in meaning to the target word and this strategy enables others to understand John's writing, it is time consuming and not a true reflection of what he intended to say.

John provided a writing sample (see page 296) about the purchase of his new motorbike. It is apparent that although he attempts to spell words phonically he has great difficulties spelling multisyllabic words, often omitting, reversing or rearranging letters. John has difficulty pronouncing words and his spelling of protection as *protesion* and comfortable as *cufnthable* indicates the link between spoken language and spelling. Put simply, John spells words the way he pronounces them.

John is disappointed with his reading ability. He reads uncomplicated text, such as selected newspaper articles and magazines about topics of interest, slowly but fluently and hesitates at multisyllabic words. John has difficulties sounding out words that are unknown, as he

>

Box 7.5 continued

MY ST1100

The reson I brort my Honda ST1100 is becauge the bike that I had befor the ST was ~~fiter~~ rwiten off after and acedend. So i had to find a bike that sooted my needs. Wich are ~~Sarftt~~ Sarft drive ~~god~~ good flue range. Good ~~&~~wind protesion & Capable of carry all my wifes and my camping gear and ~~es~~ cumthable. for Pilion & Rider.

cannot associate sounds with letters. He will often use the prefix or the initial sound to guess at a word. John remarks that he will often use a picture or the context of a story to guess words he does not immediately recognise.

John regrets not learning to read and write at primary school because it has impacted on many aspects of his life. At the same time, John acknowledges that he has learned to overcome the literacy demands daily life presents him with because he has an otherwise happy and successful life. John concludes: 'I only wish my teachers had not given up on me when I was young because they were the key to my success, I could not fix my reading problems.'

Authors: Dr Lorraine Hammond and Debbie Callcott, Special Education, Edith Cowan University, Perth, Western Australia

Some useful spelling strategies

Research and opinion suggest that the most effective way of learning to spell words is for the student to correct any errors (possibly with teacher or parent direction) immediately after finishing a personal writing or spelling task. This strategy is particularly important for personal writing, where students are more likely to be motivated to learn to spell words correctly as they want to use them.

The only difficulty with such an approach is that it requires fairly close supervision of a poor speller to ensure that errors are immediately identified and corrected. The regular classroom teacher may not have sufficient time for regular personal conferencing (Westwood, 1994), and may have to enlist the aid of parents to help identify errors and teach spelling patterns.

In attempting to spell words correctly, a variety of strategies may help (Scott, 2000). These can include:

- underlining sections of the word the student is not sure how to spell
- using parts of words already known to help with new words
- looking for known words inside the word
- writing the word in two different ways to see which looks right
- thinking of words that have the same letter–sound patterns.

Sipe (2002) suggests challenged spellers need the following:

- instruction that generalises to larger groups of words so students can see order and logic in language
- resources like spell checkers, dictionaries and editors, as well as instruction in how to use them
- learning of high-frequency words that can be emphasised through personal dictionaries, wall charts and frequent discussion
- having opportunities for multiple drafts when correctness is important
- having opportunities to play with words and developing an interest in literacy through meaningful oral and written interactions.

Computer technology and spelling

Even with much help and guidance, some children will really struggle to produce neat script and quickly tire in the process. For these students, handwritten work is a chore and may restrict the opportunity for self-expression. If children have to concentrate too much on letter formation and correct spelling, they may lose coherence and meaning in what they are writing. Use of a computer in such situations may be an important way of re-establishing confidence and enhancing self-esteem.

A number of advantages have been identified for using a computer with children who have writing and spelling problems (Thompson & Gilchrist, 1997):

- It can make the final product look more professional.
- It is easier for the teacher to read, especially as such children often have poorly spaced and ill-formed handwriting, as well as weak spelling.
- It gives the child an opportunity to demonstrate competence, which is very important if they lack confidence in writing and spelling.
- Use of a keyboard may help them to see similar letter patterns in words. They may not easily see or hear the similarities between 'match', 'catch' and 'patch', but may recognise that they use the same keys in the same order.
- The 'fun' element of learning can be stressed, and useful keyboard skills will be acquired.
- Laptops may be used for dictation and may be allowed for writing in exams.

The built-in thesaurus in word processors can be an advantage, as it can provide alternative words to use. Keying in the word 'fat' may access 'obese', 'plump' or 'corpulent', which can be transferred to the text. Computers and word processors also do not criticise and have no memory of past errors. They encourage experimentation, and allow mistakes to be easily changed. If children are competent to use a word processor and can touch type, they will also have access to a spell check and be able easily to revise text. Spell check can release children from the fear of incorrect spelling and the more they produce correctly spelled, legible work, the more they can improve literacy skills. In addition, the more they use correctly spelled words, the better spelling will become. Spell check is especially useful if it highlights and 'beeps' at a wrong spelling. When students know which word is wrong, they can often correct it. MacArthur et al. (1996) investigated the benefits and limitations of spell checkers for students with learning disabilities. The study found that approximately 65 to 75 per cent of errors were identified, and 37 per cent of the errors identified were able to be corrected, compared to only 9 per cent of words corrected without a spell checker. However, when alternative suggestions for the correct word were provided, students were able to select the correct word in 82 per cent of cases, possibly because the spell checker changed the task of spelling from one of recall to the easier task of recognition. However, spell checkers do have limitations. They may identify unusual words as errors and may be unable to identify errors where the word is spelt correctly, but is not grammatically correct for the sentence (for example, here, hear; there, their). Spell checkers thus open the door to using grammatically incorrect words and, without proofreading to check for such errors, they can lead to difficulties (Sipe, 2002).

There are some other drawbacks with the use of computer technology (Rooms, 2000), including the fact that word processing skills take time to develop. Poor keyboard skills can also cause frustrations, as word processing cannot be executed efficiently without good keyboard awareness. There is also the facility to waste time: it can be compelling to 'fiddle' with text. In addition, there is always the danger of accidentally deleting work, or not saving at the end of the lesson. Usually, relevant training and ongoing support for teachers is required if use of such technology is to be effective in the classroom.

In addition to standard word processors, a number of other technologies are being increasingly used to help students with literacy problems. These technologies include a talking word processor, which will say the letters one-by-one, the whole word, the sentence or the complete paragraph. Often, the voice options can be speeded up or slowed down to suit the word recognition or phonological processing skills of the student, with adjustment of individual words also possible to cater for dialects and different pronunciations (Keates, 2000). A talking spell checker will read the sentence that contains the misspelling and then sound out the individual words. Co-Writer is another useful aid, which predicts what students will write from its bank of words and has a built-in grammar facility. Students write in the first letter of the word they wish to write and Co-Writer then selects from its bank of words the most common words that begin with that letter. If the word the pupil wants is not selected, the student keys in the second letter of the word. The Co-Writer also reads the word out, which assists poor readers who may be unable to read the words. Co-Writer provides the words most likely to be needed and learns the vocabulary the pupil is using regularly. The student can hear the individual words with the talking word processor and have them repeated with Co-Writer. They can also be repeated again as the paragraph is read out.

Another useful aid is the speech recognition system, which converts spoken words into text. These systems are now relatively cheap and will run on most home computers. They require some training to enable them to recognise the voice of the specific user. The user reads sample sentences from cues provided on the screen and a profile of the user's voice is developed. After this is developed, which may take an hour or more, a word recognition rate of 60 to 100 words per minute is achieved. Two very common products are Dragon Naturally Speaking and Kurzweil 1000 and 3000. Kurzweil products will read out Internet messages and highlight words in different colours as they are read. It will also scan documents into the computer and then read them out, with reading occurring at various speeds.

Keates (2000) provides a good guide to parents of children with dyslexia about information communications technology. There is also a good review in the *Australian Journal of Learning Disabilities*, Volume 7(1) on pages 46 and 47.

Numeracy

Reading is usually considered a priority over mathematics when helping children with learning problems as it affects all subject areas. Rohl and Milton (2002) surveyed Australian schools and found that while many schools were implementing support programs in literacy, only a small number were implementing support programs in numeracy. However, numeracy cannot be overlooked, as it has been estimated that 6 to 10 per cent of children may have difficulties with numeracy (Rohl & Milton, 2002; Rourke & Conway, 1997; Prior, 1996). Just as problems with reading can influence a child's self-image, failure at mathematics can lead to negative attitudes to school and a general feeling of inadequacy (Heymann, 1990). Numeracy also tends to be developmental and sequential (Cawley & Miller, 1989), which means that problems with early level skills may cause difficulties in efficiently mastering other skills, particularly those developed at a later level. A good example would be the mastering of basic number facts (times tables, simple addition and subtraction combinations), which need to be known fairly automatically if a child is to work efficiently in other or later areas of numeracy (problem-solving, measurement) (Kroesbergen & Van Luit, 2003). This interdependency and the hierarchical nature of mathematics also make it relatively easy for teachers to construct a sequence of skills for mastery. When such a sequence is developed, it can be used systematically to identify likely skill problem areas, as well as providing a possible sequence of activities for teaching.

Survival mathematics

It is important to consider what level of numeracy skills is needed by children with disabilities or learning difficulties. The initial aim would be to develop sufficient skills to survive in society. Mercer and Miller (1992) claim that students with learning disabilities are often socially handicapped, as their daily living requires the application of mathematics skills which they may not have. They reported that the mean maths score for such children in Year 12 was Year 5 level, with two of every three students with learning disabilities in Year 6 and above receiving special maths instruction.

Westwood (2000) also identified a core content of essential mathematics for non-academic school leavers that included the following:

- ability to count
- a high degree of automaticity in recall of basic number facts
- ability to carry out the four basic processes, with emphasis on addition and subtraction
- ability to use a calculator for multiplication and division
- basic problem-solving using the four processes
- understanding and recognition of simple common fractions ($\frac{1}{4}$, $\frac{1}{2}$, $\frac{3}{4}$, $\frac{1}{10}$)
- awareness of meaning of 100%, 50%, 25%, 10%
- ability to measure and construct, using mm, cm and m
- ability to tell time and days of week, months of year
- time estimation for journeys
- money – coin and note recognition, performing basic processes and developing competence with simple budgeting and banking
- problem-solving – all the above skills and processes applied to solving practical problems.

The authors cited above and others emphasise the importance of problem-solving in mathematics as well as the need to understand basic number concepts and the need for basic number facts to be known (Kroesbergen & Van Luit, 2003; Van Luit & Schopman, 2000). These core competencies are necessary if the student is to develop independent living skills. These competencies will be discussed more fully in the rest of this chapter, including the language of maths, or understanding of mathematical concepts, automatic knowledge of basic number facts, and the basic principles of mathematical problem solving.

Mathematics and language

In recent years, there has been more emphasis placed on the need to ensure that students understand the language and concepts that are used in mathematics activities. Students with learning difficulties may have problems conceptualising mathematical operations, solving mathematical word problems and conceptualising and learning algorithms (Mastropieri, Scruggs & Chung, 1998). To understand maths, students need to understand concepts such as 'more than', 'less than', 'first', 'last'. If students don't understand such concepts, they may not realise how maths is used to identify which amount is 'more' or 'less' or who was 'first' or 'last'. Often these concepts are very abstract but, by teaching such concepts, the teacher is developing an understanding of the fundamentals required for all later maths work.

Language in maths is further complicated by the fact that a variety of different words may be used for the same operation. For the operation of subtraction, the following common words may be used: 'minus', 'take away', 'subtract'. However, a variety of other terms are also likely to be used including 'difference', 'less', 'reduce', 'take off' and 'from', all of which involve subtraction.

There is also the problem that, while some words used may have the same meaning in maths and everyday language (add, subtract), others have only a mathematical usage (quotient, integer, equilateral) and still others may have a different meaning in maths and everyday use (take away, odd, negative, scale, degree) (Henderson, 2001; Grauberg, 1998; Marr & Helme, 1991). The issue is further complicated by the fact that word statements in mathematics are likely to be more grammatically complex than normal reading, which in turn is more complex than oral language (Cawley et al., 2001; Munro, 1989). Prior et al. (1999) found that early reading problems might predict later maths difficulties. Reading word problems in mathematics is likely to require more precision. Skim reading or text sampling, which often occurs in other reading activities, would be inappropriate in maths. A detailed word-by-word approach is likely to be more appropriate (Henderson, 2001; Jitendra et al., 1998).

As a consequence of these potential language problems, much emphasis has been placed on building an understanding of basic mathematical language and concepts. This can be achieved by using mathematical experiences related to everyday activities. Emphasis is placed on doing things that relate to the child's life and also talking about them. To make the learning of concepts even more manageable, concrete materials are frequently used in explanations. This is particularly so when developing an understanding of basic concepts of addition, subtraction, multiplication and division.

In teaching such concepts, it may be useful to start with the children explaining mathematical activities in their own language, such as the terms 'extra', 'more' or 'put with' when working with materials related to addition. These terms may then be gradually replaced by mathematical words, such as 'plus' and 'add'. When children are comfortable with these mathematical words, the symbol '+' for these terms can be gradually introduced (Irons, 2000).

A useful sequence for developing understanding of the basic facts could be as follows:

- Learn the concept by starting with concrete materials and evolving to the more abstract materials, as outlined below:

1 Concrete	*3 Semi-abstract*
1 + 2 = □ + □□ (Blocks)	1 + 2 = | + || (Tallies)
2 Semi-concrete	*4 Abstract*
1 + 2 = ☛ + ☛☛ (Pictures)	1 + 2 = 1 + 2 (Symbols)

- Give strategies to work out facts before they are memorised; for example, the basic number fact 3 + 3 = 6 can be worked out by:
  - counting both numbers: '1–2–3/4–5–6'
  - counting from the highest number: '3–4–5–6'
  - using doubles: '2–4–6'.
- Finally, developing immediate memory (automaticity) of the basic facts through regular practice.

Basic number facts

The basic number facts involve simple (two figure) addition, subtraction and division combinations as well as multiplication tables. These facts may not be effectively learned by many children with learning disabilities (Jitendra, Di Pipi & Perron-Jones, 2002; Mastropieri, Scruggs & Chung, 1998; Mercer & Miller, 1992). They are, however, fundamental to achieving competence in most maths areas. For example, solving simple problems related to everyday activities for time, money and measurement assumes knowledge of these basic number facts.

Many students with a learning disability may understand the basic concepts, but appear to remain at the lower stage of using counting strategies, such as fingers to count or a number line, instead of memorising the basic facts. Counting strategies have been claimed to interfere with higher level multiple number operations and divert attention away from the problem to be solved (Hasselbring, Goin & Bransford, 1987). It has been claimed that fewer than 2 per cent of the basic facts are recalled automatically by children with learning disabilities, when operations involving ones (for example, $2 + 1$) and doubles (for example, 2×2) are not included (Hasselbring, Goin & Bransford, 1987).

If children are experiencing problems with the basic number facts, the specific problems need to be identified. Fortunately in maths, this is not difficult as there are many commercial and school-developed assessment methods available (for example, Mercer & Mercer, 2001). Most of these methods involve putting basic facts in a hierarchy of increasing level of difficulty, with a number of examples of each basic fact to be attempted at each level of the hierarchy, as shown in Box 7.6. Students are required to complete the activities at each level of the sequence until they start to have difficulties, which could be the starting point for any special assistance to be given. The rest of the sequence could then be used as a basic program for future teaching activities. A test of such operations as those shown in Box 7.6 may be used as a whole class screen at the start of a teaching year, or as a basis for diagnosing individual difficulties. Once the point of failure on the hierarchy identifies the area of difficulty, it does not usually take a great deal of explanation to correct the problem, or to give more practice in that area until a level of independence is gained. Practice at school could easily be supplemented by parental support at home.

A wide review of research into mathematics interventions for children with special needs (Kroesbergen & Van Luit, 2003) found the most common area of intervention involved basic mathematics skills. It was also identified as the area in which intervention was most effective, with direct teacher instruction being more effective than computer aided instruction.

Summary

This chapter outlined the nature of the reading process and the likely underlying learning disabilities related to reading. It then detailed the basic literacy and numeracy skills, as well as suggesting ways of facilitating the learning of such skills.

Emphasis was placed on the fact that many learning disabilities are not 'visible' and, as a consequence, effective support and understanding has not always been forthcoming. Reading is a very complex visual, auditory and language processing task, with minor problems in any of these areas likely to make the task much more difficult. In such situations the student may be very vulnerable to discouragement leading to lack of effort, failure and even further

Box 7.6
An addition hierarchy

1	Add two single numbers up		$4 + 5 =$
			$2 + 6 =$
2	Add three single numbers up		$3 + 2 + 1 =$
			$4 + 1 + 3 =$
3	Add two single numbers up		$9 + 8 =$
			$11 + 6 =$
4	Add three single numbers up		$6 + 7 + 4 =$
			$5 + 6 + 8 =$
5	Add a double number to a single number – no bringing across	55 + 3	82 + 6
6	Add a double number to a single number – bringing across from ones	85 + 7	64 + 8
7	Add two double numbers – no bringing across	42 + 25	57 + 31
8	Add two double numbers – bringing across from ones	49 + 34	16 + 75
9	Add two triple numbers – no bringing across	216 + 431	427 + 212
10	Add two triple numbers – bringing across from ones	158 + 239	227 + 135
11	Add two triple numbers – bringing across from tens	490 + 168	357 + 292
12	Add two triple numbers – bringing across from alternative places	635 + 547	467 + 735
13	Add three triple numbers – bringing across from all places	325 + 436 561	242 + 415 674
14	Add four double numbers bringing across from both places	26 + 43 32 32	45 + 58 16 21

discouragement. If the cause of this discouragement is not 'visible', then the subsequent lack of effort may be seen as the cause for the learning problems rather than being a consequence of the underlying learning disability.

The chapter also provided an overview of the basic word recognition skills required if effective comprehension is to occur. Emphasis was placed on the need for word identification to be 'automatic', so that attention can be directed to the construction of meaning. The basic skills involved in spelling and mathematics were also discussed.

The next chapter examines ways in which teachers and parents can help to improve the basic skills of students who are having difficulty with literacy or numeracy.

Discussion questions

1 Explain the concept of a downward learning cycle. Why is it more likely to apply to students with less obvious learning disabilities?

2 Why is 'automatic' word identification important for effective reading comprehension?

3 Phonics and phonemic awareness skills are a vital factor in the development of effective reading and spelling. However, many children and adults have great difficulty developing these skills. Why?

4 The learning of basic number facts is considered to be a very important prerequisite for developing the mathematical skills that are needed for everyday living activities. Why are the basic number facts so important?

Individual activities

1 Students with learning disabilities often feel frustrated with reading and will read as little as possible. Read the statistics section of a research journal article and ask yourself the following questions:
   a Reading:
      i On first reading, was attention directed more to word identification or to meaning (see Figure 7.2)?
      ii If asked to read this statistics section aloud to your peers and explain the meaning, would you feel confident or comfortable?
      iii If this article was required reading for a course, would you avoid reading it unless it was going to be assessed (see Figure 7.1)?

   b Language:
      i Did you understand all the words used?
      ii Is the language used in this passage different from how you would normally speak and, if so, how?

2 Students with literacy problems may have to resort to guessing words from context, and often read so slowly that text coherence is lost. Read a page of text in an area with which you are not familiar (or the statistics section of a research article) and ask yourself these questions:
   a Did you remember the beginning of the paragraph by the time you had reached the end?
   b If there were unfamiliar words, how did you deduce their meaning?
   c In trying to construct meaning of what is being read, analyse the methods you used to:
      i monitor whether you understand
      ii identify specific areas of difficulty.
   d What reading strategies did you use to help you construct meaning? Were they different strategies from those you would use when reading a novel?
   e Read the activities outlined in the section in this chapter titled 'Developing metacognitive skills' and identify whether you use any of them. Do you use other strategies?

Group activities

1   The complexities of our sound–symbol system make spelling a very difficult task for students with a learning disability. At the bottom of this question are listed some words which are very difficult to spell (demons). Get one person in the group to administer these words as a test, then get each individual to count up their errors and tell the rest of the group their score.

    a   Did anyone in the group spell all the words correctly?

    b   Read the section on 'Spelling' strategies in this chapter and discuss which techniques (if any) were used by members of the group while doing the test.

    c   Read the 'Phonics difficulties and spelling' section in this chapter and identify your phonics level (no phonics, semi-phonics, phonics, transition, correct).

    d   Discuss among members of the group how they felt if they got a low score:

        i embarrassed

       ii expected a low score (learned helplessness).

The demons: height, separate, business, sincerely, accommodation, necessary, queue, questionnaire, idiosyncrasy, diarrhoea, harassment, indispensable, buoyant, embarrassment, census.

2   Read the example of process writing below and answer the questions following.

Process writing

In Novena my mum is haveind a baby. And she hopes for a doy. Ane she haves every thig for her to go to the hospitat. Thent I will be sad. She haves got the batsennet. She got to baby soc and to Peairs of soc and she have got a blue toy and…

    a   Can this person effectively hear sounds in words?

    b   Does this person know many irregular words in spelling by sight (see heading in this chapter titled 'Difficulties in spelling irregular words')?

    c   Does this person have trouble with phonics?

3   Read the writing samples in the Box 7.5 (John), especially the sample in which he talks about the purchase of his new ST 1100 motorbike and answer the following questions:

    a   Does he appear to have any underlying visual problems or auditory problems when spelling?

    b   Does he appear to have any fine motor coordination problems when writing?

    c   Identify words he knows by sight when writing about his new bike.

4   Words used in numeracy can be confusing, as they may often have a different meaning in maths than in everyday usage. As a group, identify words that could be categorised under the following headings:

    a   words that mean the same in maths and everyday use

    b   words with only a maths meaning

    c   words that have a different meaning in maths than in everyday use.

5   Read the 'Demographic data on learning disabilities' in the example below, and:

    a   discuss the social and economic consequences of having a learning disability

    b   use the data as a basis for people in the group to discuss any personal experiences of children with learning disabilities/literacy problems and the effect it had on them.

Demographic data on learning disabilities

- Fifty per cent of juvenile delinquents tested were found to have undetected learning disabilities.
- Up to 60 per cent of adolescents in treatment for substance abuse have learning disabilities.
- Sixty-two per cent of students who are learning disabled were unemployed one year after graduating.
- Fifty per cent of females with learning disabilities will be mothers (many of them single) within 3 to 5 years of leaving high school.
- Thirty-one per cent of adolescents with learning disabilities will be arrested 3 to 5 years out of high school.
- Learning disabilities and substance abuse are the most common impediments to keeping welfare clients from becoming and remaining employed.

(Source: Turner, 1997)

6   Read the outline below of what good readers and poor readers do.

   a   Discuss how these aspects relate to processing stages in reading as outlined in Figure 7.2.

   b   Discuss within the tutorial group personal situations in which you are likely to be good or poor readers.

   c   Discuss how these aspects of good and poor readers relate to the downward learning cycle (Figure 7.1).

   d   How might you try to improve comprehension skills for poor readers with the problems outlined below?

Good readers	Poor readers
Before reading:	
Think about what they already know about a subject	Begin to read without thinking about the topic
Know the purpose for which they read	Do not know why they are reading
Are motivated or interested to begin reading	Lack interest and motivation to begin reading
Have a general sense of how the big ideas will fit together	Have little sense of how the big ideas will fit together

Good readers	Poor readers
During reading:	
Pay simultaneous attention to words and meaning	Over-attend to individual words; miss salience
Read fluently	Read slower and at the same rate of speed
Concentrate well while reading	Have difficulty concentrating, particularly during silent reading
Willing to 'risk' encountering difficult words and able to grapple with text ambiguities	Unwilling to 'risk'; easily defeated by words and text
Construct efficient strategies to monitor comprehension	Unable to construct efficient strategies to monitor comprehension
Stop to use a 'fix-it' strategy when confused	Seldom use a 'fix-it' strategy; plod on ahead, eager to finish
Reading skills improve	Reading progress is painfully slow

Good readers	Poor readers
After reading:	
Understand how the pieces of information fit together	Do not understand how the pieces of information fit together
Able to identify what's salient	May focus on the extraneous, peripheral
Interested in reading more	See reading as distasteful

(Source: Cibrowski, 1995)

References

Adams, A. (1991). Oral reading errors of readers with learning disabilities: Variations produced within the instructional and frustration ranges. *Remedial and Special Education, 12*(1), 48–55, 62.

*Adams, M. J. (1990). *Beginning to Read*, Cambridge, MA: MIT Press.

*Adams, M. J., Foorman, B. R., Lundberg, I. & Beeler, T. (1998). *Phonemic Awareness in Young Children: A Classroom Curriculum*. Baltimore, MA: Paul H. Brookes.

Alvermann, D. E. (2002). Effective literacy instruction for adolescents. *Journal of Literacy Research, 32*(4), 189–208.

Andrews, S. (1989). Psycholinguistics and reading. *New South Wales Journal of Special Education*, 10, 15–21.

Badenhop, A. (1992). Phonological awareness skills in the first two years of school. In A. Watson & A. Badenhop (Eds), *Preventing Reading Failure*, Gosford, NSW: Ashton Scholastic.

Bakker, J. & Whedon, C. K. (2002). Teaching text structure to improve reading comprehension. *Intervention in School and Clinic, 37*(4), 229–37.

Barker, K. A., Torgesen, J. K. & Wagner, R. K. (1992). The role of orthographic processing skills on five different reading tasks. *Reading Research Quarterly, 27*(4), 335–45.

Bishop, J. (2000). New developments in English literacy for indigenous students. *Newsletter of the Australian Literacy Educator's Association*, June, 1–2.

Bluestein, N. A. (2002). Comprehension through characterisation: Enabling readers to make personal connections with the literature. *The Reading Teacher, 55*(5), 431–4.

Boden, C. & Brodeur, D. A. (1999). Visual processing of verbal and nonverbal stimuli in adolescents with reading disabilities. *Journal of Learning Disabilities, 32*(1), 58–71.

Booth, J. R., Perfetti, C. A., McWhinnie, B. & Hunt, S. B. (2000). The association of rapid temporal perception with orthographic and phonological processing in children and adults with reading impairment. *Scientific Studies of Reading, 4*(2), 101–32.

Bouldoukian, J., Wilkins, A. J. & Evans, B. J. W. (2002). Randomised controlled trial of the effect of coloured overlays on the rate of reading of people with specific learning difficulties. *Ophthalmic and Physiological Optics, 22*, 55–60.

Bowey, J. A. (1996). Phonological sensitivity as a proximal contributor to phonological recoding skills in children's reading. *Australian Journal of Psychology, 48*(3), 113–18.

*Brent, M., Gough, F. & Robinson, S. (2001). *One in Eleven: Practical Strategies for Adolescents With a Language Learning Disability*. Melbourne: ACER.

Breznitz, Z. (1997). Effects of accelerated reading rate on memory for text among dyslexic readers. *Journal of Educational Psychology, 89*(2), 289–97.

Broomfield, H. & Combley, M. (1997). *Overcoming Dyslexia.* London: Whurr.

Bruce, M. & Robinson, G. L. (2002). The effectiveness of a metacognitive approach to teaching word identification skills to upper primary poor readers. *Special Education Perspectives, 11*(1), 3–30.

Burnip, L. (1994). Hearing impairment, phonological awareness, and the acoustic environment of the classroom. *Australian Journal of Remedial Education, 26*(1), 4–11.

Byrne, B., Freebody, P. & Gates, A. (1992). Longitudinal data on the relations of word reading strategies to comprehension, reading time, and phonemic awareness. *Journal of Educational Psychology, 83*(4), 451–5.

Cairns, L. (1989). Reading theory into practice: The practicalities. *Australian Journal of Reading, 12*(3), 223–31.

Caldwell, M. J. (1995). Metacognition, reading and children with special needs. *Australian Journal of Remedial Education, 24*(3), 16–21.

*Catts, H. W. & Kamhi, A. G. (1999). Causes of reading disabilities. In H. W. Catts & A. C. Kamhi (Eds), *Language and Reading Disabilities.* Boston: Allyn & Bacon.

Cawley, J. F. & Miller, J. H. (1989). Cross-sectional comparison of the mathematics performance of children with learning disabilities: Are we on the right track for comprehensive programming? *Journal of Learning Disabilities, 22*(4), 250–4.

Cawley, J. F., Miller, J. H. & Carr, S. C. (1991). An examination of the reading performance of students with mild educational handicaps or learning disabilities. *Journal of Learning Disabilities, 23*(5), 284–90.

Cawley, J., Parmar, R., Foley, T. E., Salmon, S. & Roy, S. (2001). Arithmetic performance of students: Implications for standards and programming. *Exceptional Children, 67*(3), 311–28.

Center, Y. & Freeman, L. (1998). Phonemic/phonological awareness. Literacy Discussion Paper No. 2. New South Wales Department of Education and Training.

Chan, L. (1991). Metacognition and remedial education. *Australian Journal of Remedial Education, 23*(1), 4–10.

Chard, D. J., Vaughan, S. & Tyler, B. (2002). A synthesis of research on effective interventions for building reading fluency with elementary students with learning disabilities. *Journal of Learning Disabilities, 35*(5), 386–406.

Chase, C., Ashourzadeh, A., Kelly, C., Monfette, S. & Kinsey, K. (2003). Can the magnocellular pathway read? Evidence from studies of colour. *Vision Research, 43,* 1211–22.

Cibrowski, J. (1995). Using textbooks with students who cannot read them. *Remedial and Special Education, 16*(2), 90–101.

Collins, M. (1998). Young children's reading strategies. *Australian Journal of Language and Literacy, 21*(1), 55–66.

Colteart, V. & Leahy, J. (1996). Procedures used by beginning and skilled readers to read unfamiliar letter strings. *Australian Journal of Psychology, 48*(3), 124–9.

Conlon, E. G., Lovegrove, W. J., Chekaluk, E. & Pattison, P. E. (1999). Measuring visual discomfort. *Visual Cognition, 6*(6), 637–63.

*Cordini, B. (1990). *Living With a Learning Disability* (2nd edn). Carbondale, IL: Southern Illinois University Press.

Cuevas, H. M., Fiore, S. M. & Oser, R. L. (2002). Scaffolding cognitive and metacognitive processes in low verbal ability learners: Use of diagrams in computer based training environments. *Instructional Science, 30*(6), 433–64.

Demb, J. M., Boynton, G. M., Best, M. & Heeger, D. J. (1998). Psychophysical evidence for a magnocellular pathway deficit in dyslexia. *Vision Research, 38*(11), 1555–9.

Doyle, W. (1993). Academic work. *Review of Educational Research, 53,* 159–200.

Eeds, M. A. (1985). Bookwords: Using a beginning list of high frequency words from children's literature, K–3. *The Reading Teacher, 38,* 418–23.

Ehri, L. C. (1997). Sight word learning in normal readers and dyslexics. In B. A. Blachman (Ed.). *Foundations of Reading Acquisition and Dyslexia.* Mahwah, NJ: Lawrence Erlbaum, pp.163–89.

*Ehri, L. C. (1999). The unobtrusive role of words in reading text. In L. R. Giorcelli & A. J. Watson (Eds), *Accepting the Literacy Challenge* (pp. 26–50). Sydney: Scholastic.

Ehri, L. C., Nunes, S. R., Willows, D. M., Schuster, B., Yaghoub-Zadeh, Z. & Shanahan, T. (2001). Phonemic awareness instruction helps children to learn to read: Evidence from the National Reading Panel's meta-analysis. *Reading Research Quarterly, 36*(3), 250–87.

Evans, B. J. W. (2000). *Dyslexia and Vision.* London: Whurr.

Felsenfeld, S., Broen, P. A. & McGue, M. (1994). A 28-year follow-up of adults with a history of moderate phonological disorder: Educational and occupational results. *Journal of Speech and Hearing Research, 37*(6), 1241–353.

Fields, B. & Kempe, A. (1992). Corrective feedback in whole language teaching: Implications for children with learning problems. *Australasian Journal of Special Education, 16*(2), 22–31.

Filozof, E. M., Albertin, H. K., Jones, C. R. & Steme, S. S. (1998). Relation of adolescent self-esteem to selected academic variables. *The Journal of School Health, 68*(2), 68–72.

Fink, R. P. (1996). Successful dyslexics: A constructivist study of passionate interest reading. *Journal of Adolescent and Adult Literacy, 39*(4), 268–79.

Fischer, B. & Hartnegg, K. (2000). Effects of visual training on saccade control in dyslexia. *Perception, 29,* 531–42.

Fitzgerald, M. H. & Paterson, K. A. (1995). The hidden disability dilemma for the preservation of self. *Journal of Occupational Science: Australia, 2*(1), 13–21.

Foorman, B. R., Francis, D. J., Fletcher, J. M., Schatschneider, C. & Mehta, P. (1998). The role of instruction in learning to read: Preventing reading failure in at-risk children. *Journal of Educational Psychology, 90*(1), 37–55.

Foorman, B. R., Francis, D. J., Fletcher, J. M. & Lynn, A. (1996). Relation of phonological and orthographic processing to early reading: Comparing two approaches to regression-based, reading-level-match designs. *Journal of Educational Psychology, 88*(4), 639–52.

Frith, U. (1980). *Cognitive Processes in Spelling.* London, UK: Academic Press.

*Fryburg, E. (1997). *Reading and Learning Disability.* Springfield, Ill.: Charles C. Thomas.

Galbraith, E. & Clayton, M. (1998). An investigation of oral reading fluency of Grade 4 students. *Australasian Journal of Special Education, 21*(2), 98–114.

Gardill, M. C. & Jitendra, A. K. (1999). Advanced story map instruction. *The Journal of Special Education, 33*(1), 2–17, 28.

Gaskins, I. W., Downer, M. A., Anderson, R. C., Cunningham, P. M., Gaskins, R. W., Schommer, M., et al. (1988). A metacognitive approach to phonics: Using what you know to decode what you don't know. *Remedial and Special Education, 9*(1), 36–41.

Gerber, A. (1993). *Language Related Learning Difficulties*. Baltimore, MD: Paul H. Brookes Pub. Co.

Gersten, R., Fuchs, L. S., Williams, J. P. & Baker, S. (2001). Teaching comprehension strategies for students with learning disabilities: A review of research. *Review of Educational Research, 71*(2), 297–320.

Goldsworthy, C. L. (1998). *Sourcebook of Phonological Awareness Activities*. San Diego: Singular Publishing.

Gonzalez, M. R. O., Espinal, A. I. G. & Rosquette, R. G. (2002). Remedial interventions for children with reading disabilities: Speech perception – an effective component in phonological training? *Journal of Learning Disabilities, 35*(4), 340–2.

Gordon, J., Vaughan, S. & Schumm, J. S. (1993). Spelling interventions: A review of the literature and implications for instruction for students with learning disabilities. *Learning Disabilities: Research and Practice, 8*(3), 175–81.

Graham, S., Harris, K. R. & Loynachan, C. (1994). The spelling for writing list. *Journal of Learning Disabilities, 27*(4), 210–24.

Grauberg, E. (1998). *Elementary Mathematics and Language Difficulties*. London: Whurr.

Greaney, K. (2001). An investigation of teacher preferences for word identification strategies. *The Australian Journal of Language and Literacy, 24*(1), 21–30.

Greaves, D., Coughlan, A., Souter, L. & Munro, J. (1998). The contribution of phonological processing skills to reading comprehension in grades one and three. *Australian Journal of Learning Disabilities, 3*(2), 22–6.

Gregg, N. & Mather, N. (2002). School is fun at recess: Informal analysis of written language for students with learning disabilities. *Journal of Learning Disabilities, 35*(1), 7–22.

Griffith, P. I. & Olsen, M. W. (1992). Phonemic awareness helps beginning readers break the code. *The Reading Teacher, 45*(7), 516–23.

Groinick, W. & Ryan, R. (1990). Self perception, motivation and adjustment in children with learning disabilities. *Journal of Learning Disabilities, 23*(3), 177–81.

Haller, E. P., Child, D. A. & Walberg, H. J. (1988). Can comprehension be taught: A quantitative analysis of metacognitive studies. *Educational Researcher, 17*(9), 5–8.

Halveston, E. M. (1987). Management of dyslexia and related learning disabilities. *Journal of Learning Disabilities, 20*, 414–21.

Harding, L. M., Beech, J. R. & Snedden, W. (1985). The changing pattern of reading errors and reading styles from 5 to 11 years of age. *British Journal of Educational Psychology, 55*, 45–52.

Hardman, P. K. & Morton, D. G. (1991). The link between developmental dyslexia, ADD and chemical dependency. *Environmental Medicine, 8*(3), 61–72.

*Harvey, S. & Goudvis, A. (2000). *Strategies That Work*. Portland, ME: Stenhouse.

Hasselbring, T. S., Goin, L. I. & Bransford, J. D. (1987). Automaticity. *Teaching Exceptional Children, 19*(3), 30–1.

Hawkins, E. (Ed.) (1984). *Awareness of Language*. London, UK: Cambridge Educational Press.

Heidelberger, R., Wang, M. M. & Sherry, D. M. (2003). Differential distribution of synaptotagmin immunoreactivity among synapses in the goldfish, salamander and mouse retina. *Visual Neuroscience, 30*, 37–49.

Henderson, A. (2001). Mathematically thinking. In M. Hunter-Carsch (Ed.), *Dyslexia: A Psychosocial Perspective* (pp. 219–31). London: Whurr.

Heymann, W. B. (1990). The self-perception of a learning disability and its relationship to academic self-concept and self-esteem. *Journal of Learning Disabilities, 23*(8), 472–5.

Holmes, V. M. (1996). Skilled reading and orthographic processing. *Australian Journal of Psychology, 48*(3), 143–54.

Howell, E. R. & Peachey, G. T. (1990). Visual dysfunction in learning. In S. R. Butler (Ed.), *The Exceptional Child*. Sydney: Harcourt Brace Jovanovich.

Hummel, S. (2000). Developing comprehension skills of secondary students with specific learning disabilities: A review of research. *Australian Journal of Learning Disabilities, 5*(4), 22–7.

Hunter-Carsch, M. (2001). Seeing the wood and the trees: Specific learning difficulties and dyslexia. In M. Hunter-Carsch (Ed.), *Dyslexia: A Psycho-social Perspective*. London: Whurr.

Hussey, E. S. (2002). Binocular visual sensation in reading II: Implications of a unified theory. *Journal of Behavioral Optometry, 13*(3), 66–83.

Irlen, H. (1991). *Reading By the Colors*. New York: Avery.

Irons, R. (2000). *Living and Learning: Beginning Maths*. Naragamba, QLD: Prime Education.

James, J., Charlton, T., Leo, E. & Indoe, D. (1991). A peer to listen. *Support for Learning, 6*(4), 165–9.

Jitendra, A. K., Di Pipi, C. M. & Perron-Jones, N. (2002). An exploratory study of schema-based word problems-solving instruction for middle school students with learning disabilities: An emphasis on conceptual and procedural understanding. *The Journal of Special Education, 36*(1), 26–38.

Jitendra, A. K., Hoppes, M. K. & Xing, Y. P. (2002). Enhancing main idea comprehension for students with learning problems. *The Journal of Special Education, 34*(3), 127–39.

Jitendra, A. K., McGoey, K., Bhat, P., Griffin, C. C., Gardill, M. C. & Riley, T. (1998). Effects of mathematical word problem solving by students at risk or with mild disabilities. *The Journal of Educational Research, 91*(6), 345–55.

Juel, C., Griffith, P. & Gough, P. (1986). Acquisitions of literacy: A longitudinal study of children in first and second grade. *Journal of Educational Psychology, 78*, 243–55.

Kame'enui, E. J. & Simmons, D. C. (1999). Beyond effective practices to schools as host environments: Building and sustaining a school-wide intervention model in beginning reading for all children. *Australasian Journal of Special Education, 23*(2 & 3), 100–27.

*Kamhi, A. G. & Catts, H. W. (1999). Reading development. In H. W. Catts & A. G. Kamhi (Eds), *Language and Reading Disabilities*. Boston: Allyn & Bacon, pp. 25–49.

Kearsley, I. (2002). Build on the rock: Teacher feedback and reading competence. *Australian Journal of Language and Literacy, 25*(1), 8–19.

*Keates, A. (2000). *Dyslexia and Information Communications Technology: A guide for Parents*. London: David Fulton.

Keogh, B. K. & Pellard, M. (1985). Vision training revisited. *Journal of Learning Disabilities, 18*(4), 228–36.

Kim, J. H. & Goetz, E. T. (1994). Context effects on word recognition and reading comprehension of good and poor readers: A test of the interactive–compensatory hypothesis. *Reading Research Quarterly, 29*(1), 179–87.

Kintsch, W. (1977). On comprehending stories. In M. A. Just & P. A. Carpenter (Eds), *Cognitive Processes in Comprehension*. Hillsdale, NJ: Lawrence Erlbaum.

Kitz, W. R. (1988). Adult literacy: A review of the past and a proposal for the future. *Remedial and Special Education*, *9*(4), 44–50.

Knight, B. A. & Smith, J. M. (1998). The teaching of spelling: A position paper. *Special Education Perspectives*, *7*(2), 15–27.

Kroesbergen, E. H. & Van Luit, J. E. H. (2003). Mathematics interventions for children with special needs: A meta-analysis. *Remedial and Special Education*, *24*(2), 97–114.

Landerl, I., Wilmer, R. & Trinity, W. (1997). The impact of orthographic consistency on dyslexia. *Cognition*, *63*, 315–34.

Lewis, B. A. (1990). Familial phonological disorders: Four degrees. *Journal of Speech and Hearing Disorders*, *55*, 160–70.

Lightstone, A., Lightstone, T. & Wilkins, A. J. (1999). Both coloured overlays and coloured lenses can improve reading fluency, but their optical chromacities differ. *Ophthalmological and Physiological Optics*, *19*(4), 279–85.

Liubinas, J. (2000). Understanding the reading process: An optometric viewpoint. *Australian Journal of Learning Disabilities*, *5*(4), 18–21.

Lovett, M. W. (1987). A developmental approach to reading disability: Accuracy and speed criteria of normal and deficient reading skill. *Child Development*, *58*, 234–60.

MacArthur, C. A., Graham, S., Haynes, J. B. & De La Paz, S. (1996). Spelling checkers and students with learning disabilities: Performance comparisons and impact on spelling. *Journal of Special Education*, *30*(1), 35–57.

Mailley, S. (2001). Visual difficulties with print. In M. Hunter-Carsch (Ed.), *Dyslexia: A Psycho-social Perspective*. London: Whurr.

Manning, B. H. & Payne, B. (1996). *Self-talk For Teachers and Students*. Massachusetts: Allyn & Bacon.

Marr, B. & Helme, S. (1991). *Breaking the Maths Barrier*. Canberra, ACT: Department of Employment, Education and Training.

Martin, F., MacKenzie, B., Lovegrove, W. & McNicol, D. (1993). Irlen lenses and the treatment of specific reading disability. An evaluation of outcomes and processes. *Australian Journal of Psychology*, *45*(3), 141–50.

Masters, G. N. & Forster, M. (1997). *Literacy Standards in Australia*. Canberra: Commonwealth of Australia.

Mastropieri, M. A. & Scruggs, T. E. (1997). Best practices in promoting reading comprehension in students with learning disabilities 1976 to 1996. *Remedial and Special Education*, *18*(4), 197–213.

Mastropieri, M. A., Scruggs, T. E. & Chung, S. (1998). Instructional interventions for students with mathematics learning disabilities. In B. Wong (Ed.), *Learning About Learning Disabilities* (2nd edn). (pp. 425–42). NY: Academic Press.

McCutchen, D., Abbot, R. D., Green, L. D., Beretvas, S. N., Cox, S., Potter, N. S., Quironga, T. & Gray, A. L. (2002). Beginning literacy: Links among teacher knowledge, teacher practice and student learning. *Journal of Learning Disabilities*, *35*(1), 69–86.

McGregor, M. (1989). Reading and writing maths. *Australian Journal of Reading*, *12*(2), 153–61.

McKay, M. & Neale, M. (1991). Reading strategies of very young fluent readers. *Australian Journal of Reading*, *14*(1), 29–40.

McLeskey, J. (1992). Students with learning disabilities at primary, intermediate and secondary grade levels: Identification and characteristics. *Learning Disability Quarterly*, *15*(1), 13–20.

Mercer, C. D. & Mercer, A. R. (2001) (6th edn). *Teaching Students with Learning Problems*. Columbus, Ohio: Charles E. Merrill.

Mercer, C. D. & Miller, S. P. (1992). Teaching students with learning problems in math to acquire, understand and apply basic math facts. *Remedial and Special Education*, *13*(3), 19–35.

Moore, D. C. (1994). Childhood fluctuating conductive deafness. *Australian Journal of Remedial Education*, *26*(2), 8–15.

Munro, J. (1989). Reading in maths: A subset of reading. *Australian Journal of Reading*, *12*(2), 114–28.

Munro, J. (1998). Phonological and phonemic awareness: Their impact on learning to read prose and to spell. *Australian Journal of Learning Disabilities*, *3*(2), 15–21.

Munro, J. & Munro, K. (1991). Phonemic awareness: A neglected cause in reading disability. *Australian Journal of Remedial Education*, *25*(4), 5–10.

National Schools English Literacy Survey (1997). *Mapping Literacy Achievement: Results of the 1996 National Schools English Literacy Survey*. Canberra: Department of Employment, Education and Youth Affairs.

Nathan, R. G. & Stanovich, K. E. (1991). The causes and consequences of differences in reading fluency. *Theory Into Practice*, *30*(3), 176–82.

Neilson, R. (1999). A discussion of approaches to phonological awareness. *Australian Journal of Language and Literacy*, *22*(2), 88–102.

Nopola-Hemmi, J., Myllyluoma, B., Voutilainen, A., Leitonen, S., Kere, J. & Ahonen, T. (2002). Familial dyslexia: Neurocognitive and genetic correlation in a large Finnish family. *Developmental Medicine and Child Neurology*, *44*(9), 580–6.

Oberklaid, F., Harris, C. & Keir, E. (1989). Auditory dysfunction in children with school problems. *Clinical Pediatrics*, *28*(9), 397–403.

O'Carroll, P. (1992). *The Fitzroy Readers*. Fitzroy, Vic: Fitzroy Community School.

O'Connor, R. E. (2000). Increasing the intensity of intervention in kindergarten and first grade. *Learning Disabilities: Research and Practice*, *15*(1), 55–64.

O'Connor, R. E., Notari-Syverson, A. & Vadsy, P. (1998). First-grade effects of teacher-led phonological activities in kindergarten for children with mild disabilities: A follow-up study. *Learning Disabilities Research and Practice*, *13*(1), 43–52.

Oloffsen, A. (2002). Twenty years of phonological deficits: Lundburg's sample revisited. In E. Hjelmquist, C. von Euler & M. Snowling (Eds), *Dyslexia and Literacy* (pp.151–62). London: Whurr.

Olsen, R. K. (2002). Phonemic awareness and reading: From the old to the new millennium. In E. Hjelmquist, C. von Euler & M. Snowling (Eds), *Dyslexia and Literacy* (pp.100–16). London: Whurr.

Paris, S. G. & Oka, E. R. (1986). Self-regulated learning among exceptional children. *Exceptional Children*, *53*, 103–8.

Parry, T. (1996). Multi stimuli disorganisation syndrome: Treatment and management of children with attentional disorders. *The Australian Educational and Developmental Psychologist*, *13*(1), 56–8.

Pavlidis, G. T. (1985). Eye movements and dyslexia: Their diagnostic significance. *Journal of Learning Disabilities*, *18*(1), 42–50.

Perfetti, C. (1986). Continuities in reading acquisition, reading skill and reading disability. *Remedial and Special Education*, *7*(1), 11–21.

Peters, M. L. (1985). *Spelling: Caught or Taught?* (2nd edn). London: Routledge.

Peterson, D. & Van der Wege, C. (2002). Guiding children to be strategic readers. *Phi Delta Kappan*, *83*(6), 437–9.

Pratt, C., Kemp, N. & Martin, F. (1996). Sentence context and word recognition in children with average reading ability and with specific reading disability. *Australian Journal of Psychology*, *48*(3), 155–9.

Prior, M. (1996). *Understanding Specific Learning Disabilities*. Sussex, UK: Psychological Press.

Prior, M., Sansom, A., Smart, D. & Oberklaid, F. (1995). Reading disability in an Australian community sample. *Australian Journal of Psychology*, *47*(1), 32–7.

Prior, M., Smart, D., Sansom, A. & Oberklaid, F. (1999). Relationships between learning difficulties and psychological problems in preadolescent children from a longitudinal sample. *Journal of the American Academy of Child and Adolescent Psychiatry*, *38*(4), 429–36.

Reetz, L. & Hoover, J. (1992). The acceptability and utility of five reading approaches as judged by middle school learning disabled students. *Learning Disabilities: Research and Practice*, *7*, 11–15.

Reichman, J. & Healey, W. C. (1983). Learning disabilities and conductive hearing loss involving otitis media. *Journal of Learning Disabilities*, *16*(5), 272–81.

Reid, G. (2003). *Dyslexia and Literacy: Overcoming Barriers to Learning*. Paper presented at the 13th European Conference on Reading. Tallinn, Estonia, July 6–9.

Riddick, B. (1995). Dyslexia and development: An interview study. *Dyslexia*, *1*(2), 63–74.

Robinson, G. L. & Conway, R. N. F. (2000). Irlen lenses and adults: A small scale study of reading speed, accuracy, comprehension and self-image. *Australian Journal of Learning Disabilities*, *5*(1), 4–13.

Robinson, G. L. & Foreman, P. J. (1999a). Scotopic Sensitivity/Irlen Syndrome and the use of coloured filters: A long-term placebo-controlled study of reading strategies using analysis of miscue. *Perceptual and Motor Skills*, *88*, 35–52.

Robinson, G. L. & Foreman, P. J. (1999b). Scotopic Sensitivity/Irlen Syndrome and the use of coloured filters: A long-term placebo-controlled and masked study of reading achievement and perception of ability. *Perceptual and Motor Skills*, *89*, 83–113.

Robinson, G. L., Foreman, P. J. & Dear, K. (1996). The familial incidence of symptoms of Scotopic Sensitivity/Irlen Syndrome. *Perceptual and Motor Skills*, *83*, 1043–55.

Robinson, G. L., Foreman, P. J. & Dear, K. G. B. (2000). The familial incidence of Scotopic Sensitivity/Irlen Syndrome: Comparison of referred and mass screened groups. *Perceptual and Motor Skills*, *91*, 707–24.

Rohl, M. & Milton, M. (2002). What's happening in schools for primary students with learning difficulties in literacy and numeracy? A national survey. *The Australian Journal of Language and Literacy*, *25*(1), 25–48.

Romani, A., Conte, S., Callieco, R., Bergamaschi, R., Versino, M., Lanzi, G., Zambrino, C. A. & Cosi, V. (2001). Visual evoked potential abnormalities in dyslexic children. *Functional Neurology*, *16*(3), 219–29.

Rooms, M. (2000). Information and communication technology and dyslexia. In J. Townend & M. Turner (Eds), *Dyslexia in Practice*. NY: Kluwer Academic.

Rourke, B. P. & Conway, J. A. (1997). Disabilities of arithmetic and mathematical reasoning: Perspectives from neurology and neuropsychology. *Journal of Learning Disabilities*, *30*(1), 34–46.

Samuels, S. J. (1999). Developing reading fluency in learning-disabled students. In R. J. Sternberg & L. Spear-Swerling (Eds). *Perspectives on Learning Disabilities*. NY: Westview Press.

Scarborough, H. S. (1990). Very early language deficits in dyslexic children. *Child Development*, *61*, 1728–43.

Scott, C. M. (2000). Principles and methods of spelling instruction: Applications for poor spellers. *Topics in Language Disorders*, *20*(3), 21–35.

Scott, L., McWhinnie, H., Taylor, L., Stevenson, N., Irons, P., Lewis, E., Evans, B. & Wilkins, A. (2002). Coloured overlays in schools: Orthoptic and optometric findings. *Ophthalmological and Physiological Optics*, *22*, 156–65.

Shaywitz, B. A., Fletcher, J. M. & Shaywitz, S. E. (1994). Issues in the definition and classification of Attention Deficit Disorder. *Topics in Language Disorders*, *14*, 1–25.

Siedermann, A. S. (1980). Optometric vision therapy: Results of a demonstration project with a learning disabled population. *Journal of the American Optometric Association*, *51*, 489–93.

Simmers, A. J., Gray, L. S. & Wilkins, A. J. (2001). The influence of tinted lenses upon ocular accommodation. *Vision Research*, *41*, 1229–38.

Sipe, R. (2002). *Supporting challenged spellers. Voices From the Middle*, *9*(3), 23–31.

Smith, J. (1997). Whole language and its critics: A New Zealand perspective. *The Australian Journal of Language and Literacy*, *20*(2), 156–62.

Smith, J. & Elkins, J. (1992). Coherence and the sharing of meaning: Supporting underachieving readers. *International Journal of Disability, Development and Education*, *39*(3), 239–49.

Smith, T. E. C., Dowdy, C. A., Polloway, E. A. & Block, G. E. (1997). *Children and Adults With Learning Disabilities*. Boston: Allyn & Bacon.

Snow, C. E., Burns, M. S. & Griffin, P. G. (Eds) (1998). *Preventing Reading Difficulties Found in Children*. Washington DC: National Academy Press.

Snowling, M. J. (1998). Reading development and its difficulties. *Educational and Child Psychology*, *15*(2), 44–58.

Snowling, M., Nation, K., Moxham, P., Gallagher, A. & Frith, U. (1997). Phonological processing skills of dyslexic students in higher education: A preliminary report. *Journal of Research in Reading*, *20*(1), 31–41.

Solomons, B. (1992). Phonological awareness training: A case for early intervention. *Special Education Perspectives*, *1*(2), 71–81.

Spedding, S. & Chan, L. (1994). Metacognitive abilities in word identification. *Australian Journal of Remedial Education*, *23*(3), 8–11.

Spencer, R. & Hay, I. (1998). Reading schemes and their high frequency words. *Australian Journal of Language and Literacy*, *21*(3), 222–33.

Stanovich, K. (1980). Towards an interactive compensatory model of individual differences in the development of reading fluency. *Reading Research Quarterly*, *16*, 32–71.

Stanovich, K. E. (1986). Matthew effects on reading: Some consequences of individual differences in the acquisition of literacy. *Reading Research Quarterly*, *21*, 360–407.

Stanthorpe, R. (1989). A balanced approach to the teaching of literacy. *Reading*, *23*(2), 69–79.

Sugai, G. & Evans, D. (1997). Using teacher perception to screen for primary students with high risk behaviours. *Australasian Journal of Special Education*, *21*(1), 18–35.

Talcott, J., Hansen, P. C., Assoku, E. L. & Stein, J. (2001). Visual motion sensitivity in dyslexia: Evidence for temporal and energy integration deficits. *Neuropsychologica*, *38*, 935–43.

Tan, A. & Nicholson, T. (1997). Flashcards revisited: Training poor readers to read words faster improves their comprehension of text. *Journal of Educational Psychology*, *89*(2), 276–88.

Terepocki, M., Kruk, R. S. & Willows, D. M. (2002). The incidence and nature of letter orientation errors in reading disability. *Journal of Learning Disabilities*, *35*(3), 214–33.

Thompson, P. & Gilchrist, P. (1997). *Dyslexia: A Multidiscipline Approach*. London: Chapman and Hall.

Torgesen, J. K. (1999). Assessment and instruction for phonemic awareness and word recognition skills. In H. W. Catts & A. G. Kamhi (Eds), *Language and Reading Disabilities*. Boston: Allyn & Bacon, pp. 128–53.

Torgesen, J. K. (2001). The theory and practice of intervention: Comparing outcomes from prevention and remediation studies. In A. Fawcett (Ed.), *Dyslexia: Theory and Good Practice* (pp.185–202). London: Whurr.

Torgesen, J. K., Alexander, A. W., Wagner, R. K., Rashotte, C. A., Voeller, K. S. & Conway, T. (2000). Intensive remedial instruction for children with severe reading disabilities: Immediate and long-term outcomes for two instructional approaches. *Journal of Learning Disabilities*, *34*(1), 33–58, 79.

Torgesen, J. K., Wagner, R. K. & Rashotte, C. A. (1994). Longitudinal studies of phonological processing and reading. *Journal of Learning Disabilities*, *27*(5), 276–86.

Townend, J. (2000). Phonological awareness and other foundation skills in literacy. In J. Townend & M. Turner (Eds), *Dyslexia in Practice*. NY: Kluwer.

Turner, M. (1997). *Psychological Assessment of Dyslexia*. London: Whurr.

Unsworth, L. & Lockhart, A. (1994). Literacy learning in science: What's happening in the Junior Primary School. *Australian Journal of Language and Literacy*, *17*(3), 212–25.

Van Luit, J. E. & Schopman, E. A. (2000). Improving early numeracy in young children with special education needs. *Remedial and Special Education*, *21*(1), 27–40.

Vellutino, F. R., Scanlon, D. M., Sipay, E. R., Small, S. G., Pratt, A., Chen, R. & Denckla, M. B. (1996). Cognitive profiles of difficult-to-remediate and readily-remediated poor readers: Early intervention as a vehicle for distinguishing between cognitive and experiential deficits as basic causes of specific reading disability. *Journal of Educational Psychology*, *88*(4), 601–38.

Waring, S., Prior, M., Sansom, A. & Smart, D. (1996). Predictions of recovery from reading disability. *Australian Journal of Psychology*, *48*(3), 160–66.

Watson, A. J. (1990). Cognitive skills in reading: five to nine year olds. In S. R. Butler (Ed.), *The Exceptional Child*. Sydney: Harcourt, Brace, Jovanovich.

Westwood, P. (1994). Issues in spelling instruction. *Special Education Perspectives*, *3*(1), 31–44.

*Westwood, P. (1999). *Spelling: Approaches to Teaching and Assessment*. Camberwell, Vic.: ACER.

*Westwood, P. (2000). *Numeracy and Learning Difficulties*. Camberwell, Vic.: ACER.

Whiteley, H. E. & Smith, C. D. (2001). The use of tinted lenses to alleviate reading difficulties. *Journal of Research in Reading, 24*(1), 30–40.

Wilkins, A. J., Lewis, E., Smith, F. & Rowland, F. (2001). Coloured overlays and their benefits for reading. *Journal of Research in Reading, 24*(1), 41–64.

Willows, D. M. (1998). Visual processing in learning disabilities. In B. Wong (Ed.), *Learning About Learning Disabilities* (2nd edn). NY: Academic Press.

Wong, B. Y. L. (1985). Metacognition and learning disabilities. In D. L. Forrest-Pressley, G. E. MacKinnon & T. G. Waller (Eds), *Metacognition, Cognition and Human Performance: Vol 2: Instructional Practices* (pp. 137–80). Orlando: Academic Press.

Wong, B. Y. L. (1998). The relevance of metacognition to learning disabilities. In B. Wong (Ed.), *Learning About Learning Disabilities* (2nd edn). NY: Academic Press.

Worthy, J. & Broaddus, K. (2002). Fluency beyond the primary grades: From group performance to silent independent reading. *The Reading Teacher, 55*(4), 334–43.

Worthy, J., Patterson, E., Salas, R., Prater, S. & Turner, M. (2002). 'More than just reading': The human factor in reaching resistant readers. *Reading Research and Instruction, 41*(2), 177–202.

———
*Recommended reading for this chapter

Further recommended reading

Blackman, B. A. (1997). *Foundations of Reading Acquisition and Dyslexia*. London: Lawrence Erlbaum.

Bley, N. & Thornton, C. A. (1989). *Teaching Mathematics to the Learning Disabled* (2nd edn). Austin: Pro-Ed.

Clutterbuck, P. M. (1990). *The Art of Teaching Spelling*. Melbourne: Longman-Chesire.

McLoughlin, J. & Lewis, R. E. (1994). *Assessing Special Students*. N. Y.: Macmillan.

Prior, M. (1996). *Understanding Specific Learning Disabilities*. Hove, Sussex: Psychology Press.

Roberts, J. (2001). *Spelling Recovery*. Melbourne: ACER.

Sanders, M. (2001). *Understanding Dyslexia and the Reading Process*. Boston: Allyn & Bacon.

Sternberg, R. J. & Spear-Swerling, L. (Eds) (1999). *Perspectives on Learning Disabilities*. N. Y.: Westview Press.

Swanson, H. L. (Ed.) (1991). *Handbook on the Assessment of Learning Disabilities*. Austin, Tex: Pro-Ed.

Watson, A. G. & Giorcelli, L. (Eds) (1999). *Accepting the Literacy Challenge*. Gosford, NSW: Ashton Scholastic.

Chapter 8

Developing literacy and numeracy skills

Greg Robinson

This chapter aims to:
- review methods of making literacy and numeracy learning meaningful and relevant
- outline approaches to the development of literacy and numeracy
- provide examples of successful interventions
- develop an appreciation of the importance of parents as partners in the learning process.

Introduction

For students with disabilities or learning difficulties, consistent failure in school tasks may lead to a downward cycle of lack of confidence, less motivation and even further failure (as discussed in the previous chapter). In order to encourage these students to 'try again', it is important that they see school tasks as meaningful. They also need to feel confident that they are able to complete the tasks.

There is a need for materials and activities to be specific to the students' needs and interests, with success emphasised and clearly demonstrated. Tasks need to be at an appropriate difficulty level, an appropriate interest level and their relevance made evident. It is also important that a variety of activities are involved to allow the necessary repetition for learning to occur without a loss of interest.

Activities that may be used to ensure relevance, generate success and provide repetition are discussed below.

Making literacy and numeracy meaningful

Using children's everyday experiences

Reading needs to be related to everyday experiences so that poor readers can see its relevance (O'Sullivan, 2000). Worthy et al. (2002) found that social interaction around literacy and access to relevant, interesting reading material was an important factor in successful tutoring for struggling resistant readers. Effective tutors tailored instruction to students' unique needs and interests, finding just the right materials to reach their students. Surveys of reading choices of children and adults has indicated a preference for newspapers and magazines, especially magazines about television programs (Love & Hamston, 2001; Moulton-Graham et al., 1997), with Walsh (2002) finding that more than half of children in the USA have a television in their bedroom. As a consequence, newspaper articles or magazines about popular television programs could generate a great deal of interest and provide the motivation to read for otherwise reluctant readers. Cairney and Ruger (1997) found significant differences between home and school literacy practices, with the home emphasising everyday literacy related to interests and needs, while school literacy was teacher-oriented and less relevant to children's interests. Alvermann (2002) suggests teachers capitalise on student interest in the Internet and various interactive communication technologies. Video games may also be a useful method of developing computer literacy as they allow a more interactive dialogue (Mackereth & Anderson, 2000).

There is a wide variety of settings, situations and activities in daily living that could be used to make print meaningful. The following examples could be used as a basis to generate ideas:

- Print related to the local environment:
  - street names and road maps
  - telephone books and timetables
  - railway signs
  - local shop names.

- Print related to advertising and packaging:
  - household packages and cans
  - items in the local supermarket
  - magazine and newspaper advertising
  - TV commercials and billboards
  - warning labels on poison bottles, paint tins, medicines.
- Print related to everyday activities:
  - TV guides
  - reading and filling in forms
  - reading instructional manuals for toys or appliances
  - reading recipes, menus or directions on food packets
  - reading pamphlets (health, safety)
  - getting a licence (road rules booklet)
  - family letters and greeting cards
  - shopping specials (from newspapers)
  - articles in magazines related to student interest.

Mathematics can also be related to home, school and community events, with a wide variety of activities to choose from. The following list could be used as a starting point for developing ideas. A good review is also provided by Patton et al. (1997).

- Shopping:
  - making a list and estimating costs
  - comparing prices
  - calculating best buys and calculating advertising discounts
  - checking totals and change.

- Home measurement:
  - making clothes, curtains and covers
  - fuel costs
  - rent, rates, mortgage payments
  - gardening
  - room size and furniture
  - decorating – paper, paint
  - building and repairing (shelves, fences, etc.).
- Looking up:
  - a street directory
  - a road map
  - telephone numbers
  - transport timetables.
- Travel:
  - comparing bus, train costs – cost of weekly travel
  - estimating speeds and distances
  - estimating time taken
  - car expenses (petrol, repairs, insurance)
  - holiday plans and choices.
- Cooking:
  - shopping for ingredients
  - measuring weight, volume, temperature and time.
- Sport and recreation:
  - scoring and calculating averages
  - pools, bets, weighing up odds
  - costs on a menu
  - costs to buy clothes, CDs, magazines and newspapers.
- Pay:
  - rates and comparisons
  - overtime calculations
  - understanding and totalling deductions.
- The school environment:
  - canteen – cost of items, buying multiple items
  - buildings – number of steps, number of doors and windows
  - playground – size of play areas, number of trees.
- Car park:
  - number of cars
  - number of doors, headlights, etc.
  - number of car spaces
  - size of car spaces.

Gordon (1996) describes the mathematical activities that may be involved in setting up a snack time stall at the school. The process included deciding what materials and resources were needed, deciding what funding was needed, decisions about what to cook, including recipes and drawing up an action plan, with a timeline.

Everyday problem-solving in maths

The solving of problems in everyday activities could be considered a main aim of mathematics, especially for students with learning disabilities. A number of authors have described the stages involved in the problem-solving process (for example, Westwood, 2000). The stages or skills could be summarised as follows:

- *programming* – understanding the nature of the problem and identifying the calculation involved
- *computation* – being able to calculate the answer correctly
- *estimating* – knowing whether the answer is of a sensible size as a safeguard against incorrect calculations (estimating implies an understanding of the process, not just a mechanical calculation)
- *interpreting* – being able to use the answer to solve a problem.

Many students seem to have difficulty deciding how to solve a problem, including the identification of whether addition, subtraction, multiplication or division are to be involved (Jitendra et al., 1998; Marr & Helme, 1991). The high level of reading comprehension skill required for maths word problems usually aggravates these difficulties. Word problems in maths appear to increase in reading difficulty level as a student progresses up the grades (Cawley & Miller, 1989), with children who have both a mathematics difficulty and a reading difficulty achieving more poorly on word problems (Jordan & Hanich, 2000). For students with learning disabilities, the syntax in maths word problems may be difficult to understand and the task may seem disconnected from real life settings (Cawley et al., 2001). Peters et al. (1987) suggested that children with mild developmental delays are unlikely to follow systematic strategies for solving word problems. They quote one study that found only 25 per cent of Year 4 and 62 per cent of Year 8 students correctly solved all five arithmetic word problems provided.

A useful checklist of skills for maths problem solving could be as follows:

- Can the student read the problem?
- Can the student explain the meaning (comprehension)?
- Can the student select the pertinent elements and discard irrelevant elements?
- Can the student relate one element to another?
- Can the student select the proper operation (for example, addition, division, etc.)?
- Can the student successfully complete this computation?
- Can the student estimate an answer (as a 'check' on their solution)?

There are many activities that could be used to develop problem-solving skills in mathematics. Some examples are listed below:

- Identify common situations in students' everyday activities and practise describing them in terms of numbers, for example, 3 brothers + 2 sisters = 5 children.
- Giving students a number sentence (12 – 3 =) and asking them to turn it into a word problem.
- Providing a word problem and asking the student to identify the mathematical operation involved. This could be done as a small group activity.
- Providing a word problem and asking the student to draw a picture, or create a semantic map or schema diagram, to help visualise the problem (Jitendra et al., 1998).

- Providing a word problem and asking children to identify the information required for a solution. This may involve circling or underlining the relevant sections, and may be a useful group activity. Owen and Fuchs (2002) successfully used this strategy to solve mathematic word problems with third grade students who had learning disabilities. An example of the steps that could be used in such an activity is outlined below:
  - read the problem
  - reread and underline the numbers/numerals
  - circle words asking questions
  - put a double line under the word telling what things are asked about. For example, 'John is <u>5 years</u> old and is <u>3 years</u> older than his sister Anna. How old is Anna?'

Group work may help reduce the anxiety often associated with mathematics, as students may realise that they are not the only person who has difficulties. Group work can also reduce fear by replacing competition with cooperation. It can also help develop the language associated with maths concepts and increase participation, as students working in groups may be more able to handle difficult tasks that they might not be able to do on their own (Marr & Helme, 1991). A wide review of research on teaching maths to low achieving students (Baker, Gersten & Lee, 2003) found the use of peers to provide feedback and support was consistently reported to be effective. Providing clear feedback on performance to parents, teachers and the students themselves was also important.

Contextualised problems presented on video or CD-ROM can promote discussions among students for plausible explanations (Hickey, Moore & Pelligrino, 2001). Video-based activities can also 'anchor' problems in authentic contexts and such 'anchored' instruction has resulted in low achieving adolescents being able to solve complex problems (Bottge et al., 2002).

The language experience approach and reading

This method attempts to relate reading to everyday experiences. It involves using the child's own stories as a basis for teaching of reading, and has been used successfully with adults (Thomas, 1995; Brehaut, 1994).

The method usually guarantees interest, as it is one in which the student has a very personal involvement. It is implemented with them and for them; it belongs to them. It allows the pupil to become involved in the learning process. Confidence and success are usually guaranteed, as developing your own stories based on everyday activities is likely to make the task easier to learn. Reading one's own story, for example, should be easier as writers should remember what the story was about. The method may also be useful for older age poor readers, if reading materials with a lower reading age level and older age interest level are not available.

The basic steps in the method are as follows:

- The student generates a story, or activity, either from personal interest/experience or from pictures taken from a magazine or comic.
- The story or activity is discussed with the teacher or a helper, with ample time given to talk through ideas so that frustrations or confusions are avoided at the writing stage.
- The story is dictated by the student and written or typed by the helper. In this process, the helper may still edit the story to exclude too many new words, difficult words, or complex grammar. As confidence builds, students may write or type their own text.

- Each day's work must be typed, ready for reading the next day. If it is a longer story, each day's work is directly added to the previous work until the story has been finished.
- If the story is written from a picture, the picture should be included above the typed story.
- The stories and activities can become a reading book for revision purposes, with lists of words related to each story or activity also used for revision.
- The story or activity may be read onto a tape recorder for individual revision if necessary.

Reader's theatre

Reader's theatre is an alternative method of involving children in writing and reading. The method involves rewriting a story in the form of a play. When the rewriting is finished, individual students, using the class as an audience, read out parts in the play. The poor reader can become involved if the teacher, a helper, or another student assists them, and is the scribe for their rewriting. Their part in the play can be written at a level that ensures they can read it successfully. Frequent rehearsal will also help. Allowing them to read their (well-practised) parts to the whole class should help peer group approval, as parts in the play are often much sought after.

The first attempts at this method may be very much teacher written, using a familiar text. However, as children gain confidence, sections of the play can be rewritten by individual children or small groups, with changes added to suit personal interest. The main features of the method are as follows (Hertzberg, 2000; O'Loughlin, 1997; Young, 1991):

- Identify characters to be used and write a first draft, highlighting speech in the text as a guide.
- Reread the first draft, with either the teacher or children doing the reading. Edit as necessary.
- Once the first draft is written, allocate students to read each character's part; often with more than one child allocated to each part. Make sure students are given time to practise their roles.
- The reading usually occurs with students standing up or sitting on stools facing the audience. Grouping of readers may be experimented with to give the best effect. Robertson (1990) recommends that scripts are double spaced, while larger print may be needed for poor readers.
- Activity during the play reading should be kept to a minimum. Reading should always be directed to the audience, and there should be few or no stage props. A narrator can be used to fill in any gaps or set the scene.
- Readers need to use varying pitch, rate, tone and volume in their voices to bring the characters to life.

A good example of the use of Reader's theatre is provided on the following website <www.aspa.asn.au/Projects/english/rtonion.htm>.

Case study

Larger schools take a team approach in assisting students who have difficulty in learning to read. The case study in Box 8.1 demonstrates the many elements taken into consideration by the support teacher in developing a learning support plan. For a support plan to be effective, classroom teachers must work closely with others in the team to ensure an integrated approach, which becomes part of normal classroom activity.

Box 8.1

Geraldine

Background

Geraldine is an 8-year-old Year 3 student. She has had some significant difficulties in her life, witnessing domestic violence, losing a step-father to suicide, and having a loving mother who has had mental health problems. Despite these setbacks, she is a lovely child who relates well to others and works very cooperatively with teachers. Her literacy difficulties were obvious from early on. In Year 1 she participated in the Reading Recovery program and exited that program reading at level 16. In Reading Recovery she had an individual lesson for 30 minutes each day. Her Reading Recovery teacher, who was also the Support Teacher Learning Assistance, reported that she made good gains in Reading Recovery but even then was very reluctant to use visual cues.

She received support from the Support Teacher Learning Assistance (STLA) during Years 2 and 3. In Year 2, team teaching occurred with the STLA and class teacher by dividing the class in two and continuing to use Reading Recovery strategies. Geraldine also had a peer tutor who worked with her sight words. In Year 3 she was in a small group with the STLA three times a week; in addition to reading, phonemic awareness and systematic phonics, teaching using the MULTILIT program were added. The STLA reported that few gains were made since the Reading Recovery program, but lack of attendance has to be a consideration.

The school counsellor referred Geraldine for further support for her learning for a variety of reasons. Her mother was concerned about Geraldine's anxiety before going to school; teachers were concerned about her physical health, her academic progress and her attend-ance, because in one year she was absent for one-quarter of the days. The counsellor found that Geraldine scored in the range of mild intel-lectual disability, with a verbal score slightly, but not significantly, below her manipulative skills.

Intervention

The District STLA (Literacy) responded to the request for support. She felt it was important to include the class teacher in the process of supporting Geraldine's learning, and if possible to provide that support in the classroom. The starting point for assisting students, particularly those with significant difficulty in their learning, is assessment. The class teacher was thus given half a day of release from teaching so that he could learn how to, and then administer, assess-ments that would give us more information about where Geraldine is now in her literacy skills.

At the same time, the District STLA would look at other students in the class to see if some others had some similar needs and could be taught with Geraldine. Two boys seemed appropriate candidates. They had both com-pleted the Reading Recovery program a year or two before, and were now reading at levels 13 and 9 (below the exit level of 16).

>

Box 8.1 continued

Assessment phase

Assessments used were:

Reading level, accuracy, fluency and comprehension

- *PM Benchmark Kit (An Assessment Resource for Emergent-12 Years R.A.)*, Elsie Nelley and Annette Smith, Nelson, Melbourne, 2000

This is not a standardised tool, but it is a curriculum-based measurement. There are numerous series of reading books in this kit now widely used in schools. The PM series has become very popular; it is often among the texts used by Reading Recovery teachers. As an approximate guide to what the levels might mean for students who do not have learning difficulties, it has been suggested that kindergarten children would reach levels 5 to 16 or beyond; Year 1 students, levels 14 to 20 or beyond; Year 2 students, levels 18 to 22 or beyond; Year 3 students, levels 20 to 26 or beyond; Year 4–6 students, level 30 and beyond.

The comprehension questions provided in this Kit are of both literal and inferential types.

Phonemic awareness

- *Sutherland Phonological Awareness Test* (SPAT), Roslyn Nielson, 1995

A revised edition of this test, with two parallel forms, is now available. This test has norms, but only raw scores are used in this report.

Letter–sound correspondence

- *The Phonics Handbook*, Sue Lloyd, Jolly Learning, Chigwell, Essex, 3rd edn, 1990

The Jolly Phonics approach has been used here to test students' knowledge of how to write and how to read the common letters and letter combinations of the alphabet that make up the 42 sounds in English assessed by this program.

Word attack skills

- *MULTILIT Word Attack Skills*, The MULTILIT Initiative, Macquarie University Special Education Centre, Sydney 1998

The MULTILIT Word Attack Skills Placement Test has been used. This is a curriculum-based test; the results pinpoint the knowledge and skill the student has, and indicate where in the accompanying program the student needs to start.

Spelling

- *The Waddington Diagnostic Spelling Test*, Neil Waddington Educational Resources SA

The Waddington Diagnostic Spelling Test has been used. It is normed, giving a spelling age. More useful than its norms is its diagnostic information: if the scores are noted separately for the first 20, last 20 and middle 30 words, teachers can see the student's score for

- words containing short vowels, with single consonants (cvc words, for example, cat), consonant blends (for example, shift) and consonant digraphs (for example, barn)
- the student's score for words that are irregular (like *they* and *said*)
- the student's score for words containing more difficult vowel spellings (for example, cope).

Sight words or 'tricky words'

In working with these students, the concept from *Jolly Phonics* of regular words (the ones that can be sounded out for reading and spelled by sounding out) versus 'tricky words' (the ones that are not spelled as they sound) has been used. The 60 tricky words from *Jolly Phonics* was used as a curriculum-based measure to know what the student needed to learn, and to test what they had learned at the end of the program.

Auditory processing skills

- *The Auditory Processing Assessment*, Department of Education, Employment and Training, Victoria 2001

Box 8.1 continued

The Auditory Processing Assessment was used as a rough check of auditory processing skills. The teachers can support students with poor auditory processing skills by making sure they have the student's attention; talking to the student using sentences that are the same length as used by the student and matching them; providing wait or processing time for the student; using visual supports.

Language

- *Clinical Evaluation of Language Fundamentals*, 3rd edn, 1996

A screening test was used to confirm whether there was need for a speech pathology assessment, in cases where a language difficulty was suspected. The District STLA gives this test.

Report

Here is the report written by the District STLA on the basis of the class teacher's administered assessments.

Strengths

Geraldine worked cooperatively during a long and sometimes quite demanding set of assessments. She wants what she reads to make sense and if the text is not too hard she will try to self-correct. Geraldine knows most letter sounds and a number of high-frequency words.

Areas for development

Reading accuracy

Year 3 texts are too hard for Geraldine at the moment. She is reading at about level 15. When she comes across unfamiliar words she has difficulty sounding out the letters to work out the word, preferring mostly to guess using a word that starts with the same sound. Sometimes the word is an irregular word she does not yet know. Sometimes the word she puts into the text does not make sense.

Reading fluency

Geraldine read level 15 text at 40–50 correct words per minute. For Year 3 we would like the fluency to be about 80–100 correct words per minute.

Comprehension

Geraldine finds comprehension a little difficult; this may be partly due to the effort she has to read the words on the page, but she probably also does not follow the meaning well.

Phonemic awareness

One crucial skill for learning to read and spell is to be consciously aware of all the sounds in a word. Geraldine found it difficult to say all the sounds in words like mug and seat, and of course also those with the more difficult consonant blends like snake, spoon and trip.

Letter-sound correspondence

Geraldine could give the sound of 25 individual letters or two-letter combinations; we would like her to know 42 and be able to write them all.

Word attack skills

Geraldine has considerable difficulty at the consonant-vowel-consonant level of word (for example, ate). She read 'rog', 'fig', 'gid' for 'rod', 'fid', 'god', for example. We need to work on developing these skills.

Spelling

On the Waddington spelling test, Geraldine could spell correctly three out of 20 words using just the short vowels. She could spell 'in', 'hat', 'web' but not 'yes', 'jog', 'mud', 'lamp', 'step', 'think'. She could spell correctly more irregular than regular words: she has relied on her memory for how words are spelled.

Sight words or 'tricky words'

A large percentage of the words in written texts are common, short words, many of which are not spelled exactly as they sound. Geraldine knew 60 per cent of high frequency words presented to her from a sight word test. On a test of what are called 'tricky words', because they are not spelled as they sound, Geraldine scored 52/60.

>

Box 8.1 continued

Spelling of irregular words

Geraldine knew five of 20 high-frequency irregular words on the Waddington test. She could spell 18/40 'tricky words'. These words are difficult to learn, but are so common in writing and reading that it is important to learn them well.

Language

On a language-screening test Geraldine scored below the criterion score for her age. A full assessment by a speech pathologist would tell us more about any language difficulties she may be experiencing, and give us some activities to strengthen her language skills; the school would need staffing resources to implement the programming that a speech pathologist would provide.

Auditory processing skills

On a screening test for these skills developed for kindergarten students, Geraldine scored a sentence length of 11 words (indicating that she would be able to process in her mind 11 meaningful words at a time; but probably have difficulty with longer and more complex sentences) and a digit span of five (indicating that she could probably work out a word of five sounds and blend the sounds together to make a word – a word like scrap, for example, or blend).

Planning, programming and implementing

The District STLA, the school STLA, the class teacher, the school Principal and the school counsellor attended a planning meeting.

The results of three students were looked at (see the pre-post testing table below). Two other children had similar literacy needs to Geraldine, and it was decided to teach them as a group. A schedule of teaching was worked out so that this group had a lesson each day, lasting from 30 minutes to 45 minutes, depending on what time could be made available. The Principal agreed to take the teacher's class for 30 minutes on one day so that the class teacher would be one of the people delivering the program. Both the school STLA and the District STLA would teach the group twice each week. The learning support plan developed by this group is printed below. It targets the areas of need identified by the assessments, and the starting points.

The aim was to speed progress by organising for three additional practices daily of work learned during the lesson. Because it was known that it would be a problem to expect very much, if any, practice to be done at home, the STLA arranged from the start that peer tutors from an older class would listen to the students reread their text, their list of words, their sounds and spelling twice daily. This was increased to three times in the case of one of the boys, where the home situation had never proved reliable for doing homework. Geraldine and the other boy would take their work home for a third practice.

It was planned that the group would be taught in the classroom while the rest of the class continued with their work. Staying in the classroom has the advantages that the students are still in the class; other students can often learn from what the small group is doing, and the teacher is always aware of what the small group is learning.

However, in this situation this rarely happened in practice. It often seemed easier to move to a separate space, which was quieter; the class included several challenging students; two of the small group were easily distracted; and, the tradition of withdrawal held a strong influence.

Evaluating

At the end of eight weeks' intervention, the teachers involved post-tested the three students on the measures used before the intervention. Results are recorded in the pre-post testing table. One student, T, moved from the school temporarily for three weeks during the program. There were also the expected interruptions due to student ill health and other school activities.

Box 8.1 continued

All three students improved the PM Benchmark level in relation to the goal set. The fluency goal was not reached for all students, but one approached it. Comprehension (based on teacher observation) kept pace with text level. Phonemic awareness improved for two of the students, but the score was lower for the third. Word attack skills improved, in both simple consonant-vowel-consonant words and words with consonant blends. Spelling of both regular and high-frequency irregular words and the spelling age of all students improved by at least 8 months in an 8-week program.

While all the students in almost all areas made gains, significant problems remain:

- phonemic awareness for all students, but for one in particular
- automatic and fluent knowledge of two-letter sounds both to read and to spell
- the need to extend word attack skills to words using vowel digraphs (for example, *ight*, *ain*)

- the need to spell regular words using consonant digraphs and blends (for example, barn, shop), and vowel digraphs (for example, right, train)
- reading accurately books that more closely approach their grade level
- reading fluency
- comprehension at literal and inferential levels.

Where to from here?

This appears to be a group of students whose literacy is likely to need consistent and sustained support, probably through their school years. They all do make gains, won through considerable energy and effort. The need is to provide the support, so that their literacy continues to improve, and hopefully the stage of functional literacy can be reached. The students will need teachers who can adapt their teaching to maximise their access to the wider classroom curriculum.

Box 8.1 continues on page 330 >

Other ways to develop literacy

Assisting students with their reading

Children with literacy problems are unlikely to cope with reading material at their grade level. In the long-term they are likely to need intensive assistance, preferably in a one-to-one setting (Vaughan, Gersten & Chard, 2000), to develop basic word attack skills (see Chapter 7). In the short-term, however, they will need support in reading grade-level texts (Shany & Beimiller, 1995). If the student has to spend a lot of time identifying a difficult word, it will restrict reading fluency and divert attention from story meaning (see Chapter 7). In mathematics, students may need assistance to ensure that the relevant elements of a word problem are identified.

In addition to 'assisting' readers with difficult material by supporting their reading, it is also possible to buy high interest books with a reduced reading difficulty level. For many years, books have been written that would interest older age children, but have a very easy reading level. Popular books that would interest older students have also been rewritten to reduce word difficulty and grammatic complexity, without losing the basic elements of the plot. This 'reduction' makes it more likely that these older students will gain pleasure from reading and be motivated to read. They can also be seen by their peers reading age appropriate books, rather than early level readers.

Box 8.1 continued

Learning support plan for Geraldine, Robert and Tim

Date — Present: District STLA, school STLA, class teacher, school principal, school counsellor

Needs	Specific goals	Strategies	Who will do this and when?	Monitoring – how will we know when it is achieved?
Accuracy	The students will improve reading level: E from 15 to 17; R from 13 to 15; T from 9 to 12	Daily reading of decodable text using Pause, Prompt, Praise Use Fitzroy readers Try PMs a little later	M – teacher T, W – STLA Th, F – District STLA	Use 100-word grid to monitor for accuracy Post test
Fluency	The students will read at 70 cwpm on instructional level text	Repeated reading, three times during the day, of the text read in the lesson	School STLA to organise two reads with peers daily Third read at home	Use 100-word grid to monitor for fluency Post test
Comprehension	The students will retell the main points from the text read	First student predicts what text will be about; second student reads; third student retells; teacher is the judge, but could take predict or retell role so a student is the judge	M – teacher T, W – STLA Th, F – District STLA	Record on observation sheet
Phonemic awareness	The students will learn the actions and letters for all 42 of the Jolly Phonics sounds, and be able to blend and segment three-, four- and five-sound words	When doing word attack and spelling activities, students will sound out the individual sounds in words	M – teacher T, W – STLA Th, F – District STLA	Post test with SPAT

continued

> ∨

Box 8.1 continued

Learning support plan for Geraldine, Robert and Tim

Date   **Present: District STLA, school STLA, class teacher, school principal, school counsellor**

Needs	Specific goals	Strategies	Who will do this and when?	Monitoring – how will we know when it is achieved?
Word attack skills	The students will learn the actions and letters for all 42 of the Jolly Phonics sounds, and be able to blend and segment three-, four- and five-sound words	Learn actions and graphemes for 42 sounds, using Jolly Phonics program Apply this knowledge in reading Word Boxes and in reading text	M – teacher T, W – STLA Th, F – District STLA	Check weekly which sounds are known to read and spell Post test
Spelling		Use letter tiles for blending and segmenting words Write words using the Word Boxes Write sentences		Check student work Post test
'Tricky word' reading	Students will learn to recognise all 60 'tricky words'	Practise reading the six sets of words; play Memory in pairs	M – teacher T, W – STLA Th, F – District STLA	Knowledge will be monitored 2-x week
'Tricky word' spelling	(In time) students will spell correctly 30 of the 60 'tricky words'	Test one set of words; correct errors Use games to strengthen memory, like *Look, Say, Cover, Write, Check* or use repeated writing (not copying)	M – teacher T, W – STLA Th, F – District STLA	

Jean Hooker, Assistant Principal, Support Teacher Learning Assistance, Newcastle District, New South Wales

A wide range of such books is available, including some of the classics (Dickens, Jules Verne) and titles related to adolescent themes (horror, romance, mystery), but with reading age levels of eight or nine years. These books are sometimes accompanied by 'read along' tapes to further assist word identification and fluency. In some cases, the tapes are adjusted to different reading speeds, ranging from 50 words per minute to more than 130 words per minute.

It is important that both parents and teachers can quickly estimate whether the chosen book is going to be too difficult. If students select a book that they cannot read, they may become further imprisoned in the downward cycle of demotivation, loss of confidence, less reading and low reading achievement, as described in Chapter 7. If an estimation of reading difficulty is made and the book is above the student's reading level, they can be guided to a less 'frustrating' book. If the child really wants to read a specific book no matter how hard, then a quick estimate of difficulty level will help make decisions about how much support the child will need to read the book. A simple guide, which could be used by children, parents and teachers, is outlined below:

Difficulty level guide

1 Choose the book/story
2 Count off first 50 words (passage)
3 Hear child read the passage
   0–4 errors = leisure reading (easy)
   5–10 errors = instructional level
   10+ errors = frustration level.

If the book is judged to be too difficult using this simple guide, then the child should be encouraged to either choose another book or get someone to help them read the book. There are several methods to assist children to read books that are too difficult for them, some of which are outlined below. Another good guide is provided by Thomson and Watkins (1998).

Reading along with the student

A widely used method of supporting reading is to read along with the student, to provide voice support. Zutell and Raisinski (1991) claim this method helps to emphasise natural rhythm, improves reading rate and enhances intonation, pitch and expression. One method that illustrates the procedure is called the 'neurological impress procedure'. This procedure involves the following steps (Kemp, 1987):

Neurological impress procedure

- From the first session, the instructor and student read the material aloud together, with the instructor initially reading a little louder and faster than the student, and the student taking over as confidence increases.
- Students are told not to think of reading, but to slide their eyes across the paper. No attempt is made by the tutor to correct or question the student.
- The instructor accompanies the voices by placing a finger under the words as they are read, for the student to follow.
- The material to be read should be slightly lower than the student's actual reading standard.

- An increase in reading speed should occur as familiarity with the technique is developed.
- The method requires 15 minutes per day in consecutive daily sessions for a total of eight to 12 hours.

The aim of this method is to create fluency in reading. It is also hoped that by exposing the student to a much larger number of words, more words will be learned. Students should feel confident while reading when they use this method, as they cannot make mistakes. Kemp (1987) cautions that difficulties may arise if the story is too complex, the language is too difficult, the instructor reads too quickly, too slowly or without intonation. There may also be difficulties if the session lasts too long, or the child forgets to track visually and concentrates on listening. Studies using this method have generally produced positive results for students with learning disabilities, but not always (Eldredge, 1990).

There have also been attempts to provide supported reading through tape recording of a book and getting students to follow the words as they listen to the tape. A good source of taped books is the USA-based company 'Talking Book World', which has over 75 thousand audiobooks. The website, <www.talkingbookworld.com>, gives information on the range of books available. Shany and Biemiller (1995) compared supported oral reading, in which a teacher supplies difficult words, with tape-assisted reading, and found similar significant gains in accuracy and comprehension. Welch and Sheridan (1995) advocate such a method, and give useful guidelines for recruiting readers, recording the text and for reading the text when recording. Their guidelines are outlined below:

Recruiting and training readers for tape recording

- Post announcements in the school or school newsletter and senior citizen centres.
- Ask teachers to nominate student candidates who are proficient readers.
- Ask for volunteers from parent associations.
- Create an application form to keep track of applicants.
- Hold an audition.
- Model and demonstrate voice levels, pacing and specific techniques.

Recording techniques

- Find a quiet place with rugs, upholstered furniture, and draperies to absorb ambient noise/echo.
- Sit in a comfortable seat that does not face hard surfaces such as walls, windows or doors to reduce echo or hollow-sounding tapes.
- Place the microphone or tape recorder with microphone on a table slightly below the mouth, approximately 15 to 25 centimetres away.
- Speak across the top of the microphone.

Reading techniques

- Announce the title, author of the book, as well as the title of chapters/subsections.
- Emphasise italics with your voice.
- *Briefly* describe photographs, charts, tables and graphs.
- Read study questions at the end of the chapter *prior* to reading the chapter; this way they serve as an advanced organiser for the listener.
- Take a break every 15 minutes to reduce voice fatigue.

- Read in a normal voice and pace that is not too fast or too slow.
- Put a single chapter on a tape to create a volume of tapes and mark/label each tape.

(Source: Welch & Sheridan, 1995)

Shared reading

Shared reading assists with word identification and also helps involve the student in the story. The aim is to link the story to the child's life experiences, so that they can relate to it, enjoy it and become involved with it. The tutor discusses with the student what is happening in the story and what is likely to happen. This discussion can bring in the student's own experiences and make reading more than just word recognition (Daisey, 1993). The student is thus placed at the meaning end of the reading model outlined in Figure 7.2, Chapter 7, where the individual's cultural and social experiences are also involved in developing meaning. Rhodes and Shanklin (1993) found paired reading interactions between peers helped students become more self-sufficient and less reliant on the teacher. The basic steps involved in shared reading are as follows:

- What's the book going to be about?
  - Title
  - Cover
  - Publisher's blurb
- What kinds of things happen to us when we read?
  - Reminders of things in your own life
  - Pictures in the mind of what is happening
  - Developing a feeling for the characters by placing yourself in their place
  - Predicting certain parts of the story
  - Making yourself one of the characters
- What support can be offered for reading difficulties?
  - Providing assistance with words not known
  - Reading difficult sections together
  - Reading alternate sections
  - Tutor reads a page, emphasising new and difficult words, then student reads the same page
- We're finished!
  - Sharing the excitement
  - Looking back on the story (title and cover – discuss their suitability)

One variation of shared reading developed for parents is called paired reading (Cairney & Ruger, 1997). This involves the child choosing the book and parents allocating at least five minutes nearly every day to read it. A place is found that is quiet and comfortable. While reading, some time is spent talking about the pictures and what can be told about the story from the pictures. There are two steps in the reading process:

- Reading together: The parent and child read every word aloud together. Each word is pointed to as it is read, with the parent adjusting reading pace to the child's pace.
- Reading alone: The child who feels confident may start to read certain sections without assistance, except for difficult words where the parent says the right word after 5 seconds

and gets the child to repeat it. The reading alone phase starts with some pre-arranged signal, such as a tap on the elbow. At this signal, the parent stops reading with the child and intervenes only if the child struggles for more than 5 seconds. At this stage the word is given – or reading together starts again until the child is confident to read alone.

A variety of other strategies may be used to involve children in a shared reading experience. Slavin et al. (1994) suggest the following activities could be used with reading teams in the classroom:

- *Partner reading:* Students read the story silently first and then take turns reading the story aloud with their partners, alternating readers after each paragraph.
- *Story structure:* Students are given questions related to each story, emphasising the story structure (characters, setting, problem, and solution). Halfway through the story, they are instructed to stop reading and to predict how the story will end or the problem will be resolved.
- *Story retell:* After reading the story and discussing it in their reading groups, students summarise the main points of the story to their partners.
- *Word meaning:* Students are given a list of story words that are new to them and asked to write a sentence for each word that shows they understand its meaning.
- *Partner checking:* After students complete the required activities, their partners sign a student assignment record form indicating it has been completed.

Griffin (2002) describes a wide range of paired reading activities used by collaborating first graders, including use of imagination, talking to one another and offering hints of encouragement, use of funny voices, singing, and joint construction of the text.

More recently there has been increasing development of talking books and interactive books using CD-ROMs. This information technology has allowed the development of programs that add speech to the computer-presented text, read portions of the text back to the student, create banks of alternative words to use, alter the speed at which a text may be read and highlight particular words. Having a computer that interacts with the reader is both interesting and also non-judgemental. It is able to speak, answer questions, highlight words, give sound effects, and expand facts. It can do a lot of things that an effective tutor or teacher may do to support reading (Thomson & Watkins, 1998). Pilon (1995) found that when words were accompanied by synthetic speech, reading speed, accuracy and comprehension were enhanced.

Enhancing reading comprehension

Methods of supporting reading discussed so far are mainly related to helping in one-to-one or small group situations. However, such situations may not always be possible at secondary school level with its much greater range of teachers and subjects for each child. It is less likely that the child will receive consistent help, as no one class teacher has responsibility for all subjects. While parents can help at home, the regular class teacher and support teacher may not always be available for individual assistance at school. Parents are also less likely to be involved in providing assistance at secondary level. As a consequence, the reading content of texts, worksheets and other class reading activities may need to be reduced or simplified, as was discussed in more detail in Chapter 4. It might also be useful to provide enhancements or guides to what is required when undertaking class reading tasks, to ensure that meaningful learning occurs.

Hudson, Lignugaris-Kraft and Miller (1993) have identified a variety of techniques that have been successful in enhancing reading. The main techniques suggested are as follows:

- Advanced organisers that involve providing an orientation to the lesson by providing detailed information on:
  - tasks to be performed
  - the background for the lesson
  - reasons for the lesson
  - vocabulary to be used
  - the framework of the lesson.

  This information may be discussed prior to the lesson, or provided in a written form so that parents may give supplementary aid.

- Visual displays that can be used to highlight the relationship between various pieces of information presented, including the identification of key vocabulary used, or important ideas which should be looked for in the text. This visual display often takes the form of a semantic web concept map (Bluestein, 2002). This technique has been used to help students understand relationships between key concepts (Di Cecco & Gleason, 2002), as well as to help develop an understanding of maths concepts (Ives & Hoy, 2003), or to help improve mathematical problem-solving performance (Jitendra, Di Pipi & Grasso, 2001). Semantic webs provide the student with a strategy for organising information, as is illustrated in Figure 8.1.

- Study guides that involve the use of simple statements or questions which emphasise important content information. Study guides may take the form of short answer questions reviewing key areas, or the matching of key words with their correct definitions. The cloze technique has also been used. This method involves the deletion of key words from summary passages that must be filled in by the student.

- Audio recordings of class reading assignments can also be provided, especially if parent volunteers can be used to provide these recordings. These recordings may involve a word-by-word reading of the assignment or text, or a paraphrasing of more detailed assignments to highlight critical information. They may be used in conjunction with worksheets or information highlighted in textbooks.

The use of pictures to assist poor readers improve comprehension has been suggested by Hibbing and Rankin-Erickson (2003). Pictures could include teacher and student drawings, illustrations in texts, picture books and movies. Such aids could help students who lack the ability to create mental images when reading. Hibbing and Rankin-Erickson (2003) claimed that many reluctant readers with comprehension difficulties were not able to develop pictures in their minds while reading. The authors provide a good review of methods for using external visual images based on research into mental imagery, with a summary of important points for teachers to consider when using visual images.

A technique called *visualising and verbalising* (Bell, 1991) has also been found to be very effective in helping to identify the main idea of what is being read. It is also useful for summarising information and recalling information, especially for secondary level students (Brennan & Robinson, 1998; Hummel, 2000). This process teaches students to develop visual images of each part of their reading and build up these images to form a whole picture. It involves a series of sequential steps, starting with visual images of a single word, to images of single sentences, then images of groups of sentences which form paragraphs, to images of whole pages and then images of a chapter. Once they have developed the image or picture, the student can check this picture by using cue words (for example, 'when', 'where'). Wilhelm (1995) emphasises that once students use such techniques, they are more likely to integrate information in a text to form a coherent representation of what is being presented, including connecting their own life to the literacy experience. Bell's (1991) *visualising and verbalising* uses cue words such as 'when', 'where', 'mood' and 'background' to provide the student with a strategy for understanding the text and organising information.

Manz (2002) outlines a strategy for previewing textbooks called THIEVES, which is used to identify the elements of a text that need to be thoroughly surveyed and previewed in advance of actual reading. This method should enhance the use of prior knowledge, help provide a purpose for reading and stimulate metacognitive processing. The following steps are suggested.

- *T – Title:* What do I already know about the topic? What does it have to do with the preceding chapter?
- *H – Headings:* What do they let me know about what I will be reading? How can I turn each heading into a question?
- *I – Introduction:* Does the first paragraph introduce the chapter? Do I know anything about this already?
- *E – Every first sentence in a paragraph:* These are often the topic sentences and may help to decide whether this portion of the text is relevant.
- *V – Visuals and vocabulary:* Are there photographs, drawings, maps, charts? What can I learn from them? Vocabulary may help identify the meaning of the chapter. Highlighted words may be keys to important concepts. Is there a key list of vocabulary terms? Do I know what they mean?
- *E – End of chapter questions:* These study questions may flag important points and concepts. Questions that ask 'why' may be particularly informative. What do the questions ask? What information do I learn from the questions?
- *S – Summary:* Encourage students to read the entire summary as part of the review, as it provides a frame of reference for the content of the chapter.

Knowledge of common text structures has also been identified as a means of assisting children with problems in understanding what they read. Students with learning disabilities may have a limited knowledge of different types of text organisation and structure. Gersten et al. (2000) claim such students have a limited knowledge of differences between narrative text structure (stories) and expository text structure (designed to inform or explain). Gersten et al. (2000) provide a range of strategies to assist in reading narrative text, to assist in monitoring comprehension of narrative text, and for developing questions about the text. They also review strategies for improving comprehension of expository text. Bakken and Whedon (2002) make the point that most children learn to read narrative prose, but when they get to school, they are exposed to a different kind of text called expository prose. Narrative prose has a story line of beginning, middle and end, which children are familiar with, which is easy to understand, as they know what to expect. Expository prose, however, presents facts, theories and dates, and the organisation of such a text is not predictable. If students are not familiar with different types of text structures, they may need explicit training in identifying these different types. Bakken and Whedon (2002) identify five types of expository text structure: main idea, list, order, compare/contrast, and classification. They discuss how children with a difficulty may identify these text structures and outline strategies that can be used to improve comprehension of these structures.

Hummel (2000) states that quite often examples of text to be used to develop comprehension strategies are only drawn from the subject area of English. She claims it is important that students are exposed to a full range of text types across a variety of subjects so that they gain experience of using strategies in different situations and discover which strategies may be more appropriate for different situations.

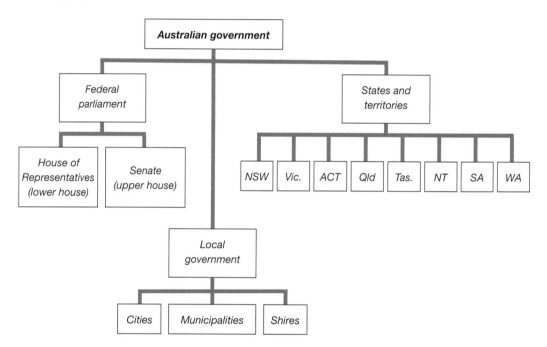

Figure 8.1 A semantic web concept map

Repeated reading

Repeated reading of the same text has also been used as a means of developing meaning of what is being read, as well as developing confidence. Frequent exposure to the same words would also help develop the 'automaticity' in word identification needed to allow the reader to concentrate on meaning (Samuels, 1999; Homan, Klesius & Hite, 1993). Elkins (1994) claims that children mainly 'automatise' reading and writing skills through massive and enthusiastic practice, largely out of school hours. He quotes evidence that suggests that repeated reading produces improvement not from memorisation, but from better orchestration of the elements of reading while performing them all together. Chard, Vaughan and Tyler (2002) reviewed 24 studies of intervention methods, including repeated reading of a familiar text. They found that repeated reading, especially when accompanied by corrective feedback, improved rate, accuracy and comprehension by enhancing automatic word identification. They claim these results support the concept that 'automaticity' allows more attention to be devoted to the meaning of what is being read, as outlined in Figure 7.2, Chapter 7.

Repeated reading of stories may often be accompanied by voice support or paired/shared reading (as discussed earlier). This voice support may involve parents reading with their children, peer tutors supporting reading, or teachers using repeated class or chorus reading with Big Books. Spreadbury (1994) reported studies which show that children, both at home and school, talk more with an adult helper when they are given support and are familiar with the story. Repeated reading can also help to build confidence, as well as improving sight vocabulary (Samuels, Schermer & Reinking, 1992; Zutell & Raisinski, 1991). Parents and teachers often report that young children ask for a story to be read over and over without a great loss of interest. Reading recovery (Clay, 1993) is one of many methods that use re-reading of familiar books as part of their strategy.

Research and opinion on repeated reading has provided the following information:

- Three to five readings of the same section or story seems to be a good goal for developing reading proficiency.
- It may be best to use short passages, with students knowing at least 85 per cent of the words at first reading.
- If used too often, there may be a lack of interest. Repeated reading may also lead to reduced exposure to a variety of words, and text types, as time spent reading the same passage reduces the number and variety of other reading passages to which the child is exposed.

Tape recordings of stories or story sections have also been used to provide supported and repeated reading in situations where other assistance may not be available (as discussed earlier in this chapter). At secondary level, tape recording of texts or of study notes may be used to provide assistance in completing assignments and preparing for exams. The method usually involves listening to a recording of the book while visually following the print, possibly followed by reading aloud in unison with the tape. The general steps are as follows:

- The student selects a book to read which a teacher, parent or volunteer helper then records on a cassette tape.
- The tape is listened to, with words followed visually in the book, possibly using the finger as a pointer. This can be repeated as often as possible at home and at school.
- After listening and following, the story is read orally in conjunction with the tape.
- As students become more proficient, they may record their own reading to be played back for practice.

Supporting writing – process writing

A common method of providing support and developing interest in writing is to involve children in identifying their areas of difficulty through conferencing and editing. The method was initially introduced at primary level, but could be particularly useful at secondary level to overcome writing problems. If students are given the responsibility for identifying their own errors in consultation with teachers and peers, they may be more committed to try to fix them. An example is the method called process writing, which aims to develop a positive attitude towards writing by giving students both a purpose for writing and an audience.

This is achieved by allowing them to identify their writing topics and emphasising that the final product should be written with the aim of being presented to an audience. The method emphasises the process as much as the product and has a series of steps that can be used to evaluate student competence. The main steps in the process are outlined below. Some students with writing difficulties may have problems with all of the steps, but others may have problems with only some of the components (West & Clauser, 1999):

- Choose a topic (from your own experience, from reading, by brainstorming of ideas).
- Think of the audience (parents, school groups), plan the story and discuss it.
- Write a draft – put your ideas on paper without paying too much attention to the mechanical aspects of grammar or spelling. This stage is likely to include reading the story aloud to a friend or friends.
- Editing – consider what listeners have said and decide whether to alter the story. Have a conference with the teacher.
- Proofread the final product, individually or with a friend.
- Publishing – think of how it will be 'published' (book, drama, etc.).
- If published, it is important that it is read by others, displayed, and a suitable reward given.

The concept of self-correction is central to this method, especially when the first draft is read to a friend or friends, and when consulting with the teacher at the editing stage. Students must ask themselves whether the sentences make sense, whether sentences have been started in different ways, whether correct grammar has been used, etc. Self-correction is also important at the proofreading stage, where children are encouraged to identify words that don't look right (underline or circle them), check capitals, full stops and other punctuation marks.

For teachers, the major difficulty with this approach has been finding time to effectively conference all children in the class. Not all products may be fully checked for punctuation and spelling, which could lead to errors being habituated. Westwood (1994) cites two surveys of spelling in Australia, which suggest that spelling levels dropped slightly between 1978 and 1993. Westwood claims that this is due to the lack of time available for teachers to personally conference all children in the class. Even when conferences occur, they may not be of sufficient depth to make children aware of all the spelling generalisations and patterns related to their errors, and spelling may thus become fragmented.

Several suggestions have been put forward to address the problem of lack of time for conferencing. Setting clearly defined skills or goals for each conference situation may be one answer. The teacher should decide what the targeted writing task is going to achieve (correct spelling, ability to recount details, grammar) and make this the single goal for the conference. It may not be possible to spend time on a number of issues with every child in one conference. The problem of lack of time for conferencing may also be addressed by whole class conferences or group conferences. Parent helpers could also be involved in individual conferencing, which may give the teacher more time for children in the class who have difficulties.

Harry

Harry is a 13-year-old student in Year 8 at a specialist high school where entry depends on successfully auditioning in the performing arts. Harry gained entry on his singing skills. He has a love of drama and performance.

Harry also has a long history of learning difficulties.

He is fortunate to have a mother who teaches adult literacy in a TAFE college and has the expertise to provide him with a high standard of guided practice at home. She has been doing so since the early grades. Harry, however, is now a teenager who needs to be taking some independent and responsible decisions about his learning.

The Support Teacher Learning Assistance at his school contacted the Learning Difficulties Coordinator to seek collaborative planning about how best to work with Harry. In the state-wide literacy test given in the first year of high schools, Harry had performed in the lowest group. The support teacher had worked with him during that year, and was quite disappointed that his results were poorer when he took the same test in Year 7; and the English faculty began to doubt the effectiveness of the work.

Harry himself talked openly and frankly about his difficulties and goals; one memorable moment came when he was asked whether he would like to 'knock over' his literacy problem or 'go around' it. He pushed the empty coffee mug in front of him over – he wanted to conquer the problem.

When the results of the two years of state testing were looked at, it became clear that in Year 7 Harry had guessed at many answers – he had answers to all the questions, but his pattern of answers showed correct answers fairly evenly distributed among both easiest and hardest questions; he had probably done quite a lot of guessing. In Year 8, he had completed only about half the test, but almost all his answers were correct. It would appear that he needs more time than other students to read and process the passages and the questions, but now has more competence and confidence to work on reading and answering carefully.

Report

The coordinator asked Harry to cooperate in doing a series of assessments to clarify what strengths and areas of need he had. Here is the report:

Strengths

Harry's persistence and determination to succeed are truly impressive. Harry reports that rather than look for ways around his reading difficulty, he wants to conquer it. In the assessment situation he demonstrated enormous patience and persistence in reading texts. He was always aware of the need for what he was reading to make sense. He would reread and apply problem-solving skills to words he did not know. In a word like 'appetite', for example, he sounded out: 'ap – et – it – ite' – 'appetite'. He worked out the word 'ancient' from a combination of sounding out, which has limited application in this word, and working on what might possibly make sense here and match the letters of the word.

Harry observed that when he needed to spend so much care working out the words, it was more of a challenge for him to keep track of the meaning. He did do so, however, on the texts read.

Harry successfully read a text we would expect Year 6 students to read with ease; for him it was very demanding.

Areas of need

Fluency
Harry's reading is very slow because so many words need careful working out. His reading would be so much more efficient if he were able to read

>

Box 8.2 continued

more quickly and automatically: not only would he get through more text, but he would also be able to comprehend more fully. On a grade-level science text, Harry read at 18 correct words per minute, and only 75 per cent accuracy. We would like students in Year 5 and beyond to be reading at 100 or more correct words per minute.

Word attack skills

On a test of word attack skills, Harry showed perfect achievement on short-vowel words, including those using consonant digraphs (sh, ch, wh, th) and blends (sl, br, tr, scr etc.). He knows the silent 'e' pattern well (he has worked on this recently with Ms R, his support teacher). There is room to develop knowledge of the major ways of representing the long vowel and vowel diphthong sounds.

Sight words

Harry scored 85 per cent correct on all three sets of 100-word sight words tests. This is not a priority for him; any confusing words he would easily solve in context.

Spelling

On the South Australian Spelling Test, Harry scored in the 7.10 – 8.5 spelling age range.

Language

A language-screening test places Harry at slightly below the criterion score for his age. It was observed that Harry took quite some time to process some questions.

Where to next?

The coordinator thought about what the results suggest, and took these suggestions for Harry to a meeting that included Harry, his mother, the support teacher and his English teacher.

The language-screening test indicates that there may be a significant language learning difficulty or disability, which could well be further diagnosed in a formal speech pathology assessment. The text *One in Eleven (One in Eleven: Practical Strategies for Teaching Adolescents with*

a *Language Learning Disability* by Mandy Brent, Florence Gough and Dsusan Robinson ACER Press 2001) suggests that the incidence of language difficulties among secondary students may be higher than we are aware; and while individual therapy is often not well-accepted by adolescents, his teachers could materially assist his learning if they were both aware of his difficulty, and had the knowledge and energy to employ supportive scaffolds such as:

- allowing him time to process
- introducing new vocabulary, planning for using vocabulary on several occasions to help new concepts to be recognised, understood, maintained and generalised
- using visual supports such as graphic organisers to assist in comprehension and planning
- providing models of what is expected – models of different text types, of acceptable answers and so on, and providing guided practice with corrective feedback before expecting Harry to produce work independently.

Suggestions for programming for Harry

Harry's stated preference is to conquer his reading difficulty.

His reading difficulties do not lie with basic reading skills; he knows how to read for meaning, to apply phonological knowledge, to monitor for making sense and to make repairs when there is an error. He rereads, reads on and sounds out to work out the word that will make sense, look and sound right. He has a good stock of common high-frequency words.

The main concern is that reading is a great effort; this is not only off-putting and draining of energy, but also a hindrance to comprehension. Improving fluency and automaticity are important goals.

Lots of practice is prescribed. Repeated reading of text (about three rereads) usually

Box 8.2 continued

results in an improvement of about 40 per cent in fluency.

Which texts to read? The choices:

- Moving from easier text to harder, and moving on when a fluency criterion is reached. The Rainbow Readers, a series of levelled texts, has tapes that go with them. Harry could read a text by himself first, then practice with the tape until he is able to read the text with the tape.
- Using current English text (very difficult level for Harry, but good for access to the English curriculum). If taped versions of text are available, he could use them to help him develop fluency.
- Using other texts across the subjects he takes – geography, science, music, art, drama, design and technology – to combine fluency practice with acquisition of curriculum content.

Including practice in word attack skills would likely be very helpful. For example, the *MULTILIT* program (*The MULTILIT Initiative*, Macquarie University Special Education Centre, Sydney 1998), which has both accuracy and fluency components. It may be useful to combine the more difficult representations of vowel sounds with actions (as in *Cued Articulation* (Jane Passy, ACER Press, 1990) or *Jolly Phonics* (*The Phonics Handbook*, Sue Lloyd, Jolly Learning Ltd 1998)) to aid recall of both sound and spelling.

A modest spelling program would logically accompany the word attack skills program.

I would advocate that if there is time, spending 20 minutes a day learning to touch type would be well worthwhile in terms of presentation of assignments, access to spelling checkers, as well as contemplating access to speech recognition programs that would read text back to the writer and to word-prediction programs.

Harry chose option 3 of the fluency options and the following individual literacy plan (on page 344) was devised in conjunction with the Support Teacher (Ms R) and the English teacher (Ms B).

>

Box 8.2 continued

Learning support plan for Harry

Present: **Date 19.6.03**

Needs	Specific goals	Strategies	Who will do this and when?	Monitoring – how will we know when it is achieved?
Fluency	Harry will improve oral reading fluency 18 cwpm to 30 cwpm	Repeated reading of text read in class Harry is timed on first reading using the conventions of taking a 1-minute read (3 seconds to work out a word); he then reads on Next day he is re-timed on the same text, and then again on new text	Mrs R; Mrs B at school Harry working with parents at home	100-word grid plus timer
Comprehension	Harry will retell the main points of what was read	In school, predicting on the basis of title, layout, headings and knowledge of text structure At home, retell after the rereading	As above	Could use a monitoring sheet if thought useful for recording and communication
Decoding skills	Harry will read vowel digraph words for long vowel sounds	Use MULTILIT Word Attack Skills, from level 9 Earlier levels could be used for fluency	Practise at home Test for mastery at school	Recording built-in to the program

continued

∨

Box 8.2 continued

Learning support plan for Harry

Present: **Date 19.6.03**

Needs	Specific goals	Strategies	Who will do this and when?	Monitoring – how will we know when it is achieved?
Spelling	Harry will spell words from the Word Attack Skills (WAS) program Harry will learn 10 high-frequency irregular words	Use phonological knowledge for WAS words (write the sounds you hear) Use repeated writing (not copying) or Look, Say, Cover, Write, Check Analyse the part of the word that is not spelled as it sounds	Dad at home	Keep workbook as record Ms R to provide list of high-frequency irregular words from Waddington test
Touch typing	Harry will learn to touch type	Mum will provide a typing tutor software program for Harry to use	Harry to practise at home Back-up will be to do this at school	Monitor cwpm using the program

Box 8.2 continued

Because Harry had a large number of pieces of work to do, a log sheet where he could recall all that he achieved was provided. It looked like this:

Recognising all the work Harry does

Task	Mon	Tue	Wed	Thu	Fri
Reading with Ms R or Ms B at school					
Comprehension – predicting what the text will be about					
Comprehension – retell the main points of what was read					
Testing word attack skills at school (accuracy) – write which number sheet					
Testing Word Attack Skills at school (fluency) – write which number sheet					
Practising touch typing skills					
Repeated reading for fluency at home, first read – time					
Repeated reading for fluency at home, second read – time					
Repeated reading for fluency at home, third read – time					
Word attack skills – accuracy sheet (list number) – at home					
Word attack skills – fluency sheet (list number) – at home					
Spelling of regular words (from word attack skills sheets)					
Spelling of all high-frequency irregular words learned so far					

Henry's comments:

Ms R's comments:

After a term (10 weeks)

Great plan! Based on analysis of need, pinpointing the areas needed to work on, constructed with the participation of all the interested parties – it should work.

But it didn't.

Mrs R began by reading a science text his science teacher was using, but Harry found it too hard and frustrating, even when Mrs R supported his reading by introducing new terms before he started reading. So they read alternative science books that were not related to his science curriculum, but that he enjoyed.

This did not last too long, because Harry was in a musical production at school and his presence at rehearsals precluded the individual work planned with Mrs R and Mrs B.

Harry found working on touch-typing a low priority and has worked at only desultorily.

Homework was rarely done.

There were, however, some insightful experiences, such as when Harry, who was working with Mrs R in a room where a younger boy was

>

Box 8.2 continued

working with a tutor on mathematics. Harry overheard their conversation, and could see he had a better explanation for the boy. Harry was given the chance to take over the maths tutoring; a productive session with positives for tutor and tutee followed.

After the musical production was over, Mrs R helped Harry with a creative writing task by acting as his amanuensis. Here are the opening paragraphs representing one eighth of his narrative.

> The house had been empty for quite a while now. It all began from the old man who used to live here. His mind must have drifted away. First he thought he was back in the war, and then he thought he was a kid running to the corner store. This happened for a fair time until they took him to a nursing home, and since then I've been here by myself.

> You ask how I got here in the first place? I was his companion, his best friend, the one who would sit by his side. I was his dog.

Where to for Harry now?

Harry has creative talents and can display an ability to manage difficult tasks that can surprise his teachers. He is not, however, a person to work systematically at a task: if something more interesting is on offer, he'll choose to do that.

Perhaps for Harry, it is time to develop strategies for 'getting around' his difficulties rather than 'knocking them over'.

Asking Harry to learn to type as an added task, and all by himself, was probably foolish and doomed from the start. Yet having touch-typing skills would allow him access to assistive technology leading to more independence in getting his narratives down on paper. We perhaps should give some thought to providing lessons in touch typing for students with learning difficulties and working with them to learn programs like *TextHelp! Read and Write, Write Out Loud, Clicker 4* or *Kurzweil 3000*.

He will be able to show much more of what he knows and can do if he has a reader/writer for assessment tasks and exams.

He needs an advocate who will explain to teachers his language difficulties and will suggest and encourage the teacher to employ scaffolding supports as described above.

Harry's story: From his mother's perspective

Harry attended the local preschool, and then his local primary school for kindergarten and Year 1. Teachers in kindy were supportive and never expressed any area of concern. In Year 1, difficulties were evident; the teacher blamed the parents and the child for him being the 'dummy' of the class. A school counsellor report was requested, but interest in supporting Harry was denied by the principal and teacher. Harry was removed to a second primary school where support was provided through an Outreach program.

At home we were implementing the recommendations of an occupational therapist (OT). We continued to read with Harry as in prior years; he loves being read to but started to show more difficulty when reading back and showed more frustration with his attempts. We persisted with the OT exercises, and they were definitely a turning point in Harry's willingness to participate in reading. He was immediately fatigued by any request to read back or when participating in any word identification.

For the next couple of years we persisted with supporting what the Support Teacher Learning Assistance (STLA) was implementing at school, in particular phonemic awareness. We employed a student teacher that Harry really liked at the school to work on maths, as this subject now appeared to be slipping, with so much attention being given to reading and writing.

It was probably around Year 4 when we just didn't say any more about his pencil grip,

>

Box 8.2 continued

and no longer persisted in the exercises. This was because of his mental state. He was fed up, stressed and showing signs of giving up on reading. This was evident in the classroom and at home. Our encouragement was to continue working hard on reading at school and we would read to him at home. Harry received an award at the end of the year for 'most books borrowed' from the library by any student in the school. As you can tell, he loved being read to, and this released any pressure he was feeling with school. His principal and teachers enjoyed their conversations with Harry and often remarked on his creativity.

We went for an assessment after hearing some good results with using Irlen filters, which we received at the end of Year 4. There was some initial improvement, especially in his willingness to participate in reading; however fluency was not developing as hoped, even with the extra support. He was still receiving the support at school, attending a tutorial centre two mornings a week and follow up at home.

In Year 5 we enrolled Harry in a small drama group to participate in some creative activity other than his drawing. He enjoyed these and his self-esteem began to improve because he was experiencing some other achievements. He wanted to try tap dancing and loved this also. He started out with drama and tap lessons, extending to jazz by Year 6. He then auditioned for drama at the performing arts high school and created his own piece, which was a story about his father singing to him from a baby. He was accepted for drama to start in Year 7. Receiving this letter was the happiest day for us all since Harry started school: we all cried.

Harry was also taking Ritalin for ADHD through Year 6. His paediatrician does not find Harry to be a serious case but the medication does help Harry to concentrate on his work.

Since starting high school, Harry has been enjoying the atmosphere of the energetic school. I met with the STLA and counsellor early in the school year to fill them in on some details about Harry. He was not taking his medication and his lack of concentration was evident to all of us. I reassured them that I thought it would take Harry half the year to settle down and by third term Harry asked me if he could go back on the medication.

Since then he has been on a program with the STLA. At home we encourage reading by supplying interest magazines (*Wheels*, etc), which he reads also at school, and by assisting with his assignments, etc. We purchased an Alphasmart so that he is encouraged to type more and he stores all his work on this before transferring to the Mac. He has maths and reading games on the Mac that he enjoys and he has a car game that he loves that also requires mathematics and analysis to succeed in. We can see improvement in his work through third term even with the distractions of the school production.

Jean Hooker, Assistant Principal, Support Teacher
Learning Assistance, Newcastle District,
New South Wales

Families as partners in the learning process

In the last decade, there has been increasing recognition of the value of using parents as a supplement to school efforts to assist students with learning problems (McCarthy, 2000). This recognition has recently focused on partnership models that include the whole family, including siblings and grandparents (Carpenter, 2003). The family-centred or ecological perspective acknowledges that the child and their environment continually influence one another, and an understanding of the dynamics between home, school and family is important in meeting the child's needs (Poole, 2003).

In particular, the family can provide additional individualised support for important school tasks. The regular class teacher usually has little time to provide individual assistance because of the large number of children in each class, and yet children with learning disabilities respond well to one-to-one intervention (Vaughan, Gersten & Chard, 2000). While there may be additional school support provided for children with problems, this support is usually not sufficient to cater for the needs of all children with difficulties. As a consequence, families can make a very valuable contribution to identifying and catering to their child's needs. Blamires, Robertson and Blamires (1997) and Carpenter (2003) suggest that parents have many areas of knowledge that would be invaluable to planning a program, including the following:

- they have extensive knowledge of the child's development from birth
- they have knowledge of family circumstances that affect the child
- they know the wider social environment in which the family lives that may influence the child
- they can supply knowledge of the child's home behaviour.

The first priority for any student with learning difficulties is to provide access to an experienced, knowledgeable and well-organised teacher. However, this may not always be possible, and in such situations, families have some advantages that can make their contribution to the school program very valuable. The first advantage is that most families should be able to allocate 10 to 15 minutes of personal time per day to a student with difficulties, which is far more than the regular teacher or even the support teacher may be able to allocate. In addition, a time for help can be chosen that is free of interruptions and is made a 'special' time, for that child only, which a regular class teacher cannot do. A further advantage is that the child will be able to work with less fear of mistakes being seen by others. In school situations, peer group judgement and comparisons are always present.

The home reading environment can have a significant impact on the development of reading skills (Molfese, Modglin & Molfese, 2003). Callaghan, Raedmacher and Hildreth (1998) also found the involvement of parents in a home-based self-management program for maths resulted in significant increases in levels of homework completion and maths achievement.

Additional school support is also unlikely to be long term (it may last no more than six to 12 months), whereas families are likely to be motivated to provide support for as long as the child may need it. Varus et al. (1992) claim that teaching reading strategies and skills to children with difficulties has limited success unless there is ongoing support. Smart et al. (2001) found in a longitudinal Australian study, that almost half of the children with reading disability at 7 to 8 years still had reading difficulties at 13 to 14 years.

The effectiveness of parents in providing support to children with learning disabilities has been well documented (Nicholas & Robinson, 1995; Furniss, 1993; Molfese, Modglin & Molfese, 2003). Henderson (1988) claims that the family, not the school, provides the primary educational environment for children, and that parent involvement is most effective when it is well planned and long lasting. Henderson also claims that family involvement at secondary level is still effective and that the average level of achievement for all students in a school may improve if families are involved both at the school and at home. Twine (1992) emphasises that when parents work with a child, praise efforts, commit themselves to help, and expect achievement, they are showing the child that school work is important, their best effort is valued and that success should follow commitment. She also claims that giving parents instruction in reading methodology leads to increased self-esteem and confidence, both for parents and children. Teachers who implemented parent support were also perceived by parents as better teachers.

The main barriers to family involvement appear to be problems of communication and confidence. A significant hereditary component has been identified for learning disabilities and reading problems, with up to an 85 per cent probability that one or both parents may have similar difficulties (Robinson, Foreman & Dear, 2000). As a consequence, it is likely that parents may have a negative history of schooling and thus lack the confidence to help (Hunter-Carsch, 2001; Coots, 1998). They may feel that they have nothing to contribute, and could have a less positive interaction with their children about school work (Young, 1995). As children grow older they may also discourage parental involvement, with secondary school families less likely to provide support (Furniss, 1993). Kearsley (2002) surveyed Year 7 students in Queensland about their reading confidence and found that while parents value the child's efforts, there was a disturbing lack of both teacher and parental feedback about their progress. Teachers may also feel uncomfortable with parental involvement, possibly seeing them as a threat (Cairney & Munsie, 1992).

Kalyanpur, Harry and Skrtic (2000), as well as Kroth and Edge (1997), identified a range of barriers to parent and family involvement, including the following:

- time – single and working parents may have difficulty finding time to help at home and to get to meetings
- intimidation – some parents feel intimidated by principals, counsellors, teachers
- don't understand the system – parents may not understand how general and special education systems work
- English as a second language – parents from non-English speaking backgrounds may have problems understanding printed materials, or teacher explanations at parent-teacher conferences
- cultural differences – manners and courtesies are different in different cultures, which may lead to unintentionally offending or embarrassing parents
- not welcomed – some parents feel they are not welcomed in the school.

Greaves (1995) surveyed parents and found the most common complaints about teachers were lack of empathy, ignoring of parent's knowledge, being patronising to parents, and dishonesty (not admitting they don't know what to do). It is important for the school to be able to see the problem from the parents' point of view, as there is much that parents know and could do that would be of great value to the child's formal education.

In relation to home–school literacy practices, McCarthy (2000) claims that mismatches between home and school environments concerning the nature and function of literacy have contributed to the development of problems with parental involvement. These problems included:

- differences in the nature of literacy practices between home and school
- differences in ways of using language between home and school
- differences in perceptions of appropriate parent-teacher roles.

McCarthy emphasises the need for the school to adjust literacy practices to accommodate home and community patterns, with a key component being the sharing of information.

A survey of home–school literacy issues in Australia by Ashton and Cairney (2001) found that despite an emphasis on partnerships, the belief among teachers is still that parents contribute little more to their child's education than perhaps help in the classroom and help with homework.

Families helping at home

There has been much written about the ways in which families may help at home, with a variety of different techniques and strategies being investigated and used. It is important that clear guidelines for home help are established, to minimise inconsistencies between home and school practices. Methods that can be used by parents to help with reading and maths are discussed below.

Helping with reading

Most of the literature has focused on help with reading, because of its importance for all school achievement. The main guidelines for home help are as follows:

- As much as possible, students should choose their own books, although selection of books of appropriate difficulty level may need to be discussed, as poor readers may pick a popular book to be like their peers, but which may require considerable reading support. Conversely, struggling readers may pick books that have been previously read at school, as they may feel confident with such a book. Such a choice, however, may be positive, as repeated reading of a familiar text can produce gains in reading (Chard, Vaughan & Tyler, 2002).
- The reading time together should be enjoyable. If frustration is creeping in, stop the session. It may be more important to keep a happy relationship than to continue practice on some nights where things are not going right.
- The helper may need, in some cases, to set a goal of remaining calm and consistently praising. If there is more than one potential home-helper, choose the helper least likely to have a personality conflict with the student.

- Make sure the atmosphere is happy, relaxed, and that reading occurs at a quiet time and place where there are no distractions.
- Sit down together so that both can see the book. Talk about the book and illustrations before reading. While reading, talk about what has happened and what might happen next.
- Smooth out any difficulties by helping with words not known. A common strategy is to:
  - give the reader time to work out the word and self-correct (5 seconds)
  - then use a prompt or read the word for them
  - use prompts to make sure the flow of reading is not disrupted
  - correct errors only if they change story meaning.
- Give lots of praise and give reward for effort, not necessarily just the outcome. Effort needs to be acknowledged.
- At the finish, talk about what is read and, if possible, relate events in the story to the child's own experience.

  Reason and Boote (1994) add a few cautions:
- avoid threatening to tell the teacher a task was not completed
- avoid showing anxiety or making reading a competition
- avoid getting angry if persistent help with the same word is needed
- don't be afraid to ask for help and advice from any of the teachers.

Families may also assist at home by tape-recording books so that children can read along with the tape in their own time. A child's reading may even be recorded and sent to school for the teacher to hear. In addition, families may be able to help the teacher identify specific words and sounds needing attention by keeping a note of these difficulties. Ortega and Ramirez (2002) describe a successful series of parent literacy workshops that were integrated with the school day. Shea and Bauer (1991) have suggested that a family resource centre be set up which could have books, pamphlets, audiotapes, cassettes, toys, and educational games. Games, in particular, are a useful way to provide practice at home in a non-stressful environment.

Helping with maths

While most attention has been directed towards reading, family assistance for mathematics is also important. Costello, Horne and Munro (1991) emphasise the strengths parents can have in helping their children. They include developing a positive attitude and developing an appropriate role model by being interested to help children with maths. Costello, Horne and Munro (1991) also suggest that parents can assist by helping children learn the skills of analysing and solving problems and encouraging them to share in home budget activities. Communication skills could be developed through speaking about budget activities, as well as by discussing graphs and tables in magazines and newspapers. The particular activities put forward by Costello, Horne and Munro (1991) include the following:

- explaining ideas as problems
- using familiar language to explain maths concepts
- using questions to help direct attention to the problem
- using diagrams and drawings
- looking for links with things children know
- encouraging children to talk about and explain school work

- accepting children's explanations, which may not be thorough, to encourage them to talk.

There are a variety of activities in the home and outdoors that could be used to help with maths, including such things as body measurements, TV activities, in the garage, playing in the park. Schools can make parents more aware of (and involved in) school maths by holding an open day, a mathematics 'display of work' evening, or a display of resources. Schools could also conduct mathematics workshops, and build a library of mathematics games and maths entertainment for parents to borrow.

Families helping at school

Families may not only be a valuable resource for learning at home, but may also provide help at school. Family volunteers could give individual assistance in class to students, as well as assisting with small group work. Helping with such activities can free teachers for other tasks. Involving parents at school may also improve home–school relationships by fostering cooperative activity and by allowing parents to appreciate the difficulties faced by the teacher. Schools may need the support of parents to help tackle special problems, to provide an extra pair of hands so that teachers can do things they might not otherwise be able to do and to help identify ways in which parents can help their children learn. Using parents as tutors for children may also have the advantage of providing them with an extra adult friend, who may have time to build a trusting relationship before the teacher can. They may also be more motivated and better behaved when with an adult tutor.

Blamires, Robertson and Blamires (1997) suggest a wide range of activities in which parents could be involved, including:

- reading stories to students or hearing them read
- assisting with spelling and writing activities including typing of stories
- helping with field trips and establishing contacts for local visits
- assisting with projects such as gardening, cooking, carpentry or classroom pets
- working puzzles and playing games with children
- helping in libraries or resource centres
- coaching sporting activities
- repairing instructional equipment and classroom materials.

At secondary level, it may be harder to get volunteers, as many parents who helped at primary school may feel that at secondary level they are not wanted. A good time to recruit volunteers at secondary school is at the orientation evening for parents of incoming students. Retired people are also a good source of assistance, as they may have the time and interest to provide effective support.

Parent support groups

As a consequence of the increasing involvement of parents, there have been extensive parent support networks developed. These networks have local branches in many areas in each state, which provide information about available support services, give parents guidelines for helping their children and provide personal advice and support. They also often have a library of books for parents to borrow and are very active in implementing and supporting changes to Commonwealth and state legislation that recognise the rights of people with learning disabilities.

Commonwealth disability discrimination legislation includes a section relating to people with any disorder or malfunction causing learning difficulties. The inclusion of this section was very much influenced by parent support networks. In most Australian states, similar legislation has now been passed which allows for 'special consideration' such as extended reading time in exams or reading and writing assistance. Possibly the best known Australian organisation for children with learning difficulties is SPELD (Specific Learning Disability Association). This was the first parent support organisation to be developed, and was started in New South Wales in 1969. It now has a network of parent support groups in all states of Australia and in New Zealand. The organisation has an extensive list of parent-oriented books and publications for sale. It is also actively involved in arranging public seminars related to learning disabilities, at which Australian and overseas authorities are invited to present their points or view. Most SPELD groups have also developed a network of remedial tutors. The main state branches are usually listed under SPELD in the telephone directory.

The large number of parent groups has helped to raise public awareness and acceptance of learning difficulties. In New South Wales, for example, the Board of Studies allows concessions for students with learning difficulties in school leaving exams. These concessions include extra reading time, writing and reading assistance, larger print exam papers and separate exam supervision. Whiting (1993) found that extra time for such students allowed them to read the questions more effectively and thus write better responses. It was also found to reduce exam pressure, which appeared to improve performance. In a further study, Whiting (1996) found that use of a writer in exams increased speed of composition, but there was a need for some prior practice to ensure that the writer and student could effectively work together. Hooker (1995) provides useful guidelines for reading exam papers to students with reading difficulties.

Parents are playing an increasingly important supportive and advisory role in public and private school education. The parent networks developed involve large numbers of people, and have been influential in ensuring that special services for children with learning difficulties have been greatly extended. There are many sites on the Internet that provide information about students with special needs. In particular, there are sites that are aimed at providing links to information, resources, services, support and discussion groups for parents and families of children with special needs. These include <www.familyvillage.wise. edu/education/kids.html> and <education.qld.gov.au>. The latter site is for the Queensland Department of Education, which provides information through disability-specific links, such as the link to students with learning disabilities.

Summary

The chapter discussed ways of making learning meaningful and relevant in the areas of literacy and numeracy. These methods included relating literacy to children's life events, as well as developing problem-solving skills for everyday activities in maths. An overview was also provided of techniques to assist students with literacy difficulties. These techniques included read along or supported reading, story sharing, and repeated reading of a story.

The chapter ended with an emphasis on the importance of involving families in the learning process. Parents in particular have the time to work in a one-to-one situation, which is not always available to the teacher. Several ways in which parents can help at home and at school were discussed.

Discussion questions

1   Surveys of choices of reading material have indicated that children and adults have a strong preference for newspapers and magazines, especially magazines about television programs. How could these choices be used to develop strategies to make literacy and numeracy meaningful for students with learning disabilities?

2   Families need to be partners with teachers in their child's education. Why is it important to involve parents and other family members? List some ways families may be effectively involved. What are some of the barriers to parental involvement?

3   Students with learning disabilities and literacy problems are now able to obtain concessions in exam situations, such as additional reading/writing time, and reading/writing assistance. Discuss the possible advantages and disadvantages of providing this assistance from an equity perspective.

Individual activities

1   Reading comprehension, especially when reading in different subject areas at secondary level, can be difficult for students with learning disabilities and literacy problems. A number of techniques have been identified in the 'Enhancing reading comprehension' section of this chapter to overcome the problem. Read this section and:
    a   identify which activities are appropriate for your area of teaching
    b   consider how these activities may be used
    c   suggest other relevant activities.

2   Read Box 8.2 – Harry – and:
    a   identify additional possible techniques which may be trialled to enhance his reading comprehension
    b   suggest ways in which parents may be further involved.

Group activities

1   In small groups, discuss recent personal activities that have involved numeracy. This discussion should concentrate on everyday activities more than on those related to academic activities. Describe the task and then outline the particular numeracy skills involved:

Example

Cooking a meal:
*   measurement of quantity, volume or weight
*   counting
*   time calculations.

Once the list is complete, ask the following questions:

a How often were the basic number facts involved?

b How often did the tasks involve very complex mathematical calculations?

c How often were paper and pencil used for these tasks?

d How often was a calculator needed?

e How often was estimation rather than actual calculation used?

Use the results from each group to discuss what could be considered the essential maths skills to function effectively in society.

2 Figure 8.1 outlines a semantic web concept map. The purpose of this map is to show how key concepts and their relationships may be graphically illustrated. In small groups:

a Identify a subsection of one chapter in this text and make up a semantic web concept map of this subsection. Discuss differences (if any) between groups in the concept map developed.

b Discuss the advantages and disadvantages of using this strategy in a regular classroom.

3 Bastiani (1989) identified the factors outlined below as contributing to a poor relationship between teachers and parents.

a Read through the factors and identify those you agree with and those you disagree with.

b Discuss possible strategies that could be put in place to overcome the problems.

Teachers	*Parents*
Don't understand total family picture	Don't have planned agendas when meeting with professionals
Don't understand parental expectations	Fail to realise or accept responsibility
Don't account for the presence of cultural or language differences of families	Don't communicate with teachers
Overwhelm parents with too much information	Look for a person or a program as a solution to their troubles
Don't involve parents in programs	Give away responsibility
Fail to develop realistic long- and short-term goals	Over protect adolescents, which fosters dependency
Don't provide parents with support and counselling	Don't carry through on programs at home
Don't coordinate services	Fail to see progress
Don't focus on positive attributes	Accept poor or inappropriate programming
Do too much for parents in the short term without helping them network with outside organisations	Think that their child is the teacher's only responsibility
Don't communicate with parents	Neglect to say 'thank you'
Don't ask adolescents about what they need	Don't ask adolescents about what they need

References

Alvermann, D. E. (2002). Effective literacy instruction for adolescents. *Journal of Literacy Research*, 34(2), 189–208.

Ashton, J. & Cairney, T. (2001). Understanding the discourses of partnership: An examination of one school's attempts at parent involvement. *The Australian Journal of Language and Literacy*, 24(2), 145–56.

Baker, S., Gersten, R. & Lee, D. (2003). A synthesis on empirical research on teaching mathematics to low-achieving students. *The Elementary School Journal*, 103(1), 51–73.

*Bakken, J. P. & Whedon, C. K. (2002). Teaching text structure to improve reading comprehension (What works for me). *Intervention in School and Clinic*, 37(4), 229–36.

Bastiani, J. (1989). *Working With Parents: A Whole School Approach*, UK: NFER Nelson.

Baumann, J. F. & Thomas, D. (1997). 'If you can pass momma's test then she knows you're getting your education'. A case study of support for literacy learning within an African American family. *The Reading Teacher*, 51(2), 108–20.

Bell, N. (1991). Gestalt imagery: A critical factor in language comprehension. *Annals of Dyslexia*, 41, 246–60.

*Blamires, M., Robertson, C. & Blamires, J. (1997). *Parent Teacher Partnerships*. London: David Fulton.

Bluestein, N. A. (2002). Comprehension through characterisation: Enabling readers to make personal connections with the literature. *The Reading Teacher*, 55(5), 431–33.

Bottge, B. A., Heinrichs, M., Mehta, Z. & Hung, Y. (2002). Weighing the benefits of anchored maths instruction for students with disabilities in general education classes. *The Journal of Special Education*, 35, 186–200.

Brehaut, L. (1994). Starting from scratch: Teaching an elderly man to read. *Good Practice in Australian Adult Literacy and Basic Education*, 25 (December), 11–13.

Brennan, S. & Robinson, G. L. (1998). Four approaches to comprehension instruction for students with literacy problems at the high school level. *Australian Journal of Learning Disabilities*, 3(4), 12–19.

Brent, M., Gough, F. & Robinson, S. (2001). *One in Eleven: Practical Strategies for Adolescents With a Language Learning Disability*. Melbourne: ACER.

Broughton, B. & Campbell, R. (1994). Promoting positive family literacy practices. *Good Practice in Adult Literacy and Basic Education*, 21, 8–9, 19.

Cairney, T. & Munsie, L. (1992). *Beyond Tokenism: Parents as Partners in Literacy*. Carlton, Vic: Australian Reading Association.

Cairney, T. & Ruger, J. (1997). *Community Literacy Practices and Schooling: Towards Effective Support for Parents*. Canberra: Department of Employment, Education, Training and Youth Affairs.

*Callaghan, K., Raedmacher, J. A. & Hildreth, B. L. (1998). The effects of parent participation strategies to improve the homework performance of students who are at risk. *Remedial and Special Education*, 19(3), 131–41.

Carpenter, B. (2003). Shifting the focus: From parent to family partnerships. *Special Education Perspectives*, 12(1), 3–16.

Cawley, J. F. & Miller, J. H. (1989). Cross-sectional comparison of the mathematics performance of children with learning disabilities: Are we on the right track for comprehensive programming? *Journal of Learning Disabilities, 22*(4), 250–4.

Cawley, J., Parmar, R., Foley, T., Salmon, S. & Roy, S. (2001). Arithmetic performance of students: Implications for standards and programming. *Exceptional Children, 67*(3), 311–28.

*Chard, D., Vaughan, S. & Tyler, B. (2002). A synthesis of research in effective intervention for building reading fluency with elementary students with learning disabilities. *Journal of Learning Disabilities, 35*(5), 386–406.

Clay, M. (1993). *Reading Recovery: A Training Guide for Teachers.* Auckland: Heinemann.

Coots, J. J. (1998). Family resources and parent participation in schooling activities for children with developmental delays. *Journal of Special Education, 31*(4), 498–520.

Costello, P., Horne, M. & Munro, J. (1991). *Sharing Maths Learning With Children.* Carlton, Vic: ACER.

Daisey, P. (1993). Three ways to promote the values and uses of literacy at any age. *Journal of Reading, 36*(6), 436–44.

Di Cecco, V. M. & Gleason, M. M. (2002). Using graphic organizers to attain relational knowledge from expository text. *Journal of Learning Disabilities, 26*(4), 306–20.

Eldredge, J. L. (1990). Increasing the performance of poor readers in third grade with a group assisted strategy. *Journal of Educational Research, 84*(2), 69–77.

Elkins, J. (1994). Helping all students become literate. *Australian Reading Association Special Interest Group No. 7, Learning Difficulties Newsletter, 2,* 8–11.

Furniss, E. (1993). Family literacy: Another fad or a new insight? *Australian Journal of Language and Literacy, 16*(2), 137–48.

Gersten, R., Fuchs, L. S., Williams, J. P. & Baker, S. (2000). Teaching reading comprehension strategies to students with learning disabilities: A review of research. *Review of Educational Research, 71*(2), 297–320.

Gordon, D. (1996). The snack time stall. *Practically Primary,* June, 18–12.

Greaves, D. (1995). Enhancing the parent-professional relationship. *Australian Journal of Remedial Education, 27*(1), 16–22.

Greenwood, G. E. & Hitchman, C. W. (1991). Research and practice in parent involvement: Implications for teacher education. *The Elementary School Journal, 91*(3), 279–88.

Griffin, M. L. (2002). Why don't you use your finger? Paired reading in first grade. *The Reading Teacher, 55*(8), 766–74.

*Hancock, J. & Lever, C. (1994). *Major Teaching Strategies for English.* Carlton, Vic: Australian Reading Association.

Henderson, A. T. (1988). Parents are a school's best friends. *Phi Delta Kappan,* October, 148–53.

Hertzberg, M. (2000). 'So we can learn something as well as doing something fun': Learning about reading through Readers' Theatre. *The Australian Journal of Language and Literacy, 23*(1), 21–35.

Hibbing, A. N. & Rankin-Erickson, J. L. (2003). A picture is worth a thousand words: Using visual images to improve comprehension for middle school struggling readers. *The Reading Teacher, 56*(8), 758–70.

Hickey, D. T., Moore, A. L. & Pelligrino, J. W. (2001). The motivational and academic consequences of elementary mathematics environments: Do constructivist innovations and reforms make a difference? *American Educational Research Journal*, 38, 611–52.

Homan, S. P., Klesius, J. P. & Hite, C. (1993). Effects of repeated reading and non-repetitive strategies on student's fluency and comprehension. *Journal of Educational Research*, 87(2), 94–9.

Hooker, J. (1995). Assessing provisions for students with learning difficulties in the print medium: Transforming official principle into practice in high school. *Special Education Perspectives*, 4(1), 45–53.

Hudson, P., Lignugaris-Kraft, B. & Miller, T. (1993). Using content enhancements to improve the performance of adolescents with learning disabilities in content classes. *Learning Disabilities Research and Practice*, 8(2), 106–26.

*Hummel, S. (2000). Developing comprehension skills of secondary students with specific learning difficulties. *Australian Journal of Learning Disabilities*, 5(4), 22–7.

Hunter-Carsch, M. (2001). Partnerships with parents. In M. Hunter-Carsch (Ed.), *Dyslexia: A Psychosocial Perspective*. London: Whurr.

Ives, B. & Hoy, C. (2003). Graphic organisers applied to higher-level secondary mathematics. *Learning Disabilities Research and Practice*, 18(1), 36–51.

Jackson, H. S. (1982). Eleven years later: A follow up of severely disabled readers. *Australian Journal of Remedial Education*, 14(1 & 2), 124–5.

Jitendra, A., Di Pipi, C. M. & Grasso, E. (2001). The role of graphic representational technique on the mathematical problem solving performance of fourth graders: An exploratory study. *Australasian Journal of Special Education*, 25(1 & 2), 17–33.

Jitendra, A. K., McGoey, K., Bhat, P., Griffin, C. C., Gardill, M. C. & Riley, T. (1998). Effects of mathematical word problem solving by students at risk or with mild disabilities. *The Journal of Educational Research*, 91(6), 345–55.

Jordan, N. C. & Hanich, L. B. (2000). Mathematical thinking in second-grade children with different forms of LD. *Journal of Learning Disabilities*, 33(6), 567–78.

Kalyanpur, M., Harry, B. & Skrtic, T. (2000). Equity and advocacy expectations of culturally diverse families participation in special education. *International Journal of Disability, Development and Education*, 47(2), 119–36.

Kearsley, I. (2002). Build on the rock: Teacher feedback and reading competence. *Australian Journal of Language and Literacy*, 25(8), 8–19.

*Kemp, M. (1987). *Watching Children Read and Write*. Melbourne: Nelson.

Kemp, M. (1993). There's more to listening than meets the ear: Interactions between oral readers and their parents as tutors. *International Journal of Disability, Development and Education*, 30(3), 197–223.

Kroth, R. L. & Edge, D. (1997). *Strategies for Communicating With Parents and Families of Exceptional Children*. Denver: Love Pub. Co.

Lane, C. H. (1990). ARROW: alleviating children's reading and spelling difficulties. In P. D. Pumfrey & C. D. Elliott (Eds), *Children's Difficulties in Reading, Spelling and Writing*. UK: Falmer Press.

Leal, D. (1993). The power of literary peer group discussions: How children collaboratively negotiate meaning. *The Reading Teacher*, 47(2), 114–20.

Love, K. & Hamston, J. (2001). Out of the mouths of boys: A profile of boys committed to reading. *The Australian Journal of Language and Literacy*, *24*(1), 31–48.

Mackereth, M. & Anderson, J. (2000). Computers, video games and literacy. What do girls think? *Australian Journal of Language and Literacy*, *23*(3), 184–96.

*Manz, S. L. (2002). A strategy for previewing textbooks: Teaching readers to become thieves. *The Reading Teacher*, *55*(5), 434–35.

Marr, B. & Helme, S. (1991). *Breaking the Maths Barrier*. Canberra, ACT: Department of Employment, Education and Training.

*Martin, B. (1989). *The Strugglers*. Milton Keynes: Open University Press.

McCarthy, S. J. (2000). Home-school connections: A review of the literature. *The Journal of Educational Research*, *93*(3), 145–63.

Molfese, V. J., Modglin, V. J. & Molfese, D. L. (2003). The role of environment in the development of reading skills: A longitudinal study of preschool and school age measures. *Journal of Learning Disabilities*, *36*(1), 59–67.

Moulton-Graham, K., Wigg, G., Kavanagh, M. & Mould, H. (1997). Functional literacies of householders: Current demands and coping strategies – a report of a pilot study. *Australian Journal of Language and Literacy*, *20*(1), 53–68.

Nicholas, K. & Robinson, G. L. (1995). Preliminary evaluation of a parent-tutor manual compared to child reading to parent in two settings: One managed from a school base and the other as a follow-up to intensive reading instruction. *Special Education Perspectives*, *4*(2), 97–108.

O'Loughlin, J. (1997). Using reader's theatre. *Practically Primary*, *2*(2), 40–2.

Ortega, A. & Ramirez, J. (2002). Parent literacy workshops: One school's parent program integrated with the school day. *The Reading Teacher*, *55*(8), 726–9.

O'Sullivan, O. (2000). Understanding spelling. *Reading*, *34*, 9–16.

Owen, R. L. & Fuchs, L. S. (2002). Mathematical problem-solving strategy instruction for third-grade students with learning disabilities. *Remedial and Special Education*, *23*(5), 268–78.

Patton, J. R., Cronin, M. E., Bassett, D. S. & Koppel, A. E. (1997). A life skills approach to mathematics instruction: Preparing students with learning difficulties for the real-life maths demands of adulthood. *Journal of Learning Disabilities*, *30*(2), 178–87.

Peters, E., Lloyd, J., Hasselbring, T., Goin, L., Bransford, J. & Stein, M. (1987). Effective maths instruction. *Teaching Exceptional Children*, *19*(3), 30–3.

Pilon, S. (1995). Computerised reading instruction: Current research. *Special Education Perspectives*, *4*(2), 87–95.

Poole, J. (2003). Dyslexia: A wider view: The contribution of an ecological paradigm to current issues. *Educational Research*, *45*(2), 167–80.

Reason, R. & Boote, R. (1994). *Learning Difficulties in Reading and Writing: A Teacher's Manual*. UK: NFER – Nelson.

Rhodes, L. & Shanklin, N. (1993). *Windows Into Literacy: Assessing Learners K–8*. Portsmouth, NH: Heinemann.

Robertson, M. (1990). True wizardry: Reader's Theatre in the classroom. *Primary English Notes* (PEN 79). Rozelle, NSW: Primary English Teacher's Association.

Robinson, G. L., Foreman, P. J. & Dear, K. (2000). The familial incidence of symptoms of scotopic sensitivity/Irlen syndrome: Comparison of referred and mass screened groups. *Perceptual and Motor Skills*, *91*, 707–24.

*Samuels, S. J. (1999). Developing reading fluency and learning disabled students. In R. J. Sternberg & L. Spear-Swerling (Eds), *Perspectives on Learning Disabilities*. NY: Westview Press.

Samuels, S. J., Schermer, N. & Reinking, D. (1992). Reading fluency: Techniques for making reading automatic. In S. J. Samuels & A. E. Farstrup (Eds), *What Research Has to Say About Reading Instruction*. Newark, Del.: International Reading Association, pp. 124–44.

Senechal, M. & Cornell, E. H. (1993). Vocabulary acquisition through shared reading experiences. *Reading Research Quarterly*, *28*(4), 361–73.

Shany, M. T. & Beimiller, A. (1995). Assisted reading practice: Effects of performance on poor readers in Grades 3 and 4. *Reading Research Quarterly*, *30*(3), 382–95.

Shea, T. & Bauer, A. (1991). *Parents and Teachers of Children with Exceptionalities*. Boston: Allyn & Bacon.

Slavin, R. E., Madden, N. A., Karwut, N. L., Dolan, L. J. & Walsh, B. A. (1994). Success for all: Getting reading right the first time. In E. M. Hiebert & B. M. Taylor (Eds), *Getting Reading Right From the Start*. Needham Heights, Mass: Allyn & Bacon, pp. 125–47.

Smart, D., Prior, M., Sanson, A. & Oberklaid, F. (2001). Children with reading difficulties: A six-year follow-up from early primary school to secondary school. *Australian Journal of Psychology*, *53*(1), 45–53.

*Spreadbury, J. (1994). *Read Me a Story*. Carlton, Vic: Australian Reading Association.

Talty, F. (1995). Small talk about big books: Interaction or conversationalisation. *Australian Journal of Language and Literacy*, *18*(1), 5–18.

Thomas, P. (1995). Keeping the ember glowing. *Good Practice in Australian Adult Literacy and Basic Education*, *28*, 10, 13.

*Thomson, M. & Watkins, E. (1998). *Dyslexia: A Teaching Handbook*. UK: Whurr.

Twine, S. (1992). *Home Team* (2nd edn). Perth, WA: Accord Publications.

Varus, M., Lehtinen, E., Kinnunen, R. & Salonen, P. (1992). Socioemotional coping and cognitive processes in training learning disabled children. In B. Wong (Ed.), *Contemporary Intervention Research in Learning Disabilities*. NY: Springer-Verlag.

Vaughan, S., Gersten, R. & Chard, D. J. (2000). The underlying message in LD intervention research: Findings from research synthesis. *Exceptional Children*, *67*(1), 99–114.

Walsh, D. (2002). Kids don't read because they can't read. *The Education Digest – Ann Arbour*, *65*(5), 29–30.

Welch, M. & Sheridan, M. (1995). *Educational Partnerships*. Orlando, Fl: Harcourt Brace.

West, C. E. & Clauser, P. S. (1999). The right stuff for reading: Assessing and facilitating written language. In H. W. Catts & A. G. Kamhi (Eds), *Language and Reading Disability*. Boston: Allyn & Bacon, pp. 259–324.

Westwood, P. (1994). Issues in spelling instruction. *Special Education Perspectives*, *3*(1), 31–44.

*Westwood, P. (2000). *Numeracy and Learning Disabilities*. Melbourne: ACER.

Whiting, P. (1993). Reasonable accommodations for learning disabled students in tertiary situations. *Australian Journal of Remedial Education*, *25*(4), 14–21.

Whiting, P. (1996). The effects of using a writer in examinations on senior students with and without learning disabilities. *Australasian Journal of Special Education*, *20*(1), 61–9.

Wilhelm, J. (1995). Reading is seeing: Using visual response to improve the literacy teaching of reluctant readers. *Journal of Reading Behaviors*, *24*(4), 467–99.

Worthy, J., Patterson, E., Salas, R., Prater, S. & Turner, M. (2002). 'More than just reading': The human factor in reaching resistant readers. *Reading Research and Instruction, 41*(2), 177–202.

Young, L. (1995). Educating children with learning difficulties and putting issues in perspective. *Australian Journal of Remedial Education, 27*(4), 26–33.

Young, T. A. (1991). Readers' Theatre: Bringing life into the reading program. *Reading Horizons, 32*(1), 33–40.

Young, T. A. & Tyre, C. (1988). *Dyslexia or Illiteracy: Realising the Right to Read.* Milton Keynes: Open University Press.

Zutell, J. & Raisinski, T. V. (1991). Training teachers to attend to their students' oral reading fluency. *Theory Into Practice, 30*, 211–17.

_____

*Recommended reading for this chapter

Further recommended reading

Bos, C. & Vaughan, S. (1997). *Strategies for Teaching Students With Learning and Behaviour Problems* (4th edn). Boston: Allyn & Bacon.

Bromfield, H. & Combley, M. (1997). *Overcoming Dyslexia: A Practical Handbook for the Classroom.* London: Whurr.

Kamhi, A. G. & Catts, H. W. (Eds) (1999). *Language and Reading Disability.* Boston: Allyn & Bacon.

Mercer, C. D. & Mercer, A. R. (2001). *Teaching Students With Learning Problems* (6th edn). Columbus: Charles E. Merrill.

Stowe, C. M. (2000). *How to Reach and Teach Students With Dyslexia.* NY: Centre for Applied Research and Education.

Taylor, G. (2000). *Parental Involvement.* Springfield, Illinois: Charles C. Thomas.

Thompson, M. E. & Watkins, E. J. (1998). *Dyslexia: A Teaching Handbook* (2nd edn). London: Whurr.

Westwood, P. (2003). *Commonsense Methods for Children With Special Needs: Strategies for the Regular Classroom.* London: Routledge Folmer.

Chapter 9

Functional communication
in the classroom

Susan Balandin and Alison Sweep

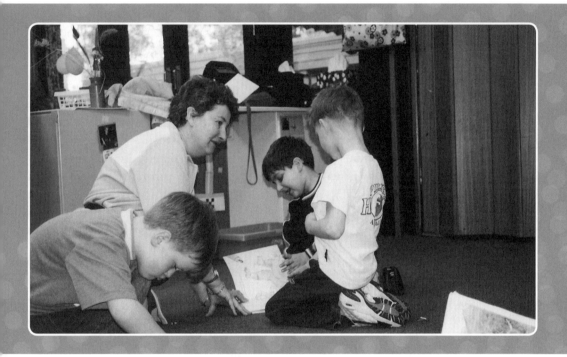

This chapter aims to:

- discuss the importance of communication in classroom and social contexts
- provide an overview of augmentative and alternative communication (AAC)
- explore the concepts of language development and functional communication
- provide a framework for assessing communication in educational settings
- consider how teachers and therapy staff can work with students and their families to improve functional communication outcomes.

Introduction

In this chapter the focus is on students who are identified as having severe speech and language delay and on those who may not be able to use speech as their primary mode of communication. This group includes all students who rely on augmentative and alternative communication (AAC) to communicate. One definition of an AAC system is that of ASHA (1991), which states that AAC is 'an integrated group of components, including the symbols, aids, strategies and techniques used by individuals to enhance communication … the system serves to supplement any gestural, spoken, and/or written communication abilities' (p. 10).

Thus, the emphasis here is on those students who need additional help with expressive language and also those who have difficulties with understanding what is said to them. It includes students who experience no cognitive deficits but who have severe motor disorder that results in them being unable to produce intelligible speech (for example, students with cerebral palsy). Some students with severe intellectual disability do not easily develop the symbolic underpinnings of language and are unable to produce spoken language. They may be referred to as having non-symbolic communication, pre-symbolic communication, or as being early communicators (Butterfield & Arthur, 1995; Granlund & Olsson, 1999; Siegel-Causey & Guess, 1989). Students who begin school with a non-symbolic communication system may go on to develop the ability to learn a formal symbol system. Whatever the cause of the speech and/or language difficulty, collaboration is one of the keys to successful intervention and support for students who are in inclusive educational settings.

The use of collaborative teams to provide communication interventions, particularly in inclusive classroom settings, increases the potential for both academic achievement and social participation for students with severe communication problems and is consistent with education legislation and good practice. Students may benefit from the use of AAC systems that support both their expressive language and their comprehension. The use of such systems will assist the students to learn within the classroom setting and will facilitate interactions with their peers and teachers, help them to make sense of their world, help them order their day, support their language comprehension and assist them to be independent within the contexts of both school and home.

This chapter explains the role of functional communication in supporting students in inclusive contexts, and how teachers and therapists can work together to develop appropriate communication opportunities for students with different communication needs. The chapter will explore recent research that has focused on students with complex communication needs in inclusive educational settings. In addition, it will provide a number of case illustrations and practical activities.

Communication, learning and inclusive settings

Communication is an integral facet of learning. The classroom is a communicative environment in which communication occurs continuously throughout the day. Teachers communicate with students formally (for example, explaining an algebraic equation) and informally (for example, asking a student how a favourite football team is progressing). Students must be able to communicate effectively with their teachers during learning activities and also with their peers during class and breaks (Hunt, Alwell & Goetz, 1991a; Kent-Walsh & Light, 2003). Indeed, the school setting provides many opportunities for social interaction and the development of friendships. Clearly, a student with communication difficulties will be disadvantaged in both learning and social activities unless every effort is made to ensure that the student has an effective and functional means of communication (Beukelman & Mirenda, 1998).

When considering communication for students in educational settings, it is important not to overlook other communicative contexts in which effective communication is important. These include communication between teaching staff, therapists, and other service providers, and communication between teachers, service providers and parents (Björck-Åkesson, Grandlund & Olsson, 1996; Duchan, 1993; Friend & Cook, 1992; Giangreco, 2000; Giangreco et al., 1993; Pugach & Johnson, 1995).

Students with complex communication needs

As many as one in seven children has a communication disorder (Harasty & Reed, 1994). Yet most of these children will enter mainstream schools and will cope in these settings with the help of a speech pathologist and possibly some additional educational support. These children may have difficulty understanding what is said or in making themselves understood. They are also at risk of problems with literacy (Bird, Bishop & Freeman, 1995; Morais, 1991; O'Connor, Notari-Syverson & Vadasy, 1996; Prior et al., 1995; Stackhouse & Wells, 1998; Watkins, 1996; Whiting, 1996). These students form part of the regular classroom population.

In this chapter the focus is on functional communication in the classroom for students with complex communication needs. Students with complex communication needs require additional time, support, resources, and classroom adaptation if they are to maximise their learning and social opportunities in the educational setting. Often they have physical disability and are unable to write or easily join in spoken language activities (Beukelman & Mirenda, 1998). If they are not proficient at using their communication system, or if their system is broken or lost, they will be unable to join in most classroom activities. Indeed, these students may spend a large part of their time in school unable to communicate or not participating in academic activities because they are still learning to use their communication systems (Beukelman & Mirenda, 1998). It is essential that the AAC team includes all the people who are involved with the student in the inclusive context. This includes teachers, the student, class peers, and parents, as well as other service providers and administrative staff. The team must understand what is required to optimise the inclusive educational experience for each of the students with complex communication needs (Beukelman & Mirenda, 1998). Full inclusion occurs when the student is fully integrated in the class, participating competitively or actively, academically and socially and is as independent as possible (Beukelman & Mirenda, 1998).

Increasingly, students with complex communication needs are attending inclusive educational settings. They may have cognitive impairment and/or physical impairments and, if they have no functional speech, will benefit from an AAC system (Beukelman & Mirenda, 1998). Initially, general education teachers may feel overwhelmed by the prospect of working with students with severe communication problems; nevertheless, many of these students are participating successfully in inclusive educational settings and achieving their educational goals (Kent-Walsh & Light, 2003).

Augmentative and alternative communication systems

In order to consider AAC and its role with students with communication disorders, it is important to define the populations most likely to use and benefit from AAC systems. AAC is appropriate for use with students with expressive and/or receptive language disorders, including students with autism spectrum disorder (Mirenda & Schuler, 1988; von Tetzchner, 1999; von Tetzchner & Martinsen, 2000); students with cerebral palsy (Dormans & Pellegrino, 1998; Frame et al., 2000; Warrick & Kaul, 1997; Willard-Holt, 1998), students with intellectual disability (Carter, 2003a; 2003b; Iacono, Waring & Chan, 1996; Rowland & Schweigert, 2002), and with students with challenging behaviours (Hunt, Alwell & Goetz, 1988; Mirenda, 1997; Sigafoos & Tucker, 2000).

AAC systems may be unaided (for example, signs) or aided (for example, picture boards, alphabet boards, electronic communication aids) and are often referred to as being either high or light technology systems. High technology communication systems, (that is, 'high tech') (Sigafoos & Iacono, 1993) utilise microcomputers and specialised software. These have the capacity to provide printed and/or voice output. A device that has voice output is referred to as a *speech-generating device (SGD)* (see glossary) because it 'speaks'. The speech may be digitised (that is, natural speech that has been recorded) or synthesised (that is, synthetic speech produced from stored digital data). Low or light technology communication systems (that is, 'light-tech') (Sigafoos & Iacono, 1993) include communication boards, books, and object boards that may be made commercially or by a service provider or family member. These systems also include devices operated by electromechanical switches. Light tech systems are used by beginning communicators, including older students with a severe level of cognitive impairment, those who are unable to access high-tech systems because of severe physical disability, and as backup systems when an individual's high tech system is under repair or unavailable. Many people who use AAC and their families and service providers, favour high-tech devices because such devices have the power of voice output and can often interface with other equipment (for example, computers, environmental control systems). However, high-tech systems are not suitable for all people who need AAC, and are usually expensive. Families may not be able to afford to buy an appropriate system and the educational facility may not have the financial resources to provide and maintain the equipment. An overview of high- and light-tech AAC systems is provided in Box 9.1.

Symbol systems

Speech consists of spoken words that are used to fulfil four purposes (Light, 1988):
- communication of needs and wants
- information transfer
- social closeness
- social etiquette.

Spoken or written words are symbols, but other types of symbols are also used for communication. Logos, road signs, pictures, and gestures are all examples of symbols that can be used for communication. All AAC systems incorporate symbols that are used to encode and decode messages. Symbol systems used on AAC systems vary in transparency (ease of deciphering what the symbol means) and it is important to match the symbol system to the student's level of cognitive ability and understanding (Mirenda & Locke, 1989). The easiest or most transparent symbols are real objects, the most difficult written words. Mirenda and Locke's hierarchy of symbols is provided in Box 9.2.

Box 9.1

An overview of high- and light-tech AAC systems

High technology	Utilises microcomputers and specialised software
	Synthesised or digitised speech
	May interface with a computer, environmental control system or telephone
	Accessed directly (for example using fingers or head pointer) or indirectly (for example, scanning using a switch)
	Requires a power source (for example, battery)
	Requires specialised repair
	Expensive to purchase and maintain
Light technology – aided	No electronic parts but can include electromechanical switches
	Accessed directly (for example, finger pointing, eye gaze) or indirectly using another person to ask which symbol is required
	Examples: letter boards; chat books; object communication systems; schedules; symbol boards
	Easy to maintain but set up and maintenance can be costly in time

Light technology – unaided	Manual signing
	Examples: Auslan; British Sign Language; Amerind; American Sign Language; Signed English

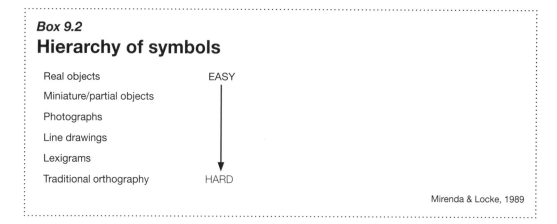

Box 9.2

Hierarchy of symbols

Real objects   EASY

Miniature/partial objects

Photographs

Line drawings

Lexigrams

Traditional orthography   HARD

Mirenda & Locke, 1989

There are many symbol systems available commercially; these include pictures, line drawings and symbol systems that are designed to provide fast and accurate access to language, for example, Boardmaker™, Compics™, Minspeak™ (Baker, 1982) and Bliss symbols (Bliss, 1965). Teachers working with students who use AAC may need to select the most appropriate system for the individual and be prepared to update the system if necessary. For example, early communicators may begin with an AAC system incorporating objects, then move on to pictures and photos, and may progress to a literacy-based system as their literacy skills develop. Ideally the AAC team will work together to select the most appropriate symbol system for the student who is using AAC but sometimes it is left to the teacher to select symbols or develop a symbol system.

One of the most common reasons for a student failing to use an AAC system is that the system is too difficult to comprehend. There has been a tendency for service providers, including teachers, to label students not using their systems as being unwilling to communicate, rather than recognising that the system may be unsuitable for the student. Careful assessment of a student's abilities is essential when introducing AAC. Communication is a distinguishing feature of humans and an essential component of adequate quality of life. Students have the right to the communication systems and supports that will help them optimise their communication skills and to learn and interact in the school environment.

Students with complex communication needs who use AAC have but one thing in common: they are unable to use speech as a primary functional communication mode. It is not known how many students use AAC or how many might benefit from the introduction of an AAC system (Bax, Cockerill & Carroll-Few, 2001). However, as noted above, most students who do use AAC have congenital disability, including intellectual disability, cerebral palsy, autism spectrum disorder, and/or severe developmental dyspraxia of speech. Some children may need AAC after acquiring a communication disorder (for example, traumatic brain injury).

Just as every student has the right to be educated in an inclusive setting, so every student has the right to the services and technology that enhance communication and assist them in participating in both academic and community activities (National Joint Committee for the Communication Needs for Persons with Severe Disabilities, 2002). Early introduction of AAC not only provides a functional means of communication, but also reduces the likelihood of the use of disruptive and/or destructive behaviours as communicative acts (Beukelman

& Mirenda, 1998; Mirenda, 1997; Sigafoos et al., 1994; Vicker, 1996). However, the introduction of AAC alone does not ensure effective communication. Students who use AAC require their communication partners to understand how to interact with someone with complex communication needs as the story in Box 9.3 by Fiona, an adult with cerebral palsy and complex communication needs, illustrates.

Box 9.3

AAC and inclusion

My education began at a school for children with special needs in 1983. My parents thought that this would be the best school for me, because of access to therapy services. Although I did benefit from this, my education suffered. The school did not cater for someone with my level of intelligence. The teachers were only prepared to teach the basics, and keep us entertained.

When I was about 8, I decided that I wanted to go to an inclusive school. Other children were integrating, but they were able to walk, and talk, easier than I could. However, I wasn't able to go because no one agreed with me. The teachers thought that it was too difficult for children who used AAC to attend a mainstream school.

In 1988 I changed school. In the beginning I attended classes in the support unit and gradually integrated more and more into mainstream classes. I went to a mainstream single-sex high school.

When I started high school, I did not have a high-tech AAC system. I had to rely on an alphabet board and typing messages into a laptop computer for people to read. This had an impact on my interactions with the teachers and other students. Socialising with the other students was difficult. I think it was because it took so much longer to communicate with me. I had an aide almost full time during my junior years at high school. The teachers and students talked to her instead of me. The aide encouraged this, as she had no formal training. She made friends with the girls, which was inappropriate. I had one teacher who walked out of the classroom as soon as he saw me, which was really demoralising for me.

I overcame some of my communication problems with the teachers over time. My social science teacher, in Year 8, noticed I answered more questions than other students. In Year 10, I got my first voice output communication device. It certainly improved my interactions with the teachers and students. It also enhanced my ability to participate in oral activities.

I would like to offer some advice to teachers who have students who use AAC in their class. First, where possible, it is very important to speak directly to the student, instead of only talking to the aide. It may be easier to ask questions requiring yes or no answers. You will need to be aware that you will need to make some adjustments to the curriculum and the student may require alternative assessments. The most important point is to treat the student as an individual.

The inclusion of students who use AAC in inclusive educational settings can have very good outcomes if the right adjustments are made and the school has the right attitude. I managed to get a good HSC result and have a law degree and an honours degree in politics. I'm now embarking on my next challenge: securing employment as a solicitor.

Fiona Given, law graduate, NSW

Teachers' experiences with students with complex communication needs in inclusive settings

To date there have been few studies that have explored the experiences of teachers with students who use AAC in inclusive settings. Soto et al. (2001) conducted a series of focus groups that explored educational teams' perceptions of the critical issues of inclusion for students who use AAC. The participants agreed that inclusion was beneficial for students who use AAC, for parents, the school community and the students' peers. They identified key indicators of successful inclusive programs that included:

- the classroom teacher welcomes and includes the student who uses AAC as a full member of the class
- the educational team works collaboratively
- all the team and school staff have appropriate training
- the presence of a support worker who is involved with the student and the program
- involvement and support from peers in class
- interactions between the student who uses AAC and peers both in and out of school time
- academic participation of the student using AAC
- the student is able to use the AAC system successfully
- adequate services and supports are available
- the student using AAC feels part of the class and school
- the classroom supports the learning of students with different needs
- the school system supports inclusion at school and area or regional level
- there is adequate support for the student within the classroom.

Although this study (Soto et al., 2001) was conducted in North America, it is applicable to Australia and New Zealand or, indeed, any school in which students who use AAC are included. Successful implementation of AAC requires a team effort (Beukelman & Mirenda, 1998; Cumley & Beukelman, 1992). In addition, there have been several research studies that have explored attitudes towards students who use AAC (Beck et al., 2000; Beck & Dennis, 1996; Blockberger et al., 1993; Fisher, Pumpian & Sax, 1998). These studies have emphasised the importance of a positive attitude in ensuring that students who use AAC are accepted and included.

The participants in Soto et al.'s study (2001) identified some barriers to successful inclusion. These included:

- lack of training in AAC
- frequent staff turnover
- lack of administrative support
- no time for collaborative team meetings
- lack of flexibility for people to move out of their individual professional roles
- case loads that were too big
- too much reliance for progress placed on the aide or support worker
- lack of opportunity for the student to participate in academic activities
- a classroom structure that marginalises the student
- lack of transition planning

- the team not feeling comfortable and confident with AAC technology
- AAC equipment breaking down and needing repair
- lack of funding for equipment
- lack of loan equipment or equipment that could be used as a back up
- limitations of the AAC system compared with natural speech.

Some of these barriers could be addressed through training; others (for example, the need for funding, limitations of the system) require major policy changes and ongoing research and development.

An interesting aspect of this study was that participants noted how their own limitations (for example, fear of failure, uneasiness about disability, feeling undervalued by the team members) have an impact on the inclusion of the student. In any collaborative team approach, time spent in planning and ensuring that all team members feel valued and have equal status on the team is well spent as it helps ensure the success of the team, particularly when there are problems to solve (Giangreco, 1996; Giangreco, 2000; Santelli et al., 1998). Soto et al. (2001) concluded that there are three keys to successful inclusion of students using AAC, adequate administrative support, AAC training for all concerned and team collaboration.

Kent-Walsh and Light (2003) interviewed 11 teachers who had taught at least one student who used AAC in an inclusive educational setting. The teachers, in common with the participants in Soto et al.'s (2001) study, were able to identify many benefits, some negative impacts, and some barriers to the inclusive experience. Participants reported that teachers, parents and peers benefited from the experience. Nevertheless, the teachers stated that some students who used AAC did not make adequate academic progress, were socially excluded and did not have equal status with their classmates. In addition, the teachers noted that the use of AAC in the classroom could be disruptive and that it was time consuming. The teachers were interested in AAC and wanted to learn more, but found that additional preparation time was sometimes difficult to schedule.

Some teachers noted that the school itself was not accessible for students with physical disability. They also indicated that large classes, particularly in high school, made it difficult to give enough individual attention to students who used AAC. In this study (Kent-Walsh & Light, 2003), the teachers expressed frustration that they were not always included as part of the AAC team and were not always involved in goal setting for the students. They also noted that their expectations were sometimes different from those of the student's parents. Teachers did not feel that they were well prepared to teach a student with complex communication needs who used AAC and that they experienced problems with setting up the equipment and assessing if the student was learning. They also noted that high tech AAC systems were beneficial to inclusion but were problematic if broken or under repair, as the student then was without a communication system. At least two of the teachers stated that they preferred their students to augment their communication with signing.

The teachers felt that there was some resistance from other teachers to include a student who used AAC, although they conceded that teachers' attitudes can improve. The teachers who participated in the study also reported negative experiences with teacher's aides similar to those reported by Fiona (Box 9.3).

Interactions between students who use AAC and their peers is consistently identified as an important issue (Arthur, Bochner & Butterfield, 1999; Blackstone & Cassatt, 1983;

Calculator, 1999; Carter & Maxwell, 1998; Hunt, Alwell & Goetz, 1991b; McConachie & Pennington, 1997; Soto et al., 2001). Kent-Walsh and Light (2003) found that slow rates of communication had a negative impact on interactions between students who used AAC and their peers. The teachers also noted that the students who used AAC were not always socially adept and that this impacted on their ability to make friends, particularly as they grew older. This highlights the need for careful preparation and training for students who use AAC and their peers prior to inclusion (Beukelman & Mirenda, 1998).

Teachers stressed the importance of students being able to access all the school buildings, classrooms and equipment. They also noted the advantages of small classes for students who use AAC. They considered it important to give the students with complex communication needs real grades for their work. The work and grading systems may be modified, but parents appreciate knowing how their child is progressing. The teachers who participated in Kent-Walsh and Light's (2003) study believed that teachers needed time to adjust to having a student who uses AAC in the class. They also spoke about the mutual support that teachers can give to each other and that this is helpful in changing teacher attitudes and encouraging other teachers to willingly accept a student who uses AAC into the class.

The teachers were in agreement with the participants in Soto et al.'s (2001) study that collaboration is a key factor in successful inclusion. The teachers considered effective communication and collaboration with other team members important, particularly at transition times when the student was moving to another class. They emphasised the importance of having time to observe a student prior to accepting that student into a class and of having detailed notes from previous teachers. Therapists, parents, special educators and other team members all provide important information and support to the teacher and are critical to the success of any inclusion program.

Participants identified three important issues relating to successful curriculum development:

- set realistic academic goals
- try to include students in some classes that are appropriate to their level of skill (for example, a lower aged class)
- some curriculums (for example, art, cooking) are easier to adapt than others (for example, maths, science).

However, it may not be appropriate to include older children with complex communication needs in classes with much younger children. This segregation heightens feelings of difference and suggests that the student using AAC does not belong in the class (Schnorr, 1990). It may be better to include all students in an activity and try to tailor the goal to each student's ability. Teacher's aides and increased time for curriculum planning may help with this.

The teachers identified a number of factors that they considered likely to facilitate inclusion for students who use AAC (Kent-Walsh & Light, 2003). These included:

- honest open communication about the inclusion experience
- developing competency in using AAC
- requesting additional planning time
- respecting the student at all times
- including the student in all activities

- matching the technology to the activity
- providing peers with information about inclusion of the student who uses AAC
- maintaining effective team collaboration
- adequate training for team members
- providing the teacher with support from the team
- implementing effective transition planning
- selecting an AAC system that is appropriate for the student.

Thus, these teachers identified the team, student peers, AAC systems and technology and the school itself as critical components of successful inclusion. The issues raised support those identified as important by specialists in AAC (for example, Beukelman & Mirenda, 1998), other researchers (Soto et al., 2001), early childhood teachers (Smith & Kenneth, 2000) and people who use AAC (see Box 9.3).

The two studies discussed here provide a clear indication of the issues that teachers and others who support students with complex communication needs consider important if the inclusion is to be successful. The case study in Box 9.4 illustrates how team members can work together to facilitate the success of the inclusion process for a young child with complex communication needs.

Box 9.4
Voices: My role as an Integration Support Teacher

Jack – a case study

My role as an Integration Support Teacher is consultancy-based, servicing preschool to Year 12. Much of my job entails resourcing classroom teachers with students who have special needs and who receive state funding for their disabilities. Transition to the first year of school can be a challenging time for all and I am often involved in the year prior to the start of school.

Jack (pseudonym) attended mainstream preschool two days per week and was starting Early Intervention (EI) class for two mornings. He had major needs in language, talked in a rapid 'off topic' staccato, did not listen well, and (in his mother's words) was 'very spaced out'. This led to temper tantrums, aversion to change, and delayed social skills. A speech pathologist diagnosed a severe receptive and expressive language disorder.

Jack's prospective teacher visited him at preschool on one of his 'bad days', and confided to the Transition Support Team that she found his difficulties very daunting! Besides the normal orientation day, I suggested Jack attend class for four mornings a week so that the teacher could get to know him in her setting. The EI teacher and an existing teacher aide agreed to support him. I also displayed a 'Going to School' transition photo album made for another student which would prepare Jack and coach him through school routines and events. His mother loved this and volunteered to take the photos. Jack would be in as many photos as possible, with personal captions.

The school counsellor suggested that Jack be referred to a paediatrician for a full assessment to see if he were eligible for other support mechanisms. I recommended an application for a behaviour support teacher to be in place for the start of the year. The EI teacher would also visit.

My base school has 'Boardmaker', a pictorial communication program, so I printed off coloured cue pictures to make a visual time-table for Jack. I prepared behaviour and direction cue pictures, cue tokens like an ice cream 'cool down' shape and a 'my turn' lollipop, and scaffolding stepping stones of 'who, why, what, where' etc. When laminated, these would become useful and fun at oral language talk time. For behaviour we decided to use five 'Smiley' circles on yellow felt. The teacher chose two resource books from a selection I provided, one on language disorders and one on behaviour. I also suggested a beanbag for positive time out that the whole class could use. The teacher was invited to a training and development morning at my base school the following week. This would give her more confidence and further resources.

The paediatrician diagnosed Jack with mild autism, probably Asperger syndrome. This diagnosis entitled Jack to apply for further support including teacher aide time and teacher release time. I subsequently arranged for the teacher to spend two mornings observing a similar student in a nearby school, and to visit a support class for students with autism. I then emailed a list of books and websites on autism. The paediatrician had also expressed concern about Jack's poor fine motor skills, so I was able to show the teacher a range of useful devices including a slope board, pencil grip, and spring-loaded scissors. These were subsequently ordered for Jack.

A gradual attendance schedule was drafted, commencing with morning-only attendance for the first two weeks. Safety contingency plans

Box 9.4 continued

were prepared in case Jack ran off from class, using examples from other schools. I left an 'induction' support booklet for the new teacher aide, and arranged for some orientation sessions at the commencement of the next school year.

All of those participating in this transition/enrolment process worked enthusiastically and collaboratively. The teacher felt more confident in her ability to manage Jack and meet his educational needs. She thanked everyone for the support and resources.

Elva Fitzgibbon,
NSW Department of Education and Training,
Gosford, NSW

Language development and functional communication

Students with complex communication needs entering inclusive educational settings are likely to have a variety of language needs and abilities. Some may have very little functional communication and severe language difficulties, whereas others may have good language skills but limited or no speech. Functional communication implies that the student will be able to communicate in a variety of contexts in the most efficient way. Many students will use a variety of communication modes (for example, vocalisations, speech, sign or gesture, facial expression or the use of a speech-generating device) to communicate different messages to different partners in different contexts. Teachers need to be flexible in their approach to communication and to accept communication attempts that are socially acceptable. This is rewarding for the student and encourages further communicative attempts. There is no one way to communicate a message – all people use a variety of communication modes (speech, gesture, written symbols).

Language and AAC

Despite recognition of the variety of communication modes that humans use and the need to be able to convey messages in the quickest and most appropriate way, teachers working with students who use or require AAC are often asked if the use of AAC will prevent a student from learning to talk or if AAC facilitates language development.

Longitudinal research on the use of AAC to promote language and communication with children and young adults with intellectual disabilities has been conducted (Romski, Sevcik & Adamson, 1997; Romski & Sevcik, 1996; Sevcik, Romski & Adamson, 1999). These researchers developed the System for Augmenting Language (SAL) and have shown that SAL can be used successfully to increase language production in primary school students and adolescents in secondary school (Romski & Sevcik, 1996).

Teachers helped students learn to use a speech-generating device (SGD) and the teachers also used the SGD when communicating with the students. Over time, the students used the SGD independently and their use of language increased. A detailed description of SAL is beyond the scope of this chapter, but interested readers can find more information in the work of Romski and Sevcik (1996).

It is important to consider intrinsic factors (that is, those that the student brings to acquiring language through AAC) and extrinsic factors (for example, AAC system) when developing a framework to understand language development and AAC (Romski, Sevcik

& Adamson, 1997). Students need to understand the relationship between the spoken word and its referent and the relationship between a spoken word and its visual symbol. Students with limited comprehension must learn the relationship between a visual symbol or sign and the referent before they can use AAC expressively. Some students may never understand this relationship and will continue to communicate using idiosyncratic gesture, vocalisation and physical manipulation of others in the environment throughout their education (Butterfield, Arthur & Sigafoos, 1995; Siegel-Causey & Guess, 1989). These students are referred to as functioning at a pre-linguistic or pre-symbolic level, or as being early communicators.

Students with lifelong disability (for example, intellectual disability) can benefit from the use of AAC to support their communication and learning (Bondy & Frost, 1994; Butterfield et al., 1992; Butterfield et al., 1995; Carr & Felce, 2000; Carter, Hotchkiss & Cassar, 1996; Cutts & Sigafoos, 2001; Goossens, Crain & Elder, 1992; Iacono, Mirenda & Beukelman, 1993; Iacono & Duncum, 1995; Musselwhite & St. Louis, 1988; Stainton & Besser, 1998). However, a number of barriers may impact on services to these students and delay the introduction of functional communication systems (National Joint Committee for the Communication Needs for Persons with Severe Disabilities, 2002). Barriers include a lack of professional staff knowledge (Balandin & Iacono, 1998) and limited or no training opportunities for communication partners (for example, families and support staff) (Light & Binger, 1998).

Students with intellectual disability

The use of sign and gesture to support the language development of people with an intellectual disability is one of the earliest reported uses of AAC (Walker, 1976). Sign and gesture are commonly used with and by students who have an intellectual disability. The use of sign provides a visual cue to comprehension and expresses a message. In a recent study of three children with Down syndrome (Chan & Iacono, 2001), the children produced different gestures for a variety of communicative functions. Limited use of gestures coupled with a lack of clarity in the child's communicative intent may predict poor spoken language and vocabulary development. Adults find it difficult to interpret the child's gestures and other behaviours, and therefore cannot provide appropriate language models (Wetherby, Warren & Reichle, 1998). Chan and Iacono (2001) reported that the children in their study used gestures common to children at similar levels of language development but failed to develop speech concurrently. This study indicated that signing may be an advantage for children with Down syndrome who are not speaking.

Students with intellectual disability may not learn sign fluently, but may benefit from the use of sign. Key word signing (Grove & Walker, 1990; Windsor & Fristoe, 1989) is often used with students who have language impairments and who may be helped by seeing a word signed as an addition to the auditory stimulus. In key word signing only the important content words are signed. The signs are supplemented with natural gesture and may include the individual's idiosyncratic signs and gestures. Key word signing is always accompanied by speech and is sometimes termed *simultaneous communication* (Beukelman & Mirenda, 1998).

It is important that those who interact with the student learning to sign (for example, teachers, teachers' aides, student peers, parents) sign consistently. It is also important that the student has the physical ability to make the signs (von Tetzchner & Martinsen, 2000). Thus, teachers and peers will need to learn the signs the student is able to use and to build up their knowledge of sign to keep pace with the student's language needs. Learning signing in school is an activity that students, particularly younger students, are likely to enjoy. However, it is an additional task for teachers. Speech pathologists or parents can often assist and provide training and resource materials.

Students learning sign will benefit from implicit and explicit teaching (von Tetzchner & Martinsen, 2000). In implicit teaching of sign, the student is exposed to a variety of signs that are meaningful within different contexts with no specific effort made to directly teach the signs. In explicit teaching, the relationship between the word and the sign is clearly identified and the student is helped to learn the sign. This includes the student practising the sign and being prompted to use it. It also includes hand-over-hand modelling.

Researchers have explored how best to select and teach signs to students who require a AAC to communicate (Iacono & Parsons, 1987; Reichle, Williams & Ryan, 1981; Spragale & Micucci, 1990). To ensure functional communication, signs should be selected for relevance to each individual student within a given communicative context (for example, the classroom, the playground, on the school bus). Signs that are most relevant and meaningful for the student and for those who interact with them will be easier to learn.

If signing is used as an aid to comprehension, it is important that all those interacting with the student use the signs consistently and that the student is rewarded for using sign. It can be argued that the onus is on those without a disability who interact with the student to learn signs and to use them in order to promote communication and language development. However, there is some reluctance on the part of some to use sign, or its use may be dropped, for example, when new staff are employed or when a student moves class. This can occur despite the fact that signing has been shown to be an effective communication tool with the particular student. Additionally, teachers need to be aware that in order to sign students must have adequate hand function to form the signs. It must also be remembered that many students who use sign may also benefit from other forms of AAC. The case study of Sarah in Box 9.5 demonstrates the important role that a teacher plays in ensuring optimal communication opportunities for a student with Down syndrome.

Box 9.5

The role of the teacher in optimising communication

Sarah is 7 years old and is in her second year of schooling. She attends her local primary school with her 9- and 11-year-old brothers. The family transferred to the area at the commencement of the year. Sarah has Down syndrome and a moderate intellectual disability. She is very sociable and settled in quickly to her new school, making a number of close friends. She likes to play soccer during lunch and dress ups during free play. She also enjoys singing and dancing.

At the beginning of the year Sarah's teacher and parents met and discussed Sarah's educational needs. Sarah's parents believed that Sarah's skills in gross motor, play and academic areas such as mathematics would be met by the class program, but were concerned about her speech and language development. Sarah received private speech pathology in the past, but the family was unable to afford further sessions. Sarah's mum became quite upset,

>

Box 9.5 continued

saying that she just wanted Sarah to be able to talk and to be liked by the other students. She expressed a willingness to assist in any way she could.

Sarah's teacher paid particular attention to Sarah's communication over the following weeks and noted that she was able to use three to four word sentences, but mainly used two to three words and inconsistently used sign language. She generally signed a main word of her utterance. For example, when Sarah asked, 'Where my book?' she only signed 'book'. Sarah's mother informed her teacher that Sarah learned the signs during private therapy and that she picked them up quickly. Sarah's teacher was usually able to understand her speech, although other teachers and some of the students said that they had difficulty understanding Sarah at times. Sarah's teacher also observed that she became frustrated when not understood and if asked to repeat herself a couple of times she would cross her arms, lower her head and refuse to repeat her words again.

Sarah followed most of her teacher's directions during class activities. Her teacher noticed, however, that Sarah watched her classmates at times and followed their lead, particularly when a new activity was introduced. Also, when Sarah's classmates spoke quickly to her and used a number of sentences together, Sarah seemed to have difficulty understanding. She would wait until she understood the conversation and then join in again.

Sarah enjoyed interacting with her classmates, but disrupted the class by talking during lessons. When asked not to speak, Sarah would stop, but refused to join in the lesson and answer any questions. The school librarian experienced the same problems and informed her teacher that Sarah found it difficult to sit and read to herself.

Each week the class wrote their news prior to presenting it to the class and Sarah recounted events when verbally prompted by her teacher. She required support to sequence the narrative. Each time Sarah was asked to present her story she would repeat a favourite one about going to the city aquarium with her family. Sarah seemed to enjoy the laughter from her classmates when asked not to talk about the aquarium.

Sarah's teacher felt overwhelmed by Sarah's speech and language needs and wasn't sure where to begin. She contacted the support teacher and arranged a joint meeting with Sarah's mother. At the meeting the integration support teacher suggested that:

- a referral be made to the local disability services for speech pathology support
- the communication needs identified by her teacher be prioritised and addressed in that order
- the school purchase Boardmaker and that she would then train Sarah's teacher and mother in its use.

Sarah's communication needs were prioritised in the following order:

- behaviour management systems – class rules and scripts
- visual work schedule with rewards built in
- use of key concept signing
- visual sequence for narratives
- chat pages for specific activities.

During the meeting the behaviour management systems were designed. The main purpose of the systems was to clearly define the expected behaviour and represent it in a way that Sarah could understand. The rewards and consequences for her behaviour also needed to be represented and incorporated into the class behaviour management strategies.

Following the Boardmaker training, Sarah's teacher represented the class rules with Picture Communication Symbols (PCS) to remind Sarah of expected behaviours. These were read with the whole class each morning and emphasised

>

Box 9.5 continued

with Sarah prior to lessons in which she had been disruptive in the past. Sarah's teacher was also able to point to them during class to remind Sarah and other students of the rules with minimal interruption to the flow of lessons.

The support teacher also made behaviour scripts to serve as a permanent reminder to Sarah of expected behaviours. The scripts were colour coded 'green' for desired behaviour and 'red' for inappropriate behaviour. Sarah's teacher kept these on Sarah's desk and found them to be very effective. Midway through the year she was able to stop using them and Sarah maintained her behaviour as long as her rewards were included in her work schedule.

Following the training on Boardmaker, Sarah's mother made behaviour scripts for use at home and also made posters consisting of PCS and signing instructions for the core vocabulary used at school. A speech pathologist began working with Sarah and was able to offer in class support to Sarah's teacher to know how to use the signs and to teach the other students. Sarah's classmates enjoyed using the signs and Sarah began to sign more, improving her communication and reducing her frustration.

The speech pathologist assessed Sarah's communication skills and designed additional AAC systems. To assist in addressing Sarah's narrative skills, a system was implemented that consisted of symbols representing 'when, who, what and where' on separate boards and Sarah was taught to select symbols and sequence them to tell her news. Sarah also kept remnants from outings to prompt her to recount different events, such as a movie ticket or lolly bag from a party, and her mum and dad began taking photos of events to serve as an additional prompt.

The speech pathologist and teacher noticed that when classmates couldn't understand what Sarah was talking about, she would some-times get out her news photos and use them to show her friends what she was talking about. The photos consisted of people and items from Sarah's home, so the speech pathologist made separate photos to represent the people and items and included other symbols to allow Sarah to talk about her family and friends at home. The symbols were organised around topics, such as Sarah's birthday party, her pet dog and ballet lessons. The speech pathologist recommended that people point to the symbols when interacting with Sarah to aid her under-standing and to model how to use language. Sarah's mother made additional pages as needed and the book assisted greatly in devel-oping Sarah's vocabulary and use of language.

Alison Sweep, Speech Pathologist, NSW

Students with physical disability

Students with physical disability may not be able to use signs as a functional communication mode as their physical disability will prevent them from making the signs accurately. They may also have communication disorders that are associated with intellectual disabilities. Other students with physical disabilities have intact language abilities but may not be able to speak because of the difficulty they experience controlling their oral musculature and breathing. Students with cerebral palsy comprise the bulk of those who have physical disabilities that affect speech. In this section we will consider students with physical disabilities who have little, if any, concomitant intellectual disability.

To date there is limited research on the language development of students who have physical disability and who use AAC. Paul (1997) suggested this was because AAC specialists have focused on ensuring that students who need AAC have functional working AAC systems rather than exploring their language development. She suggested that when working with young children with physical disabilities who use AAC the principles of normal language development are useful to consider, but noted that these children experience specific challenges. For example, if their levels of cerebral palsy are so severe that they have little functional speech, they are likely to have severe motor problems that impact on all of their motor skills including walking. As already noted, this creates problems with both learning and socialisation for students in inclusive settings (Kent-Walsh & Light, 2003; Soto et al., 2001). These students may need to rely on a wheelchair for mobility or on others to move them, and require all areas of the school to be easily accessible. They often require assistance with mealtime management and activities of daily living, and take longer to complete tasks in class. Poor hand function and lack of mobility means that they require assistance with many learning tasks and that class materials must be modified. Secondary students need additional time to complete academic work and may become fatigued when trying to keep up with the school curriculum, including homework. Teachers need to adapt teaching materials and academic curriculums to accommodate the needs of the individual student. This includes presenting materials in different formats and ensuring that the demands on the student are feasible in view of the level of physical disability.

Students may also be absent from school frequently. When young, these students may have spent much time at medical centres, therapy programs, and other appointments and so have had little time for the activities that are known to be critical in early language and reading development (for example, play and activities that foster early literacy skills) (Beukelman & Mirenda, 1998; Koppenhaver et al., 1992; Koppenhaver et al., 1995; Light, 1997). Consequently, they may require additional help with literacy skills and modified reading materials. Many students with severe physical disability have poor levels of literacy, despite having no or little cognitive impairment. Teachers in inclusive settings may feel challenged when developing an accessible curriculum for these students and will benefit if they can draw on the expertise of a collaborative team that include psychologists, therapists, and parents, and involves the student with physical disability. Any AAC system must be flexible enough for a student to transition from one level of linguistic complexity to another and from one communicative context to another (Paul, 1997).

In most cases, symbol sets on AAC systems are not a language system but rather words and phrases selected by caregivers or speech-language pathologists to support communication and meet the student's immediate communication needs (Light, 1997). These symbol sets usually consist of nouns and the communication partner must use guessing, checks, and questions in order to assist the person who uses the system to complete a sentence (Balandin, 1994; Balandin & Iacono, 1993). Communication partners, including speech-language pathologists, parents, and educators, may know exactly what vocabulary the student needs to support play, socialisation and learning (Fried-Oken, 1991; Marvin, 1994; Marvin, Beukelman & Bilyeu, 1994; McGinnis & Beukelman, 1989; Morrow et al., 1993). Thus, the AAC system may not meet all of the student's communication needs. Teachers play an important role in ensuring that students who use AAC have access to the vocabulary they need to facilitate interaction and learning across all of the school and classroom contexts (Morrow et al., 1993). It is also important that this vocabulary is regularly updated to ensure that it is relevant and current and thus meets the student's communication needs.

Finally, it is imperative that the student has access to a suitable AAC system that they can use easily and without undue fatigue. Many students have AAC systems that are not available at all times during the school day, that they cannot easily use independently, and that they are unable to switch on by themselves. Students must have access to a suitable AAC system and know how to use it. Communication partners, including teachers and peers, need to understand how to interact with students using the system. Teachers must also provide the student who uses AAC with the same opportunities for learning as their peers without disability.

Technology has changed the lives of many students with physical disability accessing inclusive educational settings. Before acquiring any technology a student will require careful assessment by a team of experts that should include educational staff who have an understanding of the student's needs within the context of school and learning. Box 9.6 provides an overview of the barriers and some solutions to inclusion experienced by Annie, a young student with cerebral palsy.

Box 9.6
Annie and her early schooling

Annie attended a state primary school in a city in rural New South Wales and was in her second year of formal schooling. She was the first child with a severe disability to enrol in this school. Annie was diagnosed with cerebral palsy at birth. She has speech dyspraxia and dysarthria, difficulty with the execution of fine motor activities and uses a walking frame. Annie successfully developed a strong social identity with her peer group and, although only partial enrolment was granted for the first three terms of the year, Annie attended the school full-time in the final term. She subsequently progressed to Year 1, receiving approximately 18 hours special-aide time per week for the school year.

Annie's ability to produce natural speech has been severely affected by oral–motor problems associated with cerebral palsy, thus resulting in an expressive-receptive language discrepancy. However, in familiar or comfortable environments it is evident that Annie comprehends most conversational language and is very quick to learn when given verbal explanations accompanied by real-life demonstrations.

Annie successfully augments her communication with a multi-modal language approach: natural gestures, some signs from the Makaton Vocabulary (Walker & Cooney, 1984), animated facial expressions, vocalisations, and a very limited repertoire of spoken words. A low-tech alternative communication system had been evolving in book and board form to assist Annie achieve the communicative functions of greeting, accepting, acknowledging, asking questions, rejecting, denying, protesting, talking about people and places, and teasing.

The contents and format of the communication book have not changed significantly since Annie commenced school. Each page was single sided with nine symbols approximately 2 cm x 2.5 cm. The index included feelings, people, food, school activities, places and holiday activities. The 'people' page had photographs of all her classmates taken from a class photograph. There were many limitations in Annie's system of communication that did not allow her to engage in the typical linguistic, phonological and conversational experiences of

>

Box 9.6 continued

other children her age. It seemed essential that her program enhanced her current participation levels, increased her communicative effectiveness and provided strategies to help support and increase her language and literacy experiences. Annie has been screened for visual perception difficulties but there was no significant problem identified.

Annie approaches the computer with a great deal of enthusiasm and confidence. She exhibits a refined coordination and understanding of the functions of a mouse. She can track easily, and demonstrates good click and drag, and drag and drop functions. Annie is familiar with a range of both educational and fun software. As a consequence of Annie's improved recognition of her letters, she can now confidently access a standard keyboard, with mainly the index finger on her left hand. She has been practising using her right hand to hold down the shift key when she wants to make a capital letter. She is familiar with a range of concept keyboard overlays, designed for literacy activities with a QWERTY layout and a programmed sticky shift.

Annie's demonstrated strengths stem from her own individual personality, willingness and determination. More opportunities need to be created for her to participate *actively* with the curriculum. Tasks need to be challenging yet achievable, encouraging her to be a proactive learner rather than a passive recipient of information.

It was important that opportunities to participate more effectively in all aspects of the school experience became a priority.

The introduction of an SGD would assist in enhancing these opportunities.

Annie has had to face a number of barriers at school. These included physical barriers such as being unable to access the room without direct assistance from an aide, if no aide was present Annie was left sitting outside the classroom. Knowledge barriers included the teacher being unwilling to acknowledge or respond to the multi-modal forms of communication used and refusing to extend a wait time for a response from Annie. Attitude barriers included no expectation that Annie could participate meaningfully on any level. Skill barriers of staff are still problematic in that there is no training available for them in implementing strategies for using an AAC device in the classroom and/or developing curriculum modifications to increase participation. There is a District Integration Officer who has provided some training in the concept keyboard but knowledge and understanding beyond this piece of equipment is limited, as is funding for any more assistance.

With the modified materials, Annie's ability to ask and answer simple questions about stories and text, and participate in writing activities has been substantially improved. As an introductory program there is evidence that the effort to focus on the overlapping features of speech, graphic symbol and print and coordinate all resources has been a successful approach with Annie's emerging literacy.

Brian Matthews and Veronica Cay, Flinders University of South Australia

Students with autism spectrum disorder

The use of AAC may benefit students with autism spectrum disorder who have no functional spoken language and those who have difficulty in comprehending language or in understanding and managing their school and home routines. AAC can be used to support both the expressive communication and also the understanding of students with autism spectrum disorder (Light et al., 1998; Mirenda, 2001). Students with autism spectrum disorder may be Gestalt processors (that is, processing the whole rather than components) (Prizant, 1983) and frequently experience difficulty in taking the perspectives of others. This inability to think of the parts of a problem or situation or consider others impacts negatively on the student's ability to learn in the classroom and to socialise with peers. AAC strategies can be used to facilitate communication development and reduce challenging behaviour (Mirenda, 1997; Sigafoos, Reichle & Light-Shriner, 1994; Sigafoos & Tucker, 2000; Stephenson, 1997). Indeed, Beukelman and Mirenda (1998) stressed the benefit of commencing AAC interventions early. However, to date there is still only a small empirically based research literature that reports the use and efficacy of AAC for students with autism spectrum disorder (Mirenda, 2001; Ogletree & Hahn, 2001).

Echolalia (repeating words and phrases that have just been uttered or uttered some time previously), self-talk, literalness of meaning, and idiosyncratic use of words are all common in students with autism spectrum disorder who do develop speech. The use of AAC may be helpful in supporting the communication of students who exhibit these linguistic behaviours. Some children with autism spectrum disorder seem to have superior visual memory and visual spatial skills and demonstrate reading or spelling skills that are at odds with their overall level of functioning (for example, the ability to find particular words in the telephone book). Such skills may cause the teacher to overlook a student's receptive language difficulty, resulting in high levels of frustration for all concerned and which may result in the student exhibiting challenging behaviours. However, teachers can capitalise on the student's visual ability by introducing AAC systems (for example, schedules and scripts) that ensure that educational activities are supplemented with visual supports.

Students with autism spectrum disorder may benefit from the use of visual AAC systems (for example, photographs, words, signs, schedules boxes and calendars) that support their comprehension and allow them to make sense of their world (Wood et al., 1998). Visual systems can assist students to be independent in the contexts of school and home. The Picture Exchange Communication Systems (PECS) can be used to improve students' spontaneous communication (Bondy & Frost, 1994; Kravits et al., 2002). The PECS program is used to encourage students with autism spectrum disorder to exchange a picture for an activity or item. There are reports that the use of PECS helps students to initiate communication and make choices (Kravits et al., 2002).

The use of a variety of communicant modes including visual timetables and behaviour scripts for an adolescent with autism spectrum disorder is described in Box 9.7.

Box 9.7

The use of AAC with Stephen, an adolescent with autism spectrum disorder

Stephen is 17 years old and has attended his local high school for five years. He has autism spectrum disorder and a mild intellectual disability. Stephen enjoys school and does well in all his subjects, but he particularly enjoys English and food technics. Stephen has an interest in cars and cooking and has had a special interest in science fiction books and movies since he was about seven years old.

Throughout Stephen's time at high school, his parents have offered regular assistance to support his education. When Stephen

>

Box 9.7 continued

commenced high school he had a great deal of difficulty settling in and found transitioning between classes and teachers extremely difficult and stressful. His parents created a visual timetable for him with symbols for each subject. Although Stephen was able to read, the symbols allowed him to interpret the timetable quickly and more easily when he was stressed. Initially, Stephen's roll-call teacher also informed him of any changes to his timetable whenever possible and Stephen noted the changes in writing on his timetable. Forewarning him in this way minimised Stephen's anxiety upon arrival at class. His parents also wrote a social story for him about coping with changes to his timetable and included strategies for him to use at these times, such as breathing slowly, counting to 10 and remembering to listen to his teacher.

During his first term at high school, Stephen's parents received a call from his English teacher informing them that although Stephen had been diligent in completing his homework, he had not completed his assignment. Stephen's parents had asked him about his assignment the week before and he had assured them that he was working on it during school time. When they questioned him and looked at his assignment, he had started it, but had not completed the final question on a book review. Stephen told his parents that he hadn't liked the book and that he wanted to review one of his science fiction books. With assistance from Stephen's English teacher, his parents wrote down a guide for him on how to review a book. They also gave him some written rules for completing his assignments and made him a rewards chart that allowed him to work towards buying a new science-fiction book each month if all his homework and assignments were completed.

Later in the same term, Stephen's parents received a phone call from the school principal who asked them to attend a meeting at school to discuss Stephen's social skills. He informed them that some of Stephen's teachers had approached him and reported difficulties with Stephen's behaviour, such as looking in other students' bags, staring at students as they changed into their sports uniform and endlessly talking about science-fiction books he had read. When Stephen's principal had spoken to him about his behaviour, he appeared to understand, but then looked at him quite seriously and told him that he had bad breath. Stephen's parents decided to seek assistance from a support service for people with autism spectrum disorder who recommended developing social stories for each of the situations.

Each year Stephen's parents and teachers have made every attempt to meet his specific learning needs as new situations were encountered and new challenges arose. This year, Stephen's final year at school, is no exception. He is studying a hospitality course at his local tertiary institution that he enjoys immensely. He travels independently to the course, but becomes extremely agitated if the train is more than five minutes late. If Stephen then arrives late to his course, he becomes quite stressed, charges into his class and from just inside the doorway loudly proclaims, 'Stephen is late. Stephen is late!' He is then unable to settle and prepare for his practical lesson. His teacher has to try to calm him and prompt him to put on his chef's uniform and check the task for the day.

One of Stephen's teachers had encountered a similar problem in Stephen's third year at school and with guidance from Stephen's speech pathologist, had written a script for him about what to do if he arrived late to class. He decided to modify the script to outline what Stephen and his hospitality teacher would say to each other. By focusing on positive behaviour and providing Stephen with a set structure to the interaction, he hoped that Stephen would be better prepared to cope with the stressful

>

Box 9.7 continued

situation and therefore be able to move onto his required tasks.

He used stick-figure characters and speech bubbles, like a comic strip, to show Stephen that he had to walk up to his teacher and speak to him in a calm voice. He used blue text for Stephen's lines, rehearsed the script with him and sent a copy to the hospitality teacher. The script lines were:

Teacher: 'Hi Stephen. Good to see you.'

Stephen: 'Hi. The train was late today. Stephen is sorry.'

Teacher: 'That's okay Stephen.' Pause 'Today we're cooking ...' Pause 'Please check your schedule.'

To complement the script he also made a schedule from Picture Communication Symbols to assist Stephen in beginning the class activities. He included: 'put uniform on', 'wash hands', 'read the recipe'. Although Stephen talked to himself as he followed his script, saying he was sorry and repeating the directions on the symbols, he soon settled down and was able to participate successfully.

Alison Sweep, Speech Pathologist, NSW

Moore, McGrath and Thorpe (2000) have suggested that computer-aided learning may be of benefit to students with autism spectrum disorder. Moore, McGrath and Thorpe (2000) suggested that a computer-aided learning system could be used to teach students to use multimedia systems to learn about appropriate social interactions, including playing with others and through observations, role plays and the use of virtual reality. Group work should also be included to prevent the student from becoming isolated from the class. These authors also suggested that computer-aided learning is also helpful for improving communication skills, in teaching symbols, non-verbal skills, and in particular conversational skills, including simulated conversations. This work is in its infancy, but the authors believe that it has the potential to facilitate inclusion for students with autism spectrum disorder in the future.

Functional assessment

The goals of AAC assessment are not only to identify a system that will be functional for the student but to select one that will allow the student to meet future communication needs and challenges (Beukelman & Mirenda, 1998; Cockerill & Fuller, 2001). It is also important to remember that ongoing assessment is a part of any AAC intervention. However, the provision of a suitable communication system does not, in itself, ensure that a student will use it or communicate more effectively. Training of both the student and communication partners is important to ensure that the student gains maximum benefit from the AAC system.

AAC assessment involves a team approach. Currently, the *Participation Model* of assessment (Beukelman & Mirenda, 1998) is used by many AAC teams. In Box 9.8 the three phases of this model are summarised.

As can been seen from Box 9.8, the emphasis is on ongoing assessment. Beukelman and Mirenda (1998) state that 'assessment is not a one-time process. Assess to meet today's needs, then tomorrow's, and tomorrow's, and tomorrow's ...' (p. 149). Because many students with complex communication needs can and do use some speech or vocalisations, it is also important to assess the student's potential to use natural speech as well as their language ability (Beukelman & Mirenda, 1998). However, assessing language is often problematic. Morse (1988) suggested that if norm-referenced standardised assessment tools are used, the assessor must note any changes and adaptations made to the testing procedures. Scores from standardised tests are not valid if adaptations are made to the assessment materials or the procedures. It is important to recognise that there are many individuals who use AAC who were wrongly diagnosed as having an intellectual disability because the testing materials were unsuitable or the individuals were physically unable to perform the tasks. Misdiagnosis can have a lasting and damaging effect on a student's educational program. AAC specialists may use observation and indepth interviewing to gain understanding of the student's communication needs and abilities. Teachers have an important role to play as they bring experience of education and specific knowledge about the student and the classroom environment to the assessment team. It is important to observe how different communication partners, including peers, interact with the student. As already discussed, it is essential that communication partners know how to interact effectively with a student who uses AAC. It is important that partners do not limit the student by being overly directive or by denying the student a wide range of communication experiences (Hunt, Alwell & Goetz, 1988, 1991a; Light, 1997).

Box 9.8

Description of the 'Participation Model' of AAC assessment and integration

Phases	*Features*
Phase I: Initial assessment for today	*Aim:* To gain a picture of the child's current level of functioning in order to develop a communication system that will meet the child's immediate needs
	Current communication needs assessed
	Physical, cognitive, language and sensory skills assessed
Phase II: Detailed assessment for tomorrow	*Aim:* To develop a system that will serve the child in a variety of contexts with varied communication partners
	System needs to facilitate a variety of interactions (for example, academic participation, social closeness)
	Future interactions and participation considered
Phase III: Follow up assessment	*Aim:* To ensure that the system continues to meet the child's needs as they mature and become involved in different activities across a variety of contexts and partners
	Frequency of follow up varies depending on the needs of the individual
	Young children developing language skills need more follow up assessment; adolescents with developed language starting work need less frequent assessment

continued >

Box 9.8 continued

Levels of involvement

Full	Same classroom with same age peers, considered part of the class – activities may vary according to student's ability
Selective	Present part of the day, attends some classes and services outside the inclusive setting
None	Not included in age-appropriate general education classes/environments
Competitive	Academic expectations and evaluation the same as for age peers – work may be adjusted
Active involved	Academic expectations lower than for peers but content is similar. Individualised assessments
Independent	Able to participate in an activity with no assistance
Set up	Can participate with assistance to set up (for example, switch on computer)
Assisted	Requires assistance from another to participate

Adapted from Beukelman and Mirenda's participation model of assessment, 1998

It is also important to assess the barriers to successful communication in order to develop strategies to overcome these. Barriers, as noted above (Kent-Walsh & Light, 2003), include negative attitudes, lack of training, limited access and lack of appropriate policies to facilitate communication (Beukelman & Mirenda, 1998).

If a student is to use an AAC device (for example, letter board, communication book, SGD), the team will also need to assess the type of device and the most suitable symbol system (Mirenda & Locke, 1989). In many parts of Australia and in other countries, the family's financial resources to purchase and maintain the devices may govern the choice of device. There are students who could use a high-tech device but who are unable to afford one and rely instead on light-tech devices (for example, communication board, communication book).

AAC assessment is a complex and time-consuming process. It usually includes a motor assessment as well as assessment of vision and hearing. Any student who uses AAC will require regular follow up assessments to ensure that the system is still appropriate for the student's communicative needs, which may change as the student moves through the educational system. This is particularly important not only because needs change but also because technology, and AAC technology in particular, is a rapidly advancing field. Currently, new technology is enabling students with severe levels of disability to ultimately lead independent lives within the communities of their choice.

Technology

Few readers of this chapter would be unfamiliar with technology and most rely on technology to facilitate their study, writing, and day-to-day activities. Such technology includes computers and word processing software, use of the Internet, and electronic diaries. Increasingly, many professionals and students alike are limited in what they can achieve if their technology fails. Recent technological advances have had a positive impact on the inclusion of students in regular schools (Parette & Marr, 1997). Assistive technology, including power chairs, switches, high tech AAC devices, page turners, joy sticks and speech readers facilitate the inclusion of students with disability in educational environments and enable them to participate in class as actively involved learners.

However, successful implementation is, to a large extent, dependent upon the knowledge, skill and commitment of the classroom teacher (White, Shelley & Donna, 2003). Throughout this chapter there has been an emphasis on teachers' needs for appropriate training and support if they are to include students with disabilities in their classes. White, Shelley and Donna (2003) suggested that higher education institutions must take some responsibility in preparing student teachers to deal with technology in the classroom setting. Assistive technology can facilitate the independence of a student and at the same reduce the one-to-one teaching load of the teacher. However, teachers must have some skill in using the technology, and appropriate support if the equipment is not working. Without this knowledge or support, students may spend a great deal of time unable to participate in the class activities or to learn. Often the technology may be tied to one particular context (for example, the general classroom) and students may not be able to use it in specialised contexts (for example, the science laboratory), thus technology can never fully replace the teacher or peers in academic learning or social interactions.

Indeed, as noted above, it is important that students who rely on technology do not become isolated from their peers at school. Beukelman and Mirenda (1998) advocated that the whole class becomes conversant with any assistive technology used by one of their peers. This approach ensures that students without disability learn more about the student with a disability, which in turn can lead to improved social interaction and peer support.

Assessment of technology is an ongoing process (Iacono & Balandin, 1992; Schutz-Meuhling & Beukelman, 1990). The student's needs and abilities may change with maturation or experience and the research and development in the fields of technology means that new technology is being developed and old superseded at a rapid rate. Thus, it is vital that students have ongoing access to appropriate assessment, funding and training and that there are policies to ensure that students are able to take advantage of the assistive technology available. Similarly, teachers require ongoing training and support to ensure that they can use the technology and facilitate the student's participation in the academic and social environment of school. The assistive technology team is an invaluable resource for teachers, parents and students and an important part of the collaborative team approach (see Chapter 10).

Working collaboratively with students, families and other professionals to improve functional communication outcomes

To meet students' functional communication needs, a clear understanding of students' abilities and support requirements is essential (Kent-Walsh & Light, 2003). Determining these areas and meeting students' needs requires the collaboration of significant people in the students' lives. Individual consultation may occur with the students, parents and other family members, people who know the students well, and other professionals. It is preferable to meet and work together in a coordinated approach (Giangreco, Edelman & Broer, 2001; Pugach & Johnson, 1995). By working collaboratively, team members are able to contribute knowledge, reflect on the input of others to enhance their own input, share responsibilities, and intervention for the student can be coordinated and interwoven into a single educational plan.

Collaboration must occur at all stages, from assessment to design of communication systems and implementation and evaluation. A commitment from each member to fulfil designated responsibilities and to respect each team member's role is essential. Ongoing communication is a crucial element to the collaborative approach (Santelli et al., 1998).

Initial planning meeting

Collaboration begins when team members meet to plan for the development of the student's communication. This may be the sole purpose of the meeting or the student's communication development could be discussed as part of an overall educational planning meeting. The purpose of the initial meeting is to discuss and document:

- the student's current communication skills and priority areas to address
- proposed strategies to support the student's communication development
- areas requiring further assessment
- the responsibilities of team members and proposed time frames for completion of tasks
- required resources and personnel
- procedures and time frames for reviewing the plan.

Each team member should receive a copy of the communication plan. The role of each team member is dependent upon their knowledge of the student, past experiences, training, time available and access to resources. Designated responsibilities should be negotiated at the initial meeting and renegotiated as required.

Role of parents in a collaborative team

Some parents coordinate the collaborative team, while others prefer to contribute to the team without leading it. Parents are able to support their child's communication development by:

- sharing knowledge of their child's current communication skills, any AAC systems that may be in place and strategies that have worked in the past
- identifying skills to be taught and long-term considerations for their child's communication, such as future employment options
- informing the team of factors that may need to be considered, such as changes in the home environment
- contributing to the design, creation and implementation of AAC systems and communication programs
- evaluating the effectiveness of programs and suggesting required changes
- supporting the acquisition of resources to support communication programs across environments.

Role of teachers in a collaborative team

Teachers usually coordinate the collaborative team and initiate the process by seeking support. Following an initial planning meeting, teachers play an ongoing role in the collaborative team by:

- completing identified responsibilities in the communication plan
- contributing to key tasks that other members may be fulfilling, such as attending interviews for assessment purposes or training sessions
- seeking ongoing information and support as required
- committing to the consistent implementation of AAC
- educating and supporting others to understand the need for AAC and how to use it
- supporting the acquisition of resources
- implementing recommendations from other professionals, such as modification of own communication style with the student.

Role of speech pathologists in a collaborative team

The speech pathologist's primary role is to offer expert guidance in the area of communication. Speech pathologists generally work as consultants within inclusive settings and the amount of support provided depends upon the complexity of students' communication needs and the resources available. Emphasis is generally placed on the development of knowledge, skills and confidence for teachers, parents and support people to be able to provide daily, ongoing support to the students within natural contexts. Speech pathologists, therefore, work side by side with teachers, implementing AAC systems and teaching strategies within the existing class activities. Current good practice is that speech pathologists working with students who have significant disability do not withdraw the students from the classroom for individual intervention. To promote the development of functional communication skills, it is essential that support be provided during usual class activities. In addition to consultations and direct guidance, speech pathologists are able to provide the following:

- Functional assessment of students' receptive and expressive communication skills. Assessment involves observation of students across contexts and with different communication partners, interviews with teachers, parents and family and other significant people and formal assessment as required.
- Reports outlining students' skills and specific recommendations on functional outcomes and implementation strategies. Functional outcomes are developed by considering a student's current abilities/strengths and the skills required to participate in priority activities that occur regularly at school, home and in the community.
- Recommendations for AAC systems.
- Demonstrations of how to use AAC and support to promote successful implementation of students' AAC.
- Training for all people involved in supporting the students' communication.
- Access to resources, including AAC systems.
- A link between home and school to promote consistency of systems and teaching strategies.

Speech pathology consultations

As mentioned previously, a key function of the collaborative team is to identify the priority areas for students' communication development. The priority areas cover receptive and/or expressive communication and are generally identified because of their significance in promoting access to the curriculum, allowing students to reach their full potential or because of their role in addressing challenging or socially inappropriate behaviours. The selected areas and proposed AAC systems are always based on the individual needs of students and although the specific layouts of systems or symbols used may differ between students, common strategies and systems are frequently employed to meet the needs of students with disabilities.

Following an initial planning meeting or as a starting point, teachers and speech pathologists should discuss the following topics and select areas to be addressed.

Environmental changes

A key purpose to modifying the students' environment is the creation of a structured learning environment that facilitates the development of communication and, if required, minimises the occurrence of challenging or inappropriate behaviours. These areas underpin the successful implementation of AAC.

Speech pathologists, for example, are able to offer suggestions to teachers on interaction and communication style. Changing the way in which people interact with the students can make significant improvements in students' comprehension. This may involve changes such as simplifying language, increasing pausing and use of natural gesture, or key concept signing for those students for whom it is important.

The physical layout of the room can also be modified. Some students may need to be seated closer to the teacher to improve attention or be moved away from distractions, such as a turning fan. Students may also need to have clearly defined areas of the classroom for different lessons or labels with corresponding symbols for classroom areas and items. Physical changes to the room may also be required, such as positioning a display board with visual systems near a student's desk.

To promote functional communication, AAC is overlayed onto an existing structure of activities. It is therefore essential that consideration be given to selection of activities, students' participation within activities and the expected outcomes for individual students. Sometimes natural indicators to the beginning and end of activities also need to be implemented, such as getting a student to put craft materials away or ringing a bell to indicate the end of free play.

Schools are environments rich in opportunities to develop communication. For students with disabilities, however, skills are unlikely to develop without specific intervention. Speech pathologists are able to assist teachers to identify opportunities for students to expand receptive and expressive communication skills. Sometimes these will need to be created, such as having an item out of reach to prompt a request or asking another teacher to pay an impromptu visit, so that a student can recount an event that they have rehearsed in class.

Ongoing support for students' communication development requires consistent input from all people who regularly interact with them. It is important that training is provided and that AAC systems are always accessible and explained to new people.

Common AAC systems

Structures and routines exist within classrooms and schools that can be augmented with communication systems to promote the learning of students with disabilities. Other common AAC systems that are initially implemented are generally components of a behaviour management plan and/or target the development of social skills.

One of the first systems usually introduced is a visual timetable. This may be for a whole class or an individual student and may represent part of a day, a whole day or a whole week. Timetables help students to know their routine, what they are expected to do, to transition between activities and can help them to attend. Changes in routine should be represented on timetables for those students who have difficulty coping with it.

An ability to make requests is a fundamental expressive communication skill. It is imperative that AAC systems are implemented to promote this skill. For younger students or students with significant disabilities, requesting usually involves the use of single symbols to ask for motivating items, such as leisure or food items. Other students may require symbols to serve as a prompt to make appropriate requests, such as a reminder to ask, 'Can you help me please?' rather than becoming upset.

A crucial system to support appropriate behaviour for students with disabilities is the visual representation of class and/or school rules and the accompanying rewards and consequences. This ensures that they have an understanding of what is expected of all students and, because it is represented visually, it serves as a permanent reminder and emphasis can be placed on appropriate behaviour.

In addition to visual class/school rules, behaviour scripts may also be required. Behaviour scripts can be used to highlight a single desired behaviour and the resulting reward through the use of symbols and an arrow between the two. The student is expected to interpret the script as 'If you do this, then this is what will happen/you'll receive.' For example, 'If you read quietly, you can use the computer.' On the reverse side of the positive script is the related negative script 'If you talk, you won't be able to use the computer'.

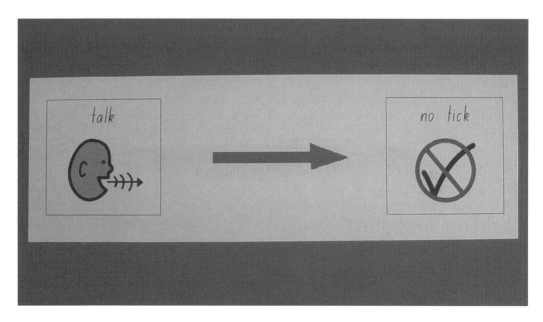

Some students may benefit from the use of social stories to teach them new skills or remind them of expected behaviour. Social stories can be utilised for those students who are able to understand a simple narrative. They outline the behaviour expected from a student in a particular situation, such as shaking the hands of opponents when losing a game, and congratulating them. Negative behaviours are not included in the stories. The desired behaviour is the sole focus and the stories largely consist of positive statements about what will happen. Social stories can be augmented with photos or picture symbols. Students read through them to help them understand what is expected, remember the expected behaviour and use it in the actual situation.

In-servicing and support for teachers

Specific areas for training and support to assist teachers in meeting students' communication needs should be identified as early as possible. Common areas are the design and use of low-tech AAC systems, use of technology, such as communication software programs or voice output devices and ways to assess communication or identify the communicative function of inappropriate behaviours. Other people may also be able to offer assistance in these areas – parents, psychologists and support teachers.

By considering these areas, teachers are able to meet a number of communicative needs for students and provide a firm basis for the implementation of further AAC systems and teaching strategies as required. Additional needs are generally identified from assessment of individual students or as students encounter new situations.

Summary

This chapter focused on communication and students with complex communication needs in inclusive settings. It included an overview of AAC and a summary of the research that has explored inclusion of students with complex communication needs.

The importance of appropriate assessments, the need for ongoing training and for academic and environmental adaptations were emphasised. Finally, the importance of a collaborative team approach and the role of the speech pathologist in supporting the student and the classroom teacher were discussed.

Discussion questions

1   Luke is a 10-year-old boy who has a mild intellectual disability and severe physical disability and he uses a speech generation device to augment his speech. His teacher believes the device sounds too robotic and is disruptive in class. The teacher frequently asks Luke to turn his device off and only use his speech. Luke tells you how frustrated he is by this and asks you to help him. What would you do?

2   What are the main reasons for using AAC with students who have poor or limited speech and/or language?

3   A high school with 850 students has four students who use AAC. Two students with cerebral palsy utilise speech generation devices and the other two students with Asperger syndrome utilise some light-tech systems. Another two students, a 12-year-old boy with autism spectrum

disorder and a 14-year-old girl with Down syndrome have recently commenced at the school and require AAC. What can be done at a whole school level to support the use of AAC at the school?

4 How can teachers of students with additional needs modify their own communication to promote students' understanding and expressive communication ability?

5 List some possible barriers to effective collaboration between students, teachers, parents and therapists.

6 AAC can be used to prevent inappropriate behaviours and as a tool to teach new skills. If a student presented with a number of inappropriate behaviours, how would you prioritise the behaviours to be addressed?

Individual activities

1 List resources required to make and utilise AAC systems.

2 Most people use visual tools, such as a calendar, or symbols, such as business logos, as part of everyday life. The tools often aid memory, comprehension and may also allow quicker processing of information or completion of actions. Make a list of common visual tools and types of symbols.

3 Indicate whether the following statements are true or false and give reasons for your answers:
   a Functional communication implies that the student is able to communicate in a variety of contexts in the most efficient way possible.
   b Supporting a student to use sign language prevents the development of speech.
   c Collaboration is a key feature in the successful inclusion of students who use AAC.
   d Speech generation devices should only be used with non-verbal students.
   e A line drawing symbol is more difficult to associate with the real item than a photo symbol.
   f A functional communication assessment should involve observations of the student and interviews with people who regularly interact with the student.
   g Early introduction of AAC reduces the likelihood of students using disruptive and/or destructive behaviours to communicate.
   h Determination of a student's AAC needs requires a one off assessment.
   i Letter boards, chat books and schedules are all types of light-technology AAC systems.
   j Students with autism spectrum disorder may become anxious if unsure of upcoming activities or if activities are changed suddenly.

4 Read the case study in Box 9.5 and identify the key factors in promoting the successful development of Sarah's communication.

Group activities

1 People communicate for a variety of purposes, such as to give information or to request assistance and also express themselves in a variety of ways. Create a list of some of the reasons *why* people communicate and *how* people communicate.

2 Read the case study in Box 9.7:

    a What factors would need to be considered when designing a visual communication system for Stephen?

    b Which aspects of Stephen's behaviour and communication are associated with autism spectrum disorder?

References

Arthur, M., Bochner, S. & Butterfield, N. (1999). Enhancing peer interactions within the context of play. *International Journal of Disability, Development, and Education, 46*, 367–82.

ASHA. (1991). Report: Augmentative and alternative communication. *ASHA, 33* (Suppl. 5), 9–12.

Baker, B. (1982). Minspeak: A semantic compaction system that makes self-expression easier for communicatively disabled individuals. *Byte, 7*, 186–202.

Balandin, S. (1994). *Symbol Board Vocabularies*. Maastricht, The Netherlands: IRV.

Balandin, S. & Iacono, T. (1993). Symbol Vocabularies: A study of vocabulary found on communication boards used by adults with cerebral palsy. In The Crippled Children's Association of SA Inc. (Ed.), *Australian Conference on Technology for People with Disabilities* (pp. 85–7). Adelaide, SA: The Crippled Children's Association of SA Inc.

Balandin, S. & Iacono, T. (1998). AAC and Australian speech pathologists: A report on a national survey. *Augmentative and Alternative Communication, 14*, 239–49.

Bax, M., Cockerill, H. & Carroll-Few, L. (2001). Who needs augmentative and alternative communication and when? In L. Carroll-Few & H. Cockerill (Eds), *Communication Without Speech: Practical Communication for Children* (pp. 65–72). Cambridge: Mac Keith Press.

Beck, A., Fritz, H., Keller, A. & Dennis, M. (2000). Attitudes of school-aged children toward their peers who use augmentative and alternative communication. *Augmentative and Alternative Communication, 16*, 13–26.

Beck, A. R. & Dennis, M. (1996). Attitudes of children toward a similar-aged child who uses augmentative communication. *Augmentative and Alternative Communication, 12*(2), 78–87.

Beukelman, D. & Mirenda, P. (1998). *Augmentative and Alternative Communication: Management of Severe Communication Disorders in Children and Adults* (2nd edn). Baltimore: Paul H. Brooks.

Bird, J., Bishop, D. & Freeman, N. (1995). Phonological awareness and literacy development in children with expressive phonological impairments. *Journal of Speech and Hearing Research, 38*, 446–62.

Björck-Åkesson, E., Grandlund, M. & Olsson, C. (1996). Collaborative problem solving in communication intervention. In S. v. Tetzchner & M. H. Jensen (Eds), *Augmentative and Alternative Communication – European Perspectives* (pp. 324–41). London: Whurr Publishers Ltd.

Blackstone, S. & Cassatt, E. L. (1983). Interaction skills in children who use communication aids. In A. Kraat (Ed.), *Communication Interactions Between Aided and Natural Speakers: An IPCAS report*. Toronto: Canadian Rehabilitation Council for the Disabled.

Bliss, C. K. (1965). *Semantography (Blissymbolics)* (2nd edn). Sydney: Semantography (Blissymbolics) Publications.

Blockberger, S., Armstrong, R., O'Connor, A. & Freeman, R. (1993). Children's attitudes toward a nonspeaking child using various augmentative and alternative communication techniques. *Augmentative and Alternative Communication, 9,* 243–50.

Bondy, A. & Frost, L. (1994). The Picture Exchange Communication System. *Topics in Language Disorders, 19,* 373–90.

Butterfield, N. & Arthur, M. (1995). Shifting the focus: Emerging priorities in communication programming for students with a severe intellectual disability. *Education and Training in Mental Retardation and Developmental Disabilities* (March), 41–50.

Butterfield, N., Arthur, M., Linfoot, K. & Phillips, S. (1992). *Creating Communicative Contexts: An Instruction Manual for Teachers of Students With Severe Intellectual Disability*: NSW Department of School Education.

Butterfield, N., Arthur, M. & Sigafoos, J. (1995). *Partners in Everyday Communicative Exchanges.* Sydney: McLennan & Petty.

Calculator, S. N. (1999). AAC outcomes for children and youths with severe disabilities: When seeing is believing. *Augmentative and Alternative Communication, 15*(1), 4–12.

Carr, D. & Felce, D. (2000). Application of stimulus equivalence to language intervention for individuals with severe linguistic disabilities. *Journal of Intellectual and Developmental Disability, 25,* 181–205.

Carter, M. (2003a). Communicative spontaneity of children with high support needs who use augmentative and alternative communication systems I: Classroom spontaneity, mode, function. *Augmentative and Alternative Communication, 19*(3).

Carter, M. (2003b). Communicative spontaneity of children with high support needs who use augmentative and alternative communication systems II: Antecedents and effectiveness of communication. *Augmentative and Alternative Communication, 19*(3), 155–69.

Carter, M., Hotchkiss, G. & Cassar, M. (1996). Spontaneity of augmentative and alternative communication in persons with intellectual disabilities: A critical review. *Augmentative and Alternative Communication, 12,* 97–109.

Carter, M. & Maxwell, K. (1998). Promoting interaction with children using augmentative and alternative communication through peer-mediated intervention. *International Journal of Disability, Development and Education, 45,* 75–96.

Chan, J. & Iacono, T. (2001). Gesture and word production in children with Down syndrome. *Augmentative and Alternative Communication, 17,* 73–87.

Cockerill, H. & Fuller, P. (2001). Assessing children for augmentative and alternative communication. In L. Carroll-Few & H. Cockerill (Eds), *Communication Without Speech: Practical Communication for Children* (pp. 73–87). Cambridge: Mac Keith Press.

Cumley, G. D. & Beukelman, D. R. (1992). Roles and responsibilities of facilitators in augmentative and alternative communication. *Seminars in Speech and Language, 13*(2), 112–19.

Cutts, S. & Sigafoos, J. (2001). Social competence and peer interactions of students with intellectual disability in inclusive high school. *Journal of Intellectual and Developmental Disability, 26*(127–41).

Dormans, J. P. & Pellegrino, L. (1998). *Caring for Children With Cerebral Palsy: A Team Approach.* Baltimore: Paul H. Brookes.

Duchan, J. (1993). Clinician-child interaction: Its nature and potential. *Seminars in Speech and Language, 14*(4), 325–33.

Fisher, D., Pumpian, I. & Sax, C. (1998). High school students' attitudes about and recommendation for their peers with significant disabilities. *JASH, 23*(3), 272–82.

Frame, A., Cleary, G., Trentepohl, D., Gallagher, V., Iacono, T. & Cupples, L. (August, 2000). *Literacy Links in Children With Cerebral Palsy.* Paper presented at the Biennial International Society for Augmentative and Alternative Communication Conference, Washington, DC.

Fried-Oken, M. (1991). Frequent single words in common: Vocabulary selected by caregivers of 3 to 6 year old, nonspeaking children with cerebral palsy and language samples from 30 matched speaking children.

Friend, M. & Cook, L. (1992). *Interactions: Collaboration Skills for School Professionals.* White Plains, NY: Longman.

Giangreco, M. F. (1996). *Vermont Independent Services Team Approach: A Guide to Coordinating Educational Support Services.* Baltimore: Paul H. Brookes Publishing Co.

Giangreco, M. F. (2000). Related services research for students with low-incidence: Implications for speech-language pathologists in inclusive classrooms. *Language, Speech and Hearing Services in Schools, 31*(3), 230–40.

Giangreco, M. F., Denis, R. S., Cloninger, C., Edelman, S. W. & Schattman, R. (1993). 'I've counted Jon': Transformational experiences of teachers educating students with disabilities. *Exceptional Children, 59*(4), 359–73.

Giangreco, M. F., Edelman, S. W. & Broer, S. M. (2001). Respect, appreciation, and acknowledgment of paraprofessionals who support students with disabilities. *Exceptional Children, 67*(4), 485–97.

Goossens, C., Crain, S. S. & Elder, P. S. (1992). *Engineering the Preschool Environment for Interactive, Symbolic Communication.* Birmingham, AL: Southeast Augmentative Communication Conference Publications.

Granlund, M. & Olsson, C. (1999). Efficacy of communication intervention for presymbolic communicators. *Augmentative and Alternative Communication, 15,* 25–37.

Grove, N. & Walker, M. (1990). The Makaton vocabulary: Using manual signs and graphic symbols to develop interpersonal communication. *Augmentative and Alternative Communication, 6,* 15–28.

Harasty, J. & Reed, V. A. (1994). The Prevalence of Speech and Language Impairment in Two Sydney Metropolitan Schools. *Australian Journal of Human Communication Disorders, 22*(1), 1–23.

Hunt, P., Alwell, M. & Goetz, L. (1988). Acquisition of conversation skills and the reduction of inappropriate social behaviors. *Journal of the Association for Persons with Severe Handicaps, 13*(1), 20–7.

Hunt, P., Alwell, M. & Goetz, L. (1991). Interacting with peers through conversation turntaking with a communication book adaptation. *Augmentative and Alternative Communication, 7*(2), 117–26.

Iacono, T. & Balandin, S. (1992). AAC for writing and conversational participation in an academic setting. *Augmentative and Alternative Communication, 8*(2), 140.

Iacono, T., Mirenda, P. & Beukelman, D. (1993). Comparison of unimodal and multimodal AAC techniques for children with intellectual disabilities. *Augmentative and Alternative Communication, 9*(2), 83–94.

Iacono, T., Waring, R. & Chan, J. (1996). Sampling communicative behaviours in children with intellectual disability in structured and unstructured situations. *European Journal of Disorders of Communication, 31*(12), 417–31.

Iacono, T. A. & Duncum, J. E. (1995). Comparison of sign alone and in combination with an electronic communication device in early language intervention: Case study. *Augmentative and Alternative Communication, 11*(4), 249–59.

Iacono, T. A. & Parsons, C. L. (1987). Stepping beyond the teaching manuals into signing in the 'real world'. *Australian Journal of Speech and Hearing Disorders, 15*(2), 101–16.

Kent-Walsh, J. & Light, J. C. (2003). General education teachers' experiences with inclusion of students who use augmentative and alternative communication. *Augmentative and Alternative Communication, 19*, 104–24.

Koppenhaver, D., Coleman, P., Kalman, P. & Yoder, D. (1992). The implications of emergent literacy research for children with developmental disabilities. *American Journal of Speech-Language Pathology, 1*, 38–44.

Koppenhaver, D., Pierce, P., Steelman, J. & Yoder, D. (1995). Contexts of early literacy intervention for children with developmental disabilities. In M. Fey, J. Windsor & S. Warren (Eds), *Language Intervention: Preschool Through Elementary Years* (pp. 241–74). Baltimore: Paul H. Brookes.

Kravits, T. R., Kamps, D. M., Kemmerer, K. & Potucek, J. (2002). Brief Report: Increasing communication skills for an elementary-aged student with autism using the picture exchange communication system. *Journal of Autism and Developmental Disorders, 32*(3), 225–30.

Light, J. (1988). Interaction involving individuals using augmentative and alternative communication systems: State of the art. *Augmentative and Alternative Communication, 4*, 66–82.

Light, J. (1997). 'Let's go star fishing': Reflections on the contexts of language learning for children who use aided AAC. *Augmentative and Alternative Communication, 13*(3), 158–71.

Light, J., Roberts, B., Dimarco, R. & Greiner, N. (1998). Augmentative and alternative communication to support receptive and expressive communication for people with autism. *Journal of Communication Disorders, 31*, 153–80.

Light, J. C. & Binger, C. (1998). *Building communicative competence with individuals who use augmentative and alternative communication.* Baltimore: Paul H. Brookes.

Marvin, C. A. (1994). Cartalk! Conversational topics of preschool children en route home from preschool. *Language, Speech, and Hearing Services in Schools, 25*, 146–55.

Marvin, C. A., Beukelman, D. R. & Bilyeu, D. (1994). Vocabulary-use patterns in preschool children: Effects of context and time sampling. *Augmentative and Alternative Communication, 10*(4), 224–36.

McConachie, H. & Pennington, L. (1997). In-service training for schools on augmentative and alternative communication. *European Journal of Disorders of Communication, 32*(3), 277–88.

McGinnis, J. S. & Beukelman, D. R. (1989). Vocabulary requirements for writing activities for the academically mainstreamed student with disabilities. *Augmentative and Alternative Communication, 5*(3), 183–91.

Mirenda, P. (1997). Supporting individuals with challenging behavior through functional communication training and AAC: Research review. *Augmentative and Alternative Communication, 13*, 207–25.

Mirenda, P. (2001). Autism, augmentative communication and assistive technology: What do we really know? *Focus on Autism and Other Developmental Disabilities, 16*, 141–59.

Mirenda, P. & Locke, P. A. (1989). A comparison of symbol transparency in nonspeaking persons with intellectual disabilities. *Journal of Speech and Hearing Disorders, 54*, 131–40.

Mirenda, P. & Schuler, A. L. (1988). Augmenting communication for people with autism: Issues and strategies. *Topics in Language Disorders, 9*(1), 24–42.

Moore, D., McGrath, P. & Thorpe, J. (2000). Computer-aided learning for people with autism: A framework for research and development. *Innovations in Education and Training International, 218*–28.

Morais, J. (1991). Phonemic awareness, language and literacy. In R. M. Joshi & C. K. Leong (Eds), *Reading Disabilities: Diagnosis and Component Processes* (pp. 175–84). Dodrecht, The Netherlands: Kluwer Academic Publishers.

Morrow, D. R., Mirenda, P., Beukelman, D. R. & Yorkston, K. M. (1993). Vocabulary selection for augmentative communication systems: A comparison of three techniques. *American Journal of Speech and Language Pathology, 2*(2), 19–30.

Morse, J. L. (1988). Assessment procedures for people with mental retardation: The dilemma and suggested adaptive procedures. In S. N. Calculator & J. L. Bedrosian (Eds), *Communication Assessment and Intervention for Adults With Mental Retardation* (pp. 109–38). London: Taylor and Francis.

Musselwhite, C. R. & St.Louis, K. W. (1988). *Communication Programming for Persons With Severe Handicaps: Vocal and Augmentative Strategies* (2nd edn). Boston: College-Hill Press.

National Joint Committee for the Communication Needs for Persons with Severe Disabilities. (2002). Supporting documentation for the position statement of access to communication and supports. *Communication Disorders Quarterly, 23*, 145–53.

O'Connor, R., Notari-Syverson, A. & Vadasy, P. (1996). Ladders to literacy: The effects of teacher-led phonological activities for kindergarten children with and without disabilities. *Exceptional Children, 63*, 117–30.

Ogletree, B. T. & Hahn, W. E. (2001). Augmentative and alternative communication for persons with autism: History, issues and unanswered questions. *Focus on Autism and Other Developmental Disabilities, 16*, 138–42.

Parette, H. P. J. & Marr, D. D. (1997). Assisting children and families who use Augmentative and Alternative Communication (AAC) devices: Best practices for school psychologists. *Psychology in the Schools, 34*(4), 337–46.

Paul, R. (1997). Facilitating transitions in language development for children using AAC. *Augmentative and Alternative Communication, 13*, 141–8.

Prior, M., Sanson, A., Smart, D. & Oberklaid, F. (1995). Reading disability in an Australian community sample. *Australian Journal of Psychology, 47*, 32–7.

Prizant, B. (1983). Language and communicative behavior in autism: Toward an understanding of the 'whole' of it. *Journal of Speech and Hearing Disorders, 46*, 241–9.

Pugach, M. C. & Johnson, L. J. (1995). *Collaborative Practitioners, Collaborative Schools*. Denver: Love Publishing Company.

Reichle, J., Williams, W. & Ryan, S. (1981). Selecting signs for the formulation of an augmentative communicative modality. *Journal of the Association for the Severely Handicapped, 6*, 48–56.

Romski, M. A. & Sevcik, R. A. (1996). *Breaking the Speech Barrier: Language Development Through Augmented Means*. Baltimore: Paul H. Brookes.

Romski, M. A., Sevcik R. & Adamson, R. (1997). Framework for studying how children with developmental disabilities develop language through augmented means. *Augmentative and Alternative Communication*, 13, 172–8.

Rowland, C. & Schweigert, P. (2002). *School Inventory of Problem Solving Skills for Children With Multiple Disabilities*: Design to Learn.

Santelli, B., Singer, G. H., Divenere, N., Ginsberg, C. & Powers, L. E. (1998). Participatory action research: Reflections on critical incidents in a PAR project. *JASH*, 23, 211–22.

Schnorr, R. F. (1990). 'Peter? He comes and goes …': First graders' perspectives on a part-time mainstream student. *The Journal of the Association for Persons with Severe Handicaps*, 15(4), 231–40.

Schutz-Meuhling, L. & Beukelman, D. (1990). An augmentative and alternative writing system for a college student with fibrositis: A case study. *Augmentative and Alternative Communication*, 6, 250–5.

Sevcik, R. A., Romski, M. A. & Adamson, L. B. (1999). Measuring AAC interventions for individuals with severe developmental disabilities. *Augmentative and Alternative Communication*, 15, 38–45.

Siegel-Causey, E. & Guess, D. (1989). *Enhancing nonsymbolic communication interactions among learners with severe disabilities*. Baltimore: Paul H. Brookes Publishing Co.

Sigafoos, J. & Iacono, T. (1993). Selecting augmentative communication devices for persons with severe disabilities: Some factors for educational teams to consider. *Australia and New Zealand Journal of Developmental Disabilities*, 16(3), 133–46.

Sigafoos, J., Reichle, J. & Light-Shriner, C. (1994). Distinguishing between socially and nonsocially motivated challenging behavior: Implications for the selection of intervention strategies. In M. F. Hayden & B. H. Abery (Eds), *Challenges for a Service System in Transition* (pp. 147–69). Baltimore: Paul H. Brookes Publishing Co.

Sigafoos, J., Roberts, D., Kerr, M., Couzens, D. & Baglioni, A. (1994). Opportunities for communication in classrooms serving children with developmental disabilities. *Journal of Autism and Developmental Disabilities*, 24, 259–79.

Sigafoos, J. & Tucker, M. (2000). Brief assessment and treatment of multiple challenging behaviors. *Behavioral Intervention*, 15, 53–70.

Smith, M. K. & Kenneth, S. E. (2000). 'I believe in inclusion, but …': regular education early childhood teachers' perceptions of successful inclusion. *Journal of Research in Childhood Education*, 14(2), 161–79.

Soto, G., Muller, E., Hunt, P. & Goetz, L. (2001). Critical issues in the inclusion of students who use augmentative and alternative communication: An educational team perspective. *Augmentative and Alternative Communication*, 17(2), 62–72.

Spragale, D. & Micucci, D. (1990). Signs of the week: A functional approach to manual sign training. *Augmentative and Alternative Communication*, 6(1), 29–37.

Stackhouse, J. & Wells, B. (1998). *Children's Speech and Literacy Difficulties: A Psycholinguistic Framework*. London: Whurr.

Stainton, T. & Besser, H. (1998). The positive impact of children with an intellectual disability on the family. *Journal of Intellectual and Developmental Disability*, 23(1), 57–70.

Stephenson, J. (1997). Dealing with the challenging behaviour of students with severe intellectual disability. *Special Education Perspectives, 6*, 71–80.

Vicker, B. (1996). *Using Tangible Symbols for Communication Purposes: An Optional Step in Building the Two-way Communication Process*. Bloomington: Indiana University, Indiana Resource Center for Autism.

von Tetzchner, S. (1999). Introduction to language development. In F. T. Loncke, J. Clibbens, H. H. Arvidson. & L. L. Lloyd (Eds), *Augmentative and Alternative Communication: New Directions in Research and Practice* (pp. 3–7). London: Whurr Publishers Ltd.

von Tetzchner, S. & Martinsen, H. (2000). *Introduction to Augmentative and Alternative Communication* (2nd edn). London: Whurr Publishers.

Walker, M. (1976). *Language Programmes for Use With the Revised Makaton Vocabulary*. Surrey: M. Walker.

Walker, M. & Cooney, A. (1984). *Line Drawings to Use With the Revised Makaton Vocabulary (Australian Version)*. Newcastle: Makaton Vocabulary Development Project.

Warrick, A. & Kaul, S. (1997). *Their Manner of Speaking: Augmentative Communication for Children and Young Adults With Severe Speech Disorders*. Calcutta: Indian Institute of Cerebral Palsy.

Watkins, R. (1996). Natural literacy: Theory and practice for preschool intervention programs. *Topics in Early Childhood Special Education, 16*, 191–212.

Wetherby, A. M., Warren, S. F. & Reichle, J. (Eds). (1998). *Transitions in Prelinguistic Communication* (Vol. 7). Baltimore: Paul H. Brookes Publishing Co.

White, E. A., Shelley, B. W. & Donna, C. (2003). Accessible education through assistive technology. *The Journal (Technological Horizons In Education), 30*(7), 24–30.

Whiting, P. (1996). Reading comprehension and dyslexia. *Australian Communication Quarterly* (Autumn), 28–32.

Willard-Holt, C. (1998). Academic and personality characteristics of gifted students with Cerebral Palsy: A multiple case study. *Exceptional Children, 65*(1), 37–50.

Windsor, J. & Fristoe, M. (1989). Key word signing: Listeners' classification of signed and spoken narratives. *Journal of Speech and Hearing Disorders, 54*, 374–82.

Wood, L. A., Lasker, J., Siegel-Causey, E., Beukelman, D. & Ball, L. (1998). Input framework for augmentative and alternative communication. *Augmentative and Alternative Communication, 14*(4), 261–76.

PART D

INSTIGATING CHANGE

Chapter 10

The role of teachers in successful inclusion

Susan Spedding

This chapter aims to:

- explore the crucial role of classroom teachers in addressing the challenges of inclusive early childhood, primary and secondary classrooms (identified in earlier chapters) and the need for teacher reflection
- identify the characteristics of effective schools and explore the need to embrace change if the needs of all students are to be met

- explore the collaborative model as a means of supporting students, families and teachers in inclusive classrooms and schools, ensuring that the most effective instructional programs to support students in achieving their maximum potential are designed and implemented

- explore the collaborative model as a means of facilitating change in classrooms and schools

- define and identify the essential principles of collaborative consultation and teamwork

- reflect on how best to establish effective partnerships between families and teachers, and between teachers and other school personnel and professionals, as a means of promoting successful inclusion

- examine action research as a powerful means of problem-solving and promoting staff development, and of bringing about change.

Introduction

The inclusion of students with very diverse needs into regular schools and classrooms has raised a number of questions about the roles and responsibilities of school personnel in implementing inclusive models of education, and the means by which they can best fulfil their roles. A substantial body of literature indicates that effective inclusion requires changes to conceptualisations of the role of professionals, changes to classroom structure, programming and instructional approaches, and the ongoing need for collaboration and teamwork. Few teachers are unaware of the challenges they face in creating positive and effective schools able to meet the needs of very diverse student populations in very diverse contexts. If they are to meet these challenges and support their students effectively, they will need to work collaboratively with students and their families, with other educators and with other professionals.

While the term inclusion is typically used to refer to the inclusion of students with disabilities in regular schools, it has relevance across a much broader population of students. Children with additional educational needs include not only those with a disability, but also those with learning difficulties and behaviour disorders, those from culturally and linguistically different backgrounds, those with chronic medical conditions, and all those who are at risk in the school environment, for whatever reason. Factors such as poverty; increases in the incidence of adolescent unmarried mothers, non-biological parents as primary caregivers (grandparents, foster carers, adoptive parents), sole parents, parents with disabilities, gay and lesbian parents, older parents, blended families, and cultural minority backgrounds; two-income families; and utilisation of long day care and respite care, may influence a child's educational needs. (The term 'families' will be used throughout this chapter to refer not only to biological parents but also to all those responsible for the development and well-being of the child, in recognition of the diversity described here). Accordingly, changes such as those referred to above may be essential if educational opportunities for *all* students are to be maximised.

Students with special educational needs share with their peers common educational goals, and their social and academic behaviours lie within a continuum shared by all. A separate educational setting or curriculum is not what is required. Rather, a common, shared curriculum is called for, one which recognises the shared goals and characteristics of all students, but within which individual needs are recognised and catered for, and success is fostered for all.

In order to accept and adjust to the new responsibilities, assume new roles, develop new competencies, and work as team members committed to providing every student with the opportunity to achieve to their potential, teachers must become aware of the philosophy and process of inclusion (see Chapters 1 and 2), and have a positive attitude to the inclusion of students with special educational needs. This will require ongoing reflection and change. For some teachers it may initially be difficult and time-consuming to explore and implement change, and they may feel themselves to be challenged both professionally and personally. However, such challenges present opportunities for teachers and schools to foster learning environments that welcome diversity and enable teachers to feel that they can make significant contributions to the school and community; in essence, that they can make a difference.

Much of the current innovation in classroom practice and curriculum has arisen as a result of the concern among teachers to find ways to manage the extremely complex and challenging task of ensuring optimal learning for every child within a large group of different, individualistic and differentiated learners (Whitaker, 1993). Whether identified as having special educational needs or not, the reality is that every child is an individual, and effective teaching involves recognising individual strengths and needs and catering for these within the classroom.

While the onus of supporting students with special educational needs has frequently fallen on the individual teacher, the inclusion of students with special educational needs is not confined to individual classrooms or teachers. All students in a school are members not only of classrooms, but also of the school as a whole. Similarly, all teachers and administrators are members of the school and have a responsibility for all students. It is, therefore, the responsibility of the school as a whole to support all members, students, teachers and families alike. Becoming truly inclusive may necessitate a great deal of reflection and substantial change by systems, schools and individuals.

Effective inclusive schools

An effective school is one that provides a comprehensive curriculum to all students, ensuring both quality and equity. One of the most damaging aspects of traditional educational concepts of the learning process has been the belief that if an individual student is failing in the schooling system, it is because of a dysfunction of the individual learner. As Whitaker (1993) has pointed out, 'it is a tragedy that given such awesome potential for growth and development so many young people in the first stage of their life's journey are made to feel failures' (p. 51). The current effective schools concept is very different from the previous traditional concept and is characterised by an underlying belief that all students can achieve.

While some may be more comfortable with the traditional approach and may perceive the current approach as unfamiliar and undesirable, the traditional approach is no longer viable, since it fails to recognise or address the increasingly complex and diverse nature of the world today. Recognising and accommodating the diversity of student skills and abilities in schools can be seen as a reflection of the increasingly diverse and complex needs of a rapidly changing world. The workplace now looks for people who demonstrate flexibility, creativity and problem-solving skills, and who are able to cooperate in the workplace, in addition to being proficient in basic skills such as reading, spelling and numeracy. The world has changed, and schools must change also. Effective schools must identify the outcomes they hope to achieve with their students, and must provide the curriculums and assessment that allow them to both achieve such outcomes and to demonstrate their achievement.

Effective schools are expected to have a dynamic vision, to meet the needs of students, their parents and families and the wider community; to constantly update curriculums that reflect future needs; to embrace technological advances; and, to be creative and innovative. In addition, they are expected to implement current approaches in learning – approaches that have seen a shift from an emphasis on content to an emphasis on learning how to learn, from learning as a product to learning as a process, from a priority on performance (compared to others) to a priority on self-concept and personal progress, from education as an age-related social necessity to a lifelong process, and from teacher as the source of all knowledge to teacher as learner and facilitator of children's learning. Obviously this is no mean feat; it requires an ongoing commitment to improvement, dedication to supporting students, their families and the community, and a belief that schools can make a difference.

Before considering how educators might go about ensuring their school is effective and inclusive, it may be helpful to consider what an effective school might look like. Stoll & Fink (1996) have developed an effective schools model in which 12 characteristics, falling into three broad categories, are outlined:

- A common mission:
  - shared values and beliefs
  - clear goals
  - instructional leadership.
- A climate conducive to learning:
  - student involvement and responsibility
  - physical environment
  - recognition and incentives
  - positive student behaviour
  - parental and community involvement and support.
- Emphasis on learning:
  - frequent monitoring of student progress
  - high expectations
  - teacher collegiality and support
  - instructional and curriculum focus.

Each of these characteristics has implications in terms of inclusion. Although it is not possible to discuss each in detail here, individual schools and teachers need to consider these carefully. As an example, the first characteristic, shared values and beliefs, must include commitment to the philosophy and implementation of inclusive practices by all school personnel, including classroom teachers, special educators and school executive. Some schools may find that current values and beliefs are not shared, nor are they inclusive. Determining values and beliefs and arriving at a consensus among all concerned may require substantial change, and may be a lengthy process.

Although there is acknowledgement that effective schools take responsibility for meeting the educational needs of all their students, in practice this is still a concept that many educational practitioners find difficult to accept (Owens, 1998). There are still some regular classroom teachers who do not have a positive attitude towards including children with special educational needs in their classroom (de Bettencourt, 1999). A substantial body of research indicates that this may be in part due to many educators, particularly general educators, questioning their knowledge and skills for planning and effectively teaching students with diverse needs. For the individual working alone, the task may seem very daunting or perhaps not achievable. However, if achieving such a goal is seen as a challenge to be met by all those involved through collegial and supportive means, all may view it as valuable and attainable.

Whereas in the past special education and regular education staff and programs have been seen as separate entities, it is essential that they now join forces to combine best practices, to examine the effectiveness of programs and curriculums being offered to students, and to change or restructure programs or services where necessary, so that all students can reach their maximum potential. This ability to work together to support students, staff and families, and to solve problems, has been identified as critical to successful inclusion (Tiegerman-Farber & Radziewicz, 1998).

Implicit in this process is an expectation of informed participation by all parties (Hobbs & Westling, 2002), with all parties providing expertise and all committed to achieving a

positive outcome for all concerned. It is not a one-way process in which the special educator advises the supposedly less expert regular teacher, although many educators share this misconception and react accordingly. It is likely that the regular educator will have had limited training in special education, while the special educator may have limited awareness, or experience, of the demands in regular classrooms. The latter may be particularly true in the secondary setting, where special educators may not have specialist subject knowledge in areas in which they are working with students and teachers. It is therefore essential that the expertise of all educators be recognised, and opportunities for sharing and for professional development be seen as important.

The earlier focus on special programs for students with special learning needs must be replaced by the development of a system of education that focuses on the best methods for all students, and the development of a school ethos in which all personnel also share responsibility for supporting every student as well as supporting their colleague teachers, parents and families. In this process all teachers are equal and all schools have the potential to be, or to become, inclusive, caring schools. Inclusive schools will be characterised by a sense of community, collaboration and collegiality, partnerships with families, flexible service delivery and commitment to professional development.

How can schools go about developing an inclusive, caring environment? Sapon-Shevin (1990) suggested positive steps include: taking the labels off the teachers, students and classrooms; establishing a school philosophy of caring; building the school as a community; honouring and celebrating diversity; thinking about curriculum in a broad sense; stressing cooperation rather than competition; and empowering everybody in the school. A final step is for teachers to work towards creating their own ideal (Sapon-Shevin, 1990).

In order for this to happen, teachers need to reflect and to talk to each other; to set individual and group goals; to team up with other teachers, parents, students, administrators, and community members; to determine what changes need to be made and what changes can be made; and to begin such a process. Simultaneous top–down and bottom–up initiatives merge, and collegiality and individuality can coexist productively.

Change and innovation in schools

While the focus of this book is the inclusion of children with special educational needs, the process of managing change effectively, of developing and enhancing teachers' professional competencies, and of working collaboratively, has relevance far beyond this focus. Technological advances, changing community needs, and new approaches to teaching and learning in general, mean that change is a constant feature of schools today. This should not be change for the sake of change, but change motivated by the need to meet new challenges and to seize new opportunities, supporting all students, staff and families effectively. As Butcher (1998) has pointed out, we are part of an increasingly seamless education environment and a more global and interrelated world. Increasingly people from schools, universities and community groups or businesses are collaborating to address the educational challenges of today. Such partnerships have the potential to maximise benefits for all stakeholders. This is the way of the future, and teachers need to be effective participants.

What do we mean by change?

Change, in this context, refers to the introduction of any innovation, whether program, process or practice, that is new to the individual or school. The innovation may not be new in the sense of having only just been developed, but rather is new to the people involved. For example, information technology is in itself not new, but its introduction into the school curriculum and ensuing technological advances may be recent innovations in some schools. The use of specific technology to support students with special educational needs may be new to staff. Those involved will need to undertake training sessions to provide them with the knowledge and skills required, and will need to work collaboratively to introduce these methods effectively on a school-wide basis.

Peer tutoring and cooperative learning (discussed in Chapter 5), or team teaching (discussed later in this chapter) are not new techniques either, but they may be new to some teachers. Introducing these techniques in their own classrooms will involve a number of changes on the part of the teachers involved. Similarly, inclusion is not a new practice, but many schools have yet to fully embrace or effectively implement inclusive practices.

It is vital to recognise change as a process, not an event. Change takes both time and commitment. This has frequently been ignored in school systems, which have tended to introduce an innovation (for example, a new curriculum or assessment technique, or a different behaviour management approach) and to believe that a change has therefore occurred. However, handing over an innovation such as a program or curriculum is an event and does not automatically ensure that change will take place.

While it is evident that the effective inclusion of students with special educational needs has required changes on the part of schools and teachers, such as changes in philosophy, organisation, physical setting, curriculum adaptations, instructional techniques and so on (depending on the individual needs of those involved), it is obvious that some schools and teachers have been better able to make the changes than others, and that this process will need to continue. Such change is a process that occurs over a period of time, often years.

From recent research into educational change, general agreement on the following characteristics of change have emerged:

- there will be more than one version of what change will be
- people have to develop their own understanding of the change through clarification and practice
- change is a personal experience
- conflict and disagreement are inevitable and fundamental
- a mix of pressure and support is needed
- top–down, bottom–up change engenders more commitment than either change imposed autocratically from above or instigated from the bottom–up alone
- change rarely involves single innovations, and one change is likely to have a ripple effect
- change requires time and persistence
- following change, a period of consolidation is needed
- there may be valid reasons for not implementing change
- not everyone will be able to change
- development is evolutionary, with adjustments made as you go along.

It must be emphasised that change for the sake of change is not desirable, nor is constant change with little or no opportunity for reflection and consolidation. Instead it is essential that change be directed to solving problems and to developing and maintaining an effective school. Furthermore, opportunities to evaluate change must be provided. Loader (1984, in Ridden 1991) suggested that excellent schools recognise their imperfections, are willing to identify causes and seek solutions, and constantly evaluate, accept criticism and adjust goals to meet the needs of their students.

Identifying problems and possible solutions, or knowing what makes an effective school, does not mean that the required changes will occur automatically or quickly. Instead, schools and individual teachers need to address the questions:

- Where are we now?
- Where would we like to be in the future?
- How best can we move in that direction?
- How do we evaluate the changes we are making?

Depending on the outcomes of this initial process, the process may later need to be undertaken again, or new goals or a different focus may be identified.

Impetus for change

While the impetus for change may come from within the school, it may also come from outside the school through such prompts as national curriculums, external assessments (such as the Basic Skills Tests in NSW), school councils or accreditation bodies, teacher appraisal processes, and quality assurance approaches. The outcomes may be student change, teacher change, or systems change. Also, as mentioned previously, change in one area may indirectly bring about change in another.

If the process is to be successful and the changes are to be long lasting, it is essential attention be given to the development of shared values, the establishment of a climate for change and maintenance of a collaborative culture. Policies, directives and guidelines can be issued from on high but it is the people in the classrooms and schools who have the greatest opportunity to bring about change.

Schools cannot improve without people working together. No one person, regardless of their position or training, can have all the answers to the complex problems faced in schools. The more that people work together, the greater the possibility of understanding complex problems and initiating change in an atmosphere of mutual respect and trust. This is easier to say than to do, of course. There are a number of barriers in schools that make change difficult to achieve.

Barriers to change

Teachers and schools have commonly been found to be resistant to change and unwilling to accommodate innovation. An extensive literature examining resistance to change in schools has identified a number of barriers to change as well as effective strategies to overcome these barriers. These will be discussed briefly.

Some barriers to change are *personal*. Two factors in particular, absence of a positive attitude to change and absence of the required skills, are key sources of resistance. Educators resist change when they can't see the point in it. There are a number of reasons this may occur. This may be because they think things are all right as they are, or they may not be able to see how a proposed change is going to improve things, either for them or for their students. They may feel that there is no real evidence that change is needed; they may see it as another directive that asks them to do more without making additional time or resources available; they may see other issues as being more important; they may see it as someone else's responsibility; they may believe that change efforts involve a lot of wasted time talking, as either nothing will come of it, or else the decision has already been made by executive staff and so talking is irrelevant; or they may see the change as being someone's attempt to gain kudos for themselves rather than being a genuine attempt to address a real need.

Resistance will also occur if those responsible for implementing change don't believe that they have the skills or knowledge required to do so. The latter has been a major source of difficulty in the inclusion of children with special educational needs.

Teachers who lack confidence in their ability to cater for children with diverse needs may fear that their incompetence will be exposed to themselves, to their colleagues and to administrators. Additionally they may fear that unreasonable demands on their time and skills will be made, that they will have to work harder or longer; they may fear the response of other parents who may feel the child makes demands on the teacher which disadvantages other class members; they may fear that the resources or support required will not be provided, or will not be ongoing; they may fear working with other professionals will mean a loss of autonomy in deciding what is best for the child; and, they may be extremely hesitant to have another person, such as an aide or support teacher, in their classroom. Fatigue, illness or inexperience may further increase perceptions of lack of competence and decrease self-esteem. For some teachers, defensiveness and lack of objectivity assessing and managing a situation interfere with their ability to effectively support some students.

Some teachers may resist utilising new strategies or adapting curriculum (such as described in Chapters 4 and 5) in the belief that these are only beneficial for students with special educational needs. Such teachers may be more willing to change if made aware that many students in the regular classroom could benefit. There is considerable research available which demonstrates that many of the so-called special education practices, such as collaborative consultation, team teaching, parent involvement and adapted instruction, benefits all students and, in some instances, the greatest benefit may be derived by regular students (for example, Saint-Laurent et al., 1998; Weiner, 2003). In reality, inclusion involves practices that are ultimately practices of good teaching.

Teachers may also be concerned that the parents and families of children without disabilities will perceive inclusion as detrimental to their children. However, research suggests that when effective instruction and inclusion are present, and when parents and families are kept involved and informed, *all* parents perceive the inclusive class setting as beneficial for *all* students (for example, Tichenor, Heins & Piechura-Couture, 2000).

Some teachers do not feel any sense of ownership of the education of students with special needs and may feel that others should address these needs. There are regular and special education teachers who have had lengthy experience of the expert model in which a specialist was considered the expert, and responsibility could be handed over to them. This experience frequently results in a perpetuation of this model.

Personal barriers, such as concern over a perceived lack of specific knowledge and skills, frequently result in active resistance to change or passive resistance in which the change is endorsed outwardly but no change in practice occurs. For example, if it were proposed that all children in grade 1 in a particular school joined in a cultural afternoon once per week, utilising a group rotation format, and involving a child who was deaf, some staff might endorse the concept in general but may feel that they must oppose its implementation because they do not have the signing skills they feel would be necessary. They may resist the change, arguing that the child requires the skills of a specific teacher, and should therefore remain with that person. Alternatively, they may agree to proceed with the proposal, but may make little or no effort to accommodate the child who is deaf. There are, of course, ways of addressing such concerns, however these are unlikely to be explored unless an atmosphere of collegiality and willingness to work together is present.

As the number of children with special educational needs in regular classrooms increases, the fears described above may be magnified accordingly for some teachers. Teachers may lack specific knowledge about the disability or special needs in question, or what knowledge they do have may be based on a medical perspective rather than an educational perspective. To address these concerns, educators may need to investigate the educational needs of the student; to rethink their expectations of and for this student accordingly; to reflect on their own competencies as teachers; and, to recognise that the real focus of the change is meeting the needs of each student, not evaluation of their teaching competence (see Box 10.1).

Box 10.1
Voices: Inclusion – a Principal reflects

After 29 years in special education I know teachers who were, are and continue to be terrified of taking students with special needs into their classes – mainly because they are scared of not being able to do a good job of supporting them and the other students. By the end of the year those same teachers are absolute supporters of inclusion. This year was no different.

Geoff was a young teacher of a Year 4 class. This class of 26 students included Sam, a lively boy with Down syndrome. Even though the learning support teacher and previous teacher had meetings with Geoff prior to the year beginning, Geoff kept asking, 'Shouldn't Sam be in a special school?' After the first week Geoff was convinced Sam should be in a special school and that far more special schools should be built!

Nevertheless, with the assistance of the learning support staff, including one and a half hours of assistant time a day, Geoff slowly began to refine his programs. More importantly, he began to know Sam as a person, and not as 'the boy with Down syndrome.' His behaviour management strategies were fine-tuned to suit Sam, and Sam began to take small but significant steps in his learning. All the students thrived.

Towards the end of the year Geoff asked to have a child with special needs in his class for the following year. He offered to speak at staff meetings about the positive experience. More importantly, he and Sam have developed a beautiful relationship based on mutual respect and love for each other.

Sally, (Acting) Principal, Catholic Regional Primary School, Queensland

As teachers become increasingly aware of the changing perception of their roles, they may become more open to accepting or facilitating change and less fearful. In contrast to previous times, today there is recognition that schools and classrooms are complex systems and that one person cannot be expected to have all the skills and knowledge that may be required. Teachers need to recognise that everyone requires assistance at some time, and that those they regard as experts (and therefore to be feared) will, at times, be seeking information or support from other colleagues, professionals, families or outside agencies. Developing partnerships through such means as successful collaborative consultation, which will be discussed later in this chapter, is one way of effectively bringing about change by decreasing resistance and by providing support for those who need it.

Other barriers to change may be termed *organisational* (or structural) barriers. In many ways schools are not structured to facilitate teachers working together. The often high degree of authority of the principal (combining both goal-setting and administrative functions), the relatively low degree of integration among teachers (particularly in the secondary school setting) and the relatively private settings in which teachers work (that is, the classroom) may all result in a degree of isolation for the teacher. Traditionally teaching has been an activity carried out by an individual in a classroom with students or, in the case of the special education teacher, on a withdrawal basis or in a resource room. Many teachers become so used to this isolation that they become uncomfortable with the idea of collaborative problem-solving and cooperative planning involving classroom activities (which could be used very effectively in the example of the Year 1 child who is deaf). This situation, in particular, often results in a lack of dissemination of good teaching practices, since the individual teacher is largely unobserved by colleagues and there is little or no opportunity to share ideas, skills or resources. In addition, there is a professional norm that emphasises non-interference by colleagues.

Being separated from one another can also result in a sense of competition among individuals or departments for resources, students and jobs. Many teachers report feeling unappreciated, overworked, not respected as professionals, undervalued and unsupported, and frustrated by the 'non-teaching' demands placed upon them. Some may begin to lack confidence in the administration, the community and themselves, eventually feeling helpless and trapped in the job, powerless to effect change. This sense of powerlessness and inevitability frequently results in inertia and resistance to the changes that could address the difficulties they are experiencing.

Other characteristics of schools that may inhibit the introduction of innovations include the general school goals and the hierarchical structure of authority. The hierarchical structure makes specific individuals responsible and accountable for the work of others. Some teachers may prefer to leave things as they are, even if they can see a need for change, rather than risk an innovation that may fail and for which they may be blamed. Sometimes those in executive positions are unwilling to consider a specific change, and those they supervise may be prevented from investigating or implementing the change in question.

Organisations such as schools can also develop strong feelings against everything from outside. There is likely to be hostility toward new ideas if those ideas are perceived to originate from an outside source (for example, if a directive is perceived to have come from the top, and staff believe they have had no say, or if the regular class teacher sees a special education teacher as imposing a change).

Many of the organisational barriers involve the type of leadership provided. Effective implementation of change requires that those involved, particularly those in leadership roles, are competent to carry out the planning and procedural tasks. Such skills might include organising time to allow for the planning involved, running meetings, or completing documentation (filling in submissions, for example).

Despite research, which has consistently demonstrated that effective leadership by school executive is crucial to the success of any change process (for example, Bernauer, 2002; Fullan, 1996; Harris & Zetlin, 1993; Mamlin, 1999; Vaughn, Schumn & Brick, 1998), there has been a tendency to focus on the roles and responsibilities of regular and special education teachers in meeting the needs of children with diverse educational needs, and to ignore or minimise the critical role of school executive. Numerous studies have reported that school executive personnel may be out of touch with the elements of inclusion most directly related to what occurs at the classroom level (for example, Daane, Bierne-Smith & Latham, 2000). Findings of a study by Brotherson et al. (2001), examining the issues confronting elementary school principals as they work with young children and their families towards inclusion, are consistent with much of the research literature in this area. In this study, a participatory action research model was used to gather information (for a description of participatory action research, see later in this chapter). Findings indicated that, despite the rhetoric, a gap continued to exist between recommended practices and the reality of early childhood inclusion in schools. Principals in this study tended not to see themselves as part of the solution for early childhood inclusion.

The tendency for some school executives to issue directives and leave it to others to implement, with no follow up to determine efficacy of practice, is not uncommon in schools. Saying that one has a policy of inclusion does not guarantee that inclusion is practised. For example, in 2003, a kindergarten child with Down syndrome enrolled in a local primary school that claimed to be inclusive, spent much of her day at a desk in the storeroom. The gap between rhetoric and reality was enormous in this case.

The physical organisation of the school may also create barriers to inclusion. The frequent location of support classes in demountable buildings at a distance from the main school building is an example of a situation which does not foster an inclusive school ethos and which may make collaboration and teacher contact very difficult. Students who use a wheelchair cannot easily access some schools and classrooms, and their opportunities for inclusion may be severely restricted. In some schools it may be difficult to accommodate large groups of students for assemblies or whole school activities, resulting in limited opportunities for students to be seen as members of the school community as a whole.

Some barriers may be described as being of an *external* origin. Examples include a lack of funding for innovations; a lack of provision for teacher training, in-service or professional development; and, a lack of physical or personnel resources. This has been a complaint (frequently justified) of many classroom teachers who feel they have been asked to include a student, or several students, with special educational needs in their classroom but have not been provided with the resources or the opportunity for professional development required to best accommodate the needs of that student. Lack of ongoing support has been identified as a major factor in lack of impact of school reforms, even when reforms are clearly based on research (Greenwood & Abbott, 2001).

For an interesting discussion of the difficulties and ambiguities experienced by schools, readers are referred to Clark et al. (1999), who report on a study of four comprehensive schools seeking to develop in a more inclusive direction. The researchers relate the findings to the current literature on educational change and inclusive schools theories, micro-political theories and current systemic educational imperatives. They argue, not surprisingly, that movement towards inclusive schooling is extremely complex.

Having said all this, many schools have initiated significant changes and innovations very successfully. With increasing recognition of factors influencing the change process in schools today has come a number of approaches to overcome these barriers.

Overcoming barriers: People and change

Change is more likely to go ahead successfully if the change effort takes into account and attempts to address the barriers that exist in the school. Some means of overcoming specific personal, organisational and external barriers have been discussed in the previous section. However, the single most important factor in any change process is the people who are involved. Recognising that change is a process, not an event, is crucial. It must be planned for, managed effectively and evaluated.

A number of approaches have been used in an attempt to bring about change despite lack of a positive attitude towards change. First, persons or groups in a position of authority (for example, school principal, Department of School Education) can simply instruct people to institute the change and gain (often grudging) compliance in this way. A major problem with this approach is that it does not involve those expected to institute the change in the decision-making process, and they may feel that they have no ownership of the process, and therefore no real commitment to it. Much has been written about the difficulties of top–down attempts at change (see the list of references and further readings at the end of this chapter).

Second, those seeking change may try to 'sell' their idea by presenting convincing arguments, either individually, in seminars or staff meetings, or by presenting written information. Sometimes such an approach is enhanced by the offer of money (such as grants) or tangible resources for participating in the process. Such approaches are often unsuccessful in the long-term if ongoing support is not provided.

Lastly, those initiating change can create the conditions whereby the responsibility for implementing change will result from those involved in analysing a current situation, agreeing on the need for change and deciding on a solution. When teachers can see a real need for change, and see that change as being both attainable and worthwhile for themselves and their students, they are more likely to become willingly involved, to be committed to the change, and to take responsibility for the outcome. A major advantage of this approach is that the participants will feel they own the change and are far more likely to be committed to it. Action research is an example of such an approach.

The strategies discussed so far are used in an attempt to overcome barriers created by an absence of a positive attitude to change. In addition, there are a number of strategies available to build up the competency levels of those involved and to overcome the barriers that may be present when people feel they lack the required skills. For example, the provision of formal learning opportunities such as inservice training has been a widely used strategy in education to develop teacher competencies. In addition, there has been increasing recognition that schools frequently have unexpected and untapped assets, such as staff with expertise in specific areas. Tapping these assets can both enhance outcomes for the school, and assist in the process of people in the school feeling they have something to offer

These approaches are useful in training task-specific skills, but do not address planning or procedural difficulties or work relationship problems. Having the initiator of the change join the group responsible for implementation of a change program in order to facilitate their exploration of the issues underlying the proposed change, and ways in which problems may be solved, has been shown to be the most effective means of developing procedural and planning skills and work relationship competencies. Collaborative consultation, described later in this chapter, is a primary means of implementing this approach.

The positive impact working together can have for teachers is demonstrated by the findings of a pilot teacher preparation program for undergraduate trainee teachers undertaken by Sprague and Pennell (2000). Prior to participation in the program, the trainee teachers involved reported that they felt unprepared for inclusive classrooms. In the pilot program, trainees participated in a special education course focusing on inclusion, and observed inclusive classrooms with an emphasis on collaborative teaching. Practical activities and suggestions for adapting materials were presented. Pre- and post-survey results revealed that initially only 30 per cent of students believed that students with special needs should be taught in a regular classroom, while at the conclusion of the program 58 per cent strongly agreed and the remainder somewhat agreed that this should happen. Initially less than 50 per cent agreed that they would be comfortable co-planning and co-teaching with special educators, while at the conclusion of the program 100 per cent agreed they would be able to co-plan and co-teach. Trainees were obviously at different stages in the change process at the time the post-survey was conducted, but all had embraced the changes to some extent (see further discussion of stages of change later in this chapter).

Facilitating change through partnership

Anyone can be a facilitator of change: principals, executive staff, classroom teachers, specialist teachers, special education teachers, parents, administrators, students, or community members. The terms 'change agent' and 'change facilitator' have been used in the literature, often interchangeably, and sometimes with a distinction made between the two. Here the terms are used interchangeably to refer to a person or persons working directly with other people in order to bring about change.

A change facilitator helps, assists, encourages, persuades or nurtures people in order to promote meaningful change. They may be a person who responds to a proposed change, a person who manages the change, or a person who initiates change. It is important that teachers are still able to see themselves as facilitators of change without having to be an initiator. The change may be someone else's idea, but other teachers may recognise its value and support its introduction and implementation.

Teachers and other school personnel may not set out specifically to promote change, but may engage in change in less formal ways. For example, teachers who reflect on their own practice will find that they are frequently engaged in a change process as they endeavour to maximise outcomes for their students and as they grow professionally. Their personal development is likely to result in changes that affect others also.

Teachers may engage with others in less formal change processes. In some cases there may be several teachers or personnel who work together as a team in order to meet a specific need. For example, a school staff may have decided that the school requires new reading materials, as current material is outdated and the needs of older poor readers are not being catered for. A group of staff members may work together to collect information on what is available, who it is relevant for, cost, advantages and disadvantages, and experiences of other schools using the materials. They may then present this information to a staff meeting, allowing the staff to consider the options and select that which they consider to be the most appropriate. It may take a considerable amount of time to reach this stage, followed by a lengthy period in which teachers introduce the new material, learn to use it effectively to instruct their students, adapt it to suit the specific needs of their students, evaluate its effectiveness, and so on.

The school referred to in Box 10.2 developed a very innovative approach to overcoming the difficulties associated with the inclusion of students with severe hearing impairments in whole school activities. In this example, all those involved in the change were required to work as a team with every team member committed to the approach adopted. On a personal level, those involved were reflective practitioners, able to analyse their own practice and committed to developing professionally. For a more detailed description of essential change agency skills and consultation competencies, readers are referred to Dettmer, Thurston and Dyck (1999), Miles, Saxi and Liberman (1988), and West, Idol and Cannon (1987).

It is not only teachers who are involved in the change process, of course. It must be emphasised that partnership with parents and families is a crucial element in providing for the needs of all students. Any successful school program, whether whole school or classroom-based, needs to acknowledge the role of parent and family involvement in the education process. At different times families may take on roles in which they initiate, facilitate, manage or respond to change. These roles are not confined to the early childhood years, but continue beyond initial placement decisions to ongoing involvement throughout their child's education.

For families of children with special educational needs, this role may be intense and long lasting. In terms of inclusion, Grove and Fisher (1999) refer to parents as 'entrepreneurs of meaning, shaping the definition and reality of inclusive education for their children' (p. 208). (See Chapter 3 for a discussion of the vital role of families and team membership).

Box 10.2

Programs: School-wide communication

A public primary school in a regional area of NSW included several support classes for students with severe hearing and language impairments. Students in these classes ranged in age from 5 to 12 years, and experienced varying levels of hearing impairment, ranging from moderate impairment to profound deafness. All students and their support teachers and teacher aide used sign language to communicate. Some students used a combination of spoken language and signing.

While students were being catered for in their classrooms, staff realised that a number of difficulties were present which made it difficult for the students to be fully included in the playground and in whole school activities. The main difficulty was that of communication – communication between students with and without hearing impairment, between other teachers and the students with hearing impairments, and between teachers and those parents and families who were hearing impaired/deaf and used sign language.

The solution adopted by the school was to include learning sign language for all students. Public primary schools in NSW include a Language Other Than English (LOTE) in their curriculum, and the introduction of sign language (while not a language other than English in the usual sense) was relevant to their school community.

The change process

Although there are some minor variations in models of change, the stages shown in Figure 10.1 are common to most.

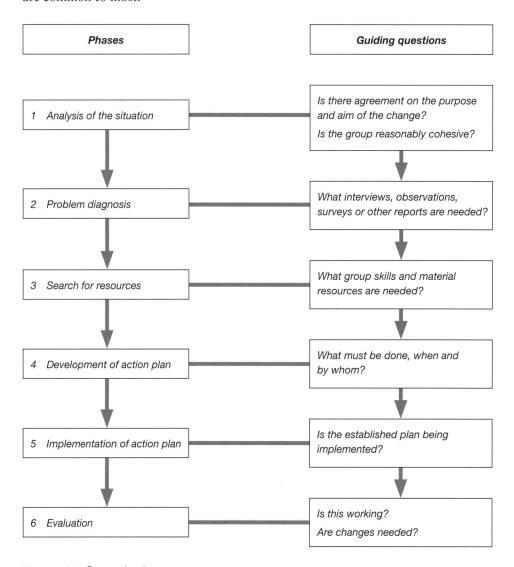

Figure 10.1 Stages in change

For change to be effective, all those involved should feel as though 'we did this ourselves'. One very effective means of bringing about change through ownership is collaborative consultation.

Collaborative consultation

Collaborative consultation has emerged as a very successful means of accommodating the diverse needs of all students, and the teachers who support them. Teachers working collaboratively can improve existing programs, develop options that might not otherwise have been available, and open lines of communication with families, students, administrators and other teachers and professionals. Consultation and collaboration among school personnel develops and enhances team accountability for all students – students become *our* students rather than *theirs*, *yours* or *mine*. Teamwork among teachers has been shown to be a critical characteristic of a successful inclusive school (Fullan & Miles, 1992; Janney et al., 1995).

According to Wideen and Grimmet (1995) the following factors underlie most collaborative effort: the pressure for change and reform in education; the increasing complexity of social systems; and the need for increased resources. These factors are all pertinent in the inclusion of students with special educational needs. Through collaborative consultation, partnerships are formed that can respond to teacher and system needs as well as student needs (Villa et al., 1990). Such collaboration has been shown to be effective in improving the performance of teachers and students, as well as being an effective means of managing the increased responsibilities that are frequently associated with inclusive education. Dettmer, Thurston and Dyck (1999, p. 6) describe collaborative school consultation as:

> interaction in which school personnel and families confer, consult and collaborate as a team to identify learning and behavioural needs, and to plan, implement, evaluate, and revise as needed the educational programs that are expected to serve those needs.

In collaborative consultation, individuals with different expertise, knowledge or experience work voluntarily together to create solutions to mutually agreed-upon problems.

West and Idol (1990) suggest that collaborative consultation may be used in schools to:

- prevent learning and behaviour problems occurring
- remediate learning and behaviour problems as they occur
- coordinate services and instructional programs.

A further use is that of supporting those who provide services to students, including special educators, regular classroom teachers and families. All types of consultation have, as their primary goals, to assist in providing a problem-solving service and to increase the skills of the participants so that similar problems can be prevented or dealt with more effectively in the future.

There are a number of advantages to working collaboratively. First, schools implementing collaborative programs can tap the expertise of all members of the school community, families and local community in order to create a supportive, caring school environment. Through collaborative consultation, solutions may be found that are better than would be any solution that a team member could produce alone (Idol, Paolucci-Whitcomb & Nevin, 1986; Salend, 1998; Tiegerman-Farber & Radziewicz, 1998).

Second, collaborative consultation allows for well-coordinated services. This is particularly important given the complexity of service delivery systems available today. For example, a student in a secondary support unit for students with mild intellectual disability may take part in activities with the regular class teacher for part of the day, a parent–tutor reading program, a program run by the Support Teacher Learning Difficulty, the school librarian, the physical education teacher (or other specialist teachers), and a speech therapist after school. Without collaboration, the potential for fragmentation of the student's program is high.

Third, there has been increasing emphasis placed on the need for early identification of students at risk of experiencing difficulty so that remedial programs can be implemented before other specialist services are required (often referred to in the literature as pre-referral intervention). Teachers working together can often provide this service for such students.

Fourth, collaboration provides opportunities for improving a teacher's ongoing practice; it offers a means of self-development. It allows teachers to share ideas, skills and resources, and to feel they have a contribution to make.

Fifth, by emphasising team accountability, it moves the onus of total responsibility from an individual to all team members. The result is shared responsibility, increased ownership of the program and a greater likelihood of individuals being prepared to go beyond their comfort zone and to take risks.

Sixth, team approaches such as co-teaching result in reduced teacher–student ratios (Austin, 2001). In addition, responsibility for programming and implementation of programs is shared, thus reducing the workload of the individual while also reducing some of the isolation commonly experienced by teachers.

Finally, as previously mentioned, it is an effective means of forging partnerships, bringing about change, and ensuring teachers feel that change belongs to them.

Collaborative consultation replaces the traditional consultation model in which the special education teacher was used as a consultant, providing indirect service delivery to assist class teachers (the consultees) who had children with special educational needs in their classrooms. The consultee then delivered a direct service, utilising that advice. In the school context, it has been customary to think of a consultation triad – the special education teacher, the classroom teacher and the student. However, this traditional and prescriptive expert-based model can foster an 'us–them' mentality.

Despite recognition of the advantages of a collaborative approach, there is still a tendency for special educators to be asked to consult. This is in large part due to the factors described in the previous section on barriers to change, for example, prior experience with the traditional consultation model. In particular, teachers have been frequently identified as being unprepared in the skills associated with collaborative consultation (Friend & Cook, 1996). However, if real change is to occur, ownership of the solution to a problem must lie with all involved, and the traditional expert model does not allow for this.

Collaborative consultation, on the other hand, emphasises the idea of a team approach in which effective partnerships are formed. While the team could consist of a special educator and a classroom teacher, it is just as likely to consist of a group of teachers working together, or several classroom teachers, a specialist teacher, a teachers' aide and parents. Earlier in this book, individualised educational programs were discussed. An optimal situation would be one in which all those involved – teachers, parents, specialist/therapists, ancillary staff and the student – interacted collaboratively in the development of the student's program, in order to maximise learning outcomes for the student. Transition to school, and vocational education and transition from school, are activities usually characterised by ongoing collaboration among school personnel and families (see Chapters 3 and 12).

In order to obtain services for a child with special educational needs in a regular classroom, a pre-referral process involving observation, assessment, and definition will be initiated. At a later stage this will involve problem identification, decisions on intervention (which may be at student, teacher, and/or systems level), implementation and evaluation. The ongoing process is likely to involve a number of personnel, and to require coordination. This, together with actual implementation, is likely to be up to the classroom teacher. Throughout this process there may be a need to collaborate with people from health care disciplines such as paediatricians or neurologists; from a variety of child development disciplines such as psychologists, occupational therapists, or speech pathologists; or from other educational disciplines, such as special educators in areas such as early intervention, learning difficulties, intellectual disability, sensory disability or behaviour disorders. From this description it can be seen that skills in collaboration are essential for regular class teachers, not just special education personnel.

Children with special needs in regular classrooms are often supported by teacher's aides. In this role, the classroom teacher and the aide are partners in accomplishing tasks and supporting the student. The teacher is responsible for overall programming and supervision of the aide, while the aide may be largely responsible for implementing the program. Each member of the team has specific roles and responsibilities, but their relationship is one of partnership.

Effective collaboration in regular classrooms should lead to a decrease in referral rates for special programs or placements (Jordan, 1994). Decreasing referral rates, however, is not an end in itself. Consider the situation in which the classroom teacher requests assessment of a child by the support teacher or school counsellor. There are two main reasons for such a referral:

- to confirm that a problem exists and therefore justify placement or program referral
- to identify where difficulties exist so that strategies can be developed and implemented in the classroom, which will assist the student to achieve.

In the former it should be noted that removing the child with the greatest difficulties from a class merely results in another child becoming bottom of the list, and the referral process may continue. Furthermore, the class teacher will not acquire the skills to adequately cater for all the children in a regular classroom, and so the difficulty will be perpetuated. On the other hand, when a classroom teacher acquires specific knowledge and skills in order to assist a student with special needs, the new knowledge and skills will enhance their future practice and their ability to maximise the learning of all students.

It must be emphasised that collaborative consultation is a problem-solving process, as well as a service delivery model (West & Idol, 1990). Not only does collaborative consultation have an application to special education in assisting students with varying needs, but it is also applicable as a school-wide process among school staff, developing partnerships in order to effectively meet the unique needs of individuals or groups within the school, or the school as a whole. While supporting students is the main focus of such processes, sometimes it is the needs of teachers or families that are the focus. The unique needs of the students, families and teachers in a particular school, the resources available to address the need, and time constraints will determine the nature of the problem-solving process and who will be involved.

Such a process involves collaborative teamwork and may involve a number of different service delivery structures according to the needs of the student, group of students, or school. For example, in some situations teachers may choose to teach together, capitalising on the individual expertise of each, in order to best meet the individual needs of students. One teacher may assist another to develop skills in a particular technique, such as cooperative learning or peer tutoring, and they may work together in the classroom. A classroom teacher may consult with a specialist teacher in order to develop and implement a specific program, such as a behaviour management program or remedial reading program. The classroom teacher may assist the special education teacher to develop a program that fits in with the class program, ensuring that the remedial program is consistent with the approach and materials used in the classroom. Together, the special education teacher and class teacher can determine the least intrusive form of assistance required to maintain students in the regular classroom. A classroom teacher, a speech pathologist and a student's family may work together to support a student experiencing speech and language difficulties, ensuring that the approach taken is consistent and maximising opportunities for the student to improve their skills.

Teachers engaged in collaborative and team approaches have reported many benefits of their collaborative approach for both the inclusion of students with special needs, and for their teaching in general (for example, Sobel & Vaughn, 1999; Stanovich, 1999). However, despite acknowledging the advantages of working together, special educators and classroom teachers have frequently reported that they are not comfortable with collaboration (Daane, Beirne-Smith & Latham, 2000). This may be due to the common misconception that special education and regular education practices vary considerably. In reality, regular and special educators have more beliefs in common about recommended practices for children with and without special needs than those that are different (Cannon, 1992; Kilgo et al., 1999), providing a basis on which to work together towards the ultimate goal of providing appropriate educational experiences for all children.

As indicated previously, it is important that families and schools work together to support students with special educational needs. Families are usually a constant in children's lives. They know the child best and have strengths and coping skills that can be identified and enhanced. Unfortunately some teachers are apprehensive about working with families, even though they acknowledge the potential benefits of doing so. In a review of research on family involvement in schools, Bennett, Deluca and Bruns (1997) found that younger teachers were more positive in general than were older, more experienced teachers.

Barriers to home–school partnerships may be related to school ethos or personnel, to family characteristics, or to program or service factors. While these cannot be examined in detail here, two caveats should be mentioned: first, school personnel who are aware of potential barriers to family–school collaboration and who have a positive attitude will be more prepared to find and utilise strategies to foster collaboration. Second, a traditional deficit approach model in which families are perceived as being deficient and in need of remediation, or the child is seen as deficient and the family is seen solely as a means of remediating the child's difficulties, is unproductive.

A true partnership between home, school and community, and the development of a team approach, is based on respect, mutual acceptance, openness, trust, and shared responsibility (Cornwell & Korteland, 1997). Hughes and MacNaughton (1999) suggest an approach to collaboration with families that actively deconstructs the hierarchical relationship which traditionally exists between teachers and families, actively replacing (reconstructing) it with a democratic relationship in and through which to increase their understandings of children, teaching, and learning. All efforts must be mindful of cultural practices and family and community needs.

If such a relationship is to be realised, consideration must be given to school and classroom practices that may either support or hinder effective collaboration. In an analysis of early intervention practices that affect collaboration, Dinnebeil, Hale and Rule (1999) found that program philosophy and climate, type of service delivery, teaming approaches, administrative policies and practices (including quality of program personnel), and community context were important variables that could either hinder or support collaboration. When collaborating with families it is essential that teachers examine their own values, initiate and actively build collaborative partnerships, individualise approaches for families, and evaluate the efficacy of the collaboration throughout. An evaluation of collaborative consultation should include evaluation in terms of the processes (including self-evaluation or reflection) and evaluation of the outcomes (solutions, interventions or approaches selected and implemented).

It is essential that teachers recognise family concerns and remember to attack the problem, not the individual or family. Perhaps a good rule of thumb is to listen at least as much or more than you talk, and be honest. Families do not respect teachers who offer solutions without listening to the problem, or who make empty promises such as offering to 'look into it and get back' but never do (so-called mirror teachers). It is more appropriate to assist families to recognise their strengths and to find their own solutions than to attempt to hand out solutions.

While the extent to which families wish to be involved varies, and their wishes must be respected, they should be provided with the opportunity to be fully involved in their child's education. It is not unusual to find that they have been relegated to roles such as canteen helpers, to listening to children read, to accompanying children on excursions, or to covering books for the school library. Such roles may be very useful and supportive of school staff and activities, but do not, by themselves, constitute an equal partnership. An egalitarian relationship includes mutual problem solving and shared decision-making. This is an issue that many teachers and schools have yet to address.

Barriers to collaboration

As with any change, barriers may exist when attempts are made to introduce collaborative consultation. Although collaborative consultation has been written about since the late 1960s, it is a relatively recent idea to some teachers, and as already discussed, some teachers may resist change. Practical barriers such as a lack of clarity about the roles of team members, lack of time, and overwhelming teacher commitments may be cited. In addition, conceptual barriers such as limited credibility of participants (such as special educators), the conflict (often imagined rather than real) between the thinking of special and regular educators, problems arising from the hierarchical relationships in schools and limitations in the knowledge base of participants may occur (Johnson, Pugach & Hammittee, 1988). In the case of family–school collaboration, a general school climate of mistrust of parents and families, lack of understanding of cultural differences, and a deficit approach model in which families are perceived as deficient in some way and educators are seen as experts, all diminish opportunity for effective collaboration and true partnerships.

Many of the barriers to change discussed earlier in this chapter have relevance here also. Barriers of a personal, organisational or external origin may be present. Of particular concern here, however, are those related to the personal characteristics of participants. When introducing collaborative consultation, the responsibilities, roles and characteristics of all participants must be considered. Variables such as age of participants, experience, orientation to collaborative consultation process, locus of control, degree of professional involvement and concern, interpersonal and communication skills, personal characteristics (such as cooperativeness, flexibility, empathy, personal adjustment, emotional stability, ability to inspire confidence, warmth and understanding), efficiency and time management skills, expectations of the process, and knowledge and skills base may constitute barriers.

The importance of personal characteristics and skills of participants was confirmed in a study by West and Cannon (1988) that sought to identify and validate essential collaborative consultation competencies needed by both regular and special educators. Skills that were rated the most highly included skills in interactive communication, collaborative problem solving, and personal characteristics. Skills in evaluating the effectiveness of consultation were also deemed important. Addressing these factors will be essential if barriers to collaboration are to be overcome.

Characteristics of collaborative consultation

Collaborative consultation is an interactive and ongoing process. It is characterised by mutual trust and respect, reciprocity, and open communication. The emphasis in collaborative consultation should be on partnerships, where cooperative problem-solving and shared responsibility for implementation of decisions are essential components. There is an assumption that all participants are equal and all contributions are of equal value, a belief that all educators can and want to learn better ways to teach students and maximise student outcomes, a belief in the capacity of all educators to design effective instructional programs and techniques as well as deliver them, a recognition that all educators, not only special educators, are responsible for students with special educational needs, and a recognition that most families want what is best for their child and have much to contribute to their child's education.

There are a number of principles, or characteristics, of collaborative consultation that are essential. These include:

- *Voluntary involvement*
  Collaborative consultation requires that all those who are involved willingly work together, and all should believe that working together will be mutually beneficial. Regardless of the specific form of collaboration (such as team teaching, partnerships with teachers' aides or other personnel, or working with families, for example) involvement must be voluntary and those involved must see the outcome to be positive for either themselves or their students, or both. No one can be forced to collaborate.
- *Equality and parity among participants*
  There must be a belief in the parity and equality of all the participants. This does not mean that the expertise of a particular team member is not recognised or utilised, or that no one has a leadership role, but rather that the contributions of each member involved in the process are of equal value and the diversity that may exist among members is valued. Differences in values, perspectives, expertise, experience, skills and interests add to the

process rather than detract from it. A perceived lack of parity by parents and families has frequently been a barrier to this process.

- *Shared expertise, knowledge or experience; reciprocity*
  Teachers involved in collaborative consultation acknowledge that the best solution will evolve from the contribution of all involved, and no one person can be expected to be the expert or to have all the answers to every problem. This is not to deny the specialised knowledge of individual members, but rather acknowledges all skills and value all contributions. It is recognised that in different situations the contribution of each member may not be equivalent (although the contributions of all members are equally valuable). It is also recognised that the pooling of experience, knowledge and ideas by the team will result in a better solution than that which could be arrived at by an individual. In this context, the expertise of families and their knowledge of their child must be acknowledged, not ignored.
- *Mutual goals, agreed upon problems*
  There must be respect for the right of all members to have their own opinions and beliefs, and agreement to the process of decision-making by consensus. Through discussion, group members must develop mutual goals towards which everyone is prepared to work.
- *Shared responsibility for participation and decision-making*
  As all participants are included as equal members, each has an equal say in decision-making. No single person, such as a member of the school executive, has a greater say than do other team members. Creating positive interdependence is essential in creating effective teams. The aim is to achieve consensus – to reach decisions agreed on by all.
- *Interactive and ongoing process*
  Because responsibility is shared, collaborative consultation involves an interactive and ongoing process. All involved must work together and, as solutions to problems require evaluation and adaptation over time, the process may be quite lengthy. It is not a 'one-off' occurrence.
- *Accountability for outcome*
  As all participants have equal say and responsibility, all are responsible for the outcome. In addition to the benefits discussed previously, such as a feeling of commitment and ownership, the sharing of responsibility evens the load among participants and alleviates some of the fears associated with risk-taking. Introducing change involves an element of risk (for example, that the change will fail or not meet its goals), but sharing the risks among participants reduces the fear of blame or failure. There has been some concern that collaborative consultation could mean that no one takes responsibility or is accountable for outcomes. However, in a truly collaborative process, all involved share responsibility and accountability for student outcomes. Collaborative consultation should be seen as an opportunity for participants to acknowledge the efforts and achievements of others, to reinforce good practice, and to support colleagues where necessary.

The advantages of the collaborative approach described above are numerous. Briefly summarised, they include:

- all participants feel ownership
- the outcome, such as a program, will be more effective and efficient as greater expertise has been utilised

- each member will have a better understanding of the purpose and implementation of the program
- members will be committed to making sure the program works most effectively
- the program can be integrated into existing programs
- all skills and expertise can be shared
- participants will acquire skills for similar problems that may be encountered in the future
- the limited educational service delivery system can be enhanced in a cost-effective way
- a multidisciplinary collaborative ethic can be developed – a very important outcome, given the emphasis on creating an inclusive, caring environment, is the sense of community that can be fostered.

The effective collaborative consultant is one who demonstrates willingness to learn from others and who respects divergent points of view. This encourages others to do the same. Unless a willingness to learn from others is present, reciprocity, an essential feature of collaborative consultation, will not develop.

An example of collaborative consultation

The following example provides a description of the stages involved in the collaborative consultation process. This example uses the more traditional view of collaborative consultation in which a special education teacher and a classroom teacher work together. Later in the chapter an example will be provided in which a group of teachers work collaboratively in order to solve a problem using a model known as action research.

Although the number and names of the stages outlined in models of collaborative consultation vary slightly, commonly acknowledged stages are those suggested by West and Idol (1990), which are used in this example.

Goal setting

Initially the roles, objectives, responsibilities and expectations of team members must be negotiated.

Example

A secondary science teacher, concerned about a student with learning difficulties in the classroom, approaches the Support Teacher Learning Difficulties (STLD) for assistance. The science teacher's concern is that the student intends to pursue a career after school which requires that he pass science in order to be eligible, but at the present time he is experiencing difficulties which may result in his failing science examinations at the end of the year, despite the amount of effort the student is obviously putting in. The class teacher is unsure what to do to help. The STLD is familiar with remedial techniques but is unfamiliar with the secondary science curriculum. They decide to work together, with the class teacher providing information on content and the STLD providing individual assistance to the student and recommending classroom strategies. The student and the student's parents will also be included in the process.

Problem identification

The nature of the presenting problems must be clearly defined. This may involve some form of assessment or collection of data.

The STLD arranges to interview the student and to observe him in the classroom on several occasions in order to find out what the problem is. From this assessment it appears that the major problems result from the student's poor reading ability, which results in him having difficulty with new vocabulary, and with reading the written material provided (including working from a text). In class he is slow to take notes, missing a lot of information, and in addition what he does write is often poorly written and almost impossible to read, making later study very difficult.

Exploration of intervention options

Potential interventions are generated and the effects of each are predicted. Brainstorming is a useful device at this stage.

Together the STLD, class teacher, parents and student decide that the class teacher will provide the STLD with lesson content in advance so that the STLD has an opportunity to grasp the subject-specific information and so that new vocabulary and content can then be discussed with the student. The STLD also undertakes to simplify written material and instructions initially, with the class teacher taking over in time. Specific classroom considerations, such as pacing, using a variety of materials and presentation modes and utilising peer cooperative learning strategies, are discussed with the STLD agreeing to work in a team-teaching situation in the classroom. It is recognised that other students in the class will benefit from these changes. Homework will be adjusted. Plans are made to organise special consideration at the time of the examinations (such as additional reading time).

Implementation of intervention

Implementation occurs according to the objectives and procedures that have been decided on.

The intervention is introduced with the STLD and class teacher meeting at the beginning of each week to discuss content for the week and progress made. The STLD joins classes indicated by the class teacher in order to assist in organising the class into groups and provide support in a team-teaching role.

Evaluation

The success of the intervention strategies is evaluated.

The STLD, class teacher, student and parents agree that there has been progress made. The student is managing in the classroom and is able to study using the notes provided. He has passed a recent class test.

Program review and evaluation

At this stage the intervention is continued, redesigned or discontinued on the basis of the evaluation.

In the example provided, it appears that little further assistance will be required. The STLD and class teacher may agree to meet at a later date for a final review, with the provision for an earlier meeting if any problems are experienced. The student and family have access to either staff member if required.

Types of service provision and collaborative consultation

The roles of the specialist teacher engaged in collaborative consultation and the service delivery structures decided upon will vary according to the strengths and needs of the teacher and school and those of the student. Collaborative programs should be dynamic, changing as needs change. The intended outcome of collaborative approaches to service provision is to better accommodate the diverse needs of students, but the means of achieving this may vary. It must be emphasised that while the focus here is on collaborative consultation between special educators and regular teachers, collaborative consultation is an effective means of developing partnerships between all stakeholders, including other school personnel, families and other professionals.

Current research points to three collaborative models of teaching:

- consultant model, in which the special educator serves as a consultant to the regular teacher in areas such as curriculum adaptation, remediation of skills and modification of assessment
- coaching model, in which the special and regular educator take turns coaching each other in areas of curriculum and pedagogy in which they have acknowledged expertise
- learning or collaborative model, in which both share equitable tasks of lesson planning, implementation, and assessment (Austin, 2001).

A growing body of research supports the latter teaming or collaborative model as most effective (for example, Boudah, Schumacher & Deschler, 1997; King-Sears, 1995; Villa, Thousand & Chapple, 1996).

Service delivery provided by the various models may be direct, indirect, or a combination. Some examples of the ways in which special and regular educators work together follow. However, it must be kept in mind that collaborative consultation is frequently blended with other approaches, or adapted to suit particular contexts or needs, and that approaches are not limited to those described in the following.

The two most common ways in which special educators provide support to students are through direct or indirect delivery. Direct services may include pullout programs, specialised learning groups, or co-teaching. Direct service delivery refers to a situation in which the collaborative consultant (in this case, the special educator) designs and implements instructional interventions directly with the student. In this example, the special education teacher and the classroom teacher may have worked together to identify the needs of a student/group of students and to develop an individualised program to address those needs. The special educator may then implement the program directly with the student/s, with ongoing evaluation of progress and consultation with the regular teacher.

Small group instruction within a classroom and team teaching are direct services that emphasise inclusion, rather than the traditional pullout model. In team teaching the special educator and regular teachers work together to jointly teach students in a specific setting. This approach requires that the teachers involved work collaboratively, planning programs and sharing responsibility for implementation and ongoing monitoring.

Indirect service delivery models are those in which maximising student outcomes is achieved in a variety of ways other than that of direct instruction. Students, teachers, parents or administrators may be supported in this way, and they may then work directly with the student. For example, indirect services may include assisting the classroom teacher to individualise instruction and plan programs, monitoring student progress, evaluating program effectiveness (see Chapter 5), encouraging appropriate behaviours (see Chapter 6), adapting instructions and materials (see Chapter 4), and utilising appropriate assessment procedures, including curriculum-based assessment (see Chapter 5). Following the collaborative problem-solving process, the classroom teacher may implement the program.

Indirect service provision may involve participation in decision-making or intervention teams, staff development, assisting parents and families, or coordinating services between school and community or the school and other agencies. Through collaborative consultation, assistance in designing and implementing peer tutoring programs or remedial reading programs utilising parent and community volunteers may be provided. Working with families (on an individual basis or through such means as family support groups or parent education programs) and coordinating services between school and community may be a key component.

In the following description of the role of an Integration Support Teacher in NSW, it can be seen that both indirect and direct service delivery are essential in this itinerant model, although indirect service delivery forms the basis of the role.

Box 10.3
Integration Support Teacher (IST)

This is a permanent position supporting students, teachers, schools and families. It is a consultancy and resource role, with one position to approximately 200 students kindergarten to Year 12, who receive state funding for disability support. The funding supports students who have moderate to high special needs in the regular classroom.

The fundamental principles of the role include the following:

- A collaborative and consultative approach is essential with families, teachers and other professionals working together as a team.
- A whole school commitment is essential to meet the needs of students with disabilities enrolled in regular classes.
- The prime responsibility for meeting the educational needs of all students lies with the school, and the IST works within this framework, advising, supporting and providing resources.

The support cycle for a student with special needs involves an appraisal by the learning support team within the school. If the needs are high and more than school resources can manage, the team may apply for state funding if the student fits the eligibility criteria. Criteria vary from year to year, but state funds are usually allocated for the school year, with longer term funding provided in some instances.

The IST is usually involved from the time when funding is granted, but sometimes may assist with the initial appraisal and programming, working collaboratively with the class teacher. Advice is given for programming, facilitating communication, developing social skills and all areas where the student may be having difficulties. The IST is based at a local school in most cases, and is one of the few services to have phone referral. This is because teachers often need a visit quickly and need support to be fast and practical.

The priority for term 1 is usually students in transition to kindergarten and high school. Programming is also greatly in demand in the first half of the year. Resourcing with information and practical materials is a constant request. In terms 2 and 3 the IST attends the official review meeting for the student and this forms a reappraisal of progress and need. Term 4 is a time to visit preschools and early intervention as part of the transition support team for the next year.

In addition, the IST may conduct training and development for groups of teachers and

>

Box 10.3 continued

works closely with the local Educational Support Centre and Regional Officers. The IST also works with teacher aides where this is needed, to advance understanding and skills. The IST liaises with parents and caregivers, particularly at transition times and during review meetings. It is a rewarding but demanding role where the IST is constantly on the road and will visit several schools each day.

The IST will usually have a post-graduate degree in special education, and experience teaching students with special educational needs as well as experience in mainstream teaching. Communication skills and the ability to work collaboratively as a team member are essential.

Elva Fitzgibbon, IST, NSW

The provision of support to students, families or other personnel is not limited to the special educator, of course. Regular classroom teachers may provide a direct service to other teachers through sharing techniques or knowledge, or they may provide an indirect service resulting from solutions at the school level (for example, curriculum modifications, school reorganisation, subject committees, mentoring). Collaborative consultation may result in a number of teachers engaging in a problem-solving process and sharing responsibility for developing and implementing solutions, thus providing a direct service to students.

For example, a school staff may recognise that they need to incorporate technology to flexibly scaffold learners as they are engaged in activities such as acquiring information, conceptualising and solving problems, communicating ideas and so on. They may recognise that for many students with disabilities, effective use of technology can improve achievement and self-esteem, provide motivation, empower students by enabling them to accomplish things that otherwise would not be possible, and free up teacher time, particularly on an individual basis. However, many staff may also realise that their current use of technology is largely limited to providing practice and developing automaticity of skills using computer software, primarily because they lack the knowledge and skills required. Teachers who have expertise in this area may then work with less proficient teachers, sharing knowledge and skills. Such an approach provides a direct service to the less proficient teachers, and an indirect service to the students.

Numerous examples are now available that detail ways in which schools across a variety of levels have implemented a formal collaborative consultation process (for example, Holmes, 1992; Lipschultz & Wood, 1989; Serge, 1990). Queensland, as part of the Projects of National Significance, established collegial groups in which professionals meet regularly in order to provide mutual support through the sharing of ideas and knowledge, respect, advice and experience. There is increasing recognition of the advantages of partnerships among prior to school settings, K–12 schools, tertiary institutions and other stakeholders which promote an interrelated application of theory, exemplary practice, continual inquiry and reflection (Vaidya & Zaslavsky, 2000).

Before proceeding, it is pertinent to note the difference between inservicing and staff development. Inservicing is usually a single event or short series of sessions on a topic of educational interest or need relevant to the school. It is usually provided by someone regarded as an expert, with goals of awareness and information. Inservicing may be one component of staff development.

Staff development, on the other hand, is a process of long-term commitment to professional growth across a broad range of school goals. It should involve most or all personnel. Goals are directed toward involvement, commitment and renewal. School personnel determine their own needs, develop steps to address those needs and evaluate their professional growth. Because the process is relevant at the local level there is greater ownership of the process and commitment to it. Collaborative consultation is an effective means of promoting staff development.

Previously in this chapter, change and innovation in schools was discussed in some depth, the role of teachers as agents of change was examined, and collaborative consultation was introduced as an effective means of promoting partnerships between stakeholders and providing staff development, all of which are essential in effective schools. One specific example of how change and staff development can be promoted through collaboration is that of action research.

Action research

Action research is a powerful form of staff development in which the focus of inquiry is the participant's own practice. By definition, action research is founded on a commitment to improvement through critical reflection and inquiry (Archer, Holly & Kasten, 2001). Fullen, Bennett and Rolheiser-Bennett (1990) argue that unless schools are places for teachers to learn, they cannot be places for students to learn. Through action research, participants may both develop professionally and bring about change.

Grundy (1995) describes action research as having two principal aims: improvement and involvement. *Improvement* targets three areas: improvement in practices; improvement in the situation in which practice is occurring; and improvement in understanding both the practice and the situation. The focus of *involvement* is on involving the practitioners, that is, those who are involved in the inquiry (Grundy, 1995). For this reason, action research has often been referred to as participatory research or participatory action research (Wadsworth, 1998).

Action research is a process of change that recognises that teaching and learning take place between and among people; therefore the emphasis is on collaboration. While it is not possible to present a comprehensive description of action research here (readers are directed to Altrichter, Posch & Somekh, 1998; Archer, Holly & Kasten, 2001; Grundy, 1995; Hopkins, 1993; Kincheloe, 1991; McNiff, Lomax & Whitehead, 1996; and Noffke & Stevenson, 1995), a brief outline follows.

Action research is a process of inquiry into and reflection about a specific aspect or need at a particular site. Action research begins with a plan resulting from a specific need. Grundy (1995) refers to the elements of the action research process as *reconnaissance*, *planning*, *acting*, *collecting evidence* and *reflecting*. An example follows that should help to illustrate and explain this process.

A school staff may be concerned about the amount of bullying occurring in the school, a considerable amount of which is directed towards several mainstreamed students who have a mild intellectual disability. Parents of these and other students in the school have indicated their concern to the principal following incidents in the playground and on the school buses. The staff may initially engage in *reconnaissance* of the situation, taking mental note of when the bullying occurs, by whom, where and so on. The staff may then *plan* what further information is needed, how they can go about getting the information (for example, through interviews with students and parents, written records of all instances of bullying) and what action to take. *Actions* may include arranging a staff development day, revising the school's discipline policy in terms of providing rewards for appropriate behaviour as well as sanctions for inappropriate behaviour, introducing social skills programs in all classes and developing further opportunities for collaborative learning. Students may be enlisted to become active participants, sharing their concerns and solutions that they believe will help.

At this stage further *evidence* will be required. It cannot be assumed, because an action has been planned and implemented, that the desired outcome has been achieved. For example, it may be that there has been a decrease in the amount of bullying occurring, but there may still be a sufficient number of incidents occurring to warrant concern. On *reflection* it may be evident that only some of the causes of the bullying have been addressed. While there has been a positive response to the reward system and teaching of social skills, and effective cooperative learning has developed, and the students with an intellectual disability are no longer being targeted specifically by others, it may be that a problem still exists because the playground is small and students are competing for space and limited equipment. The teachers and students may decide to arrange some structured activities at recess and lunch, while providing additional equipment for handball and similar games. It would then be necessary to act on this plan, to observe and reflect on the outcome, make further changes and so on.

Questions are frequently asked in schools that lend themselves to action research. Questions such as:

- What are the reading results in Years 3 and 5 (or Year 7) this year? Is this an improvement when compared to previous results? Why/why not? How can we improve further?
- How do the reading competencies of boys compare to those of girls in the secondary school? If different, why? What should or can be done?
- How can we differentiate instruction for students with diverse additional needs within each key learning area (KLA)? How can we integrate effective practices and cater for individual student needs across KLAs?
- Why are truancy rates increasing at this school? Which year levels have the highest rates? What can be done to encourage students to remain at school and to decrease truancy rates?

Some readers may question whether action research is any different from what teachers do all the time anyway. Perhaps the distinction becomes clearer when it is recognised that action research is a more purposeful, planned activity in which participants work collaboratively in order to find a solution to a particular problem. As Wadsworth (1998) says, if we are to distinguish this cycle from what we do all the time, the major distinctions are in degree rather than in kind. In action research, we are more conscious of problematising an existing problem or practice; more explicit about naming the problem; more planned and deliberate about commencing an inquiry with involved others; more systematic and rigorous in our efforts to get answers; more careful in documenting and recording action; more detailed and comprehensive in our study; more sceptical in questioning our hunches; we attempt to develop deeper understandings and more powerful and useful theory about the matters being investigated; and we change our actions in the light of the research process and findings (Wadsworth, 1998). This process is cyclical, not linear, as the results and evaluation throughout guide the ongoing process.

Action research involves both research *and* action. Too often situations occur in which a need is identified, and action is implemented, and then no inquiry (research) is pursued and evaluation does not occur. The notion of having 'critical eyes' available in order to interpret and evaluate outcomes is essential (Grundy, 1995).

Action research requires a high level of commitment from those involved. They must be committed not only to the work involved, but also to valuing the opinions of all others, and to allowing for and valuing diversity among participants. There must be an expectation that not everyone will agree on all actions, that debates may be frequent, and that not all outcomes may be positive. From such discussion, debate and reflective evaluation, comes real change – not for the sake of change, but as an improvement in the current practice.

Action research provides an opportunity for the staff to develop professionally through working collegially and purposefully to improve their practices. Action research provides an opportunity for the development of collaborative partnerships at the classroom, school, district, state or national level. A special edition of the *Australian Journal of Teacher Education* (1994) contains a series of articles about the National Schools Project, providing excellent examples of action research. In these examples, teachers, in partnership with outside researchers, investigate their work and develop, implement and evaluate initiatives designed to enhance learning outcomes for students. Principals, executive teachers, experienced and novice teachers, students and families are all involved in the decision-making.

Readers who wish to further explore the use of an action research approach relevant at state, school and classroom levels are referred to the following. Little and Houston (2003) describe a conceptual framework and specific implementation activities that the state of Florida has used to ensure that quality research-based instructional practices are implemented in schools and classrooms. This model uses a reconceptualised professional development model. An example of the use of a participatory action research approach to family–school intervention is described by Ho (2002). In this case study participatory action research was utilised in the development of a family–school partnership program in an ethnically and linguistically diverse elementary school.

As can be seen in the specific examples referred to here, action research provides an opportunity for school staffs to work collegially and collaboratively with a specific goal in mind to improve their practice. The emphasis today is on schools that can be described as a community of learners, places where teachers and students alike are involved as active learners in matters that are of importance to them and where everybody encourages the learning of others (Barth, 1990). In such schools, teachers, students, parents, administrators and the community share the opportunities and responsibilities for school improvement. Through the development of effective partnerships, schools can move towards creating a caring and inclusive environment for all within.

Summary

The movement towards inclusion requires a coordinated effort from all those involved, and can require many changes and innovations on both an individual and systems level. Throughout this chapter, the need for all teachers to share instructional expertise and to collaborate to design and implement the most effective instructional programs to assist all students in achieving their maximum potential was emphasised.

To begin with, the meaning of change and the implications involved in order for schools to be truly effective were discussed. Barriers to change were examined, and some means of overcoming these barriers were identified. The role of effective change facilitators was defined and the characteristics and essential skills required (which are the same characteristics and skills required for effective collaborative consultation) were described. Throughout it was emphasised that change is a process, not an event, and teachers are essential change facilitators.

Collaborative consultation was described as an effective means of facilitating change in classrooms and schools, and of supporting students, teachers and families. The importance of collaborative consultation in fostering partnerships and promoting inclusive school environments by instituting collaborative practices as a standard in instructional design and delivery was discussed. More specifically, collaborative consultation was defined and the goals were outlined. The stages in the collaborative consultation process were described using a specific example.

Action research was introduced as an effective means of improving professional practice through purposeful and planned reflection. A short description of a piece of action research was included as an example of a change process brought about through collaborative inquiry. Several case studies, which demonstrate the use of collaborative consultation in supporting students, teachers and families, were included.

In the next chapter, the range of human and other resources available to teachers of students with disabilities in inclusive settings is explored. The chapter includes a number of specific examples of the roles of specialist personnel, and from these descriptions the importance of collaborative consultation and teamwork is evident.

Discussion questions

1   Describe what you believe a caring, inclusive school to be.

2   From your experience in schools, list practices that act against an inclusive school environment. Now suggest some changes that could be made to improve these practices.

3   List the concerns that you feel a regular classroom teacher may have in the following situations.

   a   A new student who has Asperger syndrome has been enrolled at the school. The student will be joining the class after the school holidays.

   b   It has been decided that graphic organisers are to be trialled to plan and implement learning experiences for students. All staff teaching students in Year 3–6 and 7–10 are expected to demonstrate that they have used lesson organisers in planning their lessons and instructing students in at least one KLA.

   c   The STLD has suggested that he work with a group of students experiencing difficulty in maths (or another relevant curriculum area) in the classroom during maths lessons/periods. Previously he had withdrawn the students from the classroom for intensive remedial instruction.

   d   A new program, which involves training community members, including parents, as reading tutors so that they can assist in classroom reading programs, has been introduced by the school learning support team. On completion of training, they will assist in the classroom on a regular basis.

e   A school catering for students with high support needs has approached staff of the local primary and high schools for support in establishing a 'buddy schools' program. The program involves class groups from the special school being matched up with class groups from the primary or high school, and participation in a number of inter-school visits and community activities.

f   A class teacher has been asked to plan and implement a transition program for a student in their class who has special educational needs and who will be either entering kindergarten, or entering high school, or moving to a post-school environment, the following year.

Individual activities

1   Suggest some ways in which collaborative consultation could be utilised to address the concerns you have identified in Discussion question 3 above.

a   Compare your responses to those of others. Were they similar or different? Why?

b   Do you think the responses would differ for early childhood, primary or secondary age children/schools? Justify your answer.

2   Think about a situation you have recently been involved in with other people which resulted in you changing your beliefs and/or practices (you are likely to be able to recall many such situations from your practicum experiences).

a   Write a brief description of what happened.

b   Identify the major changes that occurred.

c   Consider why your beliefs and/or practices changed. Were there barriers that had to be overcome, and if so, what were they? What brought about the change?

d   Identify the change agent(s) involved in this situation. List the characteristics of the change agent(s) involved which influenced you to make these changes.

e   If you were given the task of being a change agent to bring about similar change in a peer or colleague (or you wish to convince others of what you have learned), how would you go about it? From your experience in this situation, are there ways in which you could be more effective?

3   List the characteristics of collaborative consultation. Now list the characteristics of a traditional model of consultation (a good example would be when you visit your doctor). What are the advantages and disadvantages of each?

4   A child with special educational needs has recently been enrolled in the school and will join your class after the holidays. You have met the parents. They are supportive and keen to be involved. A teacher aide has been appointed to assist part-time. You would like to employ a collaborative approach, and to establish a support team comprising the child, the family, the teacher aide, the STLD and yourself.

a   Describe how you would go about establishing the team. What factors would you need to consider in planning? What organisational arrangements would you need to consider?

b   Consider the process outlined in the example of collaborative consultation provided in the chapter and how it would apply in your situation. How could you ensure that the essential elements of collaborative consultation (such as voluntary involvement, equality and parity among participants, shared expertise, and so on) are maintained during this process?

5   Imagine you are a newly qualified teacher who has just been appointed to a preschool/primary school or high school (select the site most relevant to you). You have been told that you will have several students with reading difficulties and a student with a moderate intellectual disability in your class. As this is your first teaching position, and the first time you will have taught several students with differing special educational needs in a regular classroom, you may feel a little apprehensive, although you are willing to give it a go. List the concerns you would have. (Now go to Group activities, question 2.)

Group activities

1   Develop several role plays with another person or a small group. Assign roles to each member (for example, class teacher, special education teacher, parent, student, principal). Role play both a positive and negative consultation experience.

2   You are the newly qualified teacher identified in Individual activities, question 5. Share your concerns with the group.
   a   Have similar concerns been identified by others?
   b   What is the nature of these concerns? (For example, lack of expertise/knowledge, lack of resources, anxiety about parental reactions.)
   c   Discuss how these concerns could be addressed. What would effective collaborative teaching have to offer you, both personally and professionally, in this situation?

3   Identify some situations relevant to the inclusion of students with diverse needs in schools that you are aware of which would present opportunities for action research. Select one of these (group consensus) and make up a hypothetical case study. Refer to the example provided in the chapter for further guidance.
   a   Briefly describe the situation.
   b   Identify how you (group) would undertake reconnaissance, planning, acting, collecting evidence and reflecting.

4   Even if the problem is not resolved in the action research you have described in question 3, identify ways in which the process undertaken may have:
   a   contributed to the personal development or professional practice of participating members
   b   contributed to the development of a more effective school.

5   Swap hypothetical case studies (description of situation only, part (a) in question 3 above) with another group. Identify how you would undertake *reconnaissance, planning, acting, collecting evidence* and *reflecting*. Compare your plan with that of the author group. Are they similar or different? In your opinion, is one plan more likely to be successful than the other or could both be successful? Why/why not?

References

Altrichter, H., Posch, P. & Somekh, B. (1998). *Teachers Investigate Their Work*. London, U.K.: Routledge.

Archer, J. M., Holly, M. L. & Kasten, W. C. (2001). *Action Research for Teachers*. Upper Saddle River, N. J.: Merrill/Prentice Hall.

Austin, V. L. (2001). Teachers' beliefs about co-teaching. *Remedial and Special Education, 22*(4), 245–55.

Australian Journal of Teacher Education, (1994). *Special Issue: The National Schools Project and School Restructuring, 19*(1).

Barth, R. S. (1990). *Improving Schools From Within: Teachers, Parents and Principals Can Make a Difference*. San Francisco: Jossey-Bass.

Bennett, T., Deluca, D. & Bruns, D. (1997). Putting inclusion into practice: Perspectives of teachers and parents. *Exceptional Children, 64*(1), 115–31.

Bernauer, J. (2002). *Five Keys to Unlock Continuous School Improvement*. Kappa Delta Pi Record, *38*(2), 89–92.

Boudah, D. J., Schumacher, J. B. & Deschler, D. D. (1997). Collaborative instruction: Is it an effective option for inclusion in secondary classrooms? *Learning Disability Quarterly, 20*, 293–316.

Brotherson, M. J., Sheriff, G., Milburn, P. & Schertz, M. (2001). Elementary school principals and their needs and issues for inclusive early childhood programs. *Topics in Early Childhood Special Education, 21*(1), 31–45.

Butcher, J. (1998). Making a difference through effective educational alliances. Online: http://www.swin.edu.au/aare/98pap/but98364.html

Cannon, G. (1992). Educating students with mild handicaps in general classrooms: Essential teaching practices for general and special educators. *Journal of Learning Disabilities, 25*(5), 300–17.

Clark, C., Dyson, A., Milward, A. & Robson, S. (1999). Theories of inclusion, theories of schools: Deconstructing and reconstructing the 'inclusive school'. *British Educational Research Journal, 25*(2), 157–77.

Cornwell, J. R. & Korteland, C. (1997). The family as a system and a context for early intervention. In S. K. Thurman, J. R. Cornwell & S. Ridenor Gottwald (Eds), *Contexts of Early Intervention: Systems and Settings*. (pp. 93–110). Baltimore: Paul H. Brookes Pub. Co.

Daane, C. J., Beirne-Smith, M. & Latham, D. (2000). Administrators' and teachers' perceptions of the collaborative efforts of inclusion in elementary grades. *Education, 121*(2), 331–8.

De Bettencourt, L. U. (1999). General educators' attitudes toward students with mild disabilities and their use of instructional strategies: Implications for training. *Remedial and Special Education, 20*(1), 27–35.

*Dettmer, P., Thurston, L. P. & Dyck, N. (1999). *Consultation Collaboration and Teamwork for Students With Special Needs* (3rd edn). Massachusetts: Allyn & Bacon.

Dinnebeil, L. A., Hale, L. & Rule, S. (1999). Early intervention program practices that support collaboration. *Topics in Early Childhood Education, 19*(4), 225–35.

Friend, M. & Cook, L. (1996). *Interactions: Collaboration Skills for School Professionals* (2nd edn). White Plains, N.Y.: Longman.

Fullan, M., Bennet, B. & Rolheiser-Bennett, C. (1990). Linking classroom and school improvement. *Educational Leadership, 47*(8), 13–19.

Fullan, M. G. (1996). Turning systemic thinking on its head. *Phi Delta Kappan, 77*, 420–3.

Fullan, M. G. & Miles, M. B. (1992). Getting reform right: What works and what doesn't. *Phi Delta Kappan, 73*, 774–52.

Greenwood, C. & Abbott, M. (2001). The research to practice gap in special education. *Teacher Education and Special Education, 24*, 276–89.

Grove, K. A. & Fisher, D. (1999). Entrepreneurs of meaning: Parents and the process of inclusive education. *Remedial and Special Education, 20*(4), 208–15.

*Grundy, S. (1995). *Action Research as Professional Development*. Occasional Paper No 1. Innovative Links between Universities and Schools for Teacher Professional Development: A National Professional Development Project.

*Hall, G. E. & Hord, S. M. (1987). *Change in Schools: Facilitating the Process*. Albany: State University of New York Press.

Harris, K. C. & Zetlin, A. G. (1993). Exploring the collaborative ethic in an urban school: A case study. *Journal of Educational and Psychological Consultation, 4*, 305–17.

Ho, B. S. (2002). Application of participatory action research to family school intervention. *School Psychology Review, 31*(1), 106–21.

Hobbs, T. & Westling, D. L. (2002). Mentoring for inclusion: A model class for special and general educators. *The Teacher Educator, 37*(3), 186–200.

Holmes, G. (1992). Co-operative staff teams. *The Practising Administrator, 14*, 2.

Hopkins, D. (1993). *A Teacher's Guide to Classroom Research* (2nd edn). Buckingham: Open University Press.

Hughes, P. & MacNaughton, G. (1999). Who's the expert: Reconceptualising parent-staff relations in early childhood education. *Australian Journal of Early Childhood, 24*(4), 27–32.

*Idol, L., Paolucci-Whitcomb, P. & Nevin, A. (1986). *Collaborative Consultation*. Maryland: Aspen Publishers Inc.

Janney, R. E., Snell, M. E., Beers, M. K. & Raynes, M. (1995). Integrating students with moderate and severe disabilities into general education classrooms. *Exceptional Children, 61*, 425–39.

Johnson, L. J., Pugach, M. C. & Hammittee, D. J. (1988). Barriers to effective special education consultation. *Remedial and Special Education, 9*(6), 41–7.

Jordan, A. (1994). *Skills in Collaborative Classroom Consultation*. London: Routledge.

Kilgo, J. L., Johnson, L., LaMontague, M., Stayton, V., Cook, M. & Cooper, C. (1999). Importance of practices: A national study of general and special early childhood educators. *Journal of Early Intervention, 22*(4), 294–305.

Kincheloe, J. L. (1991). *Teachers as Researchers: Qualitative Inquiry as a Path to Empowerment*. New York: The Falmer Press.

King-Sears, M. E. (1995). Teamwork toward inclusion: A school system and university partnership for practicing educators. *Action in Teacher Education, 17*, 148–58.

Lipschultz, P. & Wood, S. (1989). Cooperative planning: A staff initiative. *Research Forum, 5*.

Little, M. E. & Houston, D. (2003). Research into practice through professional development. *Remedial and Special Education, 24*(2), 75–87.

Mamlin, N. (1999). Despite best intentions: When inclusion fails. *The Journal of Special Education, 33*(1), 36–49.

*McNiff, J., Lomax, P. & Whitehead, J. (1996). *You and Your Action Research Project*. London: Routledge.

Miles, M. B., Saxi, E. R. & Liberman, A. (1988). What skills do education 'change agents' need? An empirical view. *Curriculum Inquiry, 18*(2), 157–93.

Noffke, S. E. & Stevenson, R. B. (Ed.) (1995). *Educational Action Research*. New York: Teachers College Press.

Owens, R. G. (1998). *Organisational Behaviour in Education* (6th edn). Boston: Allyn & Bacon.

Ridden, P. (1991). *Managing Change in Schools*. Gosford, Australia: Ashton Scholastic.

Saint-Laurent, L., Dionne, J., Giasson, J., Royer, E., Simard, C. & Pierard, B. (1998). Academic achievement effects of an in-class service model on students with and without disabilities. *Exceptional Children, 64*(2), 239–53.

Salend, S. J. (1998). *Effective Mainstreaming: Creating Inclusive Classrooms*. Upper Saddle River, N. J.: Prentice Hall.

*Sapon-Shevin, M. (1990). Initial steps for developing a caring school. In W. Stainback & S. Stainback (Eds), *Support Networks for Inclusive Schooling: Independent Integrated Education* (pp. 241–48). Baltimore: Paul H. Brookes Pub. Co.

Serge, P. M., (1990). *The Fifth Discipline*. Doubleday Currency: New York.

Sobel, D. M. & Vaughn, N. S. (1999). Here comes the SUN team! Collaborative inclusion at work. *Teaching Exceptional Children, 32*(2), 4–12.

Sprague, M. M. & Pennell, D. P. (2000). The power of partners: Preparing preservice teachers for inclusion. *The Clearing House, 73*(1), 168–70.

Stanovich, U. J. (1999). Conversations about inclusion. *Teaching Exceptional Children, 31*(6), 54–9.

Stoll, L. & Fink, D. (1996). *Changing Our Schools. Linking School Effectiveness and School Improvement*. Philadelphia: Open Uni Press.

Tichenor, M. S., Heins, B. & Piechura-Couture, K. (2000). Parent perceptions of a co-taught inclusive classroom. *Education, 120*(3), 569–74, 546.

*Tiegerman-Farber, E. & Radziewicz, C. (1998). *Collaborative Decision Making: The Pathway to Inclusion*. Upper Saddle River, N. J.: Prentice Hall.

Vaidya, S. R. & Zaslavsky, H. N. (2000). Teacher education reform effort for inclusion classrooms: Knowledge versus pedagogy. *Education, 121*(1), 145–52.

Vaughn, S., Schumm, J. & Brick, J. (1998). Using a rating scale to design and evaluate inclusion programs. *Teaching Exceptional Children, 30*(4), 41–5.

Villa, R. A., Thousand, J. S., Paolucci-Whitcomb, P. & Nevin, A. (1990). In search of new paradigms for collaborative consultation. *Journal of Educational and Psychological Consultation, 1*(4), 279–92.

Villa, R. A., Thousand, J. S. & Chapple, J. W. (1996). Preparing teachers to support inclusion: Preservice and inservice programs. *Theory Into Practice, 35*, 42–50.

*Wadsworth, Y. (1998). What is participatory action research? Action Research International, Paper 2. Available online: http://www.scu.edu.au/schools/sawd/ari/ari-wadsworth.html

Weiner, H. M. (2003). Effective inclusion: Professional development in the context of the classroom. *Teaching Exceptional Children, 35*(6), 12–18.

West, J. F. & Cannon, G. S. (1988). Essential collaborative consultation competencies for regular and special educators. *Journal of Learning Disabilities, 21*(1), 56–63, 28.

West, J. F. & Idol, L. (1990). Collaborative consultation in the education of mildly handicapped and at-risk students. *Remedial and Special Education, 11*(1), 22–31.

West, J. F., Idol, L. & Cannon, G. (1987). *A Curriculum for Preservice and Inservice Preparation of Classroom Teachers in Collaborative Consultation*. Austin: University of Texas.

Whitaker, P. (1993). *Managing Change in Schools*. Buckingham: Open University Press.

Wideen, M. F. & Grimmet, P. P. (Eds) (1995). *Changing Times in Teacher Education*. London: The Falmer Press.

———

*Recommended reading for this chapter

Further recommended reading

Aiello, J. & Bullock, L. M. (1999). Building commitment to responsible inclusion. *Preventing School Failure, 43*(3), 99–102.

Arthur, M. (1996). The teacher as researcher in classroom and behaviour management. In Gordon, C., Arthur, M. & Butterfield, N. *Promoting Positive Behaviour: An Australian Guide to Classroom Management* (pp. 195–206). Melbourne: Thomas Nelson.

Bauwens, J., Hourcade, J. J. & Friend, M. (1989). Cooperative teaching: A model for general and special education integration. *Remedial and Special Education, 10*(2), 17–22.

Bell, J. W. & Patterson, A. (1998). *Research in Education: Does it Count?* Australian Association for Research in Education Conference, Adelaide S.A., 29 November–3 December.

Bolton, R. (1987). *People Skills*. Australia: Simon & Schuster.

Brady, L. (1996). Incorporating curriculum outcomes into teaching practice. *Curriculum Perspectives, 16*(3), 25–33.

Bricker, D. (2000). Inclusion: How the scene has changed. *Topics in Early Childhood Special Education, 20*(1), 14–19.

Butterfield, N. & Arthur, M. (1994). Addressing teacher needs and concerns in communication interventions for students with an intellectual disability. *International Journal of Disability, Development and Education, 41*(3), 201–12.

Campbell, M. (1998). *Every Day a 'Field Day': Research as a Facet of Teaching Life*. Australian Association for Research in Education Conference, Adelaide S.A., 29 November–3 December.

Carroll, D. (2001). Considering paraeducator training, roles and responsibilities. *Teaching Exceptional Children, 34*(2), 60–4.

Carter, M., Cassar, M., Dule, K., Korner, H., Weise, M. & Williams, J. (1995). A collaborative team approach to the education of students with high support needs. *Special Education Perspectives, 4*(1), 37–45.

Davis, L. & Kemp, C. (1995). A collaborative consultation service delivery model for support teachers. *Special Education perspectives, 4*(1), 17–28.

Elliot, J. (1991). *Action Research for Educational Change*. Milton Keynes: Open University Press.

Fleming, J. L. & Monda-Amaya, L. E. (2001). Process variables critical for team effectiveness: A Delphi study of wraparound team members. *Remedial and Special Education, 22*(3), 158–71.

*Fullan, M. (1993). *Change Forces. Probing the Depths of Educational Reform*. London: The Falmer Press.

Fullan, M. G. & Stiegelbauer, S. (1991). *The New Meaning of Educational Change*. New York: Teachers College Press.

Giorcelli, L. R. (1993). Creating a counter-hegemonic school. A model for the education of children with disabilities. In *Social Justice, Equity and Dilemmas of Disability in Education*, International Working Conference Proceedings, Queensland Department of Education.

Hanko, G. (1999). *Increasing Competence Through Collaborative Problem Solving*. London: David Fulton.

Hardin, B. & Hardin, M. (2002). Into the mainstream: Practical strategies for teaching in inclusive environments. *The Clearing House, 75*(1), 175–8.

Hord, S. M., Rutherford, W. L., Huling-Austin, L. & Hall, G. E. (1987). *Taking Charge of Change*. Virginia: Association for Supervision and Curriculum Development.

Hughes, J. N. (2003). Commentary: Participatory action research leads to sustainable school and community improvement. *School Psychology Review, 32*(1), 38–43.

Johnson, S. (1993). Action research as a school-level change process. *Curriculum Perspectives, 13*, 21–8.

Langerock, N. L. (2000). A passion for action research. *Teaching Exceptional Children, 33*(2), 26–34.

Lenz, B. K. Deschler, D. D. & Kissom, B. (2004). *Teaching Content to All: Evidence-based Inclusive Practices in Middle and Secondary Schools*. Boston: Pearson.

McCormick, L., Wong, M. & Yogi, L. (2003). Individualisation in the inclusive preschool: A planning process. *Childhood Education, 79*(4), 212–16.

McDonnell, J., Mathot-Buckner, C., Thorson, N. & Fister, S. (2001). Supporting the inclusion of students with moderate and severe disabilities in junior high school general education classes: The effects of classwide peer tutoring, multi-element curriculum, and accommodations. *Education and Treatment of Children, 24*(2), 141–60.

Monkhouse, T. & Henri, J. (1990). *Facilitating Change in Schools: Defining the Constants*. Orana, 26(3), 139–45.

Mostert, M. P. (1998). *Interpersonal Collaboration in Schools*. Needham Hts, Mass: Allyn & Bacon.

Newton, C. & Tarrant, T. (1992). *Managing Change in Schools. A Practical Handbook*. NY: Routledge.

Odom, S. L. (2000). Preschool inclusion: What we know and where we go from here. *Topics in Early Childhood Special Education, 20*(1), 20–33.

Owens, R. G. (1998). *Organisational Behaviour in Education* (6th edn). Boston: Allyn & Bacon.

Pellicer, L. O. & Anderson, L. W. (1995). *A Handbook for Teacher Leaders*. California: Corwin Press, Inc.

Rudduck, J. (1991). *Innovation and Change: Developing Involvement and Understanding*. Philadelphia: Open University Press.

Schoen, S. F. & Schoen, A. A. (2003). Action research in the classroom: Assisting a linguistically different learner with special needs. *Teaching Exceptional Children, 35*(3), 16–21.

Shea, T. & Bauer, A. (1991). *Parents and Teachers of Children With Exceptionalities: A Handbook for Collaboration*. Boston: Allyn & Bacon.

Smith, M. K. & Smith, K. E. (2000). 'I believe in inclusion, but …': Regular education early childhood teachers' perceptions of successful inclusion. *Journal of Research in Early Childhood Education, 14*(2), 161–80.

Tewel, K. J. (1997). *New Schools for a New Century: A Leader's Guide to High School Reform*. Florida: St Lucie Press.

Thousand, J. S. & Villa, R. A. (1990). Sharing expertise and responsibilities through teaching teams. In W. Stainback & S. Stainback (Eds), *Support Networks for Inclusive Schooling: Independent Integrated Education* (pp. 151–61). Baltimore: Paul H. Brookes Pub. Co.

Thousand, J. S., Villa, R. A. & Nevin, A. (1994). *Creativity and Collaborative Learning: A Practical Guide to Empowering Students and Teachers*. Baltimore: Paul H. Brookes Pub. Co.

Tiegerman-Farber, E. & Radziewics, C. (1998). *Collaborative Decision Making: The Pathway to Inclusion*. N. J.: Merrill.

Tindall, G., Shinn, M. R. & Rodden-Hord, K. (1990). Contextually based school consultation: Influential variables. *Exceptional Children, 56*(4), 324–36.

Turnbull, A. P. & Rutherford Turnbull III, H. (1997). *Families, Professionals and Exceptionality: A Special Partnership* (3rd edn). New Jersey: Prentice-Hall.

Turner. N. D. (2003). Preparing preservice teachers for inclusion in secondary classrooms. *Education, 123*(3), 491–5.

Walther-Thomas, C., Korinek, L. & McLaughlin, V. L. (1999). Collaboration to support students' success. *Focus on Exceptional Children, 32*(3), 1–18.

Ward, J. & Center, Y. (1999). Success and failure in inclusion: Some representative case histories. *Special Education Perspectives, 8*(1), 16–31.

Westwood., P. & Graham, L. (2000). Collaborative consultation as a component of support for students with special needs in inclusive settings: Perspectives from teachers in South Australia and New South Wales. *Special Education Perspectives, 9*(2), 13–26.

Chapter 11

Resources to support inclusion

Gordon Lyons

This chapter aims to:

- examine the range of human and other resources potentially available to support inclusion

- explain how these resources can be accessed and organised to best educational benefit

- examine the knowledge, skills and expertise about resources that all teachers need in order to plan for, implement and support successful inclusion.

Overview

The inclusion of students with additional needs in regular educational settings may increase the challenges faced by teachers, as it broadens the overall teaching and learning needs of student groups. In recognition of these increased challenges, most education authorities provide support to encourage and facilitate inclusion. The nature of this support is usually negotiated during an enrolment process that precedes placement. This negotiation is intended to ensure that all additional needs are identified, and can be met in the inclusive setting. Thorough planning and skilled implementation of appropriate individual support plans (ISPs) usually overcomes these challenges. The focus of this chapter is to identify the resources required to meet identified additional needs, and to explain how these resources can be accessed and organised to best educational benefit.

Chapters 1 and 2 explained why most students with additional needs benefit from being part of inclusive settings. Inclusive practices bring changes for teachers, students and local communities. These changes usually require additional initial effort, and often require additional resources. With thorough planning and appropriate support, inclusive settings can provide for the educational needs of most students with additional needs. The role of teachers in this planning is central. Appropriate support for the student and the school is essential. Knowing what resources are available and how they can be used is prerequisite to this planning, and consequently to successful inclusion.

This chapter examines a range of resources potentially available to support inclusion. Teaching and learning are enhanced when teachers use all available resources to support quality assessment, planning, implementation and evaluation of educational programs. A knowledge and understanding of available resources and how to access and utilise them is crucial if best practices are to be implemented, and best outcomes are to be achieved. This chapter has a very practical emphasis as it seeks to address the challenges that teachers face in their efforts to meet diverse learning needs. This chapter links to all the other chapters to provide a comprehensive approach to supporting inclusion.

The initial assessment of support needs in the enrolment of students with special needs is crucial. Some of these needs can be met through existing resources, while others will require additional resources. Some will require only initial support, whereas others will require ongoing support. This chapter seeks to develop the knowledge, skills and expertise regarding resources that all teachers need to plan for and facilitate best outcomes for all students in inclusive settings.

The first section, 'Planning for inclusion', explains common scenarios with respect to settings, transition and inclusion. Three examples of best practice in planning for inclusion are emphasised. The first is the use of a collaborative approach, centred on a school-based learning support team model. The second is comprehensive educational appraisal of educational support needs for individual students with additional needs. The third is planning for individual needs within an ecological context. An ideal inclusion scenario is suggested, wherein the importance of having the right key resources is emphasised. The second section, 'Key resources', identifies a range of potential resources to support inclusion, and suggests procedures and strategies for accessing these. The final section, 'Organising resources', brings together the first two sections in a very practical way. Six resource checklists are described and explained, assisting teachers and schools to organise resources that may support the successful inclusion of students with additional needs.

Different government systems and education authorities use different procedures and provide different resources to support inclusion. Teachers need to be familiar with the education systems within which they work. Contact information is provided at the end of this chapter.

Planning for inclusion

Introduction

This section commences with a description of six common inclusion/transition scenarios for students with additional needs. Three examples of best practice in planning for inclusion are then explained. The first best practice is the adoption of a collaborative approach to planning for inclusion, using a learning support team model. The second is appraisal of educational support needs. The third is planning for individual needs within an ecological context. Finally, an ideal inclusion/transition scenario is suggested wherein good planning, supported by the right resources, results in successful inclusion. This leads to the section on identifying and accessing these resources. Other chapters are cross-referenced for their valuable information about resources to support inclusion.

Inclusion and transition

Most children spend their early years at home, and then attend a preschool on a part-time to full-time basis. Primary school is followed by high school, then on to an adult life with part-time or full-time tertiary study and/or work. This process involves a number of stages and obvious transition periods. These changes and transitions usually occur fairly smoothly without the need for additional support or intervention.

General community acceptance of the principles of normalisation, integration and inclusion has meant that most children with additional needs are included and participate in these same transitions and life stages (Cole, 1999; Kozleski, Mainzer & Deshler, 2000). For many of these children and their families though, these changes and transitions are complex and demanding, and require additional support and resources (McRae, 1996). Children with additional needs are frequently involved in early intervention programs (Carpenter, 2002; Evans, 2002), and often participate in special programs designed to assist transition from preschool to primary to high school, and then into adult life after school (Halpern, 1993). Some parents do not want an inclusive placement and seek enrolment in a special education setting. A special education placement is a more restrictive environment, but can be the preferred placement for some students, particularly those with high support needs and challenging behaviours (Hunt & Goetz, 1997).

Common inclusive enrolment scenarios

This section describes six common inclusive enrolment scenarios for students with additional needs as they move towards adulthood.

- *Initial enrolment in an early childhood centre or preschool*
  When parents seek enrolment for their child at their local early childhood centre or preschool, a routine enrolment procedure usually occurs. Should special educational needs

be identified, an appraisal of educational support needs is conducted to supplement the regular enrolment information. Enrolment generally proceeds subject to ascertainment of any requisite resources in collaboration with the early childhood service. These are usually sourced through Commonwealth funding.

- *The first year of school*
  When parents seek enrolment for their child with additional needs in their local primary school, the school learning support team (LST) becomes involved, and an appraisal of educational support needs is conducted to supplement the regular enrolment information. Enrolment generally proceeds subject to ascertainment of any requisite resources. These resources are part of an ISP.

- *Graduation to high school*
  Enrolment for a student with additional needs in the first year of high school following attendance at a local primary school is generally considered a continuing enrolment, but is subject to a formal transition process to ensure that the student's additional needs can be met at the new school. Enrolment generally proceeds subject to assessment of any requisite resources identified as part of this transition process.

- *The new transferring student*
  When parents seek to transfer their child with additional needs to a new local primary or high school, a routine enrolment process usually occurs, followed by an appraisal of educational support needs. Enrolment generally proceeds subject to ascertainment of any requisite resources listed as part of an ISP for the student. It is usual that student records provide considerable background information for this appraisal of educational support needs. Transfers can occur at any time during the school year and can be quite challenging for all those involved.

- *The current student with 'emergent' additional needs*
  Sometimes students already enrolled in their local school may be identified as having special educational needs requiring additional support and resources. These additional needs can arise from an existing or an acquired impairment or disability. An appraisal of educational support needs is conducted and enrolment generally continues subject to ascertainment of any requisite resources listed as part of an ISP.

- *Graduation to adult education and/or the workplace*
  Transition to adult education and/or the workplace is usually subject to an extended individual transition plan over the later years of high school. Pre-employment training and preparation for more independent living are common priorities for students with additional needs and their families. Placement in an adult education or employment (training) setting is usually negotiated over the last years of high school. Appraisals of educational support needs are conducted and placement occurs subject to an extended transition/early inclusion phase as part of the transition program.

The inclusion process

Planning for inclusion means planning for transitions across settings. This planning usually takes into account three phases. The first phase, the pre-inclusion/preparation phase, focuses on the period before the child actually joins the new setting. This phase can involve preparations taking up to 18 to 24 months The second phase, the early inclusion/transition phase, focuses on the period of transition and early inclusion. This phase usually continues for around six months. This may involve part-time participation in the new setting. The third phase, the continuing inclusion/monitoring phase, involves planning for longer term or substantial inclusion. These three phases are not discrete. They 'flow' from one phase to the next to constitute the process of inclusion. It is important to emphasise that inclusion is a process – not an event or a simple point in time (Zigmond, 1997). Consequently the identification, accessing and utilisation of resources to support inclusion should be approached using these three phases as foci for analysis, as shown below:

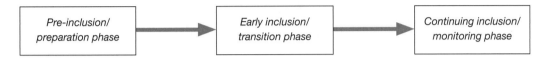

Figure 11.1 The inclusion phases

Wherever possible, the student's anticipated teachers should be involved with key others in planning for new or continuing inclusive enrolment involving the identification of necessary and additional resources as required. Current best practice in planning for the inclusion of students with additional needs emphasises the key processes of collaborative planning, appraisal of educational support needs, and individual support planning (Chalmers et al., 1998; McGregor & Vogelsberg, 1998). Brief explanations of these key processes follow.

Best practice: Collaborative planning and the LST

Collaborative consultation is an interactive and ongoing process wherein people with differing experience, knowledge and expertise work together to find solutions to mutually agreed tasks (see Chapter 10). Collaborative consultation is widely regarded as best practice when planning for the inclusion of students with additional needs (Dinnebeil & McInerney, 2001). This planning involves assessing individual support needs, and developing, implementing and evaluating ISPs. Teachers are key partners in this consultative process. The inclusion of students with special needs in local schools is a collective responsibility. The enrolment of students with special needs is an enrolment in a school, not just in a class. Class teachers do have a key role to play in ascertaining individual support needs and facilitating successful inclusion, but (new) students with additional needs, just like all students, are the responsibility of the school community as well as their parents. A 'whole school' approach, with the committed leadership of the school executive, is prerequisite to successful inclusion.

A student's additional needs differ depending upon the setting, the educational programs offered, and the people involved. Appraisals of educational support needs must be comprehensive and ongoing, with regular reviews. Education authorities have generally recognised and responded to this imperative through the establishment of the collaborative school-based LST model. LSTs function in most schools, although they may otherwise be referred to as program support groups, or student welfare, integration or inclusion committees, depending on the school system (NSW Department of Education and Training, 2003).

LSTs usually have a broad responsibility to support the learning of all students, but particularly those with learning difficulties, additional needs and disabilities. LSTs support

initiatives, programs and interventions aimed at both individuals and groups of students. The LST is a critical contributor to successful inclusion on a school-wide basis. In the case of the enrolment of a student with additional needs, a first responsibility of the LST is to conduct an appraisal of educational support needs. The LST coordinates the procurement and management of resources to support enrolment. Subsequently, on a continuing basis, the LST monitors the continuing and changing needs of this student. It is important to note that students with additional needs are not necessarily students with disabilities, and vice versa. Many students with disabilities maintain inclusive enrolments without additional resource support, as do many students with learning difficulties. At the same time, some students with learning difficulties and/or disabilities do have additional needs, and so may become eligible for additional resource support.

School LSTs have a flexible membership that depends on the focus of their support at any time. 'Core' members usually include: the school principal; the school psychologist/ counsellor; a special education/support teacher; a class teacher representative; and usually a representative from the education authority. When the team's focus is on an individual student, other members may include: key class teachers; (specialist) support teachers; teacher aides; parents; and, wherever practicable, the student. The LST's focus might otherwise be on a group of students experiencing learning difficulties who have identifiable additional needs. Membership will change accordingly.

One of the key tasks for the LST is to identify, access and coordinate a 'package' of resources to support any individual or group of students in need. The allocation and of human resources available to the LST is determined on a whole-school basis. These human resources include: other students; adult volunteers; parents; support teachers and classroom teachers; executive staff; the school psychologist/counsellor; specialist support teachers and therapists (from outside of the school); and teacher aides. The principal may authorise the LST to provide 'release days' to allow teachers to be temporarily relieved of their day-to-day teaching responsibilities. This enables them to conduct the work necessary to facilitate the team's objectives. A whole-school approach is critical to successful inclusion (Booth & Ainscow, 2002). The LST is central as it coordinates a package of resources, as part of an ISP, determined by appraisal of educational support needs.

Box 11.1

Program: Our LST

My school's LST has eight permanent members who meet fortnightly to discuss referrals from teachers and parents about students who need learning assistance. These members include executive staff, classroom teachers, the school counsellor, and specialist support staff.

It is our job to pool our knowledge and expertise to allocate the available resources to address these learning needs. We follow a flow chart for this process. Classroom teachers are expected to identify problems initially, and to seek support from their supervisors. When further assistance is required, they complete a referral form that identifies student strengths, weaknesses, prior interventions and desired outcomes. Parents are also asked to complete a form outlining developmental histories and other information to inform the LST.

Our LST uses the information provided to make recommendations about the allocation of school resources (for example, the Support Teacher Learning Assistance, Reading Recovery), district resources (for example, the Behaviour Team or Language Support Team), and to make referrals to outside agencies (for example, Health Services, Speech Pathology Services). Each referral is monitored to ensure that recommended actions are followed through.

Another role of our LST is to contribute to the development of school policy and determine priorities about learning support. At my school we always have a full agenda of referrals or reviews, and work very hard to ensure that all referrals are dealt with in a timely manner. The LST structure enables planned and prioritised action that shares resources in the most equitable manner, and builds team and school capacity to address learning needs. Smaller LSTs are established to focus on individual students, and these always include parents or carers. In these teams we share information, pass on recommendations, and discuss how parents can support their children and how school can support parents.

One example of the success of our LST was the learning support given to Craig. His teachers and mum identified that he needed a high level of literacy support if he was to make a successful transition to high school. Craig's LST – his mum, grandmother, class teacher, speech pathologist and others – met every term to plan and discuss his progress. Finding chairs and a large enough free space was difficult, but we squeezed into my office to share our progress in each of the areas identified by the speech pathologist, and to celebrate Craig's successes. Craig attended the last meeting for the year, as we recapped on our goals and achievements, and celebrated his progress.

Principal, government primary school, NSW

Best practice: Appraisal of educational support needs

Generally, all students follow the same basic process when enrolling at their local school. If special needs are identified, additional assessments are needed, with the intention of procuring adequate resources to facilitate a successful enrolment (Foreman et al., 2001). It is not possible to enrol all students in their local school, because educational authorities are not always able to meet the special educational needs of some students – particularly those with very high support needs and/or substantial additional physical access requirements (Hunt & Goetz, 1997). Nevertheless, the principle and presumption of inclusion in the least restrictive educational environment holds for all students.

As previously mentioned, a comprehensive appraisal of educational support needs is prerequisite to successful inclusion (European Agency for Development in Special Needs Education, 2000). All education authorities have policies and procedures for enrolment and for assessing individual needs. Classroom teachers may not be directly involved with formal enrolment procedures, but when potential students with known additional needs and/or disabilities require additional assessments, classroom teachers should be involved to ensure that the needs appraisal and consequent resource implications are thorough and realistic. A range of specialist personnel and organisations is available to contribute to and inform these appraisals. (See Consultancy support below.) Carriage of this assessment process is the responsibility of the school LST, not of any individual teacher. Pertinent policy and procedural documents are available from schools and education authorities.

Box 11.2

Program: Appraisal of educational support needs – a case study

Anna has autism and a moderate intellectual disability. She has very little verbal communication and her social skills need development. When she was at preschool, her mother decided that she wanted Anna to attend her local primary school. The school had not previously enrolled a student with Anna's level of support needs, and staff were unsure of how to assist her learning. The school community was, however, welcoming and accepting of Anna and her family.

District support personnel became involved when the preschool notified of the possibility of Anna attending her local school the following term. A transition plan was implemented, which included an LST forming to assess Anna's level of support needs and to then make applications for resources that might be required. This team consisted of Anna's mother, the support teacher (integration), the school's assistant principal, the preschool teacher and the school counsellor. Other personnel who were advisers to the team included the District Disabilities Program Consultant and Anna's paediatrician and therapists.

Anna had not been involved with an early intervention program and her only contact outside of home had been one day a week at preschool. A teachers' aide assisted her while she attended the preschool. The support teacher (integration) visited the preschool to observe Anna and talk with the teacher. The assistant principal also visited the preschool and spent time observing Anna.

>

Box 11.2 continued

The LST considered several options for Anna and, given her level of support needs, recommended to her mother that placement in a class for students with moderate intellectual disabilities, or in a special school be considered. These options were rejected, so the LST began planning for inclusion in kindergarten the following year.

A late application for funding support was submitted to the district office, and this resulted in the employment of a teachers' aide (special) to work in the kindergarten room. Due to the short lead time, little could be done to plan for Anna prior to her commencing kindergarten, and the results of the application for funding were not known until Anna commenced.

When Anna started kindergarten a new principal had been appointed to the school and the support teacher (integration) had taken leave, so a temporary teacher was employed. In negotiation with Anna's mother, she commenced attending for the morning only. At first it was determined that the main priority was adjusting to the new setting, and learning social skills such as sitting with the group, using the toilet and eating independently. An individual learning support plan was developed by the LST that by then consisted of the principal (who had a special education background), the class teacher, the teachers' aide (special) and support teacher (integration). Communication was the main issue for Anna, so an application to fund the purchase of a Boardmaker communication device was submitted, and a referral was made for speech therapy assistance with a support agency. The speech therapist worked in both the home and school to assist with establishing a program.

During the year some issues arose with behaviour as Anna resorted to biting, scratching and pinching to make her point. The teachers' aide (special) was bearing the brunt of this and immediate action was required. A safety assessment revealed that Anna was most vulnerable when there were changes in routine or when she was asked to move from a more desired to a less desired activity. A management plan was implemented to reduce the hazard, and modifications made to the communication program to help Anna learn to cope when there was a routine change. This was effective, and resulted in an immediate and significant reduction in incidents.

Anna is making good progress. She now attends full time, and sits with the class during group activities such as big book reading. She holds a pencil and attempts to write her name. She can recognise her name and match the names of several of her classmates. She is vocalising and has developed a small vocabulary that she uses regularly. In the playground Anna is becoming more adventurous, and although her play is still parallel, peers join her in her activities.

Anna will move on into Year 1 with support from the teachers' aide (special). She will continue to have an individual learning program that will operate within the regular classroom. Her teacher and aide will require ongoing professional development to assist Anna and this has been built into the learning support plan and budget. Her future is not known, but for now Anna is successfully learning and growing within her community.

Principal, government primary school, NSW

Best practice: An individual perspective within an ecological context

An increasing number of students with additional needs are taking their rightful place in inclusive educational settings, as a result of excellent initiatives taken by local school communities. Special needs are individual needs, so planning for inclusion must take an individual focus (Weishaar, 2001). Taking an individualised approach is widely regarded as best practice when planning for the inclusion of students with additional needs. This approach is also central to assessing individual support needs, and then developing, implementing and evaluating individual plans.

While planning for inclusion should take an individual focus, it should also occur within an ecological context. This means taking into account the broader ecology of the individual, that is, all those things that affect or are affected by the individual. Families are part of a child's ecology. In the classroom, the class teacher, other students, the learning tasks and the physical environment are all part of the individual's ecology. This approach is based on the Ecological Model of Development (Bronfenbrenner, 1979). Chapter 4 emphasises the concept of the classroom as an ecosystem, wherein the four elements of the teacher, the students, the curriculum and resources, and the physical environment interact. Chapter 5 also supports an ecological model wherein curriculum issues, instructional issues, and contextual (classroom) issues collectively impact upon effective teaching, and consequently effective learning. By extending this ecological perspective, the whole school can be viewed as an encompassing 'ecosystem' in which the additional needs of these students can be more comprehensively considered. Even further, the ecological model can take into account aspects of the school community, society in general, and other cultural influences.

This individualised approach to planning is paralleled in a number of contexts, including for example, individual transition planning, individual support planning, and individual educational planning. The ecological context is evident in the wide range of factors and issues taken into account when preparing these plans, including, for example, teacher variables, other students, family, culture, and the physical environment.

Planning for inclusion is a collaborative process and should be coordinated by a team such as an LST. At the same time, teachers are key partners in this process, and are usually primarily responsible for the design, development, implementation and evaluation of an individual education plan (IEP). An IEP is central to successful inclusion (Weishaar, 2001). Planning for individual needs within an ecological context is prerequisite and critical to successful inclusion.

An ideal inclusion scenario: Having the right resources

Imagine an ideal inclusion scenario. A family presents their child with special needs for inclusive enrolment at their local school. Following best practice, the LST adopts a collaborative approach to planning for the student's individual needs in an ecological context. An appraisal of educational support needs is conducted, and a 'package' of requisite resources is identified, accessed and organised. The transition and inclusive enrolment proceed smoothly. The student initially requires substantial support in transition. However, the student's continuing enrolment and successful inclusion are maintained with reduced but adequate and sustainable support and resources. The right package of resources for such an ideal outcome may include some of the following:

- varied and flexible 'hands-on' assistance in the classroom
- expert and timely consultancy support
- appropriate adaptation of curriculum and instructional materials
- diverse, responsive and effective teaching techniques

- facilitative and convenient assistive technology
- positive and enthusiastic student, staff and community support
- appropriate and timely physical access
- timely initial and ongoing professional development and training
- adequate 'up-front' and continuing funding support.

The above points raise a number of issues. What support, assistance and resources relate to each point? Why are they important? How can they be accessed? The next section provides more information about key resources to support inclusion. Cross-referencing with other chapters provides a comprehensive introduction to many of these resources. By drawing on the information, advice and suggestions provided in the textbook itself, and by selectively using the references and the further recommended readings provided, teachers can participate confidently in the inclusion process, and play their part in the successful inclusion of students with additional needs.

Key resources

Introduction

This section identifies a range of potential resources to support inclusion, and suggests procedures and strategies for accessing these resources. Planning for inclusion requires teachers to participate in collaborative consultation about identifying individual support needs of students, and to prepare ISPs. Consequently, teachers must be able to identify both human and other potential resources. Although both human and other key resources will differ depending on the education system and school involved, education authorities and schools generally maintain a range of resources to support inclusion.

In the classroom, where the class teacher has primary responsibility, a wide variety of human resources is available to support inclusion. These can include students, volunteers, parents, other class and support teachers, school executive staff, counsellors, consultants, therapists, and teacher aides. It is the classroom teacher's responsibility to organise these human resources to work 'as a team' (Doyle, 1997). At the school level, the LST usually coordinates these human resources. At the organisational level, consultants, specialist support teachers and other professionals are usually available. These people are usually contacted through the LST and school executive. Community groups and voluntary service organisations can also assist. Other key resources include: adapted curriculum and instructional materials; a diversity of teaching techniques; assistive technology; student, staff and community support; physical access modifications; training and professional development; and funding support. These resources variously complement and supplement the above mentioned human resources.

'Hands-on' assistance in the classroom

Students can provide valuable and continuing 'hands-on' assistance to support the inclusion of students with additional needs (Utley, Mortweet & Greenwood, 1997). There are three main ways this can occur. First, class peers can be encouraged to act as peer tutors. They are often very willing and able to do so. Second, class peers can provide regular scheduled assistance as 'buddies' to classmates with additional needs. Third, groups of students can participate in cooperative learning. Cooperative learning groups are widely used to assist students with additional needs in their academic and social development (Goor & Schwenn, 1993).

In consultation with colleague teachers, peer tutoring, buddy systems and cooperative learning groups can operate with students from other classes. This is easily arranged when classes at the same year or stage level are operating on a parallel timetable. Similar arrangements can be made with teachers of older students, including those with additional needs who can, with training, provide valuable assistance as tutors to younger students. By teaching others, they learn themselves. Students assisting others generally benefit from close and frequent supervision. It is usual that they receive formal training and practice in peer tutoring, taking a 'buddy' role, and in cooperative learning group work. Even senior high school students, as part of their course of studies, can become involved in supporting students with additional needs in the junior high school classes and at their local primary and preschools. Establishing links with colleagues in local preschools, primary schools and high schools can be most facilitative. It should be noted that these strategies benefit not only the students with additional needs; they also benefit the student's classmates, socially and academically (Shula, Kennedy & Cushing, 1999).

Adult volunteers generally, and *parents* specifically, are valuable human resources to support the inclusion of students with special needs (Brent, 2000; Burke, 2001). *Adult volunteers* usually come from the local community, and may already be members of the school community. Effective community liaison can identify and engage community volunteers. These people often have invaluable related experience and expertise, but just need some encouragement to contribute. *Parents*, as current members of the school community, can similarly be encouraged to contribute some of their time to support inclusion. These need not be parents of students in the class group. In fact parents usually prefer to work with children other than their own. It is usual for adult volunteers to participate in some preservice training focusing on child protection and confidentiality issues.

Adult volunteers and parents can take on more diverse roles than student peers. Their maturity and 'life experience' generally provides a better understanding of the basics of teaching and learning, and they can contribute greatly to the teaching/learning process. Adult volunteers, under the supervision of teachers, can work with individuals or groups of students in the classroom or in supervised withdrawal settings. Adults usually respond competently to most emerging instructional challenges and are often able to improvise solutions.

Many schools have a *support teacher* staff allocation. Depending on the number of enrolled students, education authorities allocate up to one or more full-time support teachers whose role is to support classroom teachers in providing instruction for students with additional needs and disabilities. Support teachers based in schools frequently focus on literacy and numeracy development, but this is at the discretion of the principal and in accordance with organisational policy. Support teachers provide 'hands-on' support in the classroom by team teaching alongside classroom teachers; working with individuals and small groups of students in the classroom on whole class activities; and/or by withdrawing individual or groups of students for intensive instruction.

Colleague *classroom teachers* are an invaluable source of support to all teachers in facilitating inclusion. Although most classroom teachers are full-time on their own classes, it is possible to negotiate team teaching and informal 'exchanges' to take advantage of their experience and expertise (Elliott & McKenney, 1998; Welch, Brownell & Sheridan, 1999). Team teaching arrangements, where pairs of teachers combine their classes for some or all lessons, give teachers the opportunity to see others 'in action'. This provides opportunities to learn about and draw upon their particular strengths and talents. During team teaching sessions it is possible for one teacher to take charge of the main part of the class, while the other teacher focuses on students with special needs. Informal exchanges involve 'swapping' classes on a routine or occasional basis to share expertise and experience, with a focus on students with additional needs. Both team teaching and exchanges require considerable organisation and mutual trust, but provide further enriching educational opportunities both for students and for teachers.

All larger schools have an *executive teacher* allocation. Depending on the number of enrolled students, this includes the principal and other executive staff, who have a lower 'face-to-face' teaching load to compensate for additional supervisory and administrative duties. School executive staff members are just as busy as their classroom colleagues, but they do have some flexibility in the allocation of their non face-to-face duty. This allocation includes time to support teaching staff that they supervise, particularly new teachers and those facing additional challenges in their day-to-day teaching. The school executive staff members are experienced and skilled teachers and can provide hands-on support in the classroom.

Specialist support teachers provide additional classroom support for students with additional needs. These support teachers have expertise in dealing with different disabilities, including for example, hearing impairments, vision impairments, behaviour and conduct disorders, mental health, autism, and intellectual and physical disabilities. These teachers usually support a caseload of students across a number of schools, but may provide hands-on support to individual students in the classroom or in intensive withdrawal sessions. For students with additional needs seeking enrolment in their local schools, access to specialist support teachers is usually negotiated as part of the enrolment process, and their role depends on the needs of the student and the demands of their caseload.

Some education authorities, usually in collaboration with other government departments, fund *physiotherapists*, *occupational therapists* and *speech pathologists* to deliver services for eligible students with special needs. Although primarily consultative, and usually for students with high support needs, some regular hands-on therapy support may be negotiated.

Teacher aides are probably the most utilised hands-on human resources available to support the day-to-day inclusion of students with additional needs (Wolery et al., 1995). An understanding of the diverse roles of teacher aides is important if teachers are to make best use of their assistance (Salzberg & Morgan, 1995). Teacher aides are now widely employed in primary and secondary school settings, and teachers have had to take on an increasing managerial role in supervising their work (French & Pickett, 1997; Hilton & Gerlach, 1997).

Teacher aides are generally employed to assist teachers to meet the special educational needs of individual students with a disability. Many work across classes supporting a number of students with additional needs. Some authorities allow teachers to choose between additional teacher aide time or additional off-class time to prepare teaching/learning materials for students with special needs. Others allow teachers to choose to take increased class sizes (generally arising from the inclusion of students with special needs) with an additional allocation of teacher aide time. Some school principals employ extra teacher aides rather than teachers

to provide for a better overall student–adult ratio where there is an increasing number of included students with additional needs. It is possible to employ two or more teacher aides for about the same cost as employing one additional teacher. Under some circumstances, and with the agreement of all involved, this option may provide a better teaching/learning environment for the student group as a whole.

Education authorities have diverse policies and practices relating to the roles, conditions of employment and number of teacher aides employed to support students with additional needs (French, 1999). Some students with high support needs, including students with challenging behaviours or complex physical care needs, may be individually supported by a full-time teacher aide (Giangreco, Broer & Edelman, 1999). However, this is exceptional, and is more often a transitional arrangement. Teacher aide time for students with additional needs is more often allocated as part of a package of resources to support the inclusive enrolment of students with moderate/high support needs. Depending on funding sources, it is usual that teacher aide time allocations for a number of students with additional needs are consolidated. This facilitates the employment of one or more teacher aide who then provides support across a number of settings for a number of students. This more flexible deployment of teacher aide time can better meet the often-changing needs of students and teachers with a minimum of disruptive staff turnover.

The roles of teacher aides are diverse. Teacher aides can, for example, provide assistance in academic subjects and with the teaching of functional life skills; assist with the teaching of vocational skills in community settings; collect and manage data; support students with challenging behaviours; facilitate interactions with peers; provide personal and intimate care; engage in clerical tasks; and prepare teaching/learning materials. However, it should be remembered that teacher aides are employed to implement programs, and not to develop them. They are supervised by teachers and do not have direct responsibility for students, other than that which applies under their usual duty of care to children (French, 1998).

Voices: Being teacher assistants (large class support) – 'Jack-of-all-trades'

We are teacher assistants (large class support) at a regional Catholic primary school. We are employed to support learning in classes of 30 or more students. Our role is to *help children*, and this encompasses many varied tasks.

We assist students both one-on-one, and in small groups. Much of our time is spent helping those students who have difficulties in learning. This overlaps with the work of learning support staff, but usually students with special needs are included in the one-on-one and small groups to gain extra assistance from us.

We support teachers by moving around the classes helping students with their spelling, story writing, maths, and reading. The students enjoy having adult support in the classroom. We also support teachers by being in the playground to help students during playtime.

We support classes by keeping class records like assessments and running records up-to-date, to help the teachers keep abreast of student progress. Teaching a large class is challenging, so being able to refer quickly to accurate assessment charts is very timesaving.

We also produce quality resources for class activities, photocopy, type, and mark test papers and homework. All these duties allow teachers to do what is most important, that is, to *teach*.

We always have to be flexible and respond to the ever-changing demands of the classroom. We love our work, and are rewarded with the appreciation of both the teachers and students alike.

Two 'overworked and underpaid' teacher assistants, Catholic primary school, NSW

Until recently teacher aides had very limited opportunities for professional development or training, but various authorities are now providing access to accredited training programs (Steckelberg & Vasa, 1998). Unfortunately, due to funding and enrolment variables, teacher aides are often employed on a part-time and temporary annual basis only. This provides little job security and creates difficulties for schools in trying to attract skilled teacher aides. Some authorities now provide incremental pay increases and career opportunities for experienced and qualified teacher aides.

Consultancy support

At the organisational level, education authorities usually maintain teams of consultants, specialist support teachers and therapists to support inclusion initiatives in schools.

Consultants provide support to schools enrolling and including students with additional needs. These consultants have a wide range of briefs, roles and expertise. It is usual to involve consultants who specialise in inclusion and integration; special education; (various) disabilities; and technology and equipment specialists. Access to these consultancy services is usually arranged through the school LST, and as part of a school-wide approach to facilitating inclusion. Consultants can work hands-on with students in classrooms, but more often focus their support on professional development for school staff and providing teaching resources.

Box 11.4

Program: My role as a disability program consultant

District offices provide consultancy services to assist schools to meet the educational needs of students with disabilities. A variety of personnel is available to support schools, teachers, students and parents through training and development, curriculum support, the development of models of service delivery to meet individual, school and district needs and ensuring equitable co-ordination of services.

My role as disability programs consultant is to provide advice on assessment, programming, monitoring and evaluation of learning programs, and to provide information on appropriate curriculum support materials. I work collaboratively with other consultants to coordinate training and development opportunities and to address the identified needs of teachers working with students with disabilities enrolled in mainstream classes, support classes and in special schools. I must manage the district disability programs in accordance with state policy and guidelines and make equitable recommendations regarding the allocation of available resources in the following areas:

- Coordination of the support class placement and review process and advising the district placement panel.
  Our district has a variety of support classes available to students with disabilities including intellectual, physical, hearing, autism, emotional disturbance, language, early intervention and early school support.
- Coordination of disability programs.
  Itinerant support teachers – vision, hearing, early intervention, transition and integration.
- Coordination of the funding support program (state integration program), supporting students with disabilities who are enrolled in mainstream classes.

- Making recommendations to state office in relation to special transport for students with disabilities.
- Receiving applications from school principals and making recommendations to state office in relation to properties modifications for students with disabilities.
- Processing applications for technology and equipment that will support students with disabilities to have access to the full range of curriculum experiences available in their educational setting.
- Processing special education cadetships for teachers pursuing further training in the field of special education.
- Providing advice to schools and families on support options and policy matters.
- Liaising with community agencies including health professionals and other educational services to ensure a collaborative, team approach to meeting the needs of students and their families.

In doing this I work closely with school LSTs, parents and principals, providing advice about the type and level of support students may require to achieve successful learning outcomes and to identify the most appropriate support personnel to be involved in the implementation of the student's learning program.

One of the most critical aspects of my role is working alongside parents and caregivers, encouraging them to play a major role in working with school staff to develop educational programs for their child. The Department of Education believes that parents can make a significant contribution, and are valued and essential members of the educational team as they know their child better than anyone, and have years of experience in working with their child.

>

Box 11.4 continued

It is a pleasure to work so closely with schools and families providing support to students with disabilities and to watch students reach their full potential as they progress through their school life from preschool to graduation at Year 12.

Margaret, Disability Programs Consultant

Specialist support teachers have expertise in dealing with, for example, hearing impairments, vision impairments, behaviour/conduct disorders, mental health, autism, language disorders, intellectual disabilities or physical disabilities. Specialist support teachers focus on developing the capacity of schools to provide support for these students. They may provide hands-on support in the classroom, and are available to provide consultative support and other resources on a school-wide basis. The school LST facilitates referrals for this support. Specialist support teachers should be involved on a consultative basis during the pre-inclusion/preparation phase of the inclusion process, and may participate in the initial appraisal of educational support needs phase of enrolment. They can also provide consultancy services on an ongoing basis to support the changing professional development needs of school staff.

Box 11.5
Voices: The itinerant support teacher – vision (ISTV) and Briony – a case study

Briony (pseudonym) was originally assessed as blind, severely intellectually disabled and as having cerebral palsy. She attended pre-school and was subsequently enrolled in a support class for students with severe intellectual disabilities. Briony progressed rapidly over 10 months from moving about on her bottom to a wheelchair and walking frame, to walking independently with a long cane.

Academically, Briony performed much better than her severe diagnosis suggested. This only became evident after working one-on-one in a withdrawal setting with her ISTV because in the classroom she had little opportunity to demonstrate her potential. During these withdrawal periods instruction focused on visual stimulation, literacy and numeracy skills, and Braille and tactual discrimination skills. Briony was able to read 72 point size print but developed tactile skills rapidly. Briony displayed an unexpected willingness and eagerness to learn. She developed an excellent memory and was keen to take on new challenges. Regular meetings were held with her parents and ISTV support was increased to five hours per week.

The support class teacher found it difficult to meet her educational needs in that classroom setting. She was copying inappropriate speech patterns from the other students, and behaved 'differently' in that setting. Following meetings with the LST and school executive, it was agreed that Briony should attend a regular class setting two afternoons per week, with six hours of ISTV support per week. Her program focused on orientation and mobility, social skills, speech, and eating and toileting.

Briony's continuing development and success suggested that she did not have a severe intellectual disability, so on the request of the vision team, Briony was reassessed by the counselling service. After one school term, Briony increased her enrolment to two full days

>

Box 11.5 continued

in the regular class. By this time she was also placed in the top reading group! She used a closed circuit TV that enlarged her work to an appropriate size and Braille was being taught intensely. The remaining three days per week were spent with the support class participating in gym and swimming lessons.

Numerous meetings were held as part of the inclusion process. Participants included the support unit teacher and executive, regular class teacher and executive, vision team staff, Briony's parents and district office personnel. The decision was made to move to full inclusion, and applications were placed for teacher aide support and technology assistance funding. Funding was received which allowed for one-on-one support in the regular setting, including 20 hours teacher aide time and 12 hours ISTV time.

After two terms of full-time regular class enrolment Briony is progressing rapidly using a one-handed typing program, Braille reading and using the Mountbatten Brailler. Both her social and numeracy skills are developing. She is fiercely independent and always seeking out new activities.

Briony's successful inclusion was facilitated by many factors:

- individual support from the vision team
- the flexibility of the support unit and regular education teachers
- planning through the LST
- the parents' developing understanding of their child's capabilities

- ongoing funding support for 20 hours per week teacher aide time
- 'up-front' funding support for a $6000 CCTV, and a $5000 Mountbatten Brailler
- a welcoming and supportive school principal
- a well-planned and implemented transition/ inclusion program
- regular meetings between all parties involved
- ongoing emotional support for the student and her family
- appropriate resourcing
- access to curriculum in both settings
- a very stable and supportive family
- access to and instruction in the use of technology
- carefully selected curriculum priorities
- appropriate support for the classroom teacher
- skilled specialist teachers, teacher aides and other para-professionals
- ongoing professional development
- an appreciation of the knowledge and expertise of the parents
- collaborative partnerships and team-building
- exposure to peer and personal benchmarking
- high expectations of achievement and an optimistic view of the future.

Kym Gribble, Assistant Principal (Vision), NSW government schools

Box 11.6

Voices: The itinerant support teacher – behaviour (ISTB) in rural New South Wales

My role as a specialist behaviour teacher is to provide consultancy support. I am accessed through a referral system that often differs across school districts. As an ISTB in the second largest district in NSW, the first difference between a city or coastal counterpart and myself I became aware of was the size of the engine of the car I was issued! No plastic

Box 11.6 continued

four-cylinder Japanese makes but a full Aussie Falcon for getting around road trains, and handling bulldust and potholes on dirt roads!

My day generally begins as most other teachers are considering getting out of bed. I have a 1½- to 2-hour trip to get to many schools. On arrival it is toilet and caffeine before hitting the classroom for observations or small group work, parent meetings, phone calls to support services, chasing the speech pathologist or occupational therapist referrals put in many months earlier. (The same specialist *never* visits twice due to the rapid turnover in health and community services staff.) Tracking the school counsellor for feedback about assessments, completing functional assessments or being a sounding board for stressed teachers may complete the day before the long trip home. If you're lucky, you have service from a reasonable radio station, as the Radio National afternoon art show is sure to cause you to nod off at 110 km/h!

A country ISTB is never in their base school for staff development days and is usually presenting sessions on ADHD, autism, Bill Rogers or behaviour management, often to beginning teachers due to staffing challenges in remote schools. Due to the nature of the job, ISTBs are often the easiest to send off for training and development in specialist programs such as professional assault response training (PART), non-violent crisis intervention (NVCI) or Rock and Water. Consequently we present at staff and P&C meetings, and run parenting courses. Somehow we have time for a life as well!

The biggest bugbear for rural ISTBs is the lack of, or difficulty in, obtaining support services for 'our kids' and their families. Our biggest thrill is their smiles when the kids make a week without suspension and their teachers are seeing that 'nice' child we knew was lurking below the surface.

Teachers/schools access our services through a referral process that is up to eight pages long and goes through three sets of hands. These referrals are sent to our district behaviour committee and then allocated. Our belief is that if the school perceives a problem, then it *is* a problem and deserves service. We do our best to keep our waiting lists to a minimum but misbehaviour is a growth industry …

Laraine Taylor, Itinerant Support Teacher (Behaviour), Dubbo District, NSW

Physiotherapists, occupational therapists, speech pathologists and *specialist nurses* are also generally available through most education authorities or the health system. They usually support students with high support needs, and work particularly in special education settings. Nevertheless, schools are encouraged to identify special needs and seek these additional consultancy services from their education authorities wherever possible.

The LST usually coordinates and manages the inclusion of new students with additional needs in their own school, but the wider school community also has a role to play. Community groups, disability-specific organisations and voluntary service organisations can also provide valuable support for inclusion initiatives. Organisations such as the Royal Institute for Deaf and Blind Children, The Spastic Centre and Technical Aid to the Disabled can provide (at little or no cost) expert consultancy and hands-on assistance for the assessment of support needs and modifications for students with disabilities.

Local voluntary service organisations like the Lions, Apex and View clubs may also offer the services of skilled members to assist in minor capital works initiatives for students with additional needs and disabilities. Many community groups will fundraise and provide hands-on support for individual students, as well as assistance with special facility modifications and installations for students with disabilities. Further consultancy and technical advice and support may be available from the local Department of Health and private medical services.

Best practice in collaborative planning for the inclusion of students with additional needs in local schools extends beyond 'just' the classroom and the school. Knowledge of available human resources, and how to access and manage them, is central to successful inclusion. So, too, is a knowledge of other resources. The following section explains a range of other key resources to support the inclusion of students with additional needs in local schools.

Adapted curriculum and instructional materials

For almost all students with special needs, adaptation and modification of instructional materials (coupled with more effective teaching techniques) provides improved access to the regular curriculum. This section suggests three key starting points for adapting curriculum and instructional materials.

One starting point is Chapter 4 in this textbook. Chapter 4 presents a comprehensive introduction to curriculum adaptation for the purpose of facilitating the inclusion of students with additional needs. It is an essential first resource and key reading. First, it explains the diverse nature of curriculum. Various approaches and strategies for adapting and modifying the regular primary and secondary curriculums are discussed. Subsequently, it provides rationales and strategies for adapting instructional materials, along with some valuable examples of previously adapted materials. The references and further recommended readings listed at the end of the chapter are an excellent place to start exploring professional literature. Note that it is best to read Chapter 4 in conjunction with Chapter 5, particularly the section on curriculum-based assessment.

A second starting point for locating resources to adapt curriculum and instructional materials is to investigate exemplary inclusive practices in other local schools. Although it is imperative to take an individualised approach to adapting curriculum and instructional materials, it is also inefficient to 'reinvent the wheel'. Consultants and teaching colleagues in similar schools, with similar inclusion agendas and identified student needs, can provide invaluable advice and resources for this purpose.

A third starting point for locating resources to adapt curriculum and instructional materials is to investigate exemplary practices in special education facilities. Although these are not inclusive settings, special educators generally have experience and training in developing resources for students with additional needs and/or disabilities, and may be willing to share their resources with colleagues.

A best way to facilitate the sharing of these resources with colleagues at other schools is to negotiate through your education authority's consultancy team. The development of adapted and modified curriculum and instructional materials is often best achieved collaboratively. Collaborative curriculum development days, similar to those held by stage, year and faculty teams, are highly recommended.

Chapter 4 emphasises an important relationship between the curriculum (what to teach) and teaching techniques (how to teach). That is, adaptations and modifications to what is taught are interrelated with how they are taught. This relationship links this section directly onto the next section about resources to support effective teaching techniques.

Effective teaching techniques

As previously mentioned, the regular curriculum may be inappropriate or inaccessible to some students with additional needs, particularly those students with more challenging intellectual disabilities. For almost all students with additional needs, a widened range of effective teaching techniques (coupled with adaptations to and modifications of instructional materials) facilitates the best learning.

Chapter 5 presents a comprehensive introduction to the design, development, implementation, delivery and evaluation of a range of effective teaching techniques that can facilitate effective learning for all students, including those with additional needs. Both Chapters 4 and 5 support an ecological model wherein curriculum issues, instructional issues, and contextual (classroom) issues collectively impact on effective teaching, and consequently on effective learning. An understanding of Chapter 5 is central to an understanding of resources to develop effective teaching techniques. (Note that the terms teaching and instruction are used interchangeably here, as are the terms techniques, strategies and methods. Put simply, these terms are about *how* you teach.)

This section is about developing resources that support the way teachers can bring about successful learning for their students. To identify, access and develop helpful resources, it is imperative that teachers have a sound understanding of the key elements of instruction. These are clearly and thoroughly explained in Chapter 5. These include: the process of instructional design (the DETI model is an exemplar); typical instructional cycles; individual educational programming; and curriculum-based assessment and programming (CBAP). These key elements of instruction provide a scaffold for understanding and being creative with approaches like activity-based learning, cooperative learning, problem-based learning, and outcome-based learning. Additionally, an understanding of these key elements informs the use of other instructional strategies like task analysis, mastery learning, peer tutoring, direct instruction, and computer-assisted instruction.

One starting point for identifying and developing resources is the DETI model for designing effective teaching interventions, as described in Chapter 5. Each step in the model provides a focus for resource identification and development. For example, the first two phases are about identifying and choosing long-term (annual) goals and curriculum priorities. It is essential that the LST takes a collaborative approach here. The student's teachers should then conduct a curriculum analysis and draft the IEP. Teachers need (at least) a thorough knowledge of guiding curriculums, syllabuses and support documents, and skills in conducting collaborative team meetings. Chapter 5 provides an introductory explanation to some of these issues, and further recommended readings are provided at the end of the chapter.

The other starting points for identifying and developing resources for designing effective teaching techniques are the same as those previously mentioned for adapting curriculum and instructional materials. That is, to investigate exemplary inclusive practices in other local schools, and to investigate exemplary practices in special education facilities. Similarly, relevant members of the education authority's consultancy team should be able to suggest other schools and colleagues who can assist with this task, as well as providing resource support themselves. It is important to remember that the development of effective teaching techniques is best achieved with a team of colleagues. Collaborative curriculum development days, similar to those held by year, stage and faculty teams, are highly recommended.

The development of a diversified and responsive set of effective teaching strategies is premised on a sound understanding of the key elements of instructional design.

Assistive technology

In broad terms, assistive technology is any technology that enhances human performance. For students with additional needs, it is any technology that enhances their educational performance. This usually involves overcoming barriers to learning through improved access to and participation in learning environments (Burtch, 1999). Research literature substantiates the potential benefits of assistive technology, particularly for students with disabilities (see, for example, Abbott, 2002; Brett & Provenzo, 1995; Ray & Warden, 1995).

A diverse range of materials, services, systems and devices can be regarded as assistive technology and these can be commercially purchased, adapted from and for existing technologies, or purpose built. Assistive technology includes very simple devices that are mechanically uncomplicated, inexpensive and require little training. It also includes complex equipment that is usually computer-based, expensive and requires substantial training. Ergonomic cutlery and utensils, tape-recorded books, Braille equipment, positioning and mobility equipment, communication aids, specialised computer hardware and software, medical equipment and prosthetic devices, and adaptive play equipment are all examples of assistive technology.

Identifying and accessing facilitative and appropriate assistive technology can be a difficult, time-consuming and expensive task. Nevertheless, assistive technology can be a powerful resource to facilitate and support the successful inclusion of students with additional needs (Forgrave, 2002; Lankshear, Snyder & Green, 2000; Wyer, 2001). Assistive technology can facilitate learning for students with many different special needs including sensory

impairments, physical impairments and intellectual disabilities. Specific applications of assistive technology to support students with various special needs are described in relevant chapters of this textbook, for example, Chapter 9.

Assistive technology has a wide range of potential benefits for students with additional needs. Regardless of impairment or disability, there is some form of assistive technology that can facilitate improved educational outcomes and support successful inclusion. This can result from better access to learning opportunities, improved academic skills, improved self-esteem and relationships with peers (Parette, 1997). Students with additional needs can use assistive technology to help overcome challenges such as reading difficulties, hearing and speech difficulties, fine and gross motor problems, and learning difficulties.

The selection of appropriate assistive technology should be negotiated collaboratively, as part of the appraisal of educational support needs and individual educational planning processes (Higgins, Boone & Williams, 2000). The value of assistive technology is enhanced when it finds wide application across environments. Assistive technology that 'just sits in the corner' is wasteful and counter-productive. Potential assistive technology may be assessed as 'essential' to meeting identified needs, or as 'outcome enhancing'. The cost of assistive technology assessed as essential should be funded without compromise, whereas the cost of purchasing and maintaining 'outcome-enhancing' assistive technology may be negotiated through a variety of sources.

Parette (1997) suggests some key considerations when selecting assistive technology. First, the student's current (and anticipated future) additional needs, capabilities and interests should be considered. Second, family and cultural issues are important. The success of assistive technology for students with additional needs is highly dependent on family support and involvement (Angelo, 1997). Third, technology features and service systems, such as availability, start-up and operational costs, essential training and customer support, ergonomics and safety, and funding are important.

Box 11.7
Voices: Assistive technology and Caytlin – a case study

Caytlin has a physical disability called athetoid cerebral palsy. This means she has limited coordination, which affects her ability to speak and move. Anything Caytlin wants to do happens with the help of assistive technology or the help of another person, or both. However, Caytlin doesn't let her physical limitations curb her enthusiasm for life. Caytlin attends her local high school where she has just finished the School Certificate and plans to do the HSC. She also loves to go shopping with her friends in her powered wheelchair, which is an adventure in itself when she gets stuck in the elevator! She

can surf the net and has Internet penfriends who don't know she has a disability. Caytlin communicates with her therapy team at the Spastic Centre via email, making requests for help or just to have a chat.

At school, Caytlin relies completely on technology to do her schoolwork. She uses a communication device (DeltaTalker) to speak and as the interface between her and the computer. The DeltaTalker looks a bit like a small computer, but uses icon and word keys, as well as letters, to produce a message faster than it could be done with letters alone. Caytlin accesses the

>

Box 11.7 continued

DeltaTalker using either scanning,[1] with a single switch that she activates with her head, or by directly pressing the buttons with her finger. Caytlin's athetoid movements make direct access very tiring. When she is too tired for this quicker access method, she reverts to scanning.

The DeltaTalker is connected by cable to her laptop and uses Minspeak[2] or spelling to transfer words to a program such as Microsoft Word. The DeltaTalker also allows mouse functions and keyboard commands, thus allowing her to save, print, email, Internet access, etc. Caytlin relies on a teacher's aide to set up her system in each class. Mathematics has continued to be a subject in which she requires significant input from her teacher's aide. This is because the schematic nature of mathematics is more difficult to express through the DeltaTalker and specialised software to solve this problem is hard to find.

Caytlin completes her homework on a computer, making use of the Internet. Caytlin also uses her communication device for environmental control (using TV, stereo, etc.). She reads the necessary books using an electronic page-turner, which she activates using a switch. Her school is working with Caytlin to put all of her subject material onto her computer as the page-turner struggles to turn exercise book pages.

In the past, changing from one device to another has been difficult, as she required assistance to unplug the cable from one device and plug it into another. The invention of a cordless switch now enables Caytlin to operate a number of different devices without help.

Like all teenagers Caytlin likes to talk on the phone. The phone also facilitates Caytlin's safety and independence as she likes to go out or even stay at home by herself and she needs a way of calling for help. Finding the right assistive technology to allow her to do this independently is a challenge. Caytlin currently uses her home phone via the DeltaTalker, but someone needs to hold the phone for her. We have been working with Caytlin to find a phone with a speaker function and buttons large enough that she can push for herself. The longer-term aim is to use a modified hands-free mobile phone.

Assistive technology is constantly improving and helping us to solve the problems Caytlin faces in achieving an independent lifestyle.

_____

1 'Scanning' means that items on the screen are highlighted in turn, allowing the user to choose, by clicking a switch, when the desired item is lit up. A comprehensive explanation of how scanning works can be found at <www.gusinc.com/scanning.html>

2 Minspeak is a language that uses combinations of picture icons to form words more quickly than they can be spelt.

Cheryl Jones, Occupational Therapist and Jenny Kidd, Speech Pathologist, Children's Services, Spastic Centre, NSW

Computers are a widely used assistive technology for all students, including those with additional needs (Boyd, 1999). Computers are popular because they are 'patient', allow students to work at their own pace, can be highly motivating, provide immediate feedback, and enable other people to help the student to learn (Schery & O'Connor, 1997). Conventional input and output devices may need to be modified or alternative devices added. These can be activated by sound, movement or light. Occupational therapists or physiotherapists can conduct assessments of the need for special switches or devices. Organisations such as The Royal Blind Society and the Spastic Centre also have trained therapists who may conduct these assessments.

Personal computers, with appropriate input and output devices, and quality software, have many potential educational advantages for students with disabilities. Personal computers can provide improved cognitive, physical and sensory accessibility to learning experiences for students with a disability.

Quality educational software is prerequisite to a valuable learning experience. An increasing volume of software is now being designed and marketed to meet special educational needs, but most good software has potential value if used thoughtfully and creatively. Most educational authorities review and make recommendations on quality software, but classroom teachers can conduct their own evaluations by using some general guidelines. Good educational software for students with disabilities, according to Ray and Warden (1995, pp. 96–7), should:

- make knowledge construction overt
- maintain attention to cognitive goals
- treat a student's lack of knowledge in a positive way
- provide process-relevant feedback
- encourage learning strategies other than rehearsal
- encourage multiple passes through information
- support varied ways for students to organise their knowledge
- encourage maximum use and examination of existing knowledge
- provide opportunities for reflection and take into account individual learning style
- facilitate transfer of knowledge across contexts
- give students more responsibility for contributing to one another's learning.

More specifically, when evaluating the potential value and utility of educational software (Ray & Warden, 1995, pp. 167–8), teachers should:

- identify the purpose of the instructional program, its objectives, and the validity of its content
- determine the characteristics of learners for whom the program is appropriate
- describe the format and ways information is presented to the learner
- determine the extent of student control over the program
- describe the commands required to use the material, the academic and physical demands placed on the student, and the speed and accuracy of the program
- identify the type and frequency of feedback and reinforcement provided by the program
- determine the extent of branching within the program
- identify the options that exist to enable the teacher to modify features of the program
- determine the adequacy of program documentation.

Personal computers attached to the Internet and the World Wide Web also have a great potential to enhance the quality of lives of students with disabilities, especially those with impairments that impact on their opportunity to access other people, places and activities. The Internet has a huge potential to assist students with disabilities and their teachers and parents to gather and disseminate information and to communicate effectively. Individual teachers, schools and educational authorities are now beginning to explore the many ways in which this potential can be realised with all students (Abbott, 2002).

The technology/computing consultant and the special education consultant are the best starting points for identifying assistive technology to support inclusion. These consultants are likely to provide and discuss catalogues of assistive technology devices, and advise of other schools using such technologies for students with comparable special needs.

Student, staff and community support

The success of inclusive practices is strongly influenced by the attitudes and perspectives of all members of the local school community (Cole, 1999). If students, school staff, and other school community members are supportive of initiatives to include students with additional needs as members of their school community, the likelihood of successful inclusion is strongly enhanced (Avramidis & Norwich, 2002). The leadership and commitment of the school executive is central here. A consensus of positive support is not always evident, and research has demonstrated the challenges arising from unsupportive attitudes to inclusion (Devore, 2000). These challenges are exacerbated when the students seeking inclusive enrolment have high support needs (Cowling, 2001), particularly when their special needs include challenging behaviours (Hunt et al., 2003).

To enhance student perspectives on inclusion, teachers are encouraged to focus on pertinent areas of the curriculum that relate closely to this topic. The establishment of valued student–student relationships, particularly during the transition/early inclusion phase of the inclusion process, has been demonstrated to be effective in overcoming prejudices and unfair discrimination. To enhance staff perspectives, professional development activities for the whole school staff are suggested. Presentations by guest speakers from other schools who have experienced successful inclusion are often valuable. To enhance broader school community perspectives, informative letters and after-school presentations can be helpful, particularly when parents from other schools who have been involved with successful inclusion participate as guest speakers.

A positive school climate is facilitated when school staff focus on encouraging and developing positive interactions between students, and between students and staff. There is a plethora of research providing arguments for the importance of teaching students how to interact positively (Johnson et al., 2000; Jones & Jones, 2001; Peterson, 1997). Chapter 6 explains the significant relationships between social and academic programs and learning in the context of a classroom ecosystem. Appropriate social behaviour by all members of the school community is central to the successful inclusion of students with additional needs. Chapter 6 describes the particular social challenges faced by students with additional needs in inclusive settings, and provides some guidance in overcoming these challenges. In addition, it describes some strategies for encouraging positive interaction, and recommended readings are provided at the end of the chapter.

Building a supportive and positive school climate for the inclusion of students with additional needs is an ongoing, whole school issue. Attitudes will not change overnight, but well publicised, positive, valued outcomes arising from successful inclusion initiatives will influence an improvement in a school community's support for the further inclusion of students with additional needs.

Access and mobility

Some students have significant fine and gross motor impairments, sensory impairments, physical disabilities and mobility problems. Just getting to the local school can be a major challenge. Accessibility is an issue for many students. Barriers to access can occur getting to and from school, moving around the school between rooms, using toilet facilities, and when using specialist equipment and facilities.

Modifications to school buildings and more immediate learning environments are often required to provide fair and safe access for all members of the school community. For major installations, education authorities usually have access to design and construction expertise. For smaller modifications, the expertise of physiotherapists and occupational therapists is highly recommended. Funding for improving access is usually sought by application to the responsible educational authority through the LST. The initial set-up time and costs associated with this aspect of inclusion are often substantial. Major and expensive modifications like toilet/bathroom facilities, ramps and lifts can take more than 12 months from application to installation, so pre-planning is essential. Generally though, these modifications will benefit other students with comparable needs, and often all members of the school community. For example, ramps, once installed, tend to be used by everybody.

Professional development and training

For the benefits of inclusion to be realised, all those involved should be appropriately trained, skilled and experienced. Professional development and training needs will differ over the three phases of the inclusion process. At the pre-inclusion/preparation stage, when collaborative planning is the focus activity, knowledge of the student, experience with inclusion, and diverse expertise relating to needs and requisite resources are central.

Subsequent to completion of the appraisal of educational support needs, the IEP outline and the ISP, preparations should begin for the early inclusion/transition stage. These preparations will usually include some professional development and training. This often focuses on the needs of classroom teachers, the teacher aides and the students involved in peer support roles.

During the early inclusion/transition stage, staff development is primarily 'on-the-job' and experiential, and new or changing professional development and training needs will become evident during this period. Professional development and training needs will continue into the long-term inclusion/monitoring stage, but are likely to decrease significantly. These will primarily relate to the continuing training demands of assistive technology, and the retraining of any new teachers, teacher aides, volunteers, and students involved in peer tutoring and buddy arrangements. It is important to remember that development and training needs are ongoing because a student's resource support needs change over time.

Professional development and training can be provided by colleague teachers or staff, or by colleagues from other schools with comparable experience. Education authorities will provide specialist support teachers and consultants to contribute to professional development. Disability-specific community organisations also provide consultancy and training services.

General professional development and training is also available. Professional organisations like the Australian Association of Special Education (AASE) and the Australasian Society for the Study of Intellectual Disability (ASSID) have regular publications and conferences in all states of Australia and in New Zealand. The focus of these organisations is on the professional development of members. Specialist consultants from education authorities frequently organise regular 'network' meetings and seminars for school staff involved with students with special needs and disabilities. Interested teachers can enrol in post-graduate training courses in special education or disability studies, sometimes with financial support from their employer.

These courses run at many universities at the (graduate) certificate, diploma and degree levels. Teacher aides can benefit greatly from appropriate training (Wadsworth & Knight, 1996) and may enrol in nationally accredited training courses, sometimes with financial support. A 'benchmark' course is the Certificate III in Education Support (Teacher's Aide Special).

Box 11.8
Voices: Professional development and teacher aides

For almost nine years now I have worked as a Teacher's Assistant in a Catholic high school. It is a challenging job, one that I enjoy immensely with no two days ever the same! Previously I had worked as a volunteer at the local infants school with the Reading Recovery Program.

When I first started out as a teacher's assistant I felt that I was operating very much on an instinctive basis, using my experience as a mother as a constant reference. I was, however, very eager to learn, continually asking the Learning Support Teacher for books to read on children with special needs and how best to help them in the classroom. Once in a while an in-service would come up for Teacher's Assistants, but this was very rare. I felt that working by instinct was all very well but I never felt very sure of myself, often questioning my judgement – had I got it right?

About three years ago a wonderful opportunity presented itself. The Diocese offered its teacher's assistants the chance to enrol in the Certificate III in Education Support – Teacher's Aide Special. The course involved attendance one day per fortnight during school terms for about two years. The study was extensive and ranged from Role and Responsibilities, Literacy and Numeracy Development to Social Skills Development, Communication Needs and Behaviour Management.

With each topic came the assessment tasks. As most of us were 'mature-age' students it had been a very long time since we had to write essays. We felt on very shaky ground! However,

it really made us sit down and focus on what we were doing in the classroom and gave us the depth of understanding that was perhaps, up until now, lacking. Our approach to children's learning became more of a professional one. The next step to the assessment process was having the courage to hand our work in for marking! Most nerve-racking! How did I go? Did I word it right? Am I on the right track here? (Never underestimate the impact of smiley stickers, ticks and positive comments that you, as teachers, can give!) Unless our efforts fell into the 'crashing and burning' category we *always* received a sticker. Our confidence and belief in ourselves grew.

This training also gave us the opportunity to come together and share our experiences as teacher's assistants. This was certainly an integral part of the learning process. We were very fortunate to have a wonderful lecturer. He was very generous in sharing his wealth of knowledge and experience with us, but he also valued and respected the roles we, as teacher's assistants, played in the school.

Completing the Certificate III gave us all a great deal of confidence. Today when I walk into the classroom I feel that I know what I am doing – that I can better support not only the children, but the teachers as well. I have more than just instinct to go by now. And of course we are now accredited, we have *that* piece of paper, which, incidentally is now framed and proudly hanging on the wall at home!

Teacher Assistant, Catholic regional high school

Funding support

Funding support is often a crucial component of any resource package for supporting the inclusion of students with additional needs (European Agency for Development in Special Needs Education, 2000). It is important, though, for schools to identify and utilise existing resources before seeking external resources and funding support. Resources can already be in the school, or within the school community. A number of examples are pertinent.

Students and/or community volunteers can provide 'hands-on' assistance in the classroom. Existing school staff and/or community members often have the expertise to deliver valuable consultancy support. Colleagues from the local school, and other local schools and special education facilities, may have the expertise and experience to contribute to the development of adapted curriculum and instructional materials, as well as developing additional effective teaching strategies. Local community service clubs and disability organisations are usually enthusiastic about supporting inclusion initiatives with human, material and/or financial resources.

School budgets may include allocations for inclusion and/or special education, but funding may be drawn from other areas of school budgets when expenditure can be shown to be within guidelines, and to benefit the school community. For 'non-essential' integration initiatives that seek to enhance existing outcomes, extra funding can be sought from parent and citizen groups and/or school council groups. An argument could be put that funding allocations and grants will benefit the broader school community, and not 'just' individual students with additional needs. Schools can sometimes negotiate industry partnerships with local businesses, and enter into research partnerships with local tertiary institutions, to support inclusion initiatives that benefit individuals or groups of students.

Planning for funding support should take into account whether funding is required to meet initial 'set-up' costs and/or for ongoing costs. All educational authorities have access to some annual government funds to support the inclusion of students with disabilities. All schools and education authorities have policies and procedures for seeking this funding support. The school principal and educational authority's consultant or inclusion/integration/special education program manager can advise school LSTs on the due process for funding applications. Funding is not always essential for successful inclusion, and quite often students with additional needs can be included in their local school using existing resources. Nevertheless, most inclusion initiatives do require some initial and ongoing funding support.

Box 11.9
Voices: Michael – a case study in funding support

I first met Michael and his family when they submitted a referral for support through our Transition to School Program. Michael's family was very concerned about how he might be supported at school. Michael has a physical disability, and his family was unsure of how

Michael may be received at his local school. Michael's older siblings attended their local school and his mum and dad were keen for him to have the same opportunities.

When I first contacted Michael's parents they had lots of questions and fears about how

>

Box 11.9 continued

people might respond to them and Michael, but also they wanted to be sure that they were making sound decisions on which placement would best meet Michael's needs. As part of my role as Disability Programs Consultant I attended a meeting with Michael's family, the principal and the school counsellor from his local school, Michael's preschool teacher and the occupational therapist who was working with Michael. In our department we call this the Early Learning Support Team. At this meeting we talked openly about Michael, his strengths, needs, likes and dislikes. We identified areas where Michael may require support in the school setting and other areas where he may participate independently. Michael's parents had a lot of questions about the resources available to Michael at the school, the attitudes of staff and the school community towards people with disabilities, and the expectations of the school on how they may be involved in Michael's education.

At this meeting it was identified that if Michael were to attend his local school then several modifications would be required to buildings and facilities to enable him to access all areas of the school alongside his peers. It was also apparent that Michael would need some additional technology to enable him to access the curriculum. In addition, a decision was made to apply for Funding Support (Integration Funding) to provide Michael with additional teacher aide support in the classroom. This would provide an opportunity for Michael's teacher to participate in planning meetings and training and development opportunities to enable them to better program for Michael's needs in the classroom. The appropriate paperwork for funding support, properties and equipment was completed by the school and family and Michael commenced school the following year with all supports in place.

This funding provided teacher aide support for Michael in the areas of curriculum access, communication, social participation, safety, personal care, mobility and hand motor skills. Funds from this program were also used to enable Michael's classroom teacher to participate in training and development in the use of technology to support Michael in the classroom. In addition to this it provided funds for his teacher to have release time to liaise with other professionals and Michael's family for planning and evaluation of Michael's educational plan as part of the LST.

As part of the Funding Support Program each student has a minimum of one review meeting per year. At this meeting a student's program and placement are reviewed to ensure that the current setting and resources are meeting that student's individual needs. The Itinerant Support Teacher Integration worked alongside Michael's teacher and the teacher's aide to develop appropriate educational outcomes for Michael and to support them in making adjustments to the curriculum to enable Michael's participation and inclusion in all classroom activities. The integration support teacher was also engaged to provide inservicing to the whole school community in relation to disability and inclusion of all students in the mainstream environment.

Over the past six years Michael has moved through the grades with his peers. He has achieved a high level of success and independence – both socially and academically. Michael's parents are very proud of his achievements and recognise the value of working in partnership with the school through the LST to ensure all appropriate supports are in place. Next year Michael will transition to Year 7 and the LST will liaise with his high school to ensure that appropriate supports are in place, and that all relevant information is communicated to his new school.

Margaret, Disability Programs Consultant, NSW

Finding out more information

There are a number of points of reference for finding out more information about best practices and key resources to support inclusion. The next section of this chapter is specifically about finding out more information.

One starting point is the published literature. First, the reader can review this text itself. There is a wealth of practical ideas for resourcing inclusion initiatives discussed in most of the chapters. The reader can borrow or purchase one or more of the recommended readings listed at the end of each chapter. There is, of course, much more literature focusing on best practices and key resources discussed in this chapter. Much of this literature is available on the Web. This includes education and disability research journals, and promotional and sales catalogues from manufacturers and suppliers.

A second starting point is peer or informal consultancy. Many teaching colleagues have experience and knowledge about resourcing inclusion, as well as a personal library of professional resources collected and/or developed over time. Observing good current teaching/learning practices is an invaluable experience for the beginning teacher. Colleagues' personal resource collections are often very informative, but the authors should always be given credit. Even though these resources may not be copyright, giving due recognition to the author is best professional practice.

A third starting point is professional or formal consultancy. Education authorities have teams of specialist consultants, specialist support teachers and therapists to provide consultancy services to teachers in schools. In addition, disability-specific community organisations, and many manufacturers and suppliers of teaching resources provide formal consultancy services.

In general terms, there need not be any substantial cost involved in investigating and accessing these resources. The cost of photocopying resources provided by colleagues, and of purchasing any published resources, should be negotiated with the school principal. Formal consultancy services are often free. Investigating resources to facilitate inclusion and enhance outcomes for students with additional needs can be time-consuming. However, the LST may negotiate with the school principal for 'release time' to make necessary investigations.

Organising resources

Introduction

Putting together a best practice package of resources to support the inclusion of students with additional needs can be a challenging and demanding task. This task has become more challenging as schools seek to enrol an increasing number of students with additional needs. Being well prepared and organised is essential if students with additional needs are to have the best chance of success in their local schools. The next section of this chapter looks at various ways of organising resources to support inclusion.

This section brings together the first two sections in a very practical way. Six resource checklists are described and explained. These checklists are designed to assist teachers, LSTs and schools to organise resources that can potentially support the successful inclusion of students with additional needs. These checklists help to develop a grounded and comprehensive approach to successful inclusion.

Resource checklist 1: Using this textbook as a first resource

This textbook is an excellent first resource for supporting inclusion. To assist the reader to review the text and gather information about best practices and key resources, this checklist cross-references the three best practices and nine key groups of resources discussed in this chapter against specific and informative parts of each chapter in the text. This checklist should be used in conjunction with the Contents, Glossary and Index sections of the text.

Practice/resource	Chapter											
	1	2	3	4	5	6	7	8	9	10	11	12
Best practice: Collaborative planning/LST		X	X	X	X	X		X	X		X	X
Best practice: (Continuing) appraisal of educational support needs			X	X	X	X		X	X		X	X
Best practice: An individual perspective & an ecological context		X	X	X	X	X			X	X	X	X
'Hands-on' assistance in the classroom			X	X	X	X	X	X	X		X	
Consultancy support			X	X		X		X	X		X	X
Adapted curriculum & instructional materials				X		X			X		X	X
Effective teaching strategies	X		X	X	X	X	X	X			X	X
Assistive technology			X	X	X	X			X		X	
Student, staff and community support			X	X		X		X	X		X	X
Access and mobility			X	X		X			X		X	
Professional development & training		X	X	X		X			X		X	
Funding support	X										X	

Resource checklist 2: Best-recommended literature

Each chapter includes recommended references and readings to assist with the gathering of further information. This checklist cross-references the three best practices and nine key groups of resources discussed in this chapter against best-recommended literature. This literature may include, for example: professional journals; textbooks; kits and teaching/learning resources; and/or catalogues from manufacturers and suppliers. Full reference details are available in the reference lists at the end of each of the nominated chapters. This checklist should be used in conjunction with the Contents, Glossary and Index sections of the text.

	Best-recommended literature	*Chapter*
Best practice: Collaborative planning/LST	Jitendra, Edwards, Choutka & Treadway (2002)	4
	Pugach & Johnson (1995)	9
	Dettmer, Thurston & Dyck (1999)	10
	Friend & Cook (1996)	10
	Tiegerman-Farber & Radziewicz (1998)	10
	Bolton (1987)	10
	Davis & Kemp (1995)	10
	Mostert (1998)	10
Best practice: (Continuing) appraisal of educational support needs	Choate, Enright, Miller, Poteet & Rakes (1995)	5
	Center for Effective Collaboration and Practice (CECP) (1998b)	6
	Gregg & Mather (2002)	7
	Foreman, Bourke, Mishra & Frost (2001)	11
Best practice: An individual perspective & an ecological context	McGregor & Vogelsberg (1998)	1
	Centre for Studies on Inclusive Education (2002)	2
	Arthur, Gordon & Butterfield (2003)	5
	Horner & Carr (1997)	6
	Beukelman & Mirenda (1998)	9
	Murray (2003)	12
'Hands-on' assistance in the classroom	Westwood (2003)	4
	Chard, Vaughan & Tyler (2002)	7
	Bakken & Whedon (2002)	8
	Griffin (2002)	8
	Doyle (1997)	11
	Giangreco, Edelman, Broer & Doyle (2001)	11
Consultancy support	Rice & Zigmond (2000)	4
	Dettmer, Thurston & Dyck (1999)	10

continued

	Best-recommended literature	Chapter
Adapted curriculum & instructional materials	McLeskey & Waldron (2002)	2
	Beukelman & Mirenda (1998)	9
	Jenkinson (1997)	11
	NSW Board of Studies (2003)	12
Effective teaching strategies	Bricker, Prette-Frontczak & McComas (1998)	3
	Westwood (2003)	5
	Colvin, Ainge & Nelson (1997)	6
	Bakker & Whedon (2002)	7
	Brent, Gough & Robinson (2001)	7
	Gardill & Jitendra (1999)	7
	Goldsworthy (1998)	7
	Mastropieri & Scruggs (1997)	7
	Torgesen (1999)	7
	Hibbing & Rankin-Erickson (2003)	8
	Westwood (2003)	8
	Soto, Muller, Hunt & Goetz (2001)	9
	Lenz, Deschler & Kissom (2004)	10
Assistive technology	Mull & Sitlington (2003)	5
	Parette & Marr (1997)	9
	White, Shelley & Donna (2003)	9
	Lankshear, Snyder & Green (2000)	11
Student, staff and community support	Carpenter (2003)	8
	Ortega & Ramirez (2002)	8
	Dettmer, Thurston & Dyck (1999)	10
	Turnbull & Rutherford Turnbull III (1997)	10
	Avramidis & Norwich (2002)	11
Access and mobility	Soto, Muller, Hunt & Goetz (2001)	9
Professional development & training	Eves (2001)	6
	Dettmer, Thurston & Dyck (1999)	10
	Grundy (1995)	10
	Little & Houston (2003)	10
	McNiff, Lomax & Whitehead (1996)	10
	Chalmers, Carter, Clayton & Hook (1998)	11
	French & Pickett (1997)	11
Funding support	Foreman, Bourke, Mishra & Frost (2001)	1
	Wills & Cain (2003)	1
	Cumley & Beukelman (1992)	9

Resource checklist 3: Informal consultancy

Informal consultancy with teaching colleagues and others is an excellent source of further information about resources to support inclusion. Many teachers (and other school community members) have a wealth of experience with and knowledge about inclusion, as well as personal collections of valuable resources. Observing good current teaching/learning practices is also an invaluable experience for the beginning teacher. This checklist cross-references informal consultancy support sources against types of resources potentially available from each source. Depending upon personal needs, checklists could be completed for each of the three best practices and nine key resource groups. This checklist should be used in conjunction with the Contents, Glossary and Index sections of the text.

Potential informal consultancy support source	Resources potentially available from each source				
	Discussion? Observation?	Resources: Borrow, copy, buy?	Professional development/ training?	Referral to others?	Funding/ relief days?
Teaching colleagues at school					
Other school community members (incl. parents, TAs, volunteers familiar with the student)					
Other teaching colleagues					
Special education colleagues					
Professional organisations					
Disability organisations					
Commercial suppliers					
TAFE/university colleagues					
Others					

Resource checklist 4: Formal consultancy

Professional consultants are an excellent source of key information about resources to support inclusion. Education authorities have teams of specialist consultants, specialist support teachers and therapists to provide consultancy services to teachers and schools. This checklist cross-references the three best practices and nine key groups of resources discussed in this chapter against this range of consultancy providers. Again, the checklist should be used in conjunction with the Contents, Glossary and Index sections of the text.

Key questions could include, for each of the three best practices and nine key groups of resources listed:

- What resources (literature, consultancy, funding) are available?
- Can the consultant provide/advise about further professional development and training for those involved?
- What other people can provide information and/or resources?

Discussion topics	Specialist consultancy personnel						
	Inclusion/ integration/ transition consultant	Special education consultant	Technology consultant	Early childhood consultant	Specialist support teacher/s	Therapist/s	Other
Best practice: Collaborative planning/ LST							
Best practice: Support needs assessment							
Best practice: Individual perspective & ecological context							
'Hands-on' assistance in the classroom							
Consultancy support							
Adapted curriculum & instructional materials							
Effective teaching strategies							
Assistive technology							
Student, staff and community support							
Access and mobility							
Professional development & training							
Funding support							

Resource checklist 5: Hands-on assistance in the classroom

For classroom teachers, hands-on assistance is a key element of any resource package to support the continuing inclusion of students with additional needs. Identifying and organising the best hands-on support is an important task. This checklist cross-references potential human resources who can provide this assistance against options for delivering this assistance. The classroom teacher, who is ultimately responsible for the student in the classroom, will need to: negotiate the frequency and duration of hands-on assistance at each phase of the inclusion process, and advise the LST on necessary training and instructional materials required.

Human resource	Focus of hands-on assistance							
	Classroom team teaching	Classroom group	Classroom 1 to 1	Playground group	Playground 1 to 1	Withdrawal group	Withdrawal 1 to 1
Class peers							
Age peers							
Older students							
Senior students							
Volunteers							
Parents							
Teacher aides							
Colleague teachers							
Support teachers							
Executive teachers							
Specialist support teachers							
Specialist consultants							
Therapists							
Disability organisations							
Community organisations							

Resource checklist 6: Funding support

Funding support can be a key component of a resource support package for students with additional needs. Funding, if required, should be sought first from within school resources. Determinations will need to be made whether funding support is for initial setup costs and/or for ongoing costs. There is a variety of potential funding sources to support inclusion, but needs-based essential funding should be negotiated first, with non-essential 'value-adding' funding negotiated subsequently from a broader source base. This checklist cross-references the three best practices and nine key groups of resources discussed in this chapter against potential funding sources.

Potential funding support source

Funding focus	School budget	District/education authority budget	Direct state/federal government funding	School council/parent group	Parents	Industry partners	Community groups	Setup and/or ongoing costs?	Essential or non-essential funding?
Best practice: Collaborative planning/LST									
Best practice: Support needs assessment									
Best practice: An individual perspective & an ecological context									
'Hands-on' assistance in the classroom									
Consultancy support									
Adapted curriculum & instructional materials									
Assistive technology									
Student, staff and community support									
Access and mobility									
Professional development & training									
Funding support									

Summary

This chapter has introduced readers to the wide range of potential resources available to support the inclusion of students with additional needs. Planning for inclusion is explained in terms of three best practices: collaborative planning within a learning support team model; comprehensive and ongoing appraisal of educational support needs; and an individual perspective within an ecological context. Nine key groups of resources were then described. A particular emphasis was placed on explaining the diversity and utility of hands-on resources for the classroom. The last part of the chapter presents and explains a series of resource checklists to assist teachers and schools to organise a comprehensive 'package' of resources. The chapter is cross-referenced to other chapters to ensure a comprehensive approach to inclusive planning, and successful outcomes for students with additional needs.

Discussion questions

1   Meeting the special educational needs of some students requires extensive resource allocations. Most educational authorities have a limit on resource allocations to support individual inclusive enrolments. How might this limit be determined?

2   School communities embracing inclusion are enrolling increasing numbers of students with special needs. Is the number of students with special needs enrolling in any one school or class an issue? Why?

3   Imagine you are involved in setting up an LST at a new school. What is a reasonable and fair due process for enrolling students with special needs?

4   Adapted curriculum and instructional materials and the development of effective teaching techniques are key elements in the successful inclusion of students with special needs. How could/should resources to support these activities be developed?

Individual activities

1   Go to the website for a relevant education authority. (See Education authorities: URLs below.) Find and describe 10 web pages that are relevant to the inclusion of students with special needs.

2   Using one of the scenarios in Group activities from Chapter 1, prepare a 500-word interim ISP. This should cover the pre-inclusion/pre-transition phase of the inclusion process (say one term preceding the student's enrolment), and the early inclusion/transition phase (say the first term of enrolment). Focus on identifying and organising requisite resources to facilitate successful inclusion.

3   Imagine yourself back commencing your final year of high school. Also imagine you had a serious illness during the end-of-year holidays and are confined to a wheelchair for your remaining time at school. Develop a hypothetical ISP, with an emphasis on a 'package' of resources to support you in your quest to qualify for a place at university.

4   You have been newly appointed to a class with a number of students with special educational needs. You have no information about their needs at this time. Your principal has allocated you a teacher aide for 10 hours per week for at least the first term. How could you plan to use this teacher aide time as a resource in your classroom?

5 A diverse group of children with special needs is enrolled at your new school. There appear to be no resources to support their inclusion. You mention this to your principal who responds by asking you to prepare the agenda for, and act as chairperson for, the school's next pupil-free day. All the school staff and interested school community members will be attending. The topic will be 'Supporting the inclusion of students with special needs'. Your educational authority has promised you four hours of specialist consultancy support on the day. What will your agenda be?

Group activities

1 As a group, form an LST, and prepare a preliminary resource package proposal that you believe will facilitate the successful inclusion of a (hypothetical) student with special needs.

2 As a group, conduct a role play involving five people. These are: a prospective student (with a physical disability and special needs), who is keen to enrol in the first year of high school; the student's parents, who strongly support an inclusive enrolment; the school principal, who believes that enrolment at the local school is inappropriate; and the year level adviser, who has mixed views on the enrolment. This is a first meeting to discuss the feasibility and suitability of the proposed enrolment.

3 Prepare and conduct a debate on the topic: Inclusion for students with behaviour problems is unrealistic.

4 Prepare and conduct a debate on the topic: The common curriculum is inappropriate for students with intellectual disabilities.

5 As the parents of a child with high support needs, including severe intellectual disabilities, sensory impairments and complex physical care needs, you rightfully seek their enrolment at the local school. The school principal doubts the school's ability to support this enrolment, and suggests that you enrol your child in a special education setting. You refuse, and take your child's case to the local state MP. As a group, prepare a five-minute presentation (also in writing) to the member outlining your argument for this enrolment.

References

Abbott, C. (Ed.), (2002). *Special Educational Needs and the Internet: Issues for the Inclusive Classroom*. London: Routledge Falmer.

Angelo, D. (1997). AAC in the family and home. In S. Glennen & D. DeCoste (Eds), *Handbook of Augmentative and Alternative Communication*. San Diego: Singular. pp. 523–45.

*Avramidis, E. & Norwich, B. (2002). Teachers' attitudes towards integration/inclusion: A review of the literature. *European Journal of Special Needs Education*, 17(2), 129–47.

Booth, T. & Ainscow, M. (2002). *Index for Inclusion: Developing Learning and Participation in Schools*. Bristol, England: Centre for Studies on Inclusive Education.

Boyd, S. (1999). *All Keyed Up: The Use of Computers, at Home and at School, by Children With Special Needs*. SET Special, Wellington: New Zealand Council for Educational Research.

Brent, B. O. (2000). Do classroom volunteers benefit schools? *Principal*, 80(1), 36–40, 43.

Brett, A. & Provenzo, E. F. (1995). *Adaptive Technology for Special Human Needs*. New York: State University of New York Press.

Bronfenbrenner, U. (1979). *The Ecology of Human Development*. Cambridge, MA: Harvard University Press.

Burke, M. A. (2001). Recruiting and using volunteers in meaningful ways in secondary schools. *NASSP Bulletin*, 85(2), 46–52.

Burtch, J. A. (1999). Technology is for everyone. *Educational Leadership*, 56(5), 33–4.

Carpenter, B. (2002). Defining early intervention for the 21st Century: The first steps towards social inclusion. *The SLD Experience*, (33), 8–10.

*Chalmers, S. E., Carter, M., Clayton, M. & Hook, J. (1998). Education of students with high support needs: Teachers' perceptions of possible best practices, reported implementation and training needs. *Australasian Journal of Special Education*, 22(2), 76–94.

*Cole, P. C. (1999). The structure of arguments used to support or oppose inclusion policies for students with disabilities. *Journal of Intellectual and Developmental Disability*, 24(3), 215–25.

Cowling, M. (2001). *When Does the Concept of Inclusion/Integration Become Unrealistic and Move Down the Path of Tokenism? Follow the Yellow Brick Road.* Paper presented at the Australian Society for the Study of Intellectual Disability (ASSID) 36th Annual Conference, 12–15 November, Sydney Australia.

Devore, S. (2000). 'I wanted to see if we could make it work': Perspectives on inclusive childcare. *Exceptional Children*, 66(2), 241–55.

Dinnebeil, L. A. & McInerney, W. F. (2001). An innovative practicum to support early childhood inclusion through collaborative consultation. *Teacher Education and Special Education*, 24(3), 263–6.

*Doyle, M. B. (1997). *The Paraprofessionals Guide to the Inclusive Classroom: Working as a Team.* Baltimore: Paul H. Brookes

Elliott, D. & McKenney, M. (1998). Four inclusion models that work. *Teaching Exceptional Children*, 30(4), 54–8.

European Agency for Development in Special Needs Education (2000). *A Seventeen Country Study of the Relationship Between Financing of Special Needs Education and Inclusion* [Online]. Available: http:///www.european-agency.org/publications/finance/english.html

Evans, D. (2002). *Young Children With Disabilities Transitioning to School: What Are the Critical Players Saying?* Paper presented at the 7th Annual International Hippocrates & Socrates Conference, March 15–16, CHERI Education Research Institute, Childrens' Hospital at Westmead, Sydney, Australia.

*Foreman, P., Bourke, S., Mishra, G. & Frost, R. (2001). Assessing the support needs of children with a disability in regular classes. *International Journal of Disability, Development and Education*, 48(3), 239–52.

Forgrave, K. E. (2002). Assistive technology: Empowering students with learning disabilities. *Clearing House*, 75(3), 122–6.

French, N. K. (1998). Working together: Resource teachers and paraprofessionals. *Remedial and Special Education*, 19, 357–68.

French, N. K. (1999). Topic #1 Paraeducators: Who are they and what do they do? *Teaching Exceptional Children*, 32(1), 65–9.

*French, N. K. & Pickett, A. L. (1997). Paraprofessionals in special education: Issues for teacher educators. *Teacher Education and Special Education*, 20(1), 61–73.

Giangreco, M. E., Broer, S. M. & Edelman, S. W. (1999). The tip of the iceberg: Determining whether paraprofessional support is needed for students with disabilities in general education settings. *The Journal of the Association for Persons with Severe Handicaps*, 24, 280–90.

*Giangreco, M. F., Edelman, S. W., Broer, S. M. & Doyle, M. B. (2001). Paraprofessional support of students with disabilities: Literature from the past decade. *Exceptional Children, 68*(1), 45–63.

Goor, M. B. & Schwenn, J. O. (1993). Accommodating diversity and disability with co-operative learning. *Intervention in School and Clinic, 29*, 6–16.

Halpern, A. S. (1993). *Evaluation of the Transition Process From a Qualitative Process.* Paper presented at the Second International Transition Conference, Sydney, July.

Higgins, K., Boone, R. & Williams, D. L. (2000). Evaluating educational software for special education. *Intervention in School and Clinic, 36*(2), 109–15.

Hilton, A. & Gerlach, K. (1997). Employment, preparation and management of paraeducators: Challenges to appropriate services for children with developmental disabilities. *Education and Training in Mental Retardation and Developmental Disabilities, 32*, 71–7.

*Hunt, P. & Goetz, L. (1997). Research on inclusive education programs, practices, and outcomes for students with severe disabilities. *Journal of Special Education, 31*, 3–29.

Hunt, P., Soto, G., Maier, J. & Doering, K. (2003). Collaborative teaming to support students at risk and students with severe disabilities in general education classrooms. *Exceptional Children, 69*(3), 315–32.

*Jenkinson, J. (1997). Chapter 10 Teaching and learning: Curriculum, resources and support. In J. Jenkinson (Ed.), *Mainstream or Special: Educating Students With Disabilities*, London: Routledge Falmer, pp.161–81.

Johnson, J. P., Livingston, M., Schwartz, R. A. & Slate, J. R. (2000). What makes a good elementary school? A critical examination. *Journal of Educational Research, 93*(6), 339–45.

Jones, V. F. & Jones, L. S. (2001). *Comprehensive Classroom Management.* (6th edn). Sydney: Allyn and Bacon.

Kozleski, E., Mainzer, R. & Deshler, D. (2000). Bright futures for exceptional learners: An action agenda to achieve quality conditions for teaching and learning. *Teaching Exceptional Children, 32*(6), 56–69.

Lankshear, C., Snyder, I. & Green, B. (2000). *Teachers and Techno-literacy: Managing Literacy, Technology and Learning in Schools.* Sydney: Allen and Unwin.

*Lewis, R. B. (1998). Assistive technology and learning disabilities: Today's realities and tomorrow's promises. *Journal of Learning Disabilities, 31*(1), 16–26.

McGregor, G. & Vogelsberg, R. T. (1998). *Inclusive School Practices: Pedagogical and Research Foundations: A Synthesis of the Literature That Informs Best Practices About Inclusive Schooling.* Baltimore: Paul H. Brookes.

*McRae, D. (1996). *The Integration/Inclusion Feasibility Study.* Sydney: NSW Department of School Education.

NSW Department of Education and Training. (2003). *Learning Support Teams (LST)* Retrieved 12 November, 2003 from www.schools.nsw.edu.au

Parette, H. (1997). Assistive technology devices and services. *Education and Training in Mental Retardation and Training, 32*, 267–80.

Peterson, A. M. (1997). Aspects of school climate: A review of the literature. *ERS Spectrum, 15*(1), 36–42.

Ray, J. & Warden, M. K. (1995). *Technology, Computers, and the Special Needs Learner.* Melbourne: Thomas Nelson.

Salzberg, C. L. & Morgan, J. (1995). Preparing teachers to work with paraeducators. *Teacher Education and Special Education, 18*, 49–55.

Schery, T. & O,Connor, L. (1997). Language intervention: Computer training for young children with special needs. *British Journal of Educational Technology, 28*(4), 271–9.

Shula, S., Kennedy, C. H. & Cushing, L. S. (1999). Intermediate school students with severe disabilities: Supporting their education in general education classrooms. *Journal of Positive Behavior Interventions, 1*, 130–40.

Steckelberg, A. L. & Vasa, S. E. (1998). How paraeducators learn on the web. *Teaching Exceptional Children, 30*(5), 54–9.

Taylor, J. (1998). Chapter 13 Technology for living and learning. In P. Lacey & C. Ouvry (Eds), *People With Profound and Multiple Learning Disabilities. A Collaborative Approach to Meeting Complex Needs* (pp. 156–66). London: David Fulton Publishers.

Utley, C. A., Mortweet, S. L. & Greenwood, C. R. (1997). Peer-mediated instruction and interventions. *Focus on Exceptional Children, 29*(5), 2–23.

Wadsworth, D. E. & Knight, D. (1996). Paraprofessionals: The bridge to successful full inclusion. *Intervention in School and Clinic, 31*, 166–71.

Weishaar, M. K. (2001). The Regular Educator's Role in the Individual Education Plan Process. *Clearing House, 75*(2), 96–8.

Welch, M., Brownell, K. & Sheridan, S. M. (1999). What's the score and game plan on teaming in schools? A review of the literature on team teaching and school-based problem solving teams. *Remedial and Special Education, 20*(1), 36–49.

*Wolery, M., Alerts, M., Caldwell, N., Snyder, E. & Liskowski, L. (1995). Experienced teachers' perceptions of resources and supports for inclusion. *Education and Training in Mental Retardation and Developmental Disabilities, 30*, 15–26.

Wyer, K. (2001). The great equalizer: Assistive technology launches a new era in inclusion. *Teaching Tolerance, 19*, 25–9.

Zigmond, N. (1997). Chapter 19 Educating students with disabilities: The future of special education. In J. Lloyd, E. Keemanui & D. Chard (Eds), *Issues in Educating Students With Disabilities* (pp. 377–90). Manwah, NJ: Lawrence Erlbaum Associates.

——
*Recommended reading for this chapter

Education authorities: URLs

ACT Department of Education, Youth and Family Services <www.decs.act.gov.au>

Department of Education, Science and Training (DEST) <www.dest.gov.au>

Department of Education, Tasmania <www.education.tas.gov.au>

Department of Education and Children's Services, South Australia <www.dete.sa.gov.au/decs_home.asp>

Department of Education and Training, Victoria <www.deet.vic.gov.au/deet/>

Education Department of Western Australia <www.eddept.wa.edu.au>

Education Queensland <www.education.qld.gov.au>

Northern Territory Department of Employment, Education and Training <www.education.nt.gov.au>

NSW Department of Education and Training <www.schools.nsw.edu.au>

Chapter 12

Transition to adult learning

Ian Dempsey

This chapter aims to:

- show the role of regular class teachers in preparing students for post-school life
- demonstrate ways in which teachers can assist students with additional needs to successfully transition from school
- show the importance of integrating school programs with work experience and vocational education and training.

Post-school outcomes for students with additional needs

Regardless of the level of education, all teachers are part of the process of preparing students for post-school life. Even in infant grades, teachers are attempting to establish skills such as the ability to interact appropriately with others, basic independence in a range of life activities, and basic academics, which will allow students to continue to develop throughout their school careers and in later life. Understandably, at this early level it is difficult to predict exactly what academic skills students will need to be successful when they leave school. Given the rate of change in areas such as bio-technology and information and communication technology, predicting exactly what skills students will need in 10 years time is challenging because these skills are likely to change significantly in the next decade.

For this reason, attention to what students want to do when they leave school, and how schools can assist students to achieve their post-school goals, are generally left until the middle years of high school. It is at this time that the student, their family and the school will be in a better position to judge the student's capabilities and to determine the prospects for achieving a range of possible post-school outcomes. Broadly speaking, these outcomes will cover employment, living in the community, and further education and training.

Planning for post-school life occurs for all students. For students without a disability, such planning typically includes advice on possible careers through school-based careers advisers, the opportunity for work experience in the final years of schooling, and specific advice on choice of school subjects for those students who plan to continue their post-secondary education. This level of planning is also available for students with a disability. However, a coordinated transition planning process is vital for many students with additional needs because the research literature has consistently shown that post-school outcomes for students with additional needs is poor in comparison to other students. For example, Murray et al. (2000) reported that students with learning disability in the USA have lower rates of employment, lower earnings, lower rates of post-compulsory school attendance, and lower rates of independent living than other students. In reviewing the literature in this area, Murray (2003) found that these poor outcomes extended to students with intellectual disability, and to students with severe behaviour problems who were likely to experience higher incarceration rates than the general population when they left school. In the USA, only 32.5 per cent of people with a disability aged 18 to 64 work full-time or part-time, compared to 81 per cent of the population without a disability (National Organization on Disability, 2000).

Schools are in a unique position to address some of these problems. In particular, schools are capable of providing coordinated support programs through the collaboration of classroom teachers, support teachers, counsellors and career advisers. This level of coordination is not easy to achieve once the student has left school, when their requirements may need to be addressed through many government departments at the federal, state and local level, and where a single coordinating service may not be available to meet their needs.

The literature shows that there are a number of risk factors associated with post-school outcomes. This means that there are some indicators that are strongly related to how well students do when they leave school. In relation to gender, males are more likely to be labelled with a special need than females. However, females with a disability are more likely to experience poor outcomes than their male counterparts (Benz, Yovanoff & Doren, 1997). Ethnic background is also associated with disability. This relationship is well known in the USA (US Department of Education, 2000), and in Australia (Dempsey, 2003). For example, in Australia, Aboriginal students are far more likely to be suspended from school than other students (Doherty, 2003). Socio-economic status (SES) is also related to disability status, and SES is also related to ethnic background.

While this information may be instructive to teachers, we need to be careful how we interpret these findings. Clearly, having one or more of these risk factors does not condemn a student to experience poor post-school outcomes. Students spend at least 15 000 hours at school, and schools can exert a powerful positive influence on students. In addition, the research has also identified a range of protective factors that appear to balance, and sometimes negate, risk factors (Svetaz, Ireland & Blum, 2000). Rather than concentrating on issues of risk, it is more useful to be aware of both risk and of protective factors, and to use this information in a constructive way to support students with additional needs. Examples of these factors, as they relate to schools, appear in Box 12.1.

Box 12.1

Examples of school risk factors, school protective factors, and implications for practice for students with special needs

Risk factors	Protective factors	Implications for practice
<ul><li>Poor quality instruction</li><li>Low engagement in school activities</li><li>Low level of bonding to the school</li><li>Unsafe school environment</li><li>Poor peer relationships</li><li>Dropping out of school</li></ul>	<ul><li>Positive and supporting teacher–student relationships</li><li>Focus on building academic, social and emotional skills</li><li>Focus on building self-determination and internal locus of control</li><li>Consistent home–school communication</li><li>Consistent and well-designed transition planning</li></ul>	<ul><li>Build positive relationships with students by 'knowing' them</li><li>Reflect on teaching to make it responsive to students' needs</li><li>Encourage students to set goals, act on the goals, and assess their progress</li><li>Ensure students experience success</li><li>Incorporate social problem-solving skills in all curriculums</li><li>Work with parents to develop meaningful transition plans</li></ul>

Adapted from Murray, 2003

The importance of these risk and protective factors is reinforced by much of the material that appears earlier in this book, particularly the chapters that relate to designing effective instruction and to curriculum modification. However, some of the items from Box 12.1 are most relevant to transition from school. For example, the protective factors of self-determination (which relates to enhancing students' belief that they are capable of making and following through on realistic plans), and locus of control (individuals with internal locus of control are more likely to see themselves as being responsible for much that occurs in their lives), are important qualities to encourage in all students. The importance of self-determination, in particular, as well as ways in which teachers can promote this quality for their students, is discussed in more detail later in this chapter.

The importance of the transition planning process is demonstrated in the USA through legislation in this area. The 1997 amendments to the *Individuals with Disabilities Education Act* mandate that each student must have transition services included in their individualised education program (IEP) no later than age 14. The Act also requires a systematic plan of action for vocational and other community activities for students with additional needs, and that there be greater access to the regular curriculum and assessment for these students. While there is no similar legislation in Australia or New Zealand, educational policies in these countries recognise the importance of planning for the transition from school. The important features of this planning are now discussed, with examples of the ways in which schools and teachers can assist in transition.

Key components of transition planning

In many Australian states and territories, early approaches to transition planning have operated under a fairly consistent model that comprised school and community-based teams. This model recognised the importance of collaboration between schools and the organisations in the community that students were likely to access when they left school. In New South Wales, a transition education program was established in 1989 (Riches, 1996). A transition support project was introduced into Victorian schools in 1994, which used school transition officers in metropolitan and country areas to work directly with students, parents, community groups and government departments to facilitate the transition process (Keogh, 1995). Similar models also operated in Tasmania (Department of Education, Tasmania, 1999), and other states and territories in Australia.

In recent years, the orientation of transition planning has changed in many settings in Australia. This change was prompted by a number of factors. First, there has been an erroneous assumption by staff in many schools that transition planning was essentially a separate program that students were channelled into. An unfortunate consequence of this view was that transition was seen to have little to do with regular class teachers. Second, there was also a recognition that a mix of regular school curriculum, work experience, and vocational training may be a better curriculum option for many students, rather than an entirely functional curriculum (Neubert, Moon & Grigal, 2002). A functional curriculum is a program of school study that is at a conceptually easier level than the standard curriculum. Examples of functional curriculum and their place in schools are given later in this chapter.

A result of this change in orientation is that transition planning is delivered in very flexible ways and varies widely across settings in response to the needs of the students concerned. The common feature to this planning is that a combination of school- and community-based resources and supports is used. The principles that guide the use of these resources and supports include individualised planning, making use of family and community support networks, being aware of post-school options in the community, and working with relevant community agencies. Each of these principles is now described.

Individualised planning

The names and the methods of operation of specific support services across schools in Australia and New Zealand vary. However, many schools involved in transition planning have access to a transition coordinator who may offer advice, organise services, or provide direct support to students and teachers. For example, in Victoria the *Futures for Young Adults Program* provides a number of regional support staff for schools (Victorian Department of Education & Training, 2003). These staff can facilitate the organisation of planning meetings, or suggest ways in which the school might modify the curriculum to meet the needs of older students with a disability. Many teachers in regular schools will also have access to a careers adviser who may assist in the development of school- and community-based work experience programs for students with a disability.

Depending on the policy of some schools, the support teacher or resource teacher may also be available to assist older students with additional needs in a variety of ways. For example, the support teacher may be able to accompany the student to a regular class and give that student assistance in classroom activities. The support teacher may also act as a consultant by providing the regular class teacher with resources or advice to assist in the inclusion of the student. Some school systems also provide itinerant teachers, aides and therapists who can assist in the transition process.

Regardless of the types of support available, and the names used to describe this support, there are some important strategies to follow in providing transition assistance to individual students. These strategies include developing a clear plan for the student, enhancing the student's ability to assume responsibility for their current and future plans, allowing for some flexibility in the way the student progresses through high school, and providing the student with a meaningful record of their achievements at school in cases where they may not complete the standard curriculum. Each of these strategies is now discussed.

Individualised transition plan

Coordinated transition planning is essential to optimise transition outcomes for students with additional needs. While this planning may be conducted by a small group of school staff, the nature of the planning will address many issues. For example, it may include the development of appropriate curriculum for individual students, the establishment and monitoring of an individualised transition plan (ITP), the provision of relevant information about community resources and facilities, the establishment of links with other services (for example, technical education and post-school options programs), and the provision of support and advice to regular classroom teachers.

School-based support teams can be made up of students, their parents, teachers, and representatives from community organisations and other agencies that may support the student (for example, staff from technical education colleges). As students may attend several regular high school classes, the team may wish to liaise with the teachers of these classes in supporting the student. Regardless, the aim of school-based support teams is to develop a meaningful ITP for each student, and to implement and monitor this plan.

In schools where a formal transition planning process does not operate, school-based support teams may still exist. Indeed, their operation may extend beyond the transition process. For example, in New South Wales, learning support teams may be established in schools to provide planning and support to ensure that the needs of all students are being met (NSW Department of Education & Training, 1998). In considering the support required by students to achieve planned learning outcomes, the team may address issues such as curriculum modification, teaching and management strategies, and specialised equipment and transport needs.

Understanding the student and the student's vision

The ITP is a statement of the educational goals and objectives necessary for a student to achieve a successful transition. It develops from an assessment of the student's strengths, interests and needs. In doing so, it considers the range of post-school options that may be available to the student in areas such as employment, accommodation and leisure. Programming may be provided in those areas. However, depending on the needs of the student, programming may also extend to personal management, social and interpersonal skills, and communication; or it may focus on assisting the student to continue to access the regular curriculum.

The focus of the ITP is on creating a vision of the future with the student. That vision should describe how the student will be included in a variety of different aspects of community life. This planning process is student-centred. That is, the aim of the exercise is to gain a clear picture of the student as a person (their preferences, their contributions, what they do best), to describe the student's expectations (their dream(s), their goals for the future), and a structure for achieving these expectations (Morningstar, Kleinhammer-Tramill & Lattin, 1999). Examples of key questions to ask at each stage of this planning process are shown in Box 12.2.

Box 12.2
Key questions in the ITP process

Individualised transition planning steps	*Key questions*
Creating a positive description of the student	What are the student's gifts, interests and talents?
	Who is the student?
	What is the student's story?
Developing a vision	What is the student's desired lifestyle?
	What is the student's dream?
	What are desirable images for the student's future?
Making a plan	What are the student's options and what are the most important of these?
	What people and supports may be needed to achieve these options?
	What timeline and steps are required?

Without a clear understanding of the student, their strengths, interests, needs, and their vision for the future, teachers will not be in a good position to customise what they do in the classroom to meet some of these needs. Of course, a formal planning process is not always required to develop such a plan. In the normal process of developing a positive relationship with each of the students in the class, teachers will observe students in a variety of situations, will engage them in conversation, and will get to know them as more than the 'student who sits in the second row to the left'. Regardless of the way in which a deeper understanding of the student develops, the important issue is how the teacher can make use of this information in the classroom.

Using a transition plan in the regular classroom

Regular class teachers who work with students with special needs may be required to implement one or more aspects of the student's ITP. For example, an English teacher working with a student whose ITP includes an objective to improve oral communication skills, may be able to provide opportunities for the student to be involved in activities such as discussions and verbal reports. For a student whose ITP includes the objective of developing skills to access a desired career in the building industry, the mathematics teacher may plan a range of measurement activities relevant to home construction.

A review of the ITP is conducted on a regular basis, usually at least once a year. At these reviews, new goals and objectives may be introduced, the people responsible for implementing these goals are determined, and a time frame for achieving these goals is decided.

Self-determination

> Self-determination means knowing what one wants in life and having the mechanisms to achieve these goals ... The self-determined individual knows a great deal about him or herself, has a clear vision for the future, feels a sense of control over the immediate environment and decisions, can self-advocate, and can muster the necessary supports to accomplish what he or she wants.
>
> (Whitney-Thomas & Moloney, 2001, p. 376)

Perhaps the most important outcome of transition planning should be the promotion of self-determination for all school students. That is, schools should be teaching students to be self-sufficient citizens who are capable of looking after themselves as well as making a positive contribution to society. This goal is doubly important for many students with a disability because, as discussed earlier in this chapter, the post-school outcomes for these students are poor in comparison with other students. It may be that some students with a disability at school will never be fully independent in the community. For example, they may continue to rely on their family and government supports for some aspects of their lives. Regardless, the promotion of as much independence as possible is still a worthwhile goal as a means of enhancing the self-esteem of these students, and of reducing the level of financial and other community supports that they may need in the future.

Schools provide an important context in which adolescents develop a sense of themselves, and educators can do much to promote self-determination in their students. For example, providing opportunities for choice and decision-making, problem-solving, goal setting, promoting dignity of risk, self-evaluation, self-awareness, and self-efficacy (a belief that one's actions may be successful), are all likely to promote self-determination (Wehmeyer & Shalock, 2001). Many of these components of self-determination can be integrated into learning experiences from early childhood to adult settings. Some examples of learning activities that address different aspects of self-determination follow.

Choice-making

Making a choice involves communicating a preference. The value of this activity is in experiencing some control, in understanding that not all options may be available at the time, and that choices are constrained for everyone (Wehmeyer & Shalock, 2001). The wide range of activities experienced by students at school provides many opportunities for choice-making. Following are some ways in which choice may be incorporated into learning activities:

- choosing between two or more activities
- deciding when to complete an activity
- selecting with whom to participate
- deciding where to do the activity
- having the choice not to participate in an activity.

Self-awareness and self-knowledge

Blum, Lipsett and Yocom (2002) described the use of literature circles as a self-determination strategy in a high school class with students with learning difficulties. Each circle comprises three-to-six students who are encouraged to read for a purpose, report on what they have read, and to reflect on their reading. Readers prepare themselves for discussion by assuming different roles (for example, leader, illustrator, vocabulary helper), and then complete a worksheet. Examples of these worksheets appear in Box 12.3.

This activity can be combined with a survey that students complete before they experience literature circles, and several weeks later. The survey, shown in Table 12.1, is designed to encourage the students to reflect on their reading skills as a means to understanding themselves better. This activity could be used as a precursor to the students setting learning goals for themselves.

Box 12.3
Examples of participant worksheets in literature circles

Illustrator

Your job is to draw a picture about the reading. It could be a cartoon, a sketch, a diagram, or something else. You can draw a picture of something in the book, something that the reading reminded you of or a feeling you got from the reading.

When the leader asks you to, you can show the picture to the rest of the group. One at a time, they get to guess what the picture is about. When they have finished you can tell them what the picture means to you.

Vocabulary helper

Your job is to find tricky words and phrases in the reading. These could be words that you had trouble reading, or long or complicated words. Try to use the dictionary to help you with difficult words. List the words on your sheet in large writing.

When the leader asks you to, you should show the list to the rest of the group. Read the list to them and explain why you chose the words on your list. You can ask the group if they have any other tricky words to add.

Adapted from Blum, Lipsett & Yocom, 2002

Table 12.1 Student survey used in literature circles

	Low			High	
How do you rate your reading ability?	1	2	3	4	5
	Strongly disagree			Strongly agree	
I understand what I read.	1	2	3	4	5
I remember what I read.	1	2	3	4	5
I can explain to others what I read.	1	2	3	4	5

Self-awareness may be developed more explicitly and can be used to inform the student's ITP, or can be used to supplement the student's portfolio. An example of a personal profile for a hypothetical high school student appears in Box 12.4. The student, with input from relevant teachers, has developed a list of their strengths and needs. This exercise may be useful for the student in encouraging self-awareness, and it can also be useful for teachers in helping them to understand the student more deeply and by alerting them to issues they should address in classroom activities.

Self-monitoring

Self-monitoring strategies include teaching students to observe, assess and record their own behaviour. These strategies can be readily included in a range of classroom activities and an example is shown in Figure 12.1. Here, the purpose is to encourage the student to reflect on how well they have completed the requirements for submitted assignments. Self-monitoring is an important work-related skill.

Box 12.4

Personal profile for Michael

I'm 14 years old and I attend Riverbank High School. I play football in winter, and I swim in summer. I'd like to work with engines, maybe as a mechanic. I will stay at school until at least Year 10. I will look for an apprenticeship and perhaps start studying at TAFE.

Things I'm good at

Reading
- Joining in discussions about the book
- Sharing stories with the class

Maths
- Using the calculator for basic computations
- Remembering number sequences

Science
- Using the lab equipment safely
- Rainforests and their animals

Design and technology
- Using some of the hand tools
- Understanding how engines work

Study skills
- Bringing materials to class
- Being on time for class

Social skills
- Sharing with others
- Helping others

continued

Box 12.4 continued

Things I need to work on

Reading
- My writing and spelling
- Learning some of the words in maths and science

Science
- Remembering the elements
- Physics equations

Study skills
- Completing my homework on time
- Organising my projects

Maths
- Percentages and fractions
- Metric measurements

Design and technology
- Designing jobs
- Writing up my projects

Social skills
- Not getting angry when I make mistakes

P	A	C	E	1	(Three examples of erosion)
☺	☺	☺	☺	☺	Student
☺	☺	☺	X	☺	Teacher
				2	(Picture for each example)
				☺	
				☺	
				3	(Two ways to prevent erosion)
				☺	
				X	

Figure 12.1 The PACE strategy for monitoring submission of assignments

(Adapted from Rademacher, 2000)

The basis of the approach is a mnemonic strategy that uses the word 'PACE'. In this example, the letters stand for Prompt (handed in on time), Arranged neatly (tidy, correct margins, well organised), Complete (directions followed, all questions answered), and Edited (good spelling and grammar). As shown, the student has indicated he believes he has met all the requirements (the PACE requirements and three specific requirements for the work), and the teacher has shown that two requirements were not met. To make this strategy useful to students it would need to be taught to students, and follow-up support provided as required. The teacher could:

- introduce the activity to students as a way of improving the quality of their work – students could be asked for suggestions on what 'quality work' is
- give students examples of those assignments that meet and those that do not meet quality standards
- model how students would use the strategy before and during the completion of their work

- give students ideas on how they could work to complete requirements they may not have met for a given assignment.

Self-monitoring strategies also lend themselves to supporting students with social or behavioural problems. For example, the teacher may discuss with the student the behaviours that are disrupting their learning and the learning of others in the classroom. Once these are identified, and a commitment to reducing the behaviours is obtained, the student may wish to identify a preferred activity (for example, access to free time or the computer) they can use if positive behaviour is displayed. Monitoring can occur by providing the students with a record sheet that allows them to show whether they believe they've achieved their goal for each lesson, and with space on the sheet for the teacher to also provide a rating.

Flexible progression

Some states in Australia have provided a formal mechanism by which students may vary the rate at which they complete their schooling. An example is the Pathways policy in New South Wales, which allows students to select subjects at a level that may be different from that chosen by most of their peers, if they can demonstrate that they have the prerequisite skills.

Most of the attention received by this form of flexible progression has related to students who have 'fast-tracked' their schooling. That is, students who may be completing school subjects several years in advance of their peers, or who may be enrolled in one or more university subjects while they complete their schooling. However, flexible progression also has something to offer students with additional needs. For example, a student whose work capacity is slowed by a physical disability may choose to complete a Certificate 'year' over several years. In some schools, the enrolment of mature-aged students is not uncommon. Nor is it uncommon for some students to be completing their schooling part-time, and thus be taking longer to graduate. This flexibility has the potential to advantage some students with special needs who in the past may not have considered this option because of pressure to continue to progress at the same rate as their peers.

Credentialling

A major criticism of the school system's ability to meet the needs of students with learning problems has been the incapacity of some state departments of education to provide all graduating students with the same certificate of attainment. Typically, students who have been unable to meet the curriculum requirements of a syllabus or other endorsed course from a state education department have been eligible for a special record of their achievement, but not the same award presented to other students. This has clearly disadvantaged many students, who after 10 or more years at school may receive a certificate that is not recognised by employers, which may serve to discriminate against them when they seek employment.

In 1995, the New South Wales Department of Education and Training, made the School Certificate (typically completed after 10 school years), available to all students, regardless of the course of study that they had completed at school. This option became available for the Higher School Certificate (12 school years of study) in 2000. For those students who completed a non-standard syllabus (see NSW Board of Studies, 2003), a record of achievement shows the key learning area balance in the student's program of study, and a student profile shows outcomes achieved in each of the key learning areas. For some students, this will mean that their record will indicate that they completed all non-standard subjects. For others, it will show a mix of mainstream and other subjects. An important outcome from this credentialling is that students with additional needs now receive official recognition for their school achievements.

Involvement of family and other supports

The direct involvement of families is consistently referred to in the literature on best practices in transition planning (Morningstar, Kleinhammer-Tramill & Lattin, 1999). There are several reasons for this. First, families have an intimate knowledge of the skills, interests and needs of their members. Teachers will have an understanding of the students they teach in the school environment. However, this may not be enough to adequately plan for the community adjustment of these students. Second, families will continue to advocate for their members when they leave school. If teachers are to best prepare students with additional needs for post-school life, then the involvement of families in the educational process is critical. In doing so, parents may be empowered to maintain an effective support role for their son or daughter.

Unfortunately, families are typically characterised as either uninvolved or over-involved in their child's education. For example, teachers may frequently lament that school meetings are often attended by 'the parents that you don't need to see'. That is, there is a belief that the parents who attend such meetings are those whose children are not experiencing difficulties in their academic or social skills. In addition, teachers may see those parents who take a more active role in their child's education as being 'problem' parents. Individual parents will be on a continuum of levels of involvement in their child's education. What is important is that schools provide an opportunity for parents to be as involved as they wish to be. Box 12.5 identifies some barriers to parent involvement in transition planning and some ideas on facilitating their involvement.

There are several strategies that teachers can use to promote the involvement of families. These strategies include encouraging parents to have early expectations about the community living and employment options for their son or daughter, helping parents to recognise the importance of their contributions in the educational process, providing genuine opportunities for family input into the educational program, and supporting parents in honouring the choices of their children (Buswell & Sax, 2002).

In the past, regular classroom teachers typically have collaborated little with parents in the educational process. The involvement of parents in regular schools has often been limited to parents' and citizens' associations, fundraising, parent–teacher nights, and parents acting as reading tutors or volunteers. This contrasts with parental involvement that may be typical with many students with a disability where there is much more frequent communication between home and school, where parents are consulted in the development of educational programs, and where the school may provide a range of options for collaboration between teachers and parents.

As Chapter 2 demonstrated, many state and territory special education policies in Australia recognise that the involvement of parents in the educational process is highly desirable, and that parents have the right to choose to participate. Not all parents will want to be highly involved in deciding the educational programs of their son or daughter. However, it is important that teachers and school systems provide opportunities for parents to be involved, if they choose to do so.

Barriers and opportunities for family involvement in transition planning

1 Professional and family misconceptions

Teachers may see the current level of family involvement as inappropriate, and parents may distrust the school or be frustrated by a lack of opportunity for involvement.

2 Low and conflicting expectations

On the one hand, some families are seen as having low expectations for their son or daughter (perhaps influenced by a lack of awareness of opportunities, or a genuine lack of services), or families who want different things from professionals may be seen as having 'unrealistic expectations'.

3 Lack of opportunity

Some families report being left out of planning educational supports for their son or daughter. Often planning meetings are held at a time and place that is not convenient to parents.

4 Stress during transition

While adolescence is a stressful time for many families, the situation is compounded for families with a member with a disability because transition involves moving from a time of some certainty of services at school, to uncertainty about what community services may be accessible.

1 Clarifying roles

Professionals need to consider families' needs and accept a level of involvement that the family is comfortable with. Teachers cease to be 'experts', and become 'partners'. Families cease to be 'passive recipients', and become 'active players'.

2 Provide information early and throughout planning

Families need information about what services the school can provide, and what community services they may be able to access now and in the future. This information may need to be provided more than once so the planning process should start early.

3 Establishing new opportunities

The focus of the IEP meeting is the student's and the family's vision. The meeting is 'owned' by the student and their family.

4 Developing new skills

As the transition process will continue well after the student leaves school, it makes sense for students and their families to use the planning skills they will require while they are still at school.

Adapted from Morningstar, Kleinhammer-Tramill & Lattin, 1999

Awareness of community options

Vocational education and training

The potential of vocational education and training (VET) in enhancing outcomes for students with special needs has been recognised for several decades. However, in recent years there has been a resurgence of interest in vocational education for regular education students. This increased interest reflects debate about the extent to which schools should prepare students for work, through vocational training, in addition to providing more traditional training in academic skills required for access to university. The interest has also been fuelled by a massive increase in the proportion of students remaining at Australian schools to the end of secondary schooling from 35 per cent in 1980, to 72 per cent in 2000 (Te Riele & Crump, 2002). This means that schools have a responsibility to provide meaningful curriculum in the final years of schooling not only to students who may want to continue their education at university, but also to students who want to follow a career as a technician, a tradesperson, or in other vocationally-oriented professions. Regardless of the reasons for the current popularity of vocational education in schools, developments in this area have the potential to assist many students with additional needs whose current school academic program is not meeting their requirements.

The resurgence of interest in this area is also associated with the current low rates of participation by people with a disability in VET. Perhaps the most important of the statistics in this area is that while the proportion of the Australian population between 15 and 64 years who have a disability is 16.7 per cent, just 3.6 per cent of the VET population for the same age range have a disability. Further, one in six VET students without a disability are undertaking new apprenticeships, while the ratio for students with a disability is one in 50 (Australian National Training Authority, 2000a).

Such is the concern about the poor indicators in this area that a national strategy, *Bridging Pathways*, has been put in place to address the low rates of participation in VET by people with a disability and other disadvantaged groups (Australian National Training Authority,

2000b). Schools are identified as important players in this strategy. In particular, the potential for schools to facilitate VET training while students are still at school, is highlighted.

Unfortunately, some schools have not been doing as effective a job as they might in encouraging VET options for their students. As previously noted, increased numbers of students who previously may have left school after nine or 10 years (including students with learning and social problems), are continuing to high school completion, and some school systems have been slow to change curriculum offerings to meet their needs. If wider options were more available and were accepted by teachers, 'that would mean that young people choosing VET would not be labelled as often as "at risk" students, a negative consequence of many special programs targeting alienated youth. Neither would VET programs be stigmatised as only for those relegated from the standard curriculum' (Te Riele & Crump, 2002, p. 261).

Many schools are doing an excellent job of providing vocational education options for their students, including students with a disability. In NSW, this option, TAFE-delivered VET (TVET), allows students to complete certificate level training from technical institutes while they are at school, and for this work to count towards the students' Higher School Certificate. Box 12.6 gives an example of the way in which schools can provide students with a mix of course options to meet their needs. Because the success of TVET lies in the close cooperation between schools and technical colleges, this training option is discussed in more detail later in this chapter.

Box 12.6
Paul's story

To achieve the goal of increasing opportunities for people with a disability in further education and training, Belmont High School recognises that building expectations, resilience and skills in all students to take their place as much as possible alongside same-stage peers in the mainstream delivery of courses, is a key to long-term success in the wider community. Paul (not his real name) is a case in point.

Paul has benefited from his school's approach of early supported inclusion for students with an initial support class placement. The support class teachers, while delivering some separate class instruction, also work collaboratively with Paul's mainstream teachers to aim for both social inclusion and learning inclusion for many of his subjects. The new Year 7 to 10 NSW Board of Studies syllabuses, containing life skills content and outcomes,

have begun to assist mainstream teachers to program in their specialty from the one syllabus document for the whole range of students in the class. Although much of Paul's Year 9 and 10 work met grade performance descriptors, he did not sit for the School Certificate examinations. He completed food technology and attained a B grade for his School Certificate in that subject. He consolidated those skills in the school Coffee Shop.

Currently in Year 11, Paul has developed a keen interest in the hospitality industry.

The transition to the final years of the curriculum required careful planning, but Paul was confident to make his Higher School Certificate (HSC) subject selection from a wide range of school- and TAFE-delivered offerings. He receives case management for his individual program using collaborative meetings with his

>

Box 12.6 continued

family, district transition personnel and other agencies such as the TAFE Disability Consultant and a specialised Commonwealth Employment Agency.

The school provides a life skills English and mathematics class on the timetable for Paul and other students who experience significant difficulties with the standard HSC courses in these subjects. Paul is keeping up his sporting interests with the sport, lifestyle and recreation studies course, and he is learning photography and doing a TAFE-delivered hospitality course.

He completes the mainstream 2 Unit Work Studies Course, and does work experience at a local bakery one day per week, where the Commonwealth Employment Agency is negotiating a traineeship when he finishes Year 12. The school also employs a teacher aide special who monitors and supports his community-based work. A result of this level of flexibility in course selection is that Paul has a customised program of instruction that will help him to achieve his post-school goals.

Barbara Hinchey, Support Teacher Transition

University participation

Concerns about the low participation by students with a disability in VET also extend to university training (Foreman et al., 2001). In 2002, just 3.4 per cent of the Australian university student population comprised students with a disability, a figure much less than the proportion of people with a disability in the general population (Department of Education, Science & Training, 2003a).

To address the low participation by people with a disability in university training, the Australian Vice Chancellor's Committee (1996) encourages universities to follow these guidelines:

- Universities should aim to provide students with disabilities with the opportunity to realise their individual capabilities and to gain access to and participate in university life.
- Universities should ensure that all their interactions with students with disabilities are characterised by respect of their rights to dignity, privacy, confidentiality and equality.
- Universities should seek to provide support services to students with disabilities in the interests of equality of educational opportunity.

In addition, many universities have developed action plans to encourage the participation of people with a disability, as well as detailing strategies and support services to assist students with a disability who are currently enrolled. As an example, the University of Adelaide (2003) has appointed a Disability Liaison Officer to coordinate supports to students with a disability; the provision of 'Learning and Assessment Agreements' with relevant subject coordinators when changes to standard instruction are required, including aspects of inclusive teaching in the induction program for new university teaching staff; and a range of other supports that relate to library and technology services, as well as to physical access. Most universities have similar provisions.

Employment organisations

A significant change in disability services in the last two decades has been the development of a wide range of community employment options for people with a disability. For example, 10 years ago it was not uncommon to find that the only employment option for a person with a disability was a sheltered workshop. Now, particularly in metropolitan areas, employment services may include open employment (see Box 12.7 for an example), supported employment, enclaves (small groups of workers within a larger business), work crews, small businesses and cooperatives. In addition, there are post-school options programs in many states that provide training for young people with a disability who may not currently have the skills for entry into the workforce. Employers are now offered a range of incentives to employ people with a disability, and employees with a disability are now guaranteed a minimum wage and equitable working conditions (Commonwealth Department of Family & Community Services, 2003). In several states and territories, students who are unable to find employment when they leave school are provided a place in a community access program that allows them the opportunity to continue to develop their community living skills.

Box 12.7
Programs: Adam's Story

Adam is a young man 20 years of age who fought all barriers to become a successful small business operator.

Adam was diagnosed as having ADHD as a young teenager. He attended his local high school, although he struggled constantly with his school work. In Year 10 Adam, his family and school careers adviser decided that continuation of his schooling would be of no benefit to Adam, but would rather cause him further frustration. It was at this time that the careers advisor contacted our organisation, Castle Personnel Services Inc., a specialist organisation funded by the Department of Family and Community Services to assist persons with a disability to attain and retain employment in the competitive employment market (that is, open employment).

A transition-planning meeting was organised for Adam. The meeting involved Adam, his parents, the school's careers adviser and an employment officer from Castle. At the meeting Adam expressed his dislike of being indoors and frustration with academic studies. Adam also expressed an interest in plants and gardening. As a result of the meeting Adam was released from school one day a week for the final term of school to participate in a work experience placement that had been arranged by Castle. Adam's work experience placement proved very successful, with Adam deciding that gardening was the vocation he wished to pursue.

Castle managed to secure a gardening apprenticeship for Adam with the local Area Health Service. Adam commenced his apprenticeship and was excelling in the practical applications of the course. Unfortunately, due to Adam's extremely poor literacy skills, the same could not be said for the TAFE component of the course. Adam contacted Castle expressing his frustration with not being able to understand his TAFE work.

After consultation with the TAFE, Adam was able to undertake the Adult Basic Education course and then transfer back into the mainstream horticulture course. Adam successfully completed his apprenticeship obtaining credits in all subjects. After completing his apprenticeship course work Adam undertook further study in tree surgery. In 2003 Adam was awarded the Regional Apprenticeship and Traineeship Awards – Outstanding Achievement Award. He now successfully operates his own gardening and tree surgery business.

Donna Shaw, Development and Quality Manager, Castle Personnel, Newcastle

Collaboration between agencies

The array of community organisations associated with the transition from school can be confusing for students with a disability and their families. To address this problem the Department of Education, Science and Training (2003b) employs 20 Disability Coordination Officers, and 11 Regional Disability Liaison Officers. The purpose of both these positions is to assist young people with a disability to move between school, vocational education and training, and higher education. An important activity in this process is providing linkages between schools, training organisations, universities, and other relevant government departments. The relationships between schools and technical education providers have expanded considerably in the past decade. The next section describes the nature of this expansion.

Technical and further education

The state institutes of technical and further education (TAFE) play a significant role in the tertiary education of students with additional needs. Traditionally, access to TAFE has only been available to students once they have graduated from school. However, it is now possible for students to enrol in TAFE courses as part of their school studies, or as a discrete course in its own right. Students doing this may receive credit for the work they have successfully completed if they enrol in TAFE courses at a later stage. As discussed earlier in this chapter, the acronym for this form of education is VET.

VET provides a different, adult-oriented learning environment, as an alternative to traditional school education (TAFE NSW – Illawarra Institute, 2003). Typically, each VET course would be offered for one half day each week, with the student attending school for

the remainder of the week. In NSW there is a range of options in course types. Industry Curriculum Framework courses provide discrete Certificate I or II level qualifications, and provide an entry to higher-level training following the completion of school. Examples of the areas covered in this training are business services, hospitality, construction, retail, and primary industries. In addition, students may undertake some courses that will provide them with advanced standing for future VET courses they may enrol in. If students meet the course requirements, then their VET results will count towards their final school certificate. Box 12.8 provides an example of a student who is enrolled in a TAFE course while completing her final year of school.

Box 12.8
Voices: Emily's story

Hi. My name is Emily and I am going to tell you my story when I went to Glendale TAFE in Year 11 through to Year 12. OK, here goes. When I started at Glendale TAFE in Year 11, I was afraid and a little scared because I didn't know anybody and I was all alone. I found it really difficult to fit in with the other students in my class because I was a shy thing and didn't really participate in any of the class activities, plus I don't think that I was really into the course at the time.

In Year 12, which I am in now, I get along with everyone in my class including the teacher, probably because they came through with me from Year 11. I am not as shy as I used to be. Instead I'm really talkative and I participate in everything that we do. I have opened up heaps since I started at TAFE. I am really interested in the subject now and hope to get a good career with what I have learned while I have been at Glendale TAFE.

At the TAFE my teachers have been really supportive and have encouraged me to do my best.

Emily

This year has been my first year teaching TVET. It has also been my first year teaching a student with disabilities. It was, though, Emily's second year as a TVET student. Emily was born with Apert syndrome, which, among other things, affects the shape of the skull and the formation of fingers. Her shyness and reluctance to join in was quite apparent. The other students respected Emily's shyness and she was never forced to join in. She mainly spoke to her writer, rather than other students.

In second term the students were to give a presentation. I asked Emily if she would give her presentation in front of the class rather than during her tutoring time. She agreed as long as she could go first. All the students were a little nervous giving their presentations and I think they recognised that this was a special moment for Emily. After her five-minute presentation, they all applauded her. This did wonders for Emily.

That afternoon she wrote four words on the board before she went for a break. The words were about 15 centimetres high and she wrote, 'I RULZ THE WORLD'. After that it appeared that there was no holding her back.

Ann Hogan, teacher

We have a number of students with disabilities come through TVET. Some have obvious problems, some don't. Some cope well with their study, some need much support. There are some students you wouldn't even know had a disability unless you looked up their records. Emily has a physical disability. She would sit hunched over the desk trying to look inconspicuous, and refusing to participate.

>

Box 12.8 continued

Eye contact was impossible, and any answers she was asked to give were monosyllabic. She had a writer in class, but that didn't help her in submitting assignments on time, and she didn't seem to care if her work was acceptable or not. On field trips, she kept to herself, refusing to mix with the other students or participate in practical activities unless forced. It seemed, to begin with, that she was just filling in time, occupying a space until she was moved somewhere else.

That was 18 months ago. Emily, today, is a bright, vivacious, even cheeky young lady with a great sense of humour. She not only mixes readily with her classmates, she even gives verbal presentations to the class with flair and confidence. Her written work is not only acceptable, it is above the average, and she is constantly looking for ways to improve. She is a normal, happy teenage girl, actually enjoying classes and the company of her peers. And she now has a career goal – to be a Veterinary Nurse.

What has brought about this incredible change? I believe it is due to the fact that she was taken from an environment where she was expected to fail, and put into a classroom where everyone, even she, was expected to pass, and pass with flying colours. She was not treated as an optional extra, but as an important and integral part of the team, not only by the teachers but also by the students themselves. She was encouraged to achieve along with everyone else, and while support was readily given at any time, exceptions were not! I believe Emily finally found a sense of self-worth, where she could compete on an even footing and was indeed even expected to do so. And she rose to the challenge, becoming an amazing young woman.

Chris Moxon, teacher

In Victoria, over 22 000 students were enrolled in VET during 2001 to simultaneously complete a nationally recognised vocational qualification and their Victorian Certificate of Education (Educational Outcomes Research Unit, 2002). This number had grown from under 2000 students in 1995. In 2001, 32.3 per cent of Years 9, 10 and 11 students, and 13.4 per cent of Year 12 students were enrolled in VET courses in Victorian schools.

A similar picture is apparent in Western Australia. In that state, VET grew from 683 students in 36 schools in 1997, to 13 813 students (42.5 per cent of the cohort) in 133 schools in 2001 (Department of Education, Western Australia, 2001). For some students, up to 40 per cent of their school year was involved in taking one or two units of competency, full certificate courses, or in school-based traineeships. In a state with a high proportion of Aboriginal students, over 60 per cent of these students in their final years of school undertook VET.

Clearly, this massive growth in VET holds much potential for students with a wide range of learning difficulties by providing a potentially more relevant pathway to post-school employment. However, the challenge for schools is to integrate this alternative pathway into students' school experiences, rather than seeing VET as a means of 'farming out' students who may not be interested in a traditional academic approach.

Working with government departments

A common concern of families with a member with a disability is that they find it difficult to understand how the community service system operates. Schools assist families by providing some coordination of a range of different support services. However, once students with a disability leave school there is rarely a 'one stop shop' to give this level of coordination. Instead, students and their families must deal with a wide range of agencies and organisations at the Commonwealth, state and sometimes local government levels. For this reason, it is important that school staff be aware of the service system structure and that they pass on this information to students and their families throughout their high school years.

Frequent changes in the names of government departments, and changes in the responsibility for the operation of some services contribute to this confusion (Commonwealth of Australia, 2000). However, at the time of writing, the following may be said about the operation and responsibility for community disability services in Australia. The Commonwealth government maintains responsibility for the funding of employment services for people with a disability. State governments operate accommodation, respite care, leisure and other disability services. All these services are required to follow a set of service standards that are designed to ensure that these services meet minimum requirements (Department of Family & Community Services, 2003). There is also a complaints mechanism that users of these services may utilise (for example, the Commonwealth Human Rights & Equal Opportunity Commission, and similar organisations in the states and territories). A message that schools should give to students with additional needs and their families is that to make the system work for you, you need to know how the system operates.

Working with limited resources

The long-term future of transition planning for students with additional needs in Australia remains uncertain because Commonwealth government funding to maintain specific transition programs is not consistently provided, and because not all state and territory governments have committed themselves to continuing designated funding in this area. In addition, at some schools a formal transition planning program may not operate. Nevertheless, there may be some students with additional needs at that school, who are enrolled in regular classes, who would benefit from transition planning. Continuing to provide a core curriculum to those students that focuses on the academic requirements for university education is likely to be inconsistent with the needs of those students. Although the resources and supports available to classroom teachers may be limited in such a situation, there are ways in which teachers and other school staff can prepare those students for post-school life.

Ways in which the school curriculum can be made more relevant to students with additional needs were discussed in Chapter 4. In addition, the self-determination section of the current chapter demonstrated some practical ways in which regular classroom teachers can encourage more independence from their students. If teachers are finding that the curriculum they are delivering to their students is not meeting their needs, then some changes to what is taught need to be made. For example, restructuring the curriculum to include units that relate to the students' current and future life interests can be a way to teach a range of academic skills in a more interesting manner. Such a restructured curriculum for students studying English in high school could include units on choosing a career, finding a place to live, running a household, and budgeting. Examples of content covered in the accommodation unit may be reading advertisements, translating abbreviations in advertisements, comparing and contrasting choices, assessing available accommodation, and developing questions to ask the landlord. This approach can be followed in other key learning areas. In maths, the budgeting unit could cover basic computations, use of spreadsheets, and estimations.

In schools where the career adviser or support teacher can provide some coordination, the development of a generic employment education program may assist many students with additional needs. Here, learning activities could address preparing job applications and résumés, attending interviews, getting along with co-workers, and maintaining good attendance patterns. Integrating career education into the curriculum can make the school experience more relevant, and can encourage many students with additional needs to stay at school until the end of 12 years of education, which will enhance their post-school outcomes.

To ensure that what is taught to students with special educational needs is relevant, teachers should ask themselves *why* they teach what they do. If the answer is that the content meets the current and future needs of the students, then we are justified in teaching it. Once this is done, the *what, when, where* and *how* to assess, plan and teach students logically proceed.

Summary

This chapter dealt with several issues associated with the movement of students with additional needs from school to post-school life. These issues included the post-school outcomes for many of these students in comparison with their peers, the relevance of existing curriculums for these students, school-based transition planning models, the importance of developing self-determination skills, community-based support services, and the roles of parents and families in the transition process. A theme throughout the chapter was the importance of the coordination of individual transition plans for students, and the cooperation between the key players in the transition process.

Several recent trends have had a significant impact on transition planning. One of these trends is the increase in vocational training offered through schools. Also addressed were the issues of credentialling for students who are unable to benefit from a regular curriculum, and flexible progression through the curriculum for students enrolled in regular classes.

Discussion questions

1   Is it possible for high school teachers to prepare students for life outside of school and, at the same time, to provide students with a sound education in their relevant curriculum specialisation?

2   Identify some difficulties that students A and B described in the next section may face in coping with the high school curriculum. Focus on your own area of specialisation, and explain how these students could be supported in the regular classroom.

Individual activities

1   Develop a list of:
   a   school-based transition support services that can be accessed by adolescent students with a disability, and by regular teachers of these students, in your school system

b community-based support services that may be relevant to adolescent students with a disability in your local community.

You may find that organisations such as local governments produce this information. You may also find a section on disability and welfare groups in your phone book. For the school-based support services, you may find it helpful to determine how the service is accessed and how that support person may collaborate with regular teachers.

2 Collect examples of school reports that are competency-based, from schools in your area. How well are these reporting systems meeting the needs of students with a disability? What certificate of attainment are students who do not undertake mainstream subjects, eligible to receive in your state or territory?

3 Plan a lesson for each of the students with special needs described below, in your subject area. Assume that the student described is enrolled in a regular class. In your planning, incorporate one of the components of self-determination mentioned earlier in this chapter (for example, providing opportunities for choice and decision-making, problem-solving, goal setting, self-evaluation, self-awareness, and self-efficacy).

Student A

Mary-Ellen is a Year 10 student with mild intellectual disability. She is a quiet student who needs encouragement to be actively involved in class activities. She has some basic reading skills, and can work independently. She can work in a group when given a clear task to do. Her interests are swimming and cooking, and she has a small group of friends at the school that she spends time with outside of school time.

She requires help in some practical subjects because of safety issues, staying on-task, copying information, remembering her timetable, and in working out what the task is and what to do first. Her maths skills are limited and she has difficulty completing written tasks in the time provided. Mary-Ellen is interested in working with animals, or at a plant nursery, when she leaves school.

Student B

Patrick is a Year 6 student with moderate intellectual disability who is friendly, will attempt most tasks asked of him, and can work independently if he understands what he has to do. He can copy text accurately from the board or from books, and has a reading age at the Year 1 level. There is a small group of students in Patrick's class who choose to work with him and provide him with some support to do meaningful tasks in group projects. He knows the names of all the students in his class, and he has been in this class since he started school.

Patrick needs help with reading most of the written material given to the rest of the class, understanding what his task is in individual and in group work, and coping with number work beyond counting to 20. He is unable to understand much of the conceptual material associated with topics such as measurement and geometry in mathematics and other subjects. However, he is eager to be a part of all practical activities in most of the subject areas. Patrick likes being around boats (his father owns a boat shop), playing soccer and swimming.

Group activities

1   Brainstorm for strategies to encourage the involvement of parents and families in the educational process. For example, your list may include the use of telephone contact, 'plain English' letters and notes, and interpreters. What are some barriers present in schools, that discourage parental involvement?

2   Select one of the primary or secondary school key learning areas. Identify the practical applications of this learning area to everyday living skills. For example, for science you may find some relevance in horticulture, and in understanding the effects of drugs and how a car battery works.

References

*Australian National Training Authority (2000a). *Bridging Pathways: Blueprint for Implementation*. Brisbane: Author. http://www.anta.gov.au/publication.asp?qsID=57

Australian National Training Authority (2000b). *Bridging Pathways: National Strategy*. Brisbane: Author. http://www.anta.gov.au/publication.asp?qsID=74

Australian Vice Chancellor's Committee (1996). *Guidelines Relating to Students With Disabilities*. http://www.avcc.edu.au/news/public_statements/publications/gldisab.htm#1.

Benz, M.R., Yovanoff, P. & Doren, B. (1997). School-to-work components that predict postschool success for students with and without disabilities. *Exceptional Children, 63*, 151–65.

Blum, H.T., Lipsett, L.R. & Yocom, D.J. (2002). Literature circles: A tool for self-determination in one middle school inclusive classroom. *Remedial and Special Education, 23*(2), 99–108.

Buswell, B. & Sax, C.L. (2002). The three C's of family involvement. In C. L. Sax & C. A. Thoma (Eds), *Transition Assessment: Wise Practices for Quality Lives*, (pp. 39–50). Baltimore: Paul H. Brookes Pub. Co.

*Commonwealth Department of Family and Community Services (2003). *Support for People With a Disability*. http://www.facs.gov.au/internet/facsinternet.nsf/whatfacsdoes/ESP-SupptDisability.htm

Commonwealth of Australia (2000). *Australian, State, Territory and Local Governments*. http://www.gov.au

Dempsey, I. (2003). Disproportionate representation in Australian special education. *Special Education Perspectives, 12*(1), 17–30.

Department of Education, Tasmania (1999). *Transition Education in Tasmania*. http://www.tased.edu.au/tasonline/gateways/newsletr/Dec1.htm

Department of Education, Western Australia (2001). *Review of Enterprise and Vocational Education and Training in Schools 2001*. http://www.eddept.wa.edu.au/vet/downloads/review01.pdf

Department of Education, Science and Training (2003a). *Higher Education: Report for 2003 to 2005 Triennium*. Retrieved 12 September, 2003, from http://www.dest.gov.au/highered/he_report/2003_2005/pdf/triennium2003_2005.pdf

Department of Education, Science and Training (2003b). *Disability Coordination Officer Programme*. Retrieved 15 September, 2003, from http://www.dest.gov.au/ty/dco/

Department of Family and Community Services (2003). *Quality Assurance System for Disability Employment Services.* http://www.facs.gov.au/internet/facsinternet.nsf/aboutfacs/programs/disability-qa_nav.htm

Doherty, L. (2003). State fails Aboriginal students. *Sydney Morning Herald,* 17 February.

Educational Outcomes Research Unit (2002). *Transition From the VET in Schools Program: The 2000 Year 12 Cohort.* Melbourne: University of Melbourne. http://www.sofweb.vic.edu.au/voced/pdf/research/VET2000Transistions.pdf

Foreman, P., Dempsey, I., Robinson, G. & Manning, E. (2001). Characteristics, academic and post-university outcomes of students with a disability at the University of Newcastle. *Higher Education Research and Development, 20*(3), 313–25.

Keogh, R. (1995). *Transition: Opening Pathways to Post School Options.* Paper given at the Australian Association of Special Education National Conference, Darwin.

Morningstar, M. E., Kleinhammer-Tramill, P. J. & Lattin, D. L. (1999). Using successful models of student-centered transition planning and services for adolescents with disabilities. *Focus on Exceptional Children, 31*(9), 1–19.

Murray, C. (2003). Risk factors, protective factors, vulnerability, and resilience. *Remedial and Special Education, 24*(1), 16–26.

Murray, C., Goldstein, D. E., Nourse, S. & Edgar, E. (2000). The postsecondary school attendance and completion rates for high school graduates with learning disabilities. *Learning Disabilities Research and Practice, 15,* 119–27.

National Organization on Disability (2000). *2000 N.O.D./Harris Survey on Americans With Disabilities.* Washington, DC: Louis Harris & Associates.

Neubert, D. A., Moon, M. S. & Grigal, M. (2002). Post-secondary education and transition services for students aged 18–21 with significant disabilities. *Focus on Exceptional Children, 34*(8), 1–11.

*NSW Board of Studies (2003). *Stage 6 Special Program of Study – Life Skills courses.* http://www.boardofstudies.nsw.edu.au/syllabus_hsc/sps_index.html

NSW Department of Education and Training (1998). *Special Education Handbook.* Sydney: Author.

Rademacher, J.A. (2000). Involving students in assignment evaluation. *Intervention in School and Clinic, 35*(3), 151–6.

Riches, V. (1996). A review of transition from school to community for students with disabilities in NSW, Australia. *Journal of Intellectual and Developmental Disability, 21*(1), 71–88.

Svetaz, M. V., Ireland, M. & Blum, R. (2000). Adolescents with learning disabilities: Risk and protective factors associated with emotional wellbeing: Findings from the National Longitudinal Study of Adolescent Health. *Journal of Adolescent Health, 27,* 340–8.

TAFE NSW – Illawarra Institute (2003). TVET. http://www.illawarra.tafensw.edu.au/tvet/index.htm

*Te Riele, K. & Crump, S. (2002). Young people, education and hope: Bringing VET in from the margins. *International Journal of Inclusive Education, 6*(3), 251–66.

University of Adelaide (2003). *Disability Action Plan.* http://www.adelaide.edu.au/equity/reports/dap.html#3

US Department of Education (2000). *Twenty-second Annual Report to Congress on the Implementation of the Americans With Disabilities Education Act.* Washington, DC: Author.

Victorian Department of Education and Training. (2003). *Futures for Young Adults Program.* Retrieved 1 October, 2003, from http://www.sofweb.vic.edu.au/wellbeing/disabil/futures.htm

*Wehmeyer, M. L. & Shalock, R. L. (2001). Self-determination and quality of life: Implications for special education services and supports. *Focus on Exceptional Children, 33*(8), 1–16.

Whitney-Thomas, J. & Moloney, M. (2001). 'Who I am and what I want': Adolescents' self-definition and struggles. *Exceptional Children, 67*(3), 375–89.

---

*Recommended reading for this chapter

Further recommended reading

Babkie, A. M. & Provost, M. C. (2002). Select, write and use metacognitive strategies in the classroom. *Intervention in School and Clinic, 37*(3), 173–7.

Benz, M. R., Lindstrom, L. & Yovanoff, P. (2000). Improving graduation and employment outcomes of students with disabilities: Predictive factors and student perspectives. *Exceptional Children, 66*(4), 509–29.

Daly, P. M. & Ranalli, P. (2003). Using countoons to teach self-monitoring skills. *Teaching Exceptional Children, 35*(5), 30–5.

Field, S., Hoffman, A. & Spezia, S. (1998). *Self-determination Strategies for Adolescents in Transition*. Austin: PRO-ED.

Lamb, S. (2001). *The Pathways From School to Further Study and Work for Australian Graduates*. Camberwell, Vic.: Australian Council for Educational Research.

McConnell, M. E. (1999). Self-monitoring, cueing, recording and managing: Teaching students to manage their own behaviour. *Teaching Exceptional Children, 32*(2), 14–21.

Mithaug, D. K. (2002). 'Yes' means success: Teaching children with multiple disabilities to self-regulate during independent work. *Teaching Exceptional Children, 35*(1), 22–7.

Price, L. A., Wolensky, D. & Mulligan, R. (2002). Self-determination in action in the classroom. *Remedial and Special Education, 23*(2), 109–15.

Wehmeyer, M. L., Agran, M. & Hughes, C. (1998). *Teaching Self-determination to Students with Disabilities: Basic Skills for Successful Transition*. Baltimore: Paul H. Brookes Pub. Co.

REFERENCES ON SPECIFIC DISABILITIES

It is impossible for any person to be an expert on all disabilities. Most teachers will find it helpful to consult specific references and other resources when confronted with questions about a specific disability. The Internet is an excellent source of information about disabilities. Organisations such as the Down Syndrome Association, Autism Association, Spina Bifida Association and Royal Institute for Deaf & Blind Children will have websites that contain links to other relevant sites. Most large cities have a genetic counselling unit or genetic support unit that will also be a helpful source of information, particularly in the case of rare disorders. Parents also often acquire resources and expertise related to their child's disability. Listed below are some references that contain information about specific disabilities. Websites have not been listed, as they tend to change and are easily accessed through a search engine.

Acquired brain injury

Brain Foundation Victoria. (1999). *Resource Kit for Carers of People with Neurological Conditions or Acquired Brain Injury*. Camberwell, Victoria: Author.

Glang, A., Singer, G.H.S. & Todis, B. (Eds). (1997). *Students With Acquired Brain Injury: The School's Response*. Baltimore: P.H. Brookes Pub. Co.

NSW TAFE Commission. (1999). *Guide to Teaching Students With an Acquired Brain Injury*. Granville, NSW: Access Educational Services Division.

Singer, G.H.S., Glang, A. & Williams, J.M. (1996). *Children With Acquired Brain Injury: Educating and Supporting Families*. Baltimore: P.H. Brookes Pub. Co.

Sarno, M.T. (Ed.). (1998). *Acquired Aphasia* (3rd edn). San Diego: Academic Press.

Sterling, L. (1995). *Students With Acquired Brain Injuries in Primary and Secondary Schools*. Canberra: Australian Government Publishing Service.

White, P. (1996). *Acquired Brain Injury: What Children Should Know*. The Junction, NSW: Hunter Brain Injury Rehabilitation Program.

Attention deficit disorder (ADD/ADHD)

Alban-Metcalfe, J. (2001). *Managing Attention Deficit Hyperactivity Disorder in the Inclusive Classroom: Practical Strategies for Teachers*. London: David Fulton.

Barkley, R.A. (2000). *Taking Charge of ADHD: The Complete Authoritative Guide for Parents*. New York: Guilford Press.

Cooper, P. & Bilton, K. (Eds). (1999). *ADHD: Research, Practice and Opinion*. London: Whurr.

Cooper., P. & Bilton, K. (2002). *Attention Deficit/Hyperactivity Disorder: A Practical Guide for Teachers*. London: David Fulton

Ingersoll, B. D. (1993). *Attention Deficit Disorder and Learning Disabilities: Realities, Myths, and Controversial Treatments*. New York: Doubleday.

Jones, C. B. (1994). *Attention Deficit Disorder: Strategies for School-age Children*. Tucson: Communication Skill Builders.

Kewley, G. D. (2001). *ADHD: Recognition, Reality and Resolution*. Melbourne: ACER Press.

Munden, A. & Arcelus, J. (1999). *The ADHD Handbook: A Guide for Parents and Professionals on Attention Deficit Hyperactivity Disorder*. London: Jessica Kingsley.

Nevin, R. S., Anderson, V. A. & Godber, T. (2002). *Rethinking ADHD: Integrated Approaches to Helping Children at Home and at School*. Crows Nest, NSW: Allen & Unwin.

Sandberg, S. (Ed.). (2002). *Hyperactivity and Attention Deficit Disorders of Childhood*. Cambridge, UK; New York: Cambridge University Press.

Selikowitz, M. (1995). *All About ADD: Understanding Attention Deficit Disorder*. Melbourne: Oxford University Press.

Strichart, S. S. & Mangrum, C. T. (2002). *Teaching Learning Strategies and Study Skills to Students With Learning Disabilities, Attention Deficit Disorders, or Special Needs*. Boston: Allyn & Bacon.

Weingartner, P. L. (1999). *ADHD Handbook for Families: A Guide to Communicating With Professionals*. Washington DC: Child & Family Press.

Wodrich, D. L. (1994). *Attention Deficit Hyperactivity Disorder: What Every Parent Wants to Know*. Baltimore: P. H. Brookes Pub. Co.

Zimmett, D. (2001). *Eddie Enough!*. Bethesda, MD: Woodbine House.

Autism spectrum disorders

Attwood, T. (1998). *Asperger's Syndrome: A Guide for Parents and Professionals*. London: Jessica Kingsley Publishers.

Baron-Cohen, S. & Bolton, P. (1993). *Autism: The Facts*. New York: Oxford University Press.

Blakemore-Brown, L. (2002). *Reweaving the Autistic Tapestry: Autism, Asperger's Syndrome, and ADHD*. London; Philadelphia: Jessica Kinglsey.

Cohen, D. J. & Volkmar, F. R. (Eds). (1997). *Handbook of Autism and Pervasive Developmental Disorders*. New York: J. Wiley.

Cohen, S. (1998). *Targeting Autism: What We Know, Don't Know, and Can do to Help Young Children With Autism and Related Disorders*. Berkeley: University of California Press.

Dowty, T. & Cowlishaw, K. C. (Eds). (2002). *Home Educating our Autistic Children: Paths are Made by Walking*. London: Jessica Kingsley.

Frith, U. (2003). *Autism: Explaining the Enigma*. New York: Blackwell Pub.

Fullerton, A. et al. (1996). *Higher Functioning Adolescents and Young Adults With Autism: A Teachers Guide*. Austin: Pro-Ed.

Gillberg, C. (2002). *A Guide to Asperger Syndrome*. Cambridge; New York: Cambridge University Press.

Gill-Weiss, M. J. & Harris, S. L. (2001). *Reaching Out, Joining In: Teaching Social Skills to Young Children With Autism*. Bethesda, MD; Great Britain: Woodbine House.

Harland, K. (2002). *A Will of His Own: Reflections on Parenting a Child With Autism*. Bethesda, MD: Woodbine House.

Hollander, E. (2003). *Autism Spectrum Disorders*. New York: Marcel Dekker, Inc.

Holmes, D. L. (1998). *Autism Through the Lifespan*. Bethesda, MD: Woodbine House.

Howlin, P. (1998). *Children With Autism and Asperger Syndrome: A Guide for Practitioners and Carers*. Chichester, New York: John Wiley

Howlin, P. (2003). *Autism: Preparing for Adulthood* (2nd edn). London: Brunner-Routledge.

Howlin, P., Baron-Cohen, S. & Hadwin, J. (1999). *Teaching Children With Autism to Mind-read: A Practical Guide for Teachers and Parents*. New York: J. Wiley & Sons.

Jones, G. (2002). *Educational Provision for Children With Autism and Asperger Syndrome: Meeting Their Needs*. London: David Fulton.

Jordan, R. (1999). *Autism Spectrum Disorders: An Introductory Handbook for Practitioners*. London: David Fulton.

Jordan, R. & Jones, G. (1999). *Meeting the Needs of Children With Autism Spectrum Disorders*. London: David Fulton.

Jordan, R. & Powell, S. (1995). *Understanding and Teaching Children With Autism*. New York: J. Wiley.

Kinney, J. & Fischer, D. (2001). *CoTeaching: Students With Autism K-5*. Verona, WI.: IEP Resources.

Koegel, R. L. & Koegel, L. K. (1995). *Teaching Children With Autism: Strategies for Initiating Positive Interactions and Improving Learning Opportunities*. Baltimore: P. H. Brookes Pub. Co.

Lawson, W. (2003). *Build Your Own Life: A Self-help Guide for Individuals With Asperger's Syndrome*. London: Jessica Kinglsey.

McConnell, K. & Ryser, G. (2000). *Practical Ideas That Really Work for Students With Autism Spectrum Disorders*. Austin, Tex.: Pro-Ed.

Mesibov, G. B. & Howley, M. (2003). *Accessing the Curriculum for Pupils With Autistic Spectrum Disorders: Using the TEACHH Program to Help Inclusion*. London: David Fulton Publishers.

Moyes, R.A. (2002). *Addressing the Challenging Behaviour of Children With High Functioning Autism/ Asperger Syndrome in the Classroom: A Guide for Teachers and Parents*. London; Philadelphia: Jessica Kinglsey.

Ozonoff, S., Dawson, G. & McPartland, J. (2002). *A Parent's Guide to Asperger Syndrome and High-Functioning Autism: How to Meet the Challenges and Help Your Child Thrive*. New York, NY: Guilford Press.

Posers, M. D. (1995). *Educating Children With Autism, a Guide to Selecting An Appropriate Program*. Bethesda MD: Woodbine House.

Powel, S. & Jordan, R. (Eds). (1997). *Autism and Learning: A Guide to Good Practice*. London: David Fulton.

Randall, P. (1999). *Supporting the Families of Children With Autism*. West Sussex: Eng.: Wiley.

Roe, D. (2001). *Autism Spectrum Disorder and Young Children*. Watson, ACT.: Australian Early Childhood Association.

Scott, J., Brady, M.P. & Clark, C. (2002). *Students With Autism: Characteristics and Instructional Programming for Special Educators*. San Diego, Calif.; [Great Britain]: Singular.

Siegel B. (1996). *The World of the Autistic Child: Understanding and Treating Autistic Spectrum Disorders*. New York: Oxford University Press.

Simpson, R. L. (1997). *Social Skills for Students With Autism*. Reston, Va.: Council for Exceptional Children.

Simpson, R. L. & Smith Myles, B. (Eds). (1998). *Educating Children and Youth With Autism: Strategies for Effective Practice*. Austin, Tex: Pro-Ed.

Sonders, S. A. (2003). *Giggle Time – Establishing the Social Connection: A Program to Develop the Communication Skills of Children With Autism, Asperger Syndrome and PDD*. London; Philadelphia: J. Kingsley.

Trevarthen, C. Aitken, K., Papoudi, D. & Robarts, J. (1998). *Children With Autism* (2nd edn). London: Jessica Kingsley Publishers.

Volkmar, F. R. (Ed.). (1998). *Autism and Pervasive Developmental Disorders*. New York: Cambridge University Press.

Winter, M. (2003). *Asperger Syndrome: What Teachers Need to Know*. London: Jessica Kingsley Publishers.

Cerebral palsy

Bridge, G. (1999). *Parents As Care Managers: The Experiences of Those Caring for Young Children With Cerebral Palsy*. Aldershot: Ashgate.

Dormans, J. P. & Pellegrino, L. (Eds). (1998). *Caring for Children With Cerebral Palsy: A Team Approach*. Baltimore: P. H. Brookes Pub. Co.

Finnie, N. R. (1996). *Handling the Young Child With Cerebral Palsy At Home*. Oxford, Boston: Butterworth Heinemann.

Goodman, S., Houbolt, M., Denman, K. (1998). *Coaching Athletes With Cerebral Palsy*. Belconnen: Australian Sports Commission.

Miller, G. & Clark, G. D. (Eds). (1998). *The Cerebral Palsies: Causes, Consequences and Management.* Boston: Butterworth Heinemann.

Stanton, M. (1997). *The Cerebral Palsy Handbook: A Practical Guide for Parents and Carers.* London: Vermilion.

Tyers, S.A., Bainbridge, K. & Brain, M. (1999). *Using the Opportunity: Embedding a Child's Goals Into Everyday Routines.* Coolbinia, W.A.: The Cerebral Palsy Association of Western Australia.

Deafness/hearing impairment

Bull, T. H. (1998). *On the Edge of Culture: Hearing Children/Deaf Parents: Annotated Bibliography.* Alexandria, Va.: Deaf Family Research Press.

Chute, P. M. & Nevins, M. E. (2002). *The Parent's Guide to Cochlear Implants.* Washington DC: Gallaudet University Press.

Darby, A. (1999). *Deafness in Primary Schools: Information for Teachers, Governors and All School Staff.* Derby, UK: Royal School for the Deaf.

Haring, N. G. & Romer, L. T. (Eds). (1995). *Welcoming Students Who Are Deaf-Blind Into Typical Class-Rooms: Facilitating School Participation, Learning, and Friendships.* Baltimore: P. H. Brookes Pub. Co.

Kluwin, T. N., Moores, D. F. & Guastad, M. G. (Eds). (1992). *Towards Effective Public School Programs for Deaf Students: Context, Process, and Outcomes.* New York: Teachers College Press.

Knight, P. & Swanwick, R. (1999). *The Care and Education of a Deaf Child: A Book for Parents.* Clevedon: Multilingual Matters.

Luetke-Stahlman, B. (1999). *Language Across the Curriculum: When Students Are Deaf Or Hard of Hearing.* Hillsboro, Or.: Butte Publications.

Lynas, W. (1994). *Communication Options in the Education of Deaf Children.* London: Whurr.

Lynch, C. & Kidd, J. (1999). *Early Communication Skills.* Bicester: Winslow.

Paatsch, L. (2000). *Assessing and Teaching Spoken Language to School Age Students Who Are Deaf and Hearing Impaired.* North Rocks, NSW: Renwick College.

Power, D. (Ed.). (1994). *Communicating With Deaf Students: Signing, Talking and Listening.* Brisbane: Griffith University.

Schirmer, B. R. (2000). *Language and Literacy Development in Children Who Are Deaf.* Boston: Allyn & Bacon.

Stelling, J. (1997). *The Words They Need: Welcoming Children Who Are Deaf and Hard of Hearing to Literacy.* Timonium, MD: York Press.

Tucker, B. P. (1997). *IDEA Advocacy for Children Who Are Deaf Or Hard of Hearing: A Question and Answer Book for Parents and Professionals.* San Diego, Calif.: Singular Pub. Group.

Turkington, C. & Sussman, A.E. (2004) *The Encyclopedia of Deafness and Hearing Disorders* (2nd edn). New York: Facts on File.

Watson, L., Gregory, S. & Powers, S. (1999). *Deaf and Hearing Impaired Pupils in Mainstream Schools.* London: David Fulton.

Wiltshire, C. (1997). *Psychological & Psychiatric Support for Deaf and Hearing Impaired People: An Australian Directory.* Sydney: Deaf and Hearing Impaired Unit, Dept of Psychiatry, Royal Prince Alfred Hospital.

Down syndrome

Cuskelly, M., Jobling, A. & Buckley, S. (2002). *Down Syndrome Across the Life-Span.* London: Whurr.

Dmitriev, V. (2001). *Early Education for Children With Down Syndrome: Time to Begin.* Austin, Tex.: Pro-Ed.

Kliewer, C. (1998). *Schooling Children With Down Syndrome: Toward an Understanding of Possibility.* New York: Teachers College Press.

Kumin, L. (1994). *Communication Skills in Children With Down Syndrome: A Guide for Parents.* Rockville, MD: Woodbine House.

Kumin, L. (2001). *Classroom Language Skills for Children With Down Syndrome: A Guide for Parents and Teachers.* Bethesda, MD: Woodbine House.

Miller, J. F., Leavitt, L. A. & Leddy, M. G. (Eds). (1999). *Improving the Communication of People With Down Syndrome.* Baltimore, MD: P. H. Brooks Pub. Co.

Pueschel, S. M. (2001). *A Parent's Guide to Down Syndrome: Toward a Brighter Future* (Rev'd edn). Baltimore: P. H. Brooks Pub. Co.

Rynders, J. E. & Horrobin, J. M. (1995). *Down Syndrome: Birth to Adulthood. Giving Families An Edge*, Love Publishing.

Selikowitz, Mark. (1997). *Down Syndrome: The Facts* (2nd edn). New York: Oxford University Press.

Stratford, B. & Gunn, P. (Eds). (1996). *New Approaches to Down Syndrome.* London: Cassell.

Stray-Gundersen, K. (Ed.). (1995). *Babies With Down Syndrome: A New Parents' Guide.* Bethesda, MD: Woodbine House.

Van Dyke, D. C. et al. (Eds). (1995). *Medical & Surgical Care for Children With Down Syndrome: A Guide for Parents.* Bethesda: Woodbine House.

Winders, P. C. (1997). *Gross Motor Skills in Children With Down Syndrome: A Guide for Parents and Professionals.* Bethesda, MD: Woodbine House.

Wise, L. & Glass, C. (2000). *Working With Hannah: A Special Girl in a Mainstream School.* London: RoutledgeFalmer.

Epilepsy

Baddeley, L. & Ellis, S. J. (2002). *Epilepsy: A Team Approach to Effective Management.* Oxford: Butterworth-Heinemann.

Banks, G. K. (1994). *It's Only Epilepsy.* Rushcutters Bay: Gore & Osment.

Beran, R. (1995). *Learning About Epilepsy.* Sydney: McLennan & Petty.

Beran, R. G. (1997). *Epilepsy: Facts About Fits.* Sydney: MacLennan & Petty.

Hanscomb, A. & Hughes, L. (1995). *Epilepsy.* London: Ward Lock.

Hopkins, A., Shorvon, S. & Cascino, G. (Eds). (1995). *Epilepsy.* London: Chapman & Hall.

Johnson, M. & Parkinson, G. (2002). *Epilepsy: A Practical Guide.* London: D. Fulton.

McLean., T. (1996). *Seized: My Life With Epilepsy.* London: Richard Cohen Books.

Sander, J. W. (2002). *Epilepsy: Questions and Answers.* Basingstoke: Merit.

Sander, J. W., Hart, Y. M. (1997). *Epilepsy: Questions and Answers.* Basingstoke: Merit.

Fragile X syndrome

Dew-Hughes, D. (2003). *Educating Children With Fragile X: A Multi Professional View.* New York: Routledge Falmer.

Hagerman, R. J. & Silverman, A. C. (Eds). (1991). *Fragile X Syndrome: Diagnosis, Treatment, and Research.* Baltimore: Johns Hopkins University Press.

Saunders, R. (2000). *Fragile X Syndrome: A Guide for Teachers.* London: David Fulton.

Shopmeyer, B. & Lowe, F. (Eds). (1992). *The Fragile X Child.* California: Singular Pub. Group.

Weber, J. D. (Ed.).(2000). *Children With Fragile X Syndrome: A Parent's Guide.* Bethesda, MD: Woodbine House.

Muscular dystrophy

Corrick, J. (1992). *Muscular Dystrophy*. New York: F. Watts.

Emery, A. E. H. & Emery, M. L. H. (1995). *The History of a Genetic Disease: Duchenne Muscular Dystrophy Or Meryon's Disease*. London: Royal Society of Medicine Press.

Harper, P. S. (2002). *Myotonic Dystrophy – The Facts: A Book for Patients and Families*. Oxford; New York: Oxford University Press.

Pettenuzzo, B. (1989). *I Have Muscular Dystrophy*. Sydney: F. Watts.

Sach, S. & Shield, L. (1991). *Duchenne Muscular Dystrophy: A Guide for Parents*. Ascot Vale, Vic.: Muscular Dystrophy Association.

Spina bifida

Llewellyn, G. (1990). *Living With Spina Bifida: Shared Experiences*. Chippendale: Redfern Legal Centre Publishing.

Lutkenhoff, M. (Ed.). (1999). *Children With Spina Bifida: A Parents' Guide*. Bethesda, MD.; Woodbine House.

Lutkenhoff, M. & Oppenheimer, S. G. (Eds). (1997). *Spinabilities: A Young Person's Guide to Spina Bifida*. Bethesda, MD.: Woodbine House.

Rowley-Kelly, F. L. & Reigel, D. H. (Eds). (1993). *Teaching the Student With Spina Bifida*. Baltimore: P. H. Brooks Pub. Co.

Vision impairment/blindness

Arter, C., Mason, M., McCall, S., McLinden, M. & Stone, J. (1999). *Children With Visual Impairment in Mainstream Settings*. London: David Fulton.

Barraga, N. C. & Erin, J. N. (2001). *Visual Impairments and Learning*. Austin, Tx: Pro-Ed.

Bishop, V. E. (1996). *Teaching the Visually Limited Child*. Springfield, Ill.: Charles C. Thomas.

Bowman, R. J. C., Bowman, R. F., Dutton, G. N. & Royal National Institute for the Blind. (2001). *Disorders of Vision in Children: A Guide for Teachers and Carers*. London: RNIB.

Corn, A. & Koenig, A. (1996). *Foundations of Low Vision*. New York: American Foundation for the Blind.

Davis, P. (2003). *Including Children With Visual Impairment in Mainstream Schools: A Practical Guide*. London: David Fulton.

Goodman, S. A. & Wittenstein, S. H. (Eds). (2003). *Collaborative Assessment: Working With Students Who Are Blind Or Visually Impaired, Including Those With Disabilities*. New York: American Foundation for the Blind.

Knott, N. I. (2002). *Teaching Orientation and Mobility in the Schools: An Instructor's Companion*. New York: AFB Press.

Lueck, A. H., Chen, D. & Kekelis, L.S. (1997). *Developmental Guidelines for Infants With Visual Impairment: A Manual for Early Intervention*. Louisville, Ky: American Printing House for the Blind.

Mason, H. (1998). *Guidelines for Teachers and Parents of Young People With Visual Impairment Using Low Vision Aids (LVAS)*. Birmingham, England: University of Birmingham.

Mason, H. (2001). *Spotlight On Special Education Needs: Visual Impairment*. Tamworth, UK: NASEN.

Miller, O. (1996). *Supporting Children With Visual Impairment in Mainstream Schools*. London: Franklin Watts.

Sacks, S. Z. & Silberman, R. K. (Eds). (1998). *Educating Students Who Have Visual Impairments With Other Disabilities*. Baltimore: P. H. Brooks Pub. Co.

Video (1997): *Let Me See! The Importance of Positioning for Young People With Visual Impairment and Cerebral Palsy.* Edinburgh: Moray House Educational Television for the Scottish Sensory Centre.

Walsh, M. E. (2000). *Sex Education for Students With Vision Impairment: A Guide for Visiting Teachers.* Melbourne, Vic: Dept of Education, Employment and Training.

Walsh, M.E. (2001). *Integration and Inclusion for a Student With Vision Impairment.* Melbourne, Vic: Dept of Education, Employment and Training.

Warren, D. (1994). *Blindness and Children: An Individual Differences Approach.* New York: Cambridge University Press.

Webster, A. & Roe, J. (1998). *Children With Visual Impairments: Social Interaction, Language and Learning.* London; New York: Routledge.

General

Allen, J. (Ed.). (2003) *Inclusion, Participation, and Democracy: What Is the Purpose.* Dordrect; Boston: Kluwer Academic Publishers.

Ashman, A. & Elkins, J. (Eds). (2002). *Educating Children With Diverse Abilities.* Frenchs Forest, NSW: Pearson Education.

Closs, A. (1999) *The Education of Children With Medical Conditions.* London: David Fulton.

Deiner, P. L. (1999). *Resources for Educating Children With Diverse Abilities: Birth Through Eight.* Fort Worth: Harcourt Brace College Publishers.

Farrell, P. & Ainscow, M. (Eds). (2002). *Making Special Education Inclusive: From Research to Practice.* London: David Fulton.

Frederickson, N. & Cline, T. (2002). *Special Education Needs, Inclusion, and Diversity: A Textbook.* Buckingham, [England]; Philadelphia: Open University Press.

Giangreco, M. F. (Ed.) & Erikson, K. A. (2002). *Quick-Guides to Inclusion 3: Ideas for Educating Students With Disabilities.* Baltimore: P. H. Brooks Pub. Co.

Guralnick, M. J. (Ed.). (2001). *Early Childhood Inclusion: Focus On Change.* Baltimore: P. H. Brooks Pub. Co.

Hamill, L. B. & Everinghan, C. T. (2002). *Teaching Students With Moderate to Severe Disabilities: An Applied Approach for Inclusive Environments.* Upper Saddle River, N.J.: Merrill/Prentice Hall.

Pueschel, S. M. et al. (1995). *The Special Child: A Source Book for Parents of Children With Developmental Disabilities* (2nd edn). Baltimore: P. H. Brooks Pub. Co.

Schloss, P. J., Smith, M. A. & Schloss, C. N. (1995). *Instructional Methods for Adolescents With Learning and Behavior Problems.* Boston: Allyn & Bacon.

Smith, T. E. C. (2004). *Teaching Students With Special Needs in Inclusive Settings.* Boston, MA: Allyn & Bacon.

Taylor, G. R. & Harrington, F. T. (2003). *Educating the Disabled: Enabling Learners in Inclusive Settings.* Lanham, Md: Scarecrow Press.

Tilstone, C. & Rose, R. (Eds). (2003). *Strategies to Promote Inclusive Practice.* London; New York: Routledge Falmer.

Vaughn, S., Schumm, J. S. & Bos, Candace, S. (2000). *Teaching Exceptional, Diverse, and At-Risk Students in the General Education Classroom.* Boston: Allyn & Bacon.

GLOSSARY

academically engaged time The amount of time a student is actually working on a task. In many classrooms, while students may appear to be working, the amount of academically engaged time may be low. Factors that reduce academically engaged time include interruptions, distractions, inappropriate teacher expectations and inappropriate curriculum material.

acquisition phase The initial stage of learning, during which a great amount of support for the learner may be necessary.

action research A form of staff development in which the focus of inquiry is the participants' own practice. Teachers are involved in an inquiry into a situation or practice with an aim to bring about improvement.

advocacy Assistance or support on behalf of another. Typically parents and guardians act as advocates for their son or daughter. However, it is in the interests of all students to assist them to advocate for themselves.

age-appropriate behaviour A behaviour or activity that is consistent with the behaviours and activities normally undertaken by same-aged peers. For example, a young woman playing with a toy doll would not be displaying age appropriate behaviour.

agent of change A person or persons working with other people in order to bring about change.

antecedents The events that occur before a specific behaviour occurs. For example, the behaviour may be that a student calls out abusively to another student. The antecedents may be that the other student kicked the student under the desk. The antecedent behaviours are important as they affect why the behaviour occurred.

anti-discrimination legislation Laws designed to protect individuals from being unfairly treated on the basis of some personal characteristic or trait. The *Disability Discrimination Act* is a piece of Australian legislation the purpose of which is to ensure fair treatment for people with a disability.

attention deficit disorder (ADD) A neurological disorder commonly characterised by inattentiveness and an inability to concentrate on a task. The behaviour is often linked to learning difficulties and has a strong genetic component. The term has often been misused, and has only recently been recognised by some school authorities.

attention deficit hyperactivity disorder (ADHD) A neurological disorder commonly characterised by hyperactive behaviour in which the student is unable to concentrate on a task. The behaviour is often linked to learning difficulties and has a strong genetic component. The term has often been misused, and has only recently been recognised by some school authorities.

attention-seeking A behaviour often associated with Dreikurs' four goals of misbehaviour, it involves the display of behaviours that attract attention to the individual. The behaviours are at first amusing to the observer but they soon become annoying and the person turns from the centre of positive attention to the centre of negative attention.

auditory perception The ability to understand or make sense of what is heard. In reading, it could be the ability to identify a sequence of sounds as a word in spoken language.

augmentative and alternative communication (AAC) An attempt to compensate temporarily or permanently for the impairment and disability patterns of individuals with severe communication disorders through provision of an AAC device or system.

augmentative and alternative communication system (AAC system) This is an integrated group of components used to enhance communication. The system supplements any other communication abilities the person may have.

automaticity The ability to complete a task without having to think about the steps involved. For reading, it is the ability to instantly recognise words without thinking about letters and sounds in the word.

aversives The opposite to reinforcers. When a student demonstrates inappropriate behaviour, the consequences are designed to decrease the likelihood of the behaviour occurring again. Aversives include time-out and detention.

baseline The level of a specific behaviour before a behaviour management program is implemented. The baseline level should involve the collection of data on at least three occasions, so that a stable level of behaviour can be measured. The importance of the baseline is that any change in behaviour as a result of the behaviour management program can be measured against the baseline level.

basic number facts Simple (two figure) addition, subtraction and division combinations as well as multiplication tables.

behaviour management The control of certain behaviours either by the individual or another person, usually a teacher or a parent. Often applied to a specific management program that has been developed to change unacceptable behaviours.

behaviour A general term to cover any action by a person. Although it commonly refers to social behaviours such as working in a group, it can also include academic behaviours such as reading or writing.

careers adviser A member of staff in secondary schools who provides vocational support for all students. This person may assess the vocational needs of individual students, advise students on their employment options, locate work experience placements, and monitor the placement of students at these sites.

cerebral palsy A disability, usually present at birth, resulting from damage to the motor (movement) areas of the brain. Can affect one to four limbs and speech. Effects range from mild to severe.

change The introduction of any innovation, whether program, process or practice, that is new to the person or school.

change agents See **agent of change**.

change facilitator See **agent of change**.

cognitive approaches Cognitive approaches involve the transfer of a teacher-designed strategy to the student through a series of training steps. The use of scaffolding is common. Cognitive approaches differ from metacognitive approaches, where the student is responsible for the strategy and its monitoring.

cloze A technique in which words are deleted from passages, and the student is required to identify the missing word or words. The technique can be used as a method of assessing readability or as a comprehension exercise.

cognitive ability Thinking ability, intelligence.

collaborative teaching Teachers working together to achieve a common teaching goal. In the case of teaching in an integrated setting, both the integration teacher and the class teacher must be committed to the success of the program.

collaborative consultation An interactive and ongoing process where people with differing expertise and knowledge work together in order to find solutions to mutually agreed upon problems.

collegiality When teachers talk to each other about what they do, observe each other's practice, work together on planning and implementing programs, and teach each other what they know about teaching and learning.

communication aid An object or device, such as a chart, board, communication book or computer, used to assist communication.

community-based A program, activity or service that is located in the community. Sport clubs, Special Olympics and shopping facilities are examples of community-based activities and services.

competency-based curriculum Curriculums that are designed to develop a prescribed range of abilities. In Australia, these curriculums are being used in conjunction with statements and profiles to prepare students for post-school life (especially in employment-related areas).

computer assisted instruction (CAI) The application of computers for instructional purposes. Common CAI programs include drill and practice, tutorials and simulation.

concept keyboard An expanded keyboard for people who do not have fine motor control or people who have an intellectual disability. It can either have large keys or a membranous surface. It can be programmed to allow easier input to the computer.

content enhancement The provision of additional information or strategies that assist the student to master content covered in class. Mnemonics, advance organisers, study guides and visual displays are examples of this type of support.

cooperative learning A set of instructional methods that emphasise small groups of learners working together on a shared goal. Features include planned interdependence, clearly specified roles and an emphasis on problem-solving as a learning tool.

credentialling The process of awarding students a certificate showing that they have attained a certain standard. For example, in New South Wales all school students are now eligible to receive a certificate after 10 and 12 years of schooling, regardless of the level of their ability.

cues The features of a situation that set the occasion for a response. Cues, which are necessary for behaviour, may be natural or artificial, and may include visual, auditory, tactile, olfactory or other types of stimuli. Examples include the beep on a watch that signifies the hour, the smell of a barbecue, and street signs that point to the shopping centre.

curriculum In its most general sense, the total of all that is learnt in schools. It is more commonly used as a general term to describe a course of study that has been planned with expected learning outcomes and which has a structure of learning activities and evaluation procedures (for example, the K–6 English curriculum).

curriculum adaptation Altering the quantity of curriculum content, vocabulary and assessment provided to students, to ensure that they are presented with material that they can attempt.

curriculum analysis The process of identifying and sequencing the content (skills, knowledge and attitudes) covered in a particular curriculum statement or syllabus. This information can then be used in assessing student needs and programming for individuals and groups.

curriculum-based assessment A process of class level teaching and testing designed to maximise teaching and learning outcomes. This approach emphasises careful assessment, realistic programming and frequent evaluation of student performance.

curriculum overlapping One of the three basic options in adapting curriculum for students in an inclusive classroom. It involves all students completing the same activity, with a variety of curriculum focuses. For example, all students may be working in small groups on a painting activity. One student's curriculum objective may be developing language skills, while the remainder are focusing on the art curriculum objective. See also **multilevel curriculum.**

data collection A systematic method of collection information on the behaviour patterns of a student. Data can be collected using a range of methods including observation and tests.

database management The application of computers to the creating, accessing, manipulating, storing and organisation of information in the form of electronic files

deinstitutionalisation The process of moving people with a disability from institutions and hospitals into the community to live.

direct service delivery Refers to a situation in which the collaborative consultant designs and implements instructional interventions directly with the student or group of students.

direct instruction A highly structured method of teaching that emphasises curriculum analysis, student success and cumulative learning.

disability The functional consequence of an impairment. For example, because of the impairment of spina bifida, the disability may be that a person is unable to walk without the assistance of calipers and crutches.

Down syndrome A common syndrome, usually associated with moderate or mild intellectual disability, resulting from the presence of an additional chromosome in each body cell.

early intervention In education of children with disabilities, this refers to supplying educational and therapy services from the time the disability is diagnosed, sometimes from birth.

ecological analysis/ecological inventory Method of selecting vocabulary to be taught through a careful analysis of the vocabulary used by peers in a similar environment.

empowerment A process resulting in an individual having a better understanding of their environment, the resources in their environment, and the confidence to access these resources.

environmental inventory See **ecological analysis.**

error analysis A strategy designed to assist the teacher and the student, by highlighting specific areas of difficulty experienced in the completion of a task. This information is useful in the provision of remedial support in that it allows the teacher and the student to focus on the problem area.

extinction A procedure used to stop an undesired or unwanted behaviour. The procedure used often includes planned ignoring, in which the teacher or students do not respond to the behaviour. Eventually the student demonstrating the behaviour stops, as the behaviour is not being reinforced.

failure cycle A cycle of increasing social and academic alienation that begins with a failure to learn in class which results in behaviour problems because the student is not challenged, which in turn leads to continued failure to learn and then to further behaviour problems. The cycle can be broken only by addressing both the academic and behaviour needs of the student.

flexible progression The opportunity for students to complete their schooling at a faster or slower rate than is normally the case.

fluency The stage of learning in which the learner becomes more efficient with a skill and is therefore able to perform it faster, more independently and with improved accuracy.

full inclusion The concept that all children should be in regular classes, regardless of the severity of their disability.

functional curriculum A term often applied to the curriculum used for students with special educational needs, suggesting that the curriculum topics relate directly to the needs of the students. In regular education, the term could be applied to many of the new syllabuses being taught in secondary schools such as 'Science for life' or 'Contemporary English'.

generalisation The ability to use an acquired skill under a wide range of conditions.

graphics The application of computers to the creating, editing, printing and storing of graphic materials such as figures, paintings, drawings, graphs and charts.

handicap The social or environmental consequences of a disability, for example, inability to follow television news because of deafness. The extent to which a person with a disability also has a handicap will depend on how well the environment caters for the disability.

high technology system High technology communication systems utilise computers with specialised software. Outputs can be in printed form or voice.

impairment An abnormality in the way organs or systems function. It usually refers to a medical condition, for example, short-sightedness, heart problems, cerebral palsy, Down syndrome, spina bifida, deafness.

inclusive curriculum Ensuring that all students in the classroom, including those with additional educational needs, are included in the curriculum taught in the classroom.

inclusive education The concept of inclusion is based on the notion that schools should, without question, provide for the needs of all the children in their communities, whatever the level of their ability or disability. See also **full inclusion**.

indirect service delivery Refers to a situation in which the collaborative consultant is not directly engaged in instruction, but assists to maximise student outcomes in a variety of ways. Students, teachers, parents or administrators may be supported in this way.

individual transition plan (ITP) An individualised education program whose aim is to prepare the student for post-school life. Typically, this plan would develop in secondary school.

individualised education program (IEP) An individual student's program of instruction that is based on their needs, strengths and interests. The program usually develops following consultation with the students, their parents, school staff and other relevant support persons.

instructional cycle The core elements of effective teaching, expressed as a continuous cycle. Key aspects include revision, demonstration, guided and independent practice and articulation into future learning experiences.

instructional level The instructional levels in a classroom are based on the complexity of syllabus content and vocabulary used at each of the levels:

- *teacher instructional level*—the content and vocabulary level at which the teacher talks
- *material instructional level*—the content and vocabulary level of the textbook or worksheet
- *student instructional level*—the level of content and vocabulary that the students in the classroom can comprehend.

integration The term integration is used as a broad term to refer to a child's attendance at a regular school. The term also refers to the process of transferring a student to a less segregated setting. A child who attends a regular school, but is in a separate special unit or class, can still be said to be integrated.

intellectual disability Limitation in intelligence, usually associated with an intelligence quotient (IQ) below 70 and some problems in functional behaviour. Obsolete terms are 'mental retardation' and 'mental deficiency'. In the UK, intellectual disability is referred to as 'learning disabilities'.

intelligent computer assisted instruction (ICAI) The application of computers for instructional purposes by incorporating artificial intelligence in the design of the computer assisted instruction programs.

itinerant teachers Teachers who provide support to students with a disability and their teachers at several different school sites. For example, an itinerant teacher may support students with hearing impairments and the staff supporting these students at a cluster of schools.

key learning areas (KLAs) A set of accepted areas of focus in an educational curriculum. Typically, key learning areas include content in domains such as literacy, numeracy, social and physical sciences, languages and health studies.

kindergarten In some states this refers to the first year of compulsory schooling, while in other states *kindergarten* refers to a preschool year.

koala pad An input device linked to a computer. It provides input to a computer via a pen and a touch-sensitive pad by interfacing with appropriate menus on the computer screen.

learning outcomes The measurable attainments of an individual, typically considered in the light of long-term goals and the process of program evaluation.

learning disability A disorder in one or more of the basic processes involved in using spoken or written language. This disorder may particularly show itself in problems with reading, writing, spelling, speaking, listening and mathematical calculations.

learning difficulty A difficulty in learning, usually affecting the basic skills of reading or mathematics. It may result from a difficulty in perception, vision, hearing or intelligence, or be of unknown origin.

least restrictive environment The placement of people with disabilities in environments that give them the greatest range of choices, that is, the fewest restrictions.

life-span Whole of life, from birth to death.

life-span approach An educational orientation that views the student within the context of their life-span. Using this approach, a primary school teacher of students with a disability may incorporate employment related skills in the curriculum.

logical consequences A term often associated with Dreikurs' model of misbehaviour. Logical consequences are the reasonable outcome of a behaviour. For example, if I call out in class (behaviour), I can expect to be kept in at recess (logical consequence). Students are taught that if their behaviour is inappropriate, logical consequences will result.

long-term goals A statement of intended learning outcomes for an individual, usually expressed as an annual target.

low/light technology systems Low or light technology communication systems include communication boards, choice boards and object boards. Some light tech devices are operated by electromechanical switches.

mainstreaming A student is mainstreamed while they are enrolled in or participating in a regular class.

maintenance The ability to perform a learned behaviour over time, without continuing instruction.

Makaton A language program that may be used as a systematic multimodal approach for the teaching of communication skills. It provides a source of functional vocabulary for children and adults with communication needs, and for their interactive partners.

mastery learning An approach to teaching in which new material is not introduced until prior skills or knowledge have been attained. The teacher using mastery learning principles sets specific criteria for student performance and regularly checks student progress, providing support as appropriate.

metacognitive approaches An approach in which the student develops a strategy to attempt a task. The student may receive teacher or student assistance in the initial development of the strategy, although the final strategy requires that the individual student monitors and evaluates the strategy's effectiveness.

modified curriculum A course of instruction that is different from that undertaken by most students. Some students with special educational needs may need to complete subjects that are different in content and level of difficulty from those of most other students.

multiaged grouping Children in these groups are not graded or grouped according to chronological age or academic ability, and curriculum needs are developmentally based.

multilevel curriculum One of the three basic options in adapting curriculum for students in an inclusive classroom. It involves all students carrying out the same curriculum activity but at different levels. For example, all students may be carrying out tasks on addition in mathematics, although some may be adding single digits to a total less than 10, while others may be completing multiple column addition with trading. See also **curriculum overlapping**.

national curriculum In Australia, the national curriculum is an agreement between states and territories on eight key learning areas and the use of statements and profiles to monitor the progress of students in these learning areas.

non-verbal communication Behaviour that does not involve the use of speech. It is used in behaviour management to refer to communicating without words such as through the use of gesture, signals or standing in close proximity to a student. It is an effective behaviour management tool as it does not draw attention either to the student or the behaviour.

normalisation The concept that all people, regardless of disability, should be able to live a life that is as normal as possible for their culture. In relation to education, the principle of normalisation suggests that all children should have the opportunity to attend the neighbourhood school.

pacing The rate at which tasks (and related aspects such as cues, prompts and reinforcers) are presented to the student(s) in the classroom context.

partial participation The involvement of an individual in an activity even though the individual may not be able to complete all the components of the activity. For example, assistance may be provided for one or more steps in the activity.

peer-mediated instruction The involvement of peers in various teaching and support roles, including tutoring (same or cross-age), monitoring and networking in social situations. The aim of all peer-mediated strategies is to achieve benefits for both the recipient and the support provider.

peripherals Any electronic device that is connected to a computer and under its control. Examples include mouse, printer, speakers, and microphone.

phonics The ability to identify the sounds of letters or letter clusters in a word and blend them together so that they can be recognised as a word in spoken language.

photonic wand A light pen that is worn on the head. It emits an infrared beam and controls a computer by pointing at an appropriate location on the computer screen. It is usually used by students who have good control only of their head movements.

physical disability Disability in movement, usually of the lower or upper limbs.

prompts Additional support to the learner, designed to aid learning. Examples include highlighting key points in a piece of text, physical assistance and the provision of hints that assist in solving a problem.

psychometric tests Assessments that measure mental states and processes. Examples are intelligence and personality tests.

readability The level of reading required to comprehend a passage or a textbook. It is most commonly assessed using a combination of the length of the sentences and the number of syllables in the words, although there are many other methods such as the use of cloze tests and student retelling.

reciprocal teaching Students take turns to be the instructor within a small group. It can be used to provide part of the scaffolding used in transferring skills from the teacher to the individual student. As the students use their own words (student language), they are often able to provide instruction that can be more readily understood by peers than teacher language.

regular education initiative (REI) A movement that argues that there is no place for special schools in the education system. That is, it is claimed that all students should be educated in regular schools.

reinforcer Any event or reward following a behaviour that will increase the likelihood of that behaviour re-occurring. A reinforcer can be a piece of food, an activity or a token that can be exchanged for food or an activity at a later time. The closer a reinforcer occurs to the demonstration of the behaviour, the greater the effect on the behaviour.

residential school School that includes living or boarding facilities.

response cost A behaviour management technique used as part of a token economy in which a student loses tokens for demonstrating inappropriate behaviour, while gaining tokens for appropriate behaviour.

revisualisation The ability to look at letter patterns in words and retain them.

scaffolding A technique in which there is a structured move from teacher control of the activity to student control. The scaffolding provides the framework for the transfer.

school counsellor Generally a psychologist with educational qualifications who may support schools and their students by conducting student assessments, assisting staff to design educational programs, supporting 'at risk' students, and liaising with the parents of students.

school-based A program, activity or service that is located in a school. School remedial reading programs, resource or support teachers, and school assemblies are examples of school-based activities.

scope and sequence charts A visual representation of the content and order of a curriculum, or unit within a curriculum.

scribe A person who will write a student's dictated answer to an assignment or an examination question. (Also known as amanuensis.)

self-determination A personal attribute associated with knowing what one wants in life, understanding what it may require to achieve personal goals, and having access to the resources to achieve those goals.

self-esteem The extent to which individuals value and respect themselves. Positive self-esteem is a desirable direct and indirect outcome from the school experience.

sensory disability Impairment of vision or hearing, including deafness and blindness.

short-term instructional objectives Precise statements of intended student performance. Typically, these objectives specify the learner, the behaviour or content to be achieved, the conditions under which this will occur and a criterion for successful performance.

social integration The placement of a student with special educational needs into a mainstream class where the emphasis is on the student becoming part of the class's social fabric.

social behaviour A term that is used to describe the actions of a person such as calling-out or working with others, as distinct from academic behaviour, such as completing a comprehension task. In a behaviour management program, it is important to identify the specific social behaviour that the program seeks to change (for example, remain in seat).

social interaction The ways in which students work together. In an integrated setting it commonly refers to the ways both the integrated and mainstream students accept each other when working together.

social role valorisation A reconceptualisation of normalisation by Wolf Wolfensberger that is based on the social role assumed by individuals and the value placed on that role by the society in which the individual lives.

social acceptance The degree to which mainstream students are willing to accept a student with special educational needs in their class or in the playground.

social justice A belief system that is based on equity, human rights and fairness for all.

socio-economic factors The influence of the financial and social status of the family. Often considered an important influence on the school behaviour of students with behaviour problems, particularly in the case of truancy and delinquency.

special unit Group of two or more special classes within a regular school.

speech generation device (SGD) Previously known as voice output communication aid (VOCA), an SGD or VOCA is an electronic communication device that assists people who have complex communication needs to communicate. Digital recording technology allows messages to be recorded by a person's voice. The number of messages that can be recorded depends on the amount of memory available on the device. A voice synthesiser is used to speak messages that have been typed into a device, via a keyboard.

student language The language that students use in normal conversation with their peers. It can be used as a powerful teaching tool as students can explain to each other what the teacher has said. It has the benefit that it doesn't use the middle class language structures and vocabulary of the teacher. Student language is a critical part of reciprocal teaching and cooperative learning.

syllabus A subsection of curriculum containing the specific content areas to be assessed (for example, a Year 8 syllabus in geography).

target directed learning Learning experiences in which the student can identify the purpose and application of the material being taught. The student who understands the application of number facts to everyday activities such as shopping can be considered to be participating in target directed learning.

task analysis The strategy of breaking a skill or piece of knowledge into its component parts. This information can then be used for the purposes of assessment, programming and instruction.

teacher management strategies The particular techniques that a teacher uses in managing a behaviour. These can be either positive or negative, depending on the teacher's skills in applying them.

teaching learning environment The concept that a classroom is a place in which both teaching and learning occurs throughout the lesson. The teacher teaches students while learning from the students' responses and actions. Students learn both from the teacher and each other, and through reciprocal teaching and other structured approaches, teach other students and the teacher.

telecommunication The application of computers to the transfer of information from one computer to another over relatively large distances via devices such as telephone lines, microwave, satellite and optic fibre.

transition planning Usually refers to the educational planning associated with the movement of students to post-school life. However, this planning may also occur for preschool to school, and primary to high school transitions.

vertical grouping Children are grouped according to academic level, with several different levels within the same class (for example, a class may consist of children in kindergarten, Year 1 and Year 2).

visual perception The ability to understand or make sense of what is seen. In reading, it could be the ability to distinguish between visually similar letters, such as b, d, p, q.

vocational education and training (VET) Technical education provided by colleges of further education and private providers and sometimes undertaken by students while they are in the final years of high school.

welfare policies A set of procedures that addresses the social well-being of students in a school. They commonly address areas of need for students who are disadvantaged. In some states and territories the welfare policy of the school is seen as the main focus, with discipline policy as a part of the overall welfare policy.

INDEX